KU-515-949

The **Rough Guide** to

Jordan

written and researched by

Matthew Teller

with additional contributions by

Ian J. Andrews, Tony Howard and Rana Husseini

NEW YORK • LONDON • DELHI

www.roughguides.com

Contents

Front section   1–24

Introduction 6
Where to go 10
When to go 13
Things not to miss 16

Basics   25–97

Getting there 27
Travel from neighbouring
    countries............................... 36
Red tape and visas 40
Information, websites and
    maps 42
Insurance................................. 45
Health 46
Costs, money and banks 50
Getting around......................... 54
Accommodation 60
Food and drink 63
Communications...................... 69
The media................................ 71
Opening hours and public
    holidays 73
Adventure tours and trekking... 75
Crime and personal safety 81
Shopping for crafts 82
Behaviour and attitudes........... 84
Work and study........................ 92
Travelling with children 94
Travellers with disabilities 95
Directory 96

Guide   99–425

1 Amman 101
2 The Dead Sea and
    around 169
3 Jerash and the north........ 195
4 The eastern desert........... 239
5 The King's Highway 275
6 Petra 323
7 The southern desert and
    Aqaba 379

Contexts   427–503

The historical framework........ 429
Flora and fauna...................... 459
Islam...................................... 466
Women in Jordan 471
Modern art.............................. 474
Writing from Jordan 478
Books 492

Language   505–517

Advertiser   519–540

Small print & Index   541–552

◄◄ Bedouin leaders ◄ Jeep, Wadi Rum

3

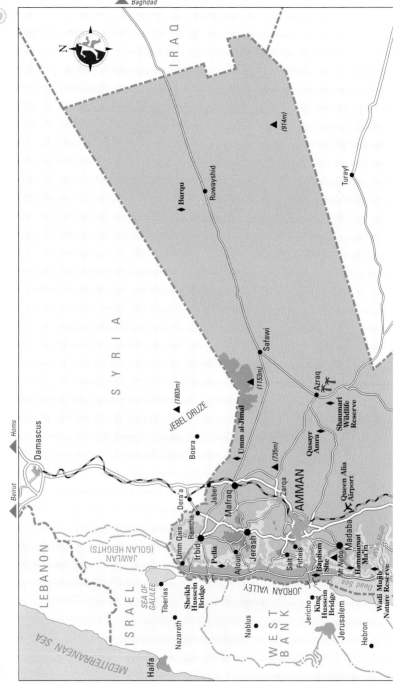

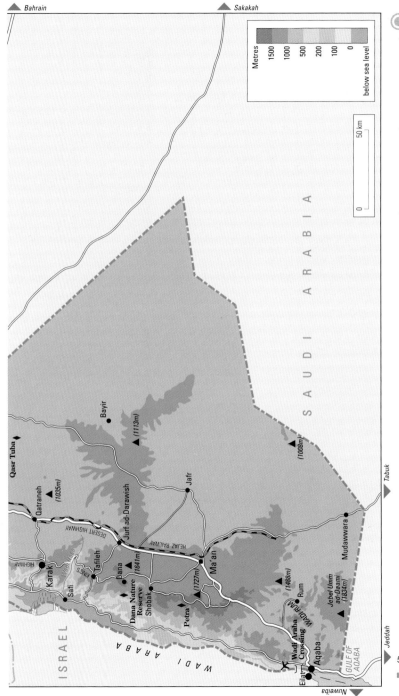

Introduction to
Jordan

Western travellers have been exploring the Middle East for well over a century, but Jordan remains a newcomer to tourism, welcoming only a fraction of the numbers who visit neighbouring Egypt and Israel. The country's popular image abroad encompasses not much more than camels, deserts and Bedouin, and there's little awareness of Jordan's mountains and beaches, castles and ancient churches, the urbanity of its people and richness of its culture.

Jordan is largely **desert**, but this one bland word covers a multitude of scenes, from the dramatic red sands and towering cliffs of the far south to the endless stony plains of volcanic basalt in the east. The northern hills, rich with olive trees, teeter over the rift of the **Jordan Valley**, which in turn runs down to the **Dead Sea**, lowest point on earth. The centre of the country is carpeted with tranquil fields of wheat, cut through by expansive canyons and bordered by arid, craggy mountains. At the southernmost tip of the country, beaches fringe the warm waters of the **Red Sea**, which harbours some of the most spectacular coral reefs in the world.

Jordan is part of the land bridge linking Europe, Africa and Asia, and has seen countless armies come and go. Greeks, Romans, Muslims, Christian Crusaders and more have left evidence of their conquests, and there are literally thousands of **ruins** and **archeological sites** from all periods in every corner of the country. In addition, Israel and Palestine, Jordan's neighbours to the west, have no monopoly on **biblical history**: it was in

6

■

Jordan that Lot sought refuge from the fire and brimstone of the Lord; Moses, Aaron and John the Baptist all died in Jordan; and Jesus was almost certainly baptized here. Even the Prophet Muhammad passed through.

▲ Nabatean sculpture

And yet the country is far from being stuck in the past. Amman is a thoroughly modern capital, and Jordan's respectable rate of economic growth means that grinding poverty is the rare exception rather than the rule. Kids may sell you cigarettes or offer to shine your shoes, but you'll see more desperate begging in the streets of any European or North American city than anywhere in Jordan. Government is stable, with leanings towards democracy under a constitutional monarchy, and manages to be simultaneously pro-Western, pro-Arab, founded on a bedrock of Muslim authority and dedicated to ongoing peace with Israel. **Women** are better integrated into positions of power in government and business than almost anywhere else in the Middle East, military conscription was abolished in 1991, and Jordanians are exceptionally highly educated: just over 2.5 percent of the total population is enrolled at university, a proportion comparable to the UK. Traditions of **hospitality** are ingrained, and taking up some of the many invitations you'll get to tea or a meal will expose you to an outlook among local people that is often as cosmopolitan and world-aware as anything at home. Though surrounded by instability, Jordan is the **safest** country in the Middle East by quite a long way, and domestic extremism is virtually non-existent.

> **Jordan is the safest country in the Middle East by a long way**

▶ Aqaba

Fact file

• The **Hashemite Kingdom of Jordan** (in Arabic, al-Mamlakeh al-Urduniyyeh al-Hashmiyyeh, or **al-Urdun**) covers an area of around 92,000 square kilometres – a little more than Portugal and a little less than Indiana. About 85 percent is desert. The highest and lowest points are Jebel Umm ad-Daami (1834m) and the Dead Sea shore (408m below sea level).

• Well over 90 percent of the **population** of around 5.5 million are **Muslim Arabs**, with small minorities of Muslim **Circassians** and **Chechens**, as well as **Christian Arabs**. The population has increased ninefold since 1952, and though its growth rate has now slowed to 2.5 percent, some 37 percent of the population is below the age of 14.

• Jordan is a **constitutional monarchy**, with universal suffrage over the age of 20. The king appoints the Prime Minister and together they appoint the cabinet. In the bicameral **National Assembly**, the forty-member Senate is appointed by the king and the eighty-member House of Representatives voted in by proportional representation. The single biggest sector in the **economy** – traditionally dependent on phosphates and potash production – is now **tourism**, which generates 13 percent of GDP.

Most people take great pride in their ancestry, whether they're present or former desert-dwellers (**Bedouin**) or from a settled farming tradition (**fellaheen**). Across the desert areas, people still live and work on their **tribal** lands, whether together in villages or apart in individual family units; most town-dwellers, including substantial numbers of Ammanis, claim tribal identity. Belonging to a tribe (an honour conferred by birth) means respecting the authority of a communal leader, or sheikh, and living in a culture of shared history, values and principles that often crosses national boundaries. Notions of honour and mutual defence are strong. Tribes also wield a great deal of institutional power: most members of Jordan's lower house of parliament are elected for their tribal, rather than political, affiliation.

▼ Jerash

The **king**, as sheikh of sheikhs, commands heartfelt loyalty among many people and deep respect among most of the rest.

National identity is a thorny issue in Jordan, which has been perennially flooded with **Palestinian** refugees since the foundation of the State of Israel in 1948. Many people from tribes resident east of the River Jordan before 1948 resent this overbalancing of the country's demography, and the fact that incoming Palestinians, having developed an urbanized, entrepreneurial culture, dominate private-sector business. For their part, Jordanians of Palestinian origin – estimated to make up as much as sixty percent of the population – often resent the "East Bank" Jordanians' grip on power in government and the public sector. All are Jordanian

Jordan's flag

Jordan's flag is a source of national pride. It is adapted from the revolutionary banner of the Great Arab Revolt of 1916–17, when Arab armies led by the Hashemites – a noble dynasty, now led by King Abdullah II of Jordan, which traces its origins back to the Prophet Muhammad himself – overthrew the rule of the Ottoman Empire in the Middle East.

The flag has three equal horizontal bands. At the top is **black**, representing the **Abbasid Caliphate** that ruled from Baghdad in the eighth and ninth centuries; in the middle is **white**, representing the **Umayyad Caliphate** that ruled from Damascus in the seventh and eighth centuries; and at the bottom is **green**, representing the **Fatimid Caliphate** that ruled from Cairo in the tenth and eleventh centuries. On the hoist side is a **red triangle** representing the **Great Arab Revolt** of 1916–17. Within the triangle is a seven-pointed **white star** which symbolizes the seven verses of the opening sura (verse) of the Quran; the points represent faith in one God, humanity, national spirit, humility, social justice, virtue and hope.

▲ Blue Sinai lizard

citizens, but citizenship tends to mean less to many of Palestinian origin than their national identity, and less to many East Bankers than their tribal affiliation. Large numbers of long-stay guest workers from Egypt muddy the issue still further. "Where are you from?" – a simple enough question in most countries – is in Jordan the cue for a life story.

Where to go

The prime attraction in Jordan is **Petra**, an unforgettably dramatic 2000-year-old city carved out of a red sandstone valley hidden behind mountain peaks in the south of the country. Its extraordinary architecture and powerful atmosphere imprint themselves indelibly on most visitors' imaginations.

Jordan has a wealth of other **historical sites**, outstanding among them the exceptionally well-preserved Roman city of **Jerash**, but also including **Umm Qais**, set on a dramatic promontory overlooking the Sea of Galilee, and **Pella**, where Jerusalem's Christians fled Roman persecution in the first century AD. **Madaba**, which became an important Christian town and regional centre for mosaic art during the Byzantine period, houses the oldest known map of the Middle East, made up of millions of mosaic stones laid on the floor of a church. After the Muslim conquest, the Umayyad dynasty built for themselves a series of retreats in the Jordanian desert, now dubbed the "Desert Castles"; most notable among them are the bath-house of **Qusayr Amra**, which features a unique set of naturalistic and erotic frescoes, and **Qasr**

◄ Petra sandstone

Hraneh, perhaps the most atmospheric ancient building in the country. Centuries later, the Crusaders established a heavy presence in southern Jordan, most impressively with the huge castles at **Karak** and **Shobak**. The Arab resistance to the Crusader invasion left behind a no less impressive castle at **Ajloun** in the north.

Even though Jordan lost the holy sites of East Jerusalem, Bethlehem and Hebron to Israel in 1967, it has continued to market itself as the "Holy Land" for its **religious sites**, most importantly the **Baptism Site** of Jesus on the banks of the River Jordan, and **Mount Nebo**, from where Moses looked over the Promised Land and where he died. John the Baptist met his death at Herod's hilltop palace at **Mukawir** after Salome's demand for his head on a platter. Nearby are **Bab adh-Dhraa**, one of the leading contenders for the site of biblical Sodom, and **Lot's Cave**, where Abraham's nephew sought refuge with his family from the destruction of Sodom and Gomorrah. Most of these, and other sites such as the **tomb of Aaron** at Petra, are holy to Muslims, Jews and Christians alike, while there are also plenty of specifically Muslim sites, including a holy tree in

The search for water

Jordan is desperately **water-poor**: current annual consumption is about 200 cubic metres per person, compared with 1800 in Syria, 7700 as the world average, and 110,000 in North America. Almost a third of the water used in Jordan comes from non-sustainable or non-renewable sources. Almost three decades of pumping

from the once-abundant **Azraq** oasis (see p.263) has brought it to the point of collapse. The **River Jordan** is already dammed in several places by Israel (which regularly reneges on its treaty obligation to provide Jordan with water from Galilee); a major tributary, the **Yarmouk**, now sports the 100-metre-high Wihdeh dam shared by Jordan and Syria; and all the major valleys leading down to the Dead Sea – including the Mujib and the Zarqa Ma'in – are now dammed in an effort to stop water draining into the salty lake. Huge reserves of sweet water locked deep beneath the deserts around **Diseh** are to be exploited from 2007 onwards, and will go some way to relieving the crisis. Another grand project – launched with Israeli cooperation – is a **canal** to bring Red Sea water from Aqaba through the desert to the Dead Sea; it will be desalinated for drinking purposes, will also generate hydroelectric power, and may help to halt the shrinkage of the Dead Sea (for more, see p.174). Meanwhile every summer Amman suffers increasingly acute **shortages**, its piped water supplies sometimes failing for days at a time.

the desert at **Biqya'wiyya**, said to have sheltered the Prophet Muhammad himself, and literally dozens of shrines and tombs in every corner of the country.

However, your most abiding memories of a visit are likely to be of Jordan's varied and beautiful natural **environment**. With its sheer cliffs and red sands, austere **Wadi Rum** – where David Lean filmed *Lawrence of Arabia* – presents the classic desert picture of Jordan, and is the starting-point for camel treks of anything from an hour to a week. Less well-known are the gentle northern hills

◀ Black Iris, Jordan's national flower

Your most abiding memories are likely to be of Jordan's beautiful natural environment

around the **Ajloun woodlands**, where you could walk for days through flower-strewn meadows and cool, shady forests without seeing another soul. In the south, the tranquil **Dana Nature Reserve** encompasses a swathe of territory from verdant highland orchards down to the sandy desert floor of the Wadi Araba, and offers extensive opportunities for bird- and wildlife-spotting. The protected **Wadi Mujib** is a giant canyon, 4km wide at the top, that narrows to a high, rocky gorge carrying a fast-flowing river down to the exceptionally salty **Dead Sea**, an inland lake too buoyant for swimming but perfect for floating, your body supported by nothing more than the density of the salty water. Way out in the east of the country, in the furnace of the Black Desert, lies a small dammed lake at **Burqu**, one

◀ Wadi Rum

of the most rewarding birdwatching sites in the entire Middle East, and there are other nature reserves at **Shaumari** (with oryx and ostrich breeding programmes) and **Azraq** (a protected wetland habitat). Last but not least, Jordan has some of the world's best diving and snorkelling in the coral-fringed Red Sea off **Aqaba**.

The appeal of the capital, **Amman**, comes from its location, spread out over a series of precipitous hills, as well as the country's major archeological museum and some of the finest restaurants in the whole Middle East. Jordan's other towns and cities are, for the most part, mundane, although **Irbid** in the north holds a fine museum of culture and **Salt**, the former capital in the Balqa hills west of Amman, has clung on to much of its elegant, late-Ottoman domestic architecture.

When to go

The high seasons for Western tourism are April, May, September and October, with tourism from Arab countries taking over in high summer, but even at peak times the only site that can get unpleasantly crowded is the main path at Petra. The weather should have more impact on your decision when to visit. Despite the small size of the country, you'll find wide variations in **climate**

Transliterating Arabic

Many sounds in **Arabic** have no equivalent in English, and any attempt to render them in English script is bound to be imprecise. Place names are the biggest sources of confusion, varying from map to map and often from sign to sign – you'll see roadsigns to Wadi Seer, Wadi El Sseir, Wadi Alsear and Wadi as-Sir, all referring to the same place. We've tried throughout to stick to a phonetically helpful, common-sense system, while also staying recognizably close to existing English renderings (exceptions are monuments which are known by a non-Arabic name). The definite article "al" and its variations have been removed from all place names other than compound ones: al-Aqaba, ar-Ramtha and as-Salt have all been shortened (Aqaba, Ramtha, Salt), but Umm al-Jimal and Shuneh al-Janubiyyeh stay as they are. For more on the intricacies of Arabic, see p.507.

whenever you arrive: the same January day could have you throwing snowballs in Ajloun or topping up your tan on Aqaba's beaches.

▶ Nubian ibex

The best time to visit is **spring** (March–May), when temperatures are toasty but not scorching, wildflowers are out everywhere (even the desert is carpeted), and the hills and valleys running down the centre of the country are lush and gorgeously colourful. The worst of the rain is over by March (it doesn't entirely peter out in Amman and the hills until late April), although Dana, at 1500m, stays blustery into May. Humidity is pleasant everywhere, and low, clear sunlight draws a spectacular kaleidoscope of colour and texture from the desert rocks. There's only one drawback – a desert wind, loaded with dust and grit, which blows regularly each spring or early summer out of the Arabian interior. It's known across the Middle East as the *khamseen* ("fifty"), after the fifty days it traditionally persists (although in Jordan it rarely lasts longer than a few days), and can darken the sky and raise the temperature by 10°C, coating everyone and everything in a layer of sand.

In **summer** (roughly June–Sept), Amman can sizzle – even up to 40°C in Downtown – and you'll find little respite in the rest of the country, although the hills around Ajloun catch some cooler breezes. Temperatures at the Dead Sea and Aqaba have been known to top a sticky 50°C, with Aqaba in particular suffering from an intolerable hot wind that makes you feel like you're basting in a fan-assisted oven. High, hazy light flattens the brown landscape and bleaches any beauty out of the desert, and you'll find

it's too uncomfortably hot countrywide to do any walking or sightseeing between noon and 4pm. Typical **autumn** weather pretty much passes Jordan by, with only a few weeks marking the shift out of high summer – if you catch it, this can be a lovely time to visit. The first rains fall in early or mid-October, making the parched countryside briefly bloom again and the torrid temperatures drop to more manageable levels. In **winter** (roughly Dec–March), Amman can be desperately chilly, with biting winds sweeping through the valleys, annual falls of snow and plenty of cold rain, although the sun is still never far away. With short days and freezing nights, visits to Petra can be taxing; exceptional lows of -8°C have been recorded. Rum is more temperate, but Aqaba is the only retreat, with sunshine and warmth even in the depths of January (average Red Sea and Dead Sea water temperatures vary little either side of a balmy 24°C all year).

The table shows elevation, average minimum and maximum temperatures and average rainfall for the month.

	Jan	Apr	July	Oct
Amman (800m)				
Average temperatures (°C)	3–12	9–23	18–32	14–27
Average Rainfall	64mm	15mm	0mm	7mm
Aqaba (sea level)				
Average temperatures (°C)	9–21	17–31	25–39	20–33
Average Rainfall	5mm	4mm	0mm	1mm
Dead Sea (400m below sea level)				
Average temperatures (°C)	11–21	19–31	27–40	22–33
Average Rainfall	13mm	7mm	0mm	1mm
Irbid (600m)				
Average temperatures (°C)	5–13	10–22	19–31	15–27
Average Rainfall	111mm	51mm	0mm	14mm
Petra (1100m)				
Average temperatures (°C)	4–12	11–22	18–36	14–24
Average Rainfall	43mm	14mm	0mm	2mm
Rum (950m)				
Average temperatures (°C)	4–15	12–25	19–36	13–29
Average Rainfall	19mm	7mm	0mm	2mm

32

things not to miss

It's not possible to see everything that Jordan has to offer in one trip – and we don't suggest you try. What follows is a selective and subjective taste of the country's highlights: outstanding natural landscapes, ancient ruins, outdoor activities and the spectacular site of Petra. They're arranged in five colour-coded categories to help you find the very best things to see, do and experience. All entries have a page reference to take you straight into the guide, where you can find out more.

01 Wadi Mujib Page **298** • Jordan's "Grand Canyon", now protected as a nature reserve.

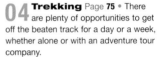

02 **Wadi Rum** Page **388** • Savour the desert ambience close-to, in the stunning company of sheer mountain giants, red dunes and vast, silent panoramas.

04 **Trekking** Page **75** • There are plenty of opportunities to get off the beaten track for a day or a week, whether alone or with an adventure tour company.

03 **Baptism Site** Page **180** • Newly discovered in the thickets flanking the River Jordan is the spot where Jesus was baptized, commemorated by dozens of Byzantine churches and hermitages.

Petra

06 **The Treasury** Page **351** • The most famous of all Petra's monuments, a huge tomb-facade chiselled out of the sheer rock face.

05 **Walking the Siq** Page **348** • The classic entry to the ancient city, picking a path between soaring cliffs into the heart of the mountain.

07 **The Monastery** Page **368** • Petra's largest facade, a gigantic mountain-top tomb only reached by an hour's hard climbing.

08 **Petra By Night** Page **346** • The most alluring way to experience Petra's magic, courtesy of a guided night-time walk to a candlelit Treasury for music, tea and story-telling.

09 **The High Place of Sacrifice**
Page **355** • The most memorable of all the "high places" carved atop strategic summits by Petra's builders, the Nabateans.

10 **Petra colours**
Page **352** • Two thousand years of blowing winds have gently eroded Petra's sandstone walls to reveal a startling kaleidoscope of colours streaking through the rock.

11 **Madaba mosaic map** Page **283** • Millions of coloured stones were laid on the floor of a church to make this, the oldest-known map of the Middle East.

12 **Qasr Hraneh** Page **251** • Jordan's most atmospheric ancient building, an eighth-century "desert castle" in the arid highlands east of Amman.

13 **Bedouin hospitality** Page **90** • The hospitality of Jordanians is legendary: whether you're out in the desert or passing through a city, you're bound to be invited in.

14 **Red Sea diving and snorkelling** Page **416** • You don't have to be a diver to come nose-to-nose with a turtle: coral reefs and multicoloured fish await just beneath the surface of this warmest and clearest of seas.

15 **Hammamat Ma'in** Page **293** • A series of natural hot springs and waterfalls in the hills above the Dead Sea makes a favourite relaxation spot for Jordanian families, and offers some spectacular canyon hikes.

20

ACTIVITIES | CONSUME | EVENTS | NATURE | SIGHTS |

16 **Dead Sea** Page **171** • Enjoy spectacular sunsets at the lowest point on earth, as you float easily on this inland lake supported only by the density of the extra-salty water.

17 **Qusayr Amra** Page **252** • Uncharacteristically erotic frescoes adorn the interior of this desert bath-house, built in the eighth century by the Umayyad caliphs.

18 **Camel-riding** Page **75** • You could barely come to Jordan and turn up the chance of shuffling off into the sands on the "ship of the desert".

19 **Umayyad Palace, Amman** Page **136** • Looming over Downtown is a very well-preserved eighth-century governor's hilltop palace, complete with domed reception hall, courtyards and a bath complex.

20 **Roman Amman** Page **129** • Bang in the heart of Downtown sit a huge Roman theatre, odeon, nymphaeum and colonnaded forum.

21 **Dana Nature Reserve** Page **313** • Jordan's flagship nature reserve, occupying a sweep of territory from highland cliffs to the sandy desert floor; whether you come for the hiking, the natural environment or the silence, you won't want to leave.

22 **King's Highway** Page **275** • Meandering its way north and south along the lonely hilltops, this most picturesque of main roads links the farming towns of southern Jordan.

24 **Jordanian cuisine** Page **143** • Amman's burgeoning in-scene boasts some of the Middle East's finest restaurants, whereas native cuisine takes much inspiration from Bedouin cooking – communal platters of meat and rice, with everyone tucking in by hand.

23 **Karak castle** Page **304** • Stoutest and starkest remnant of the Crusaders' occupation of the country.

25 Jerash Page **198** • A spectacularly well-preserved Roman city located in the hills north of Amman, complete with paved and colonnaded streets, grand temples, intimate marketplaces and Byzantine mosaic-floored churches.

26 Mount Nebo Page **289** • On the summit of the mountain where Moses looked out over the Promised Land, and where he died, stands a monastery church richly decorated with mosaics and a stylized cross.

28 Burqu Page **272** • Grasp the power of mirages at this most remote of Jordan's attractions – a sweet-water lake and ruined black castle far out in the scorching desert.

27 Pella Page **232** • You might come to explore the Roman remains, but prepare to be tempted by a plate of fresh fish and a glass of chilled white wine at the nearby Resthouse.

29 **Umm Qais** Page **224** • Atmospheric Roman and Ottoman ruins, spectacular views over the Sea of Galilee – and relatively few tourists.

30 **Jerash Festival**

Page **199** • Jordan's premier cultural happening, an annual gathering of international performers in music, cinema, dance and drama, with many events staged in the ancient ruins of Jerash.

32 **Shaumari Wildlife Reserve**

Page **264** • Stare down the ostriches at this desert breeding station, or indulge in a spot of eagle-spotting or oryx-counting.

31 **Qasr Azraq** Page **261** • Overlooking Lawrence of Arabia's "magically haunted" oasis, in the desert way east of Amman, stands a castle of black basalt that has been occupied since antiquity.

Basics

Basics

Getting there 27

Travel from neighbouring countries 36

Red tape and visas 40

Information, websites and maps 42

Insurance 45

Health... 46

Costs, money and banks 50

Getting around 54

Accommodation 60

Food and drink... 63

Communications.. 69

The media 71

Opening hours and public holidays 73

Adventure tours and trekking.. 75

Crime and personal safety.. 81

Shopping for crafts 82

Behaviour and attitudes.. 84

Work and study.. 92

Travelling with children... 94

Travellers with disabilities 95

Directory 96

Getting there

The easiest way to get to Jordan is, of course, to fly. There are daily nonstop flights from London, with services from around Britain and Ireland connecting well with London or other European airports. North America also has very convenient nonstop flights, as well as smooth transit times at midway hubs in the US or Europe. From Australasia, you're looking at a change of plane midway, but connections at major Asian hubs such as Bangkok or Dubai are good.

Fares depend on a number of factors, the most important being the **season**. The highest prices tend to apply in summer (June–Aug) and around Christmas. Fares can be slightly lower in spring (March–May) and autumn (Sept & Oct), when Jordanian weather is at its most pleasant, and lower still the rest of the year. Just as significant are the periods surrounding major **Islamic holidays** such as Eid al-Fitr and Eid al-Adha (see p.74), when thousands – or, in the case of the hajj pilgrimage to Mecca, millions – of people are on the move. For weeks before the hajj, whole planes get block-booked for pilgrims on virtually all routes into the Middle East – not only flights into Saudi Arabia, but also connections via Jordan and neighbouring countries. For two weeks after the pilgrimage, it can also be very difficult to find a spare economy-class seat out of any Middle Eastern airports. It pays to check when Islamic holidays are due to fall (see p.74); book well ahead if you want to fly at or near those times.

Amman is not a high-volume discount destination, and you'll generally find that routings are the preserve of **Royal Jordanian** (**RJ**) and your national carrier (or its code-sharing partner). The only way to cut costs on a scheduled air ticket is to fly less expensively into, say, Cairo or Tel Aviv, and then proceed overland from there (see "Travel from neighbouring countries").

Charter flights operate to Jordan – chiefly into **Aqaba** rather than Amman – from some European cities and these can be a useful way to pick up a cheap seat. In addition, there are daily short-hop shuttle flights on Royal Wings (part of Royal Jordanian) to Aqaba from Amman, and you can normally request an Amman–Aqaba add-on at the time of booking your international flight for a bargain £20/US$30 or so one-way – less than you'd pay in Jordan.

Given the relatively high fares on normal point-to-point tickets, **Round-the-World** tickets that take in the Middle East can offer good value if you have the time to make the most of some stopovers. Although few off-the-shelf itineraries take in Amman specifically, many offer a stop in Cairo or Istanbul, from where you can take a side-trip to Jordan. Alternatively, agents can easily put an itinerary together that does include Amman.

Carbon-neutral flights

Air travel is one of the leading causes of carbon dioxide emissions into the atmosphere – and carbon dioxide (or CO_2) is a major cause of global warming. Trees, however, soak up CO_2, counteracting the effects of global warming. Ⓦ **www .futureforests.com** is one of several sites offering "**carbon-neutral**" **flights**: you input details of your flight (origin and destination), and then buy enough trees in a managed forest to soak up however much CO_2 you are generating. For example, a London–Amman return flight produces 810kg of carbon dioxide per passenger, which you can offset by buying one tree (£10/US$15). A flight from Los Angeles to Amman via Paris produces 2.74 tonnes per passenger, requiring four trees.

One thing to watch when planning an itinerary and booking hotels is your scheduled **arrival time**: many European flights take off between 4pm and 8pm, arriving in Amman in the hours either side of midnight – and then departing on their return journey in the small hours. If you're on this sort of schedule, be aware that your head may not actually hit the pillow on your first night until 2am or later, and that you may have to check in at the airport before dawn on your last day. Not all schedules are this bad: a bit of flexibility when selecting your travel dates can result in more sociable flight times.

Organized tours

Many **organized tours** which include Jordan follow a fairly similar pattern – a week or so on the ground, comprising a couple of nights each in Amman, Petra and Aqaba, with sightseeing on the way and some side-trips to sites like Jerash and Wadi Rum. Others may be targeted slightly differently: maybe based at an Aqaba beach hotel instead, with options to visit Petra or Rum, but then never even reaching Amman or Jerash. In addition, it shouldn't be hard to find a Jordan add-on to an Egypt- or Israel-based tour from any number of mainstream tour operators worldwide. The advantage of these packages is that they get you a good-value flight-plus-accommodation deal; by booking a tour in advance you can end up staying in extremely comfortable places for bargain prices. The disadvantage, of course, becomes clear if you fancy an extra day or two on your own to explore Petra once you get there.

However, where fixing up an organized tour ahead of time really comes into its own is if you have a particular kind of holiday in mind. If you want to know all about Jordan's wealth of archeology, take a concentrated diving course, or if you have your heart set on sighting a Sinai rosefinch, specialist tour operators can sell you ready-made all-in packages or tailor a particular tour to suit your requirements. Adventure companies can often throw in activities such as camel-trekking, desert camping or snorkelling, and many operators specialize in pilgrimage tours to sites of biblical interest. You can also arrange worthwhile tours once you've arrived; see p.76 for a list of specialist operators in Jordan.

From the UK and Ireland

Flying to Amman from the UK or Ireland, there are daily nonstop services from London Heathrow (flight time is around 4hr 45min); from elsewhere, you'll have to change planes in London or, often more economically, in hubs such as Paris, Amsterdam or Vienna.

Flights rarely depart chock-a-block full, and the three-, six- or even twelve-month tickets offered by the big carriers are generally quite flexible, with no particular requirements for advance booking, plus either free or inexpensive date-changes permitted. However, for departures throughout spring, summer and autumn, you should book as far in advance as possible to snap up the cheapest fares.

From **London**, Royal Jordanian and British Mediterranean (a franchisee of British Airways) both fly nonstop from **Heathrow** to Amman. If you're looking to fly out of **Gatwick**, **Stansted** or **London City**, your best bet is likely to be on KLM, although you may find a bargain on Cyprus Airways from Stansted via Larnaca. From **the rest of the UK**, the most convenient options tend to be with Air France or KLM: both have plenty of flights from airports all round Britain into their hubs, from where both fly on to Amman.

Low-season return **fares** on RJ or BA for direct Heathrow flights are around £360–410; in high season add £50–80. Changing planes at a European hub can save you plenty. Rock-bottom prices on Tarom Romanian Airlines' Heathrow–Amman jaunt via Bucharest can drop to £230. Fares on Austrian, Air France, Lufthansa, KLM and Turkish tend to hover either side of £350.

Jordan's first-ever charter flights from Britain ran throughout the 2004–05 winter season – from London Gatwick **nonstop to Aqaba**. Last-minute seat-only fares on these or other package deals (advertised widely in newspaper travel sections) are likely to be very competitively priced: you could snap up full packages (return flight plus seven nights' accommodation and guided trips) for just £400–500, with late-booking deals dropping as low as £200 – well worth grabbing, even if you then abandon the itinerary and head off on your own.

From the **Republic of Ireland**, you're looking at one of the big European carriers out of **Dublin**: Austrian via Vienna, Air

France via Paris and Lufthansa via Frankfurt are all around €550–575 return high season, €450–475 low.

Airlines in the UK and Ireland

Aer Lingus UK ☏0845/084 4444, Republic of Ireland ☏0818/365 000, 🌐www.aerlingus.ie. Frequent Dublin–Heathrow shuttles.

Air France UK ☏0845/359 1000, Republic of Ireland ☏01/605 0383, 🌐www.airfrance.co.uk. Flights into Paris CDG from all round Britain and Ireland, connecting with onward service to Amman.

Austrian Airlines UK ☏0845/601 0948, 🌐www.aua.com. Shuttles from London Heathrow and Dublin to Vienna connect with onward flights to Amman.

British Mediterranean UK ☏0870/850 9850, Republic of Ireland ☏1800/626 747, 🌐www.ba.com. This British Airways franchisee operates nonstop from London Heathrow to Amman. You can book through from airports around Britain and Ireland to connect at Heathrow.

Cyprus Airways UK ☏020/8359 1333, 🌐www.cyprusairways.com. Flights into Larnaca from London Heathrow and Stansted connect well with onward Amman service.

EgyptAir UK ☏020/7734 2343, 🌐www.egyptair.com.eg. Flights from London and Manchester to Cairo, from where you can stopover on your way to Amman.

KLM UK ☏0870/507 4074, 🌐www.klm.com. Flights from Amsterdam to Amman, benefiting from a network of connections feeding into Amsterdam from all round Britain.

Lufthansa UK ☏0845/773 7747, Republic of Ireland ☏01/844 5544, 🌐www.lufthansa.com. Connections from British and Irish airports into Frankfurt for the onward Amman flight.

Middle East Airlines (MEA) UK ☏020/7493 5681, 🌐www.mea.com.lb. Lebanese carrier flies London Heathrow to Beirut, giving time to stopover before continuing to Amman.

Royal Jordanian UK ☏020/7878 6300, Republic of Ireland ☏061/474 995 or 1800/481 049, 🌐www.rja.com.jo. Nonstop from London Heathrow to Amman.

Tarom Romanian Airlines UK ☏020/7224 3693, 🌐www.tarom.ro. London Heathrow to Amman via Bucharest.

Turkish Airlines UK ☏020/7766 9300, 🌐www.thy.com. London Heathrow to Amman via Istanbul.

Travel agents in the UK and Ireland

UK

Bridge the World ☏0870/443 2399, 🌐www.bridgetheworld.com. Good-value flight deals,

round-the-world tickets and tailor-made packages, all aimed at the backpacker market.

Cheapflights 🌐www.cheapflights.co.uk. Flight deals, travel agents, plus links to other travel sites.

Co-op Travel Care ☏0870/112 0085, 🌐www.travelcareonline.com. Flights and holidays from the UK's largest independent travel agent. Non-partisan and informed advice.

ebookers ☏0870/010 7000, 🌐www.ebookers.com. Low fares on scheduled flights and package deals.

Expedia 🌐www.expedia.co.uk. Discount airfares, all-airline search engine and daily deals.

Flightcentre ☏0870/890 8099, 🌐www.flightcentre.co.uk. Rock-bottom fares.

Flights4Less ☏0871/222 3423, 🌐www.flights4less.co.uk. Good discount airfares. Part of Lastminute.com.

Flynow ☏0870/444 0045, 🌐www.flynow.com. Large range of discounted tickets.

Kelkoo 🌐www.kelkoo.co.uk. Useful price-comparison site, checking several sources of low-cost flights (and other goods and services) according to specific criteria.

Lastminute.com 🌐www.lastminute.com. Last-minute holiday package and flight-only deals.

North South Travel ☏01245/608 291, 🌐www.northsouthtravel.co.uk. Friendly, competitive travel agency, offering discounted fares worldwide. Profits are used to support projects in the developing world, especially the promotion of sustainable tourism.

Premier Travel ☏028/7126 3333, 🌐www.premiertravel.uk.com. Discount flight specialists based in Northern Ireland.

Priceline 🌐www.priceline.co.uk. Name-your-own-price website that has deals at around forty percent off standard fares.

STA Travel ☏0870/160 0599, 🌐www.statravel.co.uk. Worldwide specialists in low-cost flights, overland and holiday deals. Good discounts for students and under-26s.

Top Deck ☏020/7244 8000, 🌐www.topdecktravel.co.uk. Long-established agent dealing in discount flights and tours.

Trailfinders ☏020/7938 3939, 🌐www.trailfinders.com. One of the best-informed and most efficient agents for independent travellers.

Travel Bag ☏0870/890 1456, 🌐www.travelbag.co.uk. Discount deals.

Travel Care ☏0870/112 0085, 🌐www.travelcare.co.uk. Flights and holiday deals.

Travelocity 🌐www.travelocity.co.uk. Destination guides, hot fares and great deals for car rental, accommodation and lodging.

Republic of Ireland

ebookers ☎01/241 5689, ⓦwww.ebookers.ie.
Low fares on scheduled flights and package deals.
First Choice Travel ☎01/834 1111, ⓦwww
.firstchoicetravel.ie. Good-value flights.
Joe Walsh Tours ☎01/676 0991, ⓦwww
.joewalshtours.ie. Long-established general budget
fares and holidays agent.
Lee Travel ☎021/427 7111, ⓦwww.leetravel.ie.
Flights and holidays.
McCarthys Travel ☎021/427 0127, ⓦwww
.mccarthystravel.ie. Established travel agent, part of
the Worldchoice chain of travel shops.
Trailfinders ☎01/677 7888, ⓦwww.trailfinders
.ie. One of the best-informed and most efficient
agents for independent travellers.
USIT ☎0818/200 020, ⓦwww.usit.ie. Specialists
in student, youth and independent travel – flights,
trains, study tours, TEFL, visas and more.
World Travel Centre ☎01/416 7007, ⓦwww
.worldtravel.ie. Excellent fares.

Tour operators in the UK

General cultural/historical

Abercrombie & Kent ☎0845/070 0612, ⓦwww
.abercrombiekent.co.uk. Upmarket tours and tailor-
made trips.
Ancient World Tours ☎020/7917 9494, ⓦwww
.ancient.co.uk. Archeological, historical and cultural
itineraries around Jordan and Syria.
Andante Travels ☎01722/713800, ⓦwww
.andantetravels.co.uk. Small-scale, personalized,
expert-led archeological/historical tours around Jordan.
Arabian Odyssey ☎01242/224482, ⓦwww
.arabianodyssey.co.uk. Classic escorted cultural tour
of the country's highlights.
Bales Worldwide ☎0870/752 0780, ⓦwww
.balesworldwide.com. One of the biggest operators
to Jordan – a family-owned company offering
high-quality escorted tours as well as tailor-made
itineraries.
Cox & Kings ☎020/7873 5000, ⓦwww
.coxandkings.co.uk. Highly respected and long-
established company offering gilt-edged cultural and
historical tours to Jordan.
Dragoman ☎0870/499 4470, ⓦwww.dragoman
.co.uk. Extended overland journeys in purpose-built
expedition vehicles; itineraries such as Istanbul–Cairo
(4 weeks) pass through Jordan.
Elite Vacations ☎01707/371000, ⓦwww
.elitevacations.com. Cultural historical tours of
Jordan, in conjunction with Syria and Lebanon.
Far Frontiers ☎01285/850926. Classic 10-day
historical tours of Jordan.

Indus Tours ☎020/8901 7320, ⓦwww
.industours.co.uk. Expert-led cultural tours of Jordan,
specifically focusing on allowing time for painting and
creative art.
Kumuka Worldwide ☎020/7937 8855, ⓦwww
.kumuka.com. "Soft" adventure trips and overland
expeditions around the Middle East that include
Jordan.
Kuoni ☎01306/747002, ⓦwww.kuoni.co.uk.
Large holiday operator, with a range of trips to
Jordan.
Longwood Holidays ☎020/8551 4494, ⓦwww
.longwoodholidays.co.uk. Straightforward off-the-
peg package tours, flying in and out of Ovda airport
(outside Eilat, Israel) on charter flights.
Martin Randall Travel ☎020/8742 3355,
ⓦwww.martinrandall.com. Small-group cultural
tours, led by experts on art and archeology.
Noble Caledonia ☎020/7752 0000, ⓦwww
.noble-caledonia.co.uk. Cultural and historical tour of
the main sights in the country.
Prospect Tours ☎020/7486 5704, ⓦwww
.prospecttours.com. Small-group cultural tours.
Silk Road Tours ☎020/7371 3131, ⓦwww
.silkroadtours.co.uk. Cultural trips around the Middle
East, passing through Jordan on the way.
Somak Holidays ☎020/8423 3000, ⓦwww
.somak.co.uk. Historical and cultural adventures in
Jordan.
Steppes East ☎01285/651010, ⓦwww
.steppeseast.co.uk. Expertly prepared and presented
tailor-mades and escorted tours.
Temple World ☎020/8940 4114, ⓦwww
.templeworld.com. Tailor-made historical and cultural
holidays.
Titan HiTours ☎01293/455345, ⓦwww
.titantravel.co.uk. Classic escorted tours of major
historical sites.
Travelsphere Holidays ☎0870/240 2426,
ⓦwww.travelsphere.co.uk. Off-the-peg holidays to
Jordan, alone or in combination with Egypt.
Tribes Travel ☎01728/685971, ⓦwww.tribes
.co.uk. Tailor-made trips that explore Jordan's natural
environment, working with the Royal Society for the
Conservation of Nature.
Voyages Jules Verne ☎0845/166 7000, ⓦwww
.vjv.com. Major Jordan operator, with a range of
holiday options all round the country.

Adventure/outdoors specialists

Adventure Company ☎01420/541007, ⓦwww
.adventurecompany.co.uk. Guided "soft" adventure
trips for individuals and families.
Adventure Peaks ☎015394/47301, ⓦwww
.adventurepeaks.com. Courses in rock-climbing,
scrambling and outdoor adventures in Wadi Rum.

Arabica Travel ☎ 020/7640 2332,
ⓔ arabica@annal.dircon.co.uk. Specialists in
eco-friendly small-group trips, run by a team with
an intimate and wide-ranging knowledge of Jordan.
Works closely with the RSCN and other environmental
organizations, and donates part of its income to local
conservation charities.

ATG Oxford ☎ 01865/315678, ⓦ www.atg-oxford
.co.uk. High-quality adventure tours, concentrating
on Dana and Petra and including some excellent long
walks.

Desert Discoveries ☎ 020/7616 1091, ⓦ www
.desertdiscoveries.co.uk. Luxury tailor-made trips
into the deep desert, covering off-road terrain, from
Bayir and Jafr to Petra and Rum, in plush air-con
vehicles. Accommodation, when not in open country,
is at five-star hotels.

Discover the World ☎ 01737/218802, ⓦ www
.discover-the-world.co.uk. Well-established wildlife
holiday specialist, offering specialist-led tours for school
groups to Jordan's nature reserves and major sites.

Equitour ☎ 01606/819182, ⓦ www.equitour.co.uk.
Tours on horseback around Petra or Wadi Rum.

Exodus ☎ 0870/240 5550, ⓦ www.exodus
.co.uk. Small-group adventure tour operators, with
specialist programmes including walking, trekking,
scrambling and cycling.

Explore ☎ 0870/333 4001, ⓦ www.explore
.co.uk. A wide range of small-group tours, treks,
expeditions and safaris, staying mostly in small hotels
or Bedouin tents.

Headwater ☎ 01606/720099, ⓦ www.headwater
.com. Excellent guided walking tours, outside high
summer.

High Places ☎ 0114/275 7500, ⓦ www
.highplaces.co.uk. Great-value trekking and climbing
holidays in Wadi Rum and Petra.

Imaginative Traveller ☎ 020/8742 8612,
ⓦ www.imaginative-traveller.com. Well-respected
adventure operator with a good range of tours.

In The Saddle ☎ 01299/272997, ⓦ www
.inthesaddle.com. High-quality tours around Petra
and Wadi Rum on horseback.

Naturetrek ☎ 01962/733051, ⓦ www.naturetrek
.co.uk. Acknowledged leaders in birdwatching and
botanical holidays worldwide, operating regular
small-group tours to Jordan with sympathetic expert
guidance. Their spring and winter tours cover every
nook and cranny for birders in the country, from Dana
to the Aqaba sewage works.

Nomadic Thoughts ☎ 020/7604 4408, ⓦ www
.nomadicthoughts.com. Tailor-made trips to Jordan.

NOMADS ☎ 01457/873231, ⓦ www.nomadstravel
.co.uk. Small operation run by Tony Howard and Di
Taylor, the British climbing duo who opened up Rum to
international tourism twenty years ago. They provide

detailed, knowledgeable advice on all aspects of
independent exploration of Jordan's wilder corners.

Original Travel ☎ 020/7978 7333, ⓦ www
.originaltravel.co.uk. Diverse company focusing on
short adventure breaks, including a packed five days
in Jordan.

Ossian Guides ☎ 0870/757 6774, ⓦ www
.ossianguides.co.uk. Excellent small company
running memorable walking and climbing trips to
Jordan, specifically in and around Rum.

Ride World Wide ☎ 01837/82544, ⓦ www
.rideworldwide.co.uk. High-quality horse-riding
holidays in Wadi Rum.

Walks Worldwide ☎ 01524/242000, ⓦ www
.walksworldwide.com. Leading walking and outdoors
operator to Jordan, with a broad range of tours to suit
all levels of capability, including family trips. Highly
recommended.

Wildlife Wilderness ☎ 01625/530035, ⓦ www
.wildlifewilderness.com. High-quality tailor-made
trips, covering anything from culture and history to
Jordan's nature reserves.

Diving specialists

Aquatours ☎ 0870/442 3288, ⓦ www.aquatours
.com. Jordan diving specialist, which tags itself as
offering "adventures for the thinking diver", combining
underwater trips with classic cultural itineraries.

Scubasnacks ☎ 0870/746 1266, ⓦ www
.scubasnacks.co.uk. Well-respected dive operator,
with a variety of programmes focused on Aqaba.

Spa packages

Erna Low/Body & Soul Holidays ☎ 020/7594
0290, ⓦ www.bodyandsoulholidays.info. Luxury
spa packages to the five-star resort hotels on the
Dead Sea.

Spa Luxury ☎ 0870/747 5765, ⓦ www.spaluxury
.com. Package deals to the spa resorts on the Dead
Sea, with or without flights.

Thermalia ☎ 0870/165 9420, ⓦ www.thermalia
.co.uk. Spa specialists, with a range of deals to the
Dead Sea resort hotels.

Pilgrimage tours

Guiding Star ⓦ www.guidingstar2.com. A leading
pilgrimage operator based at offices in Jerusalem,
Bethlehem and Amman, with forty years' experience.
Combining Christian sites with adventure excursions
and cultural exploration, they are exceptionally well
connected, and can design a unique itinerary on
demand.

ITS ☎ 0870/794 3333, ⓦ www.itstravel.co.uk.
Short trips for pilgrims, added on to an Israel-based
itinerary.

Maranatha Tours ☎01753/689568, ⓦwww
.maranatha.co.uk. Specialist in biblical pilgrimage
tours to Jordan and around the Middle East.
Mastersun ☎020/8942 9442, ⓦwww.mastersun
.co.uk. Christian holidays, covering points of biblical
interest around Jordan.
McCabe Pilgrimages ☎020/8675 6828, ⓦwww
.mccabe-travel.co.uk. Pilgrim tours to Jordan, often
in conjunction with the Sinai (Egypt).
Pilgrim Travel ☎01306/375345, ⓦwww
.pilgrimtraveluk.ltd.uk. Leading operator of church
tours to Jordan and other Middle East destinations.
Sam Smith Travel ☎01446/774018, ⓦwww
.samsmithtravel.com. Small firm specializing in
pilgrimages and trips to Petra.
World Wide Christian Travel ☎0845/458 8308,
ⓦ www.christian-travel.com. Biblical and pilgrimage
tours to Jordan and around the Middle East.

From the US and Canada

The most convenient **flights** from North
America are on Royal Jordanian nonstop
to Amman out of New York, Chicago and
Detroit. RJ's codeshare deal with America
West means you can ticket through to
Amman easily from anywhere on America
West's extensive domestic network. In
addition, virtually all European airlines can
fly you from major US and Canadian cities
to Amman easily, if relatively expensively,
with a change of plane at their hub airport.
If you're weaving Jordan into a longer journey, consider choosing a less expensive
deal on a flight into another Middle Eastern
airport, notably Cairo or Tel Aviv, with a view
to grabbing a local shuttle flight or proceeding overland from there (see p.38 for more).
Flight time is eleven hours from the East
Coast, twelve hours from the central time-
zones, fifteen hours from the West Coast,
not including stops on the ground. The
sample fares we give below are round-trip,
including taxes.

From the US, Royal Jordanian offers
nonstop or one-stop flights to Amman from
JFK, Chicago and Detroit, plus code-share
routings from all round the US that require
a change of plane. A whole raft of US and
European airlines fly direct to major cities
in Europe, then separately on to Amman;
the most accessible are Air France, British Airways, Delta, Northwest/KLM and
United. From New York, high-season **fares**
on Royal Jordanian are a bargain $1200 or

so, with virtually all other carriers hovering
around $1400; in the low season, it's easy
to find fares not much higher than $900. As
an indication of fares from around the US,
on a European carrier flying out of Chicago
in the high season, you're looking at around
$1500, in the low season, around $1000;
equivalents from Los Angeles are $1900
and $1300. Generally, if you fly with RJ, you
can add on a domestic flight from Amman to
Aqaba at no extra cost.

Flying **from Canada**, it shouldn't be hard
to pick up a round-trip high-season ticket
on any of several airlines from Montréal or
Toronto for around C$1600, from Vancouver
for C$2000. Both drop by around C$200 in
the low season.

Airlines in North America

Air Canada ☎1-888/247-2262, ⓦwww
.aircanada.com. Connections into Toronto and
Montréal for flights to London, then on to Amman.
Air France US ☎1-800/237-2747, Canada
☎1-800/667-2747, ⓦwww.airfrance.com. Flights
from Toronto, Montréal and several US cities to Paris,
connecting to Amman.
America West ☎1-800/235-9292, ⓦwww
.americawest.com. Extensive US network,
codesharing with Royal Jordanian to Amman.
British Airways ☎1-800/247-9297, ⓦwww
.ba.com. Flights to London from many US and
Canadian cities, with connecting flights on to Amman.
Delta ☎1-800/241-4141, ⓦwww.delta.com.
Flights from around the US to Amman via Paris.
EgyptAir US ☎1-800/334-6787 or 212/315-0900,
Canada ☎416/960-0009, ⓦwww.egyptair.com.eg.
Flights to Cairo nonstop from New York and one-stop
from LA and Montréal, with connections to Amman.
Northwest/KLM US ☎1-800/447-4747, Canada
☎514/397-0775, ⓦwww.klm.com. Daily flights
to Amsterdam from most major cities in the US and
Canada, with good connections onward to Amman.
Royal Jordanian US ☎1-800/223-0470 or
212/949-0050, Canada ☎1-800/363-0711, ⓦwww
.rja.com.jo. Nonstop flights to Amman from New York
JFK, Chicago and Detroit, plus plenty of code-share
connections from other North American cities.
United Airlines ☎1-800/538-2929, ⓦwww
.united.com. Flights to Amman via Frankfurt.

Travel agents in North America

Air Brokers International ☎1-800/883-3273,
ⓦwww.airbrokers.com. Consolidator and specialist
in Round-the-World tickets.

Airtech ☎ 212/219-7000, ⓦ www.airtech.com.
Standby seat broker; also deals in consolidator fares.
Airtreks ☎ 1-877/AIRTREKS, ⓦ www.airtreks.com.
Round-the-World tickets. The website features an
interactive database that lets you build and price your
own itinerary.
Cheapflights ⓦ www.cheapflights.com (in US),
ⓦ www.cheapflights.ca (in Canada). Flight deals,
travel agents, plus links to other travel sites.
Cheaptickets US ☎ 1-888/922-8849, ⓦ www
.cheaptickets.com. Discount flight specialists.
Educational Travel Center ☎ 1-800/747-5551
or 608/256-5551, ⓦ www.edtrav.com. Low-cost
fares worldwide, student/youth discount offers, car
rental and tours.
Expedia ⓦ www.expedia.com (in US), ⓦ www
.expedia.ca (in Canada). Discount airfares, all-airline
search engine and daily deals.
Flightcentre US ☎ 1-866/WORLD-51, ⓦ www
.flightcentre.us, Canada ☎ 1-888/WORLD-55,
ⓦ www.flightcentre.ca. Rock-bottom fares
worldwide.
Hotwire.com ⓦ www.hotwire.com (US only).
Last-minute savings of up to forty percent on regular
published fares. Travellers must be at least 18 and
there are no refunds, transfers or changes allowed.
Log-in required.
New Frontiers US ☎ 1-800/677-0720, ⓦ www
.newfrontiers.com. Discount travel firm.
Priceline ⓦ www.priceline.com (in US). Name-
your-own-price website that has deals at around forty
percent off standard fares.
Skyauction ⓦ www.skyauction.com (in US).
Auctions tickets and travel packages to destinations
worldwide.
STA Travel US ☎ 1-800/329-9537, Canada ☎ 1-
888/427-5639, ⓦ www.statravel.com. Worldwide
specialists in independent travel; also student IDs,
travel insurance, car rental, rail passes, and more.
Student Flights ☎ 1-800/255-8000 or 480/951-
1177, ⓦ www.isecard.com/studentflights. Student/
youth fares, plus student IDs.
TFI Tours ☎ 1-800/745-8000 or 212/736-1140,
ⓦ www.lowestairprice.com. Well-established
consolidator with a wide variety of global fares.
Travel Avenue ☎ 1-800/333-3335, ⓦ www
.travelavenue.com. Full-service travel agent that
offers discounts in the form of rebates.
Travel Cuts US ☎ 1-800/592-CUTS, Canada
☎ 1-888/246-9762, ⓦ www.travelcuts.com.
Popular, long-established student-travel organization,
with worldwide offers.
Travelers Advantage ☎ 1-877/259-2691,
ⓦ www.travelersadvantage.com. Discount travel
club, with cash-back deals and discounted car rental.
Membership required (US$1 for 3 months' trial).

Travelocity ⓦ www.travelocity.com (in US),
ⓦ www.travelocity.ca (in Canada). Destination
guides, hot fares and great deals for car rental,
accommodation and lodging.
Travelosophy US ☎ 1-800/332-2687, ⓦ www
.itravelosophy.com. Good range of discounted and
student fares worldwide.
Worldtek Travel ☎ 1-800/243-1723, ⓦ www
.worldtek.com. Discount travel agency for worldwide
travel.

Tour operators in North America

Abercrombie & Kent ☎ 1-800/323-7308 or
630/954-2944, ⓦ www.abercrombiekent.com.
Plenty of top-end, fully escorted tours to Jordan and
its neighbours.
Absolute Asia ☎ 1-800/736-8187, ⓦ www
.absoluteasia.com. Luxury tours with all the
trimmings.
Adventure Center ☎ 1-800/228-8747 or
510/654-1879, ⓦ www.adventurecenter.com.
Hiking and "soft adventure" specialists.
Adventures Abroad ☎ 1-800/665-3998 or
604/303-1099, ⓦ www.adventures-abroad.com.
Small-group adventure specialists, with a range of
offerings around the Middle East.
AER World Tours ☎ 1-800/492 0254 or 612/377-
9767, ⓦ www.aertours.com. Custom-designed
travel, in small groups with private guides.
Ancient Adventures ☎ 1-800/353-4978, ⓦ www
.ancientadventures.com. A range of tours all round
the Middle East, some historical/cultural, others
incorporating diving or "soft" adventure.
Bestway Tours Canada ☎ 1-800/663-0844,
ⓦ www.bestway.com. Cultural tours all round the
Middle East, including trips devoted solely to Jordan.
Caravan-Serai Tours ☎ 1-800/451-8097 or
206/545-1735, ⓦ www.caravan-serai.com. Leading
specialists to the Middle East and North Africa, with
a range of excellent, culturally aware tours to Jordan
and all across the region – breaking new ground in
Saudi Arabia, Syria, Libya and elsewhere too. Owned
and run by the award-winning, Jordanian-born
businesswoman Rita Zawaideh.
Cox and Kings ☎ 1-800/999-1758, ⓦ www
.coxandkingsusa.com. Long-established top-of-
the-range tour operator, with several Middle Eastern
offerings.
Destinations & Adventures International ☎ 1-
800/659-4599, ⓦ www.daitravel.com. Broad range
of Middle Eastern cultural trips, including extended
itineraries around Jordan.
Educational Travel Services ☎ 1-800/929-4387
ext 1590, ⓦ www.ets.travelwithus.com. Christian
pilgrimage tours.

Elderhostel ☎877/426-8056, ⓦwww.elderhostel
.org. Specialists in educational and activity
programmes for senior travellers, including journeys
around Syria and Jordan.
FreeGate Tourism ☎1-888/373-3428, ⓦwww
.freegatetours.com. A decent range of tours to the
eastern Mediterranean, including Jordan alone or in
combination with its neighbours.
Gateways International ☎1-800/268-0900,
ⓦwww.gateways-international.com. A range of
historical tours to the Middle East, including Jordan.
HLO Tours ☎1-800/736-4456, ⓦwww.hlotours
.com. Specialists in tailor-made trips, with many years
of experience in the Middle East.
IGM Tours ☎510/727-0380, ⓦwww.igmtours
.com. Wide-ranging biblical tours.
IsramWorld ☎1-800/223-7460, ⓦwww.isram
.com. Long-established tour operator with a diverse
selection of Middle Eastern offerings.
Key Tours ☎1-800/576-1784, ⓦwww.keytours
.com. Package deals to Amman or Petra.
Maranatha Tours ☎602/788-8864, ⓦwww
.maranathatours.com. Specialist in biblical pilgrimage
tours to Jordan and around the Middle East.
Sita World Travel ☎1-800/421-5643, ⓦwww
.sitatours.com. Cultural/historical trips around Jordan,
also with options to Egypt, Dubai and elsewhere in
the Middle East, plus tailor-mades. Also with offices
in Canada.
Spiekermann Travel ☎1-800/645-3233,
ⓦwww.mideasttrvl.com. Experts on Middle Eastern
travel, with tours all round the region, including
Jordan, Syria, Lebanon, Iran, Libya and elsewhere.
TCS Expeditions ☎1-800/727-7477, ⓦwww
.tcs-expeditions.com. Extraordinarily opulent tours
– by private jet, no less – to destinations worldwide,
including stops for Petra and Rum in Jordan. Current
price for this tour: $40,000.
Travcoa ☎1-800/992-2003, ⓦwww.travcoa
.com. Luxury escorted tours include extended trips
through Syria and Jordan.
Travel In Style ☎1-888/466-8242, ⓦwww
.travelinstyle.com. Specialists in the eastern
Mediterranean, with a good range of tours to Jordan
in three price categories, added on to their basic
packages to Egypt, Syria and Israel.
Travel Plans International ☎1-800/323-7600,
ⓦwww.travelplansintl.com. Cultural and historical
tours worldwide, including to Syria, Lebanon and
Jordan.
Trek Holidays Canada ☎1-888/456-3522,
ⓦwww.trekholidays.com. Details of dozens of
small-group adventure trips to Jordan run by various
different agents – well worth a browse.
Wilderness Travel ☎1-888/368-2794, ⓦwww
.wildernesstravel.com. Cultural, wildlife and

hiking trips, including to selected Middle Eastern
destinations.
Ya'lla Tours ☎1-800/644-1595, ⓦwww
.yallatours.com. Excellent tour operator specializing
in the Middle East, with a range of trips and packages
covering Jordan.

From Australia and New Zealand

There are no nonstop or direct flights to
Amman from Australasia. Your best option is
to fly on Middle Eastern or Asian airlines via
their hub cities; even if you manage to turn
up a better deal via Europe, the flight time
will end up being exhaustingly long.

The least expensive low-season return
fares to Amman from **Australia** that you're
likely to find are around A$1800; add A$250
in high season. From **New Zealand**, fares
start at NZ$2400, rising by NZ$500 or more
during high season.

Airlines in Australia and New Zealand

Air New Zealand Australia ☎13 2476, New
Zealand ☎0800/737 000, ⓦwww.airnz.com. From
Auckland to Singapore, then changes of plane needed
to reach Dubai and Amman.
EgyptAir Australia ☎02/9241 5696, ⓦwww
.egyptair.com.eg. Direct from Sydney to Cairo via
Singapore, plus onward hops to Amman. Also code-
sharing deals out of Melbourne and Brisbane.
Emirates Australia ☎1300/303 777 or 02/9290
9700, New Zealand ☎09/377 6004, ⓦwww
.emirates.com. Direct from Sydney and Melbourne
to Dubai via Singapore, for onward connections to
Amman.
Gulf Air Australia ☎02/9244 2199, New Zealand
☎09/308 3366, ⓦwww.gulfairco.com. Direct
from Sydney and Melbourne to Bahrain, with onward
Amman shuttles.
Malaysia Airlines Australia ☎13 2627, New
Zealand ☎0800/777 747, ⓦwww.malaysia
-airlines.com. Nonstop from Sydney, Melbourne,
Adelaide, Perth and Auckland to Kuala Lumpur, where
you'll find plenty of onward connections to Amman.
Middle East Airlines (MEA) ⓦwww.mea
.com.lb; phone contact via Malaysia Airlines. Direct
from Sydney to Beirut via Kuala Lumpur, plus short-
hop shuttles from Beirut to Amman.
Qantas Australia ☎13 1313, New Zealand
☎0800/808 767, ⓦwww.qantas.com.au. A wide
choice of flights from Australian cities to Southeast
Asian hubs for onward connections.

Royal Jordanian Australia ☎02/9244 2701, New Zealand ☎03/365 3910, ⊛www.rja.com.jo. Code-sharing with Malaysian from Sydney, Melbourne and Brisbane to Kuala Lumpur, and with Thai to Bangkok, and then direct from either of those to Amman. Also nonstop to Amman from Middle Eastern hubs such as Bahrain, Beirut, Cairo and Dubai.

Travel agents in Australia and New Zealand

Cheapflights ⊛www.cheapflights.com.au. Flight deals, travel agents, plus links to other travel sites.

Flight Centre Australia ☎13 31 33, ⊛www.flightcentre.com.au, New Zealand ☎0800 243 544, ⊛www.flightcentre.co.nz. Rock-bottom fares worldwide.

Holiday Shoppe New Zealand ☎0800/808 480, ⊛www.holidayshoppe.co.nz. Great deals on flights, hotels and holidays.

Lastminute.com ⊛www.lastminute.com.au (in Australia), ⊛www.lastminute.co.nz (in NZ). Last-minute holiday package and flight-only deals.

OTC Australia ☎1300/855 118, ⊛www.otctravel.com.au. Deals on flights, hotels and holidays.

STA Travel Australia ☎1300/733 035, New Zealand ☎0508/782 872, ⊛www.statravel.com. Worldwide specialists in low-cost flights, overlands and holiday deals. Good discounts for students and under-26s.

Student Uni Travel Australia ☎02/9232 8444, ⊛www.sut.com.au, New Zealand ☎09/379 4224, ⊛www.sut.co.nz. Great deals for students.

Trailfinders Australia ☎02/9247 7666, ⊛www.trailfinders.com.au. One of the best-informed and most efficient agents for independent travellers.

Travel Australia ☎1300/130 482 or 02/9249 5444, ⊛www.travel.com.au, New Zealand ☎0800/468 332, ⊛www.travel.co.nz. Comprehensive online travel company, with discounted fares.

Travelshop ☎1800/108108, ⊛www.travelshop.com.au. Discounted flights, packages and insurance.

Zuji ⊛www.zuji.com.au. Destination guides, hot fares and great deals for car rental, accommodation and lodging.

Tour operators in Australia and New Zealand

Abercrombie & Kent Australia ☎1300/851 800, New Zealand ☎0800/441 638, ⊛www.abercrombiekent.com.au. Classy operator with a strong reputation – upmarket luxury tours.

Adventure World Australia ☎1300/363 055, New Zealand ☎09/524 5118, ⊛www.adventureworld.com.au. Agents and wholesalers for a vast array of international adventure-travel companies – well worth a browse.

Kumuka Expeditions Australia ☎1800/804 277 or 02/9279 0491, ⊛www.kumuka.com. Independent tour operator specializing in overland expeditions, as well as local and private transport tours.

Martin Randall Travel Australia ☎1300/559 595, ⊛www.martinrandall.com. British company running small-group cultural tours. Expert lecturers on art, archeology and history give specialist insight, and accommodation is always comfortable.

Passport Travel Australia ☎03/9867 3888, ⊛www.travelcentre.com.au. Tour options on the Red Sea and around the Middle East.

Peregrine Adventures Australia ☎03/9663 8611, ⊛www.peregrine.net.au. Agent for a multitude of adventure companies all over the world, taking small groups on specialist programmes that include walking, biking, overlanding, adventure and cultural trips.

Sun Island Tours Australia ☎02/9283 3840, ⊛www.sunislandtours.com.au. Package holidays and full travel arrangements for the Middle East.

World Expeditions Australia ☎1300/720 000, ⊛www.worldexpeditions.com.au, New Zealand ☎0800/350 354, ⊛www.worldexpeditions.co.nz. Australian-owned adventure company, with a broad programme of trekking and adventure expeditions, including Jordan and Syria. There's a "challenging" brochure available for hardcore adventurers, and over-fifties are well catered for with a separate brochure.

Yalla Tours Australia ☎1300/362 844, ⊛www.yallatours.com.au. Middle East specialists.

Travel from neighbouring countries

Jordan is easily accessible from surrounding countries: land borders are open from all its neighbours, there's a regular, swift boat service from nearby Egypt, and Amman is closely linked into air routes around the Middle East. Most nationalities can pick up Jordanian visas on arrival at any border crossing, except the King Hussein (Allenby) Bridge.

From Syria

Many travellers arrive in Jordan on an overland Middle Eastern odyssey between Istanbul and Cairo, and routes into the country from the Syrian capital **Damascus**, barely 100km north of the Jordanian frontier, are plentiful and undemanding.

The easiest and fastest way in is by serveece, or shared taxi. These vehicles depart 24 hours a day from the northwestern corner of the Baramkeh Terminal (Karaj Baramkeh) in central Damascus. A seat in a serveece to Amman costs S£400 (JD6), to Irbid S£300 (JD4.500); some serveeces run to the less useful destinations of Zarqa and Mafraq. If you're in a hurry or prefer some privacy, you can pay five times the per-person rate to charter the whole car. Cars bound for Amman use the Nasib/Jaber border post, where formalities are dealt with swiftly and efficiently; you'll only use the route between Dera'a and Ramtha if you're heading for Irbid. Both border crossings have 24-hour banks. The usual serveece terminus in Amman is Abdali station (in Irbid the New Amman station); however, for a few extra dollars the driver can drop you off anywhere you want in those cities. Journey times to Amman can be as little as three hours, half an hour less to Irbid.

Comfortable Karnak and JETT **buses** also leave from the Baramkeh Terminal in Damascus (☎011/212 9515) daily at 7am and 3pm, bound for Amman. The fare is US$6 or JD5; you can't pay in Syrian pounds. Reckon on a journey time of four hours, since everyone must clear customs and immigration before the bus can carry on (which is one reason to go by serveece instead). Buses terminate next to the JFTT External Lines office, uphill from Abdali station. It's wise to book seats one day ahead. In summer, extra buses are laid on – as many as six a day.

For a more peaceful journey, once-weekly **trains** – sometimes pulled by vintage steam engines – depart from the Hejaz station in Damascus every Monday and Thursday at 8am for a nine-hour meander to Amman. The fare is a rock-bottom S£150 (US$3).

Most **flights** from Damascus to Amman are awkward early morning or late-night departures, prohibitively expensive and not worth bothering with. Time spent at both ends getting to and from the airports (both are 35km out of the city) plus an hour in the air adds up to a longer journey than by road. From Aleppo, however, the ninety-minute flight is a viable way to get to Amman with minimum fuss, if you can afford about US$185 one-way. The Royal Jordanian agent is Julia Dumna Travel, at 29 Ayyar Street in Damascus (☎011/232 2014), and Saadallah al-Gaberi Street in Aleppo (☎021/226 7959).

From Jerusalem, the West Bank and Gaza

No public transport runs directly between **Jerusalem** (or any West Bank city) and Amman: the only way to go is with a combination of bus, taxi and/or serveece. All traffic is funnelled towards the single border crossing open to the public (Mon–Thurs & Sun 7.30am–midnight, Fri & Sat 7.30am–2pm; ☎02/994 2302 or 940 7444), known to the Jordanians as the **King Hussein Bridge** (Jissr al-Malek Hussein) and to the Palestinians and the Israelis as the **Allenby Bridge** (Jissr Allenby in Arabic; Gesher Allenby in Hebrew). On a good day, the journey can take as little as two hours; on a bad day, or after dark, it can be more than five. This

The Israeli stamps question

If you intend to visit Israel, the West Bank or Gaza as part of a longer journey in the region, you need to bear in mind that almost all Middle Eastern and North African countries except Egypt, Jordan, Tunisia and Morocco refuse entry to people with **evidence of a visit to Israel** in their passports. "Evidence" includes not only specifically Israeli stamps, but also entry or exit stamps from the Jordanian border-posts at the Sheikh Hussein (Jordan River) Bridge, the King Hussein (Allenby) Bridge and the Wadi Araba (Yitzhak Rabin) crossing (Aqaba–Eilat), as well as stamps from the Egyptian border-posts at Taba near Eilat, and Rafah in northern Sinai. (It formerly also included arrival stamps from Amman's second airport at Marka "Amman Civil Airport" once served by flights from Israel and Gaza – but there have been no flights from Gaza for some years, and flights from Tel Aviv now land at Amman's Queen Alia International Airport thus showing no evidence of where they originated.) **Visas** issued in Israel for travel to any country, and inbound or outbound flight tickets mentioning Tel Aviv (or TLV) will also bar you from travelling in Syria, Lebanon and elsewhere, as will anything in Hebrew discovered in your belongings: searches are common.

The best advice is to construct your itinerary so that you **visit Israel last**, after Syria and the rest. Alternatively, you can apply in your home country, well in advance, for a **second passport**: most Western countries issue these to people travelling around the Middle East as a matter of routine, but it's then up to you to ensure that your tally of entry and exit stamps in each passport adds up, and that you don't hand the wrong passport over to the wrong border official.

The only foolproof method of avoiding trouble, while holding only one passport, is to enter Jordan by air, sea or across the land borders from Syria, Iraq or Saudi Arabia, then use *only* the King Hussein (Allenby) Bridge to cross from Jordan to the West Bank and back, while making sure that your Jordanian visa does not expire in the meantime. At this bridge Israeli and Jordanian immigration officials will routinely stamp you both in and out on a **piece of paper** if you ask, thus avoiding any permanent evidence of having been "on the other side" (as many travellers refer to Israel, to avoid detection by eavesdropping officials). There are no formal borders around Palestinian-controlled areas of the West Bank and once you're over the bridge, you – as a foreigner – can come and go as you please between the West Bank, Jerusalem and Israel.

It's a well-known ploy of travellers who have unwittingly acquired evidence of an Israeli visit to **lose their passports** deliberately in Egypt or Jordan and apply for new ones from their embassies. However, after several years of stamping visas into unsullied passports, Syrian consulates have finally cottoned on to the scam. These days it's almost impossible to get a Syrian visa outside your home capital anyway, but even were you to try, an unused passport issued in Cairo or Amman is as much evidence to Syrian consular officials of a visit to "Occupied Palestine" (as Syrian visa application forms put it) as a border stamp is. Even if the loss of your old passport was genuine, you may still find yourself refused entry to Syria on this suspicion.

crossing-point is also notoriously subject to the ebb and flow of Middle Eastern politics, and is often closed at short notice.

A diplomatic anomaly left over from pre-peace-treaty days is that Jordan does not issue any **visas** to visitors entering the country via this bridge. Despite the peace treaty with Israel, and Jordan's recognition of Palestinian autonomy, a complex piece of official doublethink leads to the bridge not being viewed as an international border. The most noticeable upshot of this is that no Jordanian flags fly over the bridge, and if you don't already hold a Jordanian visa, you'll be turned back by Israeli passport control at the bridge terminal.

Israeli buses from West Jerusalem don't run to the bridge. The way to go is with the fast and convenient serveeces (shared taxis) departing frequently from **East Jerusalem** direct to the bridge; the two most efficient companies are Abdo, opposite Damascus Gate (℡02/628 3281), and Star/Nijmah, down an alley just beyond the bus station (℡02/627 6699). Bear in mind that locals set out early: you're best off either turning up first thing in the morning, or booking seats at least a couple of hours ahead. The standard serveece fare is NIS35 or JD6 per person. By mid-afternoon, when serveeces will have stopped for the day, your only certain option is a taxi for around NIS130. Depending on the political situation there may be buses running from Damascus Gate direct to the bridge, for around NIS25. If you're starting from elsewhere in the **West Bank**, serveeces and buses usually run to the bridge from most towns, including Bethlehem, Ramallah and Jericho, although transport throughout the West Bank is prone to disruption.

Once you're at the bridge terminal, signs will direct you to a small bank where you pay the exorbitant Israeli **departure tax**, currently NIS140 or JD25 or US$35 – payable in shekels only or by credit card (make sure you get a receipt). If you intend using your passport for overland travel beyond Jordan, be sure to tell the Israeli and Jordanian passport officials to stamp the loose immigration forms only – not your passport. You'll be directed to wait for a bus for which you must pay JD2 (in dinars only), which will make the short drive across no-man's-land and the bridge itself to the Jordanian arrivals terminal. Once you're through the formalities, loitering serveece drivers will nab you for the one-hour ride direct to Abdali station in Amman (JD3 per person). If you turn left from the serveece stand, left again through an unmarked door into the locals' arrivals hall, then left through the glass doors, you'll discover another serveece and bus stand; occasional buses from here take about twice as long as the serveece for the uphill grind to Abdali (JD2), while others head for Zarqa and Salt.

Gaza International Airport – opened in 1998, and formerly linked to Amman by regular flights – had its runway ripped up by Israeli bulldozers in 2002 and, at the time of writing, remains out of action.

From Tel Aviv, Nazareth and Eilat

There are two land crossing-points between **Israel** and Jordan. Buses of Trust International Transport run from Tel Aviv and Nazareth to Irbid and Amman via the **Sheikh Hussein Bridge** (Mon–Thurs & Sun 6.30am–10pm, Fri & Sat 8am–8pm; ℡04/609 3400 or 640 0670), located about 6km from the northern Israeli town of Bet She'an and also known as the Jordan Bridge or **Jordan River Crossing**. A hefty Israeli departure tax is levied here, currently NIS75 (US$17 or JD12). From **Tel Aviv**, buses depart from the Central Bus Station (daily 3.30pm except Sat; NIS150 or JD21). From Lower **Nazareth**, departures are from the Trust office (daily 4.45pm; NIS130 or JD18; ℡04/646 6660). All these buses drop off in Irbid at the Trust office near Safeway, and terminate in Amman at the Trust office next to the Royal Jordanian building off 7th Circle. It's possible to cross independently, with a shared taxi from Bet She'an to the terminal (about NIS10), a bus across the bridge itself (NIS4) and then either a taxi on to Irbid (about JD10) or Amman (JD25), or a hitch out to the main road for the minibuses running between Shuneh ash-Shamaliyyeh and Dayr Alla.

The other crossing-point from Israel is in the south, between the Red Sea resort towns of Eilat and Aqaba, known to the Israelis as the **Yitzhak Rabin** or **Arava crossing** (Mon–Thurs & Sun 6.30am–10pm, Fri & Sat 8am–8pm; ℡08/633 6811), and to the Jordanians as the **Wadi Araba** or Southern crossing. From **Eilat** Central Bus Station, it's reached most easily by taking a taxi (around NIS30) or by simply walking 2km to the border. There's an Israeli departure tax of NIS75 (US$17 or JD12). Once

Details of fees, regulations and transport for crossing into Jordan via the King Hussein/Allenby Bridge, the Sheikh Hussein/Jordan River Bridge and the Rabin/Wadi Araba border are given at the Israel Airports Authority site ⊛www.iaa.gov.il.

you're through the formalities, serveeces do the five-kilometre run into central Aqaba for JD1 per person, or JD4 for the car. Note the tip on p.41 regarding free entry visas to Aqaba.

Private vehicles can cross at the Jordan River/Sheikh Hussein bridge and the Rabin/Araba border (not at Allenby/King Hussein), with all the requisite paperwork. The fees, payable as you cross, total around JD50 for translation of registration papers, changing plates and buying compulsory Jordanian insurance for a week (JD70 for a month).

It saves a great deal of time to **fly** from Tel Aviv's Ben Gurion Airport to Amman, and this also offers the extra lure of flying low over spectacular scenery of desert hills and the Dead Sea. At the time of writing, only Royal Jordanian (℡03/516 5566) operates this route; El Al (℡03/972 2333) has suspended its service. All flights go to Amman's Queen Alia International Airport; the route to Marka Airport has been dropped. Fares are around US$100 one-way, US$175 for a three-month return, US$200 for a year's open return (taxes included). Flight time is about thirty minutes.

From Egypt

Buses do run from **Cairo** all the way through to Amman, though you'd have to have masochistic tendencies to embark on such a long ride voluntarily. Jordanian JETT and Egyptian SuperJet buses make the 21-hour trek four times weekly, departing either from the Arab Union Bus Company office (℡02/290-9017) at Midan Almaza in Heliopolis (Masr el-Gedida) or from the Turgoman Garage in Bulaq (℡02/579-8181). The fare, which includes the Nuweiba–Aqaba ferry crossing, is US$76, payable only in dollars.

However, the time-honoured method of getting from Egypt to Jordan involves a leisurely few days or more spent exploring the **Sinai**, from where there are a few possibilities for crossing into Jordan. The town of Nuweiba, 70km north of Dahab, is linked to Aqaba by a daily ferry and catamaran service operated by Arab Bridge Maritime (℡02/419-8657 or 356-2670, Ⓦwww.abmaritime.com.jo), which runs to a notoriously unreliable timetable. Although there are many **ticket outlets** in Cairo and elsewhere, it's perfectly

safe to wait to buy your ticket until you get to Nuweiba Port (℡069/520-365 or 520-216), some 8km south of Nuweiba town. Slow **ferries** depart daily around 3pm and take up to three hours to do the crossing for a fare of US$35, while the **catamaran** departs daily around 2pm and takes one hour; it costs US$46 in economy or US$66 in first-class (all are inclusive of tax, payable in dollars only). On boarding, you'll have to hand over your passport, which will be returned to you at Aqaba passport control, where all Western nationalities can get a Jordanian entry visa (for more on Aqaba visas, see p.41). Once you're through the formalities, serveeces stand poised to whisk you the 9km into Aqaba for JD1 per person.

When demand is high (during the summer, at the end of Ramadan for Eid al-Fitr, and around the hajj and Eid al-Adha), many more departures are laid on, both ferry and catamaran – and, an additional, catamaran service starts up between **Sharm el-Sheikh** and Aqaba. This departs late afternoon, currently twice a week during these peak periods, for US$55 economy or US$75 first-class. Check dates and details with Arab Bridge Maritime in Cairo (℡02/419-8657) or agents in Sharm (℡069/661-502) or Nuweiba (℡069/520-427).

An alternative option from the Sinai is to go **overland** through the Israeli resort of Eilat; this involves more bureaucracy than the boat but much less hanging around, and can be considerably cheaper too. **Taba**, on the Egyptian side of the border 70km north of Nuweiba, is well served by transport from Nuweiba, Dahab and Cairo. The border itself is open 24 hours daily, but it's almost impossible to find any transport inside Israel during the Jewish *shabbat*, so avoid crossing in the period from about 2pm on Fridays to 8pm on Saturdays. On Jewish festivals and holidays, this border can get extremely busy, with people and cars streaming south from dawn onwards, and back north again after sunset; on these days, your best bet is to cross at noon or midnight. There's a E£30 Egyptian departure tax, and Western nationals are routinely issued with free Israeli visas on arrival. Once in Israel, local city bus #16 (NIS4) runs to Eilat's Central Bus Station; change there for a bus to Kibbutz

Elot, which is a 500m walk from the Jordanian border (*hagvul ha-yardeni* in Hebrew). For details of the Israeli departure tax and crossing procedures to Aqaba, see p.38. The journey from Taba to Aqaba need not take more than three or four hours; however, although the Israelis and the Jordanians will stamp you in and out on a loose sheet, the Egyptians won't – and the Taba exit stamp in your passport will disqualify you from entering Syria, Lebanon and most other Middle Eastern countries.

Private vehicles are accepted on both the ferries and catamarans from Nuweiba to Aqaba: the fare for an ordinary car is about US$110, or a 4x4 about US$150. Driv-

ing across the Taba border into Israel, be prepared for fees totalling about US$120.

If you have limited time and can afford the extra expense, catching one of the frequent **flights** from Cairo or Alexandria to Amman is a viable option. Reasonably regular charter flights also link Hurghada and Sharm el-Sheikh with Amman, and – until Gaza airport is rebuilt – there are several flights a week to Amman from the tiny airport at El Arish in northern Sinai. Check with Royal Jordanian for details of all these, in Cairo at Zamalek Sporting Club (☎02/344-3114) or 6 Qasr el-Nil Street (☎02/575-0905), or in Sharm (☎069/602320) or Alex (☎03/487-9926). For EgyptAir call ☎02/390-3444.

Red tape and visas

Unlike in neighbouring countries, red tape in Jordan is rarely a problem: procedures have been streamlined in recent years specifically to ensure that paperwork for visitors is minimal.

Many army **checkpoints** – which were formerly set across roads in the Jordan Valley and elsewhere as a security measure – have now been removed to ease the movement of people and goods around the country. Some do remain, however; all you need to do is show your passport and you'll be waved through. You should always carry your **passport** with you as a matter of course: you'll need it to check into hotels at the least. It's also a wise precaution to photocopy the pages of your passport recording your personal details, and keep them separately.

Visas

All visitors to Jordan must hold passports valid for at least **six months** beyond the proposed date of entry to the country. Everyone other than nationals of certain Arab countries must also have a **visa** to enter Jordan, available from Jordanian embassies and consulates worldwide. EU,

US, Canadian, Australian and New Zealand nationals can also buy visas at Jordanian embassies in neighbouring countries, including Israel, Egypt, Syria and Lebanon, as well as at all land, sea and air borders apart from the King Hussein (Allenby) Bridge. If you plan to enter Jordan for the first time via this bridge, you must already hold a visa; if, however, you left Jordan via this bridge and are returning the same way, you don't need to buy another visa as long as your current one is still valid.

Visa **fees** have been unified: almost all nationalities now pay the equivalent of £11/US$17 for a single-entry visa bought in advance from embassies (or JD10 on arrival at the air, land or sea borders), or £21/US$32 for a multiple-entry visa. For **groups** of five or more people, whose journey has been arranged by a travel agent and who intend to stay in Jordan for at least four nights, visa fees and departure taxes are waived.

All Jordanian tourist visas – whether single- or multiple-entry – are initially valid for a stay of **thirty days** only. If you're planning to stay longer than that, you must **register with the police** in the last couple of days before the thirty-day period is up – a simple, free, five-minute procedure which, in effect, alters your status to that of "temporary resident" and simultaneously extends your visa to three months from the date of entry. A second three-month extension – issued only at the Directorate of Residency and Borders in Amman (see p.165) – is allowed only if an official HIV test proves negative.

You can register your visa extension at any police station in the country, but those in Amman (see p.165), Petra (p.342) and Aqaba (p.423) are most used to handling it. (However, if you entered Jordan from the West Bank or Israel and chose to keep your passport free of stamps, your extension must be registered at the Directorate.) You'll be asked a few simple questions, your passport will be stamped, and you should hang on to any bits of paper they give you. If you don't register, the **fine** is JD1.5 per day over the allotted thirty, charged in full when you depart. Take up any problems with the Ministry of the Interior (*wizarat ad-dakhliyyeh*; ☏06/569 1141) in Amman.

Aqaba: ASEZ visas

The visa situation is complicated by the status of the coastal resort of Aqaba. The city and an area around it comprise the **Aqaba Special Economic Zone (ASEZ)**, with its own rules. Special 30-day visas to enter Jordan via ASEZ are given **free** on arrival at Aqaba port, Aqaba's King Hussein International Airport, at the Wadi Araba/Yitzhak Rabin crossing from Israel and the Durra crossing from Saudi Arabia. There's no obligation to stay within the zone – you can then travel around Jordan freely. However, ASEZ visas can only be **extended** beyond their initial 30 days' permitted stay at the offices of **ASEZA** (Aqaba Special Economic Zone Authority) in Aqaba itself. If this is likely to be awkward – for instance, if you're planning to be elsewhere in Jordan on the day your ASEZ visa runs out – you should ask for a standard JD10 visa when you arrive, since these can be extended at any police station nationwide.

If you arrive in Jordan elsewhere – other than the King Hussein/Allenby Bridge – and you let the passport officials know that you intend to go directly to Aqaba, you are entitled to get a free ASEZ visa rather than a standard JD10 visa. In these cases, though, you must **register** at the ASEZA offices in Aqaba within 48 hours of your arrival in Jordan. If you miss this deadline, you become liable for the cost of the visa plus a fine of JD1.5 per day.

ASEZA's offices are marked on the map on p.408.

Jordanian embassies and consulates

Australia 20 Roebuck St, Redhill, Canberra, ACT 2603 ☏02/6295 9951, ℱ6239 7236.
Canada 100 Bronson Ave #701, Ottawa, ON, K1R 6G8 ☏613/238-8091, ℱ232-3341.
Egypt 6 Juhaini St, Doqqi, Cairo ☏02/348-7543, ℱ360-1027.
Israel Beit Oz building, 10th floor, 14 Abba Hillel St, Ramat Gan, Tel Aviv ☏03/751 7722, ℱ751 7713.
Lebanon Sakiet al-Janzir, Beirut ☏01/864950 or 922500, ℱ863794 or 922502.
Syria Jalaa St, Abu Rummana, Damascus ☏011/333 4642, ℱ333 6741.
Turkey Cinnah Cad 54/10-11-12, Ankara ☏0312/674 4161, ℱ674 0578.
UK 6 Upper Phillimore Gardens, London W8 7HB ☏020/7937 3685, ℱ7937 8795, recorded information ☏0906/550 8968, ⓦwww .jordanembassyuk.org.
USA 3504 International Drive NW, Washington DC 20008 ☏202/966-2664, ℱ966-3110, ⓦwww .jordanembassyus.org. Consulates at 12559 S Holiday Drive, Alsip, IL 60803 ☏708/272-6665; PO Box 3727, Houston, TX 77253 ☏713/224-2911; 28551 Southfield Rd #203, Lathrup Village, MI 48076 ☏248/557-4377; 972 Mission St, 4th floor, San Francisco, CA 94103 ☏415/546-1155.

Embassies and consulates in Amman

Australian ☏06/580 7000, ℱ580 7001, ⓦwww .jordan.embassy.gov.au.
Canadian ☏06/566 6126, ℱ568 9227, ⓦwww .dfait-maeci.gc.ca.
Irish ☏06/551 6807, ℱ551 6804, ⓦwww .foreignaffairs.gov.ie.
New Zealand ☏06/463 6720, ℱ463 4349, ⓦwww.nzembassy.com.
UK ☏06/590 9200, ℱ590 9279, ⓦwww.britain .org.jo.
US ☏06/592 0101, ℱ592 0136, ⓦamman .usembassy.gov.

Customs

You're permitted to buy 200 cigarettes, one litre of spirits and two litres of wine **duty-free** on arrival in the country; all borders and airports now have duty-free shops, open long hours. Personal items such as cameras are exempt from duty, but customs officials may take an interest in more expensive goods (such as camcorders). They'll only charge you duty if they think you plan to sell whatever it is in Jordan; otherwise, they'll enter a description of the item in your passport, meaning that you'll be charged duty when you leave if you don't have it with you. In theory, ordinary music CDs are liable for duty as well, so pack them deep.

The area around the southern city of Aqaba is a **Special Economic Zone**, with lower taxes and its own customs rules: on all roads into the city, you'll have to pass through a customs station. When entering the zone, it's not a bad idea to declare the "temporary entry" of high-value items like camcorders, laptops or electronic goods, so that their details can be entered in your passport. On departing the zone, there are Red and Green Channels, as in an airport. Personal items and a maximum of 200 cigarettes and one litre of alcohol that you bought in the zone are permitted – but if you're carrying anything more, including expensive items that haven't already been declared, you should head for the Red Channel.

Information, websites and maps

Accurate, up-to-date information on Jordan is relatively easy to come by before you leave home, from tourist offices and online.

The **Jordan Tourism Board** (JTB), part-affiliated to the Ministry of Tourism and part-private, publicizes the country's tourist assets abroad. In most countries, the account for handling promotion of Jordan is awarded to a local PR company, so contact details (see below) can, and do, change.

The JTB head office in Amman distributes a range of half-decent maps and generally worthwhile, professionally designed brochures, booklets and magazines, replete with glitzy photos and occasionally scholarly, interesting prose written by archeologists or journalists. In addition, press bureaus attached to the embassies in London and Washington dispense a vast range of more abstruse material on Jordan's political, industrial and economic background.

Jordan is one of the Arab world's leaders in **internet** development, borne out by the plethora of personal sites as well as by the massive amount of social, political and economic data posted online by the government.

Jordan Tourism Board

ⓦ **www.see-jordan.com**
Belgium 30 rue Herman Richir, 1030 Brussels ⓣ 02/215 36 87, ⓕ 248 29 16, ⓔ jtb.belgium @multi-mundo.com.
France 122 rue Paris, 92100 Boulogne-Billancourt, Paris ⓣ 01.55.60.94.46, ⓔ gsv@articleonze.com.
Germany Adam & Partner GmbH, Postfach 160 120, 60064 Frankfurt (Weserstr. 4, 60329) ⓣ 069/9231 8870, ⓕ 9231 8879, ⓔ jordan @adam-partner.de.
Italy Via C. Lombroso 26, 10125 Torino ⓣ 800.339198 or 011.669.0471, ⓕ 011.668.0785, ⓔ infogiordania@adam.it.
Jordan PO Box 830688, Amman 11183 ⓣ 06/567 8294, ⓕ 567 8295, ⓦ www.see-jordan.com.
Netherlands Leliegracht 20, 1015 DG Amsterdam ⓣ 020/670 5356, ⓕ 670 5357, ⓔ infojordan@travelmc.com.
Saudi Arabia & Gulf Afkar Promo Seven, Al Badriyah Towers, 1st floor, Prince Abdullah St, Jeddah ⓣ 02/606 1160, ⓕ 606 0150.
Spain 339 Bis Diagonal St. Ent. 4a, 08037

Barcelona ☎ 932 072 649, Ⓕ 932 075 691,
Ⓔ oviedo@arrakis.es.
UK Kennedy House, 1st floor, 115 Hammersmith
Rd, London W14 0QH ☎ 020/7371 6496
(brochure line 0870/770 6933), Ⓕ 7603 2424,
Ⓔ info@jordantourismboard.co.uk.
US & Canada 6867 Elm St #102, McLean, VA
22101 ☎ 1-877/SEE-JORDAN or 703/243-7404,
Ⓕ 243-7406, Ⓦ www.seejordan.org.

Useful websites

Tourism to Jordan

Ⓦ **www.see-jordan.com** Jordan Tourism Board.
Ⓦ **www.seejordan.org** JTB North America.
Ⓦ **www.mota.gov.jo** Ministry Of Tourism and
Antiquities portal, with details of the country's sites
and ongoing restoration projects.
Ⓦ **www.tourism.jo** MOTA mirror site.
Ⓦ **www.johotels.com** Jordan Hotel Association,
with a complete listing of its member hotels.
Ⓦ **www.jordanjubilee.com** Wide-ranging,
knowledgeable and entertaining personal site on
Jordan – its history, Bedouin culture, how to get
around, travellers' tips and tons more, logically set out
and well maintained.
Ⓦ **www.nomadstravel.co.uk** Run by Tony Howard
and Di Taylor, British climbers who pioneered tourism
to Wadi Rum in the 1980s, who post frequent updates
on the situation in Rum for visitors.
Ⓦ **www.andrewsi.freeserve.co.uk** Hugely
informative site for birdwatchers visiting Jordan.
Ⓦ **www.rscn.org.jo** Royal Society for the
Conservation of Nature, with excellent information on
nature reserves and Jordan's wilderness areas.
Ⓦ **www.holysites.com** Put together in 1999 for
the millennium celebrations – well out of date on the
practicalities, but still a useful and interesting digest of
Jordan's historical and religious sites.
Ⓦ **thorntree.lonelyplanet.com** Top-choice travel
forum, with a good Middle East branch: there's a lot of
dross, but also a lot of useful first-hand information.
Ⓦ **www.jmd.gov.jo** Jordan Meteorological
Department, with weather forecasts and climate data.

Jordan: news and culture

Ⓦ **www.kingabdullah.jo** Superb country
introduction, with detailed features on history, the
royal family, present-day government and politics,
and tourism.
Ⓦ **www.kinghussein.gov.jo** The late King
Hussein; biography, history and tributes.
Ⓦ **www.nic.gov.jo** Massive government database
run by the National Information Centre, presenting
information and statistics on everything from
environmental conservation projects to mortality rates.
Ⓦ **www.jordan.jo** Another arm of the National
Information system, collating access to news and official
information for Jordanians. Currently in Arabic only.
Ⓦ **www.jordantimes.com** The country's leading
English-language daily newspaper.
Ⓦ **www.star.com.jo** The weekly *Star* newspaper.
Ⓦ **www.sportupjordan.com** Sports news from
around the country.
Ⓦ **www.jiblondon.com** Jordan Information Bureau,
London, with business-oriented introductions to the
country and information digests.
Ⓦ **menic.utexas.edu** Scholarly information and a
huge list of useful links.
Ⓦ **www.turab.org** Details of Jordan's holy sites,
Islamic and Christian.
Ⓦ **www.aqabazone.com** The Aqaba Special
Economic Zone, with some useful information about
the city's development.
Ⓦ **www.mideasttravelnet.com/peace**
A collection of stunning photos by the royal
photographer Zohrab Markarian, produced for the
book *Kingdom of Peace* to celebrate the Jordan–Israel
peace treaty.
Ⓦ **www.janetaylorphotos.com** Homepage of the
acclaimed Jordan-based photographer Jane Taylor.

The Arab world and Islam

Ⓦ **www.ahram.org.eg/weekly** The Arab world's
leading English newspaper.
Ⓦ **almashriq.hiof.no** Quirky overview of Levantine
culture.
Ⓦ **www.arableagueonline.org** Excellent
background on Arab civilizations.

Jordan Jubilee

Of the array of personal websites devoted to Jordan, one stands out. Ⓦ **www
.jordanjubilee.com** is a fascinating, encyclopedic and vastly knowledgeable
collection of information for travellers of all stripes – backpackers, cultural explorers,
trekkers and armchair enthusiasts alike. Written and maintained (ad-free and not-
for-profit) by the engaging Ruth Caswell, who was born in Wales, lives in Paris and
Wadi Musa, and is often to be found exploring the wilder corners of Rum, "Jordan
Jubilee" is a true labour of love – and an invaluable resource.

Ⓦ **www.islamicity.org** Clear, intelligent and informative site on Islam.

Ⓦ **www.musalman.com** Islamic portal and search engine.

Ⓦ **www.merip.org** Outstanding left-leaning analysis of social and political trends in the Arab world.

Ⓦ **www.meionline.com** Highly respected Middle East news magazine.

Ⓦ **www.arabwomenconnect.org** The Amman-based regional office of UNIFEM, the UN development fund for women. Its partner site Ⓦ www.unifem.org. jo has a range of material on the situation for women in the Arab world.

Ⓦ **www.hrw.org** Human Rights Watch, with a detailed section on the Middle East.

Travel advisories

Ⓦ **www.fco.gov.uk** UK Foreign Office.
Ⓦ **travel.state.gov** US State Department.
Ⓦ **foreignaffairs.gov.ie** Irish Republic.
Ⓦ **www.dfait-maeci.gc.ca** Canada.
Ⓦ **www.dfat.gov.au** Australia.
Ⓦ **www.mfat.govt.nz** New Zealand.

Maps

For all general purposes, the **maps** in this book should be more than adequate. All the main international map publishers cover Jordan in one way or another, but none of their offerings has close detail and most omit newer roads and/or mark villages or archeological sites inaccurately. The widely available *GeoProjects* 1:730,000 map (third edition or later) leaves out some detail but is probably the best available outside Jordan, especially since it also has plans of Amman, Aqaba, Jerash and Petra on the back, including expanded detail of Amman city centre. You'd do just as well to wait until you arrive. The general *Jordan Tourist Map* produced by the Royal Jordanian Geographic Centre includes every village and most roads, but their fuzzy colour reproduction leaves a lot to be desired; you'd be just as well off with the JTB's free map, which pinpoints every site of touristic and religious interest. These and the smaller RJGC maps to all the major sites are almost the only maps available in Jordan itself, at bookshops and kiosks in the big hotels: there are 1:5000 maps for Petra, Rum, Jerash, Karak and Ajloun, a 1:10,000 map for Aqaba and a reasonable 1:20,000 one for Amman (around JD2.500 each).

The people who put together Ⓦwww .holysites.com for the millennium include a decent tourist map of the country online, and are also responsible for the leading fold-out map currently available in English, titled *Maps of Jordan, Amman and Aqaba* (available in Jordan only, at bookshops and in the big hotels; around JD4) – comprising an accurate and reader-friendly city map of Amman at 1:20,000 (the best around), a plan of Aqaba city centre, a decent country map at 1:655,000, and a brief rundown of Jordan's touristic highlights with photos.

Map outlets

In the UK and Ireland

Stanfords 12–14 Long Acre, London WC2E 9LP ☎020/7836 1321, Ⓦwww.stanfords.co.uk. Also at 39 Spring Gardens, Manchester ☎0161/831 0250, and 29 Corn St, Bristol ☎0117/929 9966.
Blackwell's Map Centre 50 Broad St, Oxford OX1 3BQ ☎01865/793 550, Ⓦmaps.blackwell .co.uk. Branches in Bristol, Cambridge, Cardiff, Leeds, Liverpool, Newcastle, Reading and Sheffield.
The Map Shop 30a Belvoir St, Leicester LE1 6QH ☎0116/247 1400, Ⓦwww.mapshopleicester.co.uk.
National Map Centre 22–24 Caxton St, London SW1H 0QU ☎020/7222 2466, Ⓦwww.mapsnmc .co.uk.
National Map Centre Ireland 34 Aungier St, Dublin ☎01/476 0471, Ⓦwww.mapcentre.ie.
The Travel Bookshop 13–15 Blenheim Crescent, London W11 2EE ☎020/7229 5260, Ⓦwww .thetravelbookshop.co.uk.
Traveller 55 Grey St, Newcastle-upon-Tyne NE1 6EF ☎0191/261 5622, Ⓦwww.newtraveller.com.

In the US and Canada

The giant US map wholesalers Map Link (Ⓦwww.maplink.com) has a useful list of specialist map/travel bookstores in every US state, as well as some worldwide; click on "Retail Partners".
110 North Latitude US ☎336/369-4171, Ⓦwww.110nlatitude.com.
Book Passage 51 Tamal Vista Blvd, Corte Madera, CA 94925 ☎1-800/999-7909 or 415/927-0960; 1 Ferry Plaza #46, San Francisco, CA 94941 ☎415/835-1020, Ⓦwww.bookpassage.com.
Distant Lands 56 S Raymond Ave, Pasadena, CA 91105 ☎1-800/310-3220, Ⓦwww.distantlands.com.
Globe Corner Bookstore 28 Church St,

Cambridge, MA 02138 ☎1-800/358-6013,
ⓦwww.globecorner.com.
Longitude Books 115 W 30th St #1206, New York,
NY 10001 ☎1-800/342-2164, ⓦwww
.longitudebooks.com.
Map Town 400 5 Ave SW, Suite 100, Calgary, AB,
T2P 0L6 ☎1-877/921-6277 or 403/266-2241,
ⓦwww.maptown.com.
Travel Bug Bookstore 3065 W Broadway,
Vancouver, BC, V6K 2G9 ☎604/737-1122, ⓦwww
.travelbugbooks.ca.
World of Maps 1235 Wellington St, Ottawa, ON,
K1Y 3A3 ☎1-800/214-8524 or 613/724-6776,
ⓦwww.worldofmaps.com.

In Australia and New Zealand

Map Centre ⓦwww.mapcentre.co.nz.
Mapland 372 Little Bourke St, Melbourne
☎03/9670 4383, ⓦwww.mapland.com.au.
Map Shop 6–10 Peel St, Adelaide ☎08/8231
2033, ⓦwww.mapshop.net.au.
Map World 371 Pitt St, Sydney ☎02/9261 3601,
ⓦwww.mapworld.net.au. Also at 900 Hay St,
Perth ☎08/9322 5733, Jolimont Centre, Canberra
☎02/6230 4097 and 1981 Logan Road, Brisbane
☎07/3349 6633.
Map World (NZ) 173 Gloucester St, Christchurch
☎0800/627 967, ⓦwww.mapworld.co.nz.

Insurance

It's essential to take out a good travel insurance policy to cover against theft,
loss of property and illness or injury. Before paying for a new policy, however, it's
worth checking whether you are already covered: some all-risks home insurance
policies may cover your possessions when overseas, and many private medical
schemes include cover when abroad.

Bank and credit cards often have certain
levels of medical or other insurance
included, especially if you use them to pay
for your trip. Students may find that their
student health coverage extends during
the vacations and for one term beyond the
date of last enrolment. In Canada, provincial
health plans usually provide partial cover for
medical mishaps overseas, while holders
of official student/teacher/youth cards in
Canada and the US are entitled to meagre
accident coverage and hospital inpatient
benefits.

After exhausting these possibilities, you
might want to contact a specialist travel insurance company, or consider **Rough Guides'**

Rough Guides travel insurance

Rough Guides has teamed up with Columbus Direct to offer you travel insurance
that can be tailored to suit your needs. Readers can choose from many different
travel insurance products, including a **low-cost backpacker** option for long stays; a
short break option for city getaways; a typical **holiday package** option; and many
others. There are also **annual multi-trip** policies for those who travel regularly, with
variable levels of cover available. Different **sports and activities** (trekking, skiing,
etc) can be covered if required on most policies. Rough Guides travel insurance is
available to the residents of 36 different countries with different language options
to choose from via our website – where you can also purchase the insurance. Alternatively, UK residents should call ☎0800 083 9507; US citizens should call ☎1-800
749-4922; Australians should call ☎1 300 669 999. All other nationalities should call
☎+44 870 890 2843.

own **travel insurance** deal (see box). A typical travel insurance policy usually provides cover for the loss of baggage, tickets and – up to a certain limit – cash or cheques, as well as cancellation or curtailment of your journey. Most of them exclude so-called **dangerous sports** unless an extra premium is paid: in Jordan this can mean scuba-diving, rock-climbing, parachuting, and so on. Many policies can be chopped and changed: for example, sickness and accident benefits can often be excluded or included at will. Ascertain whether medical benefits will be paid as your treatment proceeds or only after you return

home, and make sure that there is a medical emergency phone number you can call 24 hours a day. When securing baggage cover, make sure that the per-article limit – typically under £500/US$750 – will cover your most valuable possession. If you need to make a claim, you should **keep all receipts** for medicines and medical treatment, and in the event you have anything stolen you must obtain an official report from the police. Note also that very few insurers will arrange on-the-spot payments in the event of a major expense or loss; you will usually be reimbursed only after going home.

Health

No immunizations or vaccinations are required before you can enter Jordan, though you'll need a yellow fever certificate if you're arriving from equatorial Africa. However, before you travel, it's strongly recommended that you make sure you're up-to-date with immunizations against hepatitis A, polio, tetanus (lockjaw), tuberculosis and typhoid fever.

You should consult a doctor at least two months in advance of your departure date, as there are some immunizations that can't be given at the same time, and several take a while to become effective. The *Rough Guide to Travel Health* has full details.

Dehydration

Top of the list of Jordan's maladies, well ahead of the worst creepy-crawlies, is **dehydration**. This is a major threat to health, and can work insidiously over days and weeks to weaken you to the point of exhaustion without your ever showing any signs of illness. Equally – and just as dangerously – if you're sweating profusely (while on one of Jordan's many gorge-walks, for instance), even experienced walkers can go from alert and vigorous to dizzy and hopelessly lethargic in as little as half an hour, due solely to loss of body fluids. It is essential to carry *lots* of water with you on these walks: one bottle is not enough.

An adult should normally drink two litres of water a day; from day one in the Middle East, you should be drinking at least three litres – and, if you're exerting yourself in hot conditions, up to seven or eight litres. It's something of a matter of pride among the desert Bedouin not to drink water in front of foreigners, but if you copy them you're likely to make yourself ill quite quickly. Drinking to quench your thirst just isn't enough in a hot climate, since the combination of the sun's evaporation and your own sweating can pull water out of your system far quicker than your body can deliver thirst messages to your brain: you must drink well beyond thirst-quenching if you're to head off the lethargy and splitting headaches – and potentially serious physical and mental incapacity – caused by dehydration. It's also worth remembering that both **alcohol** and **caffeine** exacerbate the effects of dehydration.

The best way to check your hydration levels is to check your urine output. If you have to go reasonably frequently and your urine is pale and straw-coloured, you're OK; if you only go once or twice a day and it's dark yellow and acidic, you're not drinking enough.

Travellers' diarrhoea

A bout of **diarrhoea** is the only medical problem you're at all likely to encounter in Jordan. Few travellers, however cautious, seem to avoid it altogether, largely because the bacteria in Jordanian food are different from, and more numerous than, bacteria in the West.

For this reason, instant recourse to **drugs** such as Imodium or Lomotil that plug you up (in fact, what they do is paralyse your gut so it can't work to rid itself of infection) is inadvisable; you should only use them if you absolutely must travel (eg if you're flying). The best thing to do when diarrhoea strikes is to wait up, eat nothing for at least 24 hours and let it run its course, while constantly replacing the fluids and salts that you're flushing away. In extreme cases, you can lose so much water through diarrhoea that you can go from normal to seriously **dehydrated** in a matter of hours: maintaining fluid intake (even if it all rushes out again) is vitally important. **Oral rehydration solutions** such as Dioralyte or Electrosol are widely available in Jordan and the West, sold in sachets for dissolving in a glassful of clean water. They're often mistakenly marketed as being for babies only, but will make you feel better and stronger than any other treatment. If you can't get the sachets, make up your own solution with one heaped teaspoon of salt and twelve level teaspoons of sugar added to a standard-sized (1.5-litre) bottle of mineral water. You need to keep downing the stuff, whether or not the diarrhoea is continuing – at least a litre of the solution per day interspersed with three litres of fresh water. Bouts of diarrhoea rarely last longer than 24–48 hours, but note that they can render the contraceptive pill ineffective.

Diarrhoea complications

If watery diarrhoea lasts longer than four days, seek medical advice. Nasty but easily treatable diseases such as giardiasis and amoebiasis must be tested for by a stool examination.

If there is at any time blood in your diarrhoea, you've most likely got dysentery – this is rare, but far from unheard-of among travellers in the Middle East. The most important thing is to get a stool sample to a doctor to find out which of the two main kinds you've got (although, whichever it is, maintaining hydration levels is essential). **Bacillary dysentery** (shigella) is bacterial; symptoms are cramping abdominal pains, fever, fatigue and lethargy. You'll eventually get over it, and, for all but the most serious cases, rehydration is far more important than treatment with drugs. **Amoebic dysentery** is far nastier, and can recur over many years if left untreated, with abscesses forming in the liver. This is caused by a parasite, transmitted by tiny eggs left on food, and leads to bloody, slimy diarrhoea, fever, sweating and chills. You should be certain of the diagnosis before embarking on a course of metronidazole (sold as Flagyl). You should also see your doctor as soon as you get home to make sure you're entirely cured.

Heat exhaustion and sunstroke

Heat exhaustion is another common, but avoidable, condition. Forty-eight hours is the minimum acclimatization period to hot conditions, although you may not be entirely yourself for up to ten days. The Jordanian sun can be scorching intense, and – obvious though it sounds – you should do all you can to **avoid sun exposure**, especially if you're travelling in high summer (May–Sept). Some kind of head protection is essential, although your fashion sense may stop short of the "hat with a brim of at least 8cm" recommended by the medical profession. Lightweight light-coloured 100 percent cotton clothes that protect your skin from the sun – such as long-sleeved shirts, and long trousers or ankle-length skirts – will allow air to circulate close to your skin to keep you cool and limit both sunburn and dehydration.

Sunstroke occurs when the normal bodily processes of temperature control break down, making you feel very hot, dizzy and faint but without sweating. If you're gentle about breaking yourself into the heat, you're unlikely to succumb. If it does happen, you'll probably need medical assistance. Get out of the sun immediately, and into air conditioning and/or a cold bath as soon as possible; at the very least, douse yourself and your clothes with water.

Bites and stings

Although malaria is a small risk in a few areas of Egypt, Syria and Saudi Arabia, it's not present in Jordan, so while the local **mosquitoes** may be annoying, they aren't life-threatening. Normal precautions, such as DEET-impregnated wrist- and ankle-bands, sprays and roll-ons, will keep the critters away; for sensitive skins, citronella is a good substitute.

Sandfly bites can lead to fevers and a flu-like illness with painful eyes and muscles that lasts three or four days – alarming but not serious. Treatment is with paracetamol or aspirin to lower temperature and relieve headache, and plenty of bed rest. Sandflies are tiny, and can only fly short distances (up to 200m) from their breeding places in sand, rubbish heaps, stone walls and animal dens. DEET can repel them, and covering exposed skin after dark limits the risk of bites.

The likelihood of tangling with anything worse in Jordan is very small. **Snakes** are frightened of humans, and to see one you'll have to search stealthily; if you stomp around making slow, noisy movements, any snakes present will slither away. Jordan is home to a handful of dangerous **scorpions**; to avoid them, never walk barefoot, especially in the dark, and if you're camping always shake out your shoes and clothes before wearing them. There are also a few dangerous species of **spider**, found under stones, in bunches of fruit and in outside toilets.

If you've been bitten or stung you must get to a doctor fast. It's very important to be able to identify what bit you, preferably by killing it and bringing it with you. You should immobilize the affected limb using a splint, and wind a crepe bandage over and above the bite/sting. Tourniquets, cutting around the wound, and trying to suck out poison have all been medically proved to be either worthless or positively dangerous.

Food hygiene

The most obvious and effective way to **prevent** yourself getting ill while in Jordan is to **avoid eating contaminated food**. If you've already been travelling in Egypt or Syria, it's quite likely you'll already have gone through travellers' diarrhoea, and so will be acclimatized to the lower levels of hygiene than at home. If you haven't, or if you arrive in Jordan directly from the West or Israel, you should give your stomach a chance to get used to the conditions; lay off the street food for a few days and spend a little extra to eat in posher, but cleaner, restaurants. Everywhere from the diviest diner upwards will have a sink somewhere with soap for washing your hands: use it! (*Fee hammam?* means "Have you got a bathroom?") Beware of eateries that have no customers: their food is less likely to be freshly prepared.

Throughout your time in Jordan, you should always thoroughly **wash** all fruit, salad and vegetables in clean water before eating; some cautious souls even stick to the rule that "if you can't peel it, don't eat it". **Undercooked** or raw meat, fish or shellfish are major sources of disease and you should definitely send food back if it's anything less than well done. Unpasteurized **milk** is another danger; but unless you're out with the Bedouin – who drink milk fresh from the goat/camel – this is unlikely to arise; Jordan's dairy industry is scrupulous about pasteurization.

Although Jordanians drink **water** freely from the tap, you might do better not to; tap water is chlorinated strongly enough not to do you any harm (it just tastes bad), but the pipes it runs through add a quantity of rust and filth you could do without. It's fine for brushing your teeth and even for drinking, but bottles of local **mineral water** are available very inexpensively in all corners of the country.

Treatment in Jordan

Every town, large and small, has at least one **pharmacy** (*saydaliyyeh*), generally staffed by fluent English-speaking professionals trained to Western standards. Unless you're obviously a hospital case, these are where you should head first, since a pharmacist charges nothing for a "consultation", and can either prescribe a remedy on the spot or refer you to a local doctor. If you're given a medicine, find out explicitly from the pharmacist what the dosage is, since printed English information on the box might be sketchy.

If you need a **doctor** (*doktoor*) in Amman, you should ask your embassy to recommend one. Elsewhere, either ask a pharmacist for a recommendation or take your chances by popping into a surgery from the street. All doctors are trained in English, and so fluent; many also receive training in hospitals in the UK or US. If you're in real trouble, aim for the emergency room of a **hospital** (*moostashfa*); all large towns have one. If you need to be hospitalized longer than overnight, call the emergency helpline of your embassy (see p.41) and ask for advice. Standards of medical hygiene in giving injections and blood transfusions are as scrupulously high as in the West. Consultation fees and medical costs are much lower than back home, but you should still get signed **receipts** for everything in order to claim money back from your insurance company when you return.

Medical resources for travellers

Online

Ⓦ **www.cdc.gov** Top-choice website run by the US Centers for Disease Control and Prevention. Comprehensive information, well presented.

Ⓦ **www.tripprep.com** A database of vaccinations, as well as destination and medical service provider information.

Ⓦ **www.who.int** The World Health Organization website – a little dry in places, but with invaluable "Health Topics" giving factsheets on a range of diseases.

Ⓦ **health.yahoo.com** Information on specific diseases and conditions, drugs and herbal remedies, as well as advice from health experts.

Ⓦ **www.istm.org** The International Society for Travel Medicine, with a full list of clinics specializing in international travel health.

Ⓦ **www.fitfortravel.scot.nhs.uk** UK website carrying information about travel-related diseases and how to avoid them.

In the UK and Ireland

British Airways Travel Clinics 213 Piccadilly, London W1 (Mon–Fri 9.30am–5.30pm, Sat 10am–4pm, no appointment necessary); 101 Cheapside, London EC2 (Mon–Fri 9am–4.30pm, appointment required); Ⓣ0845/600 2236, Ⓦwww .ba.com/travel/healthclinintro. Vaccinations, tailored advice from an online database and a complete range of travel healthcare products.

Dun Laoghaire Medical Centre 5 Northumberland Ave, Dun Laoghaire, Co. Dublin Ⓣ01/280 4996. Advice on medical matters abroad.

Hospital for Tropical Diseases Travel Clinic 2nd floor, Mortimer Market Centre, off Capper St, London WC1 (Mon–Fri 9am–5pm by appointment only; Ⓣ020/7388 9600, Ⓦwww .masta.org; £15 consultation fee is waived if you have your injections here). A recorded Health Line (Ⓣ0906/133 7733; 50p/min) gives hints on hygiene and illness prevention as well as listing appropriate immunizations.

Liverpool School of Tropical Medicine Pembroke Place, Liverpool L3 Ⓣ0151/708 9393, Ⓦwww.liv.ac.uk/lstm. Walk-in clinic Mon–Fri 1–4pm; appointment required for yellow fever, but not for other jabs.

MASTA (Medical Advisory Service for Travellers Abroad) 40 regional clinics (call Ⓣ0870/6062782 for the nearest). Also operates a pre-recorded 24hr Travellers' Health Line (UK Ⓣ0906/822 4100, 60p/min), giving written information tailored to your journey by return of post.

Nomad Pharmacy Surgeries 40 Bernard St, London WC1; and 3 Wellington Terrace, London N8 (Mon–Fri 9.30am–6pm, Ⓣ020/7833 4114 to book an appointment). Advice is free if you go in person. Their helpline is Ⓣ0906/863 3414 (60p/min).

Travel Health Centre Mercers Medical Centre, St Stephen's St Lower, Dublin 2 Ⓣ01/402 2337. Expert pre-trip advice and inoculations.

Travel Medicine Services 16 College St, Belfast BT1 Ⓣ028/9031 5220. Offers medical advice before a trip and help afterwards in the event of a tropical disease.

Tropical Medical Bureau Grafton Buildings, 34 Grafton St, Dublin 2, Ⓣ1850/487 674, Ⓦwww .tmb.ie.

In the US and Canada

Canadian Society for International Health 1 Nicholas St, Suite 1105, Ottawa, ON, K1N 7B7 Ⓣ613/241-5785, Ⓦwww.csih.org. Distributes a free pamphlet, "Health Information for Canadian Travellers", containing an extensive list of travel health centres in Canada.

Centers for Disease Control 1600 Clifton Rd NE, Atlanta, GA 30333 Ⓣ1-800/311-3435 or 404/639-3534, Ⓦwww.cdc.gov. Publishes outbreak warnings, suggested inoculations, precautions and other background information for travellers. Useful website plus International Travelers Hotline on ☎ 1-877/FYI-TRIP.

International Association for Medical Assistance to Travellers (IAMAT) 417 Center St, Lewiston, NY 14092 ☎ 716/754-4883, ⓦ www .iamat.org, and 1287 St. Clair Avenue West, Suite #1, Toronto, Ontario M6E 1B8 ☎ 416/652-0137. A non-profit organization supported by donations, it can provide a list of English-speaking doctors in Jordan, climate charts and leaflets on various diseases and inoculations.

International SOS Assistance 8 Neshaminy Interplex #207, Trevose, PA 19053-6956 ☎ 1-800/523-8930, ⓦ www.intsos.com. Members receive pre-trip medical referral info, as well as overseas emergency services designed to complement travel insurance coverage.

MedJet Assistance ☎ 1-800/963-3538 or 205/595-6658, ⓦ www.medjetassistance.com. Annual membership program for travellers that, in the event of illness or injury, will fly members home or to the hospital of their choice in a medically equipped and staffed jet.

Travel Medicine ☎ 1-800/872-8633, ⓦ www .travmed.com. Sells first-aid kits, mosquito netting, water filters, reference books and other health-related travel products.

In Australia and New Zealand

Travellers' Medical and Vaccination Centres ⓦ www.tmvc.com.au. Australia: 27–29 Gilbert Place, Adelaide ☎ 08/8212 7522; 5/247 Adelaide St, Brisbane ☎ 07/3221 9066; 5/8–10 Hobart Place, Canberra ☎ 02/6257 7156; 270 Sandy Bay Rd, Sandy Bay, Hobart ☎ 03/6223 7577; 2/393 Little Bourke St, Melbourne ☎ 03/9602 5788; Level 7, Dymocks Bldg, 428 George St, Sydney ☎ 02/9221 7133. NZ: 1/170 Queen St, Auckland ☎ 09/373 3531; 15 Grand Arcade, 14–16 Willis St, Wellington ☎ 04/473 0991.

Costs, money and banks

By Western standards, Jordan is a good-value destination, with most tourist essentials more expensive than in Egypt or Syria, but way below Israeli prices. The most significant dent in your budget is liable to come from a visit to Petra, where the tourist boom has arrived with a vengeance and hotels and services are much pricier than in the rest of the country.

Currency

The Jordanian unit of currency is the **dinar**, abbreviated to JD. Its **exchange rate** is pegged to the dollar at US$1=JD0.71 and JD1=US$1.40. The current rate against the British pound is around JD1=£0.75p or £1=JD1.33. Check the latest rates at ⓦ www.oanda.com.

You won't hear many people using the name "dinar"; *jaydee* is more common in speech, and another popular name, shouted by street sellers, is *lira*. Confusingly enough, the dinar has two subdivisions: one dinar comprises either 1000 **fils** or 100 **piastres** (*qirsh*). In practice, locals always think in piastres; they only use fils when talking to foreigners. In verbal exchanges, you'll also find that people quite often leave the denomination off the end of prices; if they say something costs *"ashreen"* (twenty), it's up to you to decide whether they mean 20 fils (a throwaway amount), 20 piastres (ie 200 fils; the price of a street snack or a short bus ride), or 20 JDs (the cost of a double room in a decent small hotel). Nicknames also pop up: 100 fils is often called a *barizeh* and 50 fils is a *shilin*. Almost all written/ printed hotel and restaurant bills are in the form "14.650", meaning 14 dinars and 650 fils. Some newer outlets knock off the last digit, but "14.65" means the same as "14.650".

To avoid any more confusion than necessary, throughout the guide we've indicated all prices in dinars and fils.

Banknotes in circulation are JD50, JD20, JD10, JD5 and JD1, all with Arabic on one side and English on the other. If you can, try not to get lumbered with JD20 and JD50 notes – this is a lot of money to most Jordanians, and many places won't be able to give you change. Banknotes dated earlier than 2002 are no longer legal tender: you can change them for current notes (at one-to-one) only at the Central Bank of Jordan in Downtown Amman.

Trying to figure out the **coinage** is a real headache, with new and old designs all in circulation together. The most common coins are these four: a **half-dinar** coin that is gold-coloured, seven-sided and inset with a circular silver bit in the middle; a **quarter-dinar** coin that is also gold-coloured and seven-sided, but smaller and without the silver inset; and coins of **ten piastres** and **five piastres**, both of which are thin, round and silver. Coppers of one piastre are virtually worthless. Note that ten-piastre coins are the same size, weight and value as older **100 fils** coins which are still in circulation. Similarly, five-piastre coins have an identical twin, marked as **fifty fils**. In addition, you may also come across the following: two varieties of one-dinar coin – a large seven-sided gold version, and a smaller round gold one (like a British pound coin, except thinner); an alternative half-dinar coin that is silver, seven-sided and thick; an alternative quarter-dinar that is large and round in silver; and tiny silver coins of two and a half piastres or 25 fils.

All coins state their value on them somewhere in tiny English lettering.

Changing and carrying money

Although few banks in the West keep Jordanian dinars on hand, you should be able to **order** them with a few days' notice, and it's a good idea to bring at least JD50 or so with you in cash, to cover visa and transportation costs on arrival and a night or two in a simple hotel.

In fact, it is most economical to order as many dinars as you think you'll need for your trip beforehand, and bring the whole lot with you – that way, you avoid commission charges in Jordan and the hassle of exchange, and by taking a bit of time to shop around at home it's also not hard to find special deals or promotions giving good rates at zero commission. Other advantages of this are that Jordan has no restrictions on bringing in and taking out any amount of foreign or Jordanian currency; everyone (apart from international car-rental firms) will accept **cash** for all purchases; and, as far as **security** goes, Jordan is safer than anywhere in the West: you can carry wads of cash around in your pocket without concern. Whether on a crowded rush-hour bus or at 2am in a dark alley, you're far more likely to be invited to a stranger's home for tea than mugged, conned or pickpocketed.

All major Western currencies are freely convertible in Jordan, although you might find some resistance to the Israeli shekel. There's no black market in currency exchange. For **changing cash**, every town has a welter of banks, with no difference in exchange rates between them; all generally offer fast service. If you want to change money outside the rather limited bank opening hours (see p.73), though, you may have to sacrifice a few fils and hunt down an **exchange bureau**. Amman's Downtown is crammed with these, all of which are authorized and have comparable rates, a fraction lower than the banks' – but to get the best out of them you'll have to shop around and bargain hard over the small sums they take in commission. Other large towns generally have a few bureaux. High-denomination bills are always preferable: a single $100 bill will get you a better bureau exchange rate than a hundred $1 bills. Also make sure that the notes you're carrying are crisp and new, since many bureaux automatically reject grimy or creased bills (especially dollars) as possible forgeries; some will even refuse to take anything other than unused notes.

Unlike in some other Middle Eastern countries, merchants prefer to use the local money, and in most situations it's impossible to pay for goods or services in dollars.

Credit and debit cards

Most Jordanian hotels, shops and restaurants above the cheapest category accept some form of plastic in payment (most often Visa) – but bear in mind that paying like this when overseas can turn out to have hidden costs. Your home bank or credit-card company will not only set its own exchange rates (not necessarily to your advantage) but is also likely to impose a handling charge: relatively high for using your credit card (which is also subject to high levels of interest), slightly less so for using your debit card (which is interest-free). These charges will only become apparent later, on your monthly statement, not at the time of purchase.

Hidden exchange rates and handling charges will also turn up on your statement if you take an over-the-counter **cash advance** on your credit or debit card at a bank overseas. In Jordan, HSBC and Jordan National Bank accept Mastercard only, the Housing Bank accepts Visa only, but the Union Bank accepts both.

Easiest of all (but still liable to those charges) is to use the **cash machines (ATMs)** that are attached to banks in Amman and larger towns. HSBC Bank, to name one, has thoroughly reliable English-language ATMs that accept all cards with Visa, Mastercard, Global Access, Plus and Cirrus symbols on them (for ATM locations, click on Personal Banking at ⓦwww.jordan.hsbc .com). Many other banks are the same – but note that you may have a daily withdrawal limit of JD100 or JD300. Make sure before you leave home that you have a personal identification number (PIN) designed to work overseas. American Express card-holders can get cash and traveller's cheques and draw on personal cheques at the Amex office in Amman.

Traveller's cheques

Traveller's cheques can be an expensive way of carrying your money: you're paying for the security of a **rapid replacement service**, should you need it. The usual fee for buying the cheques is one or two percent, though this may be waived if you buy them through a bank where you have an account. It pays to get a selection of denominations. Make sure to keep the purchase agreement and a record of cheque serial numbers safe and separate from the cheques themselves. In the event that cheques are **lost or stolen**, the issuing company will expect you to report the loss forthwith to their office in Amman;

most companies claim to replace lost or stolen cheques within 24 hours. American Express are the most widely accepted brand in the Middle East, but you should have few problems with other major brands. Although the US dollar is king throughout the region, in Jordan traveller's cheques in British pounds or euros are universally acceptable.

In Jordan, all **banks** will change traveller's cheques in major currencies, but their procedures can be long-winded and they can charge excessive **commissions** (often a minimum JD5 per transaction) or insist on seeing the cheques' proof of purchase; most **exchange bureaus** in Amman, Petra and Aqaba will deal with cheques with considerably less hassle. You'll also get a slightly worse exchange rate for traveller's cheques than for cash.

Lost or stolen cards and traveller's cheques

American Express International Traders, opposite *Ambassador Hotel*, Shmeisani, Amman (daily except Fri 8am–6pm; ☎06/560 7075, ⓦwww .traders.com.jo). Outside these times, call regional head office in Bahrain ☎00973/256834; the call charge will be reimbursed to you, ⓦwww .americanexpress.com.
Mastercard and Thomas Cook Jordan National Bank, 3rd Circle, Jebel Amman (daily 24hr; ☎0800/22277 or 06/461 8412, ⓦwww.ahli .com). Alternatively, call collect (reverse-charge) to international head offices: for Mastercard ☎001-314/542-7111 in the US, ⓦwww.mastercard.com; for Thomas Cook ☎0044-1733/318950 in the UK, ⓦwww.thomascook.com.
Visa Jordan Payment Services, 3rd floor, Housing Bank Centre, Shmeisani, Amman (daily 24hr; ☎06/568 0554 or 568 0574). Alternatively, call head office in the US collect on ☎001-410/581-3836, ⓦwww.visa.com.

Wiring money

Having money **wired** from home is quick, but it's never convenient or cheap, and should be considered a last resort. Bank-to-bank transfers are another option, but involve plenty of bureaucracy and normally take two working days to arrive. Check with your bank before travelling to see if they have reciprocal arrangements with any banks in Jordan, and what information they need before making a transfer. Whether wiring or transferring, expect to pay large fees in commission.

Travelers Express/Moneygram North America ☎1-800/MONEYGRAM (666-3947), all other countries toll-free ☎+800/6663-9472, ⓦ www .moneygram.com. Jordan agents: Jordan Gulf Bank ☎06/569 3982.

Western Union UK ☎0800/833833, Ireland ☎1800/395395, US ☎1-800/325-6000, Canada ☎1-800/235-0000, Australia ☎1800/173833, New Zealand ☎09/270 0050, ⓦ www.westernunion .com. Jordan agents: Cairo Amman Bank ☎06/465 3610.

Basic costs

You'll find Jordan an inexpensive place to visit; if you have the heart to bargain a little, prices that are low to start with will plummet through the floor.

Average daily expenditure for one at rock-bottom prices, if you're eating only falafel and hummus, sharing a room in the cheapest of hotels, travelling by serveece or minibus and avoiding sights that charge admission (but paying minimal tips) is about £8/$15. Add in one square meal a day and an occasional castle visit or taxi ride, and you should plan on £11/$20. Staying in plain but adequate two- or three-star hotels, eating at the occasional nice restaurant, travelling comfortably and seeing a fair spread of sights will set you back around £25–35/$45–65 a day per person, while travelling independently in five-star luxury requires a daily budget of £110/$200 per person or more.

Amman's cheapest **accommodation** – a bed in a shared room – can be had for about £2/$3, plus 50p/90¢ for a shower; a cosier budget double is still only about twice that per person. About £15/$28 buys a comfortable, if smallish, double room with an en-suite bathroom, TV, phone and some form of air conditioning. Five-star luxury hotels have been known to sell off double rooms for as little as £50/$90 with a little encouragement, although £100/$180 is nearer their mark.

Food is extremely inexpensive. If you're prepared to eat one or other of the basic staples at every sitting, you could get by paying as little as £2/$4 for three reasonably nutritious meals. If you include one high-quality meal plus a vitamin-supplementing fresh juice, food costs would still stay below £5/$9 a day. Even at the top end of the scale, a reasonable £25/$45 covers a lavish buffet breakfast, a light lunch, and dinner (plus wine) in a good restaurant.

Entry to sites is a mixed bag. Most places around the country are either free, or £1–3/$2–5 or so. The unmissable Petra is the big exception, with a one-day pass costing a whacking £17.50/$33. You may find that admission fees are reduced in the off-season or if tourism levels are low.

If you're looking to get off the tourist trail and cover all corners of the country independently, the one thing that can really push costs up is **transport**. Jordan's public transport system leaves quite a lot to be desired, although within Amman shared taxis whisk you around town for pennies and even a crosstown ride in a metered taxi comes to little more than £1/$1.80. Travelling by bus between urban centres is inexpensive (eg Amman–Aqaba £2.50/$4), but the more remote and interesting corners of the country are poorly served by public transport – if at all – and getting to them can involve more significant expense, either hiring a taxi for the day, renting a car or chartering a four-wheel-drive vehicle to go across country. Prices obviously vary, but £35/$65 generally covers a major full-day excursion in a car or 4x4.

Almost nowhere in the country are discounts offered to students.

Hidden costs and tipping

Jordan has a **government sales tax** of 17 percent, which applies to a whole range of goods and services: bear in mind that, in most situations, the price you see (or are told) doesn't include this tax, which is only added on when you come to pay. In Aqaba, sales tax is lower, at seven percent. What's more, all hotels and restaurants above a certain quality threshold automatically add a **ten percent service charge** to all bills. They are legally obliged to state these additions somewhere, although it can be as surreptitious as a tiny line on the bottom of a menu, or just a simple "++" attached to a hotel price-list, as in "Double Room JD40++". If you try to bargain, you'll often find the "plus-plus" suddenly disappearing from view.

On larger sums, tax and service can obviously represent a hefty double-whammy

– over a quarter of the headline figure added on top. It can be a hard lesson to learn, that the price you thought you'd be paying is only three-quarters of what you'll actually have to shell out.

In a good restaurant, even when a service charge is included, it's customary to round the bill up slightly as well. Occasionally, restaurants will add the tax but leave the service charge up to you – in these situations, your meal would have to have been really awful to merit anything less than a ten percent tip. Budget local diners don't expect tips and will never press you for anything though.

In most everyday situations a 100 fils tip is a perfectly satisfactory indication of your appreciation for a service, such as a porter loading your bags onto a bus or taxi. Taxi-drivers deserve ten percent. For a bellboy in a four- or five-star hotel who brings your bags up to your room, half a dinar is nearer the mark.

 # Getting around

Jordan's public transport – of which there isn't much, other than buses – is a hotchpotch. Bus routes cover what's necessary for the locals: there is little or no provision for budget travellers wishing to visit out-of-the-way places, and it's impossible to get from one end of the country to the other without making at least two or three changes of bus. With some highly visitable places inaccessible by public transport, the best way to see the whole of Jordan is to rent a car for at least part of your stay.

As an aid to getting around the country, we've included in a box at the end of each chapter of the guide a list, in English and Arabic, of useful **place-names** – for comparison with roadsigns or bus destination signs, or for pointing to, should you get into difficulties.

Buses and serveeces

The most common way of getting between cities is by **bus**, most of which are small, privately owned fifteen- or eighteen-seater minibuses. There are a few big government-run buses and a handful of modern air-conditioned tour-buses serving as public transport, but they're rare. Throughout the guide, we've used "bus" as a catch-all term; in most cases, minibuses are the only transport option available, but we've only resorted to the term "minibus" when the distinction needs to be made between them and big buses. Virtually no timetables are in operation, and buses tend to depart only

when they're full. This means that, on less-travelled routes especially, you should factor in sometimes quite considerable waiting time for the bus to fill up. However, once you get going, journeys are rarely arduous – roads are good, and the longest single journey in the country, from Amman to Aqaba, is unlikely to take more than four hours. All buses and minibuses have their point of origin and **destination** written or painted in Arabic script just above either brake-light on the rear of the vehicle.

Bus **fares** are very low. As a guide, a half-hour hop between towns costs 150–200 fils one-way. Longer journeys – Amman to Jerash, or Zarqa to Azraq – are in the order of 400–500 fils; Amman to Karak is about 900 fils. Fares tend to be a little inflated travelling to and from the major tourist sites of Petra and Wadi Rum, but the most you'll ever pay for a single minibus ride – from Amman to Aqaba – is JD3. Minibuses always have someone employed to ride up front to keep the driver company and deal with letting

△ Downtown Amman

people on and off; at some point during the journey, he'll come round to collect fares.

The only times you'll find a choice of bus possibilities is on a handful of long-distance runs, where a few companies operate large, air-con **buses** in competition with the minibuses. Jordan Express Tourist Transport, or JETT, has timetabled services from Amman to Aqaba (and once-weekly to Hammamat Ma'in); Trust International Transport operates Amman–Aqaba and Irbid–Aqaba; Afana Tourist Transport also operates Amman–Aqaba; and Hijazi shuttles between Amman and Irbid, mainly for students attending Yarmouk University. These all offer the advantages of comfort and speed over the minibuses, and most even allow you to book in advance (in person only, at the company's office).

On most inter-city routes, shared taxis (universally known as **serveeces**) tout for business alongside the buses. These are often vintage seven- or eight-seater Mercedes – generally white – which offer, at a slightly higher price, the single advantage of speed over the same journey by bus. However, being squashed into the back seat of a suspension-challenged heap on a long journey can counter in discomfort what might be gained in time. Serveeces also operate the system of departing when full, but because there are fewer seats they leave more often than buses. If you're carrying bulky or heavy luggage, you may well find that serveece, and some minibus, drivers will charge you for the space your bags occupy, whether or not they take up seating space.

For getting around **within cities**, only Amman and Irbid are too big to walk across; details of public transport provisions in these cities are in the relevant chapters. Although most other towns have their own systems of short-hop buses and serveeces, all are small enough that you can easily walk between sights. The long, steep slopes of Wadi Musa prompt most visitors to resort to taxis for getting to and from the Petra gate.

Bus and serveece **etiquette** says that men should sit next to men and women next to women (except for married partners or siblings), and you should stick to this rule when you can. No one will be mortally offended if circumstances force you to sit next to a Jordanian of the opposite sex, but – especially for a close-quarters serveece journey – other passengers may shuffle themselves around to make a more acceptable space for you.

Hitch-hiking

Hitching a ride on well-travelled routes such as Amman to Irbid will likely take you hours, since drivers won't have a clue why you can't just get the bus like everyone else. However, in areas where buses may be sporadic or nonexistent – the eastern desert, the southern portions of the King's Highway (south of Qadisiyyeh), the link road from the Desert Highway into Wadi Rum, or just from one village to the next on quiet country roads – all moving vehicles are fair game for hitching; local drivers stick to a well-established countryside protocol about picking people up if they have space. The generally accepted way to indicate you're hitching is to lazily hold out your arm and loosely flap your index finger.

The first rule of hitching in Jordan – apart from foreign women never hitching alone – is that you should always be prepared to **pay something**, even if your money is refused when offered. Rightly or wrongly, foreigners are seen as able to pay their bus fares, and trying to freebie your way around the country will inspire contempt rather than sympathy.

Travellers who decide to hitch should do so always in pairs. The risks of assault (or worse) attached to hitching in Europe or elsewhere in the world are minuscule in Jordan, but nonetheless do exist; women should never sit next to men, and spontaneous offers of hospitality on the part of drivers should be accepted only with extreme caution, if at all. On a more prosaic note, **water** and a **hat** are vital hitching accoutrements: out on the road, you're in more danger from dehydration than anything else.

Driving

Compared with Egypt or Syria, **driving** in Jordan is a breeze; compared with the West, it's a nightmare. Cities, highways, backroads and desert tracks each pose a challenge to drivers' skills and nerve, and, apart from driving on the right and always obeying a policeman, **rules of the road** have individual interpretations. Most roads aren't marked out in lanes, so overtaking on both sides is normal – always accompanied by a blast or two on the horn – as is pulling out into fast-moving traffic without looking. There is no universally accepted pattern of **right of way**. It's wise to follow the locals and sound your **horn** before many types of manoeuvre; out in the sticks, you should look out for kids playing on the hard shoulder and give a warning honk from a long way back. **Traffic lights** are always respected – there are cameras in Amman recording red-light runners – as are most **one-ways**, although people do sometimes drive slowly the wrong way down a highway, searching for a place to U-turn. Right of way on roundabouts goes to whoever's moving fastest.

Road surfaces are generally good, although there are lots of **unmarked speed bumps** and rumble strips in unexpected places (including main highways), as well as killer potholes on minor roads. Look out also for drifting sand on roads in the desert: if you're going too fast when you hit a patch of sand, you can easily be spun off the road before you know what's happened. **Speed limits** are posted regularly, and are generally 100kph on highways and 90kph on main roads, dropping to 40kph or so in built-up areas. Mobile police radar traps regularly catch dozens of offenders, with spot fines for speeding in the order of JD15–20: it pays to stick to the speed limit.

On major roads, **directional signs** are plentiful and informative; most have English as well as Arabic. A series of large white-on-brown signs around the country specifically directs tourists to major sites, superseding older, idiosyncratically spelled white-on-blue ones. On unsigned back roads, the only failsafe method of finding the right direction is to keep asking the locals.

Night driving is considerably more scary, when speed bumps, uneven road surfaces, children or animals (or objects) in the road and potholes all become invisible. In addition, slow-moving trucks and farm vehicles often chug along in the dark without headlights, or with faulty rear lights, effectively rendering them invisible too. It's also common – if inexplicable – practice on dark country roads to flip to main beam when you see somebody coming, effectively dazzling them blind. Most

people flash their headlights to say "get out of the way", but some do it to say "OK go ahead", others merely to say hello: you must make up your own mind at the time which it is.

Although a normal **driving licence** from home is sufficient, an International Driving Permit can be useful, since it has an Arabic translation; these are available very inexpensively from motoring organizations in your home country. Without a Jordanian driving licence, you're only permitted behind the wheel of rental cars (green plates), cars registered to foreigners resident in Jordan (yellow plates) and foreign-registered vehicles; to drive the regular white-plated cars you must hold a local licence.

Renting a self-drive car

For reaching all corners of the country at your own pace, a **rental car** is a worthwhile – sometimes essential – investment. The rental market is huge, with more than 150 different companies nationwide, competition being based on price rather than quality. Local operators tend to cater much more to Jordanians' own visiting friends and family than to Westerners, and although you can get great deals from trustworthy firms, many of these tiny outfits are no more than a guy with a phone renting out old cars on the cheap with no insurance, no papers and no service. Reliable companies in Amman or Aqaba, all of which take major credit cards, are recommended in the relevant chapters of the guide.

It is possible to arrange car rental **before you arrive** but, although this buys you peace of mind, prices quoted for international reservations are invariably higher than those quoted to walk-in customers, sometimes by as much as fifty percent. Further savings can be had by going to local agencies, all of which can match or undercut the big agencies' walk-in rates, some maintaining equivalent levels of quality and service. Whether you book in advance or on arrival, international agencies can generally bring a car to you at any border crossing or airport for free (local operators may add a surcharge): Hertz offers the best coverage and service, if not the best value for money, with locations in Amman, Petra, Aqaba, Queen Alia Airport and at the Dead Sea.

Trustworthy businesses – such as Reliable Rent-a-Car in Amman (☎06/592 9676, ⊛www.reliable.com.jo) – charge about JD30 a day, for a 1- or 2-year-old car (manual or automatic) comfortable for four people, including unlimited mileage and full insurance. A "subcompact", comfortable for two, is JD3–4 less. Some form of collision damage waiver (CDW) covering all but the first JD200–300 of damage might cost a few dinars more, but, considering the Jordanian driving style, is eminently worth it. Only the international agencies offer optional extras such as zero-deductible cover, personal accident insurance (PAI) and theft protection (TP) – the last truly unnecessary in such a safe country. Before moving off, you'd do well to check that the car has a pumped-up spare tyre and a full toolkit and jack. It's also a good idea to keep a few litres of bottled water in the car, in case you have to wait for breakdown recovery in some remote spot.

A couple of agencies in Amman, and a few more in Aqaba, rent out reliable **four-wheel-drive** vehicles (universally called "four-by-fours") from about JD35 a day upwards. These are essential for getting to a handful of out-of-the-way archeological sites and quiet spots in Wadi Rum, but you should have some familiarity with 4x4 driving – and a local guide with you – before you set off into the desert. For all but the most dedicated adventurers, a normal car is fine.

In the case of an **accident**, to claim costs back from the insurance company you'll need a full written report from the police, and from the first doctor on the scene who treated any injuries.

Car rental agencies abroad

Avis UK ☎0870/606 0100, Ireland ☎01/605 7555, US ☎1-800/331-1084, Canada ☎1-800/272-5871, Australia ☎13 6333, New Zealand ☎0800/655111; ⊛www.avis.com.
Budget UK ☎0800/181181, Ireland ☎01/878 7814, US & Canada ☎1-800/527-0700, Australia ☎1300/362848, New Zealand ☎0800/652277; ⊛www.budget.com.
Hertz UK ☎0870/844 8844, Ireland ☎01/676 7476, US ☎1-800/654-3001, Canada ☎1-800/263-0600, Australia ☎13 3039, New Zealand ☎0800/655955; ⊛www.hertz.com.
Thrifty UK ☎01494/751600, US & Canada

☎1-800/847-4389, Australia ☎1300/367227, New Zealand ☎09/309 0111; ⊛www.thrifty.com.

Motoring organizations

Australia: AAA ☎02/6247 7311, ⊛www.aaa.asn.au.
Canada: CAA ☎613/247-0117, ⊛www.caa.ca.
Ireland: AA Ireland ☎01/617 9999, ⊛www.aaireland.ie.
Jordan: RACJ ☎06/585 0626, ⊛www.racj.com.
New Zealand: NZAA ☎09/377 4660, ⊛www.nzaa.co.nz.
UK: AA ☎0870/600 0371, ⊛www.theaa.com; RAC ☎0800/550055, ⊛www.rac.co.uk.
US: AAA ☎1-800/222-4357, ⊛www.aaa.com.

Fuel

Almost all **petrol** stations around the country are run by the Jordan Petroleum Refinery Company, with its distinctive red snowflake logo; most towns have at least one or two pumps. All stations have attendants to do the work for you: either hand over your dinars before he starts, or just ask for "full". Low-octane "regular" (*benzeen*, aka *aadi*) is available everywhere. Most rental agencies will tell you to fill up with high-octane "super" (*soober*, aka *khas*), but it's rarely found outside Amman – the only places you can rely on it are Aqaba and the Amman–Irbid road. Elsewhere, *aadi* will do fine. Diesel (*deezel*) is available only rarely, and there are just a handful of stations selling unleaded (*khal min ar-rasas*), most reliably near 8th Circle in Amman. You must almost always pay in **cash only** – barely a handful of stations take Visa. Pump attendants tip themselves a few fils off your change as a matter of course.

Accidents

Despite the Jordanian driving style, **accidents** are infrequent, and rarely amount to more than a prang. However, bear in mind that under Jordanian law any accident involving a car and a **pedestrian** is automatically deemed to be the fault of the driver: if you hit anybody, cause any sort of injury, or even if someone falls out of a window onto your stationary vehicle, you will be held responsible. Goats, sheep, donkeys and camels roam more or less freely on and off roads in the countryside, but if you **hit an animal,** you will also be held responsible, and will have to pay the owner compensation. With a common-or-garden goat costing 80JD or more, and a camel at least ten times as much, you'd do well to keep your eyes peeled.

If you're in any sort of accident while behind the wheel of a **rental car**, call the rental company first, since – if they're trustworthy – they will call the police on your behalf and make the situation clear (possibly serving as interlocutors) and will also arrange to come out and pick you up; otherwise, call the police/civil defence yourself on ☏199. If the accident involves serious injury to a pedestrian, and there are people around to take care of whoever you've hit, it would be prudent to retreat to your car until the police arrive (and also let your embassy know what's happened); aside from the fact that, amidst all the shock and upset at the accident, there will be a near-insurmountable barrier of language and culture between you and any bystanders, expats of many years' standing in Jordan tell alarming tales of instant revenge being exacted on hapless tourist drivers by the extended family of accident victims.

Taxis and chauffeur-driven cars

All **taxis** in Jordan are yellow with green panels in Arabic on both front doors, and they'll go anywhere if the price is right. Inexpensive and quite often essential within Amman, their good value declines the further afield you want to go; renting a taxi to cover the transport-thin eastern desert, for instance, will cost you almost twice as much as if you drove there yourself in a rental car (but, obviously, with none of the stress of negotiating the roads). As far as **fares** go, other than within Amman city limits, where taxis are metered, you'll have to negotiate with the driver before setting off. Ballpark figures for particular routes are given in the guide, but where you're inventing your own itinerary, you'd do well to ask the advice of a disinterested party (such as a hotel receptionist) beforehand. Jordanian **women** would never get in the front seat next to a male driver (there are very few

female taxi-drivers), and, wherever possible, foreign women should follow suit and sit in the back.

Most rent-a-car agencies can provide a **driver** for the day for about JD15 on top of the price of the rental; on a longer trip, JD35 a day should cover his food and accommodation costs.

Trains

At the time of writing, the only usable passenger **train** tracks in Jordan are the remnants of the Hejaz Railway (see p.383), running from the Syrian border through Mafraq, Zarqa and Amman, and on into the desert via Qatraneh to Ma'an. The only regular service is a twice-weekly train between Amman and Damascus. South of Amman, the unguarded line runs through open desert and the resident Bedouin tend to rip up the rails for building joists when no one's looking; the only services into the desert are occasional steam trains chartered by visiting enthusiasts or tour groups. For your very own fully equipped steam locomotive pulling a comfortable carriage or two on an excursion from Amman, prices start from about JD450 all-in, rising the further you want to go. Call Mr Ali Hassan Jehdullah (☏06/489 5413), Traffic Manager at the Hejaz Jordan Railway in Amman, for details of chartering your own train.

In 2004 a proposal to run a passenger train from Aqaba to Wadi Rum was approved. Freight trains carrying phosphates to port in Aqaba from mines in the desert have used the line for some years, but this is the first time it will have been used for passenger service. At the time of writing it's still unclear what the project will entail, or what timescale is involved however.

Planes

Royal Wings (☏06/487 5202, ⌘www.royal wings.com.jo), a subsidiary of Royal Jordanian, operates the single domestic passenger **air** route, between Amman and Aqaba. At JD35 one-way, this isn't prohibitively expensive, and means you can travel from city centre to city centre in just over an hour, compared with more than four bumpy hours overland. In addition, the airborne views over the desert, the Dead Sea and the Petra mountains are worth the fare in themselves; make sure you're sitting on the right-hand side of the plane heading south.

Bicycles

Propelling yourself around the country by **bicycle** is a very pleasant way to travel, although barely a handful of locals cycle (mostly in the flat Jordan Valley) – and you're quite likely to be regarded as completely potty if you try. There are no bike rental firms in Jordan, so you must bring your own; you should also make arrangements for receiving advice and spare parts while on the road from a specialist back home.

Around the country, the roads are empty enough that much of the time you'll probably have the tarmac to yourself. Even Amman's traffic is sufficiently low-key that you could negotiate the city with relatively little hassle. The major problem, though, comes in the terrain: coping with the 14 or 15 percent hills of the King's Highway, while battling the prevailing westerly winds trying to sweep you into the ravine, is no joke. The south of the country is particularly taxing: from Ma'an to Aqaba is down all the way, but to return north you either have to struggle your way 80km back up to the plateau, or alternatively pedal against the strong northerly winds blowing down the funnel of the flat Wadi Araba. Winter rains and summer heat throughout Jordan can both be deadly, and you should ideally plan a cycling tour for the three spring months of March to May.

Accommodation

Accommodation in Jordan runs the gamut from the cheapest fleapit dives all the way up to international-standard luxury five-star hotels. Amman, Petra and Aqaba have a wide choice covering all price brackets, but other towns are restricted to a few, often uninspiring mid-range options. However, Jordan's award-winning Dead Sea hotels have quickly established themselves as some of the best luxury spa resort complexes in the world.

Jordan's hoteliers have had a tough few years. From a time in 2000 when average occupancy rates were running at a healthy 80 percent-plus, and there was widespread optimism in the tourism sector, income plummeted to almost nothing: following 9/11, the Palestinian intifada and the Iraq war, average occupancy around the country was running at 20 percent or less for much of 2003. Many smaller hotels ran a skeleton operation or closed altogether. These days things are on the up again, but the market is more cautious – trying to make a quick buck has been shown to be counter-productive, and generally only the better hotels have survived. You'll find room rates in all price brackets to be very competitive, and quality of service and standards is improving across the board as investment starts to flow again.

On a **backpacker budget**, there's a network of traveller-style hotels in all the major towns, and you'll easily get onto the grapevine for bargain excursions and adventures. On a mid-level budget, you can take advantage of some excellent-value small hotels – almost all still family-run – dotted about the country, on and off the beaten track. At the top end, Jordan's finest hotels can compete on equal terms with the best in the world.

As anywhere, **room rates** vary according to the season. In general, the high season for tourism from non-Arab countries is spring (March–May) and autumn (Sept & Oct) – this is when hotels are at their busi-

Hotel price codes

Throughout this guide, hotels have been categorized according to the price codes given below, which indicate the normal price for the **least expensive double room** in an establishment during the **high season** (excluding the 17 percent tax and ten percent service charge levied in all hotels priced ❸ and above). **Single rooms** can cost anything between seventy and a hundred percent of the double-room rates. Where a hotel also offers beds in **shared rooms**, a price *per person* to share has been given.

❶ under JD10
❷ JD10–20
❸ JD20–30

❹ JD30–40
❺ JD40–50
❻ JD50–65

❼ JD65–80
❽ JD80–95
❾ over JD95

est. High summer (June–Aug) is when tourism from Arab countries – specifically the Gulf States – is at its peak, but these visitors tend to prefer to stay in self-catering apartment suites, so hotel bargains can still be had. In Aqaba charter flights continue even in the height of summer, and hotels stay busy with sun-seeking tourists all winter long (Oct–April). The luxury five-star Dead Sea hotels are a law unto themselves, and are regularly completely full – block-booked either by conference delegates or by tour groups, or frequently packed with wealthy Ammanis on weekend breaks.

The **Jordan Hotels Association** (ⓦ www .johotels.com) grades all hotels from one to five stars, with so-called "unclassified" hotels off the bottom end of the scale. All hotels above ❸ in our price-coding system tack 17 percent **government tax** onto their quoted prices and generally accept payment by credit card; some also add another ten percent **service charge** (often indicated by "++", or "plus-plus"). **Standards** vary widely within each price bracket and sometimes within each hotel: if the room you're shown isn't good enough, ask to see others.

Below our ❸ bracket, things to look out for are **air conditioning** or a ceiling fan in summer, and **heating** in winter; both are essential almost everywhere and worth paying for (although you're unlikely to need a heater in Aqaba, even in January). South- or west-facing rooms that receive direct sunshine are liable to become ovens on summer afternoons and so stay uncomfortably hot during the night; you'd do well in Aqaba to reject a sea view in favour of a cooler, north-facing balcony.

There are no **hostels** in Jordan, and the tiny number of **campsites** are all privately run and not affiliated to international organizations (see p.80).

Budget and mid-range hotels

Budget and mid-range hotels – covering the ❶–❷ price brackets – comprise the majority of hotels in Jordan.

The bottom end of the market consists of cheap **dosshouses** in the centres of all towns, catering chiefly to Egyptian, Syrian and Iraqi men come to Jordan to labour. These are universally filthy dives that are best avoided: washing facilities are likely to be spartan or nonexistent, and there might easily be only one squat toilet to share. Slightly up from these – though still well inside the ❶ bracket – are **budget** establishments aimed either exclusively at Westerners, or at both locals and Westerners; often the latter will have some means of separation, like reserving one whole floor for locals only and another for Westerners only. Quite often you'll find a choice of shared or private rooms, housing two, three or four beds, with many places also offering a choice of some en-suite rooms as well. Whatever the outward appearance of the decor, though, you'd be advised to check things out before you commit yourself: seeing if the sheets are clean, the bed is stable, the flyscreens on the windows are intact, the ceiling fan works, the water in the bathroom is hot (or at least lukewarm), the toilets don't smell too much, and so on, are all completely acceptable things to do before agreeing to pay. Once you've checked in, most places won't bother with holding on to your **passport**, but nonetheless it's a good rule to insist on keeping your passport with you at all times.

Women travelling alone or together on a rock-bottom budget will have to play things by ear most of the time, although we've given some pointers in the guide on places that are OK for foreign women. In general – although not always – hotels with price code ❶ that are geared towards Western backpackers will be safe and welcoming for women, whereas those that are mainly geared up for locals should be avoided. The security and privacy on offer in slightly pricier places have obvious advantages over coping with inquisitive late-night doorknob-rattlings or finding Peeping Toms in the communal shower area.

Breakfast is never included in hotels in the ❶ and ❷ price ranges, and – counting as an optional extra – provides some scope for bargaining in hotels priced ❸ and above.

Mid-range hotels – in the ❸, ❹ and ❺ brackets – are all generally clean and comfortable. However, Jordan has no grand, fading colonial-age piles to fall back on for a night or two of nostalgia; Amman's venerable *Philadelphia Hotel*, built in the 1920s in the heart of Downtown alongside the Roman Odeon, was rather short-sightedly bulldozed in the 1980s. Instead, the prevailing tone is one of glitz, as hordes of shiny new hotels – often featuring plenty of gilt and fake marble – jostle for position. Most of these mid-range places are priced in the ❹ and even ❺ brackets, but will often adjust their rates down to ❸ with not much prompting.

Luxury hotels

The **luxury** end of the market offers some excellent value for money. An over-concentration of hotels priced ❻, ❼, ❽ and ❾ means that, with prudent advance booking (which can bring you bed-and-breakfast for less than the room-only walk-up rate), you could quite easily bring the cost of a five-star splurge down to a half (or even a third) of what you might pay in Europe for equivalent facilities. All five-star hotels will be able to cater for **non-smoking** guests on request, either with designated rooms or frequently with whole non-smoking floors. Amman, in particular, has more five-star beds than it knows what to do with, some in long-established properties that have been renovated and upgraded, many in opulent new hotel complexes built in the last couple of years or so. The five-star resort hotels newly built in Aqaba and on the Dead Sea shore – often with world-class spa complexes on site – are extraordinarily sleek and luxurious.

Food and drink

BASICS | Food and drink

Arab tradition values home cooking over eating out, and consequently the bulk of Jordan's restaurants are simple places serving straightforward fare. Excellent restaurants do exist, but must be sought out; unadventurous travellers can easily find themselves stuck in a rut of low-quality falafel and kebabs, departing the country never having tasted the best of what's on offer.

Outside large hotels and relatively upmarket formal restaurants, you'll be **eating with your fingers** at least some of the time – generally using pieces of flat bread to scoop up dips or make one-bite sandwiches. Since the **left hand** is traditionally used for toilet purposes, Jordanians instinctively always eat only with the **right**. Using your left hand while eating from a communal platter in someone's house would be considered unhygienic and possibly rude (see p.90 for more on this kind of etiquette), but in restaurant situations, no one will be mortally offended if you use your left hand for a tricky shovelling or tearing manoeuvre. In most budget diners, the only **cutlery** you'll find will be a spoon, used for rice and soupy stews. Even where there is cutlery, flaps or pockets of flat bread count as knife and fork, for dipping, mopping up sauces and tearing meat off the bone.

Unlike in other Middle Eastern countries, **hygiene** is rarely a problem in Jordan. However, nowhere in the country can you avoid **tobacco smoke**, least of all in cafés and restaurants.

Where and when to eat

Where you choose to eat depends partly on your budget and partly on your expectations. The easiest way to escape the endless budget round of hummus, chicken and falafel – aside from plumping for burger-style Western fast food – is to take refuge in **hotel food**, ranging from a reasonable set-price buffet with a range of salads and hot dishes all the way up to high-class à-la-carte restaurants. Large towns generally have a choice of **restaurants** serving the ubiquitous basic staples; Amman's restaurants are some of the finest in the Middle East, and Aqaba has some good options too; above-average places exist elsewhere, but are rather thin on the ground. In more out-of-the-way villages, a restaurant (if there is one) is likely to be a nameless, dingy den with a couple of pots of meat stew in the back and a chicken rotisserie on the street.

The traditional Jordanian way to round off a meal is with fresh fruit, and inexpensive eateries rarely offer desserts. However, all

Hidden costs and tipping

In addition to the standard **government sales tax** of 17 percent (seven percent in Aqaba), all restaurants above a certain quality threshold automatically add to all bills a **ten percent service charge**. On larger sums, this can obviously represent a hefty surcharge. They are legally obliged to state these additions somewhere, although it can be as surreptitious as a tiny line on the bottom of a menu. Visitors from North America may be used to this, but for Europeans it can be a hard lesson to learn, that the price you thought you'd be paying is only three-quarters of what you'll actually have to shell out.

In a good restaurant, even when a service charge is included, it's customary to **round the bill up** slightly as well. Occasionally, restaurants will add the tax but leave the service charge up to you – in these situations, your meal would have to have been really awful to merit anything less than a ten percent tip. Budget local diners don't expect tips and will never press you for anything.

For a list of useful culinary terms in Arabic, see p.512.

large towns have plenty of **patisseries** for Arabic sweets, where, if they have a seating area, you can also get a coffee. It's not unknown to take a few choice sweets away in a box to munch at a nearby coffee house.

As far as **timing** goes, simple breakfasts are generally finished with by 8am. Lunch is eaten between 1 and 3pm, and you may come across locals taking a break around 6pm for coffee and sweet pastries. The main meal of the day is eaten late, rarely before 8pm; in Amman, Aqaba and the north of the country, restaurants may not even start to fill up until 9.30 or 10pm. In keeping with the Bedouin tradition of eating only at home, you'll find that even quite large towns in the Bedouin heartland of southern Jordan, such as Madaba or Karak, have a bare handful of unimpressive, often empty restaurants that do a roaring

trade in early-evening takeaways and close up by 8 or 9pm.

Throughout the guide, we've included **phone numbers** for restaurants where it's a good idea to book.

Breakfast and street snacks

The traditional Jordanian **breakfast** is a bowl of hot **fuul** (boiled fava beans mashed with lemon juice, olive oil and chopped chillis), mopped up with fresh-baked *khubez* (flat bread) – guaranteed to keep you going for hours. **Hummus**, a cold dip of boiled chickpeas blended with lemon juice, garlic, sesame and olive oil, is slightly less heavy, but harder to find first thing in the morning. Both *fuul* and hummus can be ordered to take away (*barra*) in plastic pots. Bakeries that have an open oven (*firin*) usually offer a whole selection of savoury pastries, including *khubez bayd* (a kind of small egg pizza) and a range of bite-sized pastry triangles (*ftayer*) filled with cheese (*jibneh*), spinach

---

Eating during Ramadan

For the whole month of **Ramadan** (see p.74) Muslims are forbidden by both religious and civil law from **smoking** and from **eating or drinking** anything – including water and, in the strictest interpretations, even their own saliva – during the hours of daylight. Throughout Ramadan, all coffee houses and restaurants nationwide (apart from those in big hotels) stay closed until sunset, and many choose to take the whole month off for renovations; any that do business, though, often stay open from sunset until the early hours. Markets, groceries and supermarkets are open during the day with slightly truncated hours, and all shops close for an hour or two around dusk to allow staff to break the fast with family or friends – and this is a great time to join in. Restaurants of all kinds, including those within hotels, make the sunset meal – known as **iftar** – a real occasion, with special colourful decorations, themed folkloric events or music and general merriment. Even the cheapest diners will rig up party lights and lay out tables and chairs on the street to accommodate crowds of people, all sitting down together to share the experience of breaking the day's fast. Many people have two or three light dinners as the evening goes on, moving from one group of friends or relatives to the next.

For **foreigners**, nothing serious will happen if you inadvertently light up a cigarette in public during the day, but the locals will not thank you for walking down the street munching a sandwich. All four- and five-star hotels serve both food and soft drinks to foreigners during daylight and also alcohol after dark, although you may find that they'll only do so in places out of public view; lobby or terrace coffee-shops may not serve you. If you're travelling on a tight budget and are buying picnic food for both breakfast and lunch, you'll need to exercise a good deal of tact during the day in eating either behind closed doors or well out of sight in the countryside.

Note that It is illegal for supermarkets and non-hotel restaurants to sell **alcohol** for the entire month. Businesses operated by Christians adopt the same practices.

(*sabanekh*), potato (*batata*) or meat (*lahmeh*). Larger bakeries also have a wide range of chunky breadsticks, sesame-seed bread rings (*kaak*), thick slabs of crunchy toast (*garshella*) and rough brown bread (*khubez baladi*). Along with some olives (*zaytoon*) and yoghurt – either runny (*laban*) or creamy (*labneh*) – it's easy to put together a picnic breakfast. Where breakfast is included in budget **hotel** prices, you generally get pretty poor fare, but larger hotels offer more substantial buffet choices.

The staple **street snack** in the Middle East is **falafel**, small balls of a spiced chick-pea paste deep-fried and served stuffed into *khubez* along with some salad, a blob of *tahini* (sesame-seed paste) and optional hot sauce (*harr*). Up and down the country you'll also find **shwarma** stands, with a huge vertical spit outside to tempt in customers. *Shwarma* meat is almost always lamb (only occasionally chicken), slabs of it compressed into a distinctive inverted cone shape and topped with chunks of fat and tomatoes to percolate juices down through the meat as it cooks. When you order a *shwarma*, the cook will dip a *khubez* into the fat underneath the spit and hold it against the flame until it crackles, then fill it with thin shavings of the meat and a little salad and hot sauce.

Prices are nominal. All over the country, a bowl of *fuul* or hummus costs around 300 fils, and small baked nibbles 100–200 fils. Bread is sold by weight, with a kilo of large *khubez* (about five pieces) or small *khubez* (about eleven pieces) 200–300 fils. A falafel sandwich is about 150 fils, a *shwarma* sandwich about 300 fils.

Restaurant meals

The cheapest budget **diners** will generally only have one or two main dishes on view – roast chicken or *fuul* or stew with rice – but you can almost always get hummus and salad to fill out the meal. In better-quality **Arabic restaurants**, the usual way to eat is to order a whole variety of small starters (*mezze*), followed by either a selection of main courses to be shared by everyone, or a single, large dish for sharing.

Good Arabic restaurants might have thirty different choices of **mezze**, from simple bowls of hummus or *labneh* up to dishes

of fried chicken liver (*kibdet djaj*) or wings (*jawaneh*). Universal favourites are *tabbouleh* (parsley salad), *fattoush* (salad garnished with squares of crunchy fried bread), *warag aynab* (vine leaves stuffed with rice, minced vegetables, and often meat as well) and spiced olives. *Kibbeh* – the national dish of Syria and Lebanon and widely available at better Jordanian restaurants – is a mixture of cracked wheat, grated onion and minced lamb pounded to a paste; it's usually shaped into oval torpedoes and deep-fried, though occasionally you can find it raw (*kibbeh nayeh*), a highly prized delicacy. Portions are small enough that two people could share four or five *mezze* as a sizeable starter or, depending on your appetite, a complete meal. Bread and a few pickles are always free.

Mezze are the best dishes for **vegetarians** to concentrate on, with enough grains, pulses and vegetables to make substantial and interesting meat-free meals that cost considerably less than standard meaty dishes. Virtually all of the *mezze* salads are **vegan**, as are filling dishes such as *mujeddrah* (lentils with rice and onions) and *mahshi* (cooked vegetables stuffed with rice).

Main courses are almost entirely meat-based. Any inexpensive diner can do half a chicken (*nuss farooj*) with rice and salad. Kebabs are also ubiquitous (the chicken version is called *shish tawook*). Lots of places also do lunchtime meaty stews with rice; the most common is with beans (*fasooliyeh*), although others feature potatoes or a spinach-like green called *mulukhayyeh*. Jordan's national speciality is the traditional Bedouin feast-dish of *mensaf* – chunks of boiled lamb or mutton served on a bed of fatty rice, with pine nuts sprinkled on top and a tart, yoghurt-based sauce on the side to pour over. You'll also find some delicious Palestinian dishes, including *musakhan* (chicken steamed with onions and a sour-flavoured red berry called sumac) and *magloobeh* (essentially chicken with rice). A few places, mainly in Amman and the north, do a high-quality Syrian *fatteh* (meat or chicken cooked in an earthenware pot together with bread, rice, pine nuts, yoghurt, herbs and hummus, with myriad variations). Good fish (*samak*) is rare in Jordan; Aqaba's fish restaurants and

Amman's upstart seafood places can't match the succulent St Peter's fish served fresh at the Pella Resthouse (see p.234). Pork is forbidden under Islam and only appears at expensive Chinese restaurants in Amman.

Diner meals of chicken, stew or kebabs won't **cost** more than about JD1.500 for a stomach-filling, if not a gourmet, experience. Plenty of Arabic and foreign restaurants in Amman and other corners of the country serve high-quality meals for JD5–8 per person. It's possible to dine sumptuously on *mezze* at even the most expensive restaurants in the country for less than JD10 per person, although meaty main courses and wine at these places can rapidly torpedo a bill into the JD30s per head without too much effort.

Sweets

A Western-bred, naughty-but-nice guilt-ridden attitude to confectionery can only quail in the face of the unabashedly sugar-happy, no-holds-barred Levantine sweet tooth: most **Arabic sweets** (*halawiyyat*) are packed with enough sugar, syrup, butter and honey to give a nutritionist the screaming horrors.

There are three broad categories of *halawiyyat*: large round trays of hot, fresh-made confections, often **grain-based**, which are sliced into squares and drenched in hot syrup; piles of pre-prepared, bite-sized honey-dripping **pastries** and cakes; and stacks of dry sesame-seed or date-filled **biscuits**. The best of the hot sweets made in trays is *k'naffy*, a heavenly Palestinian speciality of buttery shredded filo pastry layered over melted goat's cheese. *Baglawa* – layered flaky pastry filled with pistachios or other nuts – is available in any number of different varieties. Juice-stands often lay out tempting trays of *hareeseh*, a syrupy semolina almond-cake, sliced into individual portions. Of the biscuits, you'd have to go a long way to beat *maamoul*, buttery, crumbly rose-scented things with a date or nut filling. Everything is sold **by weight**, and you can pick and choose a mixture: a quarter-kilo (*wagiyyeh*) – rarely more than JD1.500 – is plenty for two.

Large restaurants and some patisseries also have **milk-based** sweets, often flavoured deliciously with rosewater and no less sweet than anything else. King of these is *muhallabiyyeh*, a semi-set almond cream pudding served in individual bowls, but the Egyptian speciality *Umm Ali* – served hot, sprinkled with nuts and cinnamon – runs a close second.

For seasonal treats, extra-sweet, curiously elastic **ice-cream** (*boozeh*) is a summer standard around the country; Aqaba has the best range and quality. A common sight during Ramadan is for bakeries and patisseries to make stacks of fresh *gatayyif* – traditional **pancakes** – on hotplates set up on the street; locals buy dozens of them for stuffing at home with nuts and syrup.

Fresh fruit and picnic food

Street markets all over the country groan with stacks of **fresh fruit** year round, including apples from Shobak and oranges, mandarins and bananas from Gaza and the Jordan Valley. Local bananas (or the common Somali ones) are smaller, blacker and sweeter than the bland, oversized clones imported from Latin America. In the late spring, Fuheis produces boxes of luscious peaches; local grapes – green, red and black but none seedless – come from the Balqa and Palestine. Jordan is also one of the principal markets for exquisite Iraqi dates, which are available stoned and packed all year. The best time to look out for fresh dates is in late autumn, when you'll also see mountains of small, yellow-orange fruit often still on the branch; these are *balah*, sweet, crunchy unripe dates that seldom make it to the West. Around the same time, pomegranates appear everywhere, while spring and summer are the season for local melon and watermelon.

As far as picnic **vegetables** go, carrots, tomatoes and cucumbers are year-round staples. For picnic supplements, most towns have a good range of stalls or mobile vendors selling **dried fruit** and roasted **nuts and seeds**. Raisins, sultanas, dried figs and dried apricots can all be found cheaply everywhere. The most popular kind of seeds are *bizr* (dry-roasted melon, watermelon or sunflower seeds), the cracking of which in order to get at the minuscule kernel is an acquired skill. Local almonds (*luz*) – at around JD2 per quarter-kilo – are delectable. Pistachios and roasted chick-peas are locally produced; peanuts, hazel-nuts and cashews are imported. It's often possible to buy individual **hard-boiled eggs** from neighbourhood groceries, and varie-ties of the local salty white **cheese** (*jibneh*) are available everywhere.

Tea, coffee and other drinks

The main focus of every Jordanian village, town and city neighbourhood is a **coffee house**, where friends and neighbours meet, gossip does the rounds and a quiet moment can be had away from the family. The musicians, poets and story-tellers of previous generations have been replaced everywhere by taped music and football on the TV, although a genial, sociable ambience survives. However, all are exclusively male domains and bastions of social tradition; foreign women will always be served without hesitation, but sometimes might feel uncom-fortably watched.

The national drink, lubricating every social occasion, is **tea** (*shy*), a strong, dark brew served scalding-hot and milkless in small glasses. The traditional method of tea-making is to boil up loose leaves in a pot together with several spoons of sugar to allow maximum flavour infusion. In deference to foreign taste buds, you may find the sugar being left to your discretion, but the tannins in steeped tea are so lip-curlingly bitter that you'll probably prefer the Jordanian way.

Coffee (*gahweh*), another national institu-tion, has two broad varieties. **Turkish coffee** is what you'll come across most often. Made by boiling up cardamom-flavoured grounds in a distinctive long-handled pot, then letting it cool, then reboiling it several times (tradition-ally seven, though in practice two suffices), it's served in small cups along with a glass of water as chaser. Sugar is added beforehand, so you should request your coffee unsweet-ened (*saada*), medium-sweet (*wasat*) or syrupy (*helweh*); let the grounds settle before sipping, and leave the last mouthful, which is mud, behind. Some of the best coffee comes rich and pitch-black from the twin silver pots of mobile vendors, found on street corners and highway shoulders nationwide. **Arabic coffee**, also known as Bedouin coffee, is

an entirely different, almost greenish liquid, unsweetened and pleasantly bitter, tradition-ally made in a long-spouted brass pot set in hot embers. Public coffee houses don't have it, and you'll only be served it – often, rather prosaically, from a thermos flask – in a social situation by Bedouin themselves (for exam-ple, if you're meeting with a police officer or government official).

Coffee houses also serve soft drinks and a wide range of seasonal **herbal teas**, includ-ing mint, fennel, fenugreek, thyme, sage and camomile. In colder seasons at coffee houses and street-stands, you'll also come across the winter-warmer **sahleb**, a thick milky drink made from a ground-up orchid tuber and served very hot sprinkled with nuts, cinnamon and coconut.

A coffee house is also the place to try a tobacco-filled water pipe, known by different names around the Arab world but most famil-iarly in Jordan as a **"hubbly-bubbly"**, *argileh* or *nargileh*. Many upscale restaurants offer an *argileh* as a post-prandial digestive, and it is utterly unlike smoking a cigarette: the tobacco is nearly always flavoured sweetly with apple or honey, and this, coupled with the smoke cooling as it bubbles through the water chamber before you inhale, makes the whole experience pleasant and soothing.

Mineral water

Bottles of local **mineral water** are available in all corners of the country (see p.48 for advice on tap water). All brands have the price printed on the bottle, a standard 1.5 litre size costing 300 fils if you buy them individually, or much less than that if you buy a six-pack from a supermarket or grocery. Conversely, you pay a premium in out-of-the-way places – JD1 or more inside Petra. Check that the seal is unbroken before you buy. Inexpensive diners always have jugs of drinkable tap water (*my aadi*) on the table, but in restaurants waiters will quite often bring a bottle of mineral water (normally JD1) to your table with the menu – which you're quite entitled to reject.

Fresh juice and squash

Benefiting from the wealth of local fresh fruit, most Jordanian towns have at least one stand-up **juice-bar**; these are great places for supplementing a meagre breakfast or just replenishing your vitamin C. Any fruit in view can be juiced or puréed. Sugar (*sukkr*) and ice (*talj*) are automatically added to almost everything; however, considering ice blocks are generally wheeled in filthy trolleys along the roadside and broken up with a screwdriver, you might like to give it a miss – if so, request your juice *bidoon talj* ("without sugar" is *bidoon sukkr*). Most freshly squeezed juices, and each stall's own juice cocktail, cost 300–350 fils for a "small" glass (actually quite big), double that for a pint. Exceptions are mango, strawberry and other exotic fruit, which cost a little more.

More popular, and thus easier to find, are much cheaper ready-made **fruit squashes**. Dark-brown *tamarhindi* (tamarind, tartly refreshing) and *kharroub* (carob, sweet-but-sour), or watery *limoon* (lemon squash) are the best bets; other, less common, choices include *soos* (made from liquorice root, also dark brown, supposedly medicinal and horribly bitter) and *luz* (sickly-sweet white almond-milk). All are 50 fils a glass.

Juice-bars are happy to fill an empty 1.5-litre plastic bottle with any quantity of juice or squash to take away.

Alcohol

Drinking **alcohol** is forbidden under Islam. Alcohol is widely available, but you have to look for it: the market streets and ordinary eateries of most towns show no evidence of the stuff at all. Apart from in big hotels, the only **restaurants** to offer alcohol are upscale establishments in Amman and Aqaba (Arabic and non-Arabic), resthouses at archeological sites nationwide and a couple of divey joints in Petra. Most big supermarkets and some smaller convenience stores sell alcohol, but

you'll generally be able to find dedicated **liquor stores** only in Amman, Aqaba, Madaba and Fuheis.

Drinking alcohol in public – which includes on the street, in cafés or coffee houses, in hotel lobbies, on the beach or even in the seemingly empty desert or countryside – is completely unacceptable and will cause great offence to local people. Places to drink are limited to your own hotel room, areas such as poolsides within hotel precincts, and the interiors of restaurants or bars that offer alcohol on the menu.

The predominant local **beer** is Amstel, brewed under licence and very palatable; local Henninger is better but rarer. Both come in 650ml bottles, for which liquor stores charge around JD1.500 (200 fils of which is a returnable deposit on the bottle) and Amman's upmarket bars ask JD4 or more. You'll also find cans of Guinness and Kilkenny for JD5 or so. Other finds include local brews such as Petra (whackingly strong at eight percent; JD3 per half-litre), Philadelphia (JD2.500) and Ferida (JD3), immortally labelled as "Among The Best Beer In The World".

There's quite a range of Jordanian and Palestinian **wines**, both marketed as "Holy Land". The best in both red and white comes from Latroun, although Bethlehem's Crémisan runs a close second. Mount Nebo whites, although winning no prizes, have a certain chilled appeal. The best local wines are generally JD5–7, imported European bottles much more. As for **spirits**, the top local choice is anise-flavoured *araq*, much like Turkish *raki* and generally drunk with water over ice during a meal. A bottle of high-quality Lebanese *araq* will set you back JD14 or so, more than most imported whiskies, gins and vodkas.

Communications

International communications from Jordan are simple and straightforward. Phone lines are good-quality, mobile phone coverage is excellent, there are hundreds of internet stations all over the country and the post is reliable, if slow.

Mail

Airmail **letters and postcards** can take anything up to two weeks to reach Western Europe from Jordan, a month to the USA or Australasia. Asking someone to write the destination country in Arabic can help avoid things going astray. It's safest to ignore the street postboxes and instead send your mail from larger post offices, all of which have a box for airmail (*barid jowwy*) marked in English. Stamps (*tawabe'a*) for postcards or letters to international destinations are 300–500 fils, but packets and parcels are horribly expensive – JD10–15 for 1kg.

Incoming mail (at least to Amman) is somewhat faster than outgoing: things can arrive in a matter of days from Europe. Mail addressed to "Poste Restante, Amman 11118" or "Poste Restante, Aqaba 77110" should arrive at the central post offices in those cities. Poste restante mail to any other town is unlikely to show up. Bulky envelopes or packets sent to a poste restante address will be stored out of sight, with a small slip with the addressee's name left in the tray instead; show the slip (and your passport) to collect your package. The Amex office in Amman (see p.52) will keep mail for Amex customers (ie you have to be a cardholder or carrying Amex traveller's cheques) sent to PO Box 408, Amman 11118.

International **courier** firms – and home-grown courier Aramex – are well represented in Amman and Aqaba. Prices are sky-high, but there's no danger of items going astray.

Phones

Jordan Telecom (ⓦwww.jordantelecom.jo) has been privatized, and ongoing deregulation is likely to shake up the telecoms market significantly over the next few years, with new phone companies launching and new services on offer.

Dotted around the country you'll see the forlorn remnants of **public phones**, installed in the late 1990s after privatization. Almost

---

Useful numbers and codes

Operator ☏1322
International directory enquiries ☏1213
Domestic directory enquiries ☏1212 or 06/464 0444
Emergencies ☏199 or 191

Phoning home
To the UK ☏0044 + area code without the zero + number.
To the Republic of Ireland ☏00353 + area code without the zero + number.
To the US or Canada ☏001 + area code + number.
To Australia ☏0061 + area code without the zero + number.
To New Zealand ☏0064 + area code without the zero + number.

Calling Jordan from abroad
First dial your **international access code** (00 from the UK, Ireland and New Zealand; 011 from the US and Canada; 0011 from Australia), followed by **962** for Jordan, then the Jordanian area code minus its initial zero, then the number.

none of them works any more – either vandalized or just abandoned as broken. Nobody bothers with them, since seemingly everybody now has a **mobile phone**.

The **dialling tone** is a low-pitched buzz or hum. If, after you dial, you get three persistent rising tones, a steady series of even-pitched tones, a continuous whine, a recorded message or silence, it means your number was **unobtainable** for some reason. Check the number is right and dial again: you could quite easily get through next time. The standard Arabic phone-prompt is a listless-sounding "Allo?"

Domestic codes

All landlines have a two-digit area code and seven-digit number. There are four **area codes**: 02 covers northern Jordan, 03 southern Jordan, 05 the Jordan Valley and central and eastern districts, and 06 the Amman area. **Mobile phone** numbers have eight digits, prefixed with 07. **Toll-free** numbers start with 0800.

Mobile phones

Mobile phones are massively popular in Jordan. If you want to use your own handset, you'll need to check with your phone provider in advance whether it will work in Jordan. Most **UK**, **Australian** and **New Zealand** mobiles use GSM technology, which works fine in Jordan (@www.gsmworld.com has full details), but you'll probably have to inform your phone provider before leaving the country in order to get international access, or "roaming", switched on; this may incur a charge. You're likely to be charged extra for incoming calls, and there may be different price brackets for calling to a Jordanian landline, to your home country, and globally, as well as varying peak and off-peak times. If you want to retrieve messages while you're away, you'll probably have to ask your provider for a new international access code, but texting usually works as normal. Unless a **US** or **Canadian** phone is a special triband handset, it probably won't work in Jordan; check with your provider.

An alternative is to rent or buy a **Jordanian mobile** – very straightforward to do and remarkably inexpensive. Currently two

Jordanian mobile phone providers, **Fastlink** (@www.fastlink.com.jo) and **MobileCom** (@www.mobilecom.jo), have most of the market. Both are equally efficient, offering extensive coverage across the country. They both have dozens of outlets in Amman and every other town in Jordan – see their websites for full details. You can walk in, choose any phone with a pre-pay calling plan over the counter, and within ten minutes be making and receiving calls on your Jordanian number. At the time of writing, a basic handset complete with SIM costs around JD50 to buy, with start-up credit thrown in. Compared to the West, calling and texting is very inexpensive. Top-up cards are available in every town in the country.

Home Direct service

The following Home Direct **toll-free numbers** get you straight through to an operator in your home country, so you can make calling-card or credit-card calls, as well as collect (reverse-charge) calls – all of which are very much more expensive than dialling direct. Check the Jordan Telecom website, and your home phone provider, for full details.

UK BT ☎18800 703; C&W ☎18800 441.
USA AT&T ☎18800 000; MCI ☎18800 001; Sprint ☎18800 777.

Email and internet

One of the best ways to keep in touch while travelling is to sign up for a free internet **email address** that can be accessed via the web from anywhere. The two big names are YahooMail (@www.yahoo.com) and Hotmail (@www.hotmail.com), but there are thousands of others, all of which make a living by bombarding you with ads. Once you've set up an account, you can log on from any internet café to send and receive mail via the web. Alternatively, check out Rough Guides **InTouch** travel toolkit (@www.roughguidesintouch.com) – install it on your home PC, hit the synchronize button, and then use it from any internet café in the world to stay in touch with friends and family, upload photos to your password-controlled website, and more.

If you're carrying your own **laptop** or palmtop, you may encounter some problems unless you're staying in five-star hotels (which generally have in-room access points). Internet cafés quite often rely on incomprehensible tangles of phone-wire spaghetti culminating in hard-wired wall connections, which leave you nowhere to plug in; before you travel, check out the excellent ⓦwww.kropla.com for invaluable information on how to proceed. Where there are sockets, you'll generally find either a US-style **RJ-11** or Jordan's own style of two-pin socket. **Adaptors** to allow you to use an RJ-11 plug can be found easily, but ones for the wider British-style phone plug are more elusive; make sure you pick up a

UK-to-US adaptor before you travel. The big hotels can advise on how to get online: they all generally have in-house broadband, or local dial-up service, and temporary user IDs for guests' use. Alternatively, many Jordanian ISPs issue **scratch cards** that let you get online on a temporary user ID and password via a local dial-up number. The big supermarkets in Amman, among other places, sell these cards for about JD10 (which buys 15hr of access time); printed on the back are a phone number, a user ID and, beneath a scratch-off layer, a password, all of which you key into your settings before connecting.

The media

With the widespread use of English in public life, you'll have relatively good access to news and information while in Jordan. International newspapers and magazines are on sale, and the local English-language press is burgeoning. Satellite TV is widespread.

Arabic press

Among the region's conservative and often state-owned **Arabic press**, Jordan's newspapers, all of which are independently owned, have a reputation for relatively well-informed debate, although the strict press laws – and the slow process of media liberalization – are the subject of much ongoing controversy. The two biggest dailies, *ad-Dustour* ("Constitution", founded in 1967) and *al-Ra'i* ("Opinion"; 1971), are both centrist regurgitators of government opinion. *Al-Arab al-Yawm* ("Arabs Today"; 1997), is more populist and free-thinking, while *al-Ghad* ("Tomorrow"; 2004) has rapidly gained a reputation for quality and a fresh outlook. Other dailies include *al-Diyar*, *al-Anbat* and *al-Ittijah*, with more due to launch. There's a host of weeklies, ranging from the sober to the sensational.

English-language press

Foreign newspapers are fairly widely available – from the news kiosks in all big hotels and also from some bookshops, such as the Jordan Distribution Agency shop in Amman and Redwan bookshop in Aqaba. The *International Herald Tribune* and most British dailies and Sundays are generally one or two days late, and expensive (JD2 and upwards). Plenty of magazines are also available, from *Cosmopolitan* to *The Economist*.

There's not much choice of **local newspapers** in English. The establishment **Jordan Times** (ⓦwww.jordantimes.com) is published daily except Saturdays, and features plenty of national news mingled with agency reports and pro-government comment, as well as useful what's-on information, emergency phone numbers and flat-hunting ads. Look out for the "Weekender"

Friday supplement, which often has feature articles on sites of cultural or natural interest around the country. The weekly **Star** (Ⓦwww .star.com.jo; published every Thursday) tends to be more independent-minded, but its journalistic standards can do it down. The leading English-language newspapers in the Arab world are **Al-Ahram Weekly** (Ⓦweekly.ahram .org.eg), a long-running stalwart published in Cairo and available at Amman's Jordan Distribution Agency bookshop, and Lebanon's excellent **Daily Star** (Ⓦwww.dailystar.com.lb), published as a supplement every day inside the *International Herald Tribune*.

The market for Jordanian English-language **magazines** has recently taken off, with a range of monthly titles devoted to lifestyle, home-making and business. One of the best is **JO** (Ⓦwww.jo.jo), with a good mix of articles on Jordanian society and attitudes (including some ground-breaking investigations, such as into abortion and prostitution). Also look out for interesting features in **Eye** (Ⓦwww.eyemagazine.net), and Cosmo-style home and beauty tips in the glossy, ad-packed **Living Well** (Ⓦwww.grumpygourmet.com), which also includes excellent restaurant reviews. **Y** looks at the business community, as does **Jordan Business**. Listings/what's-on magazines, including **Jordan Today** and **W2GO** (Where To Go), are available free in cafés and hotels; the latter, in particular, is a great resource for getting a handle on Amman's restaurant, café and club scene, with menu listings and discount coupons. **Al Reem** is the Royal Society for the Conservation of Nature magazine, published in English and Arabic, with well-researched articles on environmental issues; it's available only at the Wild Jordan centre in Amman.

TV

Jordanian TV isn't up to much, and is regularly slated in the press for its appalling programming. Channel 1 (Ⓦwww.jrtv.jo) is predominantly in Arabic, relying heavily on reports of the king's official engagements, studio debates and melodramatic Bedouin soaps (all glaring eyes, bushy beards and hands-on-daggers). It has some US shows and generic TV movies, as well as the main 10pm nightly news in English. There's also a

sport channel and a movie channel, variously available.

A majority of hotels, large and small, have **satellite TV**, but few of the channels are English-language: **CNN** can be had almost everywhere, as can one or two movie and light entertainment channels, but **BBC World** and anything else in English are available only sporadically, most often only in the luxury hotels. Israeli TV shows US soaps and TV dramas (and some movies) with subtitles, and Dubai TV features some English news. Other Arab and European channels are widely available – everything from the hard-hitting news coverage of Al-Jazeera and Al-Arabiya to tacky Syrian soaps, classic Egyptian melodramas and glitzy Lebanese game-shows, plus the usual array of French, German, Spanish and Italian fare.

Radio

Amman now has several English-language music **radio** stations, with many more planned. Of the current selection, **Mood 92FM** plays classic rock and pop from the 60s, 70s and 80s, while **Play 99.6FM** is chart-driven. **Radio Jordan**'s English station (Ⓦwww.jrtv.jo) is on 855kHz medium wave nationwide and 96.3FM (Amman) or 99.7FM (Aqaba), but often sounds dowdy and outdated, with an unimaginative playlist and diabolically bad DJs. It has news in English at 7am, 2pm, 7pm and 10pm.

Radio Sawa, at 98.1FM in Amman (Ⓦwww.radiosawa.com), is publicly funded by the US Congress and broadcasts to the whole Arab world from studios in Washington and Dubai – but, despite this, it is hugely popular for its innovative music policy, mixing Arabic and Western pop music in a beguiling blend of cross-cultural styles. It was set up so that the US government could broadcast its news and opinions in Arabic directly to the people of the Middle East, but it seems from reports and polls that most listeners love the music and ignore the propaganda in between. **Radio Fann**, at 104.2FM in Amman and other frequencies nationwide (Ⓦwww.radiofann.com), has similarly good Arabic music, as does **MBC FM**, at 106.7FM in Amman (Ⓦwww.mbcfm.fm), a Saudi station based In London. Also check out the music programming of **Radio Monte Carlo** (aka Radio France International) on 97.4FM, and **Amman FM** (part of Radio Jordan) on 99FM. The French service of Radio Jordan, on 90FM in Amman, broadcasts classical music during the day. The BBC's Arabic service – with news and debate – is on 103.1FM in Amman and 639kHz MW nationwide. Several Israeli music and talk stations can be picked up on FM around the country, as can some Palestinian stations. After dark, medium wave is crammed with all shades of Arabic music out of Amman, Ramallah, Damascus and Cairo.

BBC World Service (🌐www.bbcworld service.com) can be difficult to pick up in Amman's deep valleys; elsewhere it's generally pretty clear. Find it virtually all day long on 1323kHz medium wave (also at 1413kHz for short periods), and on short wave at 6.195, 9.410, 11.760, 12.095, 15.565, 15.575 or 17.640MHz. Check the web for the schedules and Middle East frequencies of **Voice of America** (🌐www.voa.gov).

Opening hours and public holidays

In Jordan, all offices are closed on Fridays, with some businesses and all government departments also taking Saturdays off.

The main thing to bear in mind is that if somebody tells you a particular attraction is open "every day", quite often they mean every day except Friday. Some Christian-run businesses close on Fridays and Sundays.

Normal town-centre **shop** opening hours are roughly 8 or 9am to 8 or 9pm, every day. In more out-of-the-way districts shops might close around 6pm. Some places might also close for two or three hours in the middle of the afternoon, and almost everywhere closes for the hour or two either side of midday prayers on Fridays. Prime shopping hours in town-centre **markets** tend to be from 6pm onwards, and most of them are open and bustling on Fridays. For advice on café and restaurant mealtimes, see p.64.

Banks tend to be open from 8.30am to about 12.30pm; some also open again from about 4 to 5.30pm. All banks are closed on Fridays, and a selection now also close on Saturdays. Normal **post office** hours are from 7 or 8am until 6 or 7pm, and quite often between 8am and 1pm on Fridays as well. **Government departments** keep standard hours of 8am to 2pm, closing on Fridays and Saturdays. All **transport services** operate seven days a week.

Where **archeological sites** have controlled opening hours, these are generally from 8am to dusk, seven days a week. Many sites, though, either have open access or are watched over by a *haris* (guardian), who lives on or close to the site and will open up as you approach. Government-run **museums** tend to open daily except Friday from 9am to 5pm; some, though, open on Fridays from 10am to 4pm. In the few cases where there are seasonal variations in opening hours, "summer" generally counts as the period from March to October.

During **Ramadan**, the Muslim holy month of fasting, everything changes. Shops, museums and offices open from 9am to about 2 or 3pm (closed Fri), while street markets do business every day but close up about half an hour before sunset. Banks and government departments may only be open for two or three hours in the morning. Some large supermarkets and a few shops might also open again for a couple of hours after dark. Large archeological sites such as Petra keep more or less normal hours, but guardians of smaller sites will want to lock up and get home an hour or so before sunset. Similarly, famished bus and serveece drivers take time off around sunset to break the fast.

Public holidays

Jordan's **secular national holidays** tend to be low-key affairs, involving either limited local celebrations or military parades in the capital; although government offices are closed, shops and businesses quite often open as normal and you could easily not notice the holiday at all. The exception is the king's birthday, which can involve a widely adopted three- or four-day break in the last week of January.

The handful of **Islamic religious holidays**, based on the Hijra calendar, are another matter, though, and are marked by widespread public observance. All shops and offices are closed and non-essential services are liable to be suspended. See p.469 for more information about Islamic religious holidays.

Jordan's **Christians** are mostly Orthodox and follow the Julian calendar, which varies from the Gregorian calendar used in the West by a couple of weeks (Jordan's Easter celebrations occur later than Easter in the West). Nevertheless, the different Christian communities have all agreed to celebrate Christmas Day together on December 25, and since 1994 that date has been marked as a national public holiday (although Muslim shops and businesses are open as normal).

Fixed public holidays

Jan 30 King Abdullah's Birthday
May 1 Labour Day
May 25 Independence Day
June 9 Accession of King Abdullah
June 10 Army Day & celebration of the Arab Revolt
Nov 14 King Hussein Remembrance Day
Dec 25 Christmas Day

Islamic holidays and Ramadan

The following dates of **Islamic holidays** are very approximate, since each holiday is announced only when the moon has been seen clearly by an authorized cleric from Jordan's Ministry of Islamic Affairs: in practice, each date could vary by a couple of days. If you're travelling close to these dates and want more detailed information in advance, the most reliable source is the nearest Jordanian Embassy. The start of the holy month of **Ramadan** is also included here; Ramadan is not a holiday in itself, but since it comprises 30 days of restricted business hours, its first day is a useful date to know.

Eid al-Adha (4 days) – begins 11 Jan 2006; 31 Dec 2006; 20 Dec 2007; 9 Dec 2008.
1st of Muharram (Muslim New Year) – 31 Jan 2006; 20 Jan 2007; 9 Jan 2008; 29 Dec 2008.
Mowlid an-Nabawi (birthday of the Prophet Muhammad) – 10 April 2006; 30 March 2007; 19 March 2008; 8 March 2009.
Eid al-Isra wal-Miraj – 21 Aug 2006; 10 Aug 2007; 30 July 2008; 19 July 2009.
Start of Ramadan – 23 Sept 2006; 12 Sept 2007; 1 Sept 2008; 21 Aug 2009.
Eid al-Fitr (3 days) – begins 22 Oct 2006; 11 Oct 2007; 30 Sept 2008; 19 Sept 2009.

Adventure tours and trekking

Although not a budget option, taking an organized tour once you arrive in Jordan can turn out to be the most rewarding way to get to some of the more isolated attractions in the hinterland.

If all you want is to be taken around Amman, Jerash and Petra quickly and without hassle, you'd do better to book a package deal from your home country in advance; see "Getting there", p.28, for details. Longer-stay special-interest holidays – such as birdwatching or diving – are also much better organized from home. However, it can be significantly more complicated to organize from home camping overnight in Burqu, for instance, or a two-day hike through Wadi Mujib, than it is to sort things out face to face with the relevant people once you arrive.

There are hundreds of Jordanian **tour operators** dealing with incoming tourism, but only

a handful can take you off the beaten track. For exploring the wilder reaches of the Dana reserve, Wadi Mujib and the Ajloun woodland reserve – and for any enquiries about getting out into Jordan's nature, guided or solo – you should talk first with the Ecotourism Unit at the Royal Society for the Conservation of Nature (RSCN). They can also direct you to particular individuals or companies that can help you get to where you want to go. Companies such as Discovery, La Beduina and Petra Moon are more than happy to set up a customized itinerary at short notice for individuals or small groups, whether your bent is archeology or ecology. And for impromptu

Camel rides

Many visitors from the West come to Jordan never having laid eyes on a **camel**, yet almost all arrive full of all kinds of ideas about the creatures; myths about the simplicity of desert life, the nobility of the Bedouin and the Lawrence-of-Arabia-style romance of desert culture all seem to be inextricably bound up in Western minds with the camel. Jordanian Bedouin, of course, long since gave up using camels either as a means of transport or as beasts of burden: Japanese pick-ups are faster, sturdier, longer-lived and less bad-tempered than your average dromedary. However, some tribes still keep a few camels, mostly for nostalgic reasons and the milk, though some breed and sell them. The Bedouin that live in or close to touristed areas such as Petra and Rum have small herds of them to rent out for walks and desert excursions. Jordan's population of camels is down from 18,000 in 1992 to about 6000 today, and moves are now afoot to have them declared a protected species.

If you're in any doubt about whether to take the plunge and have a **camel ride**, then rest assured that it's still a great experience. There's absolutely nothing to compare with the gentle, hypnotic swaying and soft shuffle of riding camel-back in the open desert. The Wadi Rum area is the best place in Jordan to try it out, with short and long routes branching out from Rum and Diseh all over the southern desert, as far as Aqaba, Ma'an or Petra; these are hefty multi-day excursions, but then again anything less than a couple of hours' riding isn't really worth it.

As a beginners' tip, the key to not falling off a camel is to hang onto the pommel between your legs; they get up from sitting with a bronco-style triple jerk back-forward-back, and if you're not holding on as soon as your bottom hits the saddle you're liable to end up in the dust. Once up and moving, you have a choice of riding your mount like a stirrupless horse, or copying the locals and cocking one leg around the pommel.

guided hikes into the wildest corners of Jordan – outside the nature reserves, and often untouched by anyone else – get onto the Adventure Jordan email list run by independent guide Yamaan Safady.

To get a good idea of the terrain, as well as some route descriptions and advice, have a look at general Jordan-enthusiast websites, such as the well-informed Ⓦwww.jordan jubilee.com and Ⓦwww.nomadstravel.co .uk. If you're in trim, you might fancy the annual **Dead Sea Marathon** (Ⓦwww .deadseamarathon.com), run for charity every April, which includes a 50km ultra-marathon course, full and half marathons and a 10km fun run. This is one of several running events that take place in various locations; others are at Rum and Aqaba.

Adventure tour operators and specialist independent guides in Jordan

Adventure Jordan/Yamaan Safady Mobile ℡07/9564 1911, Ⓔyamaan@adventurejordan .com, Ⓦwww.adventurejordan.com. A licensed tour guide (with certification in mountain search and rescue and first aid), Yamaan Safady organizes regular adventure trips to canyons and mountain sites all round Jordan for small groups on both a pre-booked and an ad-hoc basis: once you've joined the email list, you get details of his hikes a week or so in advance and can then choose to book a place or not. Most participants are foreigners resident in Amman, almost all English-speaking. Transport and tea is included, but you generally have to bring your own gear (change of clothes or shoes, sleeping bag if on an overnight trek, etc) as well as food and water. Highly recommended.
Desert Explorer Tours ℡ & Ⓕ03/202 2626, mobile ℡07/9554 8133, Ⓦwww.desertexplorer .net. Small operation based at the Bait Ali campsite on the outskirts of Wadi Rum, run by Tahseen and Susan Shinaco. Their connections with the Swaylhiyeen tribe, who occupy the lands north of Rum, cover ground that Rum guides ignore – hiking, camel safaris and horse-riding expeditions are all specialities.
Desert Guides In France Ⓕ+33 4 50.54.70.98. In Jordan ℡03/201 4131, Ⓕ201 4133, Ⓦwww .desertguides.com. Among other services for trips and climbs in the southern desert, this respected outfit run by qualified mountain guide and old Jordan hand Wilfried Colonna – based in France and at the Alcazar Hotel in Aqaba – can offer guided multi-day wilderness treks on pure-bred Arabian horses.
Discovery PO Box 840618, Amman 11184 ℡06/569 7998, Ⓕ569 8183, Ⓦwww.discovery1 .com. A softly-softly approach to sustainable tourism,

coupled with an encyclopedic knowledge of natural and historical attractions in all corners of the country. Specializing in incentive travel for companies, but with a vast range of all kinds of trips and adventure tours on offer.
Jordan Beauty Tours PO Box 8, Wadi Musa 71810. Mobile ℡07/9558 1644 or 7728 2730, Ⓕ03/215 4999, Ⓦwww.jordanbeauty.com. Run by Sufian Amarat, a specialist guide for all kinds of hiking and trekking, specifically in the Petra area, with excellent local knowledge and plenty of experience in handling groups and individuals.
Jordan Inspiration Tours ℡ & Ⓕ03/215 7317, mobile ℡07/9555 4677, Ⓦwww.jitours.com. Small, flexible company based in Wadi Musa, run by Sami Hasanat, with a wide range of tour options all round the country.
La Beduina PO Box 80, Wadi Musa 71810 ℡03/215 7099, Ⓕ215 6931, Ⓦwww .labeduinatours.com. Specialists in fully supported adventure trips and treks in and around Petra, with a broad range of itineraries including mountain-biking and horse-riding. Thoroughly professional approach to all aspects of tour leading, with the flexibility to put together any sort of itinerary at short notice.
Mahdi Hasanat ℡03/215 7893, mobile ℡07/7742 7380, Ⓔmhasanat18@hotmail.com, Ⓦmahtours.tripod.com. A guide with several years' experience in trekking and wilderness camping. Based in Wadi Musa, but ranging around the country.
Outdoors Unlimited PO Box 9177, Amman 11191 ℡06/552 7230, Ⓕ552 0240, Ⓔhjahshan @go.com.jo. Small company run by Hanna Jahshan, a guide with extensive trekking experience and particular skill in horse-riding.
Petra Moon PO Box 129, Wadi Musa 71810 ℡03/215 6665, Ⓕ215 6666, Ⓦwww.petramoon .com. A leading adventure tour operator, and unique in offering low-impact jeep trips into the remote countryside around Petra. Very well connected, they can set you up with good local guides for hikes and long-distance horse or camel rides, and give you full backup support all the way.

Recommended guides in Wadi Rum

This list comprises some of the better-known guides at Wadi Rum, all of whom are entirely reliable and trustworthy. Note that if you're intending to visit Rum, for hiking, trekking or other activities – and you're not already on a group tour – you should always book well in advance by fax or email (stating clearly the name of the guide you want: fax machines are often shared). Turning up without a booking will most likely leave you disappointed. See p.393 for more.

Ali Hamad Zalabia ⊤ & ⨍ 03/203 2574, mobile ⊤07/9567 5327, ⓔsun_rise_camp@yahoo.com. Jeep tours, hiking and some climbing and scrambling.

Aodeh Abdullah Mobile ⊤07/9561 7902, ⓔaodeh25@yahoo.com, ⓦwww.aodeh.de. Good-value budget tours by jeep and camel, plus overnight desert camping.

Atallah Sweilhin ⊤ & ⨍03/203 3508, mobile ⊤07/9580 2108, ⓔrumhorses@yahoo.co.uk. Acknowledged specialist in horse-riding trips around the Rum area.

Attayak Ali and Attayak Aouda Mobile ⊤07/9589 9723, ⨍03/203 2651, ⓔbedouinroads@yahoo.com, ⓦwww.bedouinroads.com. Two friends who have set up together as "Wadi Rum Mountain Guides", offering a broad range of activities, including hiking, trekking, camel rides, jeep trips, scrambling and rock-climbing. Highly respected, extremely accomplished, and often booked solid.

Defallah Atieq ⊤03/201 9135, ⓔdifallahz@yahoo.com. Experienced specialist in trekking and jeep trips, short and long.

Mattar Auda ⊤ & ⨍03/201 9574, mobile ⊤07/7747 2616. Trekking and hiking specialist.

Mohammed Sabah Al-Zalabeh ⊤ & ⨍03/203 2961, mobile ⊤07/7731 4688, ⓔmohammed_rum@yahoo.com, ⓦwww.mohammedwadirum.8m.com. Specializing in cut-price jeep and camel trips and basic overnight desert camping.

Msallam Sabah Ateeg Mobile ⊤07/9566 0362, ⓔmoslam_rum@yahoo.com. Jeep trips, hikes and camel-trekking, as well as specialist scrambling and rock-climbing.

Mzied Atieq Mobile ⊤07/7730 4501, ⨍03/203 2819, ⓔmziedco@yahoo.com. Mzied is a wonderful host, urbane, charming and exceptionally knowledgeable. He has many years of experience handling groups and individuals visiting Rum, and can offer a wide range of options for hiking, trekking, camel treks and jeep trips, as well as overnight stays at his excellent permanent campsite in the deep desert, complete with running water and full facilities. Regularly fully booked.

Sabbah Eid ⊤ & ⨍03/201 6238, mobile ⊤07/7789 1243, ⓔsabbah_azlapih@yahoo.com. Specialist in hiking, trekking and especially rock-climbing.

Saleem Ali al-Zalabia ⊤ & ⨍03/203 2651, mobile ⊤07/9529 8046, ⓔsaleemrum@yahoo.com.au. Jeep tours, camels and straightforward hiking.

Salem & Selim Lafi Mobile ⊤07/9512 7148 or 9529 8046, ⨍03/203 2651,

ⓔrumtrekking@yahoo.com, ⓦwww.rumtrekking.com. Brothers working together on a range of jeep and hiking trips, including some climbing and scrambling.

Zedane al-Zalabieh ⊤ & ⨍03/203 2607, mobile ⊤07/9550 6417, ⓔzedn_a@yahoo.com, ⓦwww.drschef.de/zedane. Budget-priced jeep trips and desert camping.

Local environmental organizations

Badia Research and Development Programme (BRDP) PO Box 36, Amman-Jubayha 11941 ⊤06/534 0401, ⨍533 5284, ⓦwww.badia.gov.jo. Scientific desert research station that is branching out into eco-tourism, with facilities for hosting researchers and others for trips into the eastern Badia. Part of the Higher Council for Science and Technology (ⓦwww.hcst.gov.jo).

BirdLife International c/o RSCN (see below) or ⓦwww.birdlifemed.org. The Middle East office of an international scientific organization devoted to protecting birds and their habitats.

Friends of the Earth Middle East (FoEME) PO Box 9341, Amman 11191 ⊤06/586 6602, ⨍586 6604, ⓦwww.foeme.org. Regional headquarters of the global network of environmental pressure groups, representing a coalition of Jordanian, Israeli and Palestinian NGOs working to raise awareness of sustainable development across the Middle East.

Jordan Royal Ecological Diving Society (JREDS) PO Box 831051, Amman 11183 ⊤ & ⨍06/567 6183; also in Aqaba ⊤ & ⨍03/202 2995; ⓦwww.jreds.org. Popular and successful local NGO that works to protect the marine environment.

Royal Society for the Conservation of Nature (RSCN) PO Box 1215, Amman 11941, ⓦwww.rscn.org.jo. Main office ⊤06/533 7931, ⨍534 7411. Tourism unit ⊤06/461 6523 or 461 6483 or 463 3589, ⨍463 3657, ⓔtourism@rscn.org.jo. Increasingly important and influential NGO taking the lead in pushing conservancy and environmental issues into the social and political spotlight. Their excellent website has in-depth details of their projects nationwide. Contact the Tourism Unit (which is based at the Wild Jordan centre in Amman) directly for information and guidance on getting the most out of a visit to any of Jordan's nature reserves.

Trekking

The opportunities for getting out into the country's varied landscapes are limited only by your own preparation and fitness, but it's easy for anyone of moderate ability to embark on half- or full-day **walks** from most towns. What you can't expect is any kind of trail support: no signposts, no refreshment facilities, and often no trail markers; there are also virtually no maps useful for walkers available. In recompense, you'll generally be walking alone in pristine countryside. For greater insight, and a full range of detailed route descriptions, your best bet is to get hold of almost the only book on the subject – *Jordan: Walks, Treks, Caves, Climbs and Canyons* by Di Taylor and Tony Howard, published in the US as *Walking in Jordan* (see p.496); in this section, and the walks outlined throughout this book, we've given only some background guidance as to what to expect.

Trekking in Jordan has come of age only in the unique mountains and deserts of Wadi Rum. These days, trekking plays an important role in the local economy, with – as is the case also in Petra – trekking services offered by **local people** who still proudly consider themselves Bedouin. Small tour operators based in Wadi Musa or Aqaba lead treks along ancient **caravan routes** in and out of Petra, while plenty of the best routes in and around Rum are known only to the locals.

Elsewhere, only a handful of individuals and the **RSCN** (Royal Society for the Conservation of Nature) understand the theory and practice of trekking, the latter offering facilities in its three flagship **nature reserves** of Dana, Wadi Mujib and Ajloun. These markedly different areas primarily comprise environmentally fragile, protected landscapes off-limits to visitors: trekking is allowed only on **designated trails** with qualified guides provided by the RSCN. On no account should you enter the reserves without permission, or stray off-trail.

Outside these places, in the rugged mountains north of Aqaba or the greener hills of the far north, for example, there are no marked trails and no guides. Indeed, it is highly unlikely that while walking you'll come across anyone other than locals, some of whom may be happy to guide you, but all of whom will welcome you with the full warmth of Jordanian hospitality. Offers of tea and refreshment are likely to flow thick and fast as you pass through rural villages.

Terrain

Jordan's **terrain** is spectacularly varied. Anyone expecting a desert country will be astonished by the alpine-style meadows of **north Jordan**, which are carpeted in flowers in springtime, warm breezes carrying the aromas of herbs and pine. The hills of Ajloun (see p.214) in April are simply captivating – a gentle terrain, with no real hazards other than the lack of water. The RSCN's Ajloun Woodland Reserve offers a base for access into the area.

The **Dead Sea hills**, also dubbed "The Mountains of Moab", offer a more savage prospect, gashed by wild canyons which flash-flood after rains. They require respectful treatment. Their northern reaches fall within the boundaries of the RSCN's **Mujib** reserve (see p.300), access to which is only with the permission of the RSCN, who will provide guides and transport. The RSCN have established **campsites** in the reserve. Top choice of excursion here is the spectacular descent of the Mujib gorge.

The southern part of the Moab hills around **Karak** (see p.304), also with excellent trekking and canyoning, is outside the reserve. Hiking here, alongside water in the midst of harsh desert terrain, is always a pleasure. This part of the country is still very much off the beaten track, but you may be able to find a company or a specialist guide organizing trips to the beautiful and varied canyon of Wadi ibn Hammad.

Further south is the RSCN's nature reserve at **Dana**, its ancient village perched like an eyrie above the wild Wadi Dana (see p.313). This is, understandably, the pride of the RSCN, who organize some excellent treks past oases and ancient copper mines down to their wilderness lodge in Wadi Faynan.

The fabulous city of **Petra** is concealed beyond the next range of hills to the south. While you could spend days hiking around this remarkable site, most walkers will feel the urge to explore further. Navigating paths through this craggy range of mountains is however, extremely complex, and waterholes are few: until you gain confidence in the area, you should take a local guide. There are also companies in both Wadi Musa and Aqaba offering the unique experience of excellent week-long camel- or horse-riding treks from Petra to Rum or through the more remote parts of the Rum desert.

At **Wadi Rum**, don't let the multitudes of tour buses deter you. Out in the desert, away from the very few, well-travelled, one-hour safari routes taken by day-trippers, all is solitude. The rock climbing in Rum is world-famous, but for the walker there is also much to offer, both dramatic canyon scrambles and delightful desert valleys. Again, be sure of your abilities if you go without a guide: Bedouin camps are rare and only those intimate with Rum will find water. Far better is to get to know the local Bedouin and hire a guide: a real desert experience is just as much about the people as the place. The ascent of the mighty Jebel Rum by a Bedouin hunting route such as Sheikh Hamdan's Route or the Thamudic Route – both well known to qualified guides – is a world-class experience open to any fit and confident person.

Clothing, equipment and preparation

You should take a minimalist approach to **clothing** and **equipment**. Heavy boots really aren't necessary; good, supportive trainers or very lightweight boots are adequate. Quality socks are important and should be washed or changed frequently to keep the sand out and minimize blisters. Clothing, too, should be lightweight and cotton or similar: long trousers and long-sleeved tops will limit dehydration (see p.46), and are essential on grounds of modesty when passing through villages or visiting Bedouin camps. A sunhat, proper protective sunglasses and high-factor sunblock are also essential, as are a light windproof top and fleece. Basic **trip preparation** also includes carrying a mobile phone (bear in mind that coverage can be patchy, particularly on mountains and in canyons), a watch, a medical kit and a compass, and knowing how to use them all. You should carry a minimum of three litres of water per day for an easy walk, perhaps six or eight litres per day for exertive treks or multi-day trips. On **toilet procedures**, if you're caught short in the wilds, make sure that you squat far away from trails and water supplies, and bury the result deeply. Toilet paper is both unsightly and unhygienic (goats eat anything!); the best way to clean yourself is with water, but if you must use paper, either burn it or store it in a plastic bag and dispose of it correctly when you get back to a town.

Part of your preparation for trekking in Jordan must involve familiarizing yourself with the dangers of **flash floods**, most pertinently if you intend walking in narrow valleys and canyons, even in the desert: imminent deluges are life-threatening, and the possibility that past floods will have altered the terrain to make it impassable can jeopardize the success of a trip (see, for example, the notes on Wadi Numeira on p.309). You should carry 10m of **rope** for emergency use.

There are no official search and rescue organizations, so, however straightforward your hike may seem, you must **always tell someone** responsible (such as a reliable friend or the tourist police) where you are

Aerial adventures

The **Royal Aero Sports Club of Jordan** (RASCJ; ☎03/203 3763, ✉rparaclb@go .com.jo), based at Aqaba airport, is one of the leading clubs of its kind in the Middle East. They run a whole range of **sightseeing flights** in two-seater microlights, from JD25 for a twenty-minute overfly of the beach and Aqaba's rooftops, to JD80 for a one-hour excursion around the bay. For incredible views over the desert, sturdier single- or multi-engine light aircraft can fly from Aqaba to Wadi Rum and back (or wherever you like) for JD300 per hour (5 passengers) or JD500 per hour (9 passengers). Tandem **paragliding** from 10,000 feet, done while hooked to an instructor, costs around JD135. And after a hiatus of more than a decade, the RASCJ has also restarted **hot-air ballooning** at Wadi Rum: for JD625, a minimum of five passengers can enjoy a breathtaking ninety-minute journey over the desert cliffs at dawn.

In a similar vein, the **Royal Jordanian Gliding Club** (☎06/487 4587 or 489 1401), based at Marka Airport in Amman, can take you up for a unique view of the capital from above in either a free-flying or motorized glider, for around JD15 per hour.

going. You must then follow or stick close to your stated route, and check in when you return or reach your destination.

Camping

In a reserve, the RSCN supplies everything for overnight **camping**, from tent to meals. Elsewhere you will generally be expected to supply at least your own tent and sleeping bag. In Rum, a tent is not normally necessary outside the winter months, but it can nonetheless be chilly at night year-round, and tents do keep away scorpions and other unwanted creepy-crawlies – as well as the sometimes torrential winter and spring rains. It's always preferable, of course, to sleep under the stars or arrange to spend the night with the Bedouin locals in a traditional black goat-hair tent.

Otherwise, around Jordan, you should be judicious: camping is frowned upon by the authorities, on the grounds of safety – though in practice, if you camp far away from habitation and tourist hot spots, no one is going to bother you. You should always avoid lighting fires: aside from attracting attention, they are environmentally unsound. Ideally, use a multi-fuel stove or camping gas, available in all large towns.

Hiring guides

Fees for **trekking guides** vary throughout Jordan. **RSCN rates** are fixed at around JD35 a day, which includes a guide, use of a campsite and meals. As visitor numbers to the reserves are limited, you should book your trip well in advance.

Elsewhere, guiding fees are to some extent subject to negotiation. In **Rum**, you should reckon on JD35–45 per day for a group of up to six people using one vehicle. For short walks, JD20 is a minimum, but use of a camel could cost you that much per person. Guiding on scrambles and climbs that require ropes for safety costs considerably more, in the order of JD110 per day – and rightly so; it's a responsible job. The time-honoured way to fix up a guide on the spot is simply to strike up a conversation with the locals; you'll rapidly get passed along to someone who can help you out. Rates are similar in the **Petra** area. Here, too, camels and horses are available although you'll need to make your enquiries with an established tour company rather than with local individuals.

If you've enjoyed your trip, **tipping your guide** is entirely appropriate. Ten percent would be fine, but you may want to give more – or perhaps a gift of a useful item of clothing or equipment. This is, in many respects, better than money: the camel leads and guy-lines supporting the Bedouin tents of Rum are now mostly made from climbing ropes donated by grateful climbers.

Crime and personal safety

As a tourist and a foreigner, the chance of your coming into contact with any criminal activity while in Jordan is remote. The sense of honour and hospitality to guests embedded deep within Arab culture, coupled with a respect for others, means that you're extremely unlikely to be robbed, mugged, conned or pickpocketed on holiday in Jordan. Unfortunately, these values are more often applied to men than to women, and relatively minor but tiresome sexual harassment of foreign women is an ongoing problem; see p.85 for more.

Along with the ordinary police, Jordan maintains a force of **tourist police** – identifiable by armbands with English lettering – most of whom speak good English and all of whom are the height of courtesy. Posted at all tourist sites nationwide, they can deal with requests, complaints or problems of harassment by unofficial guides or hangers-on. Any representation by a foreigner, whether to the tourist police or the ordinary local police, will generally have you ushered into the presence of senior officers, sat down and plied with coffee, with your complaint taken in the utmost seriousness. The nationwide police **emergency number** is ☎199; phone numbers for the police in larger towns are given in the relevant chapters of the guide.

Terrorism and **civil disorder** in Jordan are extremely rare. No violent group exists within Jordan that holds any grievances against the country, its people, government or tourism policy. The political and religious make-up of Jordanian society – as well as the invisible grip of the security services – makes domestic terrorism exceptionally unlikely.

Super-aware both of extremist attacks on tourists in Egypt, and of the violence in Israel and Palestine, Jordan maintains forces of protective armed police in high-profile evidence at all major tourist sites. If you're staying in the country longer than a month, you should register your presence with your embassy in Amman; every one keeps a list of its nationals resident in the country. These precautions notwithstanding, though, and regardless of the impression journalists might like to give, you'd be in no more danger travelling round Jordan than you would be sitting on your own front doorstep.

Drugs

Drugs are nothing like as prevalent in Jordan as they are in Egypt or Lebanon, and it's highly unlikely, even if you go looking for it, that you'll come across any hashish, let alone anything else. The country is principally a transit route for drugs rather than a consumers' market: desert smuggling routes lead from Syria through Jordan into the lucrative drug markets of Israel, Egypt and the Gulf States.

In Jordan, the use of hash, and all other drugs, is unquestionably beyond the pale, officially, legally and in popular thinking. By indulging, you expose yourself to the exceptionally severe penalties that exist for possession, use or trafficking, and should expect no quarter from the authorities or your embassy if you're caught. Jordanian jails are notoriously unpleasant, even for the Middle East.

Shopping for crafts

Unlike Syria, Palestine and Egypt, the trading history of Jordan mostly revolves around goods passing through rather than being produced; no city within the boundaries of modern Jordan has ever come close to matching the craftsmanship on display in the workshops and bazaars of Aleppo, Damascus, Jerusalem and Cairo.

Traditionally, people in Jordan have simply made whatever they needed for themselves – carpets, jugs, jewellery – without their skills being noticed or valued by outside buyers. Today, although a handful of individual outlets around the country sell local (and some imported) crafts, Jordan has no craft bazaars. You may come across items of aesthetic value here and there, but your chances of picking up bargain antiques are very small, and any that you might come across almost certainly originate from outside Jordan. For the record, Jordanian law forbids the purchase of any item dating from before 1700.

There are only three rules of **bargaining**: first, never to start the process unless you want to buy; second, never, even in jest, to let a price pass your lips that you're not prepared to pay; and third, never to lose your temper. However, the lack of any tradition of bazaar-style haggling in Jordan results in a reluctance among Jordanian merchants even to embark on the process. In most everyday situations, you'll rapidly be brought up short against an unbudgeable last price – which, unlike in the Cairo or Damascus bazaars, really is the last price, take it or leave it.

Embroidery and weaving

The field where Transjordanian people have the strongest tradition is in **hand-embroidered textiles**, although up to a few decades ago such fabrics tended to stay within the confines of the town producing them and generally never came onto the open market. Embroidered jackets, dresses and cushion covers are now available everywhere, in both traditional and modern styles, but relatively few are high-quality, handmade items.

Sheep's wool and goat's hair have been used since time immemorial to **weave** tents, carpets, rugs, cushions, even food-storage containers, for family use; the two fibres woven together form a waterproof barrier. Rarer camel hair went to make rugs. Up until the 1920s, natural dyes were always used: indigo (planted in the Jordan Valley), pomegranate, onion peel and mulberries were all common, as was the sumac berry (red), kermes insect dye (crimson), cochineal (pink), and even the yellowish soil. Salt, vinegar or soda were added in order to make the colours fast.

Since the 1980s, local and international development projects – Save The Children among them – have been involved in nurturing traditional **Bedouin weaving**. By doing so, and by establishing retail outlets in Amman and elsewhere for the sale of woven items, they have managed to rejuvenate a dying craft, and simultaneously create extra sources of income for the weavers, who are almost without exception rural women. The quality of **carpets**, **rugs** and **home furnishings** produced under these various projects is first-rate, although prices are concomitantly very high. The older, more traditional colours – deep reds, navy blues, greens, oranges and blacks – as well as the traditional styles of stripes and diamonds, are being augmented these days by brighter, chemically dyed colours and more modern patterns, to appeal to a new, Western-inspired clientele, but there is usually a good range of traditional and modern pieces on offer. In Madaba, Jerash and Irbid you may see carpet shops featuring upright treadle looms; these are operated only by men, and almost exclusively in the cities, to produce mainly derivative items for sale. These have their own appeal, but the huge majority of original, traditionally designed woven pieces, for domestic use as well as for sale, are made by women, who use only a ground loom, which they set up either in front of their home tent in springtime or at village workshops.

A more affordable woven craft is **weaving with straw**, a skill of northern Jordanian women, to produce large multicoloured trays, mats, storage containers or wall-hangings. Baskets made of local **bamboo**, woven by men in Himmeh (aka Mukhaybeh) on the the Yarmouk River, often find their way to Amman for sale in ritzy crafts centres.

Jewellery

Many Jordanians have inherited their parents' and grandparents' preference – stemming partly from previous generations' nomadic existence, and partly from a rural mistrust of urban institutions – for investing their money in **jewellery** rather than in banks. Until very recently, Bedouin brides wore their personal wealth in silver jewellery, and retained the right throughout their married lives to do with it what they wanted, husbands' wishes notwithstanding. Owning jewellery was – and still is – something of a safety net for women against the possibility of abandonment, divorce or widowhood.

Traditionally, the Bedouin much preferred **silver** to gold; indeed, it's just about impossible to find genuine old gold in Jordan. The **Gold Souk** – a collection of tiny modern jewellery shops all huddled together in a few Downtown Amman alleys – has excellent prices compared to the West (see p.155), but almost everything is of generic modern design.

If you're after more distinctive jewellery, you should be aware that, although there are a few Jordanian designers producing new, hand-made items, practically all the new jewellery you'll see in craft shops has been imported from Turkey, India or Italy. Chunky **Bedouin jewellery** that looks old generally turns out to have been made no more than sixty or seventy years ago, and much old "silver" is in fact a mix of eighty percent silver and twenty percent copper. Practically all the "old" necklaces on offer were strung relatively recently on nylon thread using stones

and silver beads from long-dispersed older originals. However, none of this detracts from the fact that beautiful and unique items are available; especially striking are necklaces that combine silver beads with beads of coloured glass, **amber** or semi-precious stones. Different stones have different significances: blue stones protect the wearer from the evil eye, white stones stimulate lactation during breastfeeding, and so on. You might also find rare Circassian **enamelwork**, dramatically adding to a silver bracelet or necklace's charm. However, note that all **precious stones** in Jordan are imported, mostly from Turkey. Jordan's own colourful **sandstone** is only used for sand-in-bottle novelties, sold at practically every souvenir shop and gift stall in the country.

Metalwork, wood and glass

In Amman, **copper** and **brass** items, such as distinctive long-spouted *dalleh* coffeepots, candlesticks, embossed or inlaid platters and the like, are generally unimpressive mass-produced Indian and Pakistani pieces, not to be compared to what's on offer in the Coppersmith's Bazaar in Cairo. Distinctive curved silver **daggers**, still carried by some Bedouin in the south, are still being made by a workshop in Irbid, though older Yemeni or Iraqi daggers, on sale in Amman craft shops, are much more ornate and generally of better quality.

Since antiquity, **wood** has been a scarce resource in Jordan, and although you may dig out some Jordanian-carved pieces (simple cooking implements, mostly, from the local oak and pistachio) practically all the elegant wooden furniture you'll come across – wardrobes, chairs, beautiful inlaid chests and the like – originates (and is much cheaper) in Syria. A couple of workshops in Mazar, near Karak, still produce hand-carved pieces in wood, mostly implements used in the coffee-making process such as a *mihbash*, or grinder, and a *mabradeh*, an ornamented tray for cooling the coffee beans after roasting.

It's worthwhile remembering, too, that the line between what does and doesn't count as Jordanian is not an easy one to draw. Even if you're on the lookout for strictly local items only, the links between **Palestinian** craftspeople working on the West Bank and the retail craft-shops in Amman are strong, and most people make no distinction between the two. Prices in Amman for

olive-wood or **mother-of-pearl** pieces from Bethlehem or the famous **blown glass** of Hebron (now also made in Na'ur, just outside Amman) can be half what you might pay in Jerusalem.

Behaviour and attitudes

Veterans of travel in Egypt or Morocco will be pleased to learn that, as far as hassle from the locals goes, Jordan is a breeze: your experience of Jordanian people is likely to be that they are, almost without exception, decent, honest, respectful and friendly. However, if you want to get the most out of a visit, it seems only right that you should return some of that respect in compliance with some basic tenets of Jordanian, Arab and Muslim culture.

Dress codes

Outward appearance is the one facet of interaction between locals and Western tourists most open to misunderstandings on both sides. A lot of tourists, male and female, consistently flout simple **dress codes**, unaware of just how much it demeans them in the eyes of local people: clothes that are respectable at home can come across in Jordan as being embarrassing, disrespectful or offensive. Jordanians and Palestinians place a much greater emphasis on personal grooming and style of dress than people tend to in the West, and dressing down is unthinkable. For those locals who can afford it, anything less than every hair in place, a freshly ironed shirt or top, cologne or perfume, sharp trouser-creases or skirt-pleats, and shiny shoes simply won't do – and that's just for taking a stroll. In addition, for reasons of **modesty**, Muslim men and women expose as little skin as possible. Sleeves are long and necklines high for both sexes. Men always wear long trousers, women either voluminous neck-to-ankle robes or ankle-length skirts and loose tops.

If you want to come across as being someone worth talking to, you'll have to go some distance towards conforming to local ways, or run the risk of being dismissed either as a joke or an annoyance. Walking around in

shorts and a T-shirt will cause offence, and also reinforces the sex-object stereotypes that underpin many locals' attitudes to Western women.

Male dress codes

You'll almost never see local men wearing **shorts** in public in Jordan. Western men who break this code give roughly the same impression that they would wandering around Bournemouth or Baltimore in their underpants. If you were to wear short trousers, no doubt you'd be served in shops and restaurants – since to refuse would be disrespectful – but everyone would be rolling their eyes and tutting, and you'd be the butt of countless behind-your-back sniggers. **Long trousers** are essential in the city, the country and the desert, whatever the weather; clean and respectable light cotton, denim or canvas ones (not the flimsy, brightly patterned beach-style ones) demonstrate normality and conformity – attributes high on the Jordanian social agenda.

The exceptions to the shorts rule are central Amman in the summer, and Aqaba, which can get so absurdly hot that even some locals cool their knees.

T-shirts are fine, since younger men do wear them; however, any garment that doesn't cover your shoulders and upper arms is also liable to tag you as an underwear-flaunting loony. Loose **buttoned shirts** are far more common than anything else and, in general, you'll be received more respectfully by more people if you wear a tucked-in shirt than a tucked-out T-shirt. Jordanian men never, in any situation, walk around topless.

Female dress codes

To interact as a Western woman in Jordanian society with some degree of mutual respect, you'll probably have to go to even greater lengths than men to adjust your normal style of dress, although it is possible to do so without compromising your freedom and individuality too much. **Loose-fitting, opaque clothes** that cover your legs, arms and chest are a major help in allowing you to relate normally with local men. If **shorts** appear ridiculous on men, on women they appear flagrantly sexual and provocative, as do Lycra leggings. The **nape of the neck** is considered particularly erotic and so is best covered, either by a high collar or a thin cotton scarf.

Hair is another area where conservatism helps deter unwanted attention. Jordanian women who don't wear a headscarf rarely let long hair hang below their shoulders; you might like to follow suit and clip long hair up. Walking around with **wet hair** is – for some reason – a general indication that you've just had sex, and thus may not be the kind of signal you wish to broadcast. If your hair is **blonde**, you must unfortunately resign yourself to more inquisitive, and sexualized, attention – at least while walking around in conservative town-centres – simply because of the novelty.

Foreign women: sexual harassment

The biggest problem **women travellers** face in Jordan is the perception that some local men have of them. Unless dressed modestly and accompanied by a husband, women tourists might be seen as being both morally loose and overtly contemptuous of Arab and Islamic values. The large numbers of tourists who ignore dress codes and local norms of social contact unfortunately reinforce these perceptions. Even more unfortunately, local men thus often see foreign women as fair game for **harassment**, the level of which is lower than in Egypt or Morocco, but much higher than you're likely to be used to at home.

To appreciate why harassment happens, it helps to understand that most young unmarried Jordanian men – the source of nearly all harassment – have very little chance to meet women and relate to them "normally" (in Western eyes). Dating is almost nonexistent, since the pressure on women to retain a flawless reputation for moral behaviour is intense, and most simply can't afford to be seen in public consorting with strange men; dozens of women are killed each year in Jordan by their brothers, husbands or fathers for "bringing dishonour on the family name". Women's premarital virginity is an almost universal requirement, leading many to shun personal contact with men until the big day, which may not come until their 30s. All this amounts to a religiously inspired social segregation that limits personal contact between men and women to a minimum. As might be expected, this can lead to a deep-seated sexual frustration, which acts as a spur to many encounters between local men and foreign women. Add some stereotypes garnered from the media of Western women as being sexually available, mix in the desire among some young men to marry a foreigner and so get a visa to work in a rich country, and it becomes more understandable why the sight of a Western tourist walking down the street in a halter-top and Lycra shorts can cause such an extreme, and offensive, reaction.

The single most effective way to stop harassment is to **dress modestly**; the harsh truth is that, in Jordan, the onus is on you. Although men freely look at women – and, indeed, **staring** long and hard carries none of the implications of threat that it does in the West – local women tend to scrupulously avoid **eye-contact** with men on the street. A woman looking a man in the eyes will be interpreted as inviting him to approach her. Overt friendliness or gregariousness shown to men on the street (such as smiling, chatting, joking or gesturing) may also be misinterpreted either as sexual looseness or as romantic interest.

From a woman's perspective – some sample experiences

"During my time in Jordan there was just no way to hide that I was a tourist. And no way to hide that I was a woman. But, most important of all, there was no way to prepare myself for everything that happened: not by reading any amount of books before leaving home, not even by listening to all my female friends' experiences of travel in the Middle East. Sooner or later, you'll be surprised, as I was, by people's reactions – the best preparation is just to head out with self-confidence, curiosity and a sense of humour.

It's easy for women to travel alone in Jordan. People are extremely willing to help, and almost everyone invited me for tea – a boy selling tablecloths, taxi-drivers, even the guardian in the museum. It surprised me that although a man's presence could sometimes give more assurance to explore cafés and other places where women normally didn't venture, travelling for a time with a male friend felt somehow a little unreal. Suddenly, people stopped talking to me and paid attention only to him. Although this was probably due much more to respect for me than condescension, I couldn't help being a little upset. Self-confidence or no self-confidence, I wasn't there to be the centre of attention, and anyway (I told myself) such a cold shoulder put me in the best position to indulge my curiosity and observe events.

It is vital to be able to take things lightly, for instance after having been followed by a bunch of teenage boys for at least an hour through the whole of Salt. They'd had a great time, running around and making jokes, and it'd been impossible to leave them behind; the only way out was to head for the bus station – they could tell that I was about to leave, and the game was over. Younger children I ran into were rather obstinate though; my mistake was to try and get away. I should've stayed and talked to them, lived up to my role and – best of all – taken a picture. They'd have loved that."

Anna Hohler, journalist, Geneva

"One day in Karak, I decided to do some exercises in my hotel room. The door was locked, the shades were down. Handstands against the wall, then jogging on the spot. I can imagine the sound would've been intriguing from outside: *thud thud thud* (gasp) *thud* (sigh) *thud thud*. After about twenty minutes, I happened to glance up. Above the closet there was a small set of windows (hadn't noticed them before), and, in the window, a man's face, quickly disappearing.

The following morning, when I saw Mr Peeper in the lobby, he stared right at me without an ounce of shame. Being peeped at is no surprise in any culture, but his lack of shame was a cultural lesson for me – not about relations between men

---

Most harassment never goes beyond the verbal, and unless you're sufficiently well versed in Arabic swear-words to respond in kind (worth it for the startled looks), is ignorable if tiresome. A tiny fraction of incidents are more blatant – but still usually pretty harmless – comprising the usual tedious and demeaning round of gropes, hisses, kissy noises and the like. If you take the fight to your harasser, however, by pointing at him directly, shouting angrily and slapping away his hand, you're likely to **shame** him to his roots in front of his neighbours. Accusing him of bringing himself and his country into public disrepute – *aayib!* is Arabic for "shame!" – is about the most effective

dissuasive action you could take, and many onlookers will be embarrassed and apologetic for your having suffered harassment. Unmarried or unrelated men and women never touch each other in public (apart from possibly to shake hands in a formal setting), and any man who touches you, even on the elbow to guide you, has overstepped the mark and knows it.

More serious harassment – blocking your path or refusing to leave you alone – is less common still, and actual bodily assault is extremely rare. In Jordan strangers are much more likely to help a foreigner in distress than might be the case at home, and in an emergency you shouldn't hesitate to appeal and women in Jordan (because I think Jordanian women command a great deal of respect), but rather about the general perception of American women, primarily informed by porno flicks and B-movies. I was not assumed to have inviolable bodily boundaries. I was not assumed to question the rights of men over my body.

Nonetheless, you can regulate the respect you receive according to the way you dress. Complying with the standards of the place you're visiting relieves you from harassment. It also signals your intention to understand. The assumptions about Western women are so image-based that changing your image will change your reception. It's as simple as that."

Karinne Keithley, dancer, New York

"Living and working in Jordan was rewarding and very comfortable, if trying at times; in the end, quality of life often came down to my own attitudes. Accepting the conservative nature of Jordanian culture and modifying my dress and behaviour to match social norms helped immensely. I don't mean I made radical changes to fit in. Just wearing loose clothes and long-sleeved shirts made me feel more confident and relaxed, especially in more traditional areas, and allowed local people to take me seriously. Avoiding looking into men's eyes and maintaining a serious expression and demeanour made walking around alone mostly hassle-free. Being friendly with men I didn't know inevitably got me in trouble, since they interpreted it as flirting: I tried never to smile at men on the street and to keep my interactions with waiters and shopkeepers on a reserved and businesslike footing. This doesn't mean I didn't get stared at – I did. But I came to accept that as a foreigner I was an exotic sight to be seen, as much as Jordanian people are exotic to visitors.

The flipside of avoiding men's stares and comments was that I could smile and look freely at women. Since most women adopt a serious, frozen expression on the street to deal with male attention it was a great surprise, smiling tentatively at a woman passerby or exchanging a few words of greeting, to see her face light up with a broad smile in response. I had an immediate, spontaneous connection which surpassed words and cultural differences.

My time in Amman was also made much more enjoyable by cultivating a few places as refuges from conservative and male-centred culture. Darat al-Funun, and cafés like *Books@Café* and *el-Farouki's* were relaxing places to read, write, talk with friends or meet like-minded Jordanians."

Michelle Woodward, photographer, Baltimore

directly for help to shopkeepers or passers-by, or to bang on the nearest front door.

Foreign men: sexual propriety

Male travellers have slightly more leeway when it comes to interacting with local women. In the larger cities, it's normally OK to be verbally friendly towards a woman – if she's willing to talk to you, which is rare – without breaking any taboos, although touching is strictly forbidden and many women will refuse even to shake hands. In smaller towns and rural communities, although everything might appear fine at the time, her family might take her hanging out with a foreigner as a breach of morality, and possibly give her a hard time later. If you do talk with women in these circumstances, you should make sure that you're never alone together, and that you remain in full public view the whole time – preferably on the street rather than hidden in a café. You're most unlikely to become an object of affection, but if you choose to follow up any romantic interest, you'll have to be extremely discreet in your choice of venue. Although it's a criminal offence for a Jordanian woman to share a hotel room with a man not related to her, the legal sanctions pale into insignificance beside what her family might do to her if they find out.

Couples: displaying affection

If you're visiting Jordan with your (straight) partner, you should be aware of how social attitudes can also impact on **visiting couples** travelling together. Unlike in the hinterlands of Syria, no Jordanian hotelier will demand to see wedding rings before renting out a double room. Nonetheless, **public displays of affection** between men and women are not acceptable behaviour. Even if you're married, walking arm-around-waist or arm-over-shoulder, touching each other's face or body or giving a fond peck on the lips are all seen as immoral and deeply distasteful. It is possible occasionally in Amman to see husbands and wives walking hand-in-hand, but it's rare.

Gay and lesbian Jordan

Homosexual acts are illegal in Jordan. Amman has a small underground **gay** scene, with nothing of the pizzazz of Cairo, Tel Aviv or Beirut. For the most part, gay life in the city remains invisible to outsiders (and most locals as well), with a bare handful of uptown bars serving as gay meeting-places, and shady cruising going on around the Roman Theatre in Downtown. Nationwide, social disapproval of an overtly gay lifestyle is strong: dalliances between young, unmarried men are sometimes understood as "letting off steam", but they are accepted – if at all – only as a precursor to the standard social model of marriage and plenty of kids. Although local women form very strong bonds of friendship with each other to the exclusion of men, public perception of **lesbianism** is almost nonexistent, although again Amman has a small, word-of-mouth scene. No surveys have ever been done of opinions on homosexuality within Jordan, but locals in the know talk of some large majority of Jordan's gays and lesbians – especially those living outside the capital – being unhappily married, and either in denial or unable to come out for fear of social and familial isolation. An added twist is that few people actually consider themselves gay, with a self-identification as "bi" far more common.

A by-product of the strict social divisions between men and women, though, is that visiting gay or lesbian couples can feel much freer about limited **public displays of affection** than straight couples: cheek-kissing, eye-gazing and hand-holding between same-sex friends in public is normal and completely socially acceptable.

Social interactions

Quite aside from issues of sex and sexuality, **social interaction** in Jordan is replete with all kinds of seemingly impenetrable verbal and behavioural rituals, most of which can remain unaddressed by foreigners with impunity. A few things are worth knowing, however.

The energy which Jordanians put into social relationships can bring shame to Westerners brought up on reticence and icy propriety. Total strangers greet each other like chums and chat happily about nothing special, passers-by ask each other's advice or exchange opinions without a second thought, and old friends embark on five-minute volleys of salutations and cheek-kisses, joyful arm-squeezing or back-slapping, and earnest enquiries after health, family, business and news. Foreigners more used to avoiding strangers and doing business in shops quickly and impersonally can come across as cold, uninterested and even snooty. Learning one or two of the standard forms of **greeting** (see p.509) and taking the time to exchange pleasantries will bring you closer to people more quickly than anything else.

One stumbling block for many Westerners is the number of **questions** they face from Jordanians, questions which at home would seem overly personal. Aside from "What's your name?" and "Where are you from?", absolutely everybody wants to know whether you're **married**. A couple answering "We're just good friends" – even if truthful – is likely to bring the conversation to a halt, since that means very little to many Jordanians and merely highlights the cultural divide. Being able to point to a wedding/engagement ring, even if you have no nuptials planned, makes things instantly clear and understandable. For a woman alone, a ring, indicating an absent

Gestures and body language

There's a whole range of **gestures** used in Arab culture which will either be new to you or which carry different meanings from the same gesture in your home country. Rather than nodding, **yes** is indicated by inclining your head forwards and closing your eyes. **No** is raising your eyebrows and tilting your head up and back, often accompanied by a little "tsk" noise (which *doesn't* indicate impatience or displeasure). Shaking your head from side to side means **I don't understand**. A very useful gesture, which can be used a hundred times a day in all kinds of situations, is **putting your right hand over your heart**: this indicates genuineness or sincerity, and can soften a "no thanks" to a street-seller or a "sorry" to a beggar, or reinforce a "thank you very much" to someone who's helped you. Many people in the south of Jordan will instinctively touch their right hand to their heart after shaking hands.

One hand held out with the palm upturned and all five fingertips pressed means **wait**. A side-to-side wrist-pivot of one hand at chest level, palm up with the fingers curled, means **what do you want?** If someone holds their flat palm out to you and draws a line across it with the index finger of the other hand, they're asking you for whatever **document** seems relevant at the time – a bus ticket or passport. You can make the same gesture to ask for the bill (check) in a restaurant. **Pointing** at someone or something directly with your index finger, as you might do at home, in Jordan casts the evil eye; instead you should gesture imprecisely with two fingers, or just flap your whole hand in the direction you mean. **Beckoning** with your palm up has cutesy and overtly sexual connotations; instead you should beckon with your palm facing the ground and all four fingers together making broom-sweeping motions towards yourself.

In all Arab cultures, knowingly showing the **soles of your feet or shoes** to someone is a direct insult. Foreigners have some leeway to err, but you should be aware of it when crossing your legs while sitting: crossing knee-over-knee leaves your sole pointing unobtrusively at the floor, but crossing ankle-on-knee means your sole is showing to the person sitting next to you. Equally, sitting on the floor requires some foot-tucking to ensure no one is in your line of fire. Putting your feet up on chairs or tables is not done.

Another major no-no is **picking your teeth** openly with your fingers; you'd cause less social discomfort if you were to snort, spit into a plastic bag, jiggle a finger in your ear and pick your nose. Most diners and restaurants offer toothpicks, which should be used surreptitiously behind your palm.

husband, is a powerful signifier of respectability. The next question is inevitably about **children** – how many, what are their names, why don't you have more, and so on. *Lissa* ("later") or *masha'allah* ("according to God's will") are two respectful, comprehensible ways to say you have none. Having a few snaps to pass around of parents, brothers, sisters, nephews and nieces can break the ice (if any ice needed breaking), and locals will happily show you their family pictures in return. People **shake hands** in Jordan much more than in the West, and even the merest contact with a stranger is normally punctuated by at least one or two handshakes to indicate fraternity.

Personal space

Personal space is treated rather differently in Arab cultures from in the West: for all intents and purposes, it doesn't exist. There's an apocryphal Arab saying which sums up the attitude: "Hell is where there are no people." **Queuing** is a foreign notion, and in many situations hanging back deferentially is an invitation for other people to move in front. Jordanians also relate to the **natural environment** rather differently from Westerners. Sitting alone or with a friend in even the remotest and most perfectly tranquil spot, you may well find someone coming up to you blocking the sunset and eager for a chat. It can be difficult, if not impossible, to convey your desire to be alone.

Invitations

It's almost inevitable that during your time in Jordan you'll be **invited** to drink tea with someone, either in their shop or their home, and it's quite likely too that at some point you'll be invited for a full meal at someone's house. Jordanians take hospitality very much to heart, and are honestly interested in talking to you and making you feel comfortable, so it's a good idea to take at least a few people up on their offer. However, offers tend to flow so thick and fast that it would be very difficult to agree to every one, and yet people are often so eager it can also be difficult – and potentially rude – to refuse outright.

First and foremost, whether you're interested or not, is to take the time to chat civilly; nothing is more offensive than walking on without a word or making an impatient gesture, even if they're the twentieth person that day to stop you. If you're invited and you don't want to accept, a broad smile with your head lowered, your right hand over your heart and "*shukran shukran*" ("thank you, thank you") is a clear, but socially acceptable, no. You may have to do this several times – it's all part of the social ritual of polite insistence. Adding "*marra okhra, insha'allah*" ("another time, if God wills it") softens the "no" still further, indicating that you won't

forget their kind offer *and* throwing in a reference to Allah, which is always a good thing.

Before the meal

If you're invited to eat with someone **at home** and you choose to accept, the first thing to consider is how to **repay your host's hospitality**. Attempting to offer money would be deeply offensive – what is appropriate is to bring some token of your appreciation. A kilo or two of sweet pastries handed to your host as you arrive will be immediately ferreted away out of sight and never referred to again; the gesture, however, will have been appreciated. Otherwise, presenting gifts directly will generally cause embarrassment, since complex social etiquette demands that such a gift be refused several times before acceptance. Instead, you can acknowledge your appreciation by giving gifts to the small children: pens, small toys, sweets, even picture-postcards of your home country will endear you to your hosts much more than might appear from the monetary value of such things. It's worth pointing out too that you should be much more sparing and – above all – generalized in praising your host's home and decor than you might want to, since if you show noticeable interest in a particular piece, big or small, your host is obliged to give it to you. Whole minefields of complex verbal jockeyings to maintain dignity and family honour then open up if you refuse

---

Words of welcome

Ahlan wa sahlan is the single phrase you'll hear most often in Jordan. Everyone says it, in all situations, often repeated like a mantra in long strings. As a visitor, you needn't ever say it yourself, but you'll have to field torrents of them from the locals. *Ahlan wa sahlan* is most commonly rendered as "welcome", but translates directly as "family and ease", and so might come out better in English along the lines of "relax and make yourself at home [in my house/shop/city/country]". With hospitality a fundamental part of Arab culture, there's no warmer or more openhearted phrase in the language. The proper response is *ahlan feek* or *ahlan beek* (*feeki* or *beeki* if you're talking to a woman), or you can just acknowledge it with a *shukran* ("thank you") or an informal *ahlayn!* ("double *ahlan* back to you!").

The catch-all word used to invite someone – whether welcoming an old friend into your home or inviting a stranger to share your lunch (surprisingly common) – is **itfuddal**, often said together with *ahlan wa sahlan*. Translations of *itfuddal* (*itfuddalee* to a woman, *itfuddaloo* to more than one person) can vary, depending on circumstance, from "Come in" to "Go ahead" to "Can I help you?" to "Here you are, take it".

to accept the item in question. Many people keep their reception rooms relatively bare for this reason.

If you're a **vegetarian**, you would be quite within social etiquette to make your dietary preferences clear before you accept an invitation; especially in the well-touristed areas of Petra and Wadi Rum, vegetarianism is accepted as a Western foible and there'll be no embarrassment on either side. Elsewhere, it can help to clarify what seems an extraordinary and unfamiliar practice by claiming it to be a religious or medical obligation. All their best efforts notwithstanding, though, veggies may have to prepare themselves to sit down in front of a steaming dish of fatty meat stew and tuck in heartily, while still looking like they're enjoying it.

During and after the meal

This section outlines some of the things which may happen once you **sit down to eat** with a family. It may all seem too daunting for words to try and remember everything here. The bottom line is, you don't: you'd have to act truly outrageously to offend anyone deeply. Your host would never be so unhospitable as to make a big deal about some social blunder anyway.

Once you arrive for a meal, you'll probably be handed a thimbleful of bitter **Arabic coffee** as a welcoming gesture; down it rapidly, since everyone present must drink before sociabilities can continue. Handing the cup back with a jiggle of your wrist indicates you don't want any more. The meal – often a *mensaf* – may well be served **on the floor** if you're in a tent, generally with the head of the household, his adult sons and any male friends sitting cross-legged around a large communal platter; Western women count as males for social purposes and will be included in the circle. Even if wives and daughters are present, they almost certainly won't eat with you, and indeed you may find that they all stay out of sight in another part of the tent or house. If they do, it would be grossly impertinent to enquire after them.

Once the food appears (generally served by the women), and the host has wished you

"sahtayn!" ("[May you eat] with two appetites!"), you should confine yourself to eating – strictly with your right hand only – from that part of the platter directly in front of you; your host may toss over into your sector choice bits of meat such as the **tongue** – and, as an outside possibility, the eyes – which, if they land in front of you, it would be inexplicable to refuse. Quite often, everyone present will share a single **glass of water**, so if the only glass visible is put in front of you, it's not a cue for you to down it. While eating, locals will be careful not to **lick their fingers**, instead rolling their rice and meat into a little ball one-handed and popping it in from a short distance; however, it takes ages to learn how to do this without throwing food all over yourself, and you'll have enough social leeway to subtly cram in a fistful as best you can. It's no embarrassment – in fact, it's almost obligatory – to make a horrible greasy mess of yourself. You'd be well advised to stop or slow down **before you're full**, partly because as soon as you stop eating you'll be tossed more food; partly because no one will continue eating after you – the guest of honour – have stopped (so if you sit back too soon you'll be cutting the meal short); and partly because whatever doesn't get eaten by the men counts as dinner for the women and children. Never finish all the food in front of you, since not only does this tag you as greedy, it's also a direct insult to your host, who is obliged always to keep your plate well stocked. When you've **finished**, your right hand over your heart and the words *"al-hamdulillah"* ("thank God") make clear your satisfaction.

After everyone has washed hands and face, **fresh coffee** will be served; you should take three before you return the cup with a jiggle of the wrist. There'll then be endless **tea**, along with bonhomie, conversation and possibly an *argileh* or two. It's your host's unspoken duty to keep the tea flowing whatever happens, so after you've had enough – one or two glasses at least – the best way to stem the tide is to say *"da'iman"* ("may it always be thus") and then simply to ignore your full glass.

Work and study

The chances for either work or study in Jordan aren't great. There are only a couple of decent language schools in Amman for English teachers to try their hand with, and although picking up work in other fields – specifically journalism and computer-aided design – isn't beyond the bounds of possibility, options are pretty slim and you'd be wise not to rely on anything. Jordan is a good place to study Arabic, with two universities and a handful of other places offering casual and intensive courses. The quantity of archeology being done around the country offers good possibilities to volunteer on a dig.

Teaching English

Amman's top two **language schools**, the British Council and the American Language Center, are bustling hives of activity, with continuous programmes of English teaching at all levels. Both mainly recruit their teachers outside Jordan, but vacancies do occasionally arise at short notice, so if you hold both a university degree and the RSA TEFL certificate (or equivalent), you've got nothing to lose by asking.

Smaller language schools aren't really worth bothering with, but the huge demand for English has led to a thriving scene in private **tutoring**, for which qualifications only matter if your student requires them; the noticeboards in all cultural centres are plastered with names and numbers of tutors, any of whom could probably give you an idea of how to set up.

Studying Arabic

The main thing to determine before you start checking out Arabic courses is whether you want to learn **Modern Standard Arabic** (MSA; see p.507) or the **colloquial dialect** of Jordan and Palestine, since different courses teach different kinds of Arabic.

The highest-prestige courses for foreign students are the semester- and year-long MSA programmes at Amman's University of Jordan and Irbid's Yarmouk University, which are valid for transferable credits at most American and some British universities. However, by all accounts, teaching standards at either institution aren't high. Colloquial Arabic – far more useful for the

interested traveller – is taught on a more casual basis at a handful of cultural centres in Amman, principally the British Council and the French Cultural Centre; courses at the latter are taught by trilingual Arabic/French/English teachers, mostly in English. Prices for a one-semester (four-month) part-time course are around JD150. There's also any number of better- and worse-qualified **private tutors** in Amman, many of whom will be willing to do a deal teaching you Arabic in exchange for you teaching them English; check the noticeboards in cultural centres (see p.164) for leads.

Archeological work

There are good opportunities for amateur **archeologists** to get involved on a dig in Jordan, although you'll need to plan a long time in advance (six months or more) and be prepared to have to shell out for transport and living expenses for the privilege of being allowed to work onsite. You'll be in more demand if you know the region well, have worked on digs before, or have particular skills such as photography or technical drawing to offer. In the first instance, you should write to the big archeological institutes in Amman who, if opportunities are available, can put you in contact with the directors of specific projects.

Archeological institutes and language centres

ACOR (American Center for Oriental Research) PO Box 2470, Amman 11181 ☎06/534 6117, ℉534 4181, ⊛www.bu.edu/acor. ACOR (pronounced "aykor") is a pillar of Jordan's academic establishment, which, in addition to conducting archeological investigations of its own – principally at Madaba, Petra, Aqaba, Karak and Rum – publishes books, pamphlets and newsletters on Jordan's heritage.

American Language Center PO Box 676, Amman 11118 ℡06/585 9102, ℻585 9101, ☏www .alc.edu.jo. High-quality language school run by the Cultural Office of the US Embassy.

British Council PO Box 634, Amman 11118 ℡06/463 6147, ℻465 6413, ☏www .britishcouncil.org/jordan. Very active cultural centre, with a range of activities promoting British culture in Jordan, and one of the best language schools in the country. The website has tons of material on studying and teaching abroad.

CBRL (Council for British Research in the Levant) (formerly BIAAH, the British Institute at Amman for Archeology and History) PO Box 519, Jubayha, Amman 11941 ℡06/534 1317, ℻533 7197, ☏www.britac.ac.uk/institutes. Very active in archeology around Jordan, including at Faynan, Jerash, Pella, Wadi Araba, Baydha and elsewhere.

French Cultural Centre (Centre Culturel Français et de Cooperation Linguistique) PO Box 9257, Amman 11191 ℡06/461 2658, ℻463 0061, ☏www.cccljor-jo.org. Part of the cultural office of the French Embassy, promoting French culture in Jordan as well as supporting an array of local cultural and historical projects.

IFAPO (Institut Français d'Archéologie du Proche-Orient) PO Box 5348, Amman 11183 ℡06/461 1872, ℻464 3840, ☏www .ambafrance-jo.org. Large and long-established organization attached to the cultural office of the French Embassy, with ongoing projects in Jerash, Iraq al-Amir, Wadi Musa and Wadi Rum.

Study and work programmes

UK and Ireland

Field Studies Council Overseas ℡01743/852 150, ☏www.fscoverseas.org.uk. Respected educational charity with over twenty years' experience of organizing specialized holidays with study tours visits worldwide, including to Jordan. Group size is generally limited to 10–15 people.

Habitat for Humanity ℡01295/264240, ☏www .habitatforhumanity.org.uk. Large international organization devoted to alleviating social deprivation by building houses for impoverished families, in both the developing and the developed world. Among other activities, it places volunteers with work parties building houses for low-income families in rural communities in Jordan.

US and Canada

Association for International Practical Training ℡1-800/994-2443 or 410/997-2200, ☏www.aipt.org. Summer internships in Jordan for students who have completed at least two years of college in science, agriculture, engineering or architecture.

Council on International Educational Exchange (CIEE) ℡1-800/2COUNCIL, ☏www .ciee.org. Summer, semester and academic-year programmes in Amman.

Habitat for Humanity ℡229/924-6935 ext 2551, ☏www.habitat.org. See entry above – HfH also has affiliates all round the US and Canada.

Peace Corps ℡1-800/424-8580, ☏www .peacecorps.gov. Places Americans with specialist qualifications or skills in two-year postings in Jordan.

Volunteers for Peace ℡802/259-2759, ☏www .vfp.org. Non-profit organization with links to a huge international network of "workcamps", two- to four-week programmes that bring volunteers together from many countries to carry out needed community projects. Most workcamps are in summer.

World Learning ℡1-800/257-7751, ☏www .worldlearning.org. World Learning's School for International Training (℡1-800/257-7751, ☏www .sit.edu) runs accredited college semesters in Jordan, comprising language and cultural studies, homestay and other academic work.

Australia and New Zealand

Australians Studying Abroad ℡03/9509 1955 or 1800/645 755, ☏www.asatravinfo.com.au. Study tours focusing on art and culture; AUS$500 deposit.

Australian Volunteers International ℡03/9279 1788, ☏www.ozvol.org.au. Postings for up to two years.

Travelling with children

Children are universally loved in Jordan, and travelling with your family is likely to provoke spontaneous acts of kindness and hospitality from the locals. Children are central to Jordanian society – many couples have four or five, and double figures isn't uncommon. Middle-class extended families tend to take pleasure in spoiling kids rotten, allowing them to stay up late and play endlessly, but as a counterpoint, kids from low-income families can also often be seen out on the streets at all hours selling cigarettes. The streets are quite safe and even very young children walk to school unaccompanied.

Only the cheapest hotels will bar children; most will positively welcome them, as will all restaurants, although discounts may have to be negotiated. There are a few **precautions**, however, to bear in mind when travelling with children. First and foremost is the **heat**: kids' sensitive skin should be protected from the sun as much as possible, both in terms of clothing (brimmed hats and long sleeves are essential) and gallons of sunblock. Heatstroke and dehydration can work much faster on children than on adults. Sunglasses with full UV protection are vital to protect sensitive eyes. Second is the **food**: aside from the usual questions of hygiene, the oil liberally used in Jordanian cooking may not appeal to kids' tastes (although the sweets probably will), and restaurants may not be entirely switched on to how to prepare blander meals for children – but you'll nearly always be able to get chicken and chips. Kids are also obviously much more vulnerable than adults to **stomach upsets**, and you should definitely carry rehydration salts in case of diarrhoea. Other things to watch out for include the crazy traffic (especially for

British kids, who'll be used to traffic driving on the other side of the road), stray animals that may be disease carriers, and jellyfish and poisonous corals off Aqaba's beaches. Kids don't qualify for any discounts on public transport, but availability of multi-bed hotel rooms is generally good; given a bit of notice, hoteliers will do their best to accommodate your needs.

Children will probably love taking camel rides in Wadi Rum, and even Petra's thread-bare donkeys may hold an appeal. Most of the archeological sites will probably be too rarefied to be of anything more than passing interest (aside, possibly, from the castles at Karak, Shobak, Azraq and Ajloun); Shaumari's ostriches and oryx safaris may well be a better bet, and the pedalos on the Dead Sea and glass-bottomed boats at Aqaba are perennial favourites. Children born and brought up in urban environments will probably never have experienced anything like the vastness and silence of the open desert, and you may find they're transfixed just by the emptinesses of Rum, Wadi Araba or the eastern Badia.

Travellers with disabilities

Jordan makes few provisions for its own citizens who have limited mobility, and this is obviously reflected in the negligible facilities for tourists. By far the best option is to plump for an organized tour – sightseeing is liable to be complicated enough that leaving the practical details to the professionals will take a weight off your mind. The contacts below will be able to put you in touch with any specialists organizing trips to Jordan.

If you have limited mobility, it's hard to envisage how the situation for travelling could be less accommodating than it is in Jordan. Throughout the country – from Amman's richest neighbourhoods to the tiniest rural villages – pavements are either narrow and broken or missing altogether, kerbs are high (sometimes over half a metre), stairs are ubiquitous and **wheelchair access** to hotels, restaurants and public buildings is pretty much nonexistent. Hotel staff and tourism officials, although universally helpful and sympathetic, are generally poorly informed about the needs and capabilities of tourists with mobility limitations. You'll need patience and low expectations to get the most from a visit; travelling with an able-bodied helper and being able to shell out for things like a rental car (or a car plus driver) and a medium or high grade of accommodation will make things considerably less fraught.

All Jordan's **ancient sites** are accessible only by crossing rough and stony ground for at least some short distance, and sometimes for 200m or more. Scrambling around the rubble at sites such as Jerash or Hallabat is hard enough for those with full mobility; for those without, a visit represents a major effort of energy and organization. Amra, Hraneh and the castles at Karak, Ajloun, Azraq and elsewhere are easier, but still involve rocky ground and/or steep stairs. Petra, strangely enough, though locked away behind rugged mountains, has better access: with advance planning, you could arrange to rent a horse-drawn cart to take you the entire distance from the ticket gate through to the Qasr al-Bint, from where – with written permission obtained ahead of time from the tourist

police – you could be picked up in a car and driven back via the Wadi Turkmaniyyeh road and through a checkpoint to your hotel. At Rum, if you can sit in a bouncing jeep, you can get to see, from a distance, just about anything you want with no restrictions. Some of Madaba's church mosaics and the *Resthouse* and viewing platform at Dana are made unnecessarily difficult to access by rampless stairs.

Contacts for travellers with disabilities

In the UK and Ireland

Access Travel ☎01942/888 844, ⓦwww .access-travel.co.uk. ATOL bonded tour operator that can arrange flights, transfer and accommodation.
Holiday Care ☎0845/124 9971 or 020/8760 0072, ⓦwww.holidaycare.org.uk. Provides free lists of accessible accommodation and information on financial help for holidays.
Irish Wheelchair Association ☎01/818 6400, ⓦwww.iwa.ie. Useful information provided about travelling abroad with a wheelchair.
Tripscope ☎0845/758 5641, ⓦwww.tripscope .org.uk. This registered charity provides free advice for those with a mobility problem.

In the US and Canada

Access-Able ⓦwww.access-able.com. Online resource for travellers with disabilities.
Directions Unlimited ☎1-800/533-5343 or 914/241-1700. Travel agency specializing in bookings for people with disabilities.
Mobility International USA ☎541/343-1284, ⓦwww.miusa.org. Information and referral services, access guides, tours and exchange programmes.
Society for the Advancement of Travelers with Handicaps ☎212/447-7284, ⓦwww.sath .org. Non-profit educational organization that has

actively represented travellers with disabilities since 1976. Annual membership $45; $30 for students and seniors.

Wheels Up! ☎1-888/389-4335, 🖳www .wheelsup.com. Provides discounted airfare, tour and cruise prices for disabled travellers, also publishes a free monthly newsletter and has a comprehensive website.

In Australia and New Zealand

ACROD (Australian Council for Rehabilitation of the Disabled) ☎02/6282 4333, 🖳www.acrod .org.au. Provides lists of travel agencies and tour operators for people with disabilities.

Disabled Persons Assembly ☎04/801 9100, 🖳www.dpa.org.nz. Resource centre with lists of travel agencies and tour operators.

Directory

ADDRESSES Notwithstanding the efforts of cartographers and government officials, Jordan doesn't use street addresses: any nameplates you happen to see on street corners are largely ignored by locals, who have their own names for streets and navigate by locating themselves in relation to prominent buildings or landmarks, or by asking passersby. Mail is delivered only to PO boxes at post offices, and international courier companies deliver only to their own main offices, where parcels are held for collection. If you have an appointment, it's a good idea to phone in advance to get detailed directions.

CIGARETTES AND SMOKING Under Jordanian law, smoking is banned in public places and on public transport. However, enforcement is minimal and in effect it's impossible to escape cigarette smoke anywhere in the country. The anti-smoking lobby in Jordan (headquartered obscurely in Karak) makes little headway. A large proportion of Jordanians both smoke themselves and assume everyone else does: it's not uncommon for locals to light up blithely in a crowded taxi, then close the window against the draught. Nonetheless, Jordan has now signed up to the World Health Organization Convention on Tobacco Control: media advertising of tobacco products is banned, and fines have been imposed on shopkeepers for selling cigarettes to under-18s.

CONTRACEPTIVES Imported brand-name condoms and lubricant are reliably available

in pharmacies in Amman, Wadi Musa and Aqaba. If you use other methods, you should carry enough supplies to last the duration of your trip.

DEPARTURE TAX Leaving by land or sea, you must pay JD5 in cash dinars only. Leaving by air, your departure tax is already included in the price of your ticket.

ELECTRICITY 220V AC, 50Hz (the same as in Europe); supply is pretty steady in most areas and blackouts are rare. Plug style is a real mishmash, though. Most new buildings and big hotels have British-style square three-pin sockets. Older buildings tend to have one or other of two different styles of two-pin socket: thicker-pronged (round plugs) and thinner-pronged (flat plugs). For more information, visit 🖳www.kropla.com before you go. All electrical stores are well stocked with inexpensive adaptors and converters. American equipment will also need a 220-to-110 transformer.

TAMPONS AND PADS Local women generally prefer to use pads, and both Jordanian and imported European brands are widely available at pharmacies and supermarkets, although you may not get the choice of styles you have at home. Tampons are available – most reliably in pharmacies in Amman's uptown neighbourhoods – but might be a little harder to find.

THINGS TO BRING Jordan is not the back of beyond, and most normal travel items can be found in the flashier parts of Amman (if not elsewhere). However, it pays to bring with you a few choice bits and bobs to ease the way. The following are some ideas, ranked in order of importance:

- Total sunblock, sweatproof (you'll still tan, even through Factor 50). Sunblock lip balm is another essential.

- Anything to keep the sun off your head and neck: hat, headscarf, even a collapsible umbrella.

- Lightweight light-coloured cotton clothes that protect your skin from the sun. If you're in Jordan between November and March, you'll need proper warm and water-proof winter gear.

- Water bottle or canteen (or carry plastic mineral-water bottles for refilling).

- Mosquito repellent.

- Torch/flashlight.

TIME Jordan is usually two hours ahead of London, seven hours ahead of New York and eight hours behind Sydney. Daylight Saving Time operates from the beginning of April to the end of October, although dates for the changeover aren't fixed and don't coincide with European and Israeli summer times: for a week or two in spring, Amman can run three hours ahead of London and an hour ahead of Jerusalem; and, for a week or two in autumn, one hour ahead and one hour behind respectively.

TOILETS Public ones – if you can find any – tend not to be too bad, since they almost always have a caretaker, who'll give you some toilet paper if there isn't any visible. Fifty fils is a normal tip. Quite often you get a choice between hole-in-the-ground squat toilets and Western-style sit-down ones. Whichever you use, you should never put used paper down the hole, since it's likely to block the pipes; instead, drop it in the omnipresent little basket. A working toilet will always also have a working tap and a plastic jug, since the local way is to wash yourself clean using your left hand (there are no guidelines about drying off afterwards). Squat toilets almost never flush; instead, empty a jug or two down the hole. The proper Arabic word for toilet is *hammam*, but most people will understand *twalet*.

TOURIST GUIDES Within Jordan, the government monitors all official tourist guides and gives accreditation in three categories based on an annual written exam. Guides who have been awarded Category A status are deemed to be knowledgeable enough to guide visitors around all sites nationwide. Category B implies specialist knowledge of certain major sites only, while Category C guides are permitted to give information only about one particular site. All guides must show their laminated photo-ID card at all times, and all of them also carry a "Tourist Guide Licence" showing expiry date and accreditation category, which they must produce on demand. The upshot of this rigorous system is effectively to eliminate hustlers from tourist sites, ensuring that someone who holds official ID and claims to be a guide does genuinely know his stuff – some guides hold advanced university degrees in ancient history, most speak two or three languages, and virtually all have put in time on archeological digs in Jordan or elsewhere. Payment, though, is entirely negotiable. The going rate for a Category A guide to accompany you around the country is JD30–35 a day, excluding transport (nego-tiable) and his meals and accommodation (which amount to another JD25 or so). A local guide (who may be Category A anyway) hired once you arrive at a site should be paid at least JD4/hr. The standard rate at Amman and Jerash is about JD5/hr, at Petra JD8/hr. Tips are always optional. For more informa-tion, and to book a particular guide, see ⓦwww.tourguides.com.jo.

WEIGHTS AND MEASURES Jordan uses the metric system, with all roadsigns marked in kilometres, all fresh produce sold by the kilogramme, and mineral water in 1.5-litre bottles. The only local idiosyncrasy is the dunum, an area of land equal to a thousand square metres.

Guide

Amman 101–157

The 159–191

desert and the Red Sea 193–207

The eastern desert 209–273

The King's Highway 275–321

Petra 323–377

The southern desert and Aqaba 379–423

Guide

1 Amman 101–167

2 The Dead Sea and around 169–194

3 Jerash and the north 195–237

4 The eastern desert 239–274

5 The King's Highway 275–321

6 Petra 323–377

7 The southern desert and Aqaba 379–425

1

Amman

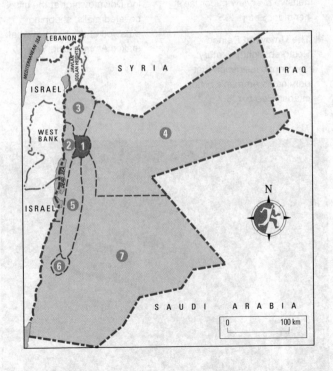

CHAPTER 1 **Highlights**

* **The Roman Theatre** Impressive ancient arena at the heart of the capital. See p.129

* **The Downtown souks** Immerse yourself in the bustle of Amman's market streets. See p.131

* **National Archeological Museum** The most comprehensive overview of Jordan's heritage. See p.135

* **The Umayyad Palace** Restored eighth-century governor's residence that dominates Amman's hilltop citadel. See p.136

* **Darat al-Funun** Cutting-edge art gallery housed in a beautiful 1920s hillside villa. See p.138

* **Arabic cuisine** Dine in style at sophisticated, elegant restaurants such as *Fakhr el-Din* or *Tannoureen*. See p.147

* **Shopping** Whether browsing Downtown or at the glitzy covered malls, shopping puts you at the heart of what makes Amman tick. See p.153

△ King Abdullah I Mosque

Amman

C onsistently overlooked and underrated by travellers to the Middle East, the Jordanian capital **AMMAN** stands in marked contrast to its raucous neighbours, with none of the grand history of Damascus, not a whiff of Jerusalem's tension and just a tiny fraction of Cairo's monuments. It's a civilized, genteel place – misunderstood by the travel writer Paul Theroux, who dismissed it in a single sentence as "repulsively spick-and-span" – with an unexpected charm, not least because it subverts many stereotypes. Taking in an art gallery or shopping in one of the big malls can give an insight into ordinary city life that most visitors, who stay fixated on museums and ruins, never get.

Amman is a thoroughly twentieth-century invention: it was no more than an unregarded, muddy farming village when Emir Abdullah chose it to be his **new capital** in 1921. The consequent sense of Amman being a village-made-good is highlighted when you spend some time on the Downtown streets. Here the weight of history that is a constant presence in the heart of most Middle Eastern cities is manifestly lacking, replaced instead by a quick-witted, self-reliant dynamism. This energy stems in large part from displacement, with a huge majority of Ammanis identifying themselves as originating somewhere else: Circassians, Iraqis and above all Palestinians have arrived in the city in large numbers, voluntarily or forcibly exiled from their homelands. The distinctive cultures they have brought are still jostling for living space with the culture of the native Transjordanian Bedouin. Indeed, scratching beneath Amman's amiable surface reveals a whole cluster of multiple personalities jockeying for supremacy: Western-educated entre-preneurs make their fortunes cheek-by-jowl with poverty-stricken refugees, Christians live next door to Muslims, Jordanians of Palestinian origin assert their identity in the face of nationalistic tendencies among "true" Jordanians, and so on. What it is to be Ammani is an ongoing dispute that shows no signs of resolution.

For the time-pressed ruin-hunter, then, there's little more than an afternoon's sightseeing to be done; however, if you're on a long, slow journey of familiar-ity you could easily spend days exploring the slopes of Amman's towering hills, getting under the city's skin while seeing nothing in particular. The capital's impressive **Roman Theatre** and eighth-century **Umayyad Palace** are the only significant monumental attractions, augmented by the country's major **archeological museum**, but of equal, if not greater, interest is contemporary Amman's burgeoning arts scene. The arts centre of **Darat al-Funun**, the **National Gallery** and regular music events can add a surprising perspective to your experience of the city's life.

Some history

The first known settlement near Amman dates from over nine thousand years ago, a Neolithic farming town near the **Ain Ghazal** spring in the hills to the northeast of the modern city. This was one of the largest such towns discovered in the region, three times bigger than contemporary Jericho. Artisans from among its two thousand inhabitants produced strikingly beautiful human busts and figurines in limestone and plaster, some of the earliest statuettes ever discovered (now on display in the Amman museum).

Around 1800 BC, during the Bronze Age, the hill now known as **Jebel al-Qal'a**, which overlooks the central valley of Amman, was fortified for the first time. According to Genesis, the area was inhabited by giants before the thirteenth-century BC arrival of the **Ammonites**, mythical descendants (along with the Moabites) of the drunken seduction of Lot by his own two daughters. By 1200 BC, the citadel on Jebel al-Qal'a had been renamed **Rabbath Ammon** (Great City of the Ammonites) and was capital of an amply defended area which extended from the Zarqa to the Mujib rivers. Rabbath – or Rabbah – is mentioned many times in the Old Testament; the earliest reference, in Deuteronomy, reports that, following a victory in battle, the city had seized as booty the great iron bed of King Og, last of the giants. Later, the book of Samuel relates that, around 1000 BC, the Israelite **King David** set messengers to Rabbah with condolences for the death of the Ammonite king. Unfortunately, the Ammonites suspected the messengers were spies: they shaved off half their beards, shredded their garments and sent them home in ignominy. In response to such a profound insult, David sent his entire army against Rabbah, although he himself stayed behind in Jerusalem to develop his ongoing friendship with Bathsheba, who soon became pregnant. On David's orders, her husband Uriah was placed in the front line of battle against Rabbah and killed. David then travelled to Rabbah to aid the conquest, threw the surviving Ammonites into slavery and returned home to marry the handily widowed Bathsheba. Their first child died, but their second, Solomon, lived to become king of Israel.

The feud between Ammon and its neighbours to the west simmered for centuries, with Israel and Judea coveting the wealth gathered by Ammon and its southern neighbours, Moab and Edom, from lucrative north–south trade routes. In the absence of military or economic might, Israel resorted to the power of prophecy. "The days are coming," warned Jeremiah in the sixth century BC, "that a trumpet blast of war will be heard against Rabbah of Ammon." The city was to become "a desolate heap" with fire "destroying the palaces". In a spitting rage at the Ammonites' celebration of the Babylonian conquest of Jerusalem in 587 BC, Ezekiel went one better, prophesying that Rabbah was to be occupied by Bedouin and to become "a stable for camels".

After Alexander the Great conquered the region in 332 BC, his successor Ptolemy II Philadelphus rebuilt Rabbah and named it **Philadelphia**, the "city of brotherly love". Turmoil reigned following the Seleucid takeover in 218 BC until the Romans restored order by creating the province of Syria in 63 BC. Philadelphia was at its zenith as the southernmost of the great Decapolis cities (see p.200), and benefited greatly from improved trade and communications along the **Via Nova Traiana**, completed in 114 AD by Emperor Trajan to link the provincial capital Bosra with the Red Sea. **The Romans** completely replanned Philadelphia and constructed grand public buildings, among them two theatres, a nymphaeum, a temple to Hercules and a huge forum, all of which survive.

In Byzantine times, Philadelphia was the seat of a bishopric and was still a regional centre when the Arabs conquered it in 635; the city's name reverted to Amman under the Damascus-based **Umayyad** dynasty, who oversaw an expansion of the city's influence. Amman became capital of the area and, around 720, its Umayyad governor developed and expanded the Roman buildings surviving on Jebel al-Qal'a into an elaborate palatial complex, which promptly collapsed in the great earthquake of 749. Following the **Abbasid** takeover shortly afterwards, power shifted east to Baghdad and Amman's influence began to wane, although it continued to serve as a stop for pilgrims on the way south to Mecca. Over the next centuries, travellers mention an increasingly desolate town; Amman had ceded regional prominence to Karak and by the time **Circassian** refugees were settled here by the Ottomans in the 1870s, Amman's hills served only as pasture-land for the local Bedouin: Ezekiel's furious prophecy come true. The Circassians, however, revived the city's fortunes, and when the **Emirate of Transjordan** was established in 1921, Emir Abdullah chose Amman to be its capital.

Modern Amman

Up to 1948, Amman comprised only a village of closely huddled houses in the valleys below Jebel al-Qal'a, with a handful of buildings on the lower slopes of the surrounding hills. But in that year, floods of **Palestinians**, escaping or ejected from the newly established State of Israel, doubled the city's population in just two weeks. Makeshift camps to house the refugees were set up on the outskirts, and, following another huge influx of Palestinian refugees from the West Bank, occupied by Israel in 1967, creeping development began to merge the camps with the city's sprawling new suburbs.

A fundamental shift in the city's fortunes came with the outbreak of the **Lebanese civil war** in 1975. Before then, Beirut had been the financial, cultural and intellectual capital of the Middle East, but when hostilities broke out, many financial institutions relocated their regional headquarters to the security of Amman. Most subsequently departed to the less parochial Gulf, but they nonetheless brought with them money, and with the money came Western influence: today there are parts of West Amman indistinguishable from upscale neighbourhoods of American or European cities, with broad leafy avenues lined with mansions, and fast multi-lane freeways swishing past strip malls and glass office buildings. A third influx of Palestinians – this time expelled from Kuwait following the 1991 **Gulf War** – again bulged the city at its seams, squeezing ever more urban sprawl along the roads out to the north-west and southwest.

When King Hussein signed a **peace treaty** with Israel in 1994, ending a state of war that had persisted since 1948, many Ammanis hoped for the opening of a new chapter in the city's life; Amman's intimate links with Palestinian markets and its generally Western-oriented business culture led many to believe wealth and commerce – not to mention Western aid – would start to flow. Building development burgeoned across the city, but for several years many of the new hotels and office buildings were white elephants, with Amman seeing little economic comeback from political rapprochement with Israel.

Since the early years of this century that situation has changed. Substantial quantities of **US aid** are starting to have an effect. Jordan's political and economic institutions are strengthening. With the government's increasing **liberalization** of the economy, confidence in Amman as a city on the up is growing. Private sector investment has rocketed, but in the face of ongoing instability across Jordan's western border, much of it is coming instead from Arab countries. With a carefully nurtured international image as the moderate and hospitable face of the modern Arab world – an image that rings true for visitors – Amman today can be said to enjoy a greater influence in the region and the world than at any time since the Romans.

Orientation

Amman is a city of hills, and any map of the place can only give half the story. Although distances may look small on paper, the reality is that traffic and people are funnelled along streets either laid on valley-beds or clinging to the side of steep hills: to reach any destinations above Downtown you'll generally have to zigzag up sharp gradients.

The area known in English as **Downtown**, in Arabic as *il-balad* (literally "the city"), is the historical core of Amman; Roman Philadelphia lies beneath its streets and as late as the 1940s this small area comprised virtually the whole of the city. Downtown forms a slender T-shape nestling in the valleys between six hills. At the joint of the T, and the heart of the city, is the imposing **Husseini Mosque**, which faces along **King Faysal Street**, the commercial centre of Downtown and home to most of its budget hotels. The other main thoroughfare of Downtown – Hashmi Street and King Talal Street, together forming the cross-piece of the T – runs in front of the mosque, passing to the west most of Amman's bustling street markets and, to the east, the huge **Roman Theatre**. Towering over Downtown are several hills, including **Jebel al-Qal'a** ("Citadel Hill"), site of a partly restored **Umayyad Palace**.

Most of Amman's explosive growth in the last sixty years has been concentrated in respectable and upmarket **West Amman**; other districts to the north, south and east are much poorer, though more populous. The various neighbourhoods of **Jebel Amman** form the heart of the city's rich western quarter. Running along the crest of the ridge is **Zahran Street**, the main east–west traffic artery, punctuated by numbered intersections known as "**circles**" (not all of them are roundabouts, and most feature overpasses and/or multi-level, crisscrossing tunnels that keep the traffic moving). Closest to Downtown, **1st Circle** marks a quiet and beautiful district with some elegant old stone buildings. The area around **2nd Circle** is less attractive, the backstreets comprising close-knit working-class neighbourhoods with rows of shops and diners. Busy **3rd Circle** is a five-way roundabout and tangle of tunnels pumping traffic around the city, though its backstreets form quiet

---

Street names

Street names in Amman are a relatively recent innovation: a few streets still have no name at all, some have had names assigned to them that no one knows but the mapmakers, and others have names that are entirely different from those published on maps or signposted on street corners. There is no system to this at all, and the only way to deal with it is to get used to it; newcomers have no way of knowing, for instance, that the street marked on all maps and signs as Sharia Abu Bakr as-Saddeeq is one and the same as the widely known Rainbow Street, or Sharia Rainbow. Common alternative names are given below; our maps use whichever name is in everyday usage.

For making sense of street names (where they exist), it helps to memorize some basic Arabic terms. *Sharia* is "street" and always precedes the name. Both *duwaar* (circle) and *maydan* (square) are used to mean "traffic intersection". Many streets are named after members of the royal family and the same titles keep cropping up: *al-malek* is "King" and *al-malka* or *al-malekah* is "Queen". Similarly, *al-amir* or *al-ameer* is "Prince" and *al-ameera* "Princess" – so "Prince Muhammad Street" translates as *Sharia al-Amir Muhammad*.

Official name	Common name
Downtown	
Quraysh Street	Saqf Sayl
Jebel Amman	
Abu Bakr as-Saddeeq Street	Rainbow Street
Omar bin al-Khattab Street	Mango Street
King Abdullah Square	1st Circle (*duwaar al-awwal*)
Wasfi at-Tall Square	2nd Circle (*duwaar al-thaani*)
King Talal Square	3rd Circle (*duwaar al-thaalith*)
Prince Ghazi bin Muhammad Square	4th Circle (*duwaar al-raabe*)
Prince Faisal bin al-Hussein Square	5th Circle (*duwaar al-khaamis*)
Prince Rashid bin el-Hassan Square	6th Circle (*duwaar al-saadis*)
Prince Talal bin Muhammad Square	7th Circle (*duwaar al-saabe*)
King Abdullah II Square	8th Circle (*duwaar al-thaamin*)
Jebel al-Lweibdeh, Shmeisani and beyond	
Khalaf Circle/Hawuz Circle	Lweibdeh Circle
Jamal Abdul-Nasser Intersection	Interior Circle (*duwaar al-dakhliyyeh*)
Suleiman an-Nabulsi Street	Mukhabarrat Street
Arar Street & Sharif Nasser bin Jameel Street	Wadi Saqra
Wasfi at-Tall Street	Gardens Street
Yubil Circle (jct Gardens/Medina St)	Waha Circle (*duwaar al-waha*)
Queen Rania al-Abdullah Street	University Street
King Abdullah II Street	Medical City Street

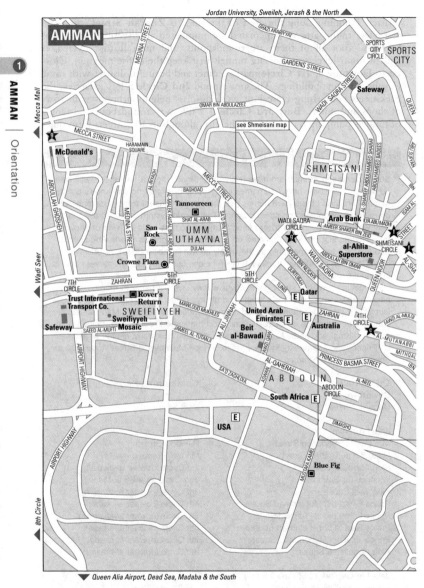

Queen Alia Airport, Dead Sea, Madaba & the South

and pleasant upscale residential districts that harbour big international hotels and fine restaurants. The slopes around **4th** and **5th Circles** are where the Prime Minister's Office and many embassies and government departments are located (as well as more big hotels); **6th Circle** is within striking distance of the cafés and boutiques of Sweifiyyeh and Umm Uthayna; **7th Circle** marks the start of the Airport Road/Desert Highway heading south, and features supermarkets, petrol stations and drive-through fast-food outlets; the

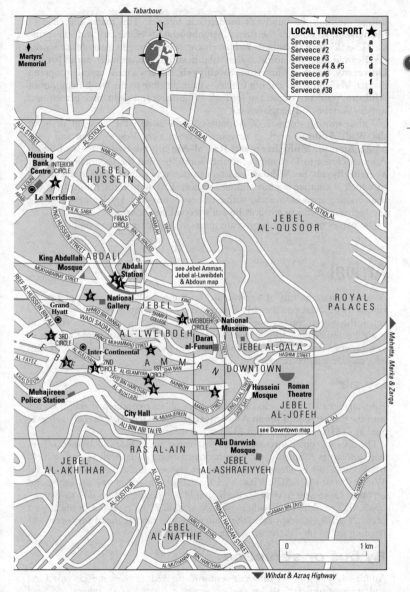

LOCAL TRANSPORT ★
Serveece #1   a
Serveece #2   b
Serveece #3   c
Serveece #4 & #5   d
Serveece #6   e
Serveece #7   f
Serveece #38   g

mundane **8th Circle** serves as the dividing line between Amman proper and Wadi Seer to the west.

The next hill over from Jebel Amman is **Jebel al-Lweibdeh**, a peaceful, monied residential neighbourhood which is home to the **National Gallery** and the arts centre, **Darat al-Funun**. Lweibdeh abuts the district known as **Abdali**, best known for its big bus and taxi station, above which a steep slope culminates in the distinctive landmark of the **Housing Bank Centre**, shaggy foliage muffling the building's modernistic terraces. This marks the edge of **Shmeisani**, still one of the ritziest neighbourhoods of the city and still sprinkled liberally with restaurants and pavement cafés serving its many office workers. Beyond here, the northwestern suburbs dribble on for miles out to **Jordan University**. South of Shmeisani, **Sweifiyyeh**, the city's most upscale shopping district, lies below 5th and 6th Circles – fittingly close to the lavish mansions of **Abdoun**, residence of most of Jordan's millionaires and night-time playground for the Porsche-and-sunglasses set.

Within spitting distance of Abdoun's tennis courts, the pungent drain of the **Wadi Abdoun** marks a division between rich West Amman and poor South Amman. **Muhajireen** and **Ras al-Ain** are the two districts of South Amman closest to Downtown; further south, beyond the mountainous **Jebel al-Ashrafiyyeh**, lies **Wihdat**, a dusty, run-down neighbourhood at the far end of which is another big bus and taxi station. East and North Amman are the least inviting areas of the city, with a ribbon of low-key development hugging the highway northeast towards Jordan's second city, **Zarqa**.

The names of all these districts are given in Arabic in the box on p.147.

Arrival

Amman's many points of **arrival** are far-flung, and unless you opt for the simplicity of a taxi you'll nearly always have a rather involved onward journey across the city to reach a hotel. However, one thing you can always count on is a generally helpful attitude from bystanders. The worst that might happen to you on your first day in Amman would be an overabundance of offers of help or a slightly inflated taxi fare.

By air

Amman has two international airports, but all intercontinental traffic comes into the pocket-sized **Queen Alia International Airport** (generally abbreviated as QAIA) – the box on p.112 has full information.

The only scheduled international flights in and out of **Marka Airport** (otherwise known as Amman Civil Airport; international code ADJ), a small airfield barely 5km east of Downtown, are short regional flights operated by Royal Wings (☎06/487 5202). **Visas** and formalities on arrival are all simple and obvious. Once you're outside, **taxis** should be waiting (about JD1 to Downtown, JD2 to Shmeisani); otherwise, if you walk 200m right out of the airport precinct to the roundabout on the main road, you can flag down **serveece** #17 heading left to the Raghadan station in Downtown.

By bus or serveece

Amman has at least six different termini scattered all over the city for local and international arrivals by bus or serveece (shared taxi): where you end up depends partly on where you're coming from, and partly on what form of transport you're using. Note the warning on p.114 about forthcoming changes.

Abdali station (pronounced *ub-d'lee*, with stress on the first syllable) is the most important point of arrival. A noisy, chaotic place occupying a big V-shaped island in the middle of King Hussein Street, it points the way down the steep slope towards Downtown. Buses, minibuses and serveeces from most

Renting a car in Amman

There are roughly 120 **car rental** firms in Amman, but few of them deserve your trust or your money. Amman's best-value and most conscientious outfit is **Reliable**, just off Princess Basma Street near 5th Circle in Abdoun (T 06/592 9676 or 592 0526 & F 06/592 9676, E reliable@nets.com.jo, W www.reliable.com.jo); they have brand-new air-con cars with unlimited mileage, insurance and collision damage waiver from about JD29 a day, less for longer periods. Cars with automatic transmission are available. They'll bring the car to you, and you can drop it off for free at the airport or anywhere in Amman, 24 hours a day.

For one-way rentals, you might do better going to **Hertz**, located at Shmeisani's *Middle East Hotel* (T 06/553 8958, F 553 8406, E hertz@go.com.jo, W www.hertz .com.jo) and on the Airport Road near Queen Alia Airport (T 06/446 0771): on rentals of three days and above, you can drop the car off for free at any of their six Amman offices, the airport, the Dead Sea, Petra or Aqaba. **Avis**, with three Amman locations including King Abdullah Gardens (T 06/569 9420, F 569 4883, W www.avis.com.jo), plus at the airport (T 06/445 9040), at the King Hussein/Allenby Bridge (T 05/358 1754) and in Aqaba, can also do one-way deals. **Dallah** is a local firm with offices in Amman (T 06/551 1112, F 551 1116, W www.dallah-jo.com) and at the airport (T 06/445 1345), while **Firas** is in Amman (T 06/461 2927, F 461 6874) and at the King Hussein/Allenby Bridge (T 05/358 1592).

Other reliable operators include: **Budget** (T 06/569 8131, F 567 3312); **Europcar** (T 06/565 5581, F 569 1505, W www.europcar.jo); **National** (T 06/560 1350, F 463 9197); and **Payless** (T 06/552 5180, F 553 2525, W www.paylessjordan.com).

If you're flying in late at night and want to be met by a car-rental firm at the airport, you'd be well advised – once you've agreed a price and finalized the details – to send them a one-page **fax confirmation**, stating your name, your flight number, where you're coming from, and what day and time you want to be met. Being left in the lurch is a bad way to start your holiday; verbal arrangements and email are probably enough, but nothing is as reliable as paper.

Jordanian towns north and west of Amman – including Jerash, Ajloun, Irbid and Salt – arrive here, as well as some minibuses from Madaba. Buses and serveeces from Damascus, from the King Hussein (Allenby) Bridge, and from Saudi Arabia, the Gulf and around the Middle East also terminate at various points nearby. There are a few hotels in and around Abdali (see p.124), but most travellers head straight for Downtown, a thirty-minute walk away. If you can't face the hike, it's easy to grab any yellow taxi heading downhill; cheaper white serveeces line up and wait for a full car before departing.

Scheduled Karnak and JETT **buses** from Damascus, as well as JETT (and partner) buses from Cairo, Baghdad, Saudi Arabia and the Gulf terminate at the **JETT depot**, about 1km uphill from Abdali. JETT buses from Aqaba drop off not in the bus parking area, but a few metres away on the street outside the company's office, from where serveece #6 runs to Downtown.

The other main transport terminus in Amman is the **Wihdat station** (aka South station, *mujemma al-janoob*), an open car park with a scattering of snack stalls, some 5km south of Downtown near Middle East Circle. This is where buses, minibuses and serveeces from the south of Jordan arrive – most usefully Aqaba, Petra, Ma'an, Karak and some from Madaba – as well as a handful of international buses. There are always taxi-drivers waiting for business, or you could take one of the three serveeces which depart from behind the buildings that stand off to one side. The most useful is #19, which runs to the Raghadan station in Downtown; long queues form for both the #27, which drops off on

Queen Alia International Airport

Amman's main **Queen Alia International Airport** (QAIA) – with the international code **AMM** – is located on the edge of the desert, 35km south of Amman and about 18km east of Madaba. It is well signposted off Jordan's main north–south highway, which is known in the south as the "Desert Highway" and in the stretches close to Amman as the "Airport Road".

The airport has two terminals, more or less identical in design and facilities, which occupy opposite halves of a single, H-shaped building. **Terminal 1** (also known as the South Terminal) is used mainly by Royal Jordanian, and **Terminal 2** (the North Terminal) is used mainly by other carriers, but these are not hard-and-fast rules. To get from one terminal to another, you simply cross the road – or, if you are already "air-side", make your way through the Duty-Free Shop, which occupies the cross-piece of the H on a bridge above the zebra crossing. Facilities within the airport are pretty simple: bucket chairs, newspaper kiosks, the odd snack bar – nothing to write home about. There are no **left luggage** facilities.

For **information** regarding arrivals or departures on Royal Jordanian call ℡06/445 3200, on all other carriers ℡06/445 2700.

Arrival

All incoming passengers – at either terminal – end up in front of a line of immigration desks. If you already have a **visa**, pick any line. If you haven't yet got a visa, look out for a small "Visa" sign on one or other of the desks (usually at the right-hand side), and wait in that line; one official will take your passport and visa fee (10JD, in dinars only), and his colleague nearby will stamp you in. (If you've arrived without dinars, skip the queue and ask an official where the nearest bank counter or ATM is; only get a small amount of dinars here, as you can find better rates in the city centre.) Once you're through the formalities, you come downstairs to ground level for baggage reclaim, where dozens of porters congregate. One will rush to help you, grabbing a trolley, identifying your bags on the carousel from the security stubs on your ticket, and even wheeling your loaded trolley out to the kerbside for you. Porter services are officially free of charge, but with the effort they go to on your behalf, you may feel a tip is in order; if so, half a dinar is fine and 1JD is generous. Beside the reclaim carousels is a small **duty-free shop**, which is open to meet incoming flights. Once you've got your bags, you just wander through customs and out to the arrivals hall, which has a sporadically staffed **information desk**.

Plenty of airport **taxis** wait just outside both terminals' arrival halls, and drivers will come up to you touting for business. In the best tradition of airport taxis the world over, they'll charge whatever they can get – as much as JD25–30 to Amman city centre, when the correct metered price is nearer JD15–18. Resist any demands for extra payments for baggage. The best way to handle all this attention is to go to the **airport taxi office** (round to the left in the arrivals area), where they'll give you a slip showing the proper, fixed price for your journey. You can also ignore taxi-drivers' claims that there are no buses: large, comfortable **Airport Express buses** leave from marked points directly outside both arrival halls to Abdali station via Shmeisani (daily: every 30min 6am–10pm; every 2hr 11pm–5am; 45min). The fare is JD1.500, including baggage; check your change carefully though and hang on to the tickets in case of inspections. Note that the overnight schedule is prone to some uncertainty: check with airport information, and be prepared to have to take a taxi anyway. There are desks for a few **car-rental** firms in the arrivals hall; shop around between them to get a decent rate – or try calling our recommendations on p.111. If you've pre-booked an airport pick-up with a car-rental firm, they should be waiting for you in the arrivals hall. All in all, reckon on an hour and a half from touchdown to your hotel room, perhaps two hours.

It's possible to go direct from the airport to other places around Jordan – specifically the nearby town of **Madaba**, where the excellent *Mariam Hotel* (see p.283) can arrange to pick you up from the airport and take you back to the hotel for JD8 (JD10 after midnight). For other destinations, you're generally looking at the official airport taxi rates: to **Petra** or **Aqaba**, reckon on anything from JD65 to JD100 or more, depending on the time of day, although if you call ahead to your hotel, they may come and collect you for slightly less than this (also check with the *Mariam* for their rates from the airport to anywhere countrywide). Note that it is possible to **fly on** to Aqaba for JD35 one-way – check schedules in advance with Royal Jordanian, since some flights depart from QAIA, others from Amman's second airport at Marka.

Departure

The easiest way to reach the airport from Amman city centre is to head west to either 7th Circle or 8th Circle and turn left (south): this road – which is the main highway south to Aqaba and the Saudi border – passes petrol stations, a turn-off for the Dead Sea and another for Madaba before reaching the clearly marked junction for the airport. **Driving time** from the city centre is about 45 minutes. Frequent **Airport Express buses** (info ☎06/585 4196) leave from beneath the distinctive square sign at the top end of Abdali station (daily every 30min 6am–10pm, then midnight, 2am & 4am; JD1.500 including baggage), picking up also from marked stops at the Housing Bank Centre and 7th Circle; be aware that the overnight schedule is not totally reliable – ask your hotel to check in advance. A **taxi** ride to the airport from anywhere within Amman should cost around JD15.

On arrival at the terminal, there's the usual hustle and bustle at the kerbside (trolleys are free of charge, but sometimes in short supply). Everyone joins one huge queue for baggage security and personal checks (women are checked separately off to one side), before heading on to the check-in desks.

After checking in, you then head across to passport control, after which an escalator takes you up to the departure lounges and the large, well-stocked **Duty-Free Shop** (credit cards accepted); gift ideas here include a sealed tin of Arabic sweet pastries, made fresh by Zalatimo (from US$10/kilo upwards), a presentation bottle of Jordanian extra-virgin olive oil (US$10–15), or locally produced crafts, ceramics and traditional design pieces, including items like *keffiyahs* and 'worry' beads. The Duty-Free Shop sits in between the two terminal buildings, which look confusingly similar – check the signs to find your boarding gate.

If you're flying with **Royal Jordanian**, you'd be well advised to avoid the queues – and accompanying chaos – at airport check-in by taking advantage of RJ's excellent **City Terminal** at 7th Circle in Amman (daily 7.30am–10pm; ☎06/585 6855). Here, anywhere **between 24hr and 3hr in advance** of your departure, you can check your bags in and receive a boarding card; a nice perk is that checking in here rather than at the airport means you have an **extra baggage allowance** of 15kg above the usual limit. If you're well ahead of your flight departure, you're then free to go back into the city; if your flight is imminent, you can take RJ's private bus direct from the City Terminal building to the airport (every 30min; JD2). You then go through a fast-track gate and proceed directly to passport control. By the time you read this, RJ's City Terminal 2, in the South Amman district of Abu Alanda – offering the same services – may already be in operation.

Coming from **elsewhere in Jordan**, it's straightforward to negotiate with a local taxi driver to take you to QAIA. From **Madaba**, the efficient *Mariam Hotel* (see p.283) does a reliable airport drop-off service on demand, for a bargain JD7. From elsewhere, it's a case of asking at your hotel and shopping around to get an idea of taxi rates for such a long-distance run. See "Arrival" above for approximate fares.

If you're dropping off a **rental car**, check the day before what your firm's procedures are: some will meet you at the airport to do the paperwork at the kerbside; others require you to drive to their office, from where you'll be shuttled to the airport by a driver.

Airport hotel

The only **hotel** on the airport grounds is the *Alia*, also known as the *Alia Gateway* (℡06/445 1000, 𝔽445 1029; ❶), located about 1km along the road linking the terminal buildings to the main highway. It was built in 1985 – and looks it – and gets most of its business from transit and stopover passengers; facilities are no more than adequate. However, if you arrive late at night this is a useful place to maximize your shut-eye, since you're cutting out the long drive into the city; also, if you want to drive south to Petra in the morning, most rental-car firms will deliver to the hotel, meaning you can avoid city traffic first thing.

Italy Street off the Saqf Sayl in the city centre, and the #27J to Abdali station via 3rd Circle.

Beside the Roman Theatre in the heart of Downtown is the large **Raghadan station**, located no more than ten minutes' walk from the budget hotels. This was completely rebuilt in 2005, thanks to funding from the Japanese government. If transport routings remain as they were before, then only buses and serveeces from Zarqa, Salt, Madaba, and districts in and around Amman stop here.

About 2km southwest of Downtown, directly beneath the hill of 3rd Circle, is the small **Muhajireen station**, arrival point for minibuses from west of Amman, including from the Dead Sea, Wadi Seer, Shuneh al-Janubiyyeh and some arrivals from Madaba. From the main road outside, yellow city bus #54 shuttles to Raghadan station in Downtown.

If you're arriving direct by bus **from Tel Aviv** or **Nazareth**, you'll end up at the office of Trust International Transport, on a shopping street near the big Safeway supermarket off 7th Circle, way out in West Amman. There are no useful minibuses or serveeces within reach, but plenty of metered taxis; the fare to Downtown is around JD1.

The next few years will see **major changes** in the Abdali area, with the new American University campus going up and complete redevelopment of the area around the parliament and King Abdullah I Mosque. Abdali bus station is to be **demolished**, with all its transport services moved to a new bus station in the northern suburb of **Tabarbour**, where Jordan Street (*sharia al-urdun*) – a main highway linking Downtown Amman with the north of Jordan – meets Yajouz Street. This may affect JETT buses too. Details remain sketchy at the time of writing.

By train

At the time of writing, only one passenger **train** operates in Jordan, a twice-weekly departure from Damascus every Monday and Thursday at 8am, which takes nine hours or so to meander into Amman's dusty old **Hejaz station** in Mahatta, to the east of the centre. Serveece #17 to Raghadan runs outside, or you should be able to flag a taxi down for the short ride into the centre – Downtown is to your right, under the bridge. Construction is under way on a new **light rail** link between Amman and Zarqa.

Information

Amman has no **tourist information** office. For brochures and other printed material, your best bet is to contact the Jordan Tourism Board in your home country before you depart. Otherwise, you'd do just as well to hole up in the nearest internet café (see p.165) to take a look at ⓦ**www.see-jordan .com** – and, while you're there, note down details for visiting Jordan's nature reserves at ⓦ**www.rscn.org.jo** and investigate the encyclopedic website of practical information and cultural background at ⓦ**www.jordanjubilee.com**. See p.43 for more websites.

To stock up on printed information, phone ahead to the offices of the **Jordan Tourism Board**, which are located alongside the Duty-Free Shop in the forecourt of the *Ammon Hotel* on Tunis Street, off the main road between 4th and 5th Circles (Sun–Thurs 8am–2pm; ℡06/567 8294). Staff won't answer enquiries for information, but they may prepare a folder of brochures for you. You can pick up good **maps** of towns around the country from any five-star hotel bookstall, and most main city bookshops too (see p.157) – these are invariably better than the free JTB handouts, which are rarely more than sketchy plans. There's more map information on p.44.

There is talk of establishing a new city tourist information office – either within the RSCN's Wild Jordan centre just above Downtown (see p.141), or as part of the redevelopment of the Downtown area centred on the National Museum (see p.133).

City transport

Due to its geography and the unplanned nature of its expansion, Amman doesn't have an integrated **transport system**: buses, minibuses and serveeces

Heavy traffic

Traffic in Amman – especially West Amman – can be horrendous. There's an estimated one car for every seven residents; with the population approaching two million, that makes for one almighty traffic jam. Add to that an influx during the summer of tens of thousands of visitors from Saudi Arabia and the Gulf, almost all of whom drive their own cars, and the problem reaches crisis levels. Summer and winter, the rush hour is under way by 7.30am, and traffic remains bad pretty much all day long, with relief only coming after about 8pm. Listing the blackspots would be pointless: traffic flows fairly well along Zahran Street from 3rd Circle to 8th Circle, but coming off at any point you'll encounter stationary jumbles of cars. All routes into, through and around Shmeisani are prone to jams that can add twenty or thirty minutes to a journey. Gardens Street is often solid. Queen Alia Street (from Interior Circle) and its extension north of Sports City, Queen Rania Street (aka University Street), are also notorious, with heavy traffic extending as far north as Sweileh. Streets in the complex Downtown one-way system are often nose-to-tail. All this isn't helped by the local driving style: lane discipline is non-existent, cars are frequently parked (or double-parked) to block the flow of traffic, roundabouts are a free-for-all, poor traffic-light phasing often leads to gridlock, and so on. The municipality vainly tries to ease the situation by continually upgrading major routes and intersections with underpasses and overpasses, and by major engineering projects such as the bridge linking 4th Circle to Abdoun, completed in 2005. The only saving grace is that the roads are fairly quiet all day on Fridays.

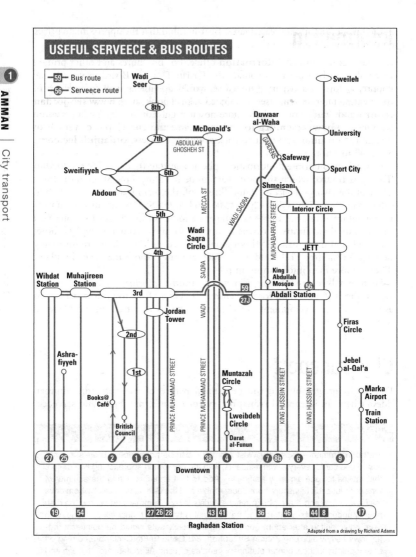

USEFUL SERVEECE & BUS ROUTES

Adapted from a drawing by Richard Adams

compete on set routes around the city (and you'll never have to wait long beside a main road to flag one or other of them down), but none runs to a timetable. Few people pay heed to the roadside bus-stop pillars that appeared in some districts recently, and for all intents and purposes buses and serveeces will stop anywhere. Most useful are the serveeces, whose routes tend to radiate out from various points in Downtown: crossing from one uptown neighbourhood to another without first passing through Downtown is virtually impossible without a taxi. A complex network of yellow, government-run city buses offers an alternative.

Fuel costs have risen significantly in Jordan in recent years – and transport operators, inevitably, have been passing those extra costs on to their customers in the form of slightly increased fares. Bear in mind that the approximate prices quoted below are likely to rise.

Serveeces

Serveeces (shared taxis) are essential for getting quickly and easily up the hills surrounding Downtown. They operate like small buses, with between four and six passengers cramming in and everyone paying a flat fare. You can get in or out wherever you like on the set route. All Amman's city serveeces are **white** cars (often Nissans or vintage Mercedes), with black stencilled panels in Arabic on both front doors stating the general district they're going to, as well as two Arabic numbers either on top of each other or separated by a slash: the top one, or right-hand one, is the route number (very important) and the bottom one, or left-hand one, is the car number (utterly irrelevant). The cars tend to form long nose-to-tail lines at the bottom of the Downtown hills; the first passengers in the queue pile into the last car in line, which then pulls out and grinds its way past all the others up the hill and away. All the rest then roll backwards one place and the same thing happens again.

Throughout this chapter, serveeces are identified by their **route number**, although, if you ask them, Ammanis will quite often have no idea about which number is which, instead identifying serveeces by the district they go to. No official information or route maps exist, but if you want to pick up a serveece partway along its route, a bunch of people forming themselves into a queue on the kerbside is a sure sign of a stop. When you want to **get out**, saying "*allah*

Major serveece routes	
1	Basman St, opposite Husseini Mosque–Prince Muhammad St–1st–2nd–3rd Circle.
2	Basman St, behind *Cliff Hotel*–Rainbow St–Mango St–Buhtari St–2nd–3rd Circle.
3	Basman St, opposite Husseini Mosque–Prince Muhammad St–Jordan Tower–3rd–4th Circle.
4 & 5	Behind Downtown Post Office–Darat al-Funun–Lweibdeh Circle–Jebel al-Lweibdeh–National Gallery.
6	Cinema al-Hussein St–King Hussein St–Abdali–JETT station–Interior Circle.
7	Cinema al-Hussein St–King Hussein St–Abdali–King Abdullah Mosque–Mukhabarrat St–Arab Bank Shmeisani.
8B	Shabsough St, junction of Hashmi St opposite Roman Theatre–King Hussein St–Abdali.
9	Shabsough St, behind Cairo Amman Bank–Jebel al-Qal'a–Jebel Hussein.
17	Raghadan–Hejaz train station–Marka Airport.
19	Raghadan–Wihdat station.
25 & 26	Saqf Sayl, near Fruit and Vegetable Market–Jebel al-Ashrafiyyeh.
27	Saqf Sayl, near Fruit and Vegetable Market–Wihdat station.
27J	Abdali–3rd Circle–Wihdat station.
38	Basman St, opposite Husseini Mosque–Prince Muhammad St–Wadi Saqra–Mecca St–Abdullah Ghosheh St.
56	Abdali Station–Interior Circle–Gardens St.

(see p.511 for Arabic numbers)

yaatik al-afyeh" ("God give you strength") will have the driver veering over to the kerb for you.

All city serveeces have a little white sign somewhere on the dashboard stating the **fare** in Arabic. Fares are generally 120–150 fils per person, except on long crosstown routes, which are around 180 fils. As for **operating hours**, the first serveeces start running daily at 5.45 or 6am. From 7.30 to 9am, the Downtown queues can be 150m long, with correspondingly lengthy waiting times. In the evening, things start to wind down after about 8pm; by 10pm there are long gaps between serveeces, and after 11.30pm any that you find will probably be operating as unmetered taxis.

Taxis

Roughly a quarter of all cars in Amman are **taxis**; the metered fares are cheap and they can whisk you to places that might take hours to get to by any other means. Unless you're starting from a remote neighbourhood, or are planning a journey in the middle of the night, enough will be roaming the streets for you never to have to **phone** for one; should you do need to set a specific pick-up time, ask your hotel receptionist or contact English-speaking Taxi al-Barq (☏06/464 1299). You should insist on the **meter** being switched on before you get going, though practically all drivers will do it anyway as a matter of course. The meters *always* work; if a driver claims it's broken and tries to negotiate a fixed fare with you, simply say "*ma'alesh*" ("forget it") and wait for another taxi to come along; note that although fares don't rise at night, the proportion of "broken" meters does. A ten-minute hop should cost something like 700 fils, with a long, crosstown journey JD1.500 or a little more. Beware the favoured con of some drivers, which is to play on foreigners' misunderstanding of the currency and reinterpret the decimal point on the meter's readout.

Although most drivers know their way around pretty well, and are keen to be helpful and courteous, no Ammani relates to street names. Unless you're

---

Walking in Amman

Walking in Amman is a mixed bag. It's absolutely the only way to get around Downtown, but once you venture further out, distances between sights lengthen and the uptown hills feel like mountain peaks.

You can walk from one end of **Downtown** to the other in about twenty or thirty minutes, staying on the flat the whole way. The trek from there to **Abdali** station, however, although not much more than 1km, is uphill and can take forty minutes or more; no local would consider walking it. **Jebel al-Lweibdeh** and the lower reaches of **Jebel Amman** (below 3rd Circle) are residential and can be explored on foot, but elsewhere, if you try to walk, you'll generally find yourself slogging along a broken kerbside beside streams of traffic in neighbourhoods designed for driving.

However, one of the most delightful discoveries of old Amman – largely ignored by visitors and locals alike – are the **flights of steps** which trace direct paths up and down the steep Downtown hills, dating from the days in the 1930s and 1940s when hillside residences were otherwise inaccessible. Countless flights – most of them undocumented and unidentifiable, many weed-ridden and crumbling – crisscross the area below 1st Circle on Jebel Amman, the nose of Jebel al-Lweibdeh, the flanks of Jebel al-Qal'a and the hills above the Roman Theatre, passing now and then through private backyards, beneath washing lines or past deserted, once-grand villas. If you're decorously dressed and sensitive to the fact that you're tramping through people's gardens – as well as to the possibility that the steps you happen to have chosen might not go anywhere – you're basically free to explore.

Major city bus routes

8	Raghadan–Abdali–Sweileh.
26	Raghadan–3rd Circle–4th–5th–6th–Sweifiyyeh–7th–8th–Wadi Seer.
27	Raghadan–3rd Circle–4th–5th–Abdoun–US embassy–Sweifiyyeh.
28	Raghadan–3rd Circle–4th–5th–6th–7th–Abdullah Ghosheh St.
36	Raghadan–Abdali–Medina St.
41	Raghadan–Wadi Saqra–Safeway.
43	Raghadan–Prince Muhammad St–Wadi Saqra–Mecca St.
44	Raghadan–Abdali–Jordan University.
46	Raghadan–Abdali–Shmeisani.
54	Raghadan–Muhajireen station.
59	Abdali–3rd Circle–Muhajireen station–Wihdat station.

going somewhere obvious, like Abdali station or the Roman Theatre, first give the name of the neighbourhood you're heading for, then, as you get closer, tell the driver which building you want, or maybe a nearby landmark: if he's not familiar with it, he'll quite likely just drive around asking passers-by for directions.

Buses

Recently a network of government-run, yellow **city buses** have started competing with serveeces – and, much to the resentment of struggling serveece-drivers, slightly undercutting them – on popular routes, mainly in and out of Raghadan station in Downtown. Their main advantage for visitors is that they display English route numbers, even though their destination boards are in Arabic only.

Accommodation

Amman has **accommodation** to suit all budgets. Hoteliers city-wide are fully primed as to the needs and expectations of Western tourists, but outside the overstocked luxury end of the market, you'll find that their margins are tight: standards in fittings and maintenance are sometimes make-do, although the welcome extended to guests is nearly always warm.

The best **inexpensive** options are in Downtown. The best **mid-range** hotels are a bit further out, on Jebel Amman, while **luxury** hotels are spread throughout the city's upscale districts. With Amman's unusual appeal – focused much more on atmosphere and gentle exploration rather than on a specific set of must-see attractions – you'll find there's an odd division to staying here. All the main sights and antiquities are in Downtown, but all the decent hotels (above budget levels) are several kilometres away in West Amman. It takes a shift in attitude to appreciate the value of this: the cafés and streetlife outside your hotel door in, say, Shmeisani can be seen as just as much an Amman "attraction" as the Roman Theatre miles away in Downtown.

In the high season (March–Oct), many places across all price brackets fill up quickly, and you'd be well advised to **book ahead**, even for the cheapest of the cheap. Cash is often the only method of payment at the lowest end of the market, but mid-range and luxury places generally take major credit cards. There are no **campsites** in or near Amman.

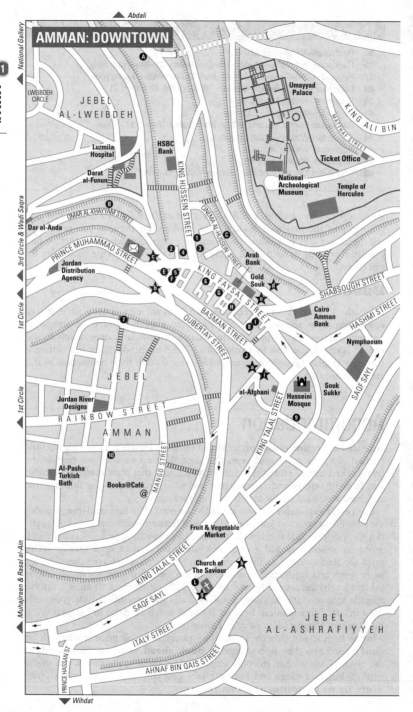

AMMAN: DOWNTOWN

▲ *Abdali*

National Gallery

LWEIBDEH
CIRCLE

JEBEL
AL-LWEIBDEH

Umayyad
Palace

KING ALI BIN

MATHAF STREET

Luzmila
Hospital

HSBC
Bank

Darat
al-Funun

National
Archeological
Museum

Ticket Office

Temple of
Hercules

3rd Circle & Wadi Saqra

OMAR AL-KHAYYAM STREET

Dar al-Anda

PRINCE MUHAMMAD STREET

1st Circle

Jordan
Distribution
Agency

KING HUSSEIN STREET

CINEMA AL-HUSSEIN STREET

Ⓐ

Ⓑ

Ⓒ

❷ ❶ ❸

Ⓔ ❺
Ⓕ
      ❻
      Ⓖ
      Ⓗ

KING FAYSAL STREET

BASMAN STREET

Arab
Bank

Gold
Souk

SHABSOUGH STREET

Cairo
Amman
Bank

HASHMI STREET

❼

QUBERTAY STREET

❽ Ⓘ

JEBEL

Jordan River
Designs

RAINBOW STREET

AMMAN

Ⓙ

al-Afghani

Husseini
Mosque

❾

KING TALAL STREET

Nymphaeum

SAQF SAYL

Souk
Sukkr

1st Circle

Muhajireen & Rasal al-Ain

Al-Pasha
Turkish
Bath

❿

MANGO STREET

Books@Café
@

Fruit & Vegetable
Market

KING TALAL STREET

Church of
The Saviour

Ⓛ

SAQF SAYL

ITALY STREET

PRINCE HASSAN ST.

AHNAF BIN QAIS STREET

JEBEL
AL-ASHRAFIYYEH

▼ *Wihdat*

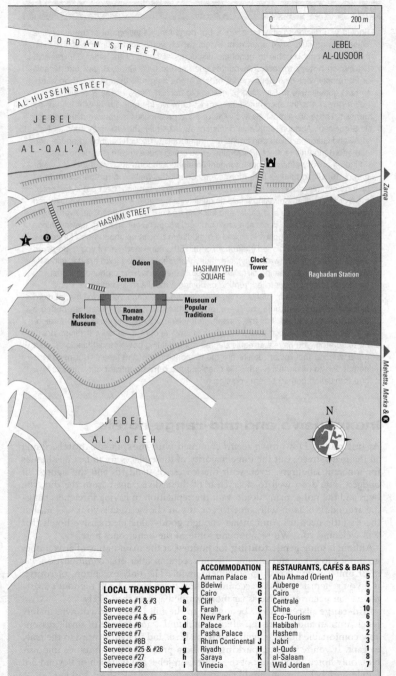

JORDAN STREET

AL-HUSSEIN STREET

JEBEL
AL-QAL'A

JEBEL
AL-QUSOOR

HASHMI STREET

▶ Zarqa

D

Odeon

Forum

HASHMIYYEH
SQUARE

Clock
Tower

Raghadan Station

Museum of
Popular
Traditions

Roman
Theatre

Folklore
Museum

▶ Mahatta, Marka & K

JEBEL
AL-JOFEH

N

0   200 m

LOCAL TRANSPORT ★

Serveece #1 & #3	a
Serveece #2	b
Serveece #4 & #5	c
Serveece #6	d
Serveece #7	e
Serveece #8B	f
Serveece #25 & #26	g
Serveece #27	h
Serveece #38	i

ACCOMMODATION

Amman Palace	L
Bdeiwi	B
Cairo	G
Cliff	F
Farah	C
New Park	A
Palace	I
Pasha Palace	D
Rhum Continental	J
Riyadh	H
Saraya	K
Vinecia	E

RESTAURANTS, CAFÉS & BARS

Abu Ahmad (Orient)	5
Auberge	5
Cairo	9
Centrale	4
China	10
Eco-Tourism	6
Habibah	3
Hashem	2
Jabri	3
al-Quds	1
al-Salaam	8
Wild Jordan	7

Long stays in Amman

Should you decide to stay for a while, but don't fancy shelling out at the numerous West Amman suite-style apartment hotels (which you'll spot on many of the main roads), you may be able to negotiate discounts at some of the small, inexpensive Downtown **hotels**: travellers' favourites such as the *Cliff*, *Farah*, *Bdeiwi* and *Vinecia* are probably your best bets (in that order). In the long run, though, you'd do better to **rent** somewhere to live. One glance in the *Jordan Times* or the *Star* will turn up half a dozen ads for accommodation, most to move in immediately with little or no deposit. These are almost always villas or huge penthouses in uptown districts such as Shmeisani, Abdoun, 4th Circle or distant suburbs near the university such as Tla'a al-Ali and Gardens. If you don't mind the impersonality of such neighbourhoods – and can afford monthly rents of JD400-plus – you could move in with little or no fuss.

Finding a cosy place in more congenial neighbourhoods such as Jebel al-Lweibdeh or 1st Circle takes a little more effort. Check the well-used **noticeboards** in all cultural centres, supermarkets and *Books@Café* first, but your best bet is to spread the word to English-speaking locals as quickly as possible. Wandering your favoured area chatting in shops and cafés, and sticking up your own "wanted" ad everywhere are good ploys. Space is not at a premium, and once you get on the grapevine things can move rapidly. It's possible to find a good flat in a quiet neighbourhood for as little as JD200 a month furnished (*mafroush*) or JD150 unfurnished; less if you're prepared to share. The costs of water (*my*), electricity (*kahraba*) and gas (*gaz*) are negligible by Western standards, heating oil (*solar*) less so. If the place has no phone, it'll cost you hundreds to get one installed; renting or buying a mobile makes more sense.

Amman is a tenants' market: under Jordanian law, once you're in, the landlord cannot raise the rent until you leave, and neither hell nor high water can budge a tenant unwilling to go. For this reason, many landlords rent exclusively to foreigners, who can be expected to leave of their own accord eventually. If things aren't up to scratch, you have a sizeable degree of bargaining power: most landlords start out assuming that minor repairs are the responsibility of the tenant, but need little persuasion to relent. It's worthwhile checking the **rental contract** out with a lawyer or a translation bureau before you sign.

Inexpensive and mid-range hotels

At first glance, Downtown seems crammed with **inexpensive hotels**, lining all the main streets, but the huge majority of these places are in fact dosshouses for itinerant labourers. Even with the lowest of standards and the tightest of budgets, you'd do well to steer clear of these dives; apart from the dirt, the bugs and the noise, many don't want the reputation of having foreigners hanging around. No harm will come to you if you choose to talk your way in, but there's little need to: Amman has enough good-value inexpensive hotels that will welcome you. We recommend some of the better ones here.

Although some gentle **touting** for business at the main points of arrival does go on, it's low-key and amiable; if you accept an offer of accommodation, it's most unlikely you'll end up anywhere awful. The only exception, of course, is if you're female, and the accommodation turns out to be in the tout's apartment – an occurrence that is far more warned against than likely.

Mid-range places tend to be located in the hills above Downtown, mainly Jebel Amman and Shmeisani. Here, you'll find a good range of small, reasonably comfortable hotels, ranging from the brisk and straightforward to the truly elegant. If you're driving, **parking** can be a problem (sometimes it's impossible): only hotels located out of the centre, on Jebel al-Lweibdeh or beyond 3rd Circle on Jebel Amman, are likely to have free, available street parking.

All hotels priced ❸ and above are safe for everybody, but some places in categories ❶ and ❷ are best avoided by **women** travelling alone or together. We've noted in the reviews below which inexpensive hotels offer women privacy and security. Key attributes wherever you end up are some form of air cooling in summer – whether a ceiling fan or full air conditioning – and heating in winter. In general, rooms on higher floors tend to be less prone to dust and traffic noise.

Downtown

If you come in on serveece #6 or #7 from Abdali station, you'll be dropped on Cinema al-Hussein Street, in the thick of **Downtown** and within five minutes' walk of most of the hotels listed here. Serveece #19 from Wihdat station drops off at Raghadan station, next to the Roman Theatre; there are a couple of cheap options nearby, or you could walk 200m or so to the prominent Husseini Mosque, which faces up King Faysal Street, crammed with hotel possibilities. The places listed below are marked on the map on pp.120–21.

Amman Palace Saqf Sayl ⓣ06/464 6172, ⓕ465 6989. Pitched firmly at a respectable Arab clientele, this is one of the highest-quality hotels in Downtown (rated as two stars), though its seventy rooms are not as clean as they should be – rather well-worn, despite air con, phone and satellite TV. Located near the Church of the Saviour. ❸

Bdeiwi Omar al-Khayyam St ⓣ06/464 3394, ⓕ464 3393. A friendly, good-quality budget hotel, on a relatively quiet street up the hill behind the post office, with clean, spartan rooms with fans. Women will feel welcome. Hot showers are free. ❶

Cairo King Faysal St ⓣ06/463 8230. Basic Downtown stalwart opposite the Arab Bank, with some quiet hot-water en-suite doubles that aren't bad. ❶

Cliff Unmarked entrance opposite *Hashem's* restaurant in an alley between Prince Muhammad St and Basman St ⓣ06/462 4273, ⓕ463 8078. With its fame spread around the Middle East, the *Cliff* has long been Amman's top backpacker hotel and meeting place, and is still well run by a jovial and patient Jerusalemite with an inexhaustible supply of sound advice on how to get around – although these days the old place is resting on its laurels just a bit. Rooms are clean, all with cold-water sinks and fans (though no heaters), but those overlooking the next-door restaurant get a little noisy and some of the beds are past their prime. Upstairs are smaller, cheaper rooms and there's a cut-price summer sleep-in on the roof. Hot showers cost 500 fils. Other features include free luggage storage and use of the kitchen, an airport pick-up service and tours to different parts of the country. Safe and comfortable for women. Book ahead or arrive early. ❶

Farah Off Cinema al-Hussein St ⓣ06/465 1443, ⓕ465 1437, ⓔfarahhotel@hotmail.com. Glossy

and ambitiously run cheapie on six floors (look for the big red signs), with hand-painted murals on every wall. Lift access, 24hr hot water, free hot showers, fans in every room, free airport pick-up/drop off and staff who are generally willing to help with car rental, tours and getting around. Quiet, comfortable and safe for women. ❶

New Park King Hussein St, opposite the law courts ⓣ06/464 8144, ⓕ464 8145. A cut above its neighbours, with OK rooms all with TV and telephone. Safe for women, despite a seedy look to the place. Comfortable and good value, with breakfast included. ❷

Palace King Faysal St ⓣ06/462 4327, ⓕ465 0603. Take the lift up to an unexpected place of quality in the heart of the bustle, more or less opposite the Gold Souk. Comfortable, top-floor rooms, each with two balconies and a spotless en-suite bathroom, are best. ❷

Pasha Palace (aka *Qasr al-Basha*) Opposite the Roman Theatre on the corner of Shabsough St and Hashmi St ⓣ06/464 5290, ⓕ464 5313. Forty-room hotel in the heart of Downtown, with adequate en-suite rooms and a rooftop terrace that's a good place to draw breath. Serveece #8b from Abdali goes to the door. ❸

Rhum Continental Basman St ⓣ06/462 3162, ⓕ461 1961. Four floors of over a hundred plain, en-suite rooms, the best ones higher up and slightly pricier. A lift, air con in every room and cleanliness raise it above its neighbours. ❷–❸

Riyadh In an alley off King Faysal St ⓣ06/462 4260. Another acceptable budget option on the main drag, with fans, hot water and welcoming staff. ❶

Saraya Al-Jaza'ir St, behind the Raghadan bus station ⓣ06/465 6791, ⓕ465 6792, ⓦwww .sarayahotel.com. One of the best Downtown choices, with good facilties, friendly, switched-on staff and some character. The proximity of the mosque loudspeakers can cause a rude awakening at dawn, but in general this is a great choice. ❷

Vinecia On an alley between Prince Muhammad St and Basman St ℡06/463 8895, Ⓕ461 6825. Travellers' favourite for its cheapness and good location beside the *Cliff*, its gloomy ambience only partly offset by the friendliness of the staff. The grimy rooms upstairs are quieter but hotter in summer. ❶

Abdali and Jebel al-Lweibdeh

The main advantage of most of the following budget and mid-range places is their proximity to **Abdali station**, useful if you arrive late at night from Jerusalem or Damascus, or if you want an early start. However, traffic noise around the station is a major problem, and none of these hotels offers particularly good value for money. The few hotels on **Jebel al-Lweibdeh**, the steep hill southeast of Abdali, are set in a residential, largely Christian area of quiet, leafy streets, with some marvellous views from its highest point over the whole of Amman. These places are shown on the map opposite.

Canary Opposite the Terra Sancta College on Jebel al-Lweibdeh ℡06/463 8353, Ⓕ465 4353, Ⓔcanary_h@hotmail.com. Peaceful two-star family hotel that gets much of its business from Western tour groups, where 21 clean, comfortable doubles come with TV, fan and breakfast – and prices for individuals are negotiable. A perfect escape from the Downtown crush. Serveece #4 runs nearby. ❸

Caravan Police College Rd near King Abdullah Mosque, just off King Hussein St ℡06/566 1195, Ⓕ566 1196, Ⓔcaravan@go.com.jo. Another good choice. Most of the 27 rooms are clean and pleasant, all with fan and some with balcony, although the dawn call to prayer from the mosque can be a drawback. Book well in advance as groups fill the place up. ❸

Cleopatra Next to Abdali station, King Hussein St ℡06/463 6959, Ⓕ465 9953. Tatty, seedy and grimy, this is the only true budget option in the Abdali area. Bargain hard. ❶

Jerusalem Jewel Building at the north end of Abdali station, top floor ℡06/464 9482, Ⓕ461 5565. Clean, quiet and airy rooms are all en suite – go for the ones with fabulous views out over Abdali towards Downtown. Continental breakfast on the covered roof terrace is included. ❸

Mirage Corner of King Hussein St and Mukhabarrat St ℡06/568 2000, Ⓕ568 8890, Ⓔmirageh@index.com.jo. Unusually high quality within spitting distance of Abdali station. Well-appointed rooms, with air con, double glazing, TV and room service, as well as a parking area and rooftop barbecue, jacuzzi and sauna. Although all a little grandiose, it's surprisingly affordable. ❹

Remal Near the Police Directorate just off King Hussein St ℡06/463 0670, Ⓕ465 5751. Quiet two-star place, safe for women; some rooms have double beds and a balcony, all are en suite with TV and fans. Mostly very clean, and set back from the main road: look for the sign on the downhill side of Abdali station. ❷

Jebel Amman

Mid-range hotels on **Jebel Amman** (there are no budget options here) are generally located in upscale residential or commercial districts, a long way from sights and attractions; your own transport – or relying on taxis – is pretty much essential. Most of these, however, can offer a gentle ambience and a quality of service that's hard to find anywhere else in the country. All these places are shown on the maps on p.120, p.125 or p.127.

Bonita On a leafy, quiet side-street opposite *El-Yassmin Suites* building, close to 3rd Circle ℡06/461 5061, Ⓕ461 5060, Ⓔbonita@nets.com.jo. Six rooms above a Spanish restaurant, small but en suite, clean and cosy; the staff are friendly and laid-back. ❺

Carlton Directly opposite the *Inter-Continental Hotel*, between 2nd and 3rd Circles ℡06/465 4200, Ⓕ465 5833, Ⓔjcarlton@joinnet.com.jo. Sixty clean, somewhat stylish rooms are bright and airy, with air con and heating, satellite TV and mini-bar. Service is good and the street-level restaurant cool and quiet. Book ahead, as it's popular with upscale tour groups. ❻

Dove Qurtubah St (a side-street midway between 4th and 5th Circles) ℡06/569 7601, Ⓕ567 4676, Ⓔdove@go.com.jo. A small Best Western hotel located in a far-flung residential district, with cool

JEBEL AMMAN, JEBEL AL-LWEIBDEH & ABDOUN

RESTAURANTS, CAFÉS & BARS

Abu Ahmad	Caffé Moka	15
New Orient	Casereccio	Pizza Hut 17
Bakehouse	Darat al-Funun	Planet Hollywood 12
Blue Fig	Fakhr el-Din	Romero 8
Bonita	Kafeteria al-Kouds	Sanabel 11
Books @ Café	Kanabayé	Snack Box 3
Café de Paris	Noodasia	Tché Tché 14
		Wild Jordan 9
		Zalatimo 1

5
16
20
6
19
14

ACCOMMODATION

Bonita	Hisham	J
Canary	Inter-Continental	F
Caravan	Jerusalem Jewel	D
Carlton	Le Royal	M
Cleopatra	Mirage	C
Dove	Remal	G
Grand Hyatt	Shepherd	H

L
K
A
I
B
E
N

Downtown & Zarqa

Jebel Hussein

Jebel Hussein

Interior Circle

Shmeisani

Shmeisani

Wadi Saqra Circle

Ashrafiyeh & Wihdat

Airport

AL-AYOUBI

AL-RAZI

KING HUSSEIN

King Abdullah Mosque

National Gallery

Abdali Station

AMERICAN UNIVERSITY IN AMMAN

SULEIMAN AL-NABULSI

ABDALI

AHMED IBN TAYMIYYAH

SHARIF AL-HUSSEIN BIN ALI

ADEEB WAHBEH

FAWZI AL-MULQI

WADI SAQRA

QUEEN NOOR STREET

WADI SAQRA

MOUSA BIN NUSAYR

AL-RIYASAH

ZAHRAN STREET

Oman

Kuwait

4TH CIRCLE

N

Ireland

New Zealand

Centre Cultural Français

LWEIBDEH CIRCLE

Green Branch

Darat al-Funun

Dar al-Anda

JEBEL AL-LWEIBDEH

IBRAHIM TOUQAN

DIHRAR BIN AL-AZWAR

AL-ZAHRAN

AHMED IBN HANBAL

MUNTAZAH CIRCLE

COLLEGE

PRINCE MUHAMMAD

1ST 9TH OF SHA'ABA

Saudi Arabia

Iraq

JEBEL AMMAN

AL-ISLAMIYAH

2ND CIRCLE

ZA'ID BIN HARETHAH

AL-BUHTARI

NOOR AL-DEEN ZANKI

Jordan River Designs

RAINBOW STREET

British Council

Al-Hussein Cultural Centre

MANGO STREET

KING TALAL

ALI BIN ABI TALEB

MUHAJIREEN

World of Argileh

City Hall

Muhajireen Station

Police

MAN BIN ZA'EDAH

AL-KULLIYAH

al-Aydi

Artisana

Zara Centre

Amman Bookshop

Police

3RD CIRCLE

PRINCE MUHAMMAD

ABDULMUNEM RIYADH

AL-MUTANABBI

MITHQAL AL-FAYEZ

ABU FIRAS AL-HAMDANI

IBN KHALDOUN

BARADA

ZAHRAN STREET

Yemen

Syria

Iran

PRINCESS BASMA STREET

AL-NEEF

Lebanon

UK

Sheraton

Entertainment Centre

ABDOUN

AL-QAHERAH

ABDOUN CIRCLE

HUSSEIN ABU AL-RAGHEB

MUSTAFA KAMEL

0   400 m

breezes and nice views. Unremarkable rooms are spacious, some with balconies; prices will halve with a little encouragement. ❹

Hisham Just off Mithqal al-Fayez St near the French Embassy, between 3rd and 4th Circles ⓣ06/464 2720, ⓕ464 7540, ⓔhishamhotel@nets.com.jo. Small, long-established residential hotel in the heart of the embassy quarter with an excellent reputation and unfailingly courteous and efficient staff. A peaceful terrace, pub, high-quality food and only 22 rooms make this the nearest thing to an English-style family hotel you'll find in Jordan. ❺–❻

San Rock International Sa'eed Abu Jaber St, behind *Crowne Plaza Hotel*, off 6th Circle ⓣ06/551 3800, ⓕ551 3600, ⓔsales@sanrock-hotel.com. An excellent mid-range tourist hotel – one of the best in the city – with spacious, comfortable rooms, good facilities (satellite TV, air conditioning, spotless bathrooms) and prompt, efficient service. It's located on a quiet backstreet near the shops and restaurants of Umm Uthayna and Sweifiyyeh, a long way out of the centre. ❺–❻

Shepherd Zaid bin al-Harith St, a backstreet midway between 1st and 2nd Circles ⓣ06/463 9197, ⓕ464 2401. Pristine and classy, this is the best choice in this price range city-wide, comfortably close to both the Downtown sights and the uptown restaurants. Rooms are pleasant and quiet, service is calm, the breakfast is good, and most rooms are free of traffic noise. Its reputation and consistently good standards bring in plenty of repeat business from tourists and businesspeople alike. ❸–❹

Shmeisani

Shmeisani has only a few hotels that aren't five stars. One of the most outgoing neighbourhoods in the city, it is still home to many of Amman's richer inhabitants and a good deal of nightlife. Shops, late-night cafés, cinemas and restaurants are all clustered along the streets behind the distinctive Arab Bank building (which overlooks the busy Shmeisani Interchange). Downtown is a twenty-minute taxi ride away. These hotels are shown on the map opposite.

Manar Al-Shareef Abdul Hamid Sharaf St ⓣ06/566 2186, ⓕ568 4329. Small, well-run place on a busy street, right in the middle of Shmeisani. Comfortable, basic rooms are clean and fairly well kept. ❸

Nefertiti 26 al-Jahed St ⓣ & ⓕ06/560 3865. Simple, spartan rooms – the only remotely budget option in this part of town, close to the *Peking Restaurant*. ❷

Al-Qasr Howard Johnson Plaza ⓣ06/568 9671, ⓕ562 0526, ⓦwww.alqasr-hojo.com. Quality upper-mid-range hotel on a quiet residential street opposite the *Peking Restaurant*, extensively refurbished by the Howard Johnson chain. Cosy rooms are very light and bright, with all the facilities – go for those on the upper floors, which have balconies and spectacular city views. One of the top choices for business-people bored with five-star isolation. Also with an excellent penthouse bar and fine restaurants. ❻

Luxury hotels

Following a glut of hotel building over the last few years, Amman now boasts a full complement of **luxury** hotels, all of them fitted out to full international standards. Since the market for top-end accommodation in the city is now hugely over-supplied, room prices are falling – if you book in advance (through a travel agent or online), you can slash these establishments' walk-in rates by up to a third. All of them offer **no-smoking rooms** on demand – most have one or two no-smoking floors – and all are shown on the maps on p.108, p.120, p.125 or p.127.

Crowne Plaza (Amra) 6th Circle, Jebel Amman ⓣ06/551 0001, ⓕ551 0003, ⓦwww.crowneplaza.com. Not a pretty building, but nonetheless upgraded by Inter-Continental to full five-star standard. Rooms are decent, if a bit generic, but the public areas are very grand and service is excellent. It's a bit out on a limb – 6th Circle is not the most prepossessing of neighbourhoods – but stands within reach of Shmeisani and Umm Uthayna, with its own facilities and shopping mall. ❼–❾

Four Seasons 5th Circle, Jebel Amman ⓣ06/550 5555, ⓕ550 5556, ⓦwww.fourseasons.com. Probably the grandest hotel in the city, perhaps in the country – a newly designed, fifteen-storey palatial landmark. The 193 guest rooms (as the

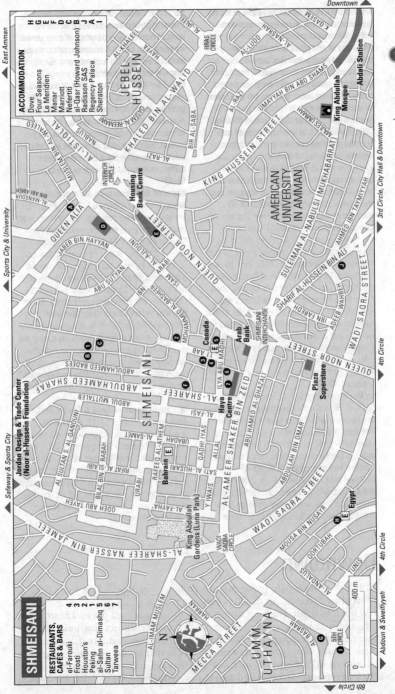

SHMEISANI

RESTAURANTS, CAFÉS & BARS

el-Farouki	4
Frosti	3
Houston's	2
Peking	1
al-Sahn al-Dimashq	5
Sultan	6
Tarweea	7

ACCOMMODATION

Dove	H
Four Seasons	G
Le Meridien	F
Manar	D
Marriott	C
Nefertiti	B
al-Qasr (Howard Johnson)	J
Radisson SAS	A
Regency Palace	I
Sheraton	E

publicity blurb declares) are the largest in the city; they're certainly exceptionally well appointed, with every detail of comfort and hi-tech gadgetry taken care of. The public areas are stunningly opulent. The second-floor spa takes in indoor and outdoor pools, as well as whirlpools, saunas and professional masseurs, and there's also a clutch of outstanding restaurants and bars. You could want for nothing more. ❾

Grand Hyatt 3rd Circle, Jebel Amman ☎06/465 1234, ⓕ465 1634, ⓦwww.amman.hyatt.com. Superbly designed monolith on the main road between 3rd Circle and Shmeisani, replete with every international business facility along with a giant fitness centre with indoor and outdoor pools, several excellent restaurants, *JJ's* nightclub, and supremely comfortable guest rooms. ❽–❾

Inter-Continental Midway between 2nd and 3rd Circles, Jebel Amman ☎06/464 1361, ⓕ464 5217, ⓦwww.intercontinental.com. One of the city's landmarks, and the standard choice for visiting journalists, diplomats and CEOs; local taxi-drivers often call it by its old name of *Funduq al-Urdun*, the *Jordan Hotel*, harking back to the days when it was the only luxury hotel in the country. Now completely renovated and extended, it has modern, spacious, well-appointed rooms and is packed with all kinds of diversions, from a crafts gallery to nightly bellydancing. Star features include the cafés in the lobby and on the rear terrace, one of the city's best bookshops and an excellent Indian restaurant. ❽–❾

Le Meridien Queen Noor St, Shmeisani ☎06/569 6511, ⓕ567 4261, ⓦwww.lemeridien.com. Lavish and luxurious, with a touch of designer style to its fittings. A good range of rooms – all superbly appointed – gives some flexibility in pricing, and there's a swathe of restaurants, bars and fitness facilities. Very near Interior Circle. ❽–❾

Le Royal 3rd Circle, Jebel Amman ☎06/460 3000, ⓕ460 3002, ⓦwww.leroyal.com. Part of a small international chain, and located within the huge cylindrical tower overlooking 3rd Circle. Guest rooms are spacious and luxurious, with formal, traditional styling; many have spectacular city views. Within the same building is a three-storey shopping mall, taking in boutiques, cafés, restaurants and even a multi-screen cinema. ❾

Marriott Issam al-Ajlouni St, near Interior Circle, Shmeisani ☎06/560 7607, ⓕ567 0100, ⓦwww.marriott.com. A popular and long-standing city landmark, rising high above Shmeisani. Weighing value against quality, this is perhaps the best of Amman's many luxury hotels – for its unfussy comfort, swift, intelligent service and excellent facilities. A great choice if five-star character matters more to you than excessive opulence. ❼–❾

Radisson SAS Hussein bin Ali St, overlooking Wadi Saqra, Shmeisani ☎06/560 7100, ⓕ566 5160, ⓦwww.radissonsas.com. High-quality luxury hotel occupying the glass block midway between 3rd Circle and Shmeisani. Fully renovated in recent years, with a good deal of care and attention paid to details of styling in the spacious and pleasant guest rooms, which now have a light, contemporary feel to them. Service is outstanding, and restaurants and public areas are faultless. ❽–❾

Regency Palace Interior Circle, Shmeisani ☎06/560 7000, ⓕ566 0013, ⓦwww.theregencyhotel.com. After a complete, top-to-toe gutting and redesigning, this long-running Amman institution has gained a new lease of life, with huge, formal, stuffily grand public areas and business-oriented guest rooms – rather generic, but ticking all the boxes. ❾

Sheraton Amman Al-Nabil & Towers 5th Circle, Jebel Amman ☎06/593 4111, ⓕ593 4222, ⓦwww.sheraton.com. Occupying an odd, rather ugly turreted monolith facing onto 5th Circle, this is nonetheless one of Amman's top five-star hotels. Guest rooms are spacious, airy and bright, styled pleasantly with light colours and fabrics and soft, luxurious textures. Public areas, and the acclaimed restaurants, are glitteringly lavish, but designed with some character. ❾

Downtown

Although you shouldn't visit Amman without spending at least some time in **Downtown**, the cramped valleys between towering hills shelter comparatively few obvious sights. Rather, Downtown is the spiritual and physical heart of the city and is unmissable for its street life. This is the district that most strongly resembles the stereotype of a Middle Eastern city – loud with traffic and voices, Arabic music blaring from tape stores, people selling clothes, coffee, cigarettes or trinkets on the street. The handful of Roman ruins that survive here have been irreverently incorporated into the everyday bustle of the city: the banked

There is a **map** of Downtown Amman on p.120.

seating of the huge **Roman Theatre** is always dotted with small groups of locals seeking refuge from the traffic noise, and the adjacent **forum** is filled with trees and cafés, a public meeting place today as it was two millennia ago.

The Roman forum

The **Roman forum**, dominating the heart of Downtown, is the best place to begin an exploration of Amman. The massive Theatre – endlessly plugged on posters, brochures and the back of every street-sweeper's overalls – was the centrepiece of Roman Philadelphia, and the initial focus for Amman's modern settlement late in the nineteenth century.

As you approach from the main Hashmi Street, winding your way through the trees, an impressively long Corinthian colonnade and some original Roman paving are the only physical remains of Philadelphia's **forum**, the marketplace which filled the gap between the Theatre and the street. What also survives, however, is the spirit of the place: this whole area is still Downtown's main hangout, as Ammanis crowd the dozens of little cafés, promenade up and down in the dappled sunshine, guzzle ice cream and sweets, meet friends and snooze on the grass.

Several nineteenth-century travellers to Amman reported seeing the remains of a large **propylaeum**, or ornamental gateway, on the edge of the forum; this still stood in 1911 but has since disappeared. If you stop in front of the Theatre and look back towards the street, high on the summit of Jebel al-Qal'a opposite you'll spot the columns of the Temple of Hercules; originally, the propylaeum stood here at what was the foot of a tremendous monumental staircase leading down from the temple, linking the religious and social quarters of the city.

The Roman Theatre

Cut into a depression in the hillside, the **Roman Theatre** (Sat–Thurs 8am–sunset, roughly, Fri 10am–4pm; JD1) is impressively huge, and the view, as well as the ability to eavesdrop on conversations between ant-like people on the stage below, definitely repays the steep climb to the top. The structure was built between 169 and 177 AD, during the reign of Emperor Marcus Aurelius, for an audience of almost six thousand, and is still occasionally filled today for concerts. Above the seating is a small, empty **shrine** with niches; the dedication isn't known, although part of a statue of Athena was discovered during clearance work. Standing on the stage or in the orchestra – the semicircle in front of the stage – you can get a sense of the ingenuity of the theatre's design: the south-facing stage is flooded with sun throughout the day, while virtually

Renovating Downtown

In 2001 the government and municipality settled on a master plan to entirely revamp Downtown Amman. At the time of writing, building works were well under way. The chaotic old **Raghadan bus station** was replaced in 2005 by a new transport terminal, with signage in the area being updated and improved – but the biggest and most prestigious project was to build by 2007 a new **Jordan National Museum** a little way west of the Roman Theatre in the district of Ras al-Ain (see p.133). There is little doubt that Downtown needs a wash-and-brush-up – and you may well find that, by the time you visit, the renovations have moved on to another target.

every spectator remains undazzled and in cool shadow. To discover the incredible acoustics, stand in the middle of the orchestra and declaim at the seating, and your normal speaking voice will suddenly gain a penetrating echo; step off that spot and there's no echo. Furthermore, two people crouching down at opposite ends of the orchestra can mutter into the semicircular stone wall below the first row of seats and easily hear each other.

To the sides of the stage are two small museums, housed in vaults beneath the auditorium. On the right as you walk in, the **Folklore Museum** (same hours & ticket) displays mannequins engaged in traditional crafts and a moderately interesting reconstruction of a sophisticated Ammani's old-style living-room. Much more worthwhile is the **Jordanian Museum of Popular Traditions**, opposite (same hours and ticket), which deftly manages to enliven the well-worn theme of traditional clothing, jewellery and customs by rooting it firmly in the present-day life of ordinary people. The vaulted rooms are full of examples of national dress, with detailed notes and occasional photographs to set them in context. Other exhibits include pieces of antique Bedouin jewellery and a fascinating range of stones used by the Bedu in healing, as well as mosaics downstairs gathered from Madaba and Jerash (and viewable up close).

The Odeon

Facing onto the forum area outside the Theatre is the Roman **Odeon** (closes 1hr earlier; same ticket). Reopened in 1997 after complete renovation, this freestanding theatre seating about five hundred dates from slightly earlier than the large theatre and was probably the venue for either parliamentary-style council meetings or small-scale drama. In antiquity, the whole building would probably have been roofed. Amman's grand old *Philadelphia Hotel*, the country's first (and, for many decades, only) hotel, was built in the 1920s beside the Odeon on the banks of the Sayl Amman, which was then a stream flowing through the city centre; sadly, the hotel was demolished in the 1980s to make way for Downtown redevelopment – which then never really took off.

The Husseini Mosque and around

From Raghadan bus station and the Roman Theatre, lively **Hashmi Street** storms west past *shwarma* stands, juice bars, patisseries and cafés towards the commercial hub of Downtown and the focal, pink-and-white-striped **Husseini Mosque**. Like everything else in Amman, this is a relatively recent construction, although a mosque has stood here since 640 (and, before that, a Byzantine cathedral). However, any remnant of the original building was erased – much to the consternation of British onlookers – when Emir Abdullah ordered the site cleared for construction of the current mosque in 1932. Renovated in 1987, it remains one of Amman's most important places of worship, and is often also the focus for political demonstrations. Although you're free to wander around the gates, whether or not you'll be allowed inside depends on the whim of the caretaker, who can normally be found sitting just inside the right-hand gate.

The building on the corner opposite the mosque formerly held Amman's best-loved coffee house, the grand old **Arab League Café** – a stalwart here for over fifty years, with its fine balcony overlooking the bustle below. In 2002, after a wrangle between the building's owners (one wanted to keep it as it was; the other wanted to rebuild), the café was closed by court order and – to the horror of seemingly everyone in the city bar the owners themselves – gutted. Its future remains uncertain, but, in this city with little enough history of its own, a piece of the past has already been lost.

However, the area around the mosque remains the heart of Amman's **bazaars**. To the east lies a bustling warren of alleys known as the **Souk Sukkr** (Sugar Market), where stalls sell everything from dates and spices to soap and mops. To the right (west) of the mosque, the main street funnelling traffic south out of Downtown is **King Talal Street**, lined with stores selling ordinary household goods, fabric and bric-a-brac; a little way down on the left, hidden behind a row of shopfronts, is the city's main fruit and vegetable market.

The main street parallel to King Talal Street follows exactly the course of the Roman *decumanus maximus*, which was formed by paving over the free-flowing stream beneath. The street – officially Quraysh Street – is still popularly known as the **Saqf Sayl** (Roof of the Stream), but these days the *sayl* is dry, having been tapped much further upstream to provide drinking water. This is the busiest and liveliest area of the city, with cobblers, tape-sellers and hawkers of soap and toothbrushes competing for space under the pavement colonnades with a dirt-cheap secondhand clothes market. There's also a small bus station here serving villages near Amman.

The Nymphaeum

On the Saqf Sayl behind the Husseini Mosque, excavation and restoration work on the Roman **Nymphaeum** has been going on for years, seemingly without end. It's very similar in design to the huge nymphaeum at Jerash, which has been dated to 191 AD; at that time, Philadelphia too was at its zenith. The site is fenced and is usually off-limits, though the guardian may not object to you exploring. However, apart from the immensity of the construction (and the shiny new reconstruction), there's not an awful lot to admire. Nymphaea – public fountains dedicated to water nymphs – were sited near rivers running through major cities throughout the Greco-Roman world. This one, facing onto an open plaza at the junction of the two principal city streets, the east–west *decumanus* and the north–south *cardo*, was originally two storeys high and must have been quite a sight, dominating the area. Colonnades of Corinthian columns would have drawn even more attention towards the concave building, which was lavishly faced in marble, with statues of gods, emperors or city notables filling the niches all around.

King Faysal Street

The Husseini Mosque faces up **King Faysal Street**, modern Amman's oldest thoroughfare, occupying the valley between Jebel Amman to the south and Jebel al-Qal'a to the north. Although it follows exactly the course of the Roman *cardo*, any trace of the ancient past has been built over: the oldest buildings, with elegant arched windows and decorated stone balconies, date only from the 1920s. One of the nicest, at no. 12 (beside the Arab Bank), has been renovated and is now open to visitors – known as the "**Duke's Diwan**" (Sat–Thurs roughly 8am–sunset; free), although there's no sign telling you that. This building, which dates from 1924, formerly served as the main post office, an annexe of the Ministry of Finance and, from the 1950s, as the Haifa Hotel (whose sign still lies in one of the rooms). In the last few years it has been renovated as a labour of love by a prominent Jordanian businessman, Mamdouh Bisharat, who owns land in the village of Mukhaybeh (see p.228) and is known as the "Duke of Mukhaybeh" – hence "Duke's Diwan" (a *diwan* is a place for meetings and gatherings). The entrance – an anonymous doorway – gives onto a long flight of steps. At the top is an atmospheric suite of seven rooms around a central hallway, decorated with old photos of Amman, paintings and cabinets of bric-à-brac. Roam around as you like; you'll inevitably be invited by the caretaker to drink tea with him on the balcony. The *diwan* now also hosts occasional informal concerts and artistic events. Opposite, another fine old building known as the **Eco-Tourism Café** – a misleading name for a perfectly ordinary locals' coffee house: indulging in a tea and an *argileh* on their luridly painted balcony is a great way to absorb the Downtown atmosphere.

Alongside the *diwan* – aside from the wonderful pastry shop **Habiba** – is the **Gold Souk**, a series of tiny jewellery shops clustered together in a little network of alleys (see p.155 for more about buying gold). Nearby is Shabsough Street, named after the Shabsough tribe of Circassians who first settled here (see box), from which stairs rise up to Jebel al-Qal'a.

The Circassians

The first people to settle in Amman in modern times were Muslim refugees from Christian persecution in Russia. The **Circassians**, who began arriving in the 1870s, trace their origins back to mountain villages above the eastern Black Sea, in the region of the **Caucasus** around present-day Georgia and Chechnya.

In the 1860s, Russian military offensives in the Caucasus forced 1.5 million people out of their homes into exile in Ottoman Turkish territory. Some headed west towards the fertile lands of the Balkans (establishing Muslim communities in and around Bosnia), while others drifted south into the Ottoman province of Syria. Stories began to filter back to those left behind of life in a Muslim land, and many Circassian and Chechen villages went en masse into voluntary exile. European governments lent their weight to the Ottoman policy of dumping the refugees on ships bound for distant Syria.

Meanwhile, Amman had been uninhabited for virtually a thousand years. In 1877, Selah Merrill, a visiting American archeologist, "spent part of one night in the great theatre... The sense of desolation was oppressive. Kings, princes, wealth and beauty once came here to be entertained, where now I see only piles of stones, owls and bats, wretched *fellahin* [peasants] and donkeys, goats and filth." The first Circassian refugees arrived the following year, setting up home in the galleries of the theatre; others founded new villages in the fertile valley of Wadi Seer to the west and among the deserted ruins of Jerash to the north. The presence of settlers caused some conflict with local tribes, but the Circassians held their own in skirmishes with the Bedu, and soon a mutual respect and a formal pact of friendship emerged between them. After 1900, Circassian labour was central to the building of the Hejaz railway line, and Circassian farmers became famed for their industry. One of their great innovations was the reintroduction of the wheel: with no roads to speak of, wheeled transport hadn't been used in Transjordan for centuries.

When, in the 1920s, Emir Abdullah established a new state and chose Amman to be its capital, he bound the Circassian community into his new administration: loyal and well-educated families were the mainstay of both the officer corps and the civil service. Over the years, however, overt expressions of Circassian culture faded: Arabic became the lingua franca, the use of national dress died out and, with the rise in land prices following the influx of Palestinian refugees in 1948, many Circassians sold their inherited farmlands around Amman for the building of new suburbs. However, their internal identity remained strong, and Circassians today form an integrated minority of 25,000. Their historians are starting to re-examine the circumstances of the exile, and the **Circassian Community Centre** on Jebel Amman (☏ 06/582 5175) often hosts theatre and dance commemorating the homeland.

Ras al-Ain

Southwest of the Husseini Mosque, King Talal Street and the Saqf Sayl meet at a large traffic intersection. To the south rises the hill of Ashrafiyyeh (see p.142), while 600m dead ahead (west) in the valley of the Sayl Amman, in an area known as **Ras al-Ain** (Source of the Spring), is Amman's **City Hall**, standing alongside the **Al-Hussein Cultural Centre**. Both of these buildings were co-designed by one of the Arab world's leading architects, Jafar Touqan, and both are light, airy and dynamic, often hosting exhibitions of contemporary art and occasional concerts, bringing affluent West Ammanis into a Downtown neighbourhood they might otherwise never visit. To reach City Hall, you walk through a delightful open colonnaded plaza featuring a huge **fountain** at its centre; on summer evenings, and after Friday prayers in the nearby mosque, this plaza and the nearby lawns fill up with promenading and picnicking families, kids squealing as they run through the fountain, the gushing water cooling, cleaning and humidifying the dry air. This regeneration of what was formerly a traffic island of dusty wasteground in a run-down neighbourhood is one of Amman's recent success stories – and it looks set to continue. Ras al-Ain is the venue for the new **Jordan National Museum** (opening in 2007), a three-storey, state-of-the-art interpretive centre, its exhibition halls showcasing Jordanian history and culture from prehistoric times to the present day.

Jebel al-Qal'a

Jebel al-Qal'a (Citadel Hill) has been a focus for human settlement since the Paleolithic Age, more than 18,000 years ago. Unfortunately, when the Romans moved in to occupy the area, they cleared away whatever they found, including the remains of the Ammonite city of Rabbath Ammon, and chucked it over the side of the hill: Bronze Age, Iron Age and Hellenistic pottery shards have been found mixed up with Roman remains on the slopes below. Of the remains surviving today, the most impressive by far is a huge **Umayyad palace** complex on the upper terrace of the Citadel, dating from the first half of the eighth century. On the middle terrace below and to the south lies the Roman **Temple of Hercules**, its massive columns dramatically silhouetted against the sky. Opposite the temple – at least, until 2007 – stands Jordan's principal **archeological museum**. East of the temple, Roman fortifications protect the grassy lower terrace, which has no visible antiquities.

The easiest way to reach the summit is by **taxi** (500 fils from Downtown). **Serveece** #9 can drop you at the crossroads below the northern tip of the Citadel, but it's still a scramble to the top from there. For the ambitious who prefer to **walk**, the ascent is extremely steep: it might only take twenty minutes, but your legs will remember it long after. About 150m along Shabsough Street as you head east, and just past the second turning on the left (which has the line of #9 serveeces heading up), another side-street has a wide flight of steps leading left up the hillside. Turn right at the top, and head up any way you can from here: there are crumbling steps most of the way, often leading through private backyards. You'll eventually arrive at the wall below the Temple of Hercules. If you're **driving**, head east out of Downtown towards Zarqa, come off at the Marka exit, pass under the highway, and rejoin it heading west again. You'll have to look hard to spot the brown sign for the Jebel al-Qal'a antiquities pointing right soon afterwards; exit here, and at the

△ Buying bread

traffic lights bear left steeply up the hill, along King Ali bin al-Hussein Street. Three-quarters of the way up is a hairpin left turn onto Matthaf Street, which brings you to the ticket office.

Admission to the whole hilltop site (Sat–Thurs 8am–7pm, winter closes 4pm, Fri 10am–4pm; JD2) includes the museum: buy **tickets** from the building located opposite the guardian's hut, where Matthaf Street ends. Keep your ticket to show to officials.

The Temple of Hercules

From the ticket office, it's a short walk up the road to the antiquities. The **Temple of Hercules**, with its towering columns that are visible from Downtown, was built in the same period as the Roman Theatre below. The temple stands on a platform at the head of the monumental staircase which formerly led up from the lower city: the blocks on the cliff edge mark the position of the staircase, and afford a tremendous panoramic view over the city centre that is particularly striking at **sunset**, when – in addition to the visual dramatics – the dozens of mosques in the city all around start broadcasting the call to prayer almost simultaneously.

There is work under way here to consolidate the hillside, and the master plan for redevelopment of Amman city centre (see p.129) involves re-establishing the ancient link between the hilltop and valley floor by means of stairways – which may mean ongoing works for some time.

The columns, which were re-erected in 1993, formed part of a colonnaded entrance to the **cella**, or inner sanctum. Within the *cella* – these days often the scene of hard-fought football games among the local kids – a patch of bare rock is exposed, which, it's thought, may have been the sacred rock that formed the centrepiece of the ninth-century BC Ammonite Temple of Milcom on this spot. The Roman dedication to Hercules is not entirely certain but, given the quantity of coins bearing his likeness found in the city below, pretty likely.

The National Archeological Museum

Opposite the temple are the steps of the **National Archeological Museum**. Until the opening in 2007 of the Jordan National Museum down at Ras al-Ain (see p.133) – which will house the entire collection – this is the major repository for archeological finds from all periods and all parts of the country. One of the reasons for building a new museum is that this one is far too small, although what's on display is of the highest quality. English noticeboards supply well-written background information on everything, and you could easily browse for an hour or two.

The collection begins before you even get inside. At the top of the steps leading up to the door you'll see an enormous marble hand, discovered in the grounds of the Temple of Hercules nearby and presumed to be part of a statue of the god-hero himself. The complete figure would have been a fittingly gigantic 9m high.

In 2007 – when the new **Jordan National Museum** opens in Ras al-Ain (see p.133) – the archeological museum on Jebel al-Qal'a will probably close permanently, although you may find that the building is put to some other use, as yet unknown. Either way, by then all the objects described here are likely to have been moved to the new museum.

Inside, you should turn right for a chronological tour of the collection. The first striking exhibits are plastered skulls, objects of veneration and worship in **Neolithic** Jericho. A couple of cabinets in the central aisle of the room hold vividly realized statuettes from the Neolithic settlement of Ain Ghazal near Amman, one of which – staring eerily at you from behind glass – is the earliest human figure ever discovered; though well over 8000 years old, it displays a surprisingly expressive grace. Back in the cabinets against the wall, another skull provides gruesome evidence of the failure of **Bronze Age** surgery techniques: this particular patient didn't just submit to having one hole drilled into his or her head (which healed up), but came back for three more – which conclusively halted the onset of any further disease. A beautifully reconstructed box in ebony and ivory from Bronze Age Pella (see p.232) is another highlight.

Bypassing the Nabatean room, the entrance to which is adorned with a replica of the Mesha Stele (see p.299), continue with the **Iron Age** cabinets, which include a fabulous limestone statuette of Yerah Azar, king of Ammon, in a characteristically stiff regal pose clutching a lotus flower to his chest. Nearby cabinets hold plenty of coins, as well as a beautiful little **Hellenistic** jug in blue and yellow. Round near the entrance, look out for a delightful **Byzantine** swan made from a seashell and carved ivory.

At this point, the chronological scheme begins to go haywire, with **Roman** figurines and glassware from Jerash dotted everywhere. At the back of the museum is an extensive collection of **Nabatean** art and pottery from Petra; its huge semicircular centrepiece represents the goddess of vegetation, taken from the temple at Khirbet Tannur (see p.310). On the left wall is the earliest mural ever discovered, from Teleilat Ghassul (see p.430); the six thousand years since it was painted have taken their toll, but figures are still recognizable. In the small room to the right is a collection of Dead Sea Scrolls.

Back in the main part of the museum, an **Islamic** room to the right displays ceramics, stone carvings and some wafer-thin gold dinars. At the back of this room, a doorway leads to two compelling Roman copies of Hellenistic statuary. Facing you is **Apollo**, beautifully slender and winsome, while in the corner stands the highlight of the whole museum – a grippingly intense **Daedalus**, reaching out to his doomed son Icarus (not pictured).

Before you leave, make time for the bust of **Tyche** in a forgotten cabinet in the middle aisle of the main room. The equivalent of the patron saint of Philadelphia, she probably had a shrine down in the lower city, now lost.

The Umayyad Palace

Climbing the path to the upper terrace from the Temple of Hercules, you'll pass a small ruined **Byzantine church** on the right, dating from the fifth or sixth centuries, which reused many of the columns from the nearby temple. The church formed part of a Byzantine town which probably covered much of the hill and which is still being excavated. About 20m further north are a huge round cistern and the remains of an olive-pressing works.

The huge **Umayyad Palace** complex stretches over the northern part of the hill. Part of the palace was built over pre-existing Roman structures, and an entire colonnaded Roman street was incorporated into it. Built after 720, when Amman was a provincial capital, the complex probably combined the residential quarters of the governor of Amman with administrative offices. It was still in use during the Islamic Abbasid (750–969) and Fatimid (969–1179) periods, although much of the brand-new palace was never rebuilt following a devastating earthquake in 749.

The first building you come to, and the most impressive, is the domed **entrance hall**, reached by crossing the first of four plazas. Built over an earlier Byzantine building (which is why it's in the shape of a cross), the hall is decorated with stucco colonnettes and Persian-style geometric patterns, set off by foliage rosettes and a hound's-tooth zigzag. A great deal of renovation has been carried out here in recent years, not all of it very subtly – the new sharp-edged stucco around the interior walls deliberately clashes with the original work, and in 1998 a new dome was hastily constructed above the building, riding roughshod over considerable archeological controversy about whether there ever was a dome here in antiquity. Between the entrance hall and the cistern is a small, newly excavated **baths**, although only a changing area and the "cold room" survive.

Beyond the entrance hall is the second large plaza, from which the **colonnaded street** leads ahead. This was the heart of the administrative quarter, surrounded by nine separate office or residential buildings (of which only four have been excavated), each in the typical Umayyad style of a self-contained *bayt* – small rooms looking onto a central courtyard. The *bayts* were constructed within the pre-existing Roman enclosure, possibly a temple, whose exterior walls are still visible in places. To the west of the courtyard is "Building F", which may have been the site of official audiences, since it was of elegant design and situated close to the entrance hall; two large *iwans* – audience rooms open on one side – with triple arcades give onto a central courtyard, from where a staircase led to an upper storey.

At the far end of the colonnaded street, a decorated doorway takes you through the Roman wall into the third plaza and the private **residential quarters** of the ruler of Amman. Rooms open from three sides, but the plaza is dominated by a huge *iwan*, which presages a domed, cruciform **throne room**, or *diwan*. According to Umayyad protocol, the ruler always stayed hidden behind a curtain during audiences – the tiny passageway between the *iwan* and the *diwan* could have served this purpose. To either side lie the largely unexcavated residential *bayts* for the ruling household. At the back of the *diwan*, a doorway leads through to the fourth and final plaza – a private affair, looking north over the massive Roman retaining wall to the hills opposite.

West Amman

Of the other quarters of the city, you're most likely to visit sprawling **West Amman**, one of the richest and most Western-oriented parts of the Arab world. It's here that you'll find practically all of Amman's nightlife, upmarket hotels and restaurants. Aside from a single, beautiful Byzantine **mosaic** in Sweifiyyeh, however, no antiquities are worth bothering with here, although the **National Gallery of Fine Arts** and the **Darat al-Funun** arts centre are worth a look.

Jebel al-Lweibdeh

Amman has a surprisingly active contemporary arts scene, and some of the best galleries are within walking distance of each other in the neat, respectable neighbourhood of **Jebel al-Lweibdeh**, overlooking the hubbub of

There is a **map** of Jebel al-Lweibdeh on p.125.

Downtown. The area has a relatively high proportion of Christian residents, and you'll find a tangibly different atmosphere from other parts of the city: many women are unveiled, there is less of a laid-back street life, and you may well hear the unfamiliar sound of church bells.

Darat al-Funun

A few minutes' walk above Downtown stands an idyllic refuge from the noise and bustle. Head for Omar al-Khayyam Street, which leads steeply up behind the Downtown post office; turning right at the first hairpin, you'll soon come in sight of a high stone wall. With gates to left and right, this wall defines the grounds of **Darat al-Funun** (Sat–Wed 10am–7pm, Thurs 10am–8pm; ℡06/464 3251, ⓦwww.daratalfunun.org; free), a lush haven of tranquillity housing a centre for contemporary Arab art (also accessible on serveece #4). The "little house of the arts", as its name translates, comprises a set of three 1920s villas in a beautiful, shaded hillside garden, within which lie the remains of the small sixth-century Byzantine **Church of St George**. The "Blue House", at the very top of the steeply terraced complex, houses changing exhibitions, and its wooden porch – a common feature of Circassian architecture, added to the building as an acknowledgment of the Circassian presence in the city – serves as a tiny **café**, Amman's most beautiful and peaceful by far. On the same level is the former home of Emir Abdullah's court poet, now a private studio for visiting artists. Below is the main building, the former official residence of Lieutenant-Colonel Frederick Peake, or "Peake Pasha", British Commander of the Arab Legion in the 1920s and 1930s. It sports a wonderful semicircular portico and has been superbly renovated by Jordanian architect Ammar Khammash to house well-lit **galleries**, studios and an excellent **art library**. Legend has it that, on his stay in late 1921 as a guest of Peake, T.E. Lawrence wrote much of *Seven Pillars of Wisdom* in this building.

Exhibitions at Darat al-Funun vary from grand overviews of contemporary Arab art to small shows from local artists, with everything publicized on the

---

Art in Amman

Aside from the four major Jebel al-Lweibdeh galleries mentioned here, there are many others to investigate: here is just a selection of commercial galleries and exhibition venues. Current shows are always publicized in the *Jordan Times*. **4Walls** (Sat–Thurs 9am–7pm; ⓦwww.4walls.org) is a spacious, contemporary gallery-cum-lecture hall located in the *Sheraton* hotel, which maintains an active programme of shows and cultural events all year round. In a similar vein, the excellent **Orfali Gallery** (ⓦwww.orfali.net), in Umm Uthayna, combines a large gallery – which also hosts concerts and other events – with a centre running art appreciation classes. **The Gallery** (daily except Tues 8am–7pm), at the *Inter-Continental Hotel*, is a long-standing favourite, displaying paintings and photographs. The **Zara Gallery** (ⓦwww.soukzara.com/zaragallery), at the *Grand Hyatt* hotel, shows contemporary art by established and up-and-coming artists from Jordan and the Arab world, while the **Broadway Gallery** (ⓦwww.broadway-gallery.com) has a three-storey exhibition space in Sweifiyyeh staging local and international shows. Most of these also sell art books, but the best selection in Amman of books on art, architecture and design is at the **Amman Bookshop** off 3rd Circle (see p.157), and it's also worth looking online at the architecture of **Ammar Khammash** (ⓦwww.khammash.com), an artist, designer and architect who has worked on several high-profile projects in the capital and nationwide. The various European cultural centres (see p.164) also often host shows of photography or painting.

gallery website. There are also plenty of **lectures and performances**, often staged atmospherically in the ruined church, and all events are free to the public. Even if art isn't your strong point, dropping in gives a sense of a flourishing side of Jordanian culture that's barely touched upon by most visitors.

Makan and Dar al-Anda
If you turn left out of the top gate of Darat al-Funun, a short walk straight ahead and then behind the al-Saadi mosque will bring you to another of Jebel al-Lweibdeh's arts centres, **Makan** (℡07/9558 8393, ⓦwww.makanhouse .net). It's a small, alternatively minded place started up by the enthusiastic Ola Khalidi that stages exhibitions and events, and also serves as a venue for informal concerts and film-screenings – links with the Amman Filmmakers' Cooperative (ⓦammanfilmmakers.alif.com) are strong. Its balcony has another spectacular view out over the city.

Further along the same street, ochre adobe walls announce the wonderful **Dar al-Anda** (℡06/462 9599, ⓦwww.daralanda.com), both a gallery and a cultural centre staging concerts, workshops and arts events. The original building, which was built in 1939, has been beautifully restored, and – along with newer buildings around the courtyard – now houses a library for children, a studio, a guest apartment for resident artists, and so on.

Whether they're staging a show or not, you may well find both Makan and Dar al-Anda open; public events at either place are advertised on posters and in the *Jordan Times*.

Jordan National Gallery of Fine Arts
Leaving from the top gate of Darat al-Funun, it's a stiff five-minute climb north past the Luzmila Hospital to the roundabout known as Lweibdeh Circle on top of the hill; the little park on the roundabout has been prettified thanks to the French Embassy and now rejoices in the name "Square de Paris". Ten minutes or so from Lweibdeh Circle on the flat along quiet, shady Shari'a College Street, past the Terra Sancta religious academy, will bring you to Muntazah Circle, an oval expanse of green lined with elegant town houses. One of these, on the right, is the newly refurbished **Jordan National Gallery of Fine Arts** (daily 9am–7pm, closed Tues & Fri; JD2; ⓦwww.nationalgallery.org), which is also accessible on serveece #4 from Downtown and on a short, signposted walk from Abdali station. This is the country's premier establishment showcase for contemporary art, with artists from Jordan, the Arab world and the wider Islamic world all represented in the fascinating 1500-work collection. Downstairs rooms feature a constantly changing selection of works from the permanent collection, while the upstairs extension features interesting temporary exhibitions. Across the Muntazah park is an annexe occupying the town house opposite, which – as well as art exhibits – stages music and other events. The stroll from one building to the other is intended to be flanked with sculpture and outdoor art installations, with a new *Art Café* alongside.

Jebel Amman: around 1st Circle

In general, West Amman is too large to attempt aimless exploratory rambling, though if you have a spare afternoon to fill, you might like to take a wander through the leafy streets **around 1st Circle** on Jebel Amman. When Amman was a small town occupying the Downtown valley-floors, this gentle neigh-

There is a **map** of Jebel Amman on p.125.

bourhood was the preserve of the elite – royalty, families wealthy through business or commerce, politicians and ambassadors, British commanders of the army, and so on. The quiet streets either side of the lower reaches of **Rainbow Street** are still lined with many fine old villas dating from the 1920s and 1930s, remnants of this time, most of them freestanding one- or two-storey buildings surrounded by walled gardens.

Along Rainbow Street

As you head east from 1st Circle, Rainbow Street – named after the Rainbow Cinema on the right – is lined with shops and boutiques preceding the walled and gated **British Council**. Beyond here, the street dips sharply; partway along on the left is a **mosque** with a fine old minaret, while an anonymous-looking town house on a minor street to the right, with a dark shade of plaster and curved Art Deco-style balcony railings, was where King Talal lived for a time before his accession, and where both the late King Hussein and his brother Prince Hassan were born.

Two of the most attractive villas in the area, both well signposted, are beside each other just off Rainbow Street about 250m east of the British Council. On the corner is an elegant symmetrical villa set back from the street and faced in local stone, with a stepped portico and tall, slender windows, that's now used as showrooms for the crafts of **Jordan River Designs** and **Bani Hamida** (see p.156). Alongside it is an even more attractive one-storey villa – home to Major Alec Kirkbride, the first British Ambassador to Jordan, among others – with a beautiful portico of pointed arches, wrought-iron window-bars, and a lovely garden centred on a star-shaped fountain. Both these houses were built in the late 1920s by Salim al-Odat, an architect originally from Karak. Just round the corner with Asfour Street is a pair of houses built for Egyptian businessman and adviser to Emir Abdullah **Ismail Bilbaysi**, a smaller one dating from the 1930s with a semi circular balcony featuring a lavishly painted ceiling visible from the street, and beside it a much larger villa designed in the 1940s in a consciously medieval Mamluke style, with bands of alternating pink and white stone and pointed arches.

Continuing down Rainbow Street past the one-time headquarters of the Jordanian Communist Party, you come to the distinctively modernistic **Mango House** on the right, at the corner with Omar bin al-Khattab Street (aka Mango Street). In smooth, reddish stone with curving, pillared balconies,

Amman's hammam

Hammams (Turkish baths) are common in Cairo, Damascus and many other Middle Eastern and North African cities, elegant and civilized places to steam the city dust out of your pores – but Amman is an exception: its short recent history means that it doesn't share the centuries-old urban traditions of its neighbours. There is, for all intents and purposes, only one *hammam* in the city, the gleaming clean and modern **Al-Pasha Turkish Bath** (daily 10am–midnight; ☎06/463 3002), located on Mahmoud Taha St, opposite the Ahlia girls' school; coming from 1st Circle along Rainbow St, it's the fifth street on the right. This was purpose-built a few years back in traditional Ottoman style and has already gained a reputation for excellence, offering two heavenly hours of soaking, scrubbing, lathering and olive-oil massaging with professional male or female therapists for under JD15. There are men-only hours, women-only hours and you can book ahead as a mixed group or a couple; call for details. Afterwards, don't miss out on herbal tea and/or a light meal of *mezze* in the beautiful garden courtyard – there are few more pleasant retreats in the city centre.

it was built in the late 1940s by Kamal and Ali Mango, members of one of Amman's most prominent business dynasties. On the other side of Rainbow Street is a long, low house, the whole facade of which is sheltered beneath an elegant Circassian-style porticoed balcony; its most famous resident was Said al-Mufti, a Circassian who was prime minister in the 1950s and also mayor of Amman. Following Mango Street to the right for 100m or so brings you to **Books@Café**, an attractive bookshop and café shoehorned into another historic old house.

Wild Jordan

Just below the Mango House, at a T-junction where Rainbow Street ends at a set of steep stairs clattering down the hill into Downtown, if you head left on Othman bin Affan Street you'll come to the striking contemporary architecture of the **Wild Jordan** centre, designed by architect Ammar Khammash for the Royal Society for the Conservation of Nature (RSCN). It is also reachable from 1st Circle by taking the fourth turning on the left and following the street round.

Inside, as well as several **internet** stations and **information** about how to explore the RSCN's various nature reserves, you'll find a **nature shop** (daily 9am–5pm) selling all kinds of pieces designed in traditional style by Jordanian craftworkers – often rural women – ranging from jewellery to painted ostrich eggs and handwoven bags. Also on sale are organic herbs, dried fruits and spices, produced on the reserves. There are often free **exhibitions** of photographs or art inspired by Jordan's natural environment. The cool, shaded balcony of the excellent **café** here (daily 11am–midnight; see p.149) – which serves only organic food, drinks and smoothies – offers one of Amman's most spectacular **views**, looking over the vast valleys of Downtown and across to Jebel al-Qal'a. Opposite, between the hills, rises a gigantic flagpole with – if the wind is low – a simply enormous Jordanian flag fluttering lazily. The pole stands a shade under 127m high, and the flag itself is 30m by 60m – an impressively dynamic visual monument for the city, but unfortunately not a world record.

Further afield

Aside from exploring the excellent shopping possibilities (for more on which, see p.153), there are few specific sights to head for in the busy, sprawling neighbourhoods of West Amman. A single, rather beautiful **mosaic** survives in the commercial district of Sweifiyyeh, while if there's time to spare you could peruse Jordan's military past at the **Martyrs' Memorial**, or the late King Hussein's passion for classic cars at the **Royal Automobile Museum**.

The Sweifiyyeh church mosaic

Out in the western suburbs, hidden among the chichi boutiques and fast-food outlets of Sweifiyyeh, is almost the only **mosaic** to be seen in Amman. Discovered in the garden of a private house by chance in 1969 and now protected under a roofed shelter (Mon–Thurs & Sat 8am–2pm; free), the mosaic, of which only the left-hand portion survives, originally formed the floor of a late sixth-century Byzantine church and is in a very good state of preservation. Bordered with foliage and various animals, it features many bucolic vignettes – a red-tongued lion, a laden donkey and more. Special care was taken with the men's faces, which are made up of tinier stones than the rest. In the corners, two striking white-bearded faces are probably personifications of the seasons.

The easiest way to get there directly is by **taxi**, or you can take a **bus** or **minibus** to 6th Circle and walk. Turn left (south) at the circle, take the first right, the second left and the fourth right, and continue past the *Boston Fried Chicken* joint; the small hangar housing the mosaic is then about 500m along, opposite the *Liwan Hotel*.

Martyrs' Memorial

Located on the northern edge of the Sports City stadium in Shmeisani is the **Martyrs' Memorial** (*Sarh ash-Shaheed;* Sat–Thurs 9am–4pm; free), Jordan's national military museum. It takes the form of a truncated pyramid in white stone, looming at the top of a slope; inside is a chronological display of military memorabilia, from the Great Arab Revolt of 1916–17 to the present day. It's a moving, worthwhile visit, as long as you're not looking for completely accurate historical coverage: several of Jordan's recent conflicts – notably those involving Israel – are somewhat glossed over. The **taxi** fare is around JD1.250 from Downtown, or you could take just about any **bus** or **minibus** bound for the University of Jordan and ask to be let out early at Sports City (see p.167 for the Arabic): the memorial is a few hundred metres' walk east from the junction.

Royal Automobile Museum

Following King Hussein's death in 1999, King Abdullah II established in his father's memory the **Royal Automobile Museum** (Mon & Wed–Sun 10am–7pm, Fri until 9pm; JD3; ⓦ www.royalautomuseum.jo). This fine building, designed by star Jordanian architect Jafar Touqan, blends in with its natural surroundings by being partly sunk into the earth and clad in untreated stone. The interior is wonderfully airy and spacious. From the entrance hall, you wander through the exhibition areas, adorned with vehicles with a royal connection, ranging from a 1916 Cadillac through some elegant Rolls-Royces (and even a 1952 Triumph Thunderbird motorbike) to a Porsche 911 turbo. Images, dioramas and noticeboards give background information to the various vehicles so beloved of King Hussein and his predecessors.

The museum is set within the **Al-Hussein National Park**, a large tract of hilly land on the western outskirts of the city, off King Abdullah II Street, reachable most easily by **taxi**. This is Amman's favourite green space, and many people come out here – especially on a Friday – to stroll, picnic or play games. At the highest point of the park is a monument to King Hussein, while alongside the Automobile Museum are set to open both a Children's Museum and a Science Museum.

South Amman

West Amman is the most accessible part of the city outside Downtown, and you're unlikely to have much reason to visit the low-income, populous neighbourhoods to the north and east. You may, however, pass through **South Amman**, either on a journey to or from the large bus terminus at **Wihdat**, or to make a pilgrimage to the far-flung **Cave of the Seven Sleepers** in Abu Alanda.

Jebel al-Ashrafiyyeh and Wihdat

Perched over Downtown to the south is **Jebel al-Ashrafiyyeh**, the highest and steepest hill in the city, topped by the peculiar black-and-white-striped **Abu Darwish Mosque**. Serveece #25 or #26 from the Saqf Sayl will take you up to the gates of the mosque, which was built in 1961 by a Circassian immigrant. On the inside, it's utterly unremarkable, but outside, it's an Alice-in-Wonderland palace, complete with a row of black-and-white chess pawns atop its walls and multicoloured fairy lights after dark. The only other reason to come up here is for the panoramic **view**, yet there are no clear sightlines from street level; you'll have to – subtly – get onto the roof of one of the apartment buildings just down from the mosque. Any effort will be amply rewarded, though, especially early in the morning or after sunset: from this high up, the entire city is laid out like a relief map at your feet.

Behind Jebel al-Ashrafiyyeh lies **Wihdat**, a low-income neighbourhood that is almost entirely Palestinian. A *wihda* is a prefab housing unit, and this is where many refugees settled in camps of temporary accommodation following their escape from the newly declared State of Israel in 1948. To this day, the UN provides aid to many Palestinian families still resident here, more than fifty years on.

Cave of the Seven Sleepers

Southeast of Wihdat, tucked away in the run-down suburb of Abu Alanda, the **Cave of the Seven Sleepers** (daily 8am–5pm; free) – known in Arabic as Ahl al-Kahf – is a pilgrimage site associated with a story recorded in the Quran about seven young Christian men who escaped Roman religious persecution by hiding in a cave. God put them to sleep for hundreds of years, and when they awoke, their attempts to buy food with ancient coins aroused incredulity. The youths were taken to the governor – by that time a Christian – who realized that a miracle had occurred, and ordered celebrations. Their work of enlightenment done, the men returned to the cave, where God put them to sleep for good.

The atmospheric cave, one of many Byzantine rock-cut tombs nearby, is set into the hillside next to a modern mosque, built to service the tide of devout Muslims who come to pay their respects. In antiquity, a small church was built literally on top of the cave: the *mihrab* of its later conversion into a mosque is directly overhead. The decorated entrance, shaded by an ancient olive tree, is topped by five medallions, one of which is a cross. Inside are alcoves with four sarcophagi, one of which has a much-worn hole through which you can peek at an eerie jumble of bones. The walls show remains of painted decoration, with a curious eight-pointed star recurring many times, which looks much like a Jewish Star of David, though it is in fact a Byzantine Christian symbol.

To reach Ahl al-Kahf by car, head 4km south from Downtown, over Jebel al-Ashrafiyyeh and through Wihdat to the major traffic intersection of **Middle East Circle** (*duwaar ash-sharq al-awsat*). Keep going south for another 2.4km to a signposted turn to Abu Alanda, which will bring you up the hill to a little roundabout in the middle of the neighbourhood. Turn right onto Ahl al-Kahf Street, and the cave is 1300m further on. By **taxi** from Downtown, expect to pay around JD5 for the return trip, with waiting time included.

Eating and drinking

Though a relatively small city, Amman has plenty of possibilities for **eating out**. There are some first-rate Arabic **restaurants**, as you might expect, but also affordable and surprisingly good Indian, East and Southeast Asian, European and international cuisine. On a tighter budget, you'll find dozens of

For a list of useful culinary terms in Arabic, see p.512

inexpensive **local diners** in Downtown while, city-wide, American-style fast food is universally popular. Ammanis also have an incorrigible sweet tooth, which they are constantly placating with visits to the city's many **patisseries**, for honey-dripping pastries and cakes, or its **coffee houses** and **cafés**, for syrupy-sweet tea and coffee (and soft drinks by the crateful).

Places where you can drink **alcohol** are scattered across the city, ranging from uptown Western-style bars and pubs, complete with draught beers and imported bottles, to covert liquor dens in Downtown back alleys.

Coffee houses, patisseries, cafés and juice bars

There are **coffee houses** tucked away in just about every alley in Downtown. These traditional places are often shunned by hip young locals, however, who prefer instead to kill their hours in newer, Western-style pavement **cafés** in Abdoun, Shmeisani and other uptown neighbourhoods, where languorous people-watching is easy and where women can feel more comfortable.

You'll also find **juice bars** (generally Sat–Thurs 7am–9pm or so) in every corner of Downtown. Two good places face each other on King Faysal Street opposite the Husseini Mosque, while the best *tamarhindi* in the city is to be had from the place just round the corner at the end of Basman Street. From here, walk towards the Roman Theatre, and you'll spot a juice bar on the right – a friendly place – which has good *luz* as well as the best-tasting *kharroub* around.

All the places listed below are marked on the maps on p.108, p.120, p.125 or p.127.

Downtown

In addition to the places listed here, unnamed, less hectic coffee houses can be found in the alleys surrounding the *Cliff Hotel* and the Cairo Amman Bank, as well as down dim staircases between shops on King Talal Street. The open cafés lining Hashmiyyeh Square near the Roman Theatre are less traditional, and a little more expensive.

Auberge Alley between Prince Muhammad St and Basman St (unmarked entrance). Small café one floor below the *Cliff Hotel* and uncompromisingly male. However, the coffee is good and the tiny balcony a great place to watch the street go by. A small backroom serving beer and *araq* adds to the air of dissipation. Daily 7am–11.30pm.

Centrale King Hussein St, at the corner with King Faysal St (entrance shared with *Hilton Bar*). The *Centrale* has never been the same since the glorious open-air terrace was ripped out for redevelopment some years back. Until work begins, it remains one large room that soaks up the morning sun: a plain, simple coffee house. Daily 7am–10pm.

Eco-Tourism Café (aka *al-Rasheed Courts*) In an alley off King Faysal St, opposite the Arab Bank. Downtown's most relaxed and foreigner-friendly coffee house, with a younger, hipper crowd than most. The balcony – Downtown's best – is a pleasant place to hang out and chat with local 20-somethings, many of whom migrate here from uptown West Amman for an after-dark *argileh* in the kind of traditional surroundings Abdoun cannot muster. Daily 9am–1am.

Habibah King Hussein St, near the corner with King Faysal St (Arabic sign only, but it's unmissably big, symmetrical blue-on-white). The best patisserie in the city, if not the country, piled high with every conceivable kind of sweetmeat, pastry and biscuit, all very affordable. There's a mixed-company café upstairs for eat-ins. Smaller pop-in branches are dotted around the city, including just off King Faysal Street next to the "Duke's Diwan". All daily 7am–11.30pm.

Jabri King Hussein St, close to *Habibah*. Another patisserie institution, with much the same stock as *Habibah*, plus OK ice-cream. Also with a mixed

upstairs restaurant for coffee and sweets or a full meal. Branches in Shmeisani and elsewhere. All daily 8am–10pm.

Jebel Amman and around

Bakehouse Just off Rainbow St, below 1st Circle, Jebel Amman. Small, one-room coffee shop tucked away in the shopping streets behind the British Council – bagels, muffins and (so many expats claim) the best cup of coffee in Amman. Daily 8am–6pm or so.

Books@Café Mango St, just off Rainbow St, below 1st Circle, Jebel Amman. A hip, Californian atmosphere unlike anywhere else in Jordan, with a bookshop downstairs and gourmet filter coffees and light meals upstairs. Highlights, in addition to internet access and no-smoking areas, are treats such as brownies, toasted sandwiches and free perusal of foreign newspapers, as well as terraces

front and back. Well worth a visit. On the serveece #2 route. Daily 10am–1am or so.

Darat al-Funun Opposite the Luzmila Hospital, Jebel al-Lweibdeh. This gallery complex and centre for the arts has the quietest, most attractive little café in Amman (see p.138). Serveece #4. Sat–Thurs 11am–6pm.

Wild Jordan Wonderful organic café with the best view in Amman. See p.141.

Zalatimo Upper end of Abdali station. Perhaps the best-loved name in the *halawiyyat* (Arabic sweets) business, with mountains of topnotch gloopy goodies at premium prices. Daily 8am–8pm, Fri closes 7pm.

Shmeisani

el-Farouki Opposite the landmark fast-food joint *Chili House*. The best and most congenial of Shmeisani's coffee houses, with good, fresh-roasted coffee (Arabic-style or filter) and a relaxed backroom where women can puff in peace. Also internet access. Daily 9am–11pm.

Frosti Beside *el-Farouki*. Amman's finest ice cream and frozen yoghurt, bar none. Daily 10am–1am.

Sultan On the main drag, An-Nahda Street. Huge, popular pavement-side café (one of several), with a big terrace to watch the people and traffic stream by. Daily 9am–11pm.

Abdoun

Blue Fig Amir Hashem bin al-Hussein St, Abdoun ℡06/592 8800, ⊕www.bluefig.com. A casual café/bar, designed by one of Jordan's top architects, that draws in a sleek, chic crowd. The ambience is cool and sophisticated, with world music and fusion beats booming out. The walls display works by local artists, and there are regular live music sessions. Daily 8.30am–1am. Booking essential on Thursday nights and Fridays (especially for breakfast/brunch). There are also Blue Fig coffee-house outlets within Mecca Mall and at the airport.

Café de Paris Sheraton Entertainment Centre, just off Abdoun Circle. Chic European-style terrace café in the centre of upscale Abdoun which – as well as churning out caffè latte, mochacino and the rest – is a good place for breakfast (around JD3):

decent bacon-and-eggs, or unlimited filter coffee plus a danish. Daily 8am–1am.

Caffè Moka Al-Qaherah St, Abdoun Circle. Rather pretentious little Italian-style café-cum-patisserie that gives itself airs and graces (and so attracts a rather snooty clientele of rich kids and ladies who lunch). Nonetheless, the food – salads, light meals and pastries – is good and the coffee is worth paying for. Daily 8am–11.30pm.

Sanabel Abdoun Circle. Chic patisserie in the heart of Abdoun, with an attractive glass-fronted eating area looking out over the bustle. Daily 8am–11pm.

Tché Tché Abdoun Circle. Relaxed postmodern-style café that attracts flocks of hip young Ammanis, male and female, who hang out, gossip and smoke hubbly-bubbly, without a trace of traditional Middle Eastern values on show. Daily noon–1am.

Restaurants

Amman's **restaurants** cover a broad spectrum, from backstreet canteens ladling meat stew to air-conditioned palaces serving international delicacies. Downtown restaurants – many of which congregate opposite the Roman Theatre

– are almost exclusively basic Arabic-style diners offering roast chicken and kebabs, but there's plenty of opportunity for cheap and tasty snacking: falafel sandwiches and bowls of *fuul* or hummus are unbeatable, and street *shwarma* stands are everywhere (Amman's **best shwarma**, however, is from the stall on 2nd Circle, on the side heading towards 3rd). All the better restaurants, and virtually all the non-Arabic places, are located in uptown districts.

Bear in mind that, in addition to the places listed here, you could copy some wealthy Ammanis, who think nothing of driving down to the big hotels on the **Dead Sea** for a special dinner: each hotel (see p.175) has several restaurants covering diverse cuisines, and the high quality of food and service – combined with the romantic setting – makes for a memorable evening out. The journey (45 minutes there, an hour coming back) takes only a bit longer than crossing Amman through heavy traffic.

Many upmarket restaurants provide **valet parking** for diners arriving by car. A minimum tip, presuming that you're not left standing around waiting for your car to reappear, is half a dinar.

All the restaurants listed below are marked on the maps on p.108, p.120, p.125 or p.127. Restaurants within hotels are identified as such in the review; in these cases, only the hotel is shown on the map.

Arabic

Budget

Cairo Down a side-street behind the Husseini Mosque, Downtown. The most convivial of a trio of celebrated Downtown diners (the others are *al-Quds* and *Hashem*), serving uncomplicated fare ranged in hot cabinets at the back. You'd have to stuff yourself to part with more than JD1.500; expect to share a table. Daily 8am–11pm.

Hashem In an alley opposite *Cliff Hotel*, Downtown. A fast-paced outdoor diner that is an Amman institution, founded by restaurateur Hashem al-Turk in the 1920s. Tables are set out all down the shaded alley, as well as in the generally locals-only interior, and there are just two dishes to choose from – *fuul* (hot beans) or hummus. Ask for *fuul* and you'll get the standard Jordanian version, but there are plenty of variations; for instance, *fuul masri* is Egyptian-style, without the chilli but with a dollop of *tahini*, while *qudsiyyeh* is Jerusalem-style – *fuul* with a blob of hummus in it. All are freshly made, tasty and just 300–350 fils. Bread, chopped onion and a sprig of mint are free (the restaurant gets through a staggering 50kg of onions a day). The stand opposite sells bags of cheap falafel balls as a side-dish, and tea-waiters periodically stride around shouting "*shy, shebab?*" (tea anyone?) – grab a glass off the tray. You can eat well for a dinar. Almost all the 17 waiters are Egyptian, earning around JD100 a month – a shade above the minimum wage. Tips are optional. Daily 24hr.

Kafeteria al-Kouds (Jerusalem) On Rainbow St, below 1st Circle, Jebel Amman. Not to be confused with the Downtown *al-Quds* restaurant (see below). This is a tiny hole-in-the-wall joint, near the British Council, that serves what many claim to be the best falafel in Amman. Catch them at busy times (say, around 6pm) when all the falafel is fresh-fried and crispy hot – and you may well agree. Daily about noon–9pm or later.

al-Quds King Hussein St, under the huge Dome of the Rock billboard next to *Habibah* patisserie, Downtown. The best restaurant in Downtown (which isn't saying much), serving a range of rather overcooked Arabic specialities, including the celebrated Bedouin speciality *mensaf* (lamb with rice). Prices are reasonable – a full meal needn't set you back more than JD2.500 or so – but the menu is in Arabic only and the waiters don't have much chatting time. Lunchtimes are more congenial. Daily 7am–11pm.

al-Sahn al-Dimashq Ilya Abu Mahdi St, near *Pizza Hut*, Shmeisani. Arabic sign only – look for the elaborate Damascene-style decoration. Solid fare at good prices, with the added attraction of half a dozen varieties of *fatteh* and *kebab halaby*. Celebrated, high-quality *shwarma*s too. Daily noon–midnight.

al-Salaam King Faysal St, opposite the Gold Souk, Downtown. Simple diner with reasonable roasted half-chickens (that's just about all they do). Rarely more than JD2. Daily 10am–10pm.

Tarweea Part of the Haya Cultural Centre, roughly opposite *KFC* in Shmeisani. The classiest low-cost Arabic restaurant in the city (*tarweea* is Lebanese dialect for "brunch"), an intimate and spotlessly clean place that is a quality alternative to Shmeisani's junk-food fixation, and streets ahead of anything Downtown. Music from the Egyptian diva Umm Kalthoum plays at a comfortable decibel level and the uniquely friendly waiters will talk you through the menu. Highlights include an excellent Lebanese *fatteh*, tasty giant-sized stuffed falafel balls and plenty of varieties of *fuul* and hummus, not to mention kebabs and a free platter of pickles, olives, mint and rocket leaves that's almost a dish in itself. Don't miss their fresh-baked *manaqeesh zaatar* bread. A meal here is unlikely to set you back more than JD4. Daily 24hr.

Mid-range and expensive

Abu Ahmad Two branches: the *Orient*, on Basman St next to the *Cliff Hotel*, Downtown; and the more formal *New Orient*, behind the *Inter-Continental Hotel*, near 3rd Circle, Jebel Amman ☏06/464 1879, the latter West Amman's oldest restaurant, opened in 1958. Well-regarded, old-fashioned places with pleasant garden terraces serving a welter of accomplished Lebanese-style dishes, especially strong on *mezze*. Around JD10 per head. Both daily 11am–midnight.

Fakhr el-Din 40 Taha Hussein St, behind Iraqi Embassy, between 1st and 2nd Circles, Jebel Amman ☏06/465 2399. Amman's premier restaurant, catering to the royal and diplomatic upper crust and housed in a tasteful 1920s villa, renovated by top architect Ammar Khammash and retaining its old-world atmosphere of understated charm. The food – formal Syrian cuisine – is as impeccable as the service, yet judicious choices can keep the bill around JD12 – not, however, if you indulge in the highly acclaimed, but expensive, raw meat platter, which includes fine *kibbeh nayeh*. Unusually for an Arabic restaurant, leave space for dessert: both the *osmaliyyeh* (crispy shredded pastry over fresh cream, doused in syrup) and *muhallabiyyeh* (rose-scented almond cream pudding) are exquisite. Reservations essential, especially in summer for dining on the patio amid the lemon trees. Daily 1–3.30pm & 8pm–midnight.

Haret Jdoudna One of Jordan's best restaurants, worth the trip to nearby Madaba. See p.289.

Houwara On King Abdullah II St (aka the Hussein Medical Centre road), north of 8th Circle towards Sweileh ☏06/535 4210. Attractive mid-priced Lebanese restaurant in an incongruous location, set back from the ring road on the very edge of town. Decor, with wooden lattice screens and art on the walls, is attractive, and the food is very good: there's a hefty range of *mezze* including a spot-on *muhammara* (a delicately spiced nut-based dip), quality *shanklish*, plus *tabbouleh* and *samakeh harra* as good as you'd expect (the latter a speciality of the Lebanese port of Tripoli, fish with onions, nuts and spiced *tahini*). The *shish tawook* is good, and the kebabs and mixed grills especially tender. In the tradition of upscale Arabic restaurants, though, the service can be over-formal, with a horde of waiters hovering to spoon out your *tabbouleh* and constantly fill your glass. Daily noon–midnight.

Reem al-Bawadi Just off Duwaar al-Waha (the junction of Medina St and Gardens St), Tla'a al-Ali, suburban West Amman ☎ 06/551 5419. Delightfully over-the-top kitsch-laden affair devoted to showy power-dining (Colonel Gaddafi has been known to drop by), complete with tent, fake castle, fountains, palm trees and neon lights. The menu is in Arabic only, but the waiters are happy to talk you through the options; few restaurants offer such untrammelled good service – formal but not stiff, warm yet subtle. The food is excellent, but you'd come as much for the atmosphere, and to take a leisurely three or four hours over lunch or dinner in a comfortable, unhurried setting. Families are welcome. Daily noon–midnight.

Sahtain At Kan Zaman tourist village ☎ 06/412 8391, ⊛ www.jtic.com. A classy out-of-town restaurant seating four hundred diners in subtly lit vaults – it's an atmospheric place to eat a superb (though overpriced) buffet, with Arabic music and dance nightly. See p.156 for details of how to reach Kan Zaman. Daily 1–4pm & 7pm–midnight.

Shehrazad At *Crowne Plaza Hotel*, 6th Circle ☎ 06/551 0001. Atmospheric restaurant with breathtaking city views from the top floor of the hotel, serving excellent Moroccan/North African cuisine. The resident Moroccan chef is slowly gaining the recognition he deserves, although you'll still have to pick out his specialities from among the menu's welter of standard Lebanese/Middle Eastern dishes. The quality *mezze*, through no fault of their own, are overshadowed by the range of topnotch, thoroughly authentic couscous dishes and *tajines* on offer, both meat and veggie. Meals from JD12 or so, plus occasional live music. Daily 7pm–midnight.

Tannoureen Shatt al-Arab St, Souk Umm Uthayna, near 6th Circle ☎ 06/551 5987. With such a vast range of contenders it's a difficult decision, but on balance, this is probably the best Arabic restaurant in Jordan – award-winning Lebanese cuisine of the highest quality in an elegant, expensive setting. Hardened restaurant critics, with an eye for a fake, declare the *mezze* here to be "out of this world" – the only difficulty is choosing from the long list of options, both hot and cold. You'll have trouble leaving space for a main course, but try: the *shish tawook* is exquisite, and the kebabs and mixed grill perfectly tender and flavour-rich. Desserts are spectacular, but not many diners make it that far. The courteous service is unusually warm and understated, as is the decor, which includes many paintings of old Jordanian and Palestinian villages. All in all, quite an experience. JD15 per head and upwards. Daily 1–4pm & 8–11pm.

Zuwwadeh Excellent Arabic restaurant in nearby Fuheis. See p.190.

European

Bonita Down a side-street opposite *El-Yassmin Suites*, very close to 3rd Circle, Jebel Amman ☎ 06/461 5061. The best Spanish restaurant in town, known for its superb fish and seafood, and three kinds of paella (one of them vegetarian). Alongside is a tapas bar with Mexican beer and dozens of cheap nibbles. A full meal could reach JD15. Restaurant daily noon–midnight, bar daily 7.30pm–midnight.

Casereccio On a side-street just off Abdoun Circle, Abdoun ☎ 06/593 4772. Casual Italian restaurant that gets jammed solid on Fridays (when the quality of food and service can suffer); on other days, you'll find the wood-fired pizzas, fresh pastas and crêpes excellent, with a meal easily affordable at JD6 or so per head. Daily noon–3pm & 7–11pm.

E.V.O.O. At *Sheraton Hotel*, 5th Circle ☎ 06/593 4111. Classy, spacious Italian restaurant with a dreadful name – it supposedly stands for *Extra*

Virgin Olive Oil. Ignore the pretension: the food is very good, with a broad selection of antipasti prepared immaculately and a long, enticing menu of main courses. The decor is elegant but not stuffy, the service calm and efficient. Expect to pay JD20 per head and more. Daily 12.30–3.30pm & 7.30–11.30pm.

L'Entrecôte At *Shepherd Hotel*, between 1st and 2nd Circles ☎ 06/464 2401. Quiet, unassuming restaurant attached to a good mid-range hotel. Classic French entrecôte steak is pretty much all they do, but they do it very well, served complete with a sauce of Dijon mustard and perfect French fries, for around JD8. Don't go expecting flair in decor or cuisine. Daily 1–3pm & 7–11pm.

L'Incontro At *Grand Hyatt Hotel*, 3rd Circle ☎ 06/465 1234. A truly elegant place to dine, with sophisticated Milanese chic decor and an attractive outside patio. The Italian food is superb, with a frequently changing menu, and the service outstanding. Bank on at least JD15 per head. Daily 12.30–3.30pm & 7.30–11.30pm.

Pizza Reef Medina St, 200m north of Duwaar al-Waha (the junction of Medina St and Gardens St), Tla'a al-Ali, suburban West Amman ☏ 06/568 7087. The best pizza in the city – thin-crust, wood-fired fresh to order and not expensive (around JD3 for two people). They can make up anything you fancy, with or without meat or cheese – their unique *labneh*-and-rocket offering with extra rosemary is delectable. Nearby sister outlet *Pizza Rimini* (turn right off Gardens at the Best supermarket before Duwaar al-Waha and go 100m, ☏ 06/568 6324) does all the same stuff including takeaways. You'll probably need a taxi and/or a detailed map to find either. Both open daily: *Reef* 4pm–midnight (closed Mon); *Rimini* noon–11pm (closed Tues).

Romero Down a side-street almost opposite the *Inter-Continental Hotel*, near 3rd Circle, Jebel Amman ☏ 06/464 4227, ⊛ www.romero-jordan. com. One of the best restaurants in the country, and the best Italian by a long streak. Service is uniquely calm and friendly, and the food outstanding, but you need not spend more than JD12 per person. Daily 1–3pm & 8–11pm.

Vinaigrette At *Al-Qasr Howard Johnson Hotel*, Shmeisani ☏ 06/568 9671. Compact little hi-tech eatery tagged as a "jazz and salad bar". The light food is fine, but even if the service is peremptory and the music sometimes too loud, you can find yourself overlooking all that for the location of this place. It is perched at the top of the hotel, which itself stands on one of the highest points in the uptown district of Shmeisani: the views all round are stunning (even more so at night). The floor-to-ceiling windows can be rather disconcerting – it sometimes feels like you're floating unsupported above the busy streets – but it's worth booking for a window table nonetheless. Daily noon–11.30pm.

Wild Jordan Othman bin Affan Street, off Rainbow St, below 1st Circle, Jebel Amman ☏ 06/ 463 3542. Wonderful café/restaurant attached to the Royal Society for the Conservation of Nature building (see p.141), with a stunning view over Downtown Amman from the balcony. Prices are high, but the food is all organic, with many ingredients grown locally on the RSCN nature reserves around Jordan. Examples include spinach and mushroom salad with hazelnut and lime dressing, smoked salmon on wild rocket, lean steak sandwich, wholewheat spaghetti with light pesto, and so on (all these JD3–4). Their smoothies are sensational – and don't miss the thirst-quenching frozen lemonade with fresh mint. Daily 11am–midnight. Booking advisable on Fridays.

Indian and East Asian

China Just off Rainbow St, 100m from Jordan River Designs, below 1st Circle, Jebel Amman ☏ 06/463 8968. Low-key place (also known as "Abu Khalil", after the owner) with a dedicated East Asian expat clientele. The food is good, and with careful selections it's easy to keep the outlay well inside single figures. Daily noon–3.30pm & 7pm–midnight.

China Town At *Le Meridien Hotel*, Queen Noor St, Shmeisani ☏ 06/569 6511. Top-quality Chinese meals in a classy, comfortable ambience, for around JD15. Also has a *teppanyaki* bar with a limited, pricey range of *sushi* and Japanese specialities. Daily 12.30–3.30pm & 7.30–11.30pm.

Indochine At *Grand Hyatt Hotel*, just off 3rd Circle ☏ 06/465 1234. Outstanding Vietnamese restaurant, furnished with louvred doors, rattan and wooden ceiling fans to evoke the colonial-era 1930s. Excellent food ranges from starters like Thai beef salad, deep-fried spring rolls and shrimp fritters to mains such as prawns and straw mushrooms in spicy lemongrass soup, ginger chicken simmered in caramel, and shrimp satay in peanut sauce. Meals from around JD20 per head. Booking essential. Daily 6.30pm–midnight.

Indu At the *Inter-Continental Hotel*, midway between 2nd and 3rd Circles, Jebel Amman ☏ 06/464 1361. Very expensive but spectacularly good Indian food, which you can watch being prepared by the Indian chefs through an archway into the kitchen, with tandoori a speciality and plenty for vegetarians. Daily noon–3pm & 7–11.30pm.

Noodasia Abdoun Circle ☏ 06/593 6999. Outstandingly good Asian restaurant. Decor is chic and contemporary, and the food authentic: the spring rolls are perhaps the best in Amman, *pad Thai* or Szechuan beef are popular staples and the sushi is outstanding. Presentation is immaculate, service efficient. Daily 12.30–3.30pm & 7–11.30pm.

Peking Opposite *al-Qasr Howard Johnson Hotel*, Shmeisani ☏ 06/566 0250. Highly regarded traditional Chinese restaurant with a long and varied menu. Highlights include a wonderful "sour peppery soup" and *ma po* tofu wok-fried to perfection. Prices are high: a full meal could set you back JD20. Daily 1–3.30pm & 7–11.30pm.

North American

Champions At the *Marriott Hotel*, Issam al-Ajlouni St, near Interior Circle, Shmeisani. A roomy, lively American diner-cum-sports-bar, crammed with TVs. Food includes nachos, burgers and fajitas, in enormous portions; wash it all down with a pitcher of beer. JD10 sees you stuffed. English football is shown live, as is every other conceivable sporting occasion. One final attraction: they serve alcohol during Ramadan. Daily noon–1am.

Cinco de Mayo At the *Inter-Continental Hotel*, between 2nd and 3rd Circles, Jebel Amman ☏06/464 1361. Tacos, burritos and fajitas, pricey but generally well prepared. Squeeze your way past the expense-account journos at the bar exchanging tales of Baghdad bravery. Daily 12.30–3.30pm & 7.30–11.30pm.

Houston's 11th of Ab Street, Shmeisani ☏06/562 0610. Casual Tex-Mex joint, crammed on weekend nights. Huge salads, draught beer and the best nachos around. Daily noon–midnight.

Planet Hollywood Orthodox Club Street, 50m east of Abdoun Circle ☏06/593 0972. Tucked back off the street, this is a surprisingly acceptable, low-key version of the global chain, with all the usual Tex-Mex offerings (nachos, burgers, etc.) not excessively priced. Daily 10am–1am.

Western fast food

Western fast food is well established in Amman, with original chains and local imitators all over the city. The only real "chippy" for takeaway French fries is *Batata*, on Rainbow Street below 1st Circle, freshly fried with a choice of sauces; it's best to request them without the snowstorm of salt/MSG. *Pizza Hut* on Abdoun Circle does home or hotel delivery (☏06/585 5555) as does the nearby *McDonalds* (☏06/582 0000 or 593 0119). Shmeisani, Sweifiyyeh and Abdoun are crammed with fast-food outlets, as are all the big West Amman malls, including Mecca Mall at the western end of Mecca Street.

Amman's best-quality cheap meals are at the *Snack Box* takeaway, owned and run by a Jordanian–Welsh couple directly opposite the blue-domed King Abdullah Mosque 200m uphill from Abdali station (Sun–Thurs noon–10pm; ☏06/566 1323) – huge stir-fries (chicken or veggie) as well as pastas, club sandwiches, giant burgers or fresh fish-and-chips for around JD3 each. Everything is freshly prepared while you wait, or you can order ahead for a takeaway. Don't miss their killer chocolate mousse.

Buying your own food and drink

The main Downtown **fruit and vegetable market**, with everything from potatoes to persimmons, is in a well-hidden back alley off King Talal Street, and there are some good general **grocery shops** in the alleys around the *Cliff Hotel*. The uptown **supermarkets** (see below) not only often undercut Downtown prices on fresh produce, but are also the sole outlets for ham and luncheon meat.

Hashem restaurant (see p.147) will give you superb **hummus** or **fuul** in plastic pots to take away – to avoid leakages, ask for it *bidoon zayt* (without oil). For something more substantial, head for the *Snack Box* takeaway (see above). Good **bakeries** can be found in every neighbourhood, all selling fresh *khubez*, rolls and breadsticks, while many of the big supermarkets have delicacies like fresh-baked baguettes and rye loaves. Exquisite Iraqi **dates** are available year-round in the Downtown Souk Sukkr.

For buying **alcohol** in Downtown, there are plenty of liquor stores selling cold beer, wine and harder stuff, both local and imported. Sweiss on Basman Street behind the *Cliff Hotel* is one of the best, and there's a good, nameless place on King Faysal Street opposite the Gold Souk. Most uptown supermarkets stock alcohol, and there's a branch of Sweiss just off Abdoun Circle. Note that many budget and mid-range hotels will object strongly to your bringing alcohol onto the premises; see p.68 for more on this.

Supermarkets

Cozmo Near Safeway, off 7th Circle ⓦwww .cozmocentre.com. A small shopping mall concentrating on chic homeware and upscale designer fashions for adults and kids. In the same complex is an excellent supermarket, with a wide range and late opening. Easy parking. Shops: Sat–Thurs 10am–10pm, Fri 11am–10pm. Supermarket: daily 8am–1am.

Plaza Superstore Next to Jordan National Bank, Queen Noor St, Shmeisani, close to 4th Circle. A well-known landmark (formerly Al-Ahlia Superstore), with a wide food range and especially good bread. Parking can be difficult. Daily 7am–11pm.

Rainbow Market Rainbow St, 100m from 1st Circle, Jebel Amman. Friendly little corner store, easy to get to from Downtown. Parking almost impossible. Daily 8.30am–8.30pm.

Safeway ⓦwww.safeway.com.jo. Three branches: in Shmeisani (on Sharif Nasser bin Jameel St near Sports City, at the foot of Gardens St); on the Airport Road (behind the Royal Jordanian building off 7th Circle); and a smaller outlet in Jubeiha. All are prominent city landmarks, known by every taxi-driver, and filled with familiar brands – as well as music stores, cobblers/key-cutters, laundry service, mobile phone stores, florists, and so on. Easy parking. All daily 24hr.

Stop & Shop Lweibdeh Circle, Jebel al-Lweibdeh ⓣ06/462 5140. Reasonably sized and close to Downtown – though none too cheap. Free delivery to anywhere in the city. OK parking. Daily 8am–8pm.

Nightlife and entertainment

As well as the wide range of **drinking and dancing** venues on the social circuit of the city's affluent crowd, Amman has a surprising amount of cultural **entertainment** to indulge in, although information, unless you call the relevant venue or sponsor in advance, is not easy to come by. Most **cultural events** are advertised on noticeboards in cultural centres, supermarkets and embassies; the *Jordan Times* lists events for that evening, and the *Star* supposedly for the week ahead, but neither is totally reliable. It's worth looking out for openings of art exhibitions at Darat al-Funun and elsewhere, some of which are accompanied by music or poetry readings.

Bars

Amman has a surprisingly wide range of **bars**, from swish upmarket hotel pubs to dingy dives well hidden in back alleys. All those in Downtown are seedy hangouts devoted to sedentary drinking, but quite a few of the uptown joints have ear-blasting sound systems and small dancefloors. Thursday is the big night out.

Your best bet for **Downtown** drinking dens is the web of alleys surrounding the *Cliff Hotel* – here you'll find the *Jordan Bar, Salamon Bar, Kit-Kat Bar* (round next to the cinema) and, further away on King Hussein Street opposite *Jabri's*, the *Hilton Bar*. All are grungy places, with no attraction whatsoever, other than the alcohol. Women, whether accompanied or not, are likely to attract a good deal of attention from slimeball barflies. There's a slightly less grisly bar attached to the *Rhum Continental Hotel*, nearby on Basman Street. Most of these places open some time in the afternoon and close around midnight; a beer is about JD1.300.

West Amman bars and pubs

Uptown neighbourhoods offer the possibility of classier drinking and – though beers are more expensive (roughly JD3 a bottle) – the added attractions of foreign imports and Amstel on draught everywhere you go. Modesty in **dress** for both men and women goes out the window in these places, and T-shirts, short skirts and the like are common.

Note that several of the places listed above as cafés or restaurants – such as *Wild Jordan*, *Bonita*, *Vinaigrette* and *Champions* – double up as drinking venues, while several others (*Sultan*, *Tché Tché*) may not serve alcohol but are just as lively and entertaining places to hang out after dark.

The Big Fellow Sheraton Entertainment Centre, just off Abdoun Circle. Behind the wall of black glass facing the street lurks a spacious, high-ceilinged Irish boozer dedicated to the "Big Fellow" Michael Collins, the Irish freedom fighter of the 1920s, recreated perfectly with lots of dark wood, old bric-a-brac and a meticulous attention to detail. Guinness, Kilkenny and Tennents are all on tap (around JD4 a pint), and there are satellite TV screens showing sport from back home. Savour your pint over a sandwich of honey-glazed Limerick ham, fish-and-chips, or My Mum's Irish Stew (around JD5). Arrive early on Thurs & Fri nights as it gets busy. Daily noon–2am or later.

Blue Fig Al-Amir Hashem bin al-Hussein St, about 1.5km south of Abdoun Circle ☎06/592 8800, ⊛www.bluefig.com. A cool fixture on West Amman's burgeoning in-scene, whose decor and young, wealthy clientele wouldn't look out of place in Soho or San Francisco. The architect-designed interior is chic and classy, taking in a couple of bars, two spacious floors of tables, plus couches dotted around, a movie room downstairs and a terrace out back for summer lounging. The food is superb if a little pricey, using loads of local and imported ingredients imaginatively in fresh-baked wrap-style dishes. Live music weekly. Daily 8.30am–1am. Booking essential for Thursday nights.

Books@Café Mango St, just off Rainbow St, below 1st Circle. This much-loved bookstore-cum-café in a beautiful part of town is simply a great place to hang out. The decor is colourful, the staff and clientele are about as hip as each other and there's always a buzz. Sit out on the front terrace, looking across the city lights, or lounge on the multi-level rear terrace (where there's often a big screen showing sports or the latest Arabic music videos). Snacks, good coffee and internet access complete the effect. Daily 10am–1am or so.

The Grenadier Beside *Liwan Hotel*, Sweifiyyeh. Amiable, informal English-style pub; an expat favourite. Also serves decent, plain pub food: go for the Dish of the Day – perhaps steak and mashed potatoes, or a curry with rice, or maybe liver and bacon. Daily 12.30pm–1am or so.

The Irish Pub Basement of the *Dove Hotel* between 4th and 5th Circles. With the arrival of *The Big Fellow* (universally dubbed the "New Irish"), this stalwart of Amman's pub scene has been unofficially renamed the "Old Irish". It's a small, appealingly gloomy basement that owes little to the Emerald Isle, but nonetheless does a good imitation of a British student bar, with lino underfoot, not enough places to sit and a cramped dancefloor. Gets packed out on hectic Thursday nights by Ammani trendies. Daily 6pm–2am or so.

JJ's At *Grand Hyatt Hotel*, just off 3rd Circle. Ultra-chic, trendy nightclub – supposedly members-only, although you're unlikely to have any difficulty getting in – featuring Amman's wealthy uptown set dancing to up-to-date music by British DJs. Mon–Sat 8.30pm–3am or so.

Kanabayé On 3rd Circle. A good daytime café and restaurant which turns into a packed, excitable nightspot – renowned for its salsa nights. Daily 11am until late.

Rover's Return Beneath *Comfort Hotel*, Sweifiyyeh, two streets behind the mosque midway between 6th and 7th Circles. An authentic, poky English pub with loud music, TVs and excellent food – including steak and kidney pie, chicken-in-a-basket and great fish-and-chips. Go early to get a seat. Daily 12.30pm–1.30am.

Saluté Opposite *Fakhr el-Din* restaurant behind Iraqi Embassy, between 1st and 2nd Circles. Feisty, trendy bar that pulls in a young crowd for long nights of sociable drinking amid loud music. Twinkly views from its plate-glass windows over the valley are an added draw. Daily 7pm–1am.

Music, dance and theatre

There's a well-established performance scene in Amman, especially of Western **classical music** – orchestras and soloists often pass through, and students from the National Music Conservatory perform regularly. The various cultural centres (see p.164) frequently sponsor performances, but **Arabic music** pops up frustratingly rarely. **Folkloric dance** is well represented, with the National Folklore Troupe (run by the Ministry of Culture; ⊛www.culture.gov.jo) leading the way. The major **venue** for everything is the **Royal Cultural Centre**

(☎06/566 1026) in Shmeisani, 300m beyond the *Regency Palace Hotel* off Interior Circle, although there are outdoor performances in summer at several locations, including Darat al-Funun and, occasionally, the Roman Theatre. Arabic-language **theatre** – both comedy and drama – is well catered for but performances in English are a rarity. For more information on the star-studded **Jerash Festival**, see the box on p.199.

Film

Although there are plenty of **cinemas** in Downtown, they're all limited to showing last year's Hollywood action blockbusters, Hong Kong gang warfare and 1970s soft porn, everything sliced to ribbons by the censor and often dubbed appallingly into Arabic; tickets are a rock-bottom JD1.500 or so. Otherwise, the main cinemas for big-name new releases (subtitled in Arabic and French, and more subtly censored) are the plush, big-screen set of the **Galleria**, in the Sheraton Entertainment Centre just off Abdoun Circle; **Ciné Le Royal**, within the *Le Royal Hotel* tower at 3rd Circle; **Century Cinemas**, in the Zara Centre on Wadi Saqra; and the seven-screen **Grand Theaters** within Mecca Mall on Mecca Street. Tickets are roughly JD5–6. With more malls being built, the number of cinemas is likely to rise. Check the *Jordan Times* for what's on.

In **other venues** around town, plenty of movie surprises are on offer – mostly on video, but all free of charge, except for the occasional projection-TV screenings at *Books@Café* (JD2 or so). The British Council and the American Center (see p.164) both have programmes of English-language films, and other cultural centres (also see p.164) often show films from their own countries, sometimes subtitled in English. Darat al-Funun regularly shows documentary films on the arts as well as some arthouse features; other centres such as Makan (see p.139) and Dar al-Anda do the same. **European film festivals** run every May and October in different cinemas around town, and there's also a Franco-Arab Film Festival every June; festival programmes are always announced in advance in the *Jordan Times*.

Shopping

Shopping is a great way to experience Jordanian culture – and it can bring you closer to understanding what makes Amman tick than almost any other activity. Many first-time visitors expect to be able to fill several days sightseeing, but Amman doesn't have that many sights; what it does have in abundance is shops. An excellent way to spend your first morning in the city would be to set yourself a modest shopping goal: a domed alarm clock that sounds the call to prayer, for instance, or a set of decorative Islamic prayer beads. Head out with a few dinars and roam the Downtown shopping streets till you have what you want: the item may be worth little, but the process of finding it and buying it will be a memorable experience.

King Talal Street, in Downtown, is lined with shops selling **household goods** where you could browse for interesting everyday items; good buys include a Turkish coffee service (a tiny pot for boiling the grounds plus six handleless cups on a tray) or an *argileh*, often steel but occasionally brass (check the joints carefully for leaks). There are many outlets near the Husseini Mosque where you could pick up a simple but attractive cotton-polyester *jellabiyyeh* (full-length robe) for less than JD10, or a *keffiyeh* (chequered or plain headcloth)

Shopping malls

The growing number of **shopping malls** in Amman can be fascinating to explore – much like their Western counterparts, these are covered, air-conditioned and packed with shops of all kinds. Several of Amman's early malls were modest affairs, but that changed with the giant **Mecca Mall** (shops Sat–Thurs 10am–10pm; Fri 2–10pm; food outlets open daily until midnight), located towards the western end of Mecca Street. Spread over five floors, this behemoth – with, of course, abundant parking – takes in literally hundreds of shops, dozens of cafés and restaurants, a seven-screen cinema, a bowling alley, a kids' adventure zone, laser gaming and more. Don't spurn it as some kind of foreign import: many ordinary Ammanis shop here, and it represents as much an authentic expression of modern Jordanian culture as the Downtown bazaars. The company that built it is already well advanced on their new Amman venture: the **Airport Mall**, located on the Airport Road south of 7th Circle, and even bigger than its predecessor.

for around JD2.500. And some **food** items can make great souvenirs, such as a kilo of fresh-roasted coffee ground with cardamom, or a box of succulent Iraqi dates.

Other fascinating areas for window-shopping include **Sweifiyyeh** and **Umm Uthayna** (the tight grid of streets to the southwest and northeast of 6th Circle, respectively), both of them packed with all kinds of shops from designer boutiques and jewellery shops to furniture stores, groceries and cafés. **Shmeisani**, around Abdul Hameed Shoman Street, is in a similar vein, with even better people-watching. The area around Firas Circle in the heart of **Jebel Hussein** has a different feel, with office workers and ordinary families browsing around. **Abdullah Ghosheh Street**, where it meets Mecca Street, is another hive of commercial activity.

Souvenirs and local crafts

Compared to Cairo, Jerusalem, Damascus and Aleppo, which all have centuries-old souks and long traditions of craftsmanship, Amman is a modern lightweight, with no memorable **bazaars** to explore. Where the city scores is in its range of **Bedouin crafts** from Jordan and Palestine at prices a fraction of Jerusalem's, and – most of all – in some amazingly inexpensive **gold**.

There's only a handful of genuine craft shops in Amman, most located around 1st and 2nd Circles, and they tend to be associated with projects to revive or nurture the skills of local craftspeople; prices are legitimately high and you're certain to be purchasing quality goods. **Souvenir shops** which are simply sales outlets for local or imported merchandise are more numerous; here prices can be high without necessarily implying a matching quality. There are many of the latter within walking distance of **Lweibdeh Circle**, and if you want to get a sense of what's available this is a good place to start.

al-Afghani Opposite the Husseini Mosque, Downtown. Sat–Thurs 9am–6pm. Also two branches on Jebel al-Lweibdeh. Amman's most famous souvenir shops, originally founded in Palestine in 1862 by a merchant from Kabul and still in the same family. The Downtown shop is a wonderful little Aladdin's cave, crammed to the ceiling with everything from Bohemian glass to ornate Cairene Ramadan lamps; serious browsing is better undertaken at the branches on al-Lweibdeh.

Artisana (Jordan Arts and Crafts Centre) Krishan St, off 2nd Circle. Sat–Thurs 9am–6.30pm. Wide range of attractive handicrafts and home furnishings, well presented for a free-spending clientele.

al-Aydi (Jordan Craft Development Centre) Just off 2nd Circle behind the *Inter-Continental Hotel*,

Jebel Amman. Sat–Thurs 9am–6pm. The best place to buy locally produced handmade crafts. Staff work as advisers and design consultants to about a hundred local craftspeople – mostly rural women – who share in the shop's profits. There's a huge variety of pieces, everything from olive-wood carving to mother-of-pearl, hand-blown glassware, textiles of all kinds (including lovely hand- and machine-embroidered jackets and dresses), jewellery, ceramics, baskets and more, both old and new. It also stocks the biggest collection of carpets in the country – Jordanian, Iraqi and Kurdish, ranging from antique pieces to newly-mades.

Badr ad-Duja 15 Abu Tammam St, off 2nd Circle, Jebel Amman Ⓦ www.badr-adduja.com.jo. Sat–Thurs 9am–6pm. Excellent range of crafts, including embroidery, rugs, jewellery, glassware, ceramics and home furnishings.

Beit al-Bawadi Fawzi Qaw St, Abdoun Ⓦ www.beitalbawadi.com. Sat–Thurs 9am–6pm. High-quality ceramics, carpets and bric-a-brac from the Jordanian Hashemite Fund for Human Development.

Buying gold

Prices for gold jewellery in Amman are some of the cheapest in the world. Not only is there a constant, massive demand in Jordan for gold, used in marriage dowries, but workmanship on gold jewellery is charged by weight here – a scheme which turns out to be very economical by world standards. The upshot is that it's well-nigh impossible to find the same quality of work or purity of gold outside Jordan for less than three or four times the Amman price. In the Downtown Gold Souk, you can be paying a measly JD5 or JD6 per gram for finished pieces in **21-carat gold** (which is very popular, partly because its orangey-yellow hue looks good against darker skin, and partly because its purity and investment value make it most desirable for dowries). You'll pay very slightly more if you go for the paler look of **18-carat gold**, principally because all the 18-carat gold in Jordan originates in Italy. Following a recent fad in Ammani high society for 18-carat **white gold**, the uptown gold shops of Sweifiyyeh and Shmeisani stock more of this than anything else, whereas the Downtown Gold Souk has stuck firm with its traditional, lower-income clientele, who prefer 21-carat yellow gold. (At the other end of the scale, the **9-carat gold** popular in the West isn't even worth an Ammani dealers' time.)

When buying, you have to know, at least sketchily, what you're looking at and what you want, and you have to be prepared to devote some hours to making a purchase. Browsing from shop to shop to get a sense of the market can be a pleasure: Jordan is mercifully entirely free of the kind of tedious hard-sell haggling for which the Middle East is notorious. Be aware that there are no hallmarks; instead, look for a stamp indicating **gold purity** in parts per thousand: "875" indicates 21-carat, while "750" is 18-carat. Any gold marked purer than 21-carat almost certainly isn't, since 23- and 24-carat gold (the latter 100 percent pure) is so soft it can be squashed in your palm. When you buy, you will be given two receipts: one for the per-gram market value of the item, another for the cost of the workmanship. The honour system among gold merchants – both in the Downtown Gold Souk and elsewhere – is very strong, and means that it is very unlikely you'll be misled.

Styles of jewellery vary from place to place – although everyone will happily make you up a necklace of a gold tag shaped with your name in Arabic – and, with prices as low as they are, commissioning a custom-made piece to your own design doesn't command the kind of absurd prices that the same thing in the West might do. One name to look out for, with a rock-solid reputation, an intimate knowledge of the market and a familiarity with Western tastes, is the company George Tawfic Khoury & Sons, trading as Tower Jewellers, with a branch in the Downtown Gold Souk and another in Sweifiyyeh (Ⓣ 06/586 2285).

As a footnote, Jordan is a bad place to buy **jewels** or precious stones, since everything is imported. However, **silver** is sold in the same way as gold, although it is much less popular and you may have to search for it; prices, though, are an absurdly low 500 fils or so per gram.

al-Burgan 12 Tal'at Harb St, behind *Inter-Continental Hotel*, 2nd Circle ✆ www.alburgan.com. Sat–Thurs 9am–6pm. Family-run business offering a good range of quality pieces at modest prices – see the excellent website for details.

The Gold Souk A network of alleys between the Arab Bank and the Cairo Amman Bank, off King Faysal St, Downtown. Most shops Sat–Thurs 8.30am–7pm. Dozens of tiny shops all next to each other, selling modern gold jewellery at highly competitive prices (see box).

The Green Branch Opposite the Centre Culturel Français, just off Lweibdeh Circle, Jebel al-Lweibdeh. Sat–Thurs 9am–6pm. The least pushy of the Lweibdeh souvenir shops, with an impressive selection of hand-embroidered jackets and dresses. No credit cards.

Jordan Design & Trade Center (Noor al-Hussein Foundation) Opposite *Amman Orchid Hotel*, Shmeisani ✆ www.nooralhussein foundation.org. Sat–Thurs 8am–7pm. Showroom for the various income-generating projects of the charitable Noor al-Hussein Foundation, which was established by Queen Noor to revive traditional crafts and which has created jobs for thousands of mostly rural women in a number of schemes around the country, producing a wide range of top-quality crafts, pottery, hand-woven rugs, embroidered home furnishings, handmade paper and more for sale. There are prominent branches around the country, including at the Petra Visitors' Centre, opposite the Aqaba fort, the Jerash Visitors' Centre and at Haret Jdoudna in Madaba.

Jordan River Designs Just off Rainbow St, below 1st Circle, Jebel Amman. Sat–Thurs 8am–7pm, Fri 10am–7pm. A project originally set up by Save The Children, selling simple, bright and pricey handmade home furnishings from a lovely old 1920s-era villa. In the same courtyard is an outlet

for superb carpets woven by women of the Bani Hamida tribe (see p.297), where you can pick up a small wall-hanging for JD20, although reasonably sized rugs start from around JD50 and large carpets can be as much as JD400.

Kan Zaman Al-Yadoudeh village, 3km off the airport road at the Madaba exit (turn left, not right to Madaba), about 10km south of Amman. Daily 10am–midnight. Kan Zaman ("Once Upon A Time") was formerly a farming estate, established in the nineteenth century – it has undergone a touristy makeover as an Ottoman village. Prices in the lavish antiques shop are sky-high. Another shop nearby sells glassware, jewellery and ceramics made by ArtiZaman (you can visit their workshops downstairs), although it's easy to find items of the same quality and design for much less elsewhere.

Wild Jordan Othman bin Affan Street, off Rainbow St, below 1st Circle, Jebel Amman. Within this centre, run by the Royal Society for the Conservation of Nature, is a "nature shop" (daily 9am–5pm), which sells pieces designed in traditional style by Jordanian craftworkers – often rural women. These range from unusual contemporary jewellery to painted ostrich eggs and handwoven bags. Also on sale are organic herbs, dried fruits and spices, produced on the reserves.

World of Argileh Ali bin Abi Taleb St, across the road from the public fountain near City Hall, Downtown (look for a big yellow shop sign in Arabic only). Daily 8am–8pm. Good-sized local shop piled high with water-pipes, in all sizes and designs. No credit cards.

al-Yousour Next to al-Aydi, just off 2nd Circle, Jebel Amman. Sat–Thurs 9am–6pm. Tiny showroom attached to a workshop, with jewellery, brass and glass decorated with Arabic calligraphy that is designed, made and sold on-site. No credit cards.

Books, newspapers and music

Dozens of places all over Amman call themselves "bookshop" or "library", but don't be fooled – somewhere along the line "stationer's" was mistranslated, for that's what all these places are, selling office supplies and nothing more literary than *Muscle Monthly*. Nonetheless, Amman does have some excellent, if well-hidden, outlets for English-language **books**.

You can pick up the *Jordan Times* and *Star* **newspapers** from Downtown pavement stalls, and a wide range of slightly dated international newspapers and magazines from all five-star hotels. There are good **music** stores for Arabic tapes in every neighbourhood in the city, but the widest selection of both Arabic and Western music on tape and CD is at Music Box, just off Abdullah Ghosheh Street a short walk down from *McDonald's* (branches also at Safeway supermarket).

Amman Bookshop Prince Muhammad St, opposite Citibank, just below 3rd Circle, Jebel Amman. Sat–Thurs 8.30am–2.30pm & 3.30–6pm. The most accessibly located big selection of books, but everything's new and a little pricey. Art, design and fiction are especially well covered.

Books@Café Mango St, just off Rainbow St, below 1st Circle, Jebel Amman. Daily 9am–midnight. See also p.145. An eclectic choice of new and used books on everything from architecture to showbiz, with plenty of classic and pulp fiction. Also international newspapers and magazines.

Inter-Continental Bookshop *Inter-Continental Hotel*, between 2nd and 3rd Circles, Jebel Amman. Daily 8am–9pm. A small, high-quality selection of books on the Middle East, plus some fiction paperbacks and a wide choice of newspapers and magazines.

Jordan Distribution Agency 9th of Sha'aban St, near the junction with Prince Muhammad St, 300m uphill from the Downtown post office. Sat–Thurs 8am–5pm. The closest true bookshop to Downtown, with a decent selection and plenty of newspapers and magazines.

Philadelphia Book Gallery Opposite the mosque halfway along Gardens St, West Amman. Daily 9am–7pm, Fri until noon. Satisfyingly large, diverse and often discounted range, with an emphasis on politics and literature, and plenty of translated Arab fiction and poetry.

Sharbain Rainbow St at 1st Circle, Jebel Amman. Sat–Thurs 8.30am–6pm, Sun closes 1pm. Tiny place with a choice of classics and others.

University Bookshop Partway along Gardens St. Sat–Thurs 9am–7pm. A wide range of titles covering all subject areas; well worth a browse. The branch opposite the main gates of Jordan University focuses on academic books.

Moving on from Amman

Amman is the centre of Jordan's **transport** network and its main link to the outside world. Where your onward transport leaves from depends partly on what your destination is and partly on how you want to get there. Awkwardly enough, there are five main bus and serveece stations – **Abdali**, **Raghadan**, **Wihdat**, **Muhajireen** and the **JETT** station – and they're all widely spaced across the city (see p.110 for location details). Fares to close-at-hand places such as Jerash and Madaba are well under 500 fils, and fares to all destinations north of Tafileh (apart from the King Hussein Bridge) are below JD1. See p.104 for some ideas for **day-trips** out of Amman.

Note that with the **redevelopment** of the Raghadan station, and major disruption at Abdali (the big bus station there is being **demolished**, with all services moved out to a new station in the northern suburbs at Tabarbour), transport details may have changed from how they're described here. You'd do well to check with your hotel what the current situation is. Also, **fuel costs** have risen significantly in Jordan in recent years – and transport operators, inevitably, have been passing those extra costs on to their customers in the form of slightly increased fares. The approximate prices quoted here are likely to rise.

To Jerash and the north

Abdali is the departure point for all buses to destinations in the north of Jordan, including **Jerash**, **Irbid**, **Ajloun** and **Ramtha**. Most leave from the upper half of the station. There are also some serveeces, generally departing from the lower half of the station, to Irbid and Ramtha. Hijazi's big, comfortable air-con buses to Irbid, catering mostly to commuting Yarmouk University students, run on a regular schedule (daily 6.15am–7.30pm every 15min). For Umm Qais and the far north, change in Irbid.

To Azraq and the east

The only direct public transport between Amman and points east are minibuses from Abdali to **Mafraq**, where you should change for Umm al-Jimal and the far desert; and minibuses from Abdali or Raghadan to **Zarqa**, from where minibuses depart to Hallabat and Azraq. There is no public transport along the Amman–Azraq highway apart from a minibus from Raghadan to **Muwaggar**, making it impossible to reach Qasr Hraneh and Qusayr Amra without your own transport; many travellers resort to hiring a taxi (see p.242).

To Petra and the south

Minibuses to **Karak**, **Shobak** and **Wadi Musa/Petra** leave from Wihdat station, also known as *mujemma al-janoob* (South station). Departures are more common in the morning (from 7am onwards) than the afternoon. Serveece-drivers tend to quote prices higher than normal to start with; some hopefuls to Petra start as high as JD8, although the real price is nearer JD5–6 (or JD4 on the bus). Getting to Petra is still much more expensive, mile for mile, than other destinations: it can cut costs to start early, take a Shobak-bound bus and change there for local onward transport. Minibuses and serveeces to **Tafileh** and **Ma'an**, and a few to **Qadisiyyeh** (for **Dana**), also leave from Wihdat.

Minibuses to **Madaba** run on various routes from Abdali, Raghadan, Muhajireen and Wihdat stations, but bear in mind that there is no direct public transport from Amman to destinations south of Madaba along the picturesque **King's Highway**: all minibuses and serveeces from Amman use the Desert Highway (see p.383). However, the *Mariam Hotel* in Madaba (see p.283) runs its own transport from Madaba to Petra along the King's Highway.

Petra scams

It's worth being aware of the **scams** used by some taxi-, serveece- and bus-drivers plying the heavily touristed route from Amman to Petra. No public buses, minibuses or serveeces from Amman to Petra follow the **King's Highway**, and any drivers who claim they do are trying to gouge you for an inflated fare. For comparison purposes, the true cost of hiring a private taxi for the day to drive you along the King's Highway to Petra is at least JD55–60.

Some of the budget hotels in Amman – such as the *Farah*, the *Cliff*, the *Vinecia* and others – take advantage of this to offer cut-price **"tours"** to Petra along the King's Highway, stopping off at various places on the way. You'll get what you pay for on these: often a driver who speaks little English, an all-day drive in a cramped, uncomfortable car, and whistle-stop photo breaks. They can, though, be an economical way to glimpse the countryside. Beware of drivers on the day claiming, for instance, that the section of the King's Highway through the Wadi Mujib canyon is closed so they have to go on the Desert Highway instead: this is invariably just a ploy to get out of a long drive. The most reliable of these King's Highway jaunts to Petra is run by the excellent *Mariam Hotel* in Madaba (see p.283).

Many Amman serveece- and taxi-drivers have understandings with certain hotels in Wadi Musa: they bring tourists directly to the hotel, and the hotel pays them **commission** for each one, passing on that cost to you in the form of a slightly higher room rate. Often the taxi driver will offer to **phone** ahead to a hotel while driving: if you're able to understand Arabic, you'll hear that, rather than asking if they have a room available, he's instead asking how much commission the hotel would pay him if he brought you to the door. If the hotel refuses to cough up, he'll then turn to you and claim they're full, before offering to try another. There are two ways to avoid all this. Either insist he hands you the phone before speaking, so you can talk to the hotel yourself, or ask that he drops you off in the middle of Wadi Musa town so you can find a hotel independently. In any case, not all hotels in Wadi Musa are recommendable: if a place isn't in our listings on p.336, there's a reason.

One or two buses leave Wihdat in the mornings for Ma'in (some going on to **Hammamat Ma'in**), and Mukawir – but you can find more reliable connections to these places from Madaba (see p.281). JETT has a weekend day-trippers' bus direct to Hammamat Ma'in from outside their office, 1km uphill from Abdali station (Fri 8.30am; JD5 return).

To Aqaba

The greatest choice is on routes to **Aqaba**. Minibuses (5hr; JD3) and serveeces (slightly quicker and more expensive) along the Desert Highway depart regularly from Wihdat, the drivers touting for business by barking "Aqabaqabaqaba!" over their revving engines. Instead, you could opt for the big buses run by one of three companies which follow the Dead Sea/Wadi Araba road; these cut the journey time to four hours. **JETT** (℡06/566 4146) has at least six fast air-con buses departing daily to Aqaba from their office 1km uphill from Abdali station (first 7am, last 5pm; JD4.300). **Afana** (℡06/568 1560) has hourly departures from Wihdat (JD3.700), although you must buy your ticket in advance from their offices at Abdali station or alongside the JETT office. **Trust** (℡06/581 3427) has more modern, comfortable air-con buses departing six times a day from their office near the Royal Jordanian building off 7th Circle (first 7.30am, last 6pm; JD4); buy tickets as you board or in advance from their booth at Abdali station.

Royal Wings (℡06/487 5202) has one or two **flights** a day from Amman to Aqaba (JD35), from either Marka Airport or Queen Alia International.

To the Dead Sea and west of Amman

Early morning minibuses (7–9am) from Muhajireen station run direct to the "Amman Beach" complex on the **Dead Sea**, but only if there's demand – guaranteed on a Friday. Others may stop short at the major crossroads town of **Shuneh al-Janubiyyeh**, about 15km north in the Jordan Valley. From the crossroads in the middle of Shuneh, frequent minibuses head to the village of **Sweimeh**, 3km northeast of the Dead Sea hotels; the driver might be willing to take you on to Amman Beach for a little extra. Transport any further south along the Dead Sea shore is erratic and unreliable: you may find one or two minibuses running to **Mazra'a**, but probably only in the early morning.

For the northern Jordan Valley, **Dayr Alla** is served by direct minibuses from Abdali; change at Dayr Alla for Pella.

Minibuses heading to towns **west of Amman** include those from Abdali or Raghadan to **Salt**; from Abdali to **Fuheis**; and from Muhajireen to **Wadi Seer**.

To neighbouring countries

Getting to some of the international departure points in Amman can be tricky, so it's advisable to ask someone to write in Arabic the name and location of where you're going to show to taxi-drivers or passers-by in case of difficulty (see p.167). The two most travelled routes – to **Damascus** and **Jerusalem** – can be complicated, and so are described in some detail; basic information is given for the others.

Needless to say, your passport and **visas** must all be in order before you buy a ticket or set out on any of these journeys, and don't forget to factor in the JD5 **departure tax** levied at every land and sea border.

Visas for nearby countries

There's little need to visit the **embassies** of Jordan's neighbours, either because visas are issued routinely on arrival in that country, or because **advance visas** – if they're actually needed – are only issued in Amman to people with full Jordanian residency. Full details are given below. If you apply in Amman but don't hold full Jordanian residency, you're often obliged to buy an expensive "letter of recommendation" from your own embassy and then wait up to two weeks while your application is scrutinized, with no guarantee of success.

If you do need to **visit** any of these embassies, the best advice is to ask your hotel to phone and get directions for handing to a taxi driver. Most are **open** for visa applications at the least from Sunday to Wednesday between 10 and 11am. Some have longer hours, but all are **closed** on Fridays, many on Saturdays and a few on Thursdays too. One or two photos are generally needed, and you can often collect your visa the same day or next. On application forms, it can sometimes cause major complications if you write anything other than "Tourism" under "What is the purpose of your visit?", or if you confess to being either a journalist or Jewish.

Egypt ☎06/560 5202. One-month "tourist visas" cost JD12 (single-entry) or JD15 (multiple-entry) for all nationalities. They're also available at entry airports and at land and sea borders (sometimes in US dollars only). A fourteen-day "Sinai-only" visa, valid only for travel along the east Sinai coast as far as Sharm el-Sheikh (including St Catherine's), is issued free at the seaport in Nuweiba, at the seaport and airport in Sharm, and at the Taba land border. This embassy is chaotic and frustrating – it's much easier to get your visa from the Egyptian consulate in Aqaba (see p.423).

Iraq ☎06/462 3175. At the time of writing no independent tourist visas were being issued, but you may find that that situation has changed by the time you read this. Check with the embassy for the latest information.

Israel ☎06/552 4686. No need to contact the embassy: tourist visas are issued free on arrival to all Western nationalities. See p.37 for details of the Israeli border stamps issue.

To Jerusalem, the West Bank and Gaza

As the crow flies, Amman and **Jerusalem** are only about 50km apart, but the Jordan Valley and a heavily fortified frontier bridge lie in the way, making the road journey tortuously long and slow. No buses or serveeces run directly between the two cities. The only way to go is with a combination of buses and taxis/serveeces, changing at the only bridge between Jordan and the West Bank that's open to the public, known to the Jordanians as the **King Hussein Bridge**, or Jissr al-Malek Hussein, and to the Israelis and Palestinians as the **Allenby Bridge** – Gesher Allenby in Hebrew, Jissr Allenby in Arabic (Sun–Thurs 7.30am–midnight, Fri & Sat 7.30am–2pm). On a good day, the journey can take as little as two hours; on a bad day, or after dark, it can be more than five. It is not unknown for the bridge to be closed by the Israeli authorities during periods of tension in the West Bank.

Presuming the bridge is open, the least arduous cheap way to go begins with a **serveece** from the southern end of Abdali station (1hr; JD2.500–3); stay on until you reach the foreigners' – *not* the locals' – terminal near the bridge. You have to sit and wait for anything up to two hours for a bus to fill up, which covers no-man's-land on either side of the bridge and drops you at the Israeli terminal (10min; JD2).

An easier but pricier option is to take the **JETT bus** from Abdali (daily 6.30am); you should book this ahead of time or turn up at their office no

Lebanon ☎06/592 9111. As with Syria, it's now almost impossible for non-Jordanian residents to get a Lebanese visa in Amman – but there's also little need, since most nationalities can buy them on arrival at the land borders or the airport. Note that there is no Lebanese embassy in Damascus.

Saudi Arabia ☎06/463 0337. Transit, business and pilgrimage visas are issued almost exclusively to Jordanian residents only. Tourists may, under certain conditions, be able to get a three-day transit visa to follow a certain land route across Saudi Arabia (such as to Kuwait) or a one-day transit visa to stopover by air in Riyadh or Jeddah – but the conditions are very strict and often change.

Syria ☎06/464 1076. It's almost impossible to get a Syrian visa in Amman unless you hold full Jordanian residency; even then, fees vary and often change without notice. If you haven't got a visa in advance, your chances of getting into Syria are virtually nil – but as long as your passport is in order (see p.37), you've nothing to lose by trying at the embassy and, if that fails (which is almost certain), you might as well head to the border anyway. One or two travellers have reported that, once there's a lull in cross-border traffic – which may take 3 or 4 hours of waiting – Syrian officials might relent and fax your visa application to Damascus to get approval. The whole process could take as long as 10 or 12 hours, but if you're prepared to wait in the border terminal area, there's the slimmest of chances that you might end up by being allowed into Syria. (If the application form, or any Syrian official, asks you if you have ever visited "Occupied Palestine", you'd be well advised to answer no.) Be under no illusions, though – it's much more likely that you'll be sent back into Jordan visa-less, whereupon the Jordanian border officials may insist you buy a new Jordanian visa. If this happens and you choose to fly from Jordan to Lebanon to continue your journey, note that there is no Syrian embassy in Beirut: your only onward options are to try your luck again at the Lebanon-Syria land border or to fly out of Beirut.

Embassies of other nearby countries Bahrain ☎06/566 4148; Iran ☎06/464 1281; Kuwait ☎06/567 5135; Oman ☎06/568 6155; Qatar ☎06/560 7311; Turkey ☎06/464 1251; UAE ☎06/593 4780; Yemen ☎06/464 2381.

later than 6am to guarantee a seat. The JD6.500 fare takes you swiftly all the way through to the Israeli terminal, but doesn't include the JD5 departure tax. Beware the bus-driver taking the passports of all the passengers to give in a huge pile to the immigration officials for stamping; if you want yours to stay unsullied, insist on taking it in to them yourself.

At passport control at the **Israeli arrivals terminal**, you should be loud and clear in asking for your passport not to be stamped: many travellers have reported the Israeli immigration officials forgetting after being asked only once. After the formalities, there's a **bank** to change money, although Palestinian businesses throughout the West Bank generally accept Jordanian dinars. A serveece (*sheroot* in Hebrew) will be waiting just outside; the one-hour ride to **East Jerusalem**, dropping you at the Damascus Gate of the Old City, costs a fixed JD6 or 35 Israeli shekels (NIS). If you walk out of the bridge terminal and to your right, you'll find the exit area from the locals' building, where you can pick up dirt-cheap buses to **West Bank** destinations such as Jericho, Bethlehem and Ramallah, though rarely Jerusalem.

Gaza International Airport – opened in 1998, and formerly linked to Amman by regular flights – had its runway ripped up by Israeli bulldozers in 2002 and, at the time of writing, remains out of action.

Amman–Jerusalem: the bureaucracy

The contradictory **bureaucracy** surrounding the journey from Amman to Jerusalem is grotesque. The **Jordanians** view the West Bank as being intimately linked with Jordan: if you have a single-entry Jordanian visa and cross the King Hussein/Allenby Bridge to spend time in the West Bank or Israel, then return *the same way* to Jordan, the Jordanians don't see you as ever having left the country and you don't need to buy a new Jordanian visa, as long as your current one is still within its validity (bear in mind, though, the crippling cost of the Israeli departure tax – see p.38). You must buy a new Jordanian visa, though, if you return to the country having used any other route out or in.

However, once you cross the King Hussein Bridge from Jordan into the West Bank, the **Israeli** authorities view you as arriving in Israel proper, and routinely issue free tourist visas on arrival, valid throughout Israeli- and **Palestinian**-administered West Bank territory and Israel itself (as yet, the Palestinians do not issue their own visas). As a foreigner, you'll be waved through any checkpoints on the "Green Line" between the West Bank and Israel proper, a border you'll find marked on Jordanian maps but not Israeli ones.

To Tel Aviv and Nazareth

Direct **buses** run from Amman to the Israeli cities of **Tel Aviv** (Sun–Fri 8.30am; JD21 or NIS150) and **Nazareth** (daily 8.30am; JD18 or NIS120). Buses drop off in Lower Nazareth, and terminate at Tel Aviv's Central Bus Station. Trust International Transport (T06/581 3427) is the Jordanian side of the operation. All buses leave from outside their office, which is located near Safeway and the Royal Jordanian building just off 7th Circle. They avoid travelling through the West Bank, instead using the northern **Sheikh Hussein Bridge**, located between Irbid (where they pick up passengers) and the Israeli town of Bet She'an. You should arrive half an hour before stated departure times for police searches.

There's normally at least one **flight** a day from Amman to Tel Aviv on Royal Wings (T06/487 5202, Wwww.royalwings.com.jo), a subsidiary of Royal Jordanian. Flights depart either from Marka Airport or Queen Alia International, depending on the day, and fares are around JD71 one-way, JD126 for a three-month return, or JD142 for an open return.

To Syria and Lebanon

There are many ways to reach **Damascus** from Amman, varying greatly in cost, duration and comfort. However, before you embark on any of them, you must have a valid entry visa for Syria: see the box on p.161 for details.

The simplest method of reaching Damascus is by **serveece** from any of the private companies lining the road either side of Abdali station. The cars are roomy 1970s-vintage Chevrolets or Dodges, and the sign of a part-filled serveece waiting for passengers is an open boot (trunk). As soon as you approach, the driver will start touting for business with "Shum, Shum, Shum!" (one of the Arabic names for Damascus). Although you may have to bargain, the real fare is JD6 per person, or JD30 for the whole car (seating five). Serveeces head out at all hours of the day and night, so you never have to wait too long, and – aside from the driver stashing a few bits and pieces on the way to sell in Syria – they go fast and direct in around three hours. You can also book a serveece one day ahead and arrange a pick-up from your hotel; a good company for this is Al-Saqer (T06/462 5576). Cars with Jordanian number-plates terminate in central Damascus at the *Karaj al-Urdun* (Jordan Garage), next to the long-distance bus station; those with Syrian plates can drop you off wherever you like for a few dollars more.

Scheduled **buses** to Damascus operated by JETT and Karnak (the Syrian state-owned bus company) are cheaper than serveeces but slower, partly since they have to wait for everyone to clear passport control before continuing. Daily departures are at 7am (JETT) and 3pm (Karnak), with up to four or five extra buses in high summer; the fare is JD5. Plenty of other companies dotted around Abdali also go to Damascus, on various schedules day and night; Afana (℡06/568 1560) is one. JETT also has a bus departing daily at 2.30pm to **Homs** (JD6), **Hama** (JD7) and **Aleppo** (JD7.500), as well as three buses a week (Sat, Tues & Thurs) to **Beirut** (JD15), for which you must already hold a valid Syrian visa. The same cities are also served by Afana and others.

The longest and least comfortable method of reaching Damascus is also the cheapest and most atmospheric: by **train**. A decrepit diesel leaves Amman's Hejaz Station (℡06/489 5413) every Monday and Thursday at 8am for the nine-hour meander to the Hejaz Station in central Damascus, stopping midway at Dera'a (from where there are frequent microbuses to the Roman ruins at Bosra). The fare is a rock-bottom JD2.750; turn up thirty minutes early to buy your ticket. As an added incentive, it has been known for a steam engine to be hooked up for the beautiful journey from the Syrian border into Damascus.

Flights from Amman to Damascus are too expensive and time-consuming to bother with. However, flying to Aleppo can save a lot of time over the equivalent road journey – Royal Wings currently operates the route, which is short but pricey (1hr 30min; JD130 one-way; ℡06/487 5202).

To Egypt, Saudi Arabia and beyond

The main Jordanian bus operator to cities around the Middle East is JETT; their "external lines" office and departure point (℡06/569 6151) is just uphill from their domestic office north of Abdali station. Afana (℡06/568 1560), with ticket offices at Abdali station and alongside the JETT external lines office, is a major competitor.

Although there are direct buses between Amman and **Cairo**, they are neither very pleasant nor very economical. Unless speed is absolutely of the essence (in which case flying is a better option), you'd do far better to break your journey in Aqaba and/or the Sinai along the way. Either way, you need a full Egyptian **visa** (see p.160). The fare on JETT (Sat, Sun, Tues & Thurs 6.30am; 21hr; US$58), payable in dollars only, includes the ferry from Aqaba to Nuweiba but not the JD5 departure tax. Buses terminate either at the office of the Arab Union Bus Company at Midan Almaza in Heliopolis (Masr el-Gedida) or at the Turgoman Garage in Bulaq. It's advisable to book up to a week ahead. Plenty of other Abdali-based companies compete (including Afana), most of them undercutting JETT in both price and comfort. Royal Jordanian and EgyptAir operate expensive daily flights to Cairo, and there are both scheduled and charter flights on Royal Wings (℡06/487 5202) to **Sharm el-Sheikh** (JD100 one-way), with flights also proposed to **Alexandria**.

Other destinations on JETT include daily buses to **Jeddah**, **Riyadh** and **Dammam** (change at Dammam for **Bahrain**, **Qatar** and the **Emirates**), less frequent buses to **Medina** and other Saudi cities, twice-weekly buses to **Kuwait** and several buses a week to **Baghdad**. Afana competes on all these routes, and you'll also find a host of private serveece and bus companies heading to Baghdad cheaply from various spots in Downtown. Several bus companies in and around Abdali are happy to quote you for seats on overland buses to cities even further afield, in **Turkey**, **Yemen** and **Libya**.

Jordan may well benefit from the growth of small **budget airlines** in the Middle East: air fares on new low-cost routes linking Amman to cities such as Sharjah, Beirut or Bahrain could compete favourably with the equivalent costs and difficulties of travelling overland.

Listings

Airlines Aeroflot ☎06/552 1643; Air Canada ☎06/463 0879; Air France ☎06/569 8317; Alitalia ☎06/462 5203; American ☎06/566 9068; Austrian ☎06/566 0449; British Airways/British Mediterranean ☎06/582 8801; Bulgarian ☎06/566 1266; Continental ☎06/568 2140; Cyprus ☎06/461 3680; Delta ☎06/464 3661; EgyptAir ☎06/463 0011; El Al ☎06/562 2526; Emirates ☎06/464 3341; Gulf Air ☎06/465 3613; IranAir ☎06/463 0879; Iraqi ☎06/463 8600; KLM ☎06/465 5267; Kuwaiti ☎06/569 0144; Lufthansa ☎06/560 1744; Malev ☎06/464 0200; MEA (Lebanese) ☎06/463 6104; Olympic ☎06/566 4871; Pakistani ☎06/462 5981; Palestinian ☎06/569 5876; Qatar ☎06/567 7414; Royal Jordanian ☎06/567 8321; Royal Wings ☎06/487 5202; Saudi Arabian ☎06/552 7755; Syrian ☎06/462 2147; Tarom ☎06/461 3670; Turkish ☎06/465 9112; Yemen ☎06/551 4165. **Airport** See p.112.

Banks and exchange For full details on changing money and using credit or debit cards, see p.50.

Children's activities The Haya Centre (Mon, Wed, Thurs, Sat & Sun 8.30am–5pm; in summer, also Tues 8.30am–2pm; ☎06/566 5195), opposite *KFC* in Shmeisani, has plays, puppet theatre, music and loads of courses and activities for children. English-speaking families are welcome to use the facilities (there's a small admission charge; unaccompanied adults are not admitted; English summary-sheet available), which include a safe and monitored sandy playground with an adjacent café for tired parents, a kids' library and a small planetarium. The Luna Park (daily 10am–10pm), in King Abdullah Gardens on Wadi Saqra Circle, has a great cable-car ride. Kids will also appreciate a visit to Mecca Mall (Sat–Thurs 10am–10pm, Fri 2–10pm), at the western end of Mecca Street, in which – among other child-friendly diversions – lies "Jungle Bungle", a great adventure activity zone. Teenagers will love paintballing in the forests north of Amman (see ⓦ www.jordanpaintball .com), while just over 12km south of 7th Circle is Amman Waves, Jordan's first aqua park, open in summer only.

Cultural centres and libraries The library of the British Council (Rainbow St, 300m from 1st Circle; Sun–Thurs 9am–6.30pm; ☎06/463 6147, ⓦ www .britishcouncil.org.jo) is a bit frumpy, though the section on Jordan has many out-of-print classics. The American Resource Center library, in the American Embassy, Abdoun (Sun–Wed 1–4.30pm, Thurs 9am–4.30pm; ☎06/592 0101, ⓦ amman .usembassy.gov) isn't bad either. Both have newspapers and magazines. Other cultural centres with libraries include: Centre Culturel Français, just off Lweibdeh Circle (Sun–Thurs 10am–6pm; ☎06/461 2658, ⓦ www.cccljor-jo.org); the Goethe Institut (German), off 3rd Circle (Sun–Wed 8.30am–2pm & 3.30–6pm, Thurs 8.30am–2pm; ☎06/464 1993, ⓦ www.goethe.de/na/amm); and the Instituto Cervantes (Spanish), behind the *Inter-Continental Hotel*, near 3rd Circle (Sun & Wed 11.30am–7pm, Mon, Tues & Thurs 11am–2pm & 4.30–8pm; ☎06/461 0858, ⓦ amman.cervantes.es). Darat al-Funun (see p.138) has a superb art library. Excellent historical libraries are run by the following: American Center of Oriental Research (ACOR) in Tla'a al-Ali (☎06/534 6117); CERMOC, a French research centre near 3rd Circle (☎06/461 1171); the Council for British Research in the Levant, Jubayha (☎06/534 1317); and the Department of Antiquities, behind 3rd Circle (☎06/464 4336).

Embassies and consulates Australian ☎06/580 7000, ⓕ580 7001, ⓦ www.jordan.embassy.gov.au; Canadian ☎06/566 6126, ⓕ568 9227, ⓦ www .dfait-maeci.gc.ca; Irish ☎06/551 6807, ⓕ551 6804, ⓦ www.foreignaffairs.gov.ie; New Zealand ☎06/463 6720, ⓕ463 4349, ⓦ www .mfat.govt.nz; UK ☎06/590 9200, ⓕ590 9279, ⓦ www.britain.org.jo; US ☎06/592 0101, ⓕ592 0136, ⓦ amman.usembassy.gov. Most are open Sun–Thurs 10am–noon at the least.

Emergencies Police ☎191; ambulance ☎193; fire ☎06/462 2090 or 461 7101; traffic police (in the city) ☎06/465 6390; traffic accidents ☎06/489 6390; highway police ☎06/534 3402.

Gliding For a paltry JD15/hr or so, the Royal Jordanian Gliding Club, based at Marka Airport, can take up one passenger at a time for a unique, silent view of Amman from above. They fly at limited times so you should call ahead to book on ☎06/487 4587.

Hospital The Khalidi Hospital (☎06/464 4281) near 4th Circle, is one of the best in Jordan, and has a 24hr emergency room.

Internet Amman has countless internet centres, offering access for about JD1–1.500/hr: the densest concentrations are near the Raghadan station in Downtown and opposite the main gates of Jordan University, though you'll have little trouble finding one in most neighbourhoods. All luxury hotels (and many mid-range and budget hotels) offer access. The two most pleasant places to surf are near each other off Rainbow St: *Books@Café* (see p.145) and the *Wild Jordan* café (see p.145), which both have music, good coffee and a pleasant smoke-free atmosphere (JD2/hr).

Laundry There are laundries all over Downtown; ask your hotel first. One of the most reliable – though not exactly speedy (normal turnaround time is at least 24hr) – is *Alf Lown wa Lown* or "The Thousand and One Colours" (Sat–Wed 8.30am–4.30pm); standing with the *Cliff Hotel* behind you, cross the street, head up the hill 10m, turn right and it's the third shop on the left. They can do a normal-sized load for about JD4, priced piece by piece, with ironing extra.

Mail The most convenient post office for everyday business is the big Downtown office (daily 7.30am–7pm, Fri until 1.30pm; hours slightly curtailed in winter) signed on Prince Muhammad St, 50m from the *Cliff Hotel*. Street vendors sell paper and envelopes nearby. This is where poste restante mail will end up. To send a parcel (Sat–Thurs 7.30am–2pm), first take it unwrapped to be checked by the Customs Department, which is through an unmarked gateway on the left halfway up the hill behind the Downtown post office. Then take it across the street to the Parcels Office, seal it up, fill out a dispatch form and pay the money. Smaller post offices, which keep the same hours as the Downtown post office, include: on 1st Circle (down the steps opposite the Saudi consulate); in the forecourt of the *Inter-Continental Hotel* between 2nd and 3rd Circles; a few doors down from the Centre Culturel Français off Lweibdeh Circle; and under the Housing Bank Centre in Shmeisani. For sending valuables, you're better off using international couriers such as Aramex (☎06/551 5111, ⓦwww.aramex.com), DHL (☎06/585 8514, ⓦwww.dhl.com) or FedEx (☎06/551 1460, ⓦwww.fedex.com).

Pharmacies The most efficient pharmacy is Jacob's on 3rd Circle (daily 8.30am–midnight). Names and numbers of doctors on night duty and 24hr pharmacies are listed daily in the *Jordan Times*.

Petrol stations There are 24hr stations all over the city, including near Downtown on Prince Muhammad St; in West Amman at 7th and 8th Circles, on the Airport Road, Gardens St, University St and near the *Regency Palace* hotel; and on the highways northeast to Zarqa and southeast to Azraq. All these have *soober*.

Police and complaints The courteous and efficient English-speaking tourist police are on duty at the Jebel al-Qal'a ruins (daily 24hr; ☎06/464 1151); their headquarters are at 8th Circle (☎06/586 1271). The Downtown police station is halfway along King Faysal St, opposite the Arab Bank, look for a plain doorway leading up some stairs; there's also a police station opposite the *Inter-Continental Hotel*. In other areas, or if you're in real distress, tell any passer-by that you want the *buleece* (police), and someone is bound to help; see also "Emergencies" opposite.

Travel agents Downtown travel agents, which can knock only a few dinars off the airlines' prices, are concentrated along King Hussein St. The best is Rainbow (☎06/462 1652), but it's worth comparing prices in Nahas (☎06/462 5535) and Pan Pacific (☎06/462 1688) on the same street. Beware of agents who take backhanders from certain airlines to promote their routes over others which may be cheaper and/or more convenient – it's worth asking around to get the full picture. You'll also spot travel agents in most West Amman neighbourhoods, including the main drag in Shmeisani.

Visa extensions To extend your visa beyond the standard thirty days, you must register with the police. If you're staying in Downtown, the relevant station is directly opposite Muhajireen bus station; if you're staying uptown, register at the Zahran police station, virtually opposite the *Inter-Continental Hotel*. However, if you entered Jordan from the West Bank or Israel and kept your passport free of stamps, you must register your visa extension instead at the Directorate of Residency and Borders, located on Majed al-Idwan street near the *Howard Johnson* hotel in Shmeisani: at the T-junction just beyond *Burger King*, turn right and it's the second street on the left. Alternatively, ask your hotel to call the Ministry of the Interior on ☎06/569 1141 for directions.

Travel details

Since most buses and all minibuses and serveeces simply depart whenever they are full, regularity of service is indicated only when a fixed timetable is in operation.

Buses, minibuses and serveeces

Abdali station to: Ajloun (1hr 30min); Dayr Alla (1hr); Fuheis (35min); Irbid (New Amman station; every 15min; 1hr 15min to 2hr); Jerash (1hr); King Hussein Bridge (1hr); Madaba (30min); Mafraq (Bedouin station; 1hr); Queen Alia Airport (every 30min; 45min); Ramtha (2hr); Salt (35min); Sweileh (15min); Zarqa (New station; 35min).

JETT office, Abdali to: Aqaba (6–8 daily; 4hr); Hammamat Ma'in (1 on Fri; 1hr 30min); King Hussein Bridge (1 daily; 1hr).

Muhajireen station to: Dead Sea ("Amman Beach"; 1hr 30min); Madaba (30min); Shuneh al-Janubiyyeh (1hr); Wadi Seer (25min).

Queen Alia Airport to: Abdali station (every 30min; 45min).

Raghadan station to: Madaba (30min); Muwaggar (30min); Salt (40min); Wadi Seer (30min); Zarqa (New station; 25min).

Wihdat station to: Aqaba (4–5hr); Hammamat Ma'in (2hr); Karak (2hr); Ma'an (2hr 30min); Madaba (30min); Shobak (2hr 45min); Tafileh (2hr 30min); Wadi Musa/Petra (3hr).

Domestic flights

Amman (Queen Alia or Marka airports) to: Aqaba (1–2 daily; 50min).

International routes

Buses and serveeces

This is a summary of principal routes.

Abdali station to: Abu Dhabi (36hr); Aleppo (10–18hr); Baghdad (10–18hr); Beirut (8–12hr); Cairo (15–28hr); Damascus (3–7hr); Dammam (28hr); Dubai (36hr); Istanbul (48hr); Jeddah (24hr); Riyadh (24hr).

JETT office, Abdali to: Baghdad (3 weekly; 15hr); Cairo (2 weekly; 21hr); Damascus (2 daily; 3hr 30min); Dammam (1 daily; 24–28hr); Jeddah (1 daily; 20–24hr); Kuwait City (1 weekly; 24–28hr); Riyadh (1 daily; 20–24hr).

Mahatta, Army Street to: Baghdad (10–18hr).

Trust office, 7th Circle to: Nazareth (1 daily; 4hr); Tel Aviv (1 daily except Sat; 6hr).

Trains

Hejaz station to: Damascus (2 weekly; 9hr).

Useful Arabic place names

Amman   عمّان

Within Amman

1st Circle	الدوار الاول	Jebel al-Qal'a	جبل القلعة
2nd Circle	الدوار الثاني	JETT station	مجمع جيت
3rd Circle	الدوار الثالث	Jordan University	جامعة الاردنية
4th Circle	الدوار الرابع	Kan Zaman	كان زمان
5th Circle	الدوار الخامس	Marka	ماركا
6th Circle	الدوار السادس	Middle East Circle	دوار الشرق الاوسط
7th Circle	الدوار السابع	Muhajireen station	مجمع المهاجرين
8th Circle	الدوار الثامن	Raghadan station	مجمع رغدان
Abdali	العبدلي	Ras al-Ain	راس العين
Abdali station	مجمع العبدلي	Sahab	سحاب
Abdoun	عبدون	Shmeisani	الشميساني
Ahl al-Kahf	اهل الكهف	Sport City	المدينة الرياضية
Downtown	وسط البلد	Sweifiyyeh	الصويفية
Hejaz train station	محطة السكة الحديد	Umm Uthayna	ام اذينة
Interior Circle	الدوار الداخلية	Tla'a al-Ali	تلاع العلي
Jebel Amman	جبل عمّان	Trust office	مكتب شركة الثقة
Jebel al-Ashrafiyyeh	جبل الاشرفية	Wihdat	الوحدات
Jebel Hussein	جبل الحسين	Wihdat station	مجمع الجنوب
Jebel al-Lweibdeh	جبل اللويبدة		

Near Amman

Baptism Site	المغطس	Queen Alia Airport	مطار الملكة علياء
Dead Sea	البحر الميّت	Sweileh	صويلح
King Hussein Bridge	جسر الملك حسين	Zarqa	الزرقاء

(For destinations further afield in Jordan, see the end of each relevant chapter).

Outside Jordan

Beirut	بيروت	Jericho	اريحا
Cairo	القاهرة	Jerusalem	القدس
Damascus	دمشق	Nazareth	الناصرة
Dera'a	درعا	Tel Aviv	تل ابيب

2

The Dead Sea
and around

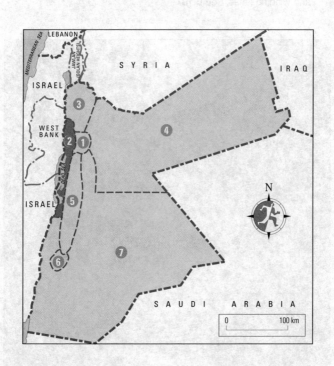

CHAPTER 2 # Highlights

* **The Dead Sea** Float your day away at the lowest point on earth. See p.171

* **Baptism Site** Widely accepted location of Jesus's baptism, on the banks of the River Jordan. See p.180

* **Salt** Elegant Ottoman-era hilltown of honeystone villas and winding lanes. See p.187

* **Fuheis** Wander the peaceful alleys of this picturesque backwater town in the scenic Balqa hills. See p.189

* **Qasr al-Abd** A white Hellenistic palace in the Amman countryside. See p.192

△ The Dead Sea

2

The Dead Sea
and around

Barely a handful of kilometres west of Amman's city limits, the rugged highlands of central and northern Jordan drop away dramatically into the Dead Sea rift. This giant valley marks a geological dividing line as well as a political one, with the Arabian plate to the east shifting a few centimetres a year northwards, and the African plate to the west moving slowly southwards. Between the two is the River Jordan, defining Jordan's western border as it flows into the large, salty inland lake of the **Dead Sea**, famed as the lowest point on earth.

This whole area is within easy reach of the capital, and serves for many visitors as an alternative base – on the shore of the Dead Sea are ranged a fistful of superb luxury hotels. It also works well as the source of some choice day-trips. Taking a dip in the Dead Sea and relaxing on its salty beaches should form an unmissable part of anyone's itinerary, and you'll also find, in the rolling hills of the Balqa region that rise towards Amman, some low-key, generally untouristed small towns and villages, such as the graceful old Ottoman capital **Salt** and its neighbour **Fuheis**, that bring a refreshing change from the hustle and bustle of the big city.

The area's main historical draw is the most authoritative and best-documented candidate for the **Baptism Site** of Jesus, located on the east bank of the River Jordan about 8km north of the Dead Sea shore. The combination of archeology, the extraordinary natural environment and the momentous religious associations of the place mean that this is one of the Middle East's most important religious destinations. Continuing the biblical theme, in the barren hills overlooking the southeastern part of the Dead Sea is **Lot's Cave**, the generally accepted location of the bolthole where Abraham's nephew sought refuge from the destruction of Sodom and Gomorrah. Nearby, tantalizing shreds of evidence for the existence of the razed cities themselves have been found.

The Dead Sea

Oppressively hot most of the year, smelly, desolate and flanked by dry, salty beaches, the amazing **DEAD SEA** (*al-Bahr al-Mayit* in Arabic) is a major

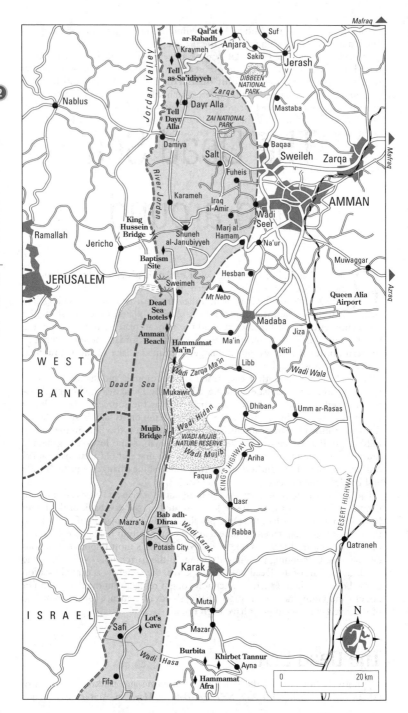

highlight of a visit to the Middle East. Swimming in it is a memorable experience, quite unlike anything else on the planet.

The lake occupies the Great Rift Valley, a deep geological cleft which can be traced from Turkey all the way into East Africa. Its shoreline – at 400m below sea level – marks **the lowest point on Earth**. The Dead Sea got its name in antiquity due to its uniquely salty water, which kills off virtually all marine life: seawater is about three or four percent salt, but Dead Sea water is over thirty percent. It is fed mainly by the River Jordan, flowing south from Galilee, but due to the geological upheavals it has no outflow; instead, water evaporates off the surface at the rate of millions of litres a day, leading to continuous precipitation of salt onto the beach and a thick atmospheric haze overhead which dampens sound down to almost nothing – there's little to hear but lapping water anyway. The haze also filters out harmful UVB sunrays, handily allowing tanning but not burning.

The major reason for a visit, though, is that the lake's high salinity makes the water so **buoyant** that it's literally impossible to sink; Olympic swimmers and hopeless paddlers alike become bobbing corks. As you walk in, you'll find your feet are forced up from under you – you couldn't touch the bottom if you tried and if you lie back you'll find the water supports you like a cradle. You ride too high in the water to swim, and should you attempt a few strokes you'll find you just splash ineffectually and are likely to get water in your eyes, which is a very unpleasant experience. The salt will also make you very aware of every little cut and open blemish on your skin. Nonetheless, the sensation of floating completely unaided and silent on a flat, hot sea surrounded by hazy mountains is worth the discomfort.

Other diversions include covering yourself in the hot, sulphurous black **mud** which collects in pools on the beach; letting it dry in the sun before washing it off will leave you with tingling muscles and baby-soft skin. However, scorching heat (well over 40°C in summer) and exceptionally low humidity make **dehydration** a real danger, and while you're out in the open you should be drinking twice or three times as much water as normal to compensate.

Practicalities

Access routes to the Dead Sea are plentiful, with a major highway from Amman branching off from the Airport Road, and several minor roads – some signed, many unsigned – heading down through the hills. With your own transport, it's easy to construct a circular day-trip route from either Amman or Madaba to take in the Baptism Site, the Dead Sea and Mount Nebo (see p.289).

Buses from Amman for the Dead Sea leave from Muhajireen station. Early-morning buses (7–9am) run direct to the "Amman Beach" complex (see p.177), but only if there's demand – guaranteed on a Friday. Others may stop short at the major crossroads town of **Shuneh al-Janubiyyeh** (see p.191), about 15km north in the Jordan Valley. You can also reach Shuneh by bus from Salt, Dayr Alla and Madaba (via Mount Nebo). From the crossroads in the middle of Shuneh, frequent minibuses head to the village of **Sweimeh**, 3km northeast of the hotel zone; the driver might be willing to take you on to Amman Beach for a little extra. The last bus direct to Amman from Amman Beach departs around 5pm, the last from Shuneh around 6pm (both an hour or two earlier in winter). If you miss these, you'll either have to get a bus to Salt, from where buses run later to Amman, or resort to the common practice on this road of hitchhiking. Marriott runs a frequent daily shuttle bus service between the *Jordan Valley Marriott* on the Dead Sea and the *Amman Marriott* hotel in the capital – in theory for guests only, but you may be able to blag a seat if you look the part.

The dying Dead Sea

Despite its name, there is life in the Dead Sea, though you won't lose your toes to it: only three species of **bacteria** and one of **algae** can withstand the concentrations of salt. The relationship between them is a neat adaptation to difficult circumstances, though human intervention is making things more difficult still. The bacteria are considerably more tolerant of high salinity levels than the algae, so when salinity in the lake rises, the algae vanish and the bacteria – which normally feed on them – are forced to rely on sunlight alone for nutrition. When salinity drops, the algae reappear and the bacteria thrive, their feeding turning the lake a beautiful purplish-pink colour. However, with the diversion of more and more water out of the Sea of Galilee and the River Jordan further upstream, the amount of sweet water reaching the lake has been dropping in recent decades and thus salinity has been steadily rising, keeping the algae away. The purplish bacterial bloom has occurred only three times since 1964, and looks increasingly unlikely ever to happen again.

Indeed, the whole future of the lake is in doubt. Since the 1960s, greater and greater inroads have been made into its **freshwater sources**, and today far more water evaporates from the lake than flows into it. There are several dams across the River Jordan (as well as across its tributary, the Yarmouk), and – as part of its national water-conservation programme – Jordan has dammed all the major rivers in its territory that formerly flowed directly into the Dead Sea (including the Zarqa Ma'in, the Mujib and the Hasa). In addition, both Israel and Jordan have developed major mineral and potash industries at the southern end of the lake which depend on large-scale evaporation for production.

In the 1950s, the lake's surface area was about a thousand square kilometres; today, it's less than seven hundred and still falling. The water level has already dropped by a massive 25m, and is continuing to fall by a metre a year. Since the 1970s, **Lynch's Strait**, a channel of water which formerly connected the northern and southern parts of the lake, has dried out, turning the Lisan Peninsula – once a promontory sticking out into the lake's southern half – into a landbridge. Dangerous sinkholes are opening up in the soft ground on both shores. If things continue as they are, the Dead Sea will dry up in a matter of decades.

This ongoing ecological disaster has, perhaps surprisingly, focused minds on cooperation. At the **Johannesburg Earth Summit** in 2002, the Israeli and Jordanian governments called for concerted action to save the Dead Sea. They launched a plan – with the Palestinian Authority – to build a conduit canal to bring seawater some 250km north from the Red Sea at Aqaba to replenish the Dead Sea: the so-called **Red-Dead Conveyance Canal**. Its 400m drop in altitude would mean that large quantities of hydro-electric power could be generated, and there would also be shared desalination plants creating up to 850 million cubic metres of potable water a year by reverse osmosis, thus substantially easing the critical shortage of water in the region. The brine residue left after desalination would then be pumped into the Dead Sea to restore its natural water level. At the time of writing, a feasibility study – funded by the World Bank – is under way.

However, not everyone is in agreement. **Friends of the Earth Middle East** (ⓦ www .foeme.org), a coalition of Israeli, Palestinian and Jordanian environmental groups, has voiced several concerns – not least that it would take ten years to implement the Red-Dead plan whereas the Dead Sea needs immediate action. In addition, as it currently stands, the Red-Dead scheme allows the unplanned exploitation of the Dead Sea's resources to continue, with no bar on the numbers of hotels being built, and no imperative for sustainable development. There have, as yet, also been no detailed environmental studies on how the addition of huge quantities of seawater might affect the Dead Sea's delicate ecological balance – or on the possible impact of a pipeline breach in the open desert. Time will tell whether the Red-Dead canal is the answer.

Note that bus routes may well change if the public beach north of the *Marriott* – alongside the old *Dead Sea Resthouse* – ever reopens.

The Dead Sea hotels and beaches

At the end of the main highway down from Amman is a T-junction: the highway bends left towards the Dead Sea shoreline hotels, while a minor road heads right to the Baptism Site (see p.180). The old road to Jerusalem formerly led straight on at this junction, but the King Abdullah Bridge which carried it over the river was bombed in the 1967 war and was never rebuilt; it has now been superseded by the King Hussein Bridge 8km upstream.

The only developed **beaches** along Jordan's shoreline are at the lake's north-eastern corner (the western shore is half in the West Bank and half in Israel) – the remainder of the long shoreline remains mostly undeveloped. The Dead Sea is a popular spot for a weekend outing, and roads and facilities all along the shore can get very crowded on Fridays. In general, foreign **women** should exercise caution before stripping off for a dip; bikinis and regular swimwear are fine at the hotel beaches and Amman Beach, but elsewhere a T-shirt and long shorts are a minimum. One thing to bear in mind, if you're planning to avoid the big hotels, is that you should take a dip near a place that supplies **freshwater showers**: Dead Sea brine is thick and oily, and leaves an uncomfortable layer of salt on your skin that you'll want to wash off quickly. Outside the developed public or hotel beaches, which offer gravelly sand and varying levels of facilities, jagged, salt-encrusted rocks line the whole length of the shore.

A high proportion of foreign visitors to the Dead Sea arrive for what's been called **therapeutic tourism**: both the waters and the mud have medically proven benefits, putting many severe skin diseases and joint problems into long-term remission. Calcium, magnesium, bromine, sulphur and bitumen – all with beneficial properties – are found in extremely high concentrations, and, in addition, the air is very highly oxygenated, due to the combination of high rates of evaporation, high temperatures, high atmospheric pressure and low humidity. Celebrated skin-care products from the Dead Sea can be bought all over the country, and internationally. Though well developed on the Israeli shore, therapeutic tourism is a relatively new field for Jordan, currently concentrated at medical centres in the big hotels, which are often booked solid for months ahead.

The first beach you come to was formerly occupied by the *Dead Sea Resthouse* – a rather shabby affair that was closed recently for complete renovations. At the time of writing its future was uncertain.

About 5km further south is Jordan's most prestigious **luxury hotel** zone, easily able to match in style, sophistication and facilities the clumps of five-star hotels which have long been a fixture on the Israeli shore, while also undercutting them considerably in price. There are now well over a thousand hotel beds in this area, all of them four- or five-star, complete with showers, bathtubs, flushing toilets and a fairly extensive acreage of irrigated and hand-watered flowers and trees, planted in what is naturally barren, salty soil. All the fresh water for this hotel strip is piped from Wadi Mujib, approval having been granted for this in the face of protests from the Royal Society for the Conservation of Nature; there is now considerable concern on the part of the RSCN and others about the damage being caused to the fragile ecosystems of the lower Mujib due to decreased flow-rates. In addition to the three big hotels listed below, there are plans for more to go up on this shoreline in the near future – including a five-star **Kempinski** and a hotels-and-aquapark complex named **Crystal City**. In such a desperately water-poor country, it's a moot point whether all this luxury development is entirely a good thing.

Jordan Valley Marriott

The northernmost hotel in the zone is the spectacular **Jordan Valley Marriott Resort and Spa** (℡05/356 0400, ℻356 0444, ⓦwww.marriott .com; ❾), built in a large U-shape around three swimming pools – including an infinity pool facing west across the Dead Sea. Its public areas are spacious, airy and well designed, while the 216 air-conditioned guest rooms are exceptional, with everything from king-size beds to high-speed internet. Twelve cafés and restaurants occupy several levels within the main reception building and seafront locations across the site, including outlets for Italian, Arabic, Asian and French brasserie-style cuisine, plus seafood and even a branch of the "Champions" sports bar, serving cold beers and Tex-Mex dishes and showing live sports events on TV. The hotel has two cinemas, as well as diversions such as beach volleyball, a tennis court and live sunset entertainment at a small amphitheatre arena. The large onsite **spa** facility has a range of offerings, from straightforward neck-rubs to multi-day treatments, many of which include exfoliation with natural Dead Sea salts, mud packs and massages. Down at the beach – which, like all along this shore, is narrow and gritty – there are full pre- and post-float facilities, including changing areas, toilets and open freshwater showers.

Dead Sea Mövenpick

Alongside – and vying with the *Marriott* for the title of best hotel in Jordan – is the extraordinary **Dead Sea Mövenpick Resort and Spa** (℡05/356 1111, ℻356 1122, ⓦwww.movenpick.com; ❾), which occupies a large swathe of land sloping from the highway several hundred metres down to the shore. It fulfils every requirement of international five-star luxury, but manages to do so with unusual taste and character. The main buildings are set back from the road, and the lobby is supremely elegant – cooled, in a piece of profound eco-folly, by a flowing artificial stream and waterfall – while the bar features a stunning wooden ceiling, hand-carved in Damascene style. The main restaurant, *al-Saraya*, has excellent buffet-style meals from about JD8 upwards. Below the main buildings, the guest rooms are housed in two-storey buildings of local stone and plaster, superbly designed to imitate and blend in with the lumpy Dead Sea landscape of low, rounded marl hills; they're arranged around a succession of quiet, village-style courtyards featuring tinkling fountains and set among exotic flower gardens, all with shaded balconies and full amenities. Further down the complex are a variety of restaurants – Italian, Asian, *haute cuisine* – plus a small amphitheatre for live music at sunset, a large open-air pool, and steps leading down to the beach. Off to one side is the ultra-chic **Zara Spa**, the largest such complex in the Middle East, with a vast range of treatments ranging from mud facials, express pedicures or full-body Swedish massages up to full-day programmes of treatments for JD100 plus.

Dead Sea Spa Hotel

Some 50m south is the four-star **Dead Sea Spa Hotel** (℡05/356 1000, ℻356 1012, ⓔdssh@nets.com.jo; ❾), which for years was out on its own here. With the recent rise in prestige value of the neighbourhood, this formerly soulless place has undergone a top-to-bottom revamp and is now a solid quality choice – especially good for day-trippers or weekenders looking to avoid splurging at the bigger hotels. Guest rooms are large and comfortable, complete with all the trimmings, and the on-site medical centre was the pioneer for therapeutic tourism in Jordan.

Amman Beach

Some 2km south of the hotel zone is the **Amman Beach** complex. Don't be fooled by the name: Amman is a good three-quarters of an hour away and over 1200m up in the hills. At the time of writing, this is the Dead Sea's only **public beach**, and it's also the most straightforward, easily accessible low-budget option for Dead Sea beach-bumming – not least because the main car park serves as the terminus for public buses from Amman and elsewhere. It's a well-run place open 24 hours a day, with trees, plenty of shade and even patches of lawn; admission for non-Jordanians is JD4. Spread around the site are plenty of facilities for children, including a play park and various beach games; there's a decent restaurant with affordably priced buffet meals available until around 10pm daily; and there are good-quality beach facilities, including separate male and female changing areas, lockers, towel-rental (JD1) and freshwater showers. You can also **pitch a tent** here (JD8).

South along the Dead Sea road

South of Amman Beach, the Dead Sea road runs along the shoreline, entering the Wadi Araba (see p.424) and eventually arriving at Aqaba 278km away. Some Amman–Aqaba **buses** use this road, but they don't stop at all; this is principally a good, fast **driving route** (as long as you take care to dodge the lumbering potash trucks, which make up the road's principal traffic). The **scenery** all the way down is spectacular, with the deep blue of the Dead Sea framed by the mountains opposite and speckled with white outcrops of salt.

After 12km you come to a series of hot-spring outflows at **Zara**, downstream from the hot waterfalls of Hammamat Ma'in (see p.293). Zara's secluded valleys are popular with day-trippers, but women should be careful to show their skin only within the small, all-female shack close to the shore (ask the locals for directions): splashing around in public in the river is the preserve only of the fully clothed or male. This is a very popular Friday outing spot, with cars lined up along the highway, and people alternating between dipping in the Dead Sea and washing the salt off in the warm spring water. A few hundred metres south of Zara are the remains of King Herod's baths and Dead Sea port at **Callirhoë**, although there's little left to see other than a handful of column drums and the remnants of a harbour wall.

Some 15km further south is the **Mujib Bridge**, a graceful 140-metre construction crossing the outflow of the River Mujib, which is the centre-piece of a protected nature reserve (for more, see p.300). A small, attractively designed building below the bridge, on the cliff side of the road, is an office

---

Gorge-walking down to the Dead Sea

The deep, lushly watered gorges that cut through the mountains east of the Dead Sea feature some of Jordan's most memorable (and testing) **gorge-walking** routes, following hot mineral springs through dramatic canyons down to the Dead Sea shore. Most of these gorges are accessed from points up in the hills – for example, **Hammamat Ma'in** (see p.294). A few, though, can be accessed from the Dead Sea side, most notably those exploring the lower stretches of the **Wadi Mujib** nature reserve (see p.301). All these gorge walks are covered in detail in the relevant passages in the King's Highway chapter, which begins on p.275.

of the RSCN (Royal Society for the Conservation of Nature), with maps and brochures (☎07/7742 2132). Staff here can advise on access routes into the reserve, and can act as guides for walks both short and long. On the lake side of the bridge, you can splash around freely in the refreshing sweet river water. Further out on the peninsula, on a quiet, north-facing beach, the RSCN established in 2004 a small, ecologically sound experimental **campsite**, with four-person tents designed to stay cool in the sunshine (which they do), plus toilets and showers. Access, however, is difficult – it's set quite a way from the road amidst tamarisk shrubs – and the tents proved to be unstable in strong winds. For now the campsite has closed, pending a redesign; check with RSCN staff for the latest news.

South of here, the Dead Sea maintains a shimmering, piercingly blue presence, the winding road hugging the salt-spattered shore below arid, rocky cliffs. Some 24km south of Mujib is **Mazra'a**, a small town located on the Dead Sea's **Lisan Peninsula**, which, with the ecological damage being wrought, is now a belt of dry land across the lake. Exploring the peninsula isn't encouraged by the Arab Potash Company, but it's still possible to turn off at the company's sign, drive out a little way and then venture into the ankle-deep soft white sand on foot. Although giving directions is impossible, you might stumble upon one of the many old **Byzantine monasteries** that lie ruined here, unexcavated, in an eerie landscape forever sultry and thick with haze.

Bab adh-Dhraa

About 1km south of Mazra'a is the turn-off leading up into the hills to Karak (see p.304). Another kilometre or so up this road, the Bronze Age *tell* of **Bab adh-Dhraa** rises to the left of the road. As far as archeological remains go, the site is more exciting for specialists than for ordinary visitors, although, after scrambling up the *tell*, you'll be able to make out a thick city wall and a handful of building foundations. However, the attraction of Bab adh-Dhraa isn't so much in investigating the ruins as in relating the place to a name. A large town which flourished around 2600 BC, with some graves in the huge **necropolis** across the road dating from as early as the fourth millennium, Bab adh-Dhraa is the leading candidate for the biblical city of **Sodom**, location of so much wickedness and depravity that God felt compelled to raze the city and rain brimstone and fire down on the heads of its inhabitants. Standing on the *tell* today, amid barren rocks on the hazy shores of a salt lake, you can only wonder what on earth the poor Sodomites must have been up to in these rooms to deserve such damnation.

These days, Bab adh-Dhraa's necropolis is the focus of international attention, not so much for its antiquities but for their plundering by modern-day grave-robbers. The huge site, which is unfenced, is pockmarked by holes dug by impoverished locals hoping to stumble on buried treasure. In truth, there's very little here of value, but rumours of the occasional find – which nearly always end up in London, the market centre for international trade in illegal antiquities – spur more and more people to try their hand. The digging has already irreparably damaged this site and others, prompting the Jordanian government to launch an international effort to cut off the trade at its source.

Lot's Cave and Museum

Under continuous excavation since 1988, **Lot's Cave** is an extraordinarily rich archeological site that has thrown up evidence of Early and Middle Bronze Age habitation, as well as Nabatean pottery, Byzantine mosaics and the earliest example of carved wood yet discovered intact in Jordan: a door that dates

Sodom and Gomorrah

The tale in Genesis of how God punished the depravity of the inhabitants of **Sodom and Gomorrah**, and how **Lot** and his wife escaped, is one of the best-known biblical stories, though some of the details may be unfamiliar – and are certainly unusual. After arriving in Canaan (Palestine), Lot and his uncle Abraham began to bicker over grazing grounds. They separated, and Lot pitched his tents at the southeastern corner of the Dead Sea near Sodom, one of the five "cities of the plain" (the others were Gomorrah, Zoar, Admah and Zeboyim). "But," as Genesis warns, "the men of Sodom were wicked and sinners before the Lord exceedingly." One evening, Lot was visited by two angels, come to warn him of the city's impending divine destruction. Lot, his wife and two daughters fled and "the Lord rained upon Sodom and Gomorrah brimstone and fire." Every one of the five cities was destroyed, and every person killed. As they were fleeing, Lot's wife disobeyed a divine order not to look back at the destruction, and was turned into a pillar of salt.

Seemingly the last people left alive in the world, Lot and his daughters sought refuge in a cave in the mountains. Calculating that, with all potential mates vaporized, they were likely to die childless, the daughters hatched a plan to get their father so drunk he wouldn't be able to tell who they were, whereupon they would seduce him and thus preserve the family. Everything worked to plan and both daughters gave birth to sons; the elder named her child **Moab**, and the younger Ben-Ammi, or "father of **Ammon**".

The last of these bizarre biblical episodes has been commemorated for centuries, and possibly millennia, at a cave-and-church complex in the hills above Safi. Ruins within Safi itself, as well as at four other scanty Early Bronze Age sites nearby (Bab adh-Dhraa, Numayra, Fifa and Khanazir), show evidence of destruction by fire – at Numayra, archeologists also found the skeletons of three men whose bones were crushed by falling masonry – so these could possibly be the five "cities of the plain". The only fly in the ointment is that they were razed around 2350 BC, several hundred years before the generally accepted era of Abraham and Lot, although archeologists are still debating the precise timescales involved.

from the seventh-century Umayyad period. The location – not to mention the notion of standing in Lot's sandalprints – is dramatic enough to warrant a visit.

Some 22km south of the Karak turning on the Dead Sea road, a sign points left to the site; 1km along this road you'll spot **Lot's Museum** (otherwise known as "The Lowest Museum on Earth") – a grand, semicircular building opened in 2005 to showcase the geological, natural and historical heritage of the whole Jordan Valley/Dead Sea area.

A track continues steeply up the hill above the museum to a parking area at the foot of steps leading up to the cave itself. The guardian will accompany you up to the site, which involves a tiring climb of **294 steps**. The Ministry of Tourism are in the process of constructing a shelter over the site, and this may be complete by the time you visit.

The first area you come to is a **court**, part of which has slipped down the hill, but which originally served to support the floor of the **church** above. The main **apse** has seating for the bishop and is slightly raised. Five **mosaics** – one dated April 606, another May 691 – have been renovated, and will be uncovered for viewing once the site shelter is complete. The **narthex** was originally entered from the right, via a doorway from the court below; this ingenious piece of design enabled visiting Jewish and Muslim pilgrims to avoid stepping inside the church and instead head straight for the holy **cave**, the entrance to which is to the left of the apse. A beautifully carved **lintel** over the cave entrance, marked with crosses, presages an interior mosaic (currently still covered for protection beneath the dirt floor), which mimics the round stones embedded in the roof. All around the church was spread a **monastery**, and the remains of six or seven isolated cells are dotted around the parched hillside. The views from the church over the Dead Sea and the nearby town of Safi are stunning.

Safi and beyond

Safi, at the southern tip of the Dead Sea, is phosphate capital of Jordan, although – under the name Zoar – it also has a history as one of the five biblical "cities of the plain", along with Sodom and Gomorrah. The southernmost portion of the Dead Sea has been corralled into huge evaporation pans for Jordan's phosphate and chemical industries and, with its neighbour, the lush farming village of **Fifa**, a bit further south, Safi shares a natural hothouse that is one of the most intensively farmed areas of Jordan, with bananas, tomatoes and other fruits as staple irrigated crops.

Just beyond Fifa is the scenic turn-off up to Tafileh (see p.312), while continuing south brings you into the long **Wadi Araba**, with drifting sand and wandering camels all the way south to Aqaba; see p.424 for details.

Bethany: the Baptism Site

The most important discovery in Middle Eastern archeology in the last few years has been the identification of a site on the east bank of the River Jordan, near the Dead Sea, as **Bethany-beyond-the-Jordan**, the place where John the Baptist lived and was active, and where he most likely **baptized Jesus Christ**. Closed off for years in a military zone along Jordan's western border, the area was reopened for investigation following the 1994 peace treaty with Israel; almost immediately, archeologists used preliminary, pre-1948 studies to uncover a wealth of sites – 21 at the last count – along **Wadi Kharrar**, a small side-valley of reeds and flowing water that runs for 2km from its source down to the River Jordan. These discoveries – eleven Byzantine churches, five baptismal pools from the Roman and Byzantine periods, caves of monks and hermits, and lodges for pilgrims – plus a wealth of medieval accounts of pilgrims and travellers to the area, very rapidly convinced both Jordanian and international opinion as to the veracity of the site, which saw in the year 2000 perhaps its greatest influx of pilgrims since antiquity. In January of that year, on Epiphany, more than forty thousand people gathered at the site in front of a convocation of notables from fifteen world churches; about a week later, King Abdullah arrived to celebrate Arbor Day; the following day, the head of the Armenian Church recognized the site as the official location of Jesus' baptism; in March of that year, Pope John Paul II celebrated open-air Mass in front of 25,000 worshippers; and so on.

All this attention could have turned the place into a tourist circus, but meticulous planning on the part of the Jordanian authorities has preserved a good proportion of the site's dignity. The Visitors' Centre has been built some kilometres away, in order to maintain the sanctity of the surroundings, and a system of shuttle buses controls the numbers entering the site, but the greatest factor mitigating against over-commercialization is the desolation of the **natural environment**. This is almost the lowest point on earth, over 350m below sea level; the air is thick, hot and heavy. On the banks of

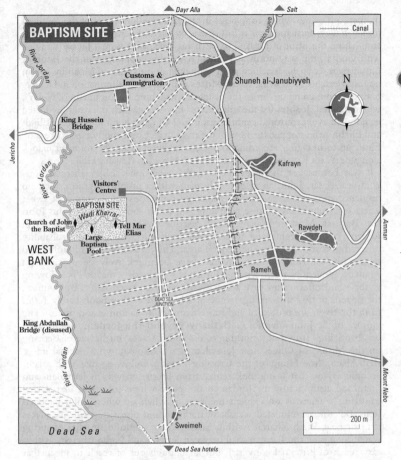

the Wadi Kharrar, you're in the midst of the biblical Plains of Moab; views across the baked ground, punctuated by the occasional dry, toughened tree, enable you to pick out individual buildings and cars in Jericho. Underfoot is a soft, starkly white, chalky marl that seems to deaden sound; only when you get close to Wadi Kharrar itself can you hear the chirping of birds and the soughing of the dense beds of reeds and tamarisk that line the watercourse. Flanking the Jordan itself is an incredible jungle-like thicket, tropically hot and humid, that is more akin to Southeast than Southwest Asia. Nowhere is movement very easy, and visiting any time outside winter means that you'll have to suffer soaring temperatures – 45°C or more in the sun – further limiting your will and capacity to explore. Don't let this put you off; for its historical resonance, natural austerity and religious power, this is an extraordinary place.

Some history

This stretch of desolate plain flanking the River Jordan has been a focus for spirituality since Old Testament times: Judaism, Christianity and Islam all recall momentous events which took place in this relatively small part of the southern Jordan Valley. First mention is in Genesis, when **Lot** separated from Abraham and "chose the plain of Jordan" to pitch his tents, after which **Jacob** wrestled with God a little way north at Penuel. A sizeable proportion of the Book of Numbers is set at the Israelites' camp, "pitched in the plains of Moab by Jordan opposite Jericho", following which **Moses** delivers a long summation in Deuteronomy before going up "from the plains of Moab unto the mountain of Nebo", where he died. **Joshua** led the tribes across the river, which miraculously halted its flow, an event mirrored centuries later in 2 Kings, when the prophets **Elijah** and **Elisha** again stopped the flow of the river, as a chariot and horses of fire took Elijah up to heaven – according to ancient tradition, from the rounded hillock alongside Wadi Kharrar now known as Tell Mar Elias (Elijah's Hill).

It was because of the associations with the prophet Elijah that, a thousand years later, John, an ascetic holy man with a prophetic vision, took up residence near the same hillock, using the numerous small springs of sweet water to symbolically cleanse people of sin; locals soon flocked to this **John the Baptist**. Most biblical mentions describe the baptisms taking place "in Jordan", which might refer to the river itself but which in all probability referred instead loosely to the general area. The Jordan, which often flooded to a width of 1km or more, would have been relatively deep, rapid (in Aramaic, *yardeen* – from which "Jordan" is derived – means "fast-flowing water") and offering no easy access from the often steep bank. By contrast, the dozens of tiny side-springs, some of which rise within pools barely 100m from the river, are protected and more manageable as immersion points. The Gospel of St John mentions "**Bethany-beyond-the-Jordan**, where John was baptizing" (the spot – nothing to do with Lazarus' birthplace of Bethany on the Mount of Olives near Jerusalem – was also known as Bethabara or Beit-Abara, "the House of the Crossing-Point"), following that with a later account saying that **Jesus** took refuge from hostile crowds in Jerusalem and "returned again across the Jordan to the place where John had first started baptizing". There is no explicit mention of when or where John baptized Jesus, but the accumulated weight of tradition and historical evidence places it in or near Wadi Kharrar, within easy reach of plentiful supplies of spring water, alongside the Roman road between Jericho and Nebo (thereby within easy reach of potential converts), but far enough out of reach to mean that John could criticize King Herod with impunity.

As early as 333 AD, a bare three hundred years after the death of Jesus, the anonymous **Pilgrim of Bordeaux** identified the site of Bethany-beyond-the-Jordan as lying five Roman miles (just under 7.5km) north of the Dead Sea, corresponding almost exactly to the point where the Wadi Kharrar enters the river: "here is a place by the river, a little hill on the far bank, where Elijah was caught up into heaven". From then on, a flood of ancient texts mention several churches in the same area on the east bank of the Jordan dedicated both to John the Baptist and his forerunner, Elijah. The sixth-century pilgrim **Theodosius** described the riverside "Church of St John, which the emperor Anastasius built [in about 500 AD]; this church is very lofty, being built above chambers on account of the flooding of the Jordan" – a description which corresponds almost exactly with one of the churches uncovered recently. Other pilgrims at this time talked of the whole valley being "full of hermits", and the place was obviously important enough to merit inclusion on the **Madaba mosaic map** (see p.283), which identifies it as "Ainon, where now is Sapsafas", another name linked in the Gospels with John's baptizing activities.

The accounts continued through the Middle Ages, with Bethany-beyond-the-Jordan taking its place in a **pilgrimage route** linking Jerusalem, Jericho, Hesban and Mount Nebo. From the twelfth to the eighteenth century, Bethany was home to **Greek Orthodox monks**, who were reported still to be present as late as the turn of the twentieth century (the whole site is still in the custody of the Greek Orthodox Church), but most ruins lay undiscovered while knowledge of the whereabouts of Bethany-beyond-the-Jordan faded from the collective memory.

Archeological investigations at Tell Mar Elias and along Wadi Kharrar had to be abandoned at the outbreak of **war** in 1948, and for almost thirty years after 1967, the site lay in a highly militarized border zone. It was only after the 1994 **peace treaty** between Jordan and Israel that the area could be swept for landmines and again opened for study. The momentous discoveries that rapidly followed convinced the Jordanian authorities, and then the broad mass of specialist opinion worldwide, that the long-lost "Bethany-beyond-the-Jordan" had been rediscovered.

Practicalities

The Baptism Site (daily 8am to one hour before sunset; JD5; Ⓦwww .baptismsite.com) is signposted from the **Dead Sea Junction**, a major T-junction at the end of the road from Amman. The highway bends left (south) to the Dead Sea hotels, while to the right (north) is a minor road to the Baptism Site. Note that if you're approaching from the Dead Sea hotels, you have to follow the highway round to the right and then make a U-turn after 200m in order to get onto the Baptism Site road. Roadsigns to the site are plentiful; you may see it marked as the Baptism Site, **el-Maghtas** (an Arabic title meaning "The Place of Dipping"), Bethany-beyond-the-Jordan, Wadi Kharrar, or possibly Ghor el-Kafrayn (which is the wider area comprising this section of the Jordan Valley).

From the Dead Sea Junction, it's 5km to a gateway across the road, where you pay the admission fee and receive a free brochure (with a map). A little ahead is the parking area in front of the low, palm-shaded **Visitors' Centre**, which has toilets, souvenir shops and kiosks selling cold drinks, and which is where the **official guides** wait. If you're visiting independently in a car (or privately hired taxi), it's a good idea to pay for a guide (roughly another 5JD), since the site is large and complex – if he has authorization, the guide may then accompany you, in your own vehicle, for a tour around the site. Private vehicles without authorization from a guide are banned within the site. Otherwise, you must wait at the Visitors' Centre for a free **shuttle bus** (every 15–20min), which makes a round trip to the three separate areas of the site.

From the Visitors' Centre, you can select which of the three areas you wish to head for: Tell Mar Elias (Elijah's Hill) is alongside **Parking 1**; the Baptism Pools and pilgrims' station are by **Parking 2**; and John the Baptist's Church down by the River Jordan is a short walk from **Parking 3**. Fresh drinking water is provided at several points throughout the site (but you should carry your own wherever possible), and there are toilets at Parking 3, as well as at the Visitors' Centre. A tour of all three areas could take up to three hours or more.

You can also elect to tackle the hot and tiring two-kilometre **walk** from the Visitors' Centre to Tell Mar Elias, in order to begin the "pilgrimage" walk on a marked trail along the south bank of the Wadi Kharrar for a further 2km to John's Church and the River Jordan itself. Ideally, you should notify the authorities in advance that you intend to do this (Ⓣ05/359 0360, Ⓕ359 0361):

this is still the international border zone, and security remains tight. Reckon on three hours' walking one-way.

If you're here to affirm your Christian faith, you can request to be taken for a religious ceremony at the two new baptism pools which have been built alongside Tell Mar Elias, the ancient baptism pool near Parking 2, or a new pool area alongside Parking 3. Someone from your own party can officiate or you can ask (in advance) for a local Greek Orthodox priest to conduct the ceremony.

Note that the pools and springs are mostly or completely dry from late May until late October.

Along Wadi Kharrar

The site comprises six square kilometres focused around the small **Wadi Kharrar**, which runs westwards for 2km on a meandering course from beside the rounded hillock of **Tell Mar Elias** down to join the River Jordan amid fourteen small springs around the **Church of John the Baptist**. Midway along is a set of ancient **baptism pools**, enhanced with the addition of a modern counterpart.

Tell Mar Elias (Elijah's Hill)

At the head of the little Wadi Kharrar, alongside **Parking 1**, stands the low **Tell Mar Elias** (pronounced "el-yass"). A few metres south of the *tell*, a number of remains have been uncovered. The most prominent sight is a large freestanding arch, raised in 1999 from 63 stones (to commemorate the death at 63 of King Hussein) over the foundations of a rectangular church dating from the fourth or fifth century. Since March 21, 2000, when the pope celebrated Mass beneath this arch and, in a gesture of reconciliation, faced west to bless Jerusalem then east to bless Mount Nebo, the site has been known as the **Church of John Paul II**. A few metres away are the foundations of a larger rectangular building, with some fragments of a mosaic floor remaining, that has been dubbed a **prayer hall**. Around here is a complicated web of water channels, pool-beds, a pear-shaped well (once circular, but distorted by earth movements) and a large **cistern**, still with its plastered interior, that formerly was covered by a barrel vault of sandstone quarried 20km away at Sweimeh topped with a mosaic floor (remnants of which have been preserved). With the level of settlement in antiquity, and the numbers of baptisms performed here, a great deal of water was needed: pipes and aqueducts channelled water to the site from several kilometres away, but still the 100-cubic-metre cistern wasn't enough, and a second, smaller cistern was built nearby.

The small *tell* features a trinity of trinities – three churches, three caves and three baptism pools – encircled by a wooden catwalk. Proceeding clockwise, on the west side of the *tell* is a cave which forms the apse of a small Byzantine **church**, with small niches to the east and south and tiny fragments of its mosaic floor. An open chapel on the northwest side leads round to the large, late Byzantine **northern church**, now sheltered from the elements, which incorporates a strange black stone into its apse to commemorate the fire which accompanied Elijah's rise to heaven. Its detailed mosaic floor includes an intriguing cross motif in diamonds and an inscription in Greek which dates it to "the time of Rhotorius" (early sixth century). Up a couple of steps on the northeastern side of the *tell* are two **pools** from the Roman period, one cut later with the addition of a fourteen-metre-deep well. Further round is a large rectangular pool, plastered, and with a line of four steps leading into it – for group baptisms, it's been suggested.

The Pilgrims' Station, Baptism Pool and caves

Paths lead down from the *tell* area to the footpath along the south side of Wadi Kharrar, which features several sites attesting to the faith of Byzantine pilgrims and ascetics. Around 500m west of the *tell* are the remains of a *lavra*, a complex of hermits' cells, while further west – near **Parking 2** – is a large **Baptism Pool**, designed to hold 300 people, built roughly on its lower courses but with well-dressed sandstone ashlars further up. Channels fed spring water to the pool; a fifth- or sixth-century building excavated on a small promontory directly above the pool, with views over the whole valley, may well have been a hostel for visiting pilgrims (it has now been dubbed the **Pilgrims' Station**).

Immediately to the west, the *ghor*, or broad valley floor, gives way to the *zor*, or narrow, deep-set flood-plain flanking the River Jordan itself. Cut into the loose marl of these cliffs, and now accessible by modern steps, are two **caves**, each featuring prayer niches; one of the caves has three interior apses. The seventh-century writer John Moschus records the pilgrimage to Sinai of a monk John, from Jerusalem; while recovering from a fever in the *lavra* of Safsafas, John the Baptist appeared to him and said, "This little cave is greater than Mount Sinai: our Lord Jesus Christ himself visited me here."

Church of John the Baptist

The Old Testament prophet Jeremiah spoke of the "**jungle of the Jordan**", and the contrast in the natural environment between Tell Mar Elias and the churches on the banks of the Jordan itself couldn't be stronger. This narrow strip flanking the river is quite unlike anywhere else in the country: paths from the wild and knobbly lunar landscape of the desert-like *zor* around **Parking 3** plunge into a wall of woody tamarisk bushes so thick that, had a way not been cut, it would be impossible to force your way through. Inside the thicket of reeds and tamarisk, the air is steamy and tropical, full of the chirruping of birds and the hum of biting insects, and marked by a constant babble of water from the fourteen springs that flow all around (indeed, the name "Kharrar" is thought to be onomatopoeic).

A five- or ten-minute walk through the "jungle" – past a number of springs and rest areas – brings you to a clearing marked by a modern pool and the sheltered remains of the sixth- or seventh-century **Church of John the Baptist**, situated alongside two more churches, which were built more or less on top of one another; the floor of the lower one, tiled in triangular, square and octagonal flags of marble, has been exposed, and there are also marble Corinthian capitals from long-fallen columns lying nearby. Beneath a shelter is the altar and mosaic floor of the main church, which was formerly raised up above the level of the river on an arched vault to protect it from flooding – exactly as medieval pilgrims recorded. Pillars from this vault still lie where they fell in antiquity, on the north side of the church building. Byzantine stairs, three of them black marble or bitumen, interspersed with white marble from Asia Minor, lead from the apse to what is still known as the **Spring of John the Baptist**. A marble fragment commemoratively marked "IOY. BATT." (a Latin abbreviation of "John the Baptist") that was found in the church will, most likely, be on display in the Visitors' Centre.

Down to the River Jordan

About 200m west of the ancient church, via a laid path through the tamarisks, stands the new Greek Orthodox **Church of St John**, completed in 2005. A Roman Catholic church may also be built nearby. Opposite, near a drinking-water fountain and across from an army position, shaded steps lead down to a wooden platform on the **River Jordan** itself – not the grand, Amazon-like spectacle of imagination, but rather a low, muddy stream, these days barely a metre deep and less than 10m wide at this point. On the opposite bank, in Israeli-occupied territory, is a grand complex known as Qasr al-Yahud – a pristine white stone terrace, complete with chapel and "baptism site". Since they were built, archeologists have struggled in vain to find historical evidence that might link the spot with biblical baptisms – and most have now given up. (Alternative Israeli baptism sites in the northern Jordan Valley are unashamedly commercial, ahistorical affairs, where "pilgrims" pay in order to line up and be dipped in quick succession into the river by a priest.) Linger awhile here, if you can: despite its modest appearance these days, the Jordan is one of the world's great rivers, with huge religious and historical significance. There are very few other places along its course where you can get this close to the water – and none has such drama.

The walk back to Parking 3 leads you on a different route via two more river lookouts, perched high above the banks.

Salt and around

The gentle hills which roll westward from Amman down to the Jordan Valley through the historic **Balqa** region – of which the graceful old town of **Salt** is

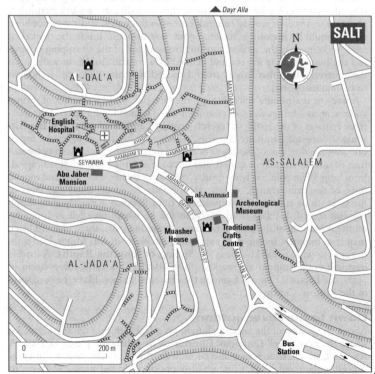

capital – are laced with lush, beautiful valleys and dotted with pleasant towns such as **Wadi Seer** and **Fuheis**, the latter with an appealing little crafts quarter. Near Wadi Seer is one of the few examples of Hellenistic architecture surviving in the Middle East: the impressive white palace of **Qasr al-Abd**, set in gorgeous countryside near an ancient cave system known as **Iraq al-Amir**. All these places are easily accessible on short bus rides from Amman. There are also good transport links to **Shuneh al-Janubiyyeh**, the main crossroads town of the **southern Jordan Valley**, which is within reach of a handful of archeological sites.

Salt

For many centuries, **SALT** was the only settlement of any size in Transjordan. A regional capital under the Ottomans, the town came into its own in the late nineteenth century, when merchants from Nablus arrived to expand their trading base east of the river. Into what was then a peasant village of shacks boxed between precipitous hills, the merchants brought sophisticated architects and masons to work with the honey-coloured local limestone; buildings were put up in the ornate Nabulsi style to serve both as grand residences and as merchandise centres. With open trade to and from Palestine, Salt's boom continued into the 1920s; the new Emirate of Transjordan was formally proclaimed in 1921 in the town's main square, but by then the railway from Damascus had reached nearby Amman and Emir Abdullah chose the better-connected town to be his capital. As quickly as Salt had flourished, so it went into decline: superseded by Amman, it was cut off by war in 1948 from its traditional trade outlet to the Mediterranean at Haifa, then again in 1967 from its Palestinian twin, Nablus. Consequently, the town has seen none of the headlong modernization that has afflicted the capital, and so much of the Ottoman architecture in the old centre has survived, as has peace and quiet, perfect for aimless exploration. A city-wide renovation project, launched in 2004 with $5 million of aid money from Japan, intends to develop Salt for tourism: you may find things have moved on by the time you visit.

Salt's name apparently derives from the ancient Greek *saltos*, meaning "thick forest", and the town has been renowned since antiquity for its natural fertility. Indeed when Salt's own variety of small, pale, very flavourful and high-quality grapes were first dried, a whole new type of raisin resulted, known, with due deference to the town, as the **sultana**.

The Town

Standing under the huge eucalyptus at the road junction a short walk up from the bus station, you are surrounded by three towering hills: to your right are the bare rocky slopes of **as-Salalem**, to the left rises the tree-adorned peak of **al-Jada'a**, and straight ahead is **al-Qal'a**, named for the Mamluke fortress on its summit which was demolished in 1840 and finally swept away recently for a white-domed mosque. Walking a little way along Maydan Street, at the main junction marked by a mosque, you'll spot the **Salt Traditional Crafts Centre** (Sun–Thurs 8am–3pm; free), an enterprise of the charitable Noor al-Hussein Foundation, concentrating on ceramics, weaving and textile-printing. You're free to wander around the workshops, which train local students (the best of whom go on to a career producing items for the foundation), and you can pick up some of their hand-worked, hand-decorated ware at the on-site shop.

Across Maydan Street, you'll spot the arched and pillared facade of the **Salt Archeological Museum** (daily 8am–6pm; free), but the displays of glass and

△ Old house in the backstreets of Salt

pottery bits and bobs are less impressive than the Ottoman-era building housing them, the former stately home of the Touqan family (King Hussein's third wife, Queen Alia, was a Touqan). A few rooms off an enchanting upstairs courtyard feature a rather lacklustre folklore museum.

Turning left at the Arab Bank a few minutes further along Maydan Street leads you into a narrow market alley, Hammam Street (the eponymous *hammam* was razed in the 1930s for lack of customers), lined with buildings – including a wonderful old mosque – which date from Salt's golden age. The street emerges at the **Seyaaha**, Salt's main plaza, dominated on one side by the graceful arched facade of the **Abu Jaber mansion** and on the other by a hideous modernistic mosque. Bending sharply to the right is tiny Khadir Street, with several flights of steps leading steeply up the face of **Jebel al-Qal'a**. Partway up you'll see the colonnaded honeystone **English Hospital**, its gates still bearing an "EH" monogram; the building is now the Middle East's first vocational training centre for people with disabilities. The view from the summit, bathed in sunshine, out over the town to the rolling Balqa hills beyond, is worth the hard climb.

Practicalities

There are plenty of **buses** direct to Salt from both Abdali and Raghadan stations in Amman, as well as from the flyover at Sweileh (the same pick-up point as for buses to Fuheis – see below). Buses from Salt also serve Dayr Alla and Shuneh al-Janubiyyeh in the Jordan Valley, and a few run to Zarqa. Meagre **information** about the town can be had from the Department of Antiquities office (℡05/355 5651) above the museum. For refreshment while wandering, there are a few **coffee houses** dotted around; one of the best spreads itself over Dayr Street next to the white-domed mosque close to the museum. **Restaurants** are exclusively in the spit-and-sawdust category, and king among them is *al-Ammad*, which has been churning out quality shish-kebabs to the Salti cognoscenti for a century or more. It's on Amaneh Street, nine doors up from the Cairo Amman Bank, with no sign in English or Arabic; spot it by the small plaque beside the door which outlines its history (in English).

If you're heading for the Jordan Valley, it's worth knowing that the road down to Shuneh al-Janubiyyeh follows the beautiful and dramatic **Wadi Shuayb**, a perpetually flowing stream lush with undergrowth all year and carpeted with wildflowers in spring; this is a much more impressive route down to the valley floor than the highway from Amman. North of Salt, on the Dayr Alla road, the **Zai National Park** is perfect picnic territory, thick forest with rough trails and plenty of wild nooks.

Fuheis

Set among rolling hills barely half an hour northwest of Amman, **FUHEIS** (pronounced "f-hayce") is a prosperous but rarely visited small town with a delightful, partially restored old quarter of rooftop restaurants and sleepy craft shops. The town is also 95 percent Christian and boasts at least five churches,

Pigeon-fancying

At sunset in towns all across Jordan, you'll see small, tight flocks of pigeons wheeling overhead. Pigeon-fancying is surprisingly popular, and has taken on something of a shady image, since the point of it is not to race the birds, but rather to kidnap prize specimens from other people's flocks. In every neighbourhood, as the sun goes down, people emerge onto the flat rooftops and open up their generally ramshackle, lean-to pigeon coops, sometimes twirling a lure on a length of rope to keep the flock dipping and swooping, sometimes holding a female bird up so that the males will circle around. Neighbours will often deliberately exercise their flocks at the same time, to try and persuade each other's birds to defect; similarly, some well-trained flocks can be enticed to fly off to another part of town to bring back new individuals. Newspapers report that enthusiasts gain three or four new birds a week – but lose roughly the same number. Fanciers generally keep their identities secret, since – for obvious reasons – they're popularly seen as being not entirely trustworthy.

three of which date back to the nineteenth century. Its easy-going atmosphere – and, in summer, the best peaches in Jordan – makes Fuheis a pleasant place to spend an afternoon.

The town has two distinct halves. The first, known as **al-Allali** (with a huge calligraphic sculpture in the central roundabout), is newer and less attractive; make sure you carry on down the steep hill to the old part of town, known as **al-Balad**. Between the two lies a vast cement factory, Jordan's biggest and Fuheis's main claim to fame: over seventy percent of the town is employed at the plant, but local people have suffered for years from clouds of cement dust and soaring rates of asthma. There have long been calls to raise standards or relocate the fifty-year-old plant away from populated areas. Several million JDs were spent recently on improving filtration systems, and in 2005 the towns-people won a battle to stop the factory switching fuels from oil to cheaper petcoke (which contains heavy metals such as lead, nickel and mercury) – yet the factory remains both a blessing and a curse for the town.

The district of quiet lanes and hundred-year-old stone cottages now known as **al-Ruwaq** – between the bus terminus in al-Balad and the deep Wadi Rahwa alongside – had been slated for demolition when, in 1992, a local character opened an art gallery here; he then bought up the cottages one by one and converted them into a self-contained arts and crafts neighbourhood (shops open daily except Tues 4–10pm). Although the crafts are a little uninspired, this quarter makes for an interesting short wander, and the tiny rural lanes come into their own in the golden light of late afternoon. During August, there's a highly acclaimed **carnival** of music and dance held in al-Ruwaq, details of which can be had from the Jordan Tourism Board and in the local press.

Practicalities

The road from Amman begins at the Sports City interchange north of Shmeisani and heads out past Jordan University. Just past the centre of **Sweileh**, a crossroads town on the northwestern fringes of Amman, a clearly marked turn-off heads off the main highway to Salt. This minor road winds through pine forest, passing the Royal Stables at Hummar before entering Fuheis. The town is served by reasonably frequent **buses** from Amman's Abdali station. If you're coming from Wadi Seer, Salt or Jerash, aim for Sweileh; dozens of bus routes from all round this area, as well as Downtown Amman, stop at or near the large roundabout beneath Sweileh's trademark flyover, from where you can pick up the Amman–Fuheis buses (ask the locals where to stand). All Fuheis buses run through al-Allali down to their terminus alongside the grandiose equestrian statue which dominates the tiny al-Balad roundabout. Note that the last bus back to Abdali leaves at around 9pm in summer, 7pm in winter.

Tucked away in a renovated old house in the lanes of al-Ruwaq, barely 50m down from the bus terminus, are a couple of Arabic **restaurants** – the best is the excellent and very reasonably priced *Zuuwadeh* (☏06/472 1528; daily 10am–midnight), housed in an atmospherically renovated old house shaded by a giant eucalyptus tree. This is a favourite informal out-of-town dining spot for affluent Ammanis; the fact that Fuheis is Christian gives it an allure of decadence for urbanite Muslims seeking to let their hair down a little, and on weekend nights in particular the place is crowded with families and groups of friends. *Zuuwadeh*'s kebabs and *fatteh* are superb, but you could choose from their inventive list of *mezze* (in English) and dine lavishly for little more than JD5. One speciality of the house, which is likely to put an interesting spin on your journey back to Amman, is an alcoholic *argileh* – it looks the same as the ordinary version, but instead of water in the bubble chamber the management substitute *araq*.

The southern Jordan Valley

Roads follow lush and beautiful valleys west through the Balqa hills from Salt and Fuheis down into the southern stretches of the **Jordan Valley**. The main settlement here, at the foot of the Wadi Shuayb road from Salt among the farming villages of the valley floor, is the crossroads market town of **Shuneh al-Janubiyyeh** (South Shuneh), its ramshackle town centre marked by traffic lights; **taxis** line up to ferry travellers west to the King Hussein Bridge, while **buses** run south to the Dead Sea and into the hills to Mount Nebo and Madaba, north along the Jordan Valley road to Dayr Alla (see below), as well as east to Salt or Amman. If you're driving to the capital, pick up the main road by heading south through Shuneh to a signposted junction. A short distance southwest of Shuneh, near the village of **Kafrayn**, is the major draw of the Baptism Site (see p.180).

North of Shuneh, the Jordan Valley road cuts a straight path through simple villages and past huge swathes of farmland. Points of interest are few and far between down here: the culture is all rural and agricultural and the archeological sites – though plentiful – are strictly for scholars: barely one stone stands upon another in any of them. A few kilometres beyond Shuneh lies the humdrum town of **Karameh**, best known today for its huge dam project, but still resonant in local minds as the location for one of the few military victories enjoyed by combined Jordanian-Palestinian forces over Israel. On March 21, 1968, the Israeli army – recent conquerors of the West Bank – launched a raid against Palestinian commandos in Karameh, and were repelled during a fierce battle in which Jordanian artillery and the Palestinian *fedayeen* worked side by side. The Palestinian crowds that later went out onto the streets of Amman to celebrate marginalized the Jordanian army's role and claimed the victory entirely for their own cause, fuelling the fire that was to become Black September (see p.449). About 16km north of Karameh is an old roadsign pointing west to the Palestinian town of Nablus, harking back to the days before 1967 when territory on both sides of the river was Jordanian (the side-road leads to a bridge over the Jordan now reserved for agricultural traffic).

Dayr Alla and around

Some 26km north of Karameh is the bustling market town of **DAYR ALLA**, served by buses from Amman, Salt and valley destinations. Rising beside the road about 1km north of the town – whose name translates as "High Monastery" and has nothing to do with Islam or Allah – is the large **Tell Dayr Alla**. Some historians link this site with biblical Penuel, where Jacob wrestled with God; others associate it with Succoth, site of an ironworks that produced pieces used in the Temple of Solomon in Jerusalem. One excavation uncovered an inscription in red and black ink on plaster, dated around 800 BC, relating tales of prophecy by Balaam, a seer also mentioned in the Bible (Numbers 22–24). Heading down the street that hugs the south flank of the *tell* will bring you to a small research station, centre for all archeological research in the Jordan Valley; as well as providing information and impromptu refreshment, the staff can unlock the small **museum** (daily except Fri 8am–1pm & 2–5pm; free), which houses a collection of interesting bits and bobs from sites throughout the valley as well as an explanation of the Balaam text. The *tell* itself, punctured by deep excavation trenches exposing anonymous walls and rooms, is barely worth the effort of the climb.

Around 9km north of Dayr Alla is the town of **Kraymeh**, served by buses from Ajloun as well as the valley villages north and south. Just before the town, opposite an isolated mosque with a stone minaret, a road branches west towards the huge mound of **Tell as-Sa'idiyyeh**, some 2km away. Occupied in the Early Bronze Age, up to about 2800 BC, the *tell* was also home to a large city in the Late Bronze Age, during the thirteenth and twelfth centuries BC. Halfway along the right-hand slope of the *tell*, a reconstructed Iron Age **stone staircase** leads up from a spring-fed **pool** to the summit; here a few excavation trenches display remnants of an Egyptian-style **public building** (Sa'idiyyeh may have been a northern outpost of the Egyptian empire) and a substantial **city wall**. The *tell* gives stunning views along the length of the valley, though the River Jordan itself, only a few hundred metres away, is still invisible in its gorge. The lower mound to the west, outside the walls, comprised a huge Late Bronze Age **cemetery**.

North of here, buses follow the valley road for 20km or so to the town of Mshare'a, access point for the ancient site of Pella in the hills to the east (see p.232).

Wadi Seer

Though barely 12km from central Amman, the town of **WADI SEER** – small and peaceful, filled with trees and birdsong – has the atmosphere of a country village. Add to the natural beauty a couple of small-scale archeological gems and the area definitely merits an exploratory picnic, although, if you choose a Friday for your outing, you'll discover that most of Amman has had the same idea. **Buses** from Amman depart from Muhajireen station and drop off at Wadi Seer's bus station, perched above a roundabout in the town centre.

Originally settled by Circassian immigrants in the 1880s, Wadi Seer boasts many nineteenth- and early twentieth-century Ottoman stone buildings in the streets around the centre, including a red-roofed mosque of yellowish limestone with one of the most beautifully carved minarets in the country. It's worth making time to hunt down a nameless, sporadically open shop tucked away on a backstreet close to the mosque, where a local craftsman makes and sells brightly coloured hand-woven carpets.

Wadi Seer is the staging-post for a journey out to the striking Hellenistic palace of **Qasr al-Abd**, located 10km west alongside the village of Iraq al-Amir. It's easy to charter a **taxi** in Wadi Seer to take you to the *qasr*, wait and bring you back (JD3), or to wait for the **minibus** (see below) to fill up for the journey to the *qasr* gates, but this is a lovely part of the country in which to dawdle, and the **walk** along the road from Wadi Seer to Iraq al-Amir slopes gently downhill all the way, hugging the side of a fertile valley and passing through a series of villages. The scenery is soft on the eye, the valley thick with fig, olive, cypress and pomegranate trees and watered by a perpetually flowing stream; springtime sees a riot of poppies and wild iris. There are plenty of **picnic** spots and even a peaceful café partway along, although you should banish thoughts of riverside footpaths and unspoilt nature – the walk is all on the tarmac road and litter is a major problem in some parts. For a shorter walk, consider taking the bus that runs along the road for some of the way, perhaps as far as the café, and walk from there. If you're picnicking you should really bring food with you from Amman, although a few shops in Wadi Seer sell simple groceries and falafel.

Iraq al-Amir

If you stand at the bus station roundabout in Wadi Seer with your back to the video store, the road leading down into the wadi is to the left, signed "Iraq al-Ameer Street". About 4km out of Wadi Seer town, the road reaches the valley floor and passes a **Roman aqueduct**; the simple *al-Yannabeea* **café** occupies a perfect spot on the grassy bank here (daily 7am–midnight) – you could do a lot worse than suck on a cold Pepsi with your feet dangling in the stream, although the café toilets are nose-wrinklingly bad.

Just before the café, a detour for the energetic leads steeply up to the left; after about 500m, a fork to the left gives access to rough paths up the hillside. A short scramble will bring you to two eerie caves known as **ad-Dayr** (meaning "the monastery"). They look rather like a medieval pigeon-fanciers' den: the interiors are lined with small triangular niches, and stone grilles are still in place over the cave windows.

Beyond the *al-Yannabeea* café, the road continues straight – apart from one left fork marked in English – for another 6km or so to **IRAQ AL-AMIR** (meaning "Caves of the Prince"). Just before you reach the village, you'll spot the smoke-blackened **caves** high up to the right of the road. However, if you scramble up to them, you'll find very little to get excited about: most are malodorous, and there's nothing to see but the view across the fields and a single ancient Hebrew inscription beside one of the cave entrances, referring to the family who built the white palace visible down in the valley. In the village itself, in an old Ottoman-built quarter, is a **handicrafts project** (daily except Fri 8am–3pm) founded by the Noor al-Hussein Foundation to help revive the local economy by giving women their own source of income; the complex, which has been restored, now houses workshops for a variety of different skills, including the manufacture of handmade paper (the only such centre in Jordan), weaving, the production of foods such as *zaatar* and olives, ceramics and more, all of which are on sale here and in Noor al-Hussein Foundation shops around the country.

Qasr al-Abd

After passing through Iraq al-Amir village, the road ends about 1km further on at the gates of the **Qasr al-Abd**, a strikingly beautiful pre-Roman country villa set on a platform above the fields. The villa was begun in the years around 200 BC by Hyrcanus, a member of the powerful Tobiad family, as the centre-piece of a lavish, cultivated estate; its name, meaning "Palace of the Servant", derives from a fifth-century BC member of the clan, who is mentioned in the Old Testament as being a governor, or "servant", of Ammon. Hyrcanus died in 175 BC and the palace was never completed; indeed, for some reason the huge limestone building blocks – some up to 25 tonnes in weight – were originally laid precariously on their half-metre edges, and dutifully collapsed at the first earthquake, in 365 AD. Since then, the building has been only sporadically occupied, possibly during the Byzantine period by Christian monks. It was only in the 1980s that the palace could be partially reconstructed by industrial cranes; before then, the fallen masonry was too heavy to be reassembled.

When you arrive, the guardian will probably materialize to unlock the gates. Inside, only a few courses of the internal walls still stand, although picture windows still ring the building and stairs lead up to a now-collapsed second storey. The main attractions, though, are outside. Around the walls are elegant carvings of wild animals, appropriate for such a rural setting although it's unlikely such beasts roamed the area even in antiquity. At ground level on both sides of the building are dolomite leopards doubling as fountains, and around the top of the walls are eagles and lions. The best of all, high up on a back corner, is a lioness – complete with mane for some reason – suckling her cubs.

Off to one side of the villa is a small modern building housing a **museum** (open on demand), housing photos of the site and some informative notes, including translations of a text by the first-century Roman historian Josephus describing the villa and its animal carvings in uncannily accurate detail. If the electricity is on, the guardian will play the excellent historical slide-show for you; even if it's off, he still deserves a tip.

Travel details

Since most buses and all minibuses and serveeces simply depart whenever they are full, regularity of service is indicated only when a fixed timetable is in operation.

Buses, minibuses and serveeces

Dayr Alla to: Amman (Abdali station; 1hr).
Dead Sea (Amman Beach) to: Amman (Muhajireen station; 1hr 30min); Shuneh al-Janubiyyeh (30min).
Fuheis to: Amman (Abdali station; 35min); Sweileh (20min).
Iraq al-Amir to: Wadi Seer (20min).
King Hussein Bridge to: Amman (Abdali station; 1hr).
Salt to: Amman (Abdali station; 35min); Amman (Raghadan station; 40min); Dayr Alla (40min); Shuneh al-Janubiyyeh (30min); Sweileh (20min); Zarqa (New station; 45min).
Shuneh al-Janubiyyeh to: Amman (Muhajireen station; 1hr); Dayr Alla (40min); Dead Sea (Amman Beach; 30min); Madaba via Mount Nebo (1hr); Salt (30min).
Sweileh to: Amman (Abdali station; 15min); Fuheis (20min); Salt (20min); Wadi Seer (15min).
Wadi Seer to: Amman (Muhajireen station; 25min); Amman (Raghadan station; 30min); Iraq al-Amir (20min); Sweileh (15min).

Useful Arabic place names

Bab adh-Dhraa	باب الذراع	Mazra'a	المزرعة
Baptism Site	المغطس	Qasr al-Abd	قصر العبد
Dayr Alla	دير علا	Safi	الصافي
Dead Sea	البحر الميت	Salt	السلط
Fifa	فيفة	Shuneh al-Janubiyyeh	الشونة الجنوبية
Fuheis	الفحيص		
Iraq al-Amir	عراق الامير	Sweileh	صويلح
Kraymeh	كرعمة	Sweimeh	سوعمة
Lot's Cave	كهف النبي لوط	Wadi Seer	وادي السير

3

Jerash and the north

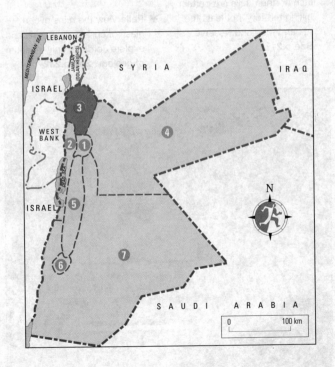

CHAPTER 3 # Highlights

* **Jerash** Explore the Roman streets, then watch the spectacle of chariot racing in the restored hippodrome. See p.198

* **Ajloun** A half-ruined Saracen castle, lording it over the rolling countryside. See p.214

* **Walking in the hills** Jordan's lush northern hills are perfect hiking territory, not least the Ajloun Woodland Reserve. See p.217

* **Umm Qais** One-time haunt of Roman poets and philosophers, perched on a cliff edge with magnificent Galilee views. See p.224

* **The Yarmouk Gorge road** One of Jordan's great scenic drives, with spectacular views of the Golan Heights. See p.229

* **Pella** View the ruins over a glass of chilled white wine and explore Jordan's only museum of geology. See p.232

△ The North Theatre at Jerash

3

Jerash and the north

The rolling hills of the **north** of Jordan hold some of the loveliest countryside in the whole Middle East, acres of olive and fig trees, patches of ancient pine forest and fields of wheat, interspersed with deep, fertile, cultivated valleys pointing the way west down to the immense Jordan Valley. This is the most densely populated part of the country, and every hill and wadi has its village; many of the local people are Jordanian, but plenty of towns also have a significant population of Palestinians, who continue to farm the East Bank of the Jordan much as they did the West Bank and Galilee before they were forced to flee in the wars of 1948 and 1967.

In biblical and classical times, this was the greater part of the area known as the **Decapolis** (see p.200 for more on the Decapolis), and extensive ruins of important Roman cities survive, most notably at **Jerash**, to the north of Amman, and at **Umm Qais**, on the border overlooking the Sea of Galilee. West of Jerash, the fairytale ruins of an Arab-built Crusader-period castle dominate the hills above **Ajloun**, which is now also the location for one of Jordan's loveliest nature reserves, set in isolated forests of evergreen oak.

The largest settlement in northern Jordan is **Irbid**, a workaday university city; for travellers its highlight is an engaging historical and craft museum. The natural boundary between Palestine and Transjordan – still an international border today – is the swelteringly subtropical **Jordan Valley**, the floor of which is more than 200m below sea level. This carries the trickling River Jordan south to the Dead Sea and is today the scene of intensive year-round agricultural production. Ongoing excavations at the Decapolis city of **Pella**, which was built around a spring just above the valley floor, have revealed continuous habitation for at least five thousand years before the Romans arrived.

Transport links around northern Jordan are good, with **buses** linking all towns and – with less regularity – just about every village. On inter-city runs, a handful of serveeces can cut down journey times, but distances are short enough that the bus is no hardship.

Jerash deserves at least a full day, but with no hotels in the town itself you'll probably want to base yourself in Amman, Irbid or Ajloun: from any of these you can be in Jerash in an hour. A **car**, of course, would be a major boon, allowing you to explore backroads and get to more remote sites like Himmeh or Pella without having to rely on a sporadic bus service.

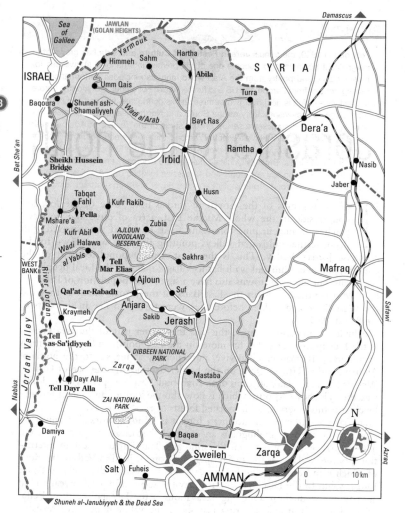

Shuneh al-Janubiyyeh & the Dead Sea

Jerash

One of the best-preserved, most dramatic and explorable Roman cities in the Middle East, set in the bowl of a well-watered valley about 50km north of Amman, **JERASH** is the principal focus of a trip into northern Jordan. With its monumental and sophisticated public buildings tempered by charmingly human touches, the city is likely to inspire even if you are on the jaded final leg of a ruin-hopping tour of the region.

Jerash is a huge site, and you could easily spend a full day here; if you have only a couple of hours, you could rapidly absorb the **Oval Plaza** buildings, the **Cardo** (the main thoroughfare), the **Sacred Way** leading up to the **Temple of Artemis** and the **North Theatre**, but without really doing the place justice.

The Jerash Festival

Founded in 1980, the annual **Jerash Festival of Culture and Arts** has grown from insignificant beginnings to become one of the premier international showcases for music, dance and poetry from the Arab world, and also includes performances by visiting troupes from Europe, the US and further afield. For a couple of months before the festival – which is held over two or three weeks during late July and early August – the ruins see feverish activity as the South and North Theatres are prepared for performances, and stages are set up on the steps of the Temple of Artemis, near the Oval Plaza and at other sites dotted among the stones and columns. Recent visitors to the festival have included orchestras from Eastern Europe, dance troupes from Japan and India, Britain's Original Shakespeare Company and a wealth of local performers, including singers, poets and Circassian folkloric dancers. Star performers from the Arab world – principally Lebanon, Egypt and Iraq – attract audiences of thousands, who pack the theatres and public spaces much as the spectators of pagan festivals in antiquity must have done. All along the Cardo and in the Oval Plaza, artisans from around Jordan and as far afield as Lebanon and North Africa set up shop to sell their crafts direct to the promenading visitors. Performances and celebrations start in the afternoon and continue late into the night; JETT lays on special buses to and from Amman throughout the festival.

Check Ⓦ**www.jerashfestival.com.jo** for more information and a schedule of performances, or contact the festival administration in Amman on ☏06/567 5199. If you're in Jordan at the time, you should definitely not miss it.

On a longer visit, the less energetic could skip the northern reaches of the city and the reservoir at Birketayn without missing out.

After Petra, the largest chunk of public and private money spent on Jordan's ancient sites is lavished on Jerash. Consequently, archeologists are working continuously at several different digs within the city, and facilities for visitors are being overhauled at a rapid rate, attracting busloads of tourists, both foreign and Jordanian. Especially in the mid-morning hours before lunch, the more accessible sights – the Oval Plaza area, and the Cardo up to the Temple of Artemis – can get overcrowded (school-trip day is Wednesday), but it takes only a minute's wandering off the beaten track to sidestep the hubbub. During late July and early August, the popular **Jerash Festival** occupies the entire city, with craft markets and an impressive line-up of evening performances.

With no hotels in immediate striking distance apart from the hard-to-reach *Olive Branch* (see p.200), nowhere to leave heavy bags while you explore, and no buses departing after 6pm, you're most likely to want to treat Jerash as a **day-trip**: Amman is the obvious place to base yourself; Irbid with its good transport connections around the north makes good sense too; but for peace, fresh air and beautiful hilly countryside, Ajloun is far preferable. Pending the success of new Roman-style **chariot racing** (see box, p.206), there are plans afoot to redevelop the modern town of Jerash and build two new hotels on the hills overlooking the ruins, but these may take some years to come to fruition.

Some history

Set in the fertile hills of **Gilead**, which is mentioned frequently in the Old Testament as being a populated and cultivated region, the Jerash area has attracted settlement since prehistory: Paleolithic and Neolithic implements have been uncovered nearby, and archeological investigation around the South Gate of the city has revealed evidence of settlement going back to the Middle Bronze Age (around 1600 BC).

The Decapolis

From the time of Alexander the Great, a group of around ten important cities of the region began to be associated together. Bastions of urban **Greek** culture in the midst of a **Semitic** rural population, these cities were founded or re-founded during or following Alexander's consolidation of power in the Levant in the late fourth century BC. **Decapolis** means "Ten Cities" in Greek, but classical authors disagreed on both the number and identity of the ten: a reasonably authoritative list, from the first century AD, comprises, in modern-day Jordan, Philadelphia (Amman), Gadara (Umm Qais), Gerasa (Jerash) and Pella; in modern Syria, Damascus, Raphana, Hippos, Dion and Canatha; and in Israel, Scythopolis (Bet She'an). Although it's tempting to imagine the Decapolis cities working together in a formal league of cooperation, no records survive of such a pact, and it seems instead that the term was used simply to refer to the geographical area of northern Transjordan and southern Syria: the gospels of Matthew and Mark, for example, mention the Decapolis only as a region. All that can be said for sure is that the Decapolis cities shared a common history and culture.

After the **Roman** armies arrived in 63 BC, the area enjoyed a sizeable degree of both affluence and autonomy. The population within the cities – by this stage predominantly of Middle Eastern origin – spoke much more Greek than Latin (the latter was only used on formal occasions, in official documents and correspondence), and were almost certainly also fluent in **Aramaic**, the language spoken in the countryside. Even in its heyday, Jerash, for instance, remained at core a Semitic society, its ancient local traditions overlaid with a thick veneer of Greco-Roman ideas and political structures.

By the second century, the Decapolis appears to have expanded; a list from this period names eighteen cities, including Abila (Qwaylbeh), Arbela (Irbid) and Capitolias (Bayt Ras, near Irbid). However, historical confusion between authors subsequently reigns supreme, with some indicating the Decapolis to be a part of Syria, others seeming to show that Syria was a part of the Decapolis, and still more including within the Decapolis cities that seem to have played no part in the common history and culture of the original ten. It was **Emperor Trajan** who effectively broke the cultural bonds in the Decapolis and sowed the seeds of this confusion. His Province of Arabia, newly created in 106 AD, included only some of the cities, but Pella and Scythopolis, for instance, remained within the Province of Syria. Bosra became the new provincial capital, and although Decapolis centres such as Gerasa and Philadelphia subsequently experienced a golden age in culture and sophistication, Trajan's reorganization ensured that their horizons now encompassed more than merely their own region: they were bonded firmly into the greater Roman order. By the time of the division of empire into east and west under **Diocletian** at the end of the third century, the notion of a special, parochial link between the cities of the Decapolis was dead.

Gerasa (the ancient name for Jerash) was founded around 170 BC, the relatively small city of the time focused around the Temple of Zeus and the low hill opposite. Very little evidence of this Hellenistic period survives today. It was at some point around this time that the idea of the **Decapolis** first emerged (see box). Gerasa and its Decapolis neighbours were "liberated" by the Romans under Pompey in 63 BC and granted autonomy under the higher authority of the **Province of Syria**. The century which followed saw unprecedented growth and stability in Gerasa, and it was during the first century AD that the basic town plan as it survives today was laid down: a colonnaded north–south axis cut by two colonnaded side-streets, along with a temple to Zeus (built over the pre-existing temple) fronted by an oval plaza, expansion of the temple to Artemis and construction of the South Theatre.

In 106, when **Emperor Trajan** reorganized Roman authority in the region around his new Province of Arabia, Gerasa lost its autonomy and was governed from the provincial capital, Bosra. Gerasa gained a link by a branch road to Trajan's new highway running between Bosra and the Red Sea, while other main roads linked the city with Philadelphia and Pella. Suddenly, the city found itself not only close to the provincial capital but also astride the highly lucrative trade routes that had been jealously guarded by the Nabateans for so long. In 129–130, Gerasa briefly became the absolute centre of the Roman Empire, as Trajan's successor, **Hadrian**, wintered in the city; in his honour, the Gerasenes built a new monumental arch outside the city's southern walls, and embarked on major expansion works, including widening of the main street and renovation of temples and public buildings. Hadrian's visit ushered in a golden age for the city, and Gerasa's population may have touched 25,000 during the later second and early third centuries.

Civil disorder in Rome in the 190s heralded the end of the boom. Taxation increased to help cover greater military expenditure – which fuelled further resentment, as well as crippling inflation – and the Persian **Sassanians** began to whittle away at the eastern flanks of the empire. Trade was seriously affected, and in Gerasa the lavish programme of public works was cut back.

A sea change took place in the early fourth century, when in 324 **Christianity** became the official religion of the eastern empire. Gerasa embraced the new religion shortly afterwards, and during the fifth and sixth centuries dozens of churches went up, though the Byzantine style of architecture was very different from the rigorously ordered Roman style preceding it; many pre-existing buildings were ransacked for stones and columns, giving a botched, make-do feel to many of Gerasa's churches. By the late seventh century, the city was literally crumbling under the twin blows of shoddy workmanship and lack of maintenance; at one point, even the water supply failed. **Persian** forces were able easily to occupy the once-grand metropolis for a dozen years or so from 614, their only significant legacy an adaptation of the Hippodrome into a polo field.

After the Muslim victory over the Byzantines in 636, it was long theorized that Gerasa – subsequently arabized into Jerash – had slipped into anonymous decline: a small, jerry-built **Umayyad** mosque and a handful of kilns were the only evidence from the Islamic period in the city. However, one of the most exciting recent digs has uncovered a large congregational **mosque** from the Umayyad period in the heart of the city centre, with what has been suggested is a Governor's House attached. Work is ongoing, but it seems Jerash may have been stronger and more populous in the early Muslim period than was previously thought. Nonetheless, the cataclysmic earthquake of 749 seems to have brought the city to its knees, and for a thousand years Jerash lay deserted.

At the beginning of the nineteenth century, **European** explorers – including, on a four-hour visit, Burckhardt – were taken around the ruins by local Bedouin, and news of the "discovery" of the ancient city of Gerasa spread rapidly to the West. Throughout the nineteenth century, and up until the present day, archeological investigation at Jerash has been continuous and wide-ranging, although large areas still remain untouched beneath the grass. In modern times, a new lease of life for the ancient city came from an unexpected quarter. In 1879, in the same process of migration and resettlement that brought **Circassian** settlers to the deserted ruins of Amman, the Ottoman authorities directed refugee Circassians to settle in the ruins of Jerash. They occupied what is believed to have been the Roman residential quarters, on the east bank of the river, and the bustling town which has since grown up there, now capital of its own governorate, still has Circassians in the majority.

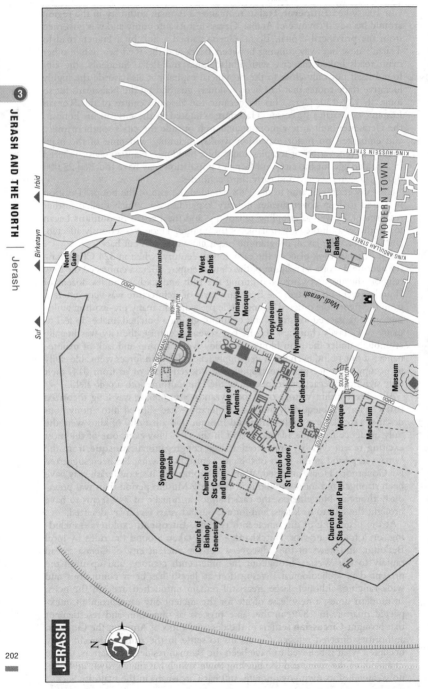

JERASH

N

Suf ▲   Birketayn ▲   Irbid ▲

CARDO

North Gate

Restaurants

West Baths

NORTH TETRAPYLON

Umayyad Mosque

North Theatre

NORTH DECUMANUS

Propylaeum Church

Nymphaeum

Temple of Artemis

Cathedral

Fountain Court

Church of St Theodore

SOUTH DECUMANUS

Church of Sts Cosmas and Damian

Synagogue Church

Church of Bishop Genesius

Church of Sts Peter and Paul

SOUTH TETRAPYLON

Mosque

Macellum

Museum

East Baths

Wadi Jerash

MODERN TOWN

KING ABDULLAH STREET

KING HUSSEIN STREET

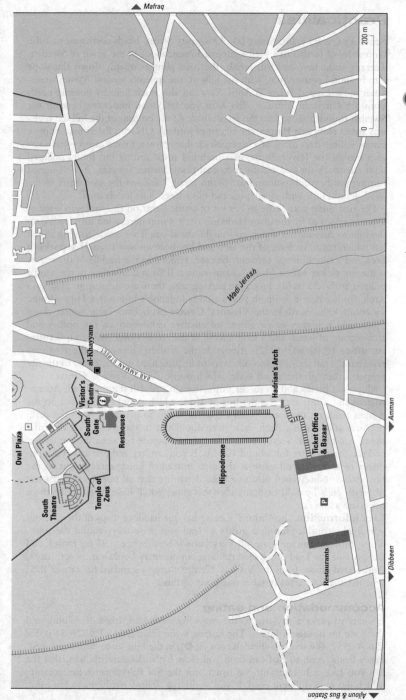

▲ Mafraq

200 m

0

Wadi Jerash

al-Khayyam

BAB AMMAN STREET

Visitor's
Centre

South
Gate

Resthouse

Oval Plaza

South
Theatre

Temple of
Zeus

Hadrian's Arch

Hippodrome

Ticket Office
& Bazaar

P

Restaurants

▼ Amman

▼ Dibbeen

◄ Ajloun & Bus Station

Practicalities

Amman's Queen Rania Street (aka University Street) heads northwest past the University of Jordan to a well-signposted roundabout in the town of Sweileh. Turning right here towards Jerash, the road plunges steeply down the slope into beautiful countryside, with the hills on the horizon around Ajloun sometimes snow-capped as late as April. You can also reach here by heading north from 8th Circle in Amman; after 8km you follow an underpass beneath the Sweileh roundabout to join the Jerash road. At the bottom of the hill the highway passes alongside **Baqaa**, the largest of Jordan's UN-run Palestinian refugee camps – these days more of a breezeblock shanty town than a camp – and soon after crosses the River Zarqa, in a beautiful rustic setting but foully polluted with chemicals spewed out by industrial plants further upriver. A well-signed turning just beyond (pointing to "South Jerash") follows the west bank of the Wadi Jerash, lush with eucalyptus and olive trees, into Jerash itself.

The first thing you come to is a set of traffic lights on the southern edge of town overlooked by the giant Hadrian's Arch. From here, a left turn leads over the hills to Ajloun, but if you go straight ahead you'll see a side-turning to the left which passes in front of the arch and heads down to a large, free **parking area** and a fake touristic souvenir **bazaar**. Hidden in the middle of the bazaar is the site **ticket office** (daily 7.30am–sunset; JD5) and an office of the tourist police (☎02/635 0670). From the parking area, there are steps up to Hadrian's Arch, from where a footpath passes alongside Jerash's impressive Hippodrome for about 400m north to the **Visitors' Centre** (daily 8am–7pm; winter closes 5pm), which houses an excellent, informative exhibition on the history and architecture of Jerash and a large model of the ruins, along with a small **tourist office** (☎02/635 1272). Alongside the Visitors' Centre is the *Resthouse* restaurant, a gift shop, and an office co-ordinating local guides. Entry to the site proper is through the South Gate, which overlooks the Visitors' Centre.

All public **buses** and serveeces from Amman's Abdali station, Irbid, Ajloun, Mafraq and Zarqa arrive at the **bus station**, which is awkwardly sited on the Ajloun road, on the southwestern edge of town: to get there from the main junction at Hadrian's Arch, head west for 800m to the second set of traffic lights, and turn left. Serveece minibuses shuttle people between the bus station and the town centre for around 100 fils. If you can, try and persuade your bus driver to drop you off early at the arch instead of going directly out to the bus station. Note when planning your departure that all public transport out of Jerash ends by 5.30 or 6pm; after that time, you'll have to either hitch or negotiate a taxi fare.

For **information**, the Visitors' Centre has free handout maps of the site, and you might consider hiring a **guide** to lead you personally around the ruins. These professionals are generally very knowledgeable (see p.97 for more), and can provide the kind of detailed running commentary books can never match. Authorized guides from the Visitors' Centre charge a standard flat rate of JD5, whether the tour actually takes one hour or three.

Accommodation and eating

It's easy to make a day-trip to the ruins from Amman, Irbid or Ajloun, and there are no **hotels** in Jerash. The nearest is the *Olive Branch* (☎02/634 0555, ⓕ634 0557, ⓦwww.olivebranch.com.jo; ❹), in the hills some 8km northwest. Buses from Jerash to **Suf** can drop you close by; make sure, though, that the bus you take is heading for Suf town, not the Suf Palestinian refugee camp, which lies on a different road. If you're driving, follow roadsigns to Suf until,

7.5km from Jerash, you'll spot a sign pointing left to Sakib and Katta (this is where you should ask the bus to drop you). From the sign, a minor road winds 1500m through olive groves directly to the hotel, which is set in a lovely, peaceful location offering an enormous panorama out over the hills as far south as Amman. (Another route to the hotel comes off the Jerash–Ajloun road: take an Ajloun minibus and ask to be dropped at a sign for the hotel, which is 2km along the turn-off.) A taxi-fare from Jerash is about JD2.500. The hotel's airy, pleasant rooms are all en suite, comfortable and very clean, with great views and some with balcony. You can camp in their spacious grounds for JD4 (they'll rent you a tent for JD1 extra), or copy the locals and bring steaks and hot dogs for an open-air picnic: the hotel rents out barbecue sets for JD1. Access to the swimming pool costs JD5 for non-guests.

Eating options in Jerash aren't bad, although virtually no foreign visitors bother to explore beyond the touristy snack bars in the parking area. The most straightforward option is the lunchtime buffet at the air-conditioned *Resthouse* (daily 8am–8pm), located alongside the Visitors' Centre; this costs a hefty JD7 for the full range of *mezze* plus main meat course, or JD5 for *mezze* only – you're paying for the location rather than the excellence of the cuisine. They also have an à la carte menu. Spread along the road near the ruins are a string of Arabic food gardens, all of them characterized by plastic furniture, loudspeakers in the trees and reasonable fare. A decent choice is the *Lebanese House* (☎02/635 1301, daily 10am–11pm), 750m south of Hadrian's Arch (take the first, unmarked turn south off the Ajloun road), a somewhat shabby joint which rests on its long-outdated reputation as one of Jordan's best Lebanese restaurants; these days it is nothing of the kind, although it can still rustle up a decent *tabbouleh* and *shish tawook*. Virtually opposite the Visitors' Centre is the *al-Khayyam* (same times), with a standard range of kebabs, half-chickens and ordinary *mezze* making a meal for about JD3, while at the Irbid junction in the northern part of town are several more that are worth checking out.

Hadrian's Arch and the Hippodrome

The first monument you see as you approach Jerash from Amman is the huge **Hadrian's Arch**, poised over a main traffic junction to the south of town. The eleven-metre-high triple-arched gateway, which originally stood to almost 22m and which has been restored and partially reconstructed, was built to honour the visit of the Roman emperor Hadrian to Jerash in 129–130 AD. The huge arches, which probably had wooden doors, are flanked by engaged columns unusually decorated with capitals at the bottom rather than the top. Seemingly out on a limb, over 400m from the city walls, the positioning and structure of the arch in fact point to a grandiose scheme for southward expansion of Jerash at the zenith of its power. It would appear that the municipal authorities were envisioning the arch as an enormous city gate, since its side walls were left untrimmed to enable tight bonding with new perimeter walls. The plan remained unrealized, however, and when it became clear, maybe a century or so later, that Gerasa wasn't going to expand any more, two small side-pavilions, with niches mirroring the arch's side entrances, were added.

On the west side of Hadrian's Arch, an array of small arches belongs to the reconstructed south wall of the **Hippodrome**, which has undergone extensive renovation work by Swiss, French and Jordanian teams of archeologists. This was the scene of ancient Gerasa's sporting festivals and chariot races, and is due again to stage Roman-style games and races after a gap of some 1500 years (see box). At 244m long, and seating up to 15,000 spectators, it is impressively large for Jerash,

Chariot racing

Jerash is now the scene for a revival of the Roman sport of **chariot racing**, with choreographed contests and Roman wargames planned to be staged in the restored Hippodrome. Swedish, British and Jordanian enthusiasts have set up the company RACE (Roman Army and Chariots Experience) to organize the reconstructions, which have been based on extensive research by academics and enthusiasts – including such luminaries as the technical adviser for the Oscar-winning movie *Gladiator*, and an actor who drove chariots in the 1950s epic *Ben Hur* who still lives in Rome with his collection of 29 chariots. After surveying Roman hippodromes around the world, experts settled on Jerash as being the most suitable, for its modest size, relatively good state of preservation and well-touristed setting. Some original seating survives, and there's an area of restored seats as well as a bank of modern, sympathetically disguised bleacher-style seating; RACE is aiming for a capacity audience of about five hundred.

From the earliest days of Classical Greece, around 650 BC, right through to the fall of Constantinople in 1453, chariot races followed a broadly similar format – four chariots competing around seven anticlockwise laps of the arena – and the Jerash re-enactment will follow the same guidelines. *Ben Hur* summons up images of gleaming, armour-plated war-chariots racing improbably quickly behind four horses, but in reality the Romans (unlike the Britons and the Celts) used chariots only for racing, not in battle, so they built much less visually impressive, but much faster, fifty-kilogram wickerwork chariots, drawn by two horses. The new Jerash chariots fall somewhere between Hollywood romanticism and the flimsy, but historically accurate, truth.

The format of events at Jerash has yet to be finalized, but they are likely to be preceded by displays of Roman military capability, with forty or so armed legionnaires firing catapults of flame-bombs from amid a procession of trumpeters and standard-bearers making their way through the ruins to the Hippodrome. Pomp and pageantry are everything, and the chariot "races" will, for obvious reasons of safety, be meticulously staged and choreographed. All the chariots, costumes and battle equipment have been manufactured in Jordan; local equestrian specialists are on hand to advise on cavalry techniques and look after the teams of horses; and RACE is employing about fifty permanent staff, all Jerash locals, to act as legionnaires and gladiators.

There will be shows five or six days a week between March and October. Preliminary studies have suggested a ticket price of about JD15 per person, and seats may be bookable in advance from abroad. For information, ask around in Jerash itself, check with the Jordan Tourism Board or consult ℗ **www.jerashchariots.com**.

but is nonetheless the smallest hippodrome so far discovered in the Roman Empire: by contrast, the Circus Maximus in Rome could accommodate over 157,000 people – far more than the largest football stadium in the world today. Jerash's arena has garnered international attention, though, for the preservation of remnants of its original starting-gates as well as some areas of original seating.

Walking from the arch north towards the gleaming Visitors' Centre takes you past a series of shops built into the Hippodrome on the left, and the small, ruinous Byzantine **Church of Bishop Marianos** on the right, erected in 570 among Roman and Byzantine tombs on what was then the main Gerasa–Philadelphia road.

The southern part of the ancient city

Beyond the Visitors' Centre stands the reconstructed **South Gate**, the principal entry point into the ancient city. It seems from the wheel ruts on the thresholds that the west door was reserved for wheeled traffic, and that the central and east doors were used principally by pedestrians. Near the gate is a section of the three-metre-thick wall which originally ran for over 3.5km around the city, a fourth-century strengthening of the original, thinner first-century wall.

Beyond the gate, the split-level **South Street** runs between what is believed to be a Hellenistic settlement on the right, and the restored vaults supporting the lower terrace of the **Temple of Zeus** complex to the left. It gives onto what is one of the most impressive pieces of Roman urban design in the world, the **Oval Plaza**. The plaza comprises a large central paved area enclosed by two curving colonnades, both irregular bent ellipses and of different lengths, forming an elegant, smooth entry into the city proper while deftly linking the east–west axis of the Temple of Zeus with the north–south axis of the main street, the Cardo. Approaching from the south, the shorter western arm of the colonnade draws your eye and your feet towards the opening of the Cardo, which may well originally have been marked by a prominent triple arch. Beautiful stone paving swirls around the plaza following the curve of the Ionic colonnades. Two slightly wider intercolumnar spaces on the west show where small side-streets led in from residential districts. The column in the centre of the plaza was put up recently to celebrate the Jerash Festival, but the podium it stands on is original and may have supported a statue instead. In the seventh century, a water tank was built around the podium, and pipes are still visible set into the paving.

The South Theatre

From the plaza a track climbs west up to the **South Theatre**, the most magnificent of all Jerash's monuments and the largest of the city's three theatres. Now extensively restored, it was built in the 90s AD to seat over three thousand, the cost of construction partly offset by contributions from wealthy Gerasenes. Inscriptions record such generosity, and lower seats on the shadier western side of the auditorium are numbered (notable citizens could presumably reserve these prime spots). You enter the theatre into the orchestra, and, as with all theatres, there are plenty of acoustic games to play: talking while standing at the midpoint of the orchestra gives an effect as good as a PA system, and if two people at opposite ends stick their heads into the round indentations below the seats they can hear each other's mutterings quite clearly. The stage has been restored in stone – it was probably wood originally – and the *scaenae frons*, or backdrop, would have had another storey on top of the elaborate and beautifully carved detail that exists today.

The Temple of Zeus

Adjacent to the theatre on the same hill, the **Temple of Zeus** in its heyday must have towered over the city, and, like its sister temple of Artemis in the city centre, was intended to be visible from all parts of Jerash. Originally surrounded on all four sides by gigantic Corinthian columns 15m high (the three that are standing now were re-erected in 1982 in the wrong place), the temple was built in 162–163 AD on the foundations of a first-century predecessor, which itself replaced a temple from the second century BC. The inner sanctum is plain and simply decorated, and the massive front wall is 4.5m thick to accommodate stairs up to the roof. In front of the temple, huge dismembered columns have lain untouched since the day of some cataclysmic earthquake in antiquity; the slope they lie on, now covered with earth and overgrown, probably conceals a monumental staircase. From above, the layout of the *temenos*, or sacred terrace, below the temple is clear, with remains of an altar to the left; the far side of the *temenos* is supported on the restored vaults visible from South Street. What is also clear from here is the vast extent of ancient Gerasa: as well as the entire sweep of the ancient ruins, much of modern Jerash is visible. Behind a minaret in a distant space between buildings in the town, you can spot a surviving remnant of the eastern city wall.

The temple is due for major reconstruction over the next few years, and so access may be limited or forbidden while the archeologists work.

The ancient city centre

The colonnaded **Cardo**, the main boulevard of Jerash, leads north from the Oval Plaza into the city centre. Some 800m long, the street was originally laid out with Ionic columns, but at some point during the remodelling of the city in the second century, it was widened as far as the Temple of Artemis and the columns updated to the grander Corinthian order. Along the Cardo the columns supported a continuous architrave, and a wide covered pavement on both sides gave access to shops behind. Because of the gentle gradient, each column stands a few centimetres higher, and is slightly shorter, than the last; where the column height would have been too small to maintain strict architectural proportion, the architrave was halted, bracketed into the side of the next column and begun again at a higher level. The diagonal street paving is marked by deep grooves worn by centuries of metal-wheeled traffic, while round drain covers give access to an underground sewerage system.

The four tallest columns in this section mark the entrance on the left to the **macellum**, the ancient food market, an octagonal courtyard built around a central fountain and surrounded by small shops. Originally there were massive tables in four corners of the courtyard; strikingly carved supports survive in the farthest corner. Opposite the *macellum*, steps lead up to the small site **museum** (daily 8.30am–5pm; Nov–March closes 4pm), the garden of which is dotted with carved sarcophagi and chunks of statuary. Inside are exhibits tracing the settlement of Jerash from Neolithic times, including a good display and explanation of ancient coinage.

The South Tetrapylon

A little way further, the Cardo meets the first of Jerash's two major cross-streets, the **South Decumanus**, at an intersection known as the **South Tetrapylon**. At the centre of this circular plaza are four freestanding podia, each of which was decorated with shell niches and held four columns topped by a square entablature. A statue probably stood between the four columns of each podium. This impressive structure was designed to turn a simple street junction into a grand meeting point flanked with shops, while not impeding traffic circulation from street to street. To the east, the South Decumanus crossed the river into what were probably Gerasa's residential neighbourhoods at the **South Bridge**. The bridge has been restored, but a modern fence bars access.

On the southwest corner of the junction, new excavations have revealed a large congregational **mosque** from the eighth-century Umayyad period, set crooked to the street so that its three *mihrabs* faced south towards Mecca. What has been suggested is a Governor's House stands alongside to the southwest, indicating that this spot may well have been the nexus of power in the city at the time. Investigation is continuing, but this building is already providing a fascinating link between the pagan Gerasa of the ancient world and modern, Muslim Jerash. Rather prosaically, beneath it has been discovered a Byzantine bath-house.

△ Oval Plaza, Jerash

The Nymphaeum

From the South Tetrapylon, the Cardo was expanded to its widest extent, and Byzantine raising of the pavement included the addition of small niches down at ankle level, either for small statues or, possibly, streetlights. The wheel-ruts from chariot traffic are particularly pronounced in this section. Eight tall columns on the left mark the entrance to the Cathedral (see p.212), while beyond, fronted by four even taller columns, is Gerasa's extraordinarily lavish **Nymphaeum**. Completed in 191 AD, and dedicated to dancing, singing water nymphs, the Nymphaeum was nothing more than a huge and grandiose public fountain, but the sight and sound of water splashing in abundance from such a finely carved monument must have been delightful. Even today, dry, the carving which survives on the two-storey semicircular recess is impressive. Originally, the lower storey was faced in green marble, while painted plaster covered the upper storey; traces of the green and orange design survive in the topmost niche on the left. Concealing the holes in the lower niches, statues were probably designed to appear to be pouring water into the basin below, from which lion's-head fountains spat water into shallow basins at pavement level (one of Jerash's most endearing small details is the basin carved as four fish kissing, their eyes serving as drainage holes). The huge red granite laver in front is a Byzantine embellishment.

Beyond the Nymphaeum, thirteen ordinary-sized columns presage four gigantic ones marking the entrance to the Temple of Artemis.

The Temple of Artemis complex

The most important edifice in the ancient city, the **Temple of Artemis** was approached via a long east–west **Sacred Way** which originated somewhere in the residential eastern quarters and cut across the Cardo at the point marked by the four huge columns. The best way to discern the route is to pick a path to the east through the jumble of rubble opposite the four columns and stand on top of the apse of what is called the **Propylaeum Church**, ingeniously created from elements of the Roman street. In the sixth century, when the cult of Artemis had passed into historical memory, the Christian inhabitants of Gerasa sealed off the old Sacred Way with the apse and used the colonnades of the street as the divisions within the church between nave and aisles. Between here and the Cardo, a plaza – decorated with beautiful spiral-twisted columns topped with a delicately carved architrave that now lies in chunks nearby – became the atrium of the new church. Behind, down below the Propylaeum Church, a Roman bridge carrying the Sacred Way once spanned the river; one of the few monuments of Gerasa to survive in modern Jerash is the huge East Baths building, which you can see opposite.

Back on the west side of the Cardo, a portico leads you to the **Propylaeum** itself, a massive, ornately decorated gateway dedicated in 150 AD, which gives onto a monumental staircase of seven flights of seven steps. At the top – but still well below the temple proper – is a terrace with the foundations of a small **altar**; from here, another monumental staircase, originally over 120m wide, takes you up to the level of the sacred courtyard, or *temenos*, with a dramatic view of the temple.

The temple

The Temple of Artemis is set far back in a vast **courtyard** some 161m deep and 121m wide, which was originally lined on all four sides with a colonnade and is now cluttered with the ruins of Byzantine and Umayyad pottery kilns and workshops. The temple has clung onto its huge **portico**, whose clustered limestone columns have been burnt an impressive peachy bronze over the centuries. Inserting a long stick or a key between the drums of any of them (the fourth on the left is a favourite) demonstrates how these mammoth pillars were designed to sway gently, in order to absorb the effects of earth tremors and high winds – and have been doing so for almost two millennia without toppling.

The **cella**, or inner sanctum, is today exposed, but would originally have been surrounded by a peristyle of six columns across each short side, eleven on each longer side; the capitals of those that stand are still in place, but some elements of the entablature have never been found, pointing to the possibility that the temple was never completed. The inner walls of the *cella* would have been richly decorated with slabs of marble supported on hooks fitting into the holes all round the walls, which were pilfered during the Byzantine period to adorn churches. At the back is the single focus of all this wealth of extraordinary architecture along the Sacred Way: the niche which once housed the image of Artemis, daughter of Zeus and goddess of the forests, who cared for women and brought fertility to all creatures.

The northern part of the ancient city

From the Temple of Artemis courtyard, a track leads north to the back of the restored **North Theatre**. Much smaller than its southern twin, this was originally constructed in the 160s AD to be a small performance space or council chamber; many of the seats in the lower rows are marked with Greek names, referring to tribes which voted in the city council. On the two ends of the semicircular orchestra wall, lovely little stone reliefs show women and boys dancing and playing different musical instruments. Upper rows of seats were constructed early in the third century to give a total capacity of around 1600, but by the fifth century the building seems to have gone out of use as a theatre. Much reconstruction and renovation work has been done here, not least in the orchestra, with its beautiful marble flooring. The restored theatre saw its first public performance in more than 1500 years when, at the opening of the 1997 Jerash Festival, the hugely popular Palestinian writer Mahmoud Darwish gave a poetry reading in front of thousands.

In front of the theatre is a reconstructed **plaza**, with huge Corinthian columns on one side of the street faced by an equally huge colonnade on the other that is flanked by unusual double columns ingeniously knitted into the walls of the theatre itself. To the right of the plaza, the **North Decumanus** meets the main Cardo at a rebuilt junction-point known as the **North Tetrapylon**. Simpler than the South Tetrapylon, this dates from the late second-century remodelling of Gerasa and comprises arches on all four sides leading into a small, domed central space.

On the eastern side of the Cardo rise the huge arches of the **West Baths**, the building itself unexcavated and tangled with undergrowth. It's possible to scramble among the chest-high weeds through the different rooms – changing area, hot and cold baths – but the highlight is a room fronted by two columns on the northern edge of the complex which has somehow clung onto its elegantly constructed domed brick roof. A fraction south of the baths, a small area of ruins close to the Cardo is a small **Umayyad mosque**, with a reused Roman shell niche serving as a makeshift *mihrab*.

Beyond the tetrapylon, the northernmost section of the Cardo is the quietest and most intimate part of the city. Ignored during the city's second-century facelift, this part of the street retains its original, plain Ionic colonnade, and is the same width as when initially laid out in the first century AD. The peaceful walk ends after some 200m at the **North Gate**, dating from 115 AD, from which a road led on to Pella. The gate is a cleverly designed wedge shape, in order to present a square facade both to the Cardo and to the Pella road. From here, you can either continue your northerly progress for 1500m to visit Birketayn (see opposite), or retrace your steps partway down the Cardo to explore the Cathedral and surrounding ruined churches.

The Cathedral and the western churches

Fifteen Byzantine **churches** have so far been uncovered in Jerash, and wending a path through the largely unexcavated southwestern quarter of the ruins to visit nine of them, starting with the Cathedral and ending up near the South Theatre, brings you out of the main crush of the central sights.

The **Cathedral Gateway**, marked by eight large columns on the Cardo just south of the Nymphaeum, is a large, elaborate construction which originally presaged a now-vanished second-century temple, thought to have been dedicated to Dionysus. During the fourth century, the old temple was converted by the Christian Gerasenes into the large church which survives today, at the head of a monumental **staircase**. The walls flanking the stairs originally supported high enclosed and roofed colonnades on both sides, but earthquakes toppled the lot. The old pagan temple probably faced west – as does the Temple of Artemis – but the new church had to face east: the Byzantine architects seem to have been less concerned about aesthetic harmony than their Roman predecessors, and calmly plonked the apse of the new church square across the head of the staircase. To provide some focus for the ascent, a small shell-niche **Shrine to Mary** was placed on the blank exterior wall of the apse. Originally dedicated to "Michael, Holy Mary and Gabriel", it's still possible to read the Greek for Gabriel in red paint on the right of the band beneath the shell.

Left or right from the shrine, the narthex brings you round into the **Cathedral** itself, a shadow of its former self. Very little is known about this building, and its dedication or even the supposition that it was Gerasa's cathedral remain unconfirmed. Colonnades, of which only bits and pieces remain scattered about, divided the nave and the aisles, and the high side walls were decorated with elaborate glass mosaics. Although very little of the stone paving of the nave has survived, pale pink limestone flags remain in the aisles. To the south of the cathedral is a small **chapel**.

Immediately west of the cathedral, a portico beautifully paved in red and white octagons and diamonds leads into the atrium, known as the **Fountain Court** after the square fountain in its centre fed by water brought from the great reservoir at Birketayn (see opposite). Roman historians, including Pliny, hinted that Gerasa held festivals to Dionysus (the god of wine) at which water miraculously turned into wine, and the idea must have been a tenacious one: after the Dionysian temple here had been converted into a church, it duly became the venue for festivals celebrating Jesus's performance of the same feat at Cana. During these festivals, so the historian Epiphanius records, the square fountain in this court miraculously began to flow with wine.

To the side of the paved portico is a small room known as the **Glass Court**, named for the enormous quantity of glass fragments discovered there during clearance work. The weeds and rubble carpeting its floor conceal beautiful mosaics, reburied for protection.

Left (west) of the Glass Court, a staircase leads up to the tiny **Sarapion Passage**, its octagonal flags running beneath precarious lintels out to the

Stepped Street. Turning left up the street brings you past the maze of tiny rooms forming the Byzantine **Baths of Placcus**, which date from an unusually late 455 AD, evidence that luxurious Roman bathing habits died hard. Dominating the baths to the left are the majestic twin colonnades of the **Church of St Theodore**, dating from 496. Nothing remains of the main superstructure of the building, the marble paving of the nave and aisles or the glass mosaics which covered both the interior walls and the semi-dome over the apse; all that does remain is the huge apse itself, nosing out dramatically above the Fountain Court one terrace below.

The western churches

A path from St Theodore's leads west over scrubby hillocks, reaching after 150m a group of three interconnected churches built between 529 and 533. On the right, the **Church of Saints Cosmas and Damian** houses the best of Jerash's viewable mosaics, although the only way to see them is to lean over the high wall around the church; the church doors are locked and covered in barbed wire. Cosmas and Damian were doctors, twin brothers born in Arabia in the late third century, who studied medicine in Syria and became famous for always providing their services for free. Their church is floored with a large mosaic open to the elements, which shows birds and animals in a geometric grid of diamonds and squares. Just below the chancel screen, the dedicatory inscription is flanked by portraits of the donors of the church; to the left is Theodore swinging a censer in his official robes as a kind of church trustee, and to the right his wife Georgia, her hands upraised.

From here, it's possible to work your way back easily to the *Resthouse* through the adjacent circular **Church of John the Baptist** and **Church of St George**, both with fragments of floor mosaics surviving. Alternatively, you could make your way up to the high ground north of Cosmas and Damian, where stands the ruined **Synagogue Church**, invisible from below. A Jewish synagogue originally stood here, oriented westwards towards the Temple in Jerusalem, with a floor mosaic depicting the Flood and various Jewish ritual objects. On its conversion into a church in 530 or 531, during a period of Jewish persecution under Emperor Justinian, a new geometric mosaic was laid over the original, and the orientation of the building reversed, with an apse laid in what was formerly the synagogue's vestibule.

South of here, and west of Cosmas and Damian, lie the untended ruins of the **Church of Bishop Genesius**, built in 611 just three years before the Persian invasion and featuring a prominent benched apse. On a hill 300m south, tucked just inside the southwestern city walls not too far from the South Theatre, the **Church of Saints Peter and Paul** and, close by, the **Mortuary Church** are slowly being reclaimed by Mother Nature.

Birketayn

Branching off the main route north to Irbid, two smaller roads pass in front of Gerasa's North Gate. The road on the left climbs towards Suf, but an easy walk along the other, leading directly away from the gate, brings you after 2km to **Birketayn** (Arabic for "two pools"). Set in a beautiful shaded valley in a crook of the road, this is a Roman double reservoir – restored in the 1960s – which fed water into Gerasa. Birketayn was the venue for the notorious Maiumas festivals, nautical celebrations of ancient origin which involved, among other things, the ritual submersion of naked women. By the time of Gerasa's heyday, the festivals seem to have become thinly veiled excuses for open-air orgies, and were duly banned by the city's early Christian rulers. In 396 AD the powers-that-be relented, and reinstated the festivals, provided that they follow "chaste customs"; however, the pleasures of the flesh seem to have proved irresistible, since three years later the ban was reimposed. Some 130 years passed before the festival was again resurrected by the Gerasenes and incorporated into their Christian faith as a kind of harvest celebration, purged of sensuality.

Overlooking the reservoir stands the thousand-seat **Festival Theatre** and, beyond, a path leads through the trees to the ruined and atmospheric **Tomb of Germanus**, standing amid sown fields, some columns upright and others – along with the empty sarcophagus – entwined in thistles down the slope.

Around Jerash

Jerash is set amid rolling, verdant hills cut through by countless lush valleys, and even in the height of summer, when the hills are baked brown and dry, you'd miss a good deal of the beauty of Jordan if you neglected the chance for a trip into the countryside around the ruins. In ancient (and not-so-ancient) times, these slopes were covered with thick forests of pine, oak and pistachio, which survived largely undamaged until the early 1900s, when large swathes of forest were felled to provide timber for the Hejaz Railway, both for track-building and for fuel. Enough forest has survived, though, in the areas around **Ajloun** and **Dibbeen** – both within half an hour's drive of Jerash – to give plenty of walking and picnicking possibilities in what is the most southerly area of complete pine forest in the world. Ajloun also has a strikingly photogenic Crusader-period castle perched among olive groves on a hilltop just outside the town.

Ajloun

A thriving market town and capital of its own governorate, **AJLOUN** (pronounced "adge-loon"), 27km west of Jerash, has been a centre of population for a thousand years or more. Marking the centre of the town, 150m along the market street from the bus station, is a **mosque** that probably dates from the early fourteenth century. The square base of its minaret, as well as the simple prayer hall and carved Quranic inscriptions set into the walls, are original, and the guardian is quite willing to show you around inside.

Ajloun castle (Qal'at ar-Rabadh)

The history of Ajloun is bound up in the story of the castle – in Arabic, the **Qal'at ar-Rabadh** – which towers over it from the west. A perfect location, with bird's-eye views over the whole of the surrounding countryside and over three major wadis leading to the Jordan Valley, the hill on which the castle sits, Jebel Auf, is said to have formerly been the site of an isolated Christian monastery, home to a monk named Ajloun. By 1184, in the midst of the Crusades, the monastery had fallen into ruin, and an Arab general and close relative of Salah ad-Din, **Azz ad-Din Usama**, took the opportunity to build a fortress on the ruins, partly to limit expansion of the Crusader kingdoms (Belvoir castle stands just across the Jordan to the west and the Frankish stronghold of Karak is ominously close), partly to protect the iron mines of the nearby hills and partly to show a strong hand to the squabbling clans of the local **Bani Auf** tribe. Legend has it that, to demonstrate his authority, Usama invited the sheikhs of the Bani Auf to a banquet in the newly completed castle, entertained and

Ajloun development

There are big plans for Ajloun. In recent years the Jordanian government has ploughed a good deal of development money into the region, in recognition of its largely unrealized potential – fertile, cultivated land, populous, with outstanding natural beauty and notable historic and religious attractions. King Abdullah and Queen Rania have been taking a personal interest, urging politicians to take steps to improve the region's infrastructure and even reportedly buying land for a royal retreat in the area. The **Ajloun Master Plan** has been set up to promote sustainable social development in the governorate, and one of the first benefits has been the **Woodland Reserve** (see p.216), an ecotourism project set up jointly by the Royal Society for the Conservation of Nature (RSCN) and the Jordan River Foundation (JRF). In addition, the JRF is working to improve **environmental education**, as well as pioneering new employment opportunities for local people – not least through Jordan's first large-scale programme for **organic farming**, introducing new agricultural technologies and developing wider markets for produce to boost local incomes. **Ajloun castle** has been extensively renovated and the Christian pilgrimage site of **Anjara** (see p.218) may be next in line.

fed them, then threw them all into the dungeons. The new castle also took its place in the chain of beacons which could transmit news by pigeon post from the Euphrates frontier to Cairo headquarters in twelve hours. From surviving records, it seems that Ajloun held out successfully against the Franks.

Expanded in 1214–15 by Azz ad-Din Aybak (who also worked on Qasr Azraq), Ajloun's castle was rebuilt by **Baybars** after being ransacked by invading **Mongols** in 1260. Ottoman troops were garrisoned here during the seventeenth and eighteenth centuries, but when the explorer Burckhardt came through in 1812, he found the castle occupied only by forty members of a single family. Severe earthquakes in 1837 and 1927 caused a great deal of damage, and major consolidation and preservation work on the surviving structures is ongoing.

These days, the castle (daily: April–Oct 8am–7pm; Nov–March 8am–5pm; JD1) is entered from a hideous modern parking area, seemingly designed to stick out like a sore thumb against the fine old stonework of the castle walls. A **moat bridge** cuts through the east wall. A long, sloping passage leads up to an older, arched entrance, decorated with carvings of birds, and just ahead stands the original entrance to Usama's fortress. Although the warren of chambers and galleries beyond is perfect for scrambled exploration, with all the rebuilding over the centuries it's very difficult to form a coherent picture of the castle's architectural development; there's even – in this Muslim-built, wholly Muslim-occupied castle – one block carved with a cross, presumably part of the monk Ajloun's monastery. However, a climb to the top of any of the **towers** gives breathtaking views over the rolling landscape, and these more than make up for any historical confusion.

Off to the side of the castle road, behind the *Bonita* restaurant (see below) and all around the castle itself, are acres of olive groves, carpeted in spring with wildflowers and perfect **walking** territory.

Practicalities

Buses run to **Ajloun** from Amman, Irbid, Jerash and Kraymeh (in the Jordan Valley), but the road from Jerash is the most beautiful way to approach, loping over the hills among stands of pine and olive trees, with the castle in plain view silhouetted on the horizon for at least half the way. If you're driving from Jerash, don't miss the turning right (north) to Ajloun in the town of Anjara. A shuttle **bus** makes the run between Ajloun bus station and the castle for pennies, infrequently during the week but usually pretty regularly on Fridays and Saturdays. The going rate for a **taxi** up is 500 fils, or JD2 for him to wait and bring you down again. If you fancy the stiff three-kilometre **climb**, start from the town-centre roundabout (topped with a kitsch model of the castle) near the old mosque, and head up the road with the minaret on your left.

There are two **hotels** on this quiet castle road, neither of them remarkable, but both pleasant enough with amenable and welcoming staff. The first is the *Qal'at al-Jabal* or *al-Jabal Castle* (☎02/642 0202, ℱ06/463 0414; ❸–❹), with a lovely garden in front; all rooms are spotless, en suite and with balconies, and some have stunning castle views. A few hundred metres further up is the smaller *Ajloun Hotel* (☎02/642 0524, ℱ642 1580; ❸–❹), much the same in style. If you're planning to stay over a weekend between April and October, or any time in July or August, it's a good idea to book.

Restaurant options are limited either to basic diners clustered around the town-centre roundabout, or the formal *Bonita* (daily 11am–11pm; ☎02/642 0981), almost at the top of the hill, with an open-air balcony and superb views. During the day, they have a good buffet of salads, cold *mezze* and hot chicken or kebab mains (JD6 for everything, or JD4 without the hot dishes), while in the evening they switch to à la carte (750 fils per *mezze*, JD3 for a kebab). On Thursdays and Fridays, the *Bonita*, the slopes around the castle and the castle itself are all crowded with carloads of locals enjoying a day out – not a good time to find peace or solitude.

You can get a pamphlet about the castle from Ajloun's **tourist office** (Sun–Thurs 8am–2pm; ☎02/642 0115), located in the same building as the *Bonita*, though they can't tell you much that isn't already in plain view.

Around Ajloun

For drivers, the major route down to the **Jordan Valley** from Ajloun is via Anjara and Kufranjeh, but there is a much more beautiful back way down between the hills. Turn off the castle road at the *al-Rabad Castle Hotel*, fork left after 4km and right 4km further. The rustic village of **Halawa** appears after another 7km, in the middle of which there's a steeply sloping fork; the road to the left (which runs past the post office) will eventually deliver you after 10km of gorgeous countryside around **Wadi al-Yabis** to the Jordan Valley highway.

Ajloun Woodland Reserve

One of the most beautiful and peaceful retreats in the whole of Jordan is the Royal Society for the Conservation of Nature's **AJLOUN WOODLAND RESERVE**, situated on a remote, isolated hillside above the Wadi Ain Zubia about 9km north of Ajloun town. This is lovely countryside, situated at around 1200m above sea level – the coolness in air temperature in these hills compared to Jerash is noticeable, and when it's sweltering a short drive away in the Jordan Valley it can be balmy and fresh up here. The reserve comprises a modestly sized area of rolling Mediterranean woodland, comprising mainly evergreen oak, with some pistachio, carob and wild strawberry trees along with olive groves. It is completely fenced: a few years back, the RSCN moved their breeding programme for the locally extinct **roe deer** to here from nearby Zubia, and they are still monitoring the possibility of releasing deer into the

Walking in northern Jordan

Outside the winter months when there may be considerable rain or even snow, the gentle terrain of north Jordan allows **walkers** to make their own explorations – preferably in the springtime, when the flowers are at their best. There are no marked trails, so you're free to wander at will over the verdant hills, and although you may meet no one while out walking you'll almost certainly be inundated with offers of tea and refreshment in any villages you pass through.

A **two-day trek** that encapsulates the best of north Jordan is a 36-kilometre walk from the twelfth-century Arabian fortress of **Ajloun** down to the ruins of the Greek city of **Pella** in the Jordan Valley. Bring plenty of water, since places to replenish supplies are widely spaced. From the castle walls at Ajloun you can see the line of the route: west along the ridge, then down right into the thickly forested valley and up west to a saddle between rounded hills, on the far side of which is concealed the **Wadi al-Yabis**. The walk down this long and varied valley is particularly beautiful, first passing through natural forests to reach a knoll on its right side, with Ottoman ruins; this makes for an idyllic campsite, with a view to the setting sun behind the hills of Palestine.

The second day covers about 20km, with a pleasant morning walk down the dale through ancient olive groves. If the stream is flowing you may get wet feet, as the path crosses and re-crosses its course, until a larger stream enters from the right after a couple of hours. Cross the confluence and take a track north through well-tended orchards where sunbirds dart between bright orange pomegranate blossoms in spring. The trail rises steeply to the hilltop village of **Kufr Abil**, where you may be faced with an obstacle course of people inviting you for tea. Various options down 6km of country lanes then take you almost to the Jordan Valley. As the hills level out, tracks cross their lower slopes northwards to emerge above the village of **Tabqat Fahl** at the ruins of **Pella** (see p.232), where there's an excellent resthouse with accommodation.

A memorable **one-day** alternative comprises a twelve-kilometre descent of Wadi Yabis. The best start is from 14km along the road between Ajloun and Kufr Abil, where the road crosses a tributary of the Yabis. A lane follows the stream down left (west) though orchards to the confluence mentioned above. From there, simply follow the stream down through ever-changing scenery – olive groves, a limestone dale, a small gorge, then steeply down to the floor of the Jordan Valley, from where buses run to Dayr Alla and then Amman.

Both these walks, and many others in the region around Umm Qais, Ajloun, Pella and the King Talal Dam just south of Dibbeen, are described in more detail in Tony Howard's book *Jordan: Walks, Treks, Caves, Climbs, Canyons* (see p.496).

wild. The **fauna** of the reserve covers some very European names: wild boar, foxes and badgers are all common, as are **birds** such as tits, finches and jays. Staying a night or two in the well-equipped **campsite** – or even just dropping in for a meal and a walk – can give an alluring perspective to this so-called desert land.

There are two **walking trails** heading out from the reserve headquarters, both of which (since they pass within the strictly protected area of the reserve) can only be done accompanied by an RSCN guide. The **Scenic Viewpoint Trail** (2km; 1–2hr; JD6 per person) is a short circuit heading up to a nearby hilltop – especially beautiful in springtime when wildflowers carpet the ground – and back again on a different route through the woods. The **Rockrose Trail** (8km; 4–5hr; JD15 per person) is a scenic countryside walk of moderate difficulty, crossing wooded valleys and ridges on a looping path through the reserve and the nearby villages.

Practicalities

There's no **public transport** anywhere near the reserve: you'll have to either **drive** yourself or hire a **taxi** (JD3–4 from Ajloun). There are distinctive brown signposts pointing the way to the reserve from the main road. From Ajloun town centre, with the castle road on your left, head straight on (north) up the hill on the road towards Irbid. After 4.7km, turn left towards Ishtafeina (or Eshtafena) village at a junction which has a fuel station on the corner. (If you're coming the other way, this junction lies 24.5km south of the Yarmouk University campus in Irbid city centre.) Just 300m from the junction down this side-road, fork right. After another 600m fork right again; the road drops down into woodland. After 600m turn left and climb up to the village of **Umm al-Yanabi**. After 900m turn left, and then after another 1.4km follow the asphalt road up to the reserve buildings.

The reserve is **open** for day visits all year round; **admission** is 3JD. However, it's only possible to **stay** here in the summer months (April–Oct): in winter, bad weather is common along with freezing temperatures and snow. Whatever you're planning, you should always contact the RSCN **in advance** to find out what's possible: turning up on spec may well leave you disappointed. Either contact the reserve staff directly (☎02/647 5672, ℉647 5673) or get in touch with the RSCN's Tourism Unit in Amman (see p.77). The reserve headquarters includes a small **restaurant** with a balcony view over the woods, where the staff – if they know you're coming – can prepare a meal. On clear days, you can see from here across to the West Bank and even as far as the snowcapped mountain Jebel ash-Sheikh in southern Lebanon.

In the trees behind the reserve building is the **accommodation**, comprising ten permanent, solidly built tented lodges arranged around a small clearing. The sleeping arrangements are excellent: the wooden lodges have canvas walls, but are built above ground on stilts, with proper floors, and each has four single beds inside. Shared bathroom facilities (showers and toilets) are nearby, alongside the main building. Charges (which include breakfast) are on a sliding scale: 20JD for one person, going down to 15JD each in a party of five or more. Whatever money you spend here helps to fund the RSCN's pioneering work protecting Jordan's natural environment.

Anjara

The small market town of **ANJARA** sits 3km south of Ajloun on the main road up from the Jordan Valley towards Jerash. Its only claim to fame is a local legend that Jesus, Mary and the disciples once stopped overnight en route to Jerash at a cave near the town, from where Jesus gave a sermon. There's nothing in the Bible about this, but it is known that Jesus crossed the Jordan many times, and since Anjara then (as now) straddled a major junction, it is plausible that a traveller heading east would stop over here. The exact location of the cave being unknown, in the 1920s an Italian Catholic priest, Father Foresto, decided a piece of land in the town would have to do for a commemorative church, and arranged for a 150-year-old life-size wooden statue of the Madonna to be brought over from Italy. The church went up in the 1950s, and then in 1971 Father Nimat – who is still the chief cleric in Anjara – built a shrine for the statue in the churchyard, known as **Sayyidat al-Jebel** (or **Our Lady of the Mountain**), and had its walls decorated with endearingly kitsch murals. Following the seal of approval from the Vatican that this is indeed a sanctified site, Christian pilgrims now flock to Anjara, more than eight thousand a year; indeed, the diminutive shrine in its rubbly artificial grotto was declared one of Jordan's five pilgrimage sites for the Jubilee Year 2000. From Anjara's central junction, the square steeple of the Catholic church, with its distinctive red roof, is clearly visible just below the main road; if the gates aren't open, ask around locally, since Father Nimat lives very nearby, and will be more than willing to unlock the shrine for you.

Tell Mar Elias

Another holy site, this time sacred to Muslims as well as Christians, lies tucked away in the hills west of Ajloun and hard to reach without your own transport. **Tell Mar Elias** is generally accepted as the birthplace of the prophet Elijah, who is named in 1 Kings as "Elijah the Tishbite" (Tishbe has long been associated with Listib, a region lying 8km west of Ajloun) and who is also proclaimed in the Quran as "a messenger". The visitable archeological remains are of a vast church on a windswept, inaccessible hilltop, but the route, along a beautiful, quiet country lane clinging to the contours of the forested slopes, is just as memorable. From Ajloun centre, head up the hill towards the castle, then turn off at the *Qal'at al-Jabal* hotel. At a crossroads after 1km, go steeply down to the left. After 4km, a junction is marked with a sign to Mar Elias (and another to the village of **Wahadneh**, where there's a modern church dedicated to Elijah); head right at the sign for just under 2km, then turn left and drive for exactly 1km, then take an unsigned dirt track left uphill for 400m to the small parking area at the foot of the *tell*.

The guardian will probably emerge to greet you as you make the short scramble up the rough stairs to the hilltop, where you'll find the ruins of a huge, cruciform **church**, roughly 33m by 32m. Only the foundations and a course or two of stones are left, and very little archeological work has been done here, but it seems that the church was built in the seventh century; one of the exposed floor **mosaics**, in white letters on a red background, has been dated to 622 AD – a time of upheaval in Jordan, with the Byzantine forces in full retreat in the face of the Islamic armies sweeping northwards. There has been, as yet, no satisfactory reason put forward as to why the authorities were building churches amid such political instability though. Beside the apse is a **sacristy**, floored with a plain mosaic, and there are some beautiful mosaic designs surviving against the north wall, including multicoloured chevrons and an elaborate drinking vessel with grapes. At the western end of the church is a section on a slightly lower level, possibly a narthex, which incorporates a deep **well** beside an ancient oak. Many of the trees in the area are bedecked with strips of cloth, tied round the branches by devout pilgrims – both Christian and Muslim – as a mark of respect for the prophet; a good time to visit is on Elijah's commemoration day of July 21, when there are special celebrations.

Dibbeen Forest Reserve

A large area of cool, fragrant, pine-forested hillside southwest of Jerash, the **Dibbeen Forest Reserve** – like its neighbour near Ajloun – is one of the most beautiful, and remote, getaways in the whole of the north, despite (or perhaps because of) the fact that there are virtually no facilities for visitors and no buses run here. If you haven't got any transport, it's hard to justify the effort of getting to the park; with a rental car, of course, a visit is much easier. From Saturday to Wednesday, the forest is largely deserted, and you could wander for hours along dappled tractor tracks through stands of Aleppo pine and evergreen oak, with expansive views of the hills all around; Thursdays and Fridays – family outing days – see a major influx of barbecues, portable radios and football matches. In 2004 this was declared Jordan's seventh nature reserve, under the protection of the RSCN, who have launched a four-year programme to enforce environmental protection measures and launch initiatives with local people for sustainable development of the area.

Until the RSCN can fund redevelopment and build more eco-friendly facilities, the institutional *Dibbeen Resthouse* (☎02/633 9710 or 635 2413, ℉635 1146) remains walled off in the middle of the forest, with a **restaurant** of sorts. In years gone by you could stay here too, but that has been halted for now. It remains a beautiful spot for walks and picnics, and its fledgling status as a protected reserve bodes well for the future.

A new road is being built to connect Dibbeen with the Amman–Jerash highway, climbing from the River Zarqa up into the hills. Until it is open, the *Resthouse* can be reached on a backroad which winds through the forest off the Jerash–Ajloun road. Coming from Jerash, a **taxi** is about JD4, or you could take a **minibus** to the nearby village of Burma and see if the driver will detour to the *Resthouse* for an extra dinar or so. If you're **driving**, follow a sign for the park pointing left off the Ajloun road 100m from Hadrian's Arch in Jerash; this road continues straight, through the Ghazza Palestinian refugee camp and down into the gorgeous Wadi Haddada and the reforestation projects at Jamla. The park road branches right at a signpost 11km from Jerash; you could stop anywhere along here and take off into the trees. The *Resthouse* is 2km further on; to return to the Jerash–Ajloun road, continue straight through the park for another 14km or so.

Irbid

Although **IRBID** has been inhabited since Chalcolithic times and has also been identified as the Decapolis city of Arbela, the *tell* rising above downtown – now home to a police station and flea market – is all that's visitable of the city's ancient past. Irbid today is unlikely to set your pulse racing, a humdrum city most often visited as a staging-post for journeys into the far north of the country or down into the Jordan Valley.

Lightening the mood of the place is **Yarmouk University**, one of Jordan's – and the Middle East's – best. Located on a campus well south of the town centre, Yarmouk has generated around itself a funky quarter of inexpensive restaurants, music stores and internet cafés. Savouring the lively student atmosphere here beats the rather mundane experience of mooching around the bustling streets and markets downtown. The university is also the rather incongruous home to one of the country's best historical and archeological museums.

Museum of Jordanian Heritage

Yarmouk University's small **Museum of Jordanian Heritage** (Sat–Wed 10am–5pm; free) – far from being a dusty collection of objects with accompanying notes – amounts to a superbly presented showcase of information, fleshed out with a few, carefully chosen objects. The approach is such that you can readily grasp the sequence of historical eras and the cultural trends that accompanied them; it's easy to spend an engaging hour or more exploring the displays. To get there from the main gate of the university, continue straight ahead until the second roundabout, and the museum is the second building to the right, part of the Institute of Archeology and Anthropology.

The **ground floor** rooms are more or less chronological, beginning from prehistory (with some of the 9000-year-old statuettes discovered at Ain Ghazal

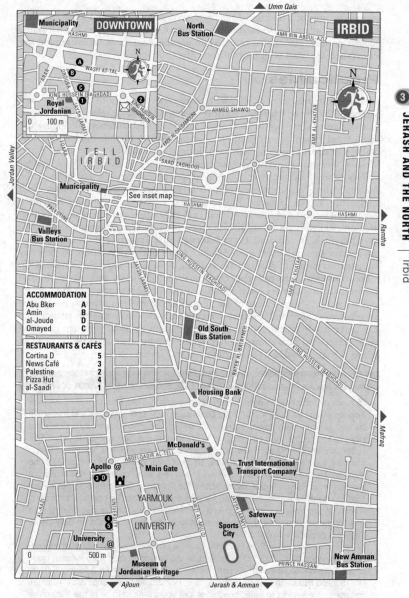

near Amman), plus excellent informative background on such topics as Jordan's external relations in 2000 BC and the development of territorial states. All periods of Jordan's history, from the Bronze and Iron ages, through the "forgotten" centuries of Jordan under the Mamlukes and Ottomans, up to the present day, are explained clearly, and subtly illustrated with interesting artefacts, including reconstructions of a traditional medieval apothecary's shop and a blacksmith's. **Upstairs**, displays are devoted to informative explanations of traditional crafts, such as pottery, glass and textiles, while the old stone-built rooms around the **courtyard** are filled with tools of rural life.

Practicalities

Irbid has four **bus** stations, of which three serve destinations other than local villages. The **New Amman station** (*mujemma amman al-jdeed*), 200m or so east of Sports City, has buses serving Amman's Abdali station (including the fast air-con Hijazi vehicles), Ajloun, Jerash, Mafraq, Ramtha and Zarqa. The **Valleys station** (*mujemma al-aghwar*), located off Palestine Street about 500m west of downtown, serves destinations in the Jordan Valley and the smaller valleys running down to it; the only places of interest here are likely to be Mshare'a (for Pella; only one or two buses a day go direct to Tabqat Fahl itself), the Sheikh Hussein Bridge, Shuneh ash-Shamaliyyeh and Kraymeh. Some 1.5km north of downtown on Fadl al-Dalgamouni Street is the **North station** (*mujemma ash-shomali*), with buses to Umm Qais, Himmeh and Hartha via Qwaylbeh. In addition, **Trust International Transport** runs comfortable, air-con no-smoking buses from its office south of the centre near the Safeway supermarket direct to Aqaba (daily 8.30am, 3.30pm & 5pm; 5hr 30min; JD6).

For **transport around the city**, serveece minibuses link all of the bus stations, although unless you read Arabic it's impossible to tell these from inter-city minibuses – you'll have to ask around for where you want to go. Similar serveece minibuses and ordinary serveece taxis also serve the bus stations and the university from different points along Hashmi Street downtown. Plenty of (often meterless) taxis prowl all main streets and bus stations; a negotiated fare across the city shouldn't come to more than 750 fils.

Moving on to Syria or Israel

To move on from Irbid **to Syria**, plenty of serveeces run day and night from the New Amman station to **Dera'a** (JD2.500), **Damascus** (JD4.500) and points further afield (as well as some destinations in Lebanon); book at the office diagonally opposite the Hijazi ticket counter and be prepared to show your passport and Syrian visa. This is the simplest way to get there, but if you need to save every fils, you could take a bus from the same station to **Ramtha**, on the border some 20km east of Irbid (the main border-post at Jaber is further away and less easy to get to). Serveeces run regularly from Ramtha's bus station across the frontier to Dera'a for JD2, but it's not hard to **hitchhike** across the border: jump off the bus before you get to Ramtha bus station, at a roundabout on the outskirts of town, and stand on the road bearing right which bypasses the town and leads straight to the border, which is open daily (24hr). There's a **departure tax** of JD5.

The easiest way to get from Irbid **into Israel** is with the buses run by Trust International Transport (⊕02/725 1878), located on the approach road from Amman close to the Safeway supermarket. Departures are to **Tel Aviv** (Sun–Fri 9.15am; JD21 or NIS150) and **Nazareth** (daily 9.15am; JD18 or NIS120). All buses originate in Amman, so timings are subject to traffic conditions (but you still need to be at the Trust office 30min in advance), and all cross via the **Sheikh Hussein Bridge**, where you pay a **departure tax** of JD5. A more laborious method is to take a bus or serveece from Irbid's Valleys station – preferably early in the morning – direct to the bridge terminal (JD2). A shuttle covers no-man's-land between the two customs posts for about 700 fils, and from the other side there are buses or shared taxis to the Israeli town of **Bet She'an**, a few kilometres west, for about 10 shekels.

There's no tourist office in Irbid. The downtown **post office** (daily 7am–7pm, Fri until 1.30pm; hours curtailed slightly in winter) is on King Hussein Street (popularly known as Baghdad Street). Irbid has dozens of **Internet** cafés, many located on the strip outside the university (nominally Arshaydat Street, but known to all as **University Street**). Most aren't cafés at all, just office spaces crammed with as many PCs as will fit, but prices, unsurprisingly, are lower here than anywhere else in the country (500 fils to JD1 per hour) and most are open day and night. The most pleasant and relaxed is the *News Café* (see below), with music and gourmet coffees, while the best-known is the huge *Apollo*, housed in a complex beside the roundabout along with *Planet Donuts*.

Accommodation

In keeping with the schizophrenic split between the city centre and the university district, Irbid's cheapest **hotels** are all clustered together in the heart of downtown, while the single more attractive option – and the best hotel in town – is close to the Yarmouk campus.

Abu Bker Just off Orouba St ℡ 02/724 2695. On the second and third floors, so a little quieter than the competition, and kept clean. Free showers. JD2 to share. **❶**

Amin Orouba St ℡ 02/724 2384. Revamped and well-cared-for cheapie, with good showers (which cost 750 fils), clean rooms and attentive management. JD2 to share. **❶**

al-Joude Off University St ℡ 02/727 5515, ℻ 727 5517. Hidden at the end of Manama St, a side-alley opposite the university mosque. Best value for money: clean and spacious en-suite rooms, friendly service and the excellent *News Café* downstairs (who provide an extensive room-service menu). Rooms are quiet, all with satellite TV. **❸**

Omayed Above Irbed Supermarket, Baghdad St ℡ & ℻ 02/724 5955. Comfortable rooms on the second floor with big windows; those at the back are quiet and have ceiling fans. JD2 to share. **❷**

Eating and drinking

Irbid wins no awards for its **restaurants**. Downtown, you're restricted to plain Arabic fare, most easily had from the myriad falafel and *shwarma* stalls on every street. Sit-down places range from basic diners that are often full to proper restaurants that are invariably empty. The *Palestine*, close to the post office on King Hussein (Baghdad) Street, is the best of the former, with a good range of the usual standard dishes; and the gloomy *al-Saadi*, opposite the *Omayed* hotel, best of the latter. All are open for lunch, but most are closed by 9pm.

Better choices by far can be found on the honky-tonk strip outside the **university**, buzzing during lunchtimes and until about 10pm (later on Thursday and Friday nights). Virtually every establishment is an eating house of some kind, although many are plastic-tablecloth places indistinguishable from one another. The best food, in the biggest portions, is at the *News Café* under the *al-Joude* hotel just off the strip – as well as featuring proper espressos and filter coffee, MTV, internet access, a pool table and a trendy student clientele, they serve beer to wash down their range of wood-fired pizzas, pasta dishes, burgers, sandwiches and great salads (ask them to hold the rather gloopy dressings, though); you can walk out replete for only a couple of JDs. Elsewhere on the strip, just copy the locals and wander till you find something that appeals. The Italian restaurant *Cortina D* is calm, with an air of formality, though they can't stretch to much more than pasta and pizza along the lines of *Pizza Hut* up the road. Completing the picture are the likes of *Chilli House, Mankal Chicken Tikka* and *Popeye's Chicken and Biscuits*. For self-catering and picnic ingredients, the large **supermarket** Safeway (daily 24hr) isn't far away, on the main Jaysh (Army) Street.

The far north

The land hard up against the Syrian border in the **far north** of Jordan is hilly farming country, especially beautiful in springtime when a riot of colour covers the fields between groves of olives and figs. The ancient trees around the picturesque village of **Umm Qais**, perched on the very edge of the Transjordanian plateau, are famed for producing some of the choicest olives in the region, although the village is best known for the atmospheric ruins of Gadara, one of the Decapolis cities, and for spectacular views out over the Sea of Galilee. Below Umm Qais is the dramatic gorge of the **River Yarmouk**, which flows west to meet the River Jordan just south of the Sea of Galilee, and which now marks the border between Jordan and the Israeli-occupied Golan Heights (Jawlan in Arabic). Travel along the gorge is restricted, but nestled among palm trees and banana plantations below the heights is **Himmeh**, graced with hot springs and a laid-back air that belies the Israeli watchtowers within shouting distance. Further east, tucked away in the peaceful Wadi Qwaylbeh north of Irbid, lie the part-excavated ruins of **Abila**, another of the Decapolis cities, featuring a hillside rock-cut cemetery decorated with some startlingly fresh Byzantine frescoes.

Umm Qais

Off the beaten track 30km northwest of Irbid, tucked into the angle of borders formed by Jordan, Israel and the Golan, the windswept village of **UMM QAIS** is well worth the effort of a long journey, whether you visit on a day-trip from Irbid or stay overnight to relish the still twilight and fresh, chilly morning. The main attraction is exploring the remote, widespread ruins of the Decapolis city of **Gadara**, some of which are jumbled together with the striking houses of black basalt and white limestone of an abandoned Ottoman village.

Since the foundation of the State of Israel in 1948, Palestinians who were expelled from or fled their homes have come to Umm Qais specifically to savour the spectacular **views** over their former homeland from the terrace of the *Resthouse* (see p.228) – the waterfront city of Tabariyyeh (the Arabic name for Tiberias), the dark and choppy lake, and the villages and lush countryside of the Galilee. The tradition is continued today by many Palestinian Jordanians, who either refuse to travel into Israel on principle or who have been denied entry visas. You should bear in mind that the site is a popular choice for Friday outings, when the parking area can be filled with family cars and youth-club buses, and the ruins swamped by teenagers more interested in having a raucous good time than absorbing the atmosphere. Umm Qais is unmissable, but do pick your moment to visit.

Some history

After the death of Alexander the Great in 323 BC, Gadara was founded by the **Ptolemies** as a frontier station on their border with the Seleucids to the north (*gader* is a Semitic word meaning "boundary"). In 218 BC, the Seleucids took the city, but came under siege a century later from the Jewish Hasmoneans; when the Roman general **Pompey** imposed order throughout Syria in 63 BC, he personally oversaw the rebuilding of Gadara as a favour to one of his favourite freedmen, a Gadarene. The city won a degree of autonomy, and became a prominent city of the **Decapolis** (see box p.200).

Gadara's main claim to fame centres on a story recounted in the **New Testament** books of Matthew, Mark and Luke, of Jesus crossing the Sea of Galilee.

The following version is at Matthew 8:28–32: "And when he came to the other side, to the country of the Gadarenes, two demoniacs met him, coming out of the tombs, so fierce that no one could pass that way. They cried out, 'What have you to do with us, O Son of God? Have you come here to torment us before the time?' Now a herd of many swine was feeding at some distance from them. And the demons begged him, 'If you cast us out, send us away into the herd of swine.' And he said to them, 'Go.' So they came out and went into the swine; and the whole herd rushed down the steep bank into the sea, and perished in the waters."

Roman rule – particularly following Trajan's annexation of the Nabatean kingdom in 106 AD – brought stability and prosperity to the Decapolis. As at Jerash, Gadara saw large-scale public building works during a second-century **golden age**, including construction of the great baths at Himmeh. Literary sources describe Gadara at this time as a city of great cultural vitality, a centre for philosophy, poetry and the performing arts, where pleasure-seeking Romans came from all over the empire. As early as the third century BC, a native of the city, **Menippos**, allegedly a slave who had earned his freedom, had risen to become renowned in Greece as a Cynic philosopher and satirist. By the second century AD, the city's Cynic streak was flourishing in the hands of **Oenomaos**, a nihilist and critic, although perhaps the city's best-known sons are **Philodemus**, a mid-first-century BC Epicurean philosopher, and **Meleager**, a highly regarded love poet (see box). **Theodoros of Gadara** was a famous rhetorician of the first century BC, who taught the Emperor Tiberius. Later, two Gadarenes of the third century AD stand out: **Apsines** taught rhetoric in Athens; and the scientist **Philo** refined Archimedes' calculations of mathematical pi.

By 325 AD Gadara was the seat of a **bishopric**, but its proximity to the decisive battles at Pella and Yarmouk, when Muslim armies defeated the Christian Byzantines, led to the establishment of Muslim rule over the city well before the foundation of the Umayyad caliphate in Damascus in 661. However, a series of **earthquakes** not long afterwards destroyed much of Gadara's infrastructure, and the town went into rapid decline. At some point in the Middle Ages, its name changed to Umm Qais, possibly derived from the Arabic *mkes* (frontier station) or *maqass* (junction).

In 1806, the German traveller Ulrich Seetzen identified the ruins as those of Gadara, and since then excavation and restoration work has proceeded slowly: Umm Qais has never had the kind of attention or funds that Jerash has commanded. During the 1890s, a small **village** grew up on the Roman ruins, the inhabitants reusing the pre-cut stones to build their homes around graceful courtyards. A modern village soon developed nearby, but people continued to occupy the Ottoman cottages right through until 1986, when the 1500 inhabitants accepted payment from the Ministry of Tourism to leave their homes, in order to enable archeologists to clear the site for excavation.

However, since then not a single square of village land has been cleared. In the mid-1990s the ministry changed its tune, backing instead a project to convert the Ottoman cottages into a **tourist village** and chalet-style hotel. A handful of houses were renovated – among them the buildings now housing the *Resthouse* and the Museum – but work then stalled. Needless to say, the former residents were none too happy at having been ousted under false pretences. Then it was announced in 2001 that there was to be a new, 120-room **hotel** constructed in Umm Qais and that the hot springs down the hill at Himmeh were to be turned into the centrepiece of a five-star **spa** complex, with luxury hotel and full facilities. Shortly after, 9/11 struck and all tourism

Meleager, Gadarene poet

Born in Gadara in the second century BC, the Greek poet **Meleager** moved in his youth to Tyre, in modern Lebanon, and spent time in different towns around Syria, ending his life on the Greek island of Kos. As well as writing satirical social criticism, he was one of the first authors ever to compile a poetry anthology – *The Garland*, comprising works from 41 poets (including himself), each of whom was compared with a different flower or plant. He is best known for his short, lyrical elegies on love and death, which effortlessly blend the strictness of formal Greek verse with the passion of the culture into which he was born. One of his most entertaining poems threatens vengeance on those who would disturb his sweetheart's sleep:

Shrill mosquitoes, shameless blood-suckers, two-winged monsters of the night, for a little, I beseech you, leave Zenophile to sleep a quiet sleep, and make your feast of flesh from my limbs instead. But why am I talking into the air? even relentless wild beasts take delight in nestling on her delicate skin. I say it again, you evil bastards, cut it out – or you'll know the force of jealous hands.

But his languorous nature poetry suits perfectly the atmosphere of a warm afternoon at his native Umm Qais:

You noisy cricket, drunk on dew, making your music perched on the edge of the leaves, sawing on your sunburnt skin with rough legs like a lyre: your country songs are shattering the silence! Sweet thing, play a new tune – something like Pan's, something to make the wood nymphs happy – so I can take a break from loving and have a snooze here, lying under the shady plane-tree at noon.

investment was shelved. At the time of writing, Umm Qais slumbers on. Until the plans are dusted off again, the abandoned Ottoman village and its once-grand Roman neighbour stand quiet for much of the year, tour groups sweeping in and rapidly out again, weeds growing higher and dustdevils infiltrating the long narrow streets.

The site

The **site** (daily 7am–sunset; JD1) occupies a hill on the west side of the modern village of Umm Qais, with the **ticket office** up some steps from the car park on the south side of the hill. On the way, in a hollow at the turn-off from the modern village, you'll pass two **Roman tombs**; the basalt doorways are beautiful, but, disappointingly, there's nothing to see inside.

Following the street along from the ticket office will bring you into the abandoned Ottoman village, where you can wander freely in and out of the weed-ridden courtyards and dusty alleys. The street leads to the evocative **West Theatre**. The theatre is built entirely of basalt, and its three thousand spectators – including VIPs in free-standing high-backed power chairs – had a fine view west over the city (now a grassy hill dotted with olive trees). North of the theatre is Gadara's most dramatic space, the **Basilica Terrace**, cut into the bedrock on one side and supported by vaulted **shops** below on the other. Its main feature, closest to the theatre, is a square Byzantine church dating from the fifth or sixth century. A small narthex opens into an outer circular passageway, still paved with coloured geometric tiles, which encloses a central octagon demarcated by basalt columns which probably supported a dome. Within the octagon, a small depression and apse housed the altar, behind which stands a thin, pink marble column carved with a cross. On the north side of the terrace,

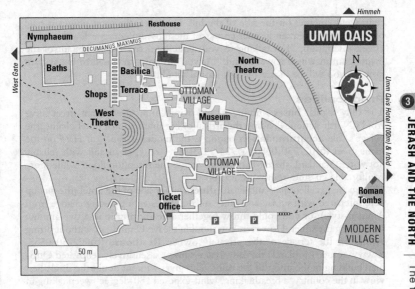

the white limestone paving and columns of the atrium stand in stark contrast to the black columns of the church. The atrium gives onto Gadara's main, paved street, the **Decumanus Maximus**, the clear line of which can be traced east and west.

Above the terrace to the east rise the restored arches of the *Resthouse*, but the rest of the city extends for the best part of a kilometre westward, largely unexcavated beneath the fields. About 100m west of the terrace is a ruined **nymphaeum**. Opposite, fences enclose a **baths** complex, once excavated but now forlornly overgrown. Some 250m further on is a colonnaded section of the street, and away to the left are the unexcavated remains of some unknown building to explore. After another 200m you'll spot a circular structure, foundations of the tower of a gate across the street, within which steps lead down into a locked underground mausoleum. Gadara's **West Gate**, with an exposed section of basalt street, is 200m further on. Alongside the modern tarmac road (which formerly ran to Tiberias) are the remains of a **hippodrome**, culminating, 500m further on, in a partly reconstructed **monumental gateway** to the city, designed to impress visitors approaching from the Jordan Valley below. Looking back from here gives an idea of the enormous size of Gadara in its heyday, and the impossible archeological task of excavating it all.

Back at the Basilica Terrace, following the Decumanus around the edge of the hill brings you to the grassy bowl of the **North Theatre**, its stones plundered to build the Ottoman cottages. Above, behind a grand gateway, is the site **museum** (daily: April–Oct 8am–5pm; Nov–March 8am–4pm), occupying the former residence of the Ottoman governor, an elegant building on two storeys, with a portico and a lovely, peaceful internal courtyard. Highlights of the collection include a headless marble statue of Tyche found in the West Theatre, mosaics from around the city and, adorning the courtyard, carved sarcophagi and capitals. The museum caretaker can come with you to explore a chill **underground aqueduct**, accessed down rickety stairs and just high enough to stand up in, which winds a tortuous course beneath much of the city centre and emerges on the side of the hill. However, the most poignant relic of Gadara lies forgotten in a far corner of the museum courtyard, a three-line Greek inscription. "I'm talking to you, passerby," says the inhabitant of the mausoleum in which it was found. "As you are now, so I used to be; as I am now, so you will be. Treat life as a mortal should."

Practicalities

The only regular **buses** running to and from Umm Qais's main street serve Irbid's North station. Pending the arrival of big international hotel chains, the village's sole **accommodation** option is the modest *Umm Qais Hotel* on the main street (℡02/750 0080, Ⓕ724 2313; ❷) – cosy, clean and with reliably hot water. Standard, shared-bath rooms are on the reception floor, while more comfortable en-suite rooms are up above.

There are excellent *fuul*-and-falafel **diners** either side of the hotel (the *fuul* up here, prepared with sumac and other spices, makes an interesting change from Amman-style), or you could throw together a hearty **picnic** in a two-minute stroll along the street. However, you shouldn't leave Umm Qais without sitting awhile on the terrace of the privately owned **Resthouse** (℡02/750 0555, Ⓦwww.romero-jordan.com; daily 10am–sunset), a sensitively renovated Ottoman building in the midst of the ruins. This gives without doubt the single best **view** in the country, a breathtaking, wind-exposed 180-degree sweep taking in the Jordan Valley, the Sea of Galilee (with the Israeli city of Tiberias in plain view), the Yarmouk gorge and, most impressive of all, the Golan Heights, pointing the way north towards snow-capped Jebel ash-Sheikh (Mount Hermon) on the Lebanese border, sometimes visible in the far distance. A meal here costs around JD10 (tax and service included) and, since the place is under the same management as Amman's *Romero* restaurant, the food is very good. During the week, the *Resthouse* closes around sunset, but on Thursdays and Fridays you can book ahead for dinner on the terrace after dark – a meal that, given the surroundings, you're unlikely to forget.

Himmeh

In its day, Gadara's lavish baths complex, built around the seven hot springs at **HIMMEH**, was grand enough to bear comparison with the fabulous imperial Roman baths at Baiae, near Naples. Modern Himmeh – also known as **Mukhaybeh** – is a shadow of its former self, and has been divided by modern boundary-drawing: most Roman remains are now in fact in what the locals call "Syrian Himmeh", on the north bank of the Yarmouk in territory currently occupied by Israel, and there is little or no historical interest in what is universally signposted hereabouts as "**Jordan Himmeh**". Hemmed in by mountains, and lying some 200m below sea level, the tiny village is crowded with palm trees and banana plants that thrive year-round in the tropical conditions. In winter and spring, there's a weekly influx of local day-trippers and overnighters, come to dip in the warm, slightly sulphurous **waters** and gawp at the massive heights dwarfing the village. The rest of the year, Himmeh is **swelteringly hot**, making the prospect of a warm dip considerably less appealing, although viewing the towering Golan – with its easily visible Israeli jeep patrols – is reason enough to visit.

Over ninety percent of the village land is owned by a single member of a wealthy Jordanian family, one Mamdouh Bisharat, whose private villa in the village – behind the tall blue gates – has its own spring and Roman pool; ask at the *Sah al-Noum* hotel to be shown around this gloriously lush and tranquil retreat. The village's tenant farmers, many of whom are of African descent and sport Egyptian-style robes and headgear, receive the standard wage of JD3 a day (for men, that is; women get half and working children a quarter), so buying some small item from the impromptu markets set up by the locals can help the village economy more than you might realize.

Practicalities

Irregular **buses** leave from Irbid's North station and pause to pick up in Umm Qais before heading down to Himmeh. Taxis do the run from Umm Qais for about JD2. If you're driving, head straight over the crossroads at the foot of the Umm Qais hill; Himmeh is 4km further, and – if business is good – charges a **toll** of 300 fils per car. With the success of luxury spa hotels at the Dead Sea, Hammamat Ma'in and elsewhere, developers are currently in negotiation to completely overhaul the facilities on offer at Himmeh, and the village may change out of all recognition in the next few years.

Until then, the springs are focused around the *al-Hameh Restaurant and Recreation*, a complex (admission 500 fils, or JD1 at peak times) comprising a large **pool**, a nondescript air-con **restaurant** (both open daily 6am–8pm), and a **hotel** (℡02/750 0512; ❷) with well-worn three- or five-bed rooms, all with balcony, ceiling fan and air con. The rather grungy pool (entry JD1.100) operates on a two-hour shift system, alternating between men-only and women-only. Bear in mind that the pool is open and public: however much the management claims that Western-style swimsuits are acceptable, women wearing a costume any less modest than long shorts and a baggy T-shirt are likely to cause a stir. A warmer welcome is to be had at the *Sah al-Noum* hotel (℡02/750 0510; ❶) – wander left at the fork in the village – where everything is very basic, rooms all equipped with ceiling fan and a private hole-in-the-ground bathroom. Out back, a rushing flow of hot spring water is channelled into a small pool.

Thursdays and Fridays are the big days here, when the spring and bedrooms at *Sah al-Noum* are generally full, and the *al-Hameh* fills up fast. If you can, visit during the rest of the week, when the village is at its most peaceful.

The Yarmouk Gorge road

Himmeh is as far east along the Yarmouk as you're allowed to venture, but with your own transport you can head west alongside a portion of the deep and dramatic **Yarmouk Gorge** (all buses go back up the hill to Umm Qais). There are checkpoints aplenty down here, for which you should always be ready to show your **passport**, and although you may be able to snatch a photo or two of the extraordinary scenery, or of the **wrecked bridge**, bombed in the 1967 war and still hanging twisted over the gorge, remember you are under constant surveillance here from both the Jordanian army and the Israeli army. The huge **Wihdeh Dam** on the Yarmouk a little further upstream – completed in 2005 as a joint venture between the governments of Jordan and Syria – is another sensitive site. Nonetheless, the **views** on this most tense of three-way frontiers are spectacular (if anything, they're better heading east than they are going west), looking down into the Yarmouk, across to the Sea of Galilee and up to the Golan Heights towering overhead. After 6km of this you come to a junction where the only option is to turn left, and this road delivers you after another 7.5km to the town of **Shuneh ash-Shamaliyyeh** (North Shuneh), at the head of the Jordan Valley, a pleasant enough little market town. The village of Tabqat Fahl – alongside the ancient site of **Pella** – is a short drive south (see p.234).

Baqoura

Northwest of Shuneh is the signposted "**Baqoura Restored Lands**". This tiny sliver, less than a kilometre square sandwiched between the Jordan and Yarmouk rivers at their confluence, was occupied by Israel in 1967 and returned to Jordan under the 1994 peace treaty. It is still controlled by the Jordanian army. Visiting isn't easy and you can't explore independently, but it's popular as a local beauty spot and retains an intriguing cross-border identity. From the Shuneh junction, head north for 3.4km to a checkpoint, where they may let you through to drive another 1.2km to the end of the road at an army base, where you must park your car. If you explain that you're interested in seeing Baqoura, an officer may find some transport and accompany you: they won't let you explore here alone. From the base a road heads down for about 1km and crosses the Yarmouk on a rickety bridge alongside a half-ruined hydroelectric station – the first in the Middle East, built in 1927 by Russian engineer Pinchas Rutenberg and damaged by Iraqi shelling in 1948. Up above is a hilltop parking area known as the "**Island of Peace**", with a breathtaking view over the meandering River Jordan: from here you can see the confluence point of the Yarmouk and the Jordan just below, with the cultivated fields of the Israeli kibbutz Ashdot Yaakov all around, the route of the old railway line from Haifa to Damascus visible and cars passing on the Israeli highway opposite. In a most unusual situation, as part of the 1994 peace treaty local Israeli farmers are permitted to rent land here – in Jordan – until 2019: you may well pass Israeli pick-ups on these roads. This car park, and the surrounding area, was formerly where Israeli and Jordanian day-trippers mixed freely, until 1997 when a Jordanian soldier, Ahmed Daqamseh, shot dead seven Israeli schoolgirls here. A rapid, high-profile trial (which had the effect of whipping up much public feeling against the treaty) convicted Daqamseh of murder, but his mental instability controversially saw the death penalty commuted to life with hard labour. His name remains notorious, a blight on Baqoura.

Abila

Lying virtually unknown in the cradle of the lush Wadi Qwaylbeh, 12km north of Irbid, the lonely ruins of the Decapolis city of **Abila** have only just begun to be excavated from the grassy fields and, although atmospheric, aren't immediately gripping. In sharp contrast, the city's Roman-Byzantine **cemetery**, comprising dozens of tombs cut into a neighbouring hillside, has to be explored to be believed: at least six tomb caves, each of which held dozens of bodies, are still adorned with their original frescoes, some patchy and damaged, some in startlingly fresh, near-perfect condition. The experience of stumbling across portraits of long-dead Abilenes gazing back into your torchlight from the rock-cut coffins that once held their bones is one to be remembered. Bear in mind that you're on your own here: there's no development of the site at all, and no facilities for visitors.

By **car**, follow signs from Irbid for Umm Qais until you reach a set of traffic lights about 7km north of the city, where the main Umm Qais road branches off left. Continue straight on here until you reach a quiet fork in the road, which divides in front of an isolated domed mosque close to Wadi Qwaylbeh (11km north of Irbid). **Buses** running from Irbid's North station towards **Hartha** bear left at this fork, which is a good place to get out, since the best way to approach Abila is to head right at the fork; walk or drive exactly 900m along this road, and then walk left straight across the fields. This will bring you to a dry-stone wall, teetering over the steep flank of the Wadi Qwaylbeh.

Prominent against the sky on a hilltop opposite is a columned seventh-century church, while the slope below the wall shelters Abila's necropolis. Very near the wall, but not immediately visible, are two of the beautifully painted **tomb caves**, while plenty of others are scattered at different levels across the slope, without signs; it would be impossible to describe their locations, and persistent exploration is required. The tomb caves which hold frescoes are gated and locked, but it's highly likely that the guardian (a local shepherd) will wander up and lead you around. Bear in mind, though, that (aside from a torch) essential exploration equipment is a steady nerve: the caves are all dank, pitch-dark, deathly quiet and very spidery. The **frescoes** themselves, however, are in remarkably good condition, delightful portraits of men and women, flowers and fruits, and one a spectacular scene of dolphins covering the ceiling.

Working your way north (right) along the cave-dotted slope brings you, after about 2km, to a modern building which overlooks the original Roman **bridge** across the stream, leading into the ancient city centre past the remains of a large Byzantine church. The site is still being excavated, although you can easily make out the bowl of a **theatre** next to a section of basalt-paved Byzantine **street**. Exploration of Tell Abila, opposite the theatre, is barely worth it, and instead you should follow the track curling up the steep hill; after climbing over a barbed-wire fence, you'll be able to explore the hilltop **church**, with its alternating basalt and limestone columns, seen from the necropolis slope opposite. Olive groves conceal the Hartha road from the church; once on the road, you could hitch a ride back to Irbid, or wait for the (infrequent) buses.

The northern Jordan Valley

The deep cleft of the **Jordan Valley** carries the River Jordan south from the Sea of Galilee (some 200m below sea level) to the Dead Sea (400m below), a distance of only 104km as the crow flies, but the meandering river twists and writhes for more than three times that length. Set down in a deep gorge flanked by a desolate flood plain (the *zor*), the river is never visible from the main road, which sweeps south through the *ghor*, or cultivable valley floor, well to the east. Flanked by 900-metre-high mountains on both sides and enjoying a swelteringly subtropical climate of low rainfall, high humidity and scorching temperatures, the valley with its fertile alluvial soil is perfect for **agriculture** on a large scale: this vast open-air greenhouse can these days produce crops up to two months ahead of elsewhere in the Middle East and can even stretch to three growing seasons annually. As early as five thousand years ago, foodstuffs from the valley were being exported to nearby states, and irrigation systems and urban development progressed hand-in-hand soon after. Throughout the centuries since, agriculture has been at the heart of the valley economy, from the wheat, barley, olives, grapes and beans of the Bronze Age to an extensive sugar-cane industry under the Mamlukes. For three hundred years up to the late nineteenth century, the valley was almost deserted, but since then rapid and concentrated development – and, in particular, the building of the **King Abdullah Canal** in the 1960s to irrigate the eastern *ghor* – has led to a burgeoning agricultural industry that supplies most of Jordan's tomatoes, cucumbers, bananas, melons and citrus fruits, as well as producing a surplus for export.

The southern part of the Jordan Valley is covered on p.191.

In contrast to the prosaic vistas of concrete piping, plastic greenhouses and farm machinery that characterize the area today, well over two hundred **archeological** sites have been catalogued in the valley, although – with the notable exception of the Roman-Byzantine remains at **Pella** – almost all of them are Neolithic or Bronze Age settlements on the summits of *tells*, with very little to see other than one or two courses of stone foundations. South of Pella, a few kilometres from the river's outflow into the Dead Sea lies the **Baptism Site** of Jesus, covered on p.180.

Transport in the valley is mostly restricted to buses shuttling north and south along the highway between the main hubs of Shuneh ash-Shamaliyyeh, Kraymeh, Dayr Alla and Shuneh al-Janubiyyeh, stopping at all points in between. Bearing in mind the excessive heat – summer temperatures regularly top 45°C – and the lack of tourist facilities, the best way to see the valley is in your own vehicle. By bus, you could devote either a half- or a full-day to the trip, starting from Irbid and heading south to end in Amman, or vice versa. The only **accommodation** comprises a few rooms at Pella.

Pella and around

For archeologists, **PELLA**, comprising a large *tell* overlooking a well-watered valley protected by hills, is quite thrilling, possibly the most significant site in all of Jordan; evidence has been found of human activity in the area for nearly a million years, with extensive remains from almost all periods from the Paleolithic through to the Mamluke. The *tell* itself has been occupied for the last six thousand years almost without interruption. However, though it's definitely worth the journey, Pella can appear rather underwhelming to non-archeologists, with – in effect – little more than three ruined Byzantine churches to divert attention from the beautiful hill-walking all around. One attraction, in addition to a well-run Resthouse (with restaurant), is an excellent **museum**, conceived and designed by the Jordanian architect Ammar Khammash.

Some history

The reasons for Pella's long history have much to do with its location on the junction of major trade routes: north–south between Arabia and Syria, and east–west between the Transjordanian interior and the Mediterranean coast. With its positioning almost exactly at sea level – the Jordan Valley yawns below – the city has a comfortably warm climate and is watered both by the gushing springs in the bed of the Wadi Jirm and by a reasonable annual rainfall, all ensuring perfect conditions for agriculture. In addition, the city was surrounded in antiquity by thick oak forests, since felled, which at more than one point provided the backbone of the city's economy.

From artefacts discovered near Pella, it seems that **Stone Age** hunters roamed the area's forests and savannahs up to a million or so years ago, bagging native game such as elephants, deer and lions. By five thousand years ago, a **Neolithic** farming village was spread out above the springs in the main Wadi Jirm, and remains have been uncovered of a larger, terraced **Chalcolithic** settlement just below Jebel Sartaba, southeast of the *tell*. By the early third millennium BC, during the **Bronze Age**, there was a thriving city at Pella, extensive evidence of which has been excavated from the *tell*: pieces dating from at least four main periods of occupation around the sixteenth and fifteenth centuries BC include luxury items imported from Egypt, Syria and Cyprus – indicating well-established trade links – such as bronze pins, stylized sculpture, gold thread, alabaster bottles, cuneiform clay tablets and beautiful inlaid ivory boxes. In the thirteenth century BC, Pella was the principal supplier to Pharaonic Egypt of wood for chariot spokes. **Iron Age** cities flourished on the *tell* up to the seventh century BC, but during the Persian period (539–332 BC) it seems that the area was abandoned.

The **Hellenistic** period is the first for which the name of Pella can be attested from historical records, and was a time of considerable affluence for the city. In 218 BC, the Seleucid king Antiochus captured Pella on a sweep through Palestine and Transjordan, and thereafter occupation of the site spread over the *tell*, the slopes of Tell Husn opposite, the so-called "Civic Complex" area on the valley floor and the peak of Jebel Sartaba.

In 83 BC, the Jewish **Hasmonean** leader Alexander Jannaeus crossed into Transjordan from Palestine and sacked pagan Pella and its neighbours Gadara, Gerasa and others. The arrival twenty years later of Pompey and the **Roman** army imposed order in Pella as elsewhere in the Decapolis region, and the city settled down to a period of stability, minting its own coins and embarking on a programme of building. However, one legacy of the city's location above a perpetually flowing spring is that, due to a rise in alluvium levels, it's been impossible to excavate in the valley bed. Consequently, virtually nothing of the Roman period apart from a small theatre survives, although coins found here show a nymphaeum, various temples, probably a forum, a baths and lavish public buildings dotted throughout the city.

A massacre of twenty thousand Jews in a single hour at Caesarea in Palestine in 66 AD fuelled a widespread Jewish revolt against Roman rule, and amid the turmoil the nascent **Christian** community of Jerusalem fled en masse to the relative safety of Pella – though they returned by the time of the rebuilding of Jerusalem, around 130 AD. Pella reached its zenith during the **Byzantine** fifth and sixth centuries, with churches, houses and shops covering the slopes of the *tell* and Tell Husn, and pottery from North Africa and Asia Minor indicating significant international trade. However, by the seventh century, the city was again in decline; in 635, **Muslim** forces defeated the Byzantine army near Pella, and the city reverted to its pre-Hellenistic Semitic name of Fahl. The devastating earthquake of 749 destroyed most of Pella's standing structures, and the city lay abandoned for several centuries, small groups of farmers coming and going throughout the Abbasid and Mamluke periods.

The site

Although there may not be much romance left to Pella, it's certainly in a beautiful location. Sweet spring water cascades out of the ground on the floor of the **Wadi Jirm**; and the imposing bulk of the sheer **Tell Husn** to one side, the long, low *tell* on the other and **Jebel Abu al-Khas** between them (on which stands the modern, triple-arched *Resthouse*) enclose the little valley with high slopes of green, leaving only the stunning vista westwards over the Jordan Valley. The abundant spring water, however, has proved irresistible to modern agriculture, and 100m beyond the antiquities stands a pumping station serving a lush area of irrigated farmland. You may well find constantly chugging machinery coupled with a reek of agrichemicals limiting your appreciation of the natural and historical drama of the site.

Before you reach the main site, you'll see the remains of the **West Church** behind barbed wire on the edge of the modern village. The church was built in the late fifth or early sixth centuries, in Pella's prime, and, although overgrown and in a poor state of repair, is one of the largest Byzantine churches uncovered in the entire Middle East. There's a gate through the site fence a few hundred metres further on, which gives access to the rest of the ruins. The main valley is dominated by the standing columns of the **Civic Complex Church** on the edge of the bubbling spring. All the re-erected columns belong to the church's atrium; to the east, in front of a finely paved portico, are two exquisite columns of green swirling marble, one of which cracked in two as it fell in antiquity. The church itself, its columns collapsed like a house of cards, has three apses, and was originally decorated with glass windows, glass mosaic half-domes, stone mosaics on the walls and floor, and chancel screens of marble. The **monumental staircase** in front was added in the seventh century, when the valley floor was some 2–3m below its current level. To one side of the church is the bowl of a small Roman **theatre**, built in the first century AD to seat about four hundred; many of its stones were plundered to build the church staircase. Across the whole area of the modern springs, there may once have stretched a forum, with the stream channelled below through subterranean vaulting, some of which is still visible.

The **tell** itself – on the left as you face the Resthouse – is likely to excite only archeologists. Although several different excavations have revealed dozens of levels of occupation over millennia, all there is to see for the layperson are the crisscrossing foundations of coarser and finer walls at different levels and a couple of re-erected columns. Of most accessible interest is a small **Mamluke mosque** close to the modern dig-house, with a plaque commemorating the decisive Battle of Fahl of 635. Excavations just beside it have unearthed the massive stone blocks of a **Canaanite temple** dating to 1480 BC, the largest yet discovered from that period. You'd have to be very keen to scale the precipitous **Tell Husn** opposite in order to poke around the sixth-century Byzantine fortress on its summit.

The steep path between the Civic Complex ruins and the *Resthouse* coils up the hillside past the columns of the small, atmospheric **East Church**, built in the fifth century overlooking the lower city and originally accessed by a monumental staircase from below. The atrium has a small pool in the centre.

Behind the *Resthouse*, the innovative Jordanian architect Ammar Khammash has built the **Pella Museum** of geology and paleontology (ⓦwww .pellamuseum.org) – ask at the *Resthouse* for access. Khammash's idea was to focus on an exploration of Jordan's history before archeology, ending 250,000 years ago, and the museum showcases his vast knowledge of Jordan's natural environment, with fossils that he's picked up around the country and geological formations displayed and explained in an attractive setting. The website is erudite and wide-ranging, and gives fascinating insight into Khammash's imaginative way of seeing Jordan's landscapes.

Practicalities

The ruins of Pella are situated close to the modern village of **TABQAT FAHL**, about 2km up a steep hill from the town of **Mshare'a** on the valley-floor highway. There are one or two **buses** running direct to Tabqat Fahl village from Irbid's Valleys station, but departures from Irbid are much more frequent to Mshare'a, from where it's not difficult to hitch or even hike up the hill. Plenty of buses heading north along the valley-floor highway from Kraymeh (a connection point from Ajloun) and Dayr Alla (easily reached by bus from Amman) stop at Mshare'a, as do buses south from Shuneh ash-Shamaliyyeh.

About 1km beyond the entrance gate to the site, on the hillside of Jebel Abu al-Khas, is the wonderfully cool and shady **Pella Resthouse** (ⓣ07/9557 4145, ⓦwww.romero-jordan.com; daily 8am–sunset). This oasis of a place, designed by Ammar Khammash with a spectacular terrace perched high above the ruins, is worth a visit on its own merits. Its fresh-squeezed juices and cold beers are an obvious attraction in a place as sultry as Pella, but the main draw is a plate of the best and freshest fish in Jordan, plucked daily from the river and served up with *mezze* for a bargain JD6 (their grilled chicken is a succulent alternative). An accompanying chilled bottle of Crémisan white wine from Bethlehem (JD11) might persuade you to leave ruin-hunting in the hot sun until next time.

The friendly *Resthouse* manager – whose family have been in the area since 1885 – operates the only place to **stay**, the small but highly recommended *Countryside Hotel*, set among peaceful olive groves on the edge of Tabqat Fahl (℡07/9557 4145, ℻02/656 0899; ❷). In the main house are one double and one triple sharing a shower, and in its own separate annexe is a lovely en-suite double room. All are simple but very clean, with the alluring appeal of genuine hospitality and a good breakfast thrown in.

Around Pella

Longer exploration of the area around Pella can take the form of a combination of ruin-hunting and adventure hiking – but you should definitely discuss your plans first with the *Resthouse* manager, who knows both the history and the topography of the area intimately. If you head past the East Church to curve up behind the *Resthouse*, you'll find rough trails leading across the hills for an hour or more out to the peak of **Jebel Sartaba**; here stands a Hellenistic fortress, rather less dramatic in itself than the remoteness of the location and the stunning views across the hills and valleys west into Israel/Palestine and east towards Ajloun.

Kahf il-Messih

Equally explorable is the route by car or on foot northwards into the hills to a little-explored site known as **Kahf il-Messih**, or the Jesus Cave. Access is straight along the approach road from the Jordan Valley (instead of taking the side-turn up to the *Resthouse*); the road is rocky and bad, but taken slowly is easily passable in an ordinary car.

Some 200m beyond the *Resthouse* junction is a fork; straight on, after 1.6km, you'll arrive at a highly photogenic **rock arch** through which flows the warm Wadi Hemmeh. Circle around to view it from the other side, where you'll also spot a small building which once housed the hot spring itself, now reduced to a stagnant pool. Back at the fork, the other road heads uphill for 2.4km; turn right here, then continue on, ignoring small roads which join from the side. After 7.3km, in the middle of the village of **Kufr Rakib**, take the right fork. As you leave the village, beneath the twin arches, take the right fork again, then a small road on the right after 1km, and left after another 1.3km into the locality of **Bayt Eidiss**. About 300m further is a spreading **oak tree**, marking the site of the Jesus Cave, with its arched entrance facing north. Local legend – thoroughly unsubstantiated – has it that Jesus stayed in the cave for some days before going to meet John for his baptism, and it has, in the Roman style, *loculi*, or alcoves for bodies, cut side-by-side into the bedrock. The oak tree is also the object of some veneration by the locals. Beside it is a flat rectangular area for treading grapes, complete with rock-cut channels and pools for collecting the juice.

The rolling hills all around are beautiful and quiet, many of them laced with extensive networks of caves and dotted with the odd archeological ruin (a small mosaic-floored church has been unearthed on one of the hills opposite). The village of **Kufr Abil**, a stop on the long walk between Ajloun and Pella (see p.217), is only a few kilometres south of here.

Sheikh Hussein Bridge (Jordan River Crossing)

Well-signposted off the valley highway north of Pella is the **Sheikh Hussein Bridge** (or Jordan River Crossing), which heads into Israel; about 5km north of Mshare'a is the turn-off for cars and buses, which share a newer terminal (Sun–Thurs 6.30am–10pm, Fri & Sat 8am–8pm), while trucks use the old terminal, signposted 4km further north. Buses from Amman and Irbid use the bridge on their way to and from Tel Aviv and Nazareth (see p.162), but it's also relatively simple to make the crossing yourself (see p.222). Arriving from Israel at this bridge, you can pick up a taxi to Amman for around JD25 for four people, or hitch a ride to the valley highway for JD1.

Travel details

Since most buses and all minibuses and serveeces simply depart whenever they are full, frequency of service is indicated only when a fixed timetable is in operation.

Buses, minibuses and serveeces

Ajloun to: Amman (Abdali station; 1hr 30min); Irbid (New Amman station; 45min); Jerash (30min); Kraymeh (30min); Qal'at ar-Rabadh (10min); Zarqa (Old station; 1hr 15min).

Dayr Alla to: Amman (Abdali station; 1hr); Kraymeh (10min); Mshare'a (30min); Salt (50min); Shuneh al-Janubiyyeh (40min); Shuneh ash-Shamaliyyeh (50min).

Himmeh to: Irbid (North station; 1hr); Umm Qais (15min).

Irbid (New Amman station) to: Ajloun (45min); Amman (Abdali station; every 15min; 1hr 15min–2hr); Jerash (35min); Mafraq (Fellahin station; 45min); Ramtha (20min); Zarqa (Old station; 1hr).

Irbid (North station) to: Himmeh (1hr); Qwaylbeh (20min); Umm Qais (45min).

Irbid (Trust office) to: Aqaba (3 daily; 5hr 30min).

Irbid (Valleys station) to: Mshare'a (45min); Sheikh Hussein Bridge (1hr); Shuneh ash-Shamaliyyeh (30min); Tabqat Fahl (1hr).

Jerash to: Ajloun (30min); Amman (Abdali station; 1hr); Irbid (New Amman station; 35min); Mafraq (Fellahin station; 40min); Zarqa (Old station; 40min).

Kraymeh to: Ajloun (45min); Dayr Alla (10min); Mshare'a (20min).

Mshare'a to: Dayr Alla (30min); Irbid (Valleys station; 1hr); Kraymeh (20min); Shuneh ash-Shamaliyyeh (20min); Tabqat Fahl (15min).

Qal'at ar-Rabadh to: Ajloun (10min).

Qwaylbeh to: Irbid (North station; 20min).

Ramtha to: Irbid (New Amman station; 20min); Mafraq (Fellahin station; 30min).

Sheikh Hussein Bridge to: Irbid (Valleys station; 1hr).

Shuneh ash-Shamaliyyeh to: Dayr Alla (50min); Irbid (Valleys station; 30min); Mshare'a (20min).

Tabqat Fahl to: Irbid (Valleys station; 1hr 15min); Mshare'a (15min).

Umm Qais to: Himmeh (15min); Irbid (North station; 45min).

International buses and serveeces

Irbid (New Amman station) to: Damascus (2hr); Dera'a (50min).

Irbid (Trust office) to: Nazareth (1 daily; 3hr); Tel Aviv (6 weekly; 5hr).

Ramtha to: Damascus (1hr 40min); Dera'a (30min).

Sheikh Hussein Bridge to: Nazareth (1 daily; 2hr); Tel Aviv (6 weekly; 4hr).

Useful Arabic place names

Ajloun	عجلون	Mukhaybeh	المخيبة
Dibbeen	دبين	Pella	طبقة فحل
Irbid	اربد	Qal'at ar-Rabadh	قلعة الربض
– New Amman station	مجمع عمّان الجديد	Ramtha	الرمثا
– North station	مجمع الشمالي	Shuneh ash-Shamaliyyeh	الشونة الشمالية
– Trust office	مكتب شركة الثقة	Suf town	بلد سوف
– Valleys station	مجمع الاغوار	Sweileh	صويلح
Jerash	جرش	Tabqat Fahl	طبقة فحل
Halawa	حلاوة	Tell Mar Elias	تل مار الياس (خربة الوهادنة)
Hartha	حرثا		
Himmeh	الحمة	Umm Qais	ام قيس
Kufr Abil	كفر ابيل	Wadi Qwaylbeh	وادي قويلبة
Kufr Rakib	كفر راكب	Wadi al-Yabis	وادي اليبس
Mshare'a	المشارع	Yarmouk University	جامعة اليرموك
		Zubia	زوبيا

4

The eastern desert

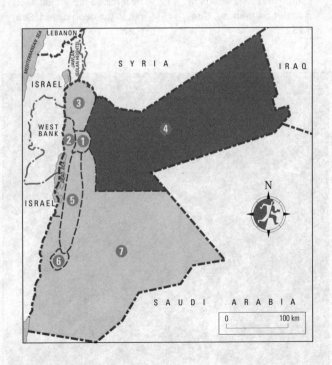

CHAPTER 4 # Highlights

✳ The Eastern Desert Circuit Take a full day from Amman to follow a looping route around the best of the "desert castles". **See p.242**

✳ Qasr Hraneh Atmospheric "desert castle", cool, dark and musty. **See p.251**

✳ Qusayr Amra Bawdy eighth-century frescoes adorning a desert bath-house. **See p.252**

✳ Azraq Palm-fringed oasis town, with an eye-popping wetland reserve on its outskirts. **See p.256**

✳ Shaumari Remote desert wildlife reserve, replete with oryx and ostrich. **See p.264**

✳ Burqu Wander on the shores of a mirage-like lake guarded by a ruined black castle, out in the deep desert. **See p.272**

△ Serving coffee

The eastern desert

or hundreds of kilometres east of Amman, the grey and stony **Eastern Desert** plains extend unbroken to the Iraqi border – and beyond, clear to Baghdad. This is the harshest and least populated part of the country, with a bare handful of roads linking small, dusty towns and frontier villages. The two exceptions are **Zarqa**, an industrial city and transport hub, and **Mafraq**, amiable but remote-feeling capital of the northeast. East of Mafraq, in the black basalt desert hugging the Syrian border, sit the stark ruins of **Umm al-Jimal**, enormously romantic in the cool evening.

The plains east of Zarqa are dotted with a string of atmospheric early Islamic inns and hunting lodges, dubbed the "Desert Castles", at least one of which, **Qusayr Amra**, is unmissable.

The highlight of a journey, though, is the castle and twin villages of **Azraq**, Lawrence of Arabia's chosen headquarters, set in a once-majestic oasis in the heart of the **eastern Badia**, which stretches from the populated central belt of the country east and north to the Syrian and Iraqi borders. Here the small, unremarkable town of **Safawi** gives access to a host of desert attractions, including the holy tree of **Biqya'wiyya** and the spectacular **Qasr Burqu**, a ruined black castle on the shores of a mirage-like lake, which lies remote in the far desert, just 50km from the Iraqi border.

Transport practicalities

Transport in the desert is predictably thin. However, Zarqa and Mafraq have good connections with Amman and other northern towns, and both

---

The Desert Castles

There are dozens of archeological sites – palaces, forts, bath-houses, inns and farmhouses of varying ages and sizes – scattered throughout the semi-arid, steppe-like desert plains to the east of Amman, most of them barely identifiable ruins. Following their rediscovery by European and American archeologists in the late nineteenth century, they were collectively tagged as "**Desert Castles**" and the title stuck, despite the fact that it's a misnomer. Not only are few of the buildings true castles, but many were built on what were then the semi-fertile fringes of the desert. In the 1200 years since their abandonment, both **Qasr Hallabat** (which actually is a fortress) and **Qasr Mushatta** (a palace) have seen the desert encroach right up to their walls. Even the remote **Qusayr Amra** (a bath-house) had an area of well-watered agricultural land surrounding it to feed its permanent staff. In recent years, archeologists have suggested titles to replace "Desert Castles" – desert complexes, country estates, farmsteads – but none exactly fits the bill.

serve as the starting points for journeys east. Azraq's main bus connection is with Zarqa. For Umm al-Jimal, Safawi and the far desert, buses run only from Mafraq.

Many of the major attractions in the eastern desert lie on a **circular route** which starts and finishes in Amman, with Azraq as its furthest point. On or close to this circuit lie, running clockwise, Qasr Hallabat, Hammam as-Srah, Qasr Azraq, Qusayr Amra, Qasr Hraneh and Qasr Mushatta. Only the first three are accessible by bus; the others have no public transport running even close. For this reason, many travellers **rent a taxi** for the day from Amman to cover the entire circuit in one go. Your hotel can help find one and conduct negotiations with the driver about your requirements and payment; the going rate is about JD45–50 for the whole car, not including a tip. Of the budget hotels in Amman, the *Cliff* and the *Farah* are the most helpful, and both run tours for around JD10–15 per person, but you must book with them at least a day or two ahead (you don't have to be staying at the hotel). Should you prefer to strike out alone, Taxi al-Barq (☎06/464 1299) is a

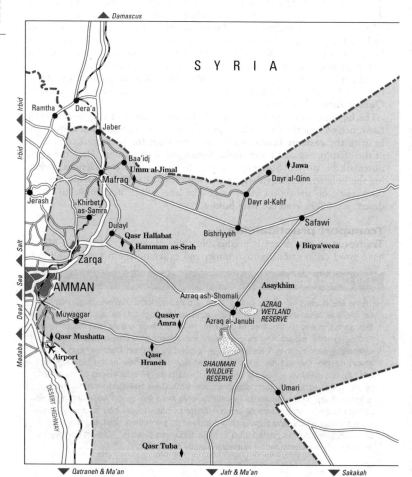

trustworthy company with which to negotiate. You could just about cover the main circuit in a hurried half-day – diverting to Mushatta adds an hour or more – but it's much more satisfying to start early, break the journey in and around Azraq, and aim to be back in Amman by nightfall. Other possibilities, including going by bus to Azraq and renting a taxi there, or hitchhiking all or part of the route, are detailed in the text. However, if you hold a driving licence, by far the most convenient option is to slash the taxi fare and **rent a self-drive car** for the day (see p.111).

Although both Qasr Burqu (see p.272) and Qasr Tuba (see p.255) can be grouped archeologically with the sites on the desert circuit, they are so far off any beaten tracks that it's only possible to reach them with a local guide and an **off-road 4x4 vehicle**. Simple directional details are given in the text, but for anyone bar the most experienced desert drivers, the best option is to go through an adventure tour operator with local knowledge; see Basics (p.75) for details.

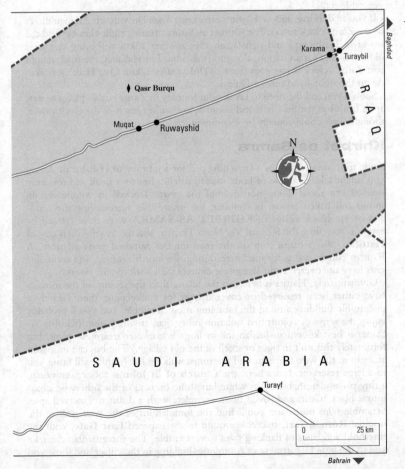

Zarqa and around

Some 20km northeast of Downtown Amman, and connected to the capital by a ribbon of suburbs, **ZARQA** is Jordan's second-largest city and its principal industrial centre. Although some older buildings survive in the ugly breezeblock jungle, there's no reason to spend any time here except to catch an onward bus – to nearby **Khirbet as-Samra**, with its Roman-Byzantine ruins; **Hallabat**, at the start of the "Desert Castles" circuit; or direct to **Azraq**.

Zarqa has two **bus stations**, 1km apart, within walking distance of the clock tower in the centre of town. The **New Station** serves Amman – either Abdali or Raghadan stations – as well as Salt and southern destinations such as Madaba and Karak. A shuttle bus runs from here to the **Old Station** but you can walk the 1km easily: head left on the main road under the canopy for 500m and then aim for the clock tower. Most buses from the Old Station serve only nearby villages, including Khirbet as-Samra and Hallabat, although there are other useful connections to Mafraq, Jerash, Irbid and Ajloun. Buses to Azraq leave from the very back of the station on the right, behind the row of vegetable stalls.

If you're **driving**, follow Hashmi Street east from Downtown Amman direct to the Zarqa clock tower. For Khirbet as-Samra, turning right 4km beyond the tower to Hashmiyya and right again after another 13km will bring you after 6km to Samra's train station, alongside the ruins. For Hallabat, the road straight past Zarqa's clock tower goes through Dulayl after 22km; Qasr Hallabat is 7km down the right-hand turn at Dulayl.

Should you feel the need to break your journey in Zarqa, viable places to **eat**, apart from bus station falafel and *shwarma,* are within reach of the clock tower, though none could actually be recommended.

Khirbet as-Samra

Aside from using Zarqa as a launching pad for a journey to Hallabat or Azraq, you might take a couple of hours out to catch a bus to a small and forlornly isolated site about 20km northeast of the town. Decked in wildflowers in spring and baked brown in summer, the grassy hills surrounding the mud-and-breeze-block village of **KHIRBET AS-SAMRA** were once crossed by caravans travelling the Roman Via Nova Traiana, and the town – then named **Hattita** – was a major stop on the road for five hundred years or more. A Roman cohort was garrisoned here during the fourth century, and archeologists have uncovered eight Byzantine churches, all with mosaic floors.

Unfortunately, Hattita is better in the telling than the seeing: all the mosaics have either been removed or covered over for safekeeping, there's barely a discernible building among the rambling mess of rubble, and you'll probably enjoy the sense of countrified isolation more than anything else. (Khirbet as-Samra is best known in Jordan for its huge wastewater treatment plant, but fortunately this isn't in sight or smell of the old village.) The bus can drop you at a gap in the wire fence around the ruins; walking left (south) will bring you to a large reservoir. From here, the **Church of St John** is about 50m north, a tiny place identifiable by its white limestone (instead of the otherwise ubiquitous black basalt) and paved floor, complete with a distinctive curved apse. Scramble 60m north and you'll find the foundations of the west wall of the original **Roman fort**, traceable around to the exposed **East Gate**, with the threshold and bases of flanking twin towers visible. The site guardian can take you to the blue Department of Antiquities building in the village and show you a map and photos from the French excavation team (Ⓦwww.afasr.org) who spend a few weeks here each year, but there's little else to keep you.

Qasr Hallabat

The main reason for passing through Zarqa is to head out on a circuit of the eastern desert, first stop on which is **Qasr Hallabat**. Perfectly situated on a small hill roughly 30km east of Zarqa, Hallabat is one of the most elaborate of the "Desert Castles", but also the most ruinous. A black basalt Roman fort was built on this site in the second century to guard the Azraq road, and parts of it still survive, but much of the present remains date from an eighth-century Umayyad restoration in contrasting white limestone, when the beautiful mosque to one side was added and mosaic floors laid. Although jumbled and broken, Hallabat is far from a washout; it's exciting to scramble around and make sense of the place.

HALLABAT village has two separate halves – Hallabat al-Gharbi (West) and Hallabat ash-Sharqi (East). There's virtually nowhere to **eat or drink** in either, so at the least bring plenty of water with you. Buses from Zarqa drop off at a roadsign 50m from the *qasr* gates in Gharbi. It's a two-hundred-metre walk over stones from the gate (where the guardian hangs out in a Bedouin-style tent) to the ruins. You first see the small **mosque**, just next to the fort, the beautiful patterned decoration cut into the arch over its doorway standing out a mile with the sky behind it. The mosque's renovated *mihrab* is to the left.

The fort lies to the right of the mosque. A wobbly **entrance arch** – one shake and it'd be rubble – leads into the stone-flagged **courtyard**, full of reused inscribed blocks jammed higgledy-piggledy everywhere and lined in black and white; a path leads left across the courtyard into a room with a roughly carved basalt lintel filled with bits of Greek and Latin. A scramble to the highest point of the ruins will help orientate you; visible in the nearby walls are very old blocks from the tiny original **Roman fort** which occupied this corner. Opposite, a water channel runs under the stairs, carrying rainwater from the roof to cisterns under the courtyard and outside the walls. If you sweep away dust from the floors of nearby rooms, well-preserved fragments of the Umayyad mosaics peep out.

Hammam as-Srah

The Umayyads also built a small bath-house, **Hammam as-Srah**, in Hallabat ash-Sharqi, roughly a three-kilometre walk or hitch from the fort. Similar to, though smaller than, Qusayr Amra, its *caldarium* (hot room) is nearest the road, followed by the *tepidarium* (warm room) with the hypocaust system of under-floor heating and terracotta flues in the walls. The *apodyterium* (changing room) is furthest away, next to the original entrance, where there's some decorative cross-hatching on the walls. Although these days it's a lonely refuge for birds and lizards, it's easy to imagine the *hammam* in its heyday, and the pleasure of a cool, quiet day spent here bathing, away from the hectic fort on the hill.

The *hammam* stands alongside a minor T-junction. If you're moving on to Azraq, head down the leg of the T with the *hammam* on your right: the main highway, where you can flag down a bus, is only 2km away.

Mafraq and around

Barely 12km south of the Syrian border lies the small, ramshackle town of **MAFRAQ**. Squeezed between it and the Jordan Valley, 50km to the west, is the whole of the northern Jordanian agricultural and industrial heartland, but to the east yawns the open desert, and the mood within the town is of a tussle with the elements scarcely won. Dust fills the long, empty streets, the buildings are squat and ranged close together; many people wear the billowing robes of desert dwellers. Close by in southern Syria, and often visible, is the extinct volcano of Jebel Druze, rising to 1800m and surrounded for hundreds of kilometres in all directions by blisteringly hot plains of basaltic lava known as the **Hawran**. Around Mafraq, irrigated fields temper the monotony, but further east – and south as far as Azraq – the desert is shadowy and grimly blackish, stark bedrock overlaid by dark boulders and glassy basalt chips too hot to touch.

Mafraq, like Zarqa, has nothing in itself to tempt you, but it's the main staging-post for journeys east, and you may well find yourself having to change buses here. Frustratingly enough for a one-horse town, it has two **bus stations**, 1.5km apart. You're likely to arrive at the large, open **Bedouin station**, so called because it serves mostly desert destinations, from where buses depart to Umm al-Jimal, Dayr al-Kahf, Safawi and Ruwayshid, as well as Zarqa and Amman's Abdali station; occasional serveeces could get you to Zarqa more rapidly. Local serveeces can shuttle you to the **Fellahin station**, serving agricultural areas; buses from here run to Irbid (which lies 45km northwest on a fast road), Jerash and Ramtha, and, in theory, a few also go to Dera'a in Syria and Damascus – ask in an office against the far wall. Town life is centred on the Fellahin station, with shops and cafés in surrounding streets, but you'll find little to **eat** beyond chicken and hummus. The Al al-Bayt University, located on the edge of town – as well as, more specifically, its hundreds of international exchange and summer-school students – give rise to a prolific array of **internet** stations, dotted throughout the town centre.

Umm al-Jimal

In 1913, the American archeologist H.C. Butler wrote: "Far out in the desert, in the midst of the rolling plain, there is a deserted city all of basalt, [rising] black and forbidding from the grey of the plain." The romance and sense of discovery accompanying a visit to **UMM AL-JIMAL** (literally "Mother of Camels") today is still memorable, even though the plain is now irrigated, and a modern village with good roads has grown up around the ruins. At first glance a mass of rubble, the site has been well excavated and is actually very easy to explore – you could happily spend a couple of hours or more here, although the combination of sun and basalt can sometimes be intolerable. Bring water with you, and plan to visit either before 11am or after 4pm; the hours just before sunset are the best, with low light casting shadows among the warm stones.

As far as the town's **history** goes, Umm al-Jimal was occupied for seven hundred years up to about 750 AD. In the first part of its existence, it was a rural village that lived more or less undisturbed under Roman authority. Following Queen Zenobia of Palmyra's rebellion against Rome in the third century, the village was rebuilt as a military station on the fortified frontier of the Roman Empire. From the fifth century on, the town prospered as an agricultural and commercial centre, and a sixth-century conversion to Christianity resulted in fifteen churches going up. However, a 150-year onslaught of plague, war, the Muslim conquest and a massive earthquake led to the town's abandonment. For well over a millennium it lay deserted, until a community of Druze fleeing

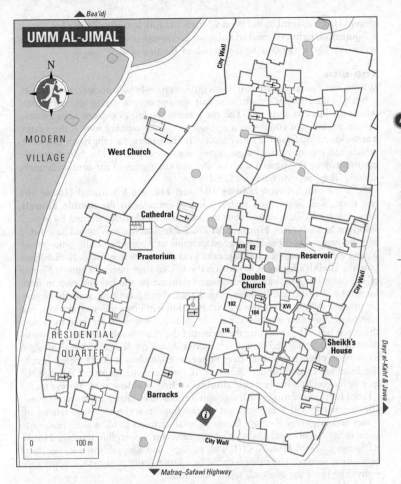

Map labels:
UMM AL-JIMAL
N
Baa'idj
City Wall
MODERN VILLAGE
West Church
Cathedral
Praetorium
XIII 82
Reservoir
Double Church
102
104
XVI
116
RESIDENTIAL QUARTER
Sheikh's House
Barracks
City Wall
City Wall
Dayr al-Kahf & Jawa
0   100 m
Mafraq–Safawi Highway

political upheavals in Syria passed through in the 1920s, occupying the ghost town for a few years and rebuilding here and there.

The appeal of Umm al-Jimal lies in its ordinariness. Although it is roughly contemporary with the grand city of Jerash, only a day's ride westward, Umm al-Jimal has no temples or monumental buildings and nothing impressive to commemorate an emperor's visit. There's not even any evidence of the town's original Roman name, which remains unknown. The archeologist who excavated the ruins, Bert de Vries, perceptively explained Umm al-Jimal's appeal as "a symbol of the real life of Rome's subjects".

A little west of the site, a well-preserved stretch of the Roman **Via Nova Traiana** survives just outside the unpronounceable village of **Baa'idj**, pointing the way across the fields north (right) towards Bosra and south (left) towards Amman. The road was cambered, with a central spine and carefully laid kerbstones, and, originally, the rough stony surface would have been covered with earth beaten flat. Drivers aiming for Baa'idj should take the perimeter road around Umm al-Jimal to the West Church and fork left; after 7km, a left turn at a T-junction, right at a small roundabout and straight on at a bigger roundabout will bring you after 600m to the stretch of Roman road.

The site

Where the modern road cuts through Umm al-Jimal's ancient town walls, a rarely staffed tourist information hut sits opposite a gap in the site fence, where the bus can drop you. The site is really too big to explore in its entirety in one go, but you could start a one- or two-hour walking tour at the nearby **barracks**, dating from the fifth century. In the eastern wall the basalt slab door, which still moves on its hinges, gives onto a courtyard. The late Byzantine **corner tower** is inscribed with crosses and the names of the four archangels: Gabriel, Raphael, Michael and Uriel.

Picking a path between **Houses 102 and 116**, and left around **House 104** (see map), will deliver you to the tumbled entrance to the **double church**, two adjacent basilicas tucked into the houses around them, fronted by a small ablutions basin. Nearby **House XVI**'s lockable double doors would have fitted together snugly, and inside is a good example of a corbelled ceiling, the strong basalt beams supporting a much greater load than limestone could. Back behind you, the **sheikh's house** is outside on the left. Its large internal courtyard is one of the town's finest, with a cantilevered staircase on the left and two in front forming a V-shape; stables were ranged around the courtyard, while bedrooms lay upstairs. Above you in the wall are two different lintel-relieving devices, one a window, the other a minuscule slot of an arch: both were designed to protect the lintels below by deflecting the weight of the heavy basalt wall onto the door-posts instead. You'll find such devices above doorways all over Umm al-Jimal; in a couple of places where they haven't been used, such as at the Double Church, the lintel has cracked under the strain. If you leave the courtyard through the gate here, you'll spot a beautiful **double-arched window** three storeys up.

From here, wandering north through a residential district strewn with loose, clinking basalt will bring you out to the huge **reservoir** – now fenced off – that was originally Roman. Umm al-Jimal's farmers lived in close proximity with their animals and, just west of the reservoir, a scramble through **House 82** brings you into **House XIII**, with mangers and a superb interlocking stone ventilation screen – partially obscured by a Druze-built twentieth-century arch – dividing space for livestock within the house.

It's a 150-metre walk across town to the four graceful and strikingly silhouetted arches of the **West Church**. The structure that remains is the division between the nave and a side-aisle, and beautiful Byzantine crosses are carved on the arches. A little way south the **cathedral** sports a reused lintel stone mentioning Valens, Valentinian and Gratian, co-emperors in 371 AD. Close by is the **praetorium**, with a triple doorway. One of the rooms nearby has strings of barbed wire across its entrances and is now the pen for a herd of beautiful white camels belonging to the local sheikh. From here, your starting point at the Barracks is nearby, or you can go on to explore the dense southwestern **residential quarter** of the town.

East from Amman to Azraq

The highway east **from Amman to Azraq** is fast, more or less straight, and runs right past two of the best archeological sites in Jordan, **Qasr Hraneh** and

△ The white camels of Umm al-Jimal

Qusayr Amra. There's nothing else to detain you along this road, which was only completed in 1985 – no public transport, no towns, no petrol stations; only the desert. If you happen to be hitching the circuit anticlockwise, you could start from the last settlement **Muwaggar**, beyond Amman's outskirts and served by a bus from Raghadan station, but, although you might find something simple to eat or drink in Muwaggar, don't rely on it – you should definitely bring sustenance with you. For advice on getting to Amra and Hraneh from Azraq, see p.260; both sites have guardians who can help out if you run out of water.

The huge and ruined **Qasr Mushatta**, beside Queen Alia Airport south of Amman, can't be reached by bus; it's best visited as an adjunct to a driving tour, tacked on either at the beginning or the end of the "eastern desert circuit". Yet more remote is the great, ruined **Qasr Tuba**, in the deep desert south of Hraneh.

Qasr Mushatta

The largest of all the "Desert Castles", **Qasr Mushatta** (Arabic for "Winter Palace") may be the last thing you ever see in Jordan, or it may be the first: the high-arched palace lies just beyond the north runway of Queen Alia Airport and is clearly visible on both takeoff and landing. The howl of nearby jet engines does tend to detract from a visit, but you may be lucky and arrive during a lull in air traffic. The guardian, should you need him, lives in a hut at the back of the site.

Mushatta dates from later than both its near-neighbours Hraneh and Hallabat – probably the 740s – and is moderately well preserved, although it was never finished. The site is enclosed by a square wall 144m along each side, with collapsed towers all round and portions of amazingly intricate classical-style **carving** surviving on the exterior. Similar pieces at one time covered all of the exterior, but as a sop to Kaiser Wilhelm of Germany before World War I, the Ottoman sultan Abdul Hamid II had most of them stripped off and presented to the Pergamon Museum in Berlin, where they still lie. The whole site is littered with unfinished work, capitals and column drums; along with the carving, everything hints at a splendour of design and execution that was never fully realized.

As you walk in, remnants of a **mosque** lie to the right, its *mihrab* set into the external wall. The palace buildings themselves are massive, built of unusual burnt brick above a stone base. The triple-arched **entrance hall** has a colonnade of beautiful swirling greenish marble columns which are still standing, very striking against the reddish brick; ahead is the huge triple-apsed **reception hall**. All around are *bayt*s, complexes of interconnected rooms, some of which still have their high, barrel-vaulted ceilings in place; if you decide to explore, tread loudly and heavily to warn any resident snakes of your presence. Behind the impressive arched *iwan*s, at the back of the hall on both sides, ancient **toilets** stick out of the wall, complete with runoff drain.

Practicalities

The simplest way to reach Mushatta is to **drive**: follow signs to the airport and, just past the *Alia* hotel, turn right at the roundabout. This is the perimeter road, and you must drive 11km around three sides of a square to reach Mushatta. You'll have to go through several checkpoints, one of which will hold onto your **passport** until you return. If you have no transport, you might try taking an Airport Express bus from Abdali station in Amman to the *Alia* hotel and hitching from there, but the perimeter road is long and quiet. Otherwise, a **taxi** from the airport terminal would probably oblige – at a price. Airport security won't let you walk the couple of kilometres from the terminal buildings.

Muwaggar

The **Amman–Azraq highway** begins from Sahab, a southern industrial district of the capital. The easiest way to find it is to **drive** south out of Amman Downtown along Prince Hassan Street (aka Madaba Street) through Wihdat into the industrial zone around Sahab. About 5km south of the major intersection Middle East Circle *(duwaar ash-sharq al-awsat)*, you'll come to the flyover which carries the road from Azraq. Heading left (east) on this road for about 17km, beyond the factories and heavy-industrial plants and into the sandy-coloured desert, brings you to the small village of **MUWAGGAR** sitting on top of a hill, terminus for a handful of minibuses from Amman's Raghadan station. A central crossroads – with unexpected speed bumps – is marked by a sign pointing the way left to the tiny, ruined **Qasr Mushash**, 24km into the desert by 4x4 and truthfully not worth the effort. About 700m further on the outskirts of the village on the right is a huge **Umayyad reservoir**, dating from the early 720s AD and still in use today. A ten-metre column formerly stood in the reservoir to mark the water level; its capital, carved with dense Kufic calligraphy, is now in the Amman archeological museum. Muwaggar's **petrol station** is the last before Azraq, a good 75km further east.

Qasr Hraneh (Qasr Kharana)

Beyond Muwaggar, there's nothing to disturb the monotony of the desert drive. After a rather alarming stretch where the road widens out and has runway markings on it (to be used in an emergency if Queen Alia Airport is out of action), you'll be able to make out a shimmering, heat-hazy shape on the horizon, which eventually resolves itself into **QASR HRANEH** (often signposted wrongly in English and/or Arabic as "**Kharaneh**" or "**Kharana**"), 38km east of Muwaggar.

Of all the inns, bath-houses and forts in the eastern desert, Hraneh – whose name derives from the stony *harra* desert in which it sits – was probably the one which gave rise to the misnomer "Desert Castles". Standing foursquare to the south of the highway, and visible for miles around, it looks like a fortress built for wholly defensive purposes, with round corner towers, arrow slits in the wall and a single, defendable entrance. However, on closer examination, you'll find that Hraneh's towers are solid (and thus unmannable) and that only three-metre giants with extra-long arms could fire anything out of the arrow slits. Rather, it seems most likely that Hraneh – positioned at the meeting-point of many desert tracks – was a kind of country conference centre, occasionally used by the Umayyad rulers of the day as a comfortable and accessible place to meet with local Bedouin leaders, or even as a site where the Bedouin themselves could meet on neutral ground to iron out tribal differences. The alternative theory, that Hraneh was a continually occupied inn or caravanserai, is thrown into doubt by the fact that it only lies near, not on, a major trade route and that it has no obvious cisterns or forms of water storage to support passing caravans. Although the date of construction is unclear, the late seventh century seems most likely; a few lines of graffiti in an upper room were written on November 24, 710.

The site

Marvellously cool and perfectly still inside, Hraneh is one of the most atmospheric and beautiful ancient buildings in Jordan. You could easily soak up the peace and quiet for a couple of hours or more. It is open every day, during daylight hours.

Walking around the building to reach the entrance, the first thing you'll notice is the distinctive band of diagonal bricks up near the top of the walls, a decorative device still in use on garden walls all over Jordan today. If the guardian doesn't meet you to unlock the gate, he's probably relaxing in the small concrete hut about 200m away to one side. As you enter the *qasr*, to left and right are long, dark rooms probably used as stables. The **courtyard** is surprisingly small, and it's here you realize how deceptive the solid exterior is: the whole building is only 35m square, but its doughty towers and soaring entrance make it seem much bigger. An arched **portico** originally ran round the courtyard, providing shade below and a corridor above – when it was in place, virtually no direct sunlight could penetrate into the interior. All the rooms round the courtyard, including those upstairs, are divided into self-contained units, each called a *bayt*, comprising a large central room with many smaller rooms opening off it. This is typically Umayyad, and the same system was used in the palace at Amman, as well as at Mushatta and Tuba. Weaving in and out, you can explore your way around the deliciously musty and cool ground floor to get a sense of how the maze-like *bayt* system works. Each *bayt* most likely held a single delegation – the central, well-lit room used for meetings or socializing, the flanking, darker rooms for sleeping or storage. Hraneh had space for a total of eight delegations and their horses.

Of the two staircases, the left-hand one as you came in delivers you to the more interesting **upper western rooms**; at the top of the stairs, it's easy to see the springs of the portico arches below. The room immediately to your left upstairs is lined with stone **rosettes** very similar to those lying around in the rubble at Hallabat. Next door, a more ornate room holds the few lines of eighth-century **graffiti** which help to date the *qasr* (as well as many more modern examples). In black painted Kufic script in the far left-hand corner above a doorway, they say, simply enough, "Abd al-Malik the son of Ubayd wrote it on Monday three days from Muharram of the year 92." All around are graceful and elegant blind arcades and friezes of rosettes, with the semi-domed ceiling supported on squinches.

The **northern bayts**, which are open to the sky, give onto the large **east room**, with a simple hound's-tooth design also used in the palace at Amman (you might also be lucky and spot the family of white owls that live here). From the southeast corner there's a nice view along the whole width of the *qasr* through alternately lit and dark areas, and it's clear that the so-called arrow slits couldn't be anything but thin windows to give ventilation and indirect light. The **southern room**, with a row of little arched windows over the court-yard, isn't part of a *bayt* and has the only large window, looking out above the entrance: this was either a watchpost or possibly a public reception area. One of the small, dark rooms on the south wall has a unique **cross-vaulted ceiling**, with decorated squares and diamonds not found elsewhere. Take the stairs up again to the **roof** to watch the dustdevils spinning across the flat, stony plain and to wonder in passing what on earth possessed the Jordanian government to build a major highway, an electricity plant and a huge broadcasting station all within metres of a beautiful ancient monument – as if pressed for space in the desert. Proposals have recently been put forward to return both Hraneh and its near-neighbour Amra to the tranquillity of the open desert by rebuilding the highway several kilometres away out of earshot.

Qusayr Amra

If you're not ready for it, you might easily miss the squat shape of **QUSAYR AMRA** (daily: summer 7am–7.30pm; winter 8am–4.30pm; free) down in the low Wadi Butm, just to the north of the Amman–Azraq highway, 15km east of Hraneh. A small bath-house, Amra was built to capitalize on the waters of the wadi, named after the *butm* (wild pistachio) trees which formerly grew here in abundance and which in springtime still form a ribbon of fertility winding through the desert, now arbitrarily cleft by the highway. A short walk in the wadi-bed beyond Amra can transport you within minutes into total silence among the trees. However, what makes Amra unmissable, and what prompted its inclusion on UNESCO's list of World Heritage Sites, is neither its natural environment nor the building itself, but the extensive **frescoes** covering every centimetre of the bath-house's interior. Joyously human, vivid and detailed, they were painted as a celebration of the good things in life, and stand in stark contrast to the windswept emptiness of the desert all around. Recently restored, they're in good condition, and you could easily spend an hour enjoying them. Alongside the parking area is an **interpretation centre**, with some good information boards and an illustrative model, although the scholarly notes, written in Arabic and French, have been translated frustratingly carelessly into English.

Some history

Amra was probably built between 711 and 715 by the **Umayyad** caliph **Walid I**. In the few years before, Walid and his predecessors had overseen the construction of the Great Mosque in their capital Damascus and the majestic Dome of the Rock in Jerusalem, and were firmly established as the new defenders of the new Islamic orthodoxy. But a hard-pressed caliph needs some time to relax. Down in the desert, far from prying eyes in Damascus, Amra was where the Umayyad establishment came to let its hair down. In a hugely entertaining counterpoint to the gorgeous mosaics of the Great Mosque, which depict a heavenly paradise for the faithful, the apparently solemn and learned Umayyads had Amra's walls painted with an earthly paradise of luscious fruits and vines, naked women, cupids, musicians, hunters and the kings of the lands they'd just conquered. The first Islamic edict ordering the destruction of images came from one of Walid's successors, when Amra's frescoes were just 5 years old, but for some reason they were overlooked and have managed to survive 1300 years of fire and graffiti.

The site

As you approach the building, what you see first is the water supply system – a cistern, a deep well and the *saqiya*, or turning circle (an ox or a donkey went round and round this circle to draw water up from the well). The main door into the bath-house is opposite.

The main hall

The main door opens southwards into the **main hall**, which is divided into three aisles; facing you at the back is a small suite of rooms probably reserved for the caliph. At first sight, the frescoes are disappointingly sparse, scratched with graffiti and – after the blinding brightness of the desert sun – almost invisible. But if you wait a few minutes to let your eyes adjust, the frescoes become much easier to see, and much more rewarding to linger over.

On the sides of the arches facing you, setting the tone of the place, are a topless woman holding up a fish [**e** on the map] and a nude female dancer welcoming visitors [**f**]. Above the entrance is a woman on a bed [**a**], with figures by her side, a pensive woman reclining with a winged angel [**b**] and a female flautist, a male lute-player and a dancer [**c**], with another nude woman [**d**]. The central aisle that you're standing in mostly has real or fantasized scenes

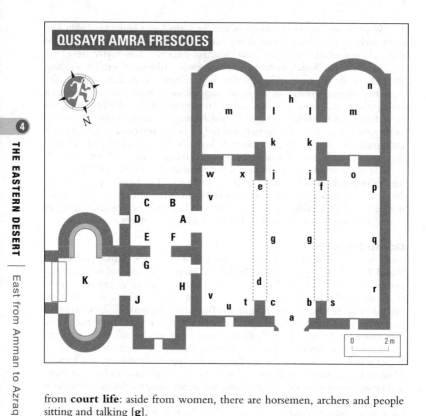

QUSAYR AMRA FRESCOES

from **court life**: aside from women, there are horsemen, archers and people sitting and talking [**g**].

At the far end of the right-hand (west) aisle [**o**], a woman reclines on a golden couch beneath an awning, with a male attendant and a woman seated on the ground nearby; at the head of the couch is a **bearded man** who pops up in many of the murals and who, archeologists have surmised, might have been in charge of the bath-house. Above the figures are two peacocks and a Greek inscription referring to victory. Below is what looks like a walled city, and below that, a decorative geometric pattern runs at eye level around the room. Near the corner – and unfortunately very difficult to make out – are **six kings** [**p**], all conquered by Walid: the Byzantine emperor, the last Visigothic king of Spain, the Persian emperor, the king of Abyssinia and two others, now obscured (the king of India, the emperor of China or the Turkish khan). Next to them is a large and strikingly clear **nude female bather** [**q**], surrounded by onlookers, one of whom is the bearded man; he's also watching male gymnastics [**r**]. Above, wild asses, their ears pricked, are being driven into nets. Much of the rest is damaged, but round near the entrance there are some grapes and fragments showing curled toes [**s**].

If you move into the suite at the back – sometimes called the **throne room** – you'll first see leopards [**j**] and fruit trees [**k**] decorating the side walls. On either side of where the throne would probably have stood are male and female figures with very clear faces, one, very pregnant, representing fertility [**l**]. Dominating the back wall is a **seated king** [**h**], possibly Walid; two attendants with fans or fly whisks keep him happy and there's a frieze of partridges around his head. On either side, and now kept locked, are presumably royal withdrawing rooms, with mosaic floors [m] and murals of fat grapes, giant pomegranates, acanthus leaves and peaches or heart-shaped fruit [n].

Back in the main hall, the east aisle is mostly devoted to male pursuits. Starting near the entrance there's a huge leaf design [t] next to **hunters** killing and disembowelling asses inside huge nets [u]. The whole of the east wall is devoted to a long hunting scene of Saluki hounds chasing and capturing asses [v]. At the far end are the muses of History and Philosophy [w], alongside Poetry [x]. Dominating the aisle, though, are a series of very clear everyday scenes overhead, depicting metalworkers, carpenters, blacksmiths, hod-carriers and jolly working camels.

The baths

The door in the east wall leads into the **baths**, which have a different style of decoration, probably the work of a different artist. The first room you come to is thought to have been a changing room (*apodyterium*) or a cool room (*frigidarium*); whichever it is, it was originally floored in marble and had benches on two sides. Above the door is a luxuriantly reclining woman, gazed on by a stubbled admirer and a cupid [A]. The south wall has a sequence of little figures in a diamond pattern, including a monkey [B] applauding a bear playing the lute [C]. Opposite the door is a woman with a very 1960s hairdo [D]; next to her are a flautist [E] and a female dancer [F]. On the ceiling overhead, blackened by smoke, is a fabulous sequence showing **the three ages of man**, with the very penetrating gaze of the same man in his 20s, 40s and 60s. Next door is a *tepidarium*, with a plunge pool and a hypocaust system to allow warm air to circulate beneath the floor and up flues in the wall. Beside the door is a tableau of three nude women [G], one of them holding a child; if you follow the picture round to the right, a woman is pouring water [H] and is about to bathe the child [J].

The last room, a domed **steam room**, or *caldarium*, is next to the furnace; the holes in the wall all around supported marble wall slabs, and there are a couple of plunge pools. Above is the earliest surviving representation of the **zodiac** on a spherical surface [K]. Dead ahead you can easily identify Sagittarius, the centaur, with the tail of Scorpio to the left. Ophiuchus the serpent-holder is above Scorpio and below an upside-down, club-wielding Hercules. From Scorpio, follow the red band left to Gemini, the twins, and Orion. The whole map is centred on the North Star; just to the left of it is the Great Bear. Above and at right angles is the Little Bear, and twisting between the two is Draco, the snake. Just to the right, Cepheus is shrugging his shoulders, next to Andromeda with outspread arms. Cygnus the swan is just by Andromeda's left hand.

Qasr Tuba

Way off any road in the depths of the desert, about 110km southeast of Amman, **Qasr Tuba** is the most southerly of the Umayyads' "Desert Castles", and, though ruined, is the only one which still has its original atmosphere of a grand estate reached after a long and difficult journey. However, you won't make it without a 4x4 and a reliable **guide** – either a local villager who knows Tuba, or a nature or archeology specialist from Amman or Azraq who's been there before. There are three possible access **routes**: best known is the rough desert track heading due south 47km from Hraneh to Tuba, with a more difficult alternative being the track heading 30km west from an unmarked point on the Azraq–Jafr road (see p.260). A road branching east off the Desert Highway about 14km north of Qatraneh (see p.384) signposts Tuba, but the tarmac runs out after about 30km, leaving you to negotiate the last 40km or so across the stony desert. As you get close, keep an eye out for the **barrel vaults** of the buildings, visible from some way off on the south side of the Wadi al-Ghadaf.

Although utterly remote these days, Tuba was intended to be a **caravanserai** on the route between Syria, the Hawran, Azraq and northern Arabia. It was begun around 743 AD, the same time as Mushatta, and in a similar style, with bricks built up on a stone foundation. Tuba's bricks, though, are of sunbaked mud, unique among the Desert Castles. The complex is very large and was originally planned as two seventy-metre-square enclosures linked by a corridor, but only the northern half was completed. You can still make out **towers** around the external wall, and around the entrance there are corridors, courtyards, passageways and rooms still surviving. The arched **doorways** are particularly striking, even if all the beautifully carved stone lintels have been smashed or taken away.

Birders who take the trouble to get to Tuba will probably also want to head some 35km due east from the *qasr*, into the stark and roadless desert close to the Saudi border. This area, known as **Thlaythwat**, is the sole Jordanian nesting place of the very rare **Houbara bustard**, a large, improbable-looking, flightless bird that can, by half-flapping and half-running, outpace a Saluki hound.

Azraq and around

As in antiquity, **AZRAQ**, 25km east of Amra (and 100km east of Amman), is today a crossroads for international traffic. In the past, its location at the head of the Wadi Sirhan, the main caravan route from Arabia to Syria (known as the Wadi al-Azraq before its settlement by the Bedouin tribe of Sirhan), meant that Azraq was both a vital trading post and a defensive strongpoint for the populated areas to the north and west. The focus of settlement was **Qasr Azraq**, originally built by the Romans and continuously renovated over the succeeding centuries; in 1917, the old castle was chosen by Lawrence of Arabia to be his headquarters.

Azraq means "blue" in Arabic, and the reason why it was such an essential caravan crossroads is that it used to be the only permanent **oasis** in thirty thousand square kilometres of desert. Fed by aquifers draining millions of cubic metres of filtered rainwater into a massive shallow basin, Azraq was surrounded by expansive freshwater pools and forests of palm and eucalyptus. Literally millions of migrating birds stopped off every year to recuperate in the highly improbable lushness on their long desert flights between Central Asia and Africa, and water buffalo and wild horses were common. Azraq was – and still is – protected under a global treaty safeguarding wetland habitats. A successful breeding programme at the **Shaumari Wildlife Reserve** to the south of town has produced large numbers of oryx and ostrich. However, after just twenty or so years of pumping from the aquifers to supply ever-growing Amman with drinking water, the oasis is today near collapse. Although ragged palms survive, in 1992 the springs dried up, the buffalo died and migrating birds headed for Galilee instead. Work in the last few years by the Royal Society for the Conservation of Nature (RSCN) to conserve and rejuvenate the **wetlands** is ongoing, and has seen a good deal of success, but faces an uphill struggle. Dust storms are more common today than ever before. The underground reservoirs, exploited almost to exhaustion, are slowly turning brackish.

Winston's hiccup

Azraq is situated near the crook of the strange angle formed by Jordan's eastern border with Saudi Arabia, which zigzags here for no apparent reason. Demarcation of this border was the work of Winston Churchill, then British Colonial Secretary, who boasted of having created the new Emirate of Transjordan with a stroke of his pen one Sunday afternoon in 1921. A story grew up that, after a particularly liquid lunch that day, he had hiccuped while attempting to draw the border and – Winston being Winston – had refused to allow it to be redrawn. Thus the zigzag has been written into history as **"Winston's hiccup"**.

Unfortunately, on closer examination, the truth is rather less engaging: Churchill in fact carefully plotted the zigzag to ensure that the massive Wadi Sirhan – holding a vital communications highway between Damascus and the Arabian interior – ended up excluded from the territory of the new emirate. Jordan's resulting "panhandle", a finger of desert territory extending east from Azraq to the Iraqi border, also had a profound significance: with the French installed dangerously nearby in Syria, it meant that Britain was able to maintain a direct, and friendly, air corridor between the Mediterranean and India at a time, immediately post-World War I, when aircraft were taking a leading role in military and civilian communication. The fact that the new, ruler-straight borders cut arbitrarily across tribal lands in the remote desert presented the colonial planners with no dilemmas of judgement.

Lawrence wrote of Azraq's numinous power, of its being "magically haunted", but only concerted effort from the RSCN and politicians in Amman can now save this uncelebrated desert outpost from ecological breakdown. **Visiting** – and staying – is not easy, but can still be a rewarding experience in the short time left before the once-lush oasis becomes just another truck stop in the desert.

Some history

Large numbers of **Paleolithic** hand axes and flint tools have been discovered around Azraq oasis, indicating a substantial settlement up to 200,000 years ago. Archeological work only began in earnest relatively recently and is ongoing: in 2000, a survey found that in the Paleolithic and Neolithic eras large quantities of **malachite** were being brought from as far away as Ain Ghazal near Amman to be worked at Azraq into delicate and beautiful earrings. The **Romans** built a fort on the site of the present Qasr Azraq in the third century, roughly when the nearby forts of Uwaynid and Asaykhim were also occupied, although archeologists have found milestones near Azraq dating from a hundred years earlier. Qasr Azraq was also used by the **Byzantines** and the **Umayyads**, and was rebuilt in 1237 by the **Ayyubid** governor Azz ad-Din Aybak, fifty years or so after the Ayyubid leader Salah ad-Din had expelled the main Crusader force from east of the Jordan. Still in use under the **Mamlukes** and the **Ottomans**, the *qasr* was occupied during the winter of 1917–18 by **Lawrence** and the forces of the Arab Revolt; their final attack on Damascus, which saw the collapse of Ottoman power, was launched from here

Just after World War I, wandering **Druze**, from Jebel Druze nearby in southern Syria, occupied the castle for a while, also founding the village outside the walls in the area of two large springs of sweet water. The volcanic plains spreading south from Jebel Druze engulf the castle, and their village was – and still is – dominated by hard black-grey basalt, which is very difficult to cut and dress, giving a lumpy, unfinished look to the older parts of the village. Although some Druze became farmers, most earned their livelihood from salt (see the box on p.262), and today Azraq is home to half the Druze in Jordan.

Barely a decade later, **Chechens** arrived at Azraq following a great emigration in 1898 from Russian military and religious persecution in their homeland in the Caucasus. They settled some 7km south of the Druze village, on flat ground near three equally large springs feeding a huge area of wetland marsh. The basalt runs out in a remarkably clear line of scarps about 4km south of the Druze village and the new settlement instead lay in an area of limestone. Most of the Chechen émigrés became farmers and fisherfolk, and, to differentiate between the two villages, the first became known as **Azraq Druze**, the second as **Azraq Shishan**.

In the 1950s, Palestinians and Syrians arrived in Azraq, blurring the clear ethnic boundaries between the two villages. In an attempt to reflect the new mix, Azraq Druze officially renamed itself **Azraq ash-Shomali** (North Azraq) and Azraq Shishan became **Azraq al-Janubi** (South Azraq), but the old names still survive in the minds of most locals. Today, the two Azraqs have a combined population of only about six thousand, not including the large contingents of Jordanian and US air force personnel quartered at the huge airbase just outside the town. Although fishing died with the oasis, farming is still carried on here and there, but the town now mainly exists by serving the traffic on the international highways from Iraq, Saudi Arabia and Syria.

The Royal Society for the Conservation of Nature (RSCN) has also taken an active role in the town, initiating conservancy projects, launching low-impact tourism and creating socio-economic programmes to boost local incomes. An excellent way to give perspective to your time in Azraq is to join the RSCN's **"Druze and Shishan Cultural Experience"**, a half day spent touring the workshops of income-generating projects in both halves of the town and talking to local craftspeople, after which you are hosted for a traditional meal in a village home. For details and bookings, contact the RSCN at the *Azraq Lodge* (see below) or at the Tourism Unit in Amman (see p.77).

Arrival

The main **minibus** route to Azraq is from Zarqa, although there are others from Mafraq and even a few from Irbid. The main roads from Zarqa and from Amman meet 9km west of Azraq. All traffic is then funnelled towards a T-junction, from where the restaurants of Azraq al-Janubi are visible to the right, extending for about 1km southwards. To the left, some 7km down the road, lie Qasr Azraq and the garages and workshops of Azraq ash-Shomali (and, 54km further on, Safawi). **Buses** wander through Janubi first, then turn round and head for Shomali, dropping off here and there before terminating at the open area opposite the post office. If you tell the driver where you want to be dropped beforehand, he'll take you to the door.

Although there are some local minibuses between the two halves of Azraq, most local people just flag down any vehicle heading in the right direction; a simple "Shomali?" or "Janubi?" to the driver suffices. The standard fare to offer, minibus or hitchhike, is 100 fils.

A couple of banks at the north end of Azraq ash-Shomali can **change money**, traveller's cheques and do Visa advances. There are two **post offices**: one behind the Janubi petrol station (Sat–Thurs 8am–7pm), the other on the Shomali crossroads (same times, also Fri 8am–2pm). Janubi has 24-hour English-speaking **pharmacies** in plain view on the main street.

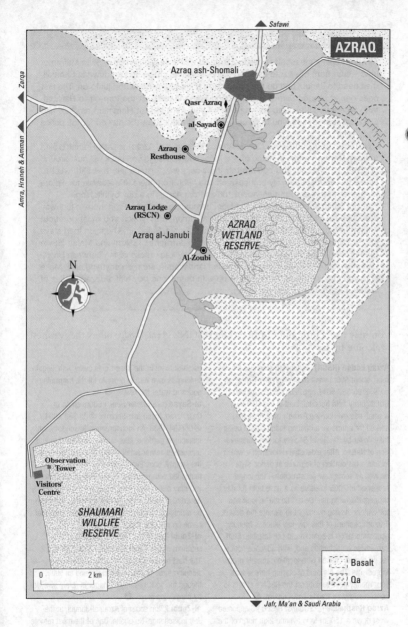

Safawi

AZRAQ

Azraq ash-Shomali

Qasr Azraq

al-Sayad

Azraq
Resthouse

Zarqa

Amra, Hraneh & Amman

Azraq Lodge
(RSCN)

Azraq al-Janubi

Al-Zoubi

*AZRAQ
WETLAND
RESERVE*

N

Observation
Tower

Visitors'
Centre

*SHAUMARI
WILDLIFE
RESERVE*

0   2 km

Basalt

Qa

Jafr, Ma'an & Saudi Arabia

Accommodation

Most tourists don't stop in Azraq, but the evenings and early mornings are
the best times to enjoy the place. The problem is that the few **hotels** here get
most of their business from Saudi or Gulf families passing through, and tend to
view Westerners as bringing down the tone: although it's easy to find a bed,

Moving on from Azraq

All **minibuses** – the regular ones to Zarqa, as well as less common ones to Mafraq or Irbid – start from the Azraq ash-Shomali post office, cruise up and down in Shomali, then head to Janubi and do the same. Stop them at any point and jump on. The first ones depart around 6am, the last around 5pm. All run past the turn-off to Hallabat, from where you'll have to walk or hitch if you want to visit Hammam as-Srah and Qasr Hallabat. Buses tend to fill up quickly on Wednesday, the day off for the police and military.

No public transport serves Qusayr Amra (25km west of Azraq) or Qasr Hraneh (15km further). **Renting a taxi** in Azraq to see these two and bring you back will cost around JD15–20. Otherwise, you could **hitch** the whole way, or take any bus 9km west to where the Amman highway branches off and hitch from there. It's feasible to explore both sites and reach Amman (about 100km from Azraq) in a day by hitching.

About 23km south of Azraq is a major interchange of **roads**. From here, a highway branches southeast to the **Saudi border** at Umari, after which you must go about 450km to reach the first big town inside Saudi Arabia, Sakakah. The main road stays inside Jordan, heading south into the desert to **Jafr** (after 185km) and Ma'an (58km further on). This is the route used almost solely by Iraqi trucks plying between Baghdad and Aqaba port – long on silent desert landscapes, short on anything else. Make sure you check your oil and tyres, fill up with petrol, and buy half a dozen bottles of water in Azraq before you get going.

---

you may feel a little out of place. The RSCN's *Azraq Lodge* offers the warmest welcome by far.

Azraq Lodge (RSCN) Signposted south up a side-road, about 600m west of the highway T-junction ☏ & ℱ 05/383 5017 or 5225 or 5425. An old British army field hospital, built in the 1930s on a small rise overlooking Azraq's mud flats, that served for a time as a hunting lodge before being taken over by the Royal Society for the Conservation of Nature. After extensive renovation – which included restoration of features in period style as well as some new construction – the lodge reopened in 2005 to serve as a base both for day-trippers following the 'Desert Castle" circuit and for visitors staying overnight to explore the desert. The atmosphere of this low-key place is friendly; accommodation is spartan but comfortable. Staff can advise on activities and, with advance notice, lay on meals, cooked with local organically grown ingredients. The big plus of staying here is that your money goes to support the RSCN's efforts to conserve Azraq's fragile environment. ❸

Azraq Resthouse (aka *Tourist Resort*) Signposted west down a 1500m-long avenue 2km north of the highway T-junction ☏ 05/383 4006, ℱ 383 5215. Comfortable, good-value chalet-style rooms around a pool that are aimed very definitely at the upscale Saudi market, and are difficult to reach without transport. Prices and food are reasonable, but you'd be justified in wondering how a government owned

establishment in the desert gets away with illegally sinking its own well in order to fill the swimming pool and water the lawns. ❸

al-Sayad (aka *Hunter Hotel*) 500m south of Qasr Azraq, Azraq ash-Shomali ☏ 05/383 4094, ℱ 06/464 4988. An incongruously kitsch folly, with manicured gardens, fake-Islamic architecture and untouched, rather small rooms; the best overlook the (empty) pool. Every corner of the place is festooned with paintings by the Bulgarian owner; you may bump into her striding around the creepily deserted corridors. The restaurant menu seems to be a product of the same fanciful imagination that came up with the decor. ❹

al-Zoubi Behind the *Refa'i* restaurant at the southern end of Azraq al-Janubi ☏ 05/383 5012. The best budget choice in town. Simple rooms – all sleeping three or four – are clean and en suite, though the sour, grumpy manager is rarely swayed by bargaining ploys. ❷

al-Zoubi 23km south of Azraq al-Janubi, at the Jafr interchange. No phone. One of the most remote hotels in the country, expertly located alongside the junction of the long roads in from Saudi Arabia and southern Jordan. Inside, huge photographic murals of blue seaside scenes and lush green gardens contrast comically with the barren views out of the window. Spartan rooms are large and clean. ❷

Qasr Azraq

We hurried up the stony ridge in high excitement, talking of the wars and songs
and passions of the early shepherd kings, with names like music, who had loved
this place; and of the Roman legionaries who languished here as garrison in yet
earlier times. Then the blue fort on its rock above the rustling palms, with the fresh
meadows and shining springs of water, broke on our sight.

T.E. Lawrence, *The Seven Pillars of Wisdom*

Lawrence will be turning in his grave at the fate of his "blue fort", **Qasr
Azraq**. Leaving aside the 1927 earthquake, which shook some height from
the walls and towers, new apartment buildings now loom over the castle,
the meadows have vanished and the "shining springs of water" have been
diverted to keep Amman alive. Adding insult to injury, the main highway
from Baghdad thunders past the walls, slicing the castle away from the oasis
that inspired it, drowning out the rustling palms and masking the warm, dry
breeze with motor oil. Nonetheless, the *qasr* is still a romantic and explorable place, with marvellous sunsets, and all the more poignant for its modest
fame and the town's recent travails. A Druze family – currently in the third
generation – have acted as guardians of the castle since the days of Lawrence
and, as you approach, one or other of them will probably materialize to
guide you round.

As you enter the dogleg gatehouse, machicolation and an Arabic **inscription**
commemorating the 1237 renovation of the castle are above your head. The
massive basalt slab front door still swings on its hinges. Inside the gatehouse are
carved stone images of animals found nearby (which are probably Umayyad),
and Roman milestones and inscribed blocks; on one of them "Ioviorum"
refers to the emperor Diocletian. Down at your feet, a double row of seven
indentations in a threshold stone is for a gatekeeper's solitaire-type game using
pebbles.

Inside the courtyard, the rooms immediately to the left were patched up with
palm fronds either by Lawrence's men or by later Druze occupiers. Further
around, the west wall is dominated by a massive **tower**, at the base of which is
a three-tonne basalt slab door, barely swingable to and fro: Lawrence described
the whole west wall trembling as it was slammed shut. The supposed **prison** in
the northwest corner features a locking hole in the door-frame rubbed smooth
and shiny by centuries of curious fingers. To the north are the smoke-blackened
kitchens and the elegant **dining hall**, and, beside them, the **stables**, supported
by oddly shaped arches. A seven-metre **well** in the east wall was filled with water
until the mid-1980s, but is now dry; these days the water table has dropped way
deeper. Sitting skewed in the middle of the courtyard is a remarkably graceful
little three-aisle **mosque**, probably built during the Ayyubid renovations. The
inevitable highlight, though, is the room above the gate you entered by: this was
Lawrence's room, accessed by stairs and in a plum position to look out over
the courtyard and the palms. In *Seven Pillars* he wrote:

In the evening when we had shut-to the gate, all guests would assemble... and
coffee and stories would go round until the last meal, and after it, till sleep came.
On stormy nights, we brought in brushwood and dung and lit a great fire in the
middle of the floor. About it would be drawn the carpets and the saddle-sheep-
skins, and in its light we would tell over our own battles, or hear the visitors'
traditions. The leaping flames chased our smoke-ruffled shadows strangely about
the rough stone wall behind us, distorting them over the hollows and projections
of its broken face.

Azraq salt

Strangely enough for a freshwater oasis, Azraq has separate, extensive underground pockets of extremely salty water, which for sixty years allowed the village to supply much of the **table salt** used in Jordan and Iraq. However, UN sanctions imposed on Iraq in 1991, and the growth of the Dead Sea salt works at Safi (which is a far bigger and more efficient operation, and, unlike Azraq's, enjoys tangible government support), mean that there is no longer any profit in producing salt in Azraq. These days, only a few locals head out to the **saltpans** east of the village in the broiling heat of summer to set up shanties – they stay there for weeks, sinking wells to draw up the brine, much thicker and more concentrated than sea water, and draining it into shallow evaporating lagoons where the sun does the work. This is repeated several times until a thick crust of salt remains, which is raked over, collected and bagged. A single pan of 25m by 10m can yield more than twenty thousand kilos of salt, and the only thing that can disturb production is rain: in 1994, an unexpected early September shower washed away twenty million kilos of harvestable salt.

The failure of Azraq's salt business, which once provided the major source of income and employment for the village, has major **ecological implications** for Jordan and its neighbours. Azraq's brine is seeping into the extensive freshwater aquifers beneath the desert and is turning Amman's drinking water brackish (see box opposite for more on the oasis). Even worse, Safi's vast evaporation ponds have already been a major contributor to the shrinkage of the Dead Sea and, should salt again be exported from Jordan to Iraq, Safi will no doubt step up its operations, causing further harm. It makes eminent ecological – even if not economic – sense to share Jordan's salt production between Safi and Azraq, to limit environmental damage at both sites and to distribute potential profits evenly. To do so, however, requires vision and political will in Amman.

Azraq Wetlands Reserve

Spreading east of Janubi village is the **Azraq Wetlands Reserve** (Ⓦwww.rscn .org.jo), a sadly depleted shadow of its former self. Before the oasis dried up, this whole area of marshes and lakes, in the midst of Azraq's *qa*, or depression, was the scene of vibrant life. Well over a hundred water buffalo roamed the area, along with wild horses and small livestock. In the winter of 1967, a staggering 240,000 ducks landed here, along with 180,000 teals, 100,000 pintails, 40,000 coots, 20,000 wigeons and 2000 mallards. Insects, molluscs and hundreds of thousands of frogs thrived; there's even a particular species of fish, the killifish, that is endemic to Azraq's pools. By 1992, though, after disastrous human intervention, there was very little left apart from some more or less deserted reed beds and low muddy pools.

In 1998, the RSCN stepped in, and since then has launched a programme to protect the wetland area and focus international effort on conservation. A signpost opposite the petrol station in Azraq al-Janubi points the way down a side-street to the wetland reserve's **Visitors' Centre**, open daily from an hour after sunrise to an hour before sunset (JD2; joint ticket with Shaumari Reserve JD3). Inside, as well as a small shop, is a well-presented **interpretation room**, leading you past information boards (in English) outlining the various factors that have brought Azraq to its knees – including an illustrative tank of tiny striped killifish.

From the terrace behind the wetland reserve's Visitors' Centre, the marked circular **Marsh Trail** (1.5km) heads off into the reed beds. Brisk walkers could cover the circuit and be back at the Visitors' Centre in ten minutes; dawdlers could find enough out there to keep them interested for hours. Boards supply good information alongside the trail, as you emerge from the reeds to look over a flat, shabby area that was once a huge lake fed by a spring, Ain Soda, or walk over a low ancient wall that is variously thought to be Umayyad or

Death of an oasis

Before 1975, Azraq positively gushed with **water**, fed to the village from all points of the compass. Rain falling on Jebel Druze 80km or so to the north takes just a few years to filter through the basalt to Azraq's aquifers. Five springs (two in Shomali and three in Janubi) poured 34 million litres of water every day into Azraq's pools. In addition, a total of ten river beds feed into Azraq's qa, including the mighty Wadi Sirhan from the southeast and Wadi Rajil from the north, draining surface rainwater (separate from the underground aquifers) towards Azraq. In rainy years, the entire qa – fifty square kilometres in the midst of a parched and burning desert – was flooded to a depth of a metre or more with sweet water.

The abundance was too tempting to resist. In 1963, a small amount of **pumping** began from Azraq to Irbid; the oasis could replenish itself and no damage was done. But, following the 1967 war with Israel, the population of Jordan – and of Amman in particular – was swollen by hundreds of thousands of Palestinian refugees, and the national water infrastructure of the time couldn't cope. In 1975, large-scale pumping to Amman began, Azraq alone supplying a quarter of the city's water. In addition, Syria dammed the Wadi Rajil, depriving the qa of a third of its runoff water and severely damaging Azraq's ecosystem. To ensure that the quantity of water being pumped to Amman didn't drop, Jordan then tapped Azraq's aquifers deeper, this time fatally. While signing Azraq's death warrant with one hand, in 1977 Jordan signed with the other an international treaty protecting wetland habitats.

During the 1980s, Azraq gained a reputation as an attractive and fruitful place to farm: people began to move to the area and sank illegal private **wells** to irrigate their fields. Whereas in previous years such wells needed to be only 3m or so deep, by this time drilling ten times deeper produced no water. In 1992, after just seventeen years of abuse, the fragile wetlands dried up. Over ten years later, 25 million cubic metres (mcm) of Azraq water is still being pumped annually to Amman – a city which, it's been claimed, loses 55 percent of its water through leaky pipes – while as much as a further 50mcm is drawn off by an estimated 700 illegal local wells. Rainfall can only contribute under half of this amount, and at this rate the underground reservoirs have barely twenty more years' supply. Yet this shortfall is only one of Azraq's ticking time bombs. Normally, a natural balance in water pressure exists between the freshwater aquifers and the underground brine, whose presence gave rise to Azraq's salt industry (see box opposite). However, with the pumping, pressure has been dangerously lowered in the aquifers. **Seepage of salt** is already making creeping inroads into the freshwater supply, and is irreversible: once brackish, an aquifer stays brackish forever.

The problems of Azraq aren't going unregarded. Since 1998, the Royal Society for the Conservation of Nature (RSCN) has managed to ensure that 1.5mcm is returned to Azraq's pools each year in an attempt to limit the damage. This is a start, but it's scant recompense. If things continue the way they are, the dying oasis will be lost to the desert in a matter of years. Almost the only lifeline is the new pipeline bringing drinking water to Amman from **Diseh** (near Rum), recent recipient of a $600 million grant from Libya. Diseh has its own ecological problems – its reserves of sweet "fossil" water, trapped underground for millennia, are limited and non-renewable – but the surplus it generates may then mean that less water is pumped to Amman from Azraq. The Diseh pipeline is due to begin operation in 2007. Time will tell whether Azraq can claw its way back from the brink.

Roman. The water which you can see gushing into the pools has come from Amman: it's the minuscule amount that the government is pumping back into the wetlands as a gesture towards eco-friendliness. Near the end of the trail is a **hide** built of mudbrick, from where you can look over a waterhole and watch the birdlife; keen twitchers should aim to be installed there soon after sunrise. If you're there towards sunset, you might be extremely lucky and see one of the **water buffalo** which were reintroduced to the wetlands by the RSCN in 1998 in an attempt to control the reed-beds and expose more open water to attract birds – although the beasts spend most of their time 9 or 10km away in the furthest reaches of the reserve.

Serious birders will be aware that the best times of year to visit the wetlands are outside high summer: how much you see depends on how much water has accumulated in the pools. Birding at dawn and dusk will mean a night in Azraq, most likely at the RSCN's *Azraq Lodge* (see p.260), and you can also arrange a **Rare Birds of Jordan expedition** (4hr, including 2km hiking), taking in both the Azraq Wetlands and Shaumari (see below). For bookings, prices and up-to-date information contact either the reserve office (☎05/383 5425 or 383 5225), or the RSCN's Tourism Unit in Amman (see p.77) well in advance.

Eating and drinking

Azraq al-Janubi's main drag is lined with **restaurants**, most of them pretty basic and all serving standard truckers' fare of meat stew, chicken and/or hummus. As soon as you're spotted looking around, you'll be beckoned in; the restaurants that don't call to you (and that don't have English signs) tend to be better. There's a good falafel stand next to *Brown Chicken*, but the choice establishment is *al-Kahf*, or The Cave (no English sign), a sunken den made of basalt stones, with a row of neon spiders and a giant *dalleh* coffeepot outside; their *mezze* and kebabs are excellent. With advance notice, the RSCN *Azraq Lodge* (see p.260) can rustle you up a filling and tasty meal for around JD6–8, even if you're not staying there.

In Azraq ash-Shomali, the dowdy *Azraq Resthouse* restaurant (daily 6am–midnight) seems to be used mainly as a residential pub and nightspot by Saudis popping across the border: the menu has more alcohol than food. Nonetheless, they can do a frill-free meal for JD6 or so. Just north of the signpost to the *Resthouse*, the *Azraq Palace Tourist Restaurant* (daily 11am–3pm) has a JD6 lunch buffet – JD4 if you don't have the *mensaf* and *maqloubeh* hot dishes – but the decor, synth-player and fake Bedouin tent are likely to appeal to only the most jaded of tour groups. The most atmospheric place to eat in town is the *al-Montazah Falls* restaurant (daily 10am–11pm); there's a sign just opposite the *qasr* pointing off the road, and it's the building at the first crossroads. Set among a grove of palms, it's shady, cool and quiet, but it too has its own illegal well and staff have a penchant for turning on the tap when visitors arrive in order to seduce them with precious spring water babbling through their lush gardens and down the drain. You have a perfect right to ask them to turn it off. North of the post office in Shomali are a couple of inexpensive diners, including the passable *al-Arez*.

Shaumari Wildlife Reserve

Out on the baking desert south of Azraq, where the highest point of land for miles around is the road, raised a bare metre or two above the dust, you'll find the RSCN **Shaumari Wildlife Reserve** (daily 8am–7.30pm, closes 3.30pm in winter; JD2; joint ticket with Azraq Wetlands Reserve JD3; ⊛www.rscn.org.jo).

Before you approach the place, you should banish thoughts of African big-game reserves: there are no breathtaking vistas here, no drama. Shaumari comprises 22 square kilometres of the flat, bare desert and although there are some majestic animals, money for tourist development is running low. If you're familiar with the struggle faced by Jordanian environmentalists to raise public awareness of ecological issues, the place will seem like a breath of fresh air; if you come expecting some grand entertainment, you'll be disappointed.

Shaumari was officially designated a reserve in 1975 and was selected as the reception area for returning **Arabian oryx** to the wild. Oryx had been extinct in Jordan since 1921, but a few had been saved from the wild before the last animal was shot by hunters in Oman in 1973. Four years later, the World Wildlife Fund brought four oryx from San Diego Zoo to Shaumari for breeding; unfortunately, it took six months before anyone realized they were all males. The following year four females were brought from San Diego, as well as three more from a zoo in Qatar in order to mix the genes of the herd, and the first foal was born in 1979. By 1983, there were 31 animals, and by the turn of the century there were over 200 – too many, since the reserve was only designed for a maximum of 120. A combination of deaths from stress due to overcrowding, seizures of young oryx by the jackals that roam the reserve, and a recent gift of oryx to Saudi Arabia, the Emirates and Qatar means that today the herd numbers a comfortable 80 or so. In 2002 a small herd of oryx were transported to a large enclosure in the Wadi Rum desert, as the first phase of a programme to release them into the wild.

Also resident at Shaumari are **ostrich**. Wild Arabian ostrich were common in Azraq as late as the 1920s, but were also hunted to extinction. In 1986, two blue-necked ostriches were brought to Shaumari from Oklahoma Zoo, and some of their offspring are still alive among Shaumari's total of around 30 birds, although three red-necked ostriches, a gift from Israel, never truly adapted to the harshness of Shaumari's desert environment and all died. The reserve also has a herd of **onagers** (a kind of wild ass) and five different species of **snake**, as well as sand rats, lizards, the occasional caracal, jackal or wildcat, plus plenty of **birdlife**, with over three hundred species logged.

Practicalities

No public **transport** runs close to Shaumari; if you don't have a car, you can ask at any of the restaurants or shops in Azraq al-Janubi for a lift. The going rate is JD3.500, or more than twice that if you want someone to wait and bring you back. About 7km south of Azraq al-Janubi is a sign for the reserve, with the entrance located 6km along a sometimes rough turn-off road. The grove of trees around the reserve's buildings stands out on the horizon, visible for miles around.

Just inside the gates, the excellent **Visitors' Centre** is kitted out with informational boards and models to explain the habitat and lifestyles of Shaumari's oryx, gazelle and ostrich. The reserve's dusty buildings are set among a small grove of eucalyptus, which is a marvellously cool and peaceful escape from the merciless desert all around, and perfect for a shady picnic. To stay overnight, there's a small **campsite** (❸), fully equipped with mattresses, pillows, sheets and blankets, with nearby showers, toilets and kitchen facilities. You should **book in advance** to stay here with the Azraq Wetlands Reserve office (see opposite) or the RSCN Tourism Unit (see p.77).

Near the buildings is a complex of pens housing baby oryx, ostrich and gazelle, and on the edge of the trees is a ten-metre **observation tower** – the staff can lend you binoculars to search for oryx or do some eagle-spotting.

The dauntingly imperious adult ostriches roam around a wide area near the base of the tower. The highlight of a visit, though, is an **oryx safari** (JD10 per trip, for up to ten people), a 4x4 expedition out into the reserve to get close to the oryx, check out any ostrich nests, and see what the desert flora looks like when not nibbled down by sheep and goats. In summer, when the oryx stay close to the water troughs near the buildings, a safari might only take an hour or two; at other times of year, the oryx roam further out into the reserve where there's a plentiful supply of runoff water, and a safari can take half a day. With advance booking, staff will take you on a two-hour **night safari** (JD3 per person), a thrilling chance to get out into the desert after dark to view the nocturnal wildlife – and the astonishingly clear night skies, full of stars.

The Eastern Badia

Jordan tends to be defined as a desert land, yet most people – locals as well as visitors – don't ever get to know the desert, spending virtually all their time in the fertile, relatively well-watered strip of hilly territory running down the western part of the country. Although the sandy areas around Wadi Rum in the so-called Southern Badia are now well known, much less is understood about the vast stony deserts which occupy more than eighty percent of Jordanian territory, the **Eastern Badia** – covering, roughly, everything east of Amman and Mafraq, and south almost to Jafr. The Badia (pronounced "bad-ya"; from the same root as the word "Bedouin") entirely lacks the drama of Rum's soaring cliffs and red sand dunes, yet holds some of the most memorable and extraordinary natural scenery in the country, from the boulder-strewn, volcanic Black Desert, or *harra*, close to Syria's Jebel Druze, out to the *hamad*, or undulating limestone plateau and grasslands in the farthest corners of the country near Iraq.

Desert travel is perhaps inevitably seen as a process of combating the tedium while getting from A to B, but you'll have much more satisfaction if you abandon your itinerary and treat the desert as a destination in its own right. With suitable preparation, adventurous explorers out here will be rewarded with an extraordinary diversity of environments and some stunning natural drama.

This wedge of desert is praised by naturalists as being one of the most fascinating and rewarding areas for **birdwatching** in the whole of Jordan. Recent notable **animal** sightings have included the sand cat, the Levantine viper and Tilbury's Spring-Footed Lizard, all of them rarities, and ongoing investigations have turned up 49 **plant** species new to science. In addition, there's a handful of relatively minor archeological sites that serve as a useful hook on which to hang a visit.

Everything centres on the region's "capital", the small, dusty town of **Safawi**. From here, the longest, straightest road in Jordan points east into the open desert towards Baghdad, which is only about 700km away – a day's drive by car, or two days in the massive lumbering trucks and oil tankers which are the road's principal traffic. North of Safawi, tight up against the Syrian border, are the mysterious ruins of **Jawa**, a long-abandoned city; south of Safawi is the **holy tree of Biqya'wiyya**, a full-grown pistachio beside a waterhole in the deep desert that, legend has it, once sheltered the Prophet Muhammad; and, most dramatic of all, barely 50km from the Iraqi border, is the astonishing, mirage-like apparition of the glittering lake and ruined black castle of **Burqu**.

Developing the Badia

The arid areas of Jordan, known as the **Badia**, cover approximately 85 percent of the country, yet are home to only five percent of the population. Although its annual rainfall is less than 200mm, the Badia provides Jordan with over half its groundwater needs and almost a quarter of national GDP: today, these arid regions are seen as the country's agricultural and industrial resource base. With Jordan's ongoing population explosion, urban areas are unable to cope, and in recent years growing numbers of people have abandoned the cities and moved out to make a life in the Badia.

Traditionally, the Badia was home to the nomadic Bedouin, but the growing power of urban communities in the twentieth century increasingly affected Bedouin social life as well as the physical environment. Key **resources** were exploited mainly for the urban population's benefit, and services and products generated by the urban community became integrated into the lifestyle of the Bedouin, reducing their sense of responsibility for the environment. Vegetation was destroyed, erosion increased, groundwater was tapped, and scarce resources were squandered. The Bedouin became alienated from the central authorities.

Sheep have been a constant problem – a traditional small-scale livelihood for the Bedouin that now severely threatens land resources through overgrazing by hugely expanded flocks. In one sector of the eastern Badia, roughly 18,000 people live in an area of 11,000 square kilometres; in 1996, after a rainy winter, they shared the land with 1.5 million sheep. And yet, perversely, the local sheep industry is almost nonexistent: Jordan imports most of its mutton from Australia, and wool is a non-starter, with most farmers shearing with hand-clippers for domestic use only. Another significant problem is **education**: a third of the Badia's children aren't enrolled in school at all. Graduates – especially women – have great difficulty finding jobs in the Badia, so the best local teachers tend to move to Amman. Badia schools give students little grounding in either the arts or vocational sciences such as agriculture or engineering; almost half the Badia's population over the age of 19 is illiterate, and just three percent are university graduates.

However, notions of the Badia and Bedouin life plug directly into the Jordanian psyche. In 1992, in an attempt to address these issues, Jordan's Higher Council for Science and Technology, with the backing of Britain's Royal Geographical Society and Durham University, established the **Badia Research and Development Programme** (BRDP; Ⓦ www.badia.gov.jo), with the specific remit to investigate the Badia's human and natural resources and the possibilities for sustainable development. Working on a shoestring budget, the BRDP has identified vast potential in the Badia, ranging from mineral resources to ecotourism, traditional crafts and renewable energy. Badia bees, for example, can produce twice as much honey as those in Ajloun, Jordan's traditional beekeeping centre; in 2001, the BRDP launched a scheme to kick-start production by private-sector Badia apiaries.

Government ministers and even the king make a point of regularly coming out to Safawi for an update, and the BRDP's research results have more than once resulted in a shift in national policy. The organization is now attempting to limit the number of sheep per household to just twenty, instead of thousands, and to turn around the priorities of farmers, who devote land and precious water to crops such as tomatoes and watermelon while simultaneously importing vast quantities of animal feed. Jordan's first ever **information technology** centre was established recently in Safawi, in response to the BRDP's campaigning and, in addition, the BRDP will administer a **micro-loan programme** to offer skills training and start-up loans to Badia residents, with a specific focus on supporting **women** in business and home-based industries. Given Jordan's rapidly expanding population, further development of the Badia is inevitable: having spent a decade laying foundations, the BRDP can now take a leading role in the implementation of sustainable policies for the Badia's future.

Practicalities

Needless to say, transport in this most remote, untouristed area of Jordan is difficult, and requires considerable forward planning. Relying on **public transport** won't get you far; there are minibuses from Mafraq to Safawi, with fewer heading on to Ruwayshid, and a handful on to the Iraqi border at Turaybil, but none goes anywhere near sites of interest. Even if you reach, say, Ruwayshid, your chances of being able to get out to Burqu independently – or get back from it – are virtually nil.

The way to go in the desert is with a **4x4**, well equipped with spares, communications equipment, food and plenty of drinking water, plus a local guide who knows the area well. A handful of local and foreign tour operators organize excellent **birdwatching and eco-tours** that can get you to all kinds of remote crannies, notably the lake at Burqu. If you haven't booked anything from home in advance, or if you've rented your own 4x4 and need a guide, your first point of contact should be the RSCN, either at their Tourism Unit in Amman (see p.77) or at the *Azraq Lodge* in Azraq. It would be equally worthwhile seeking advice from the Badia Research and Development Programme (BRDP; see box and p.267); they have some low-key, culturally aware eco-tourist services in the Badia to complement their extensive facilities for visiting scientists. Programmes for groups vary (email ⓔsafawi@nic.gov.jo for details), but might typically include demonstrations by local women of skills such as weaving, wheat-grinding and bread- and yoghurt-making, followed by a full meal in a traditional Bedouin tent, live music performances and overnight accommodation.

Otherwise, there are few places **to stay** in the area; Azraq is by far the best base. The RSCN has been known to organize some rough, wilderness **camping** on the shores of the lake at Burqu, but this is not to be undertaken lightly: you must arrange it in advance, and should always be accompanied by people with local knowledge. Camping at Burqu is dangerous in autumn and winter, when flash floods can strike. As far as **eating** goes, although you may be able to find the odd diner at Safawi and Ruwayshid, you shouldn't consider driving around the desert without also carrying enough food and water to keep you going for several days.

A word of warning: because of the harshness of the country and its proximity to the Syrian border, the Badia is one of the principal smuggling routes for Lebanese hashish bound for Israel, Egypt and the Arabian Peninsula. You'll come across a handful of **checkpoints** on back-country roads and at Safawi, and although everyone is very friendly, if you're not with a local guide on an organized trip they'll be interested to know why you're cruising around the countryside. You should carry your passport and be prepared for lengthy jovial cups of tea.

Safawi

The major town of the Eastern Badia is **SAFAWI**, 75km east of Mafraq and 53km north of Azraq. It's an oil-stained, engine-roaring kind of place that's unlikely to inspire: there are no hotels, no banks and just a handful of eating-places, with the main drag guarded at one end by a police post. Patching tyres and roasting chickens for dinner are the sole entertainments.

You may spot roadsigns to Safawi that include "H5" in brackets; this number refers to a pumping station along the route of an **oil pipeline** constructed in the 1930s, which prompted the later construction of the highway along its length. Only operational for fifteen years up until the declaration of the State of Israel in 1948, the pipeline originated in Kirkuk, Iraq, with one branch running through Syria to Tripoli on the Lebanon coast, and the other through Jordan to Haifa, now in Israel. All the pumping stations along the Haifa branch were numbered with the prefix "H": H4 is just before Ruwayshid, while H2 (over the border) became infamous during the 1991 Gulf War as the firing point for Iraqi Scud missiles directed at Israel. The town of Safawi developed around the H5 pumping station, the buildings of which are now part-occupied by the **Jordan Badia Research and Development Programme**. Another major recent arrival has been a state-of-the-art information technology centre, the first of its kind in Jordan, intended to help train the community in IT and give a boost to the local economy.

North of Safawi

Sandwiched between Safawi and the Syrian border are the hilly expanses of the **Hawran**, the black desert of igneous rocks spewed out in antiquity by the now-extinct volcano of Jebel Druze, just over the border. Within this strip, east of Umm al-Jimal, are a string of rural communities and a handful of ancient sites accessible only by **car**, the most spectacular – Jawa – only by 4x4. A bus does occasionally run out here on the back roads from Mafraq, but it's barely worth the time and effort considering the inaccessibility and low-key nature of the sites.

About 20km west of Safawi you'll spot off to the side of the road the twin hills of **Aritayn**, or Two Lungs; shortly after, the road swings northwest towards Mafraq around the aptly named **Jebel al-Asfar**, or Yellow Mountain, towards the jutting scarp of Tell ar-Remah. At the settlement of Bishriyyeh, a side-road branches northeast for 15km to **Dayr al-Kahf**. On the edge of the village, less than 5km from the Syrian border, is a substantial, well-preserved Roman **fort**, dating from 306 AD. (Coming from Umm al-Jimal, drive 7km past the site's information hut, turn left at the T-junction and then right after 22km; Dayr al-Kahf's fort comes into view 26km further.) The fort was one of many situated on the Strata Diocletiana, a frontier road designed by Emperor Diocletian to link Bosra with Azraq. The basalt walls of the overgrown fort are still standing, and some have been restored. A wander around the quiet, atmospheric court-yard reveals ground-floor stables and remnants of carved columns dumped in the plastered **cistern**. In the east wall one perfect arch survives; inside nearby rooms you'll find internal supporting arches and intact corbelling. Opposite, in the west wall, is a rebuilt arched section; going through, and then looking back, reveals reused Roman columns either side of the elegant doorway. On the north side of the fort is a small **tower** overlooking a reused Roman **reservoir**.

The road east from Dayr al-Kahf heads on to the hamlet of **Dayr al-Qinn**, with its own crumbling Roman fort, more ruinous than its neighbour, with only a few original walls still standing. All along the west wall of the fort is a line of small, internally partitioned rooms, with a hinge and a door lock still present in one surviving door-frame. At the rear of the site (north), climb up onto the highest point of the ruins to look over the large **reservoir** onto the rolling hills; the nearby white shack is the Jordanian army's frontier post, and beyond it is a square white building marking the Syrian army position. From the same spot, you can look west over one of the fort's surviving lintels to easily make out on the horizon the Roman tower at Ghrarba in Syria.

Jawa

About 25km east of Dayr al-Kahf – and only accessible with a 4x4 with a local guide – lie the bleak and mysterious ruins of **Jawa**, a town constructed five thousand years ago from the local basalt by an unknown people, occupied for only fifty years then abandoned. The rubbly, hard-to-decipher site stands desolate on a rocky hill; non-archeologists will probably find themselves in awe more of the spectacular surroundings of the Black Desert than of the ruins themselves. In these vast expanses of basalt, the silence and sense of ominous open space are overwhelming.

Some 2km out of Dayr al-Qinn, follow a rough track heading right off the road along the right-hand bank of the large Wadi Rajil for 5km into the desert. The substantial **walls** of Jawa will soon come into view ahead, fortifying an impressive craggy outcrop above the deep wadi, which describes a dramatic curve around the ancient city. You can park alongside a modern reservoir at the foot of Jawa's hill, and scramble up. Without specialist interpretation, it can be very hard to make sense of the site's expanse of tumbled ruins, although the division into lower and upper districts is clear; well over a thousand years after its construction, a citadel of sorts was built in the upper town during the Middle Bronze Age, presumably to serve as a caravanserai on the routes between Syria and Mesopotamia to the north and Palestine, Egypt and Arabia to the south. Scrambling around the hill, in and out of the closely packed **houses** – tiny, irregularly shaped one-room shacks – is just as impressive as stopping and listening to the silence of the surroundings, broken only by the occasional bird-call and the sound of the wind sweeping up the defile of the Wadi Rajil.

South of Safawi

On the western edge of Safawi town is the junction of the roads to Mafraq and Azraq. Almost exactly 15km along the Azraq road – but without any signs or noticeable landmarks – a side-track branches off the highway on one of the loveliest journeys you can take in this region of the Eastern Badia, towards the **holy tree of Biqya'wiyya**, well worth the tough, 35-minute ride by 4x4 across open country.

In his youth, the Prophet Muhammad is said to have travelled at the behest of a wealthy widow Khadija (who later became his wife) from his hometown of Mecca north across the desert to Syria. Accompanying Muhammad on this trading mission was Khadija's slave, Maysarah. During the journey the caravan stopped for a break near the remote home of a Christian monk named **Bahira**. While Muhammad rested under a wild pistachio tree, Bahira came up to Maysarah and asked, "Who is that man?" – to which Maysarah replied, "That is one of the tribe of Quraysh, who guard the Kaaba in Mecca." In a reply which has passed into folklore, Bahira then said, "No one but a Prophet is sitting beneath that tree." Islamic tradition holds that the particular tree beneath which Muhammad rested still lives; although there are competing claims, the prime candidate stands far out in the desert south of Safawi. The fact that dendro-chronologists have estimated the tree's age at only around 500 years detracts from the power of the legend not one jot.

As soon as you leave the Safawi–Azraq highway, the track deteriorates to reveal an ancient, five-metre-wide cambered pilgrims' roadway, possibly Ottoman, although known to some locals as the "British Road", made of fieldstones packed together, with defined kerbstones, a proper kerb and a central spine. This leads dead straight out across the undulating desert, visible for miles ahead without diversion. Watch for kilometre markers all along the side of this route: the first, just off the highway, is 978; after 3km of a very bumpy ride on the stony pilgrims' road, you pass a modern brick hut marked with "Km 975". Around 1500m further across the barren, black stony desert is a gentle rise, on the far side of which – in a memorable flourish of natural drama – stretches a vast area of fertile rolling **grassland**, often dotted with standing water, soft on the eye and echoing with the calls of swooping birds. A little after Km 970 is another small rise, which gives onto more gentle countryside in the area known as **Biqya'wiyya**, and shortly after you'll be able to see the **holy tree** itself, which lies about 300m past Km 967 in a beautiful setting on the edge of a flowing stream feeding a modern reservoir. It's the only tree within view – indeed, just about the only tree visible on the entire journey from Safawi – in an exceptionally peaceful and pleasant spot, from where stretch out vast panoramas across the open desert. Bear in mind, however, that this is a holy place, and that the local Bedouin as well as pilgrims from around Jordan and elsewhere make the long journey here specifically in order to pray and spend time alone or with their families in the presence of the Prophet. Frivolity, or stripping off to go bathing in the temptingly cool water, would be most disrespectful, as would tampering in any way either with the tree itself or with the strips of cloth which pilgrims leave tied to the lower branches as a mark of respect.

Asaykhim

Some 39km south of Safawi – just past the experimental Tell Hassan renewable energy station (complete with wind pump and solar panels) – or 15km north of Azraq ash-Shomali, are the hilltop ruins of the Roman fort at **Asaykhim**, definitely worth the effort to reach for the extraordinary views and ravishing sunsets. As usual in this region, you can only get here with a 4x4 and a guide: it's a tough half-hour drive east from the Safawi–Azraq road across stones and up steep gradients, although the hilltop ruins are clearly visible from some distance away. Asaykhim was one of the string of fortified stations built along the road between Azraq and Bosra, probably in the third century AD, to protect the empire's exposed eastern frontier, and it occupies a commanding position. A scramble up to the summit will reveal a series of small rooms built around a **courtyard**, the walls twelve courses high in places, with a **gatehouse** and some arched ceiling supports still standing. The arch in one room on the west wall has lost the ceiling it once supported, and stands alone facing the setting sun, perfectly framing one of Jordan's top photo-ops. It's the breathtaking 360° **panorama** that makes Asaykhim memorable, far more than the ruins: locals say that you can see all the Badia from up here, and Asaykhim is certainly a fine place to get a flavour of the vast Badia landscape.

Another reason for embarking on a 4x4 trek out here is to be able to wander on foot in the natural **Safaitic art** gallery of the rugged basalt desert to the east of the hill. A surprising number of the boulders and rocks here feature some kind of prehistoric inscription or drawing, most of which are probably at least ten thousand years old: in this once-lush land, anonymous shepherds and farmers from past eras drew stylized people, camels and other animals, geometric patterns and random unknown markings on the only canvas they had available – basalt. The article "Safaitic art" by Jordanian artist Ammar Khammash, found under "Geology Tourism" at Ⓦwww.pellamuseum.org explains more.

East of Safawi

A short way east of Safawi, the highway crosses the **Wadi Rajil**, which feeds water falling on Jebel Druze in Syria south to Azraq. Soon after, you pass alongside the prominent **Jibal Ashqaf** mountains, looming on both sides above the rolling slopes of black rocks overlaying yellowish sand which fill the immensely long sightlines in all directions. The Ashqaf area marks a watershed, since the large **Wadi Ghsayn** which runs alongside the road further east drains water into the flat Qa Abul Ghsayn and then to Burqu and north into Syria. As you head on east, you cross the dividing line between the black stony *harra* desert and flatter limestone *hamad*, which stretches east to the Iraqi border and is much more soothing on the eye. Some 90km east of Safawi is a lazy checkpoint at **Muqat**, starting point for a journey north along the Wadi Muqat into the roadless desert towards Burqu (see below).

About 10km east of Muqat is the last settlement of any size in Jordan, **RUWAYSHID**, another shabby but bustling town boasting a couple of truckers' motels – including the last-chance saloon *al-Yobeil al-Dahabi* (T02/629 2453, F629 2450; ❷) – a pharmacy or two, a few diners (*Broasted Chicken Quick Meal* is about the best you'll find) and even a place selling Amstel beer. After the 2003 invasion of Iraq, Ruwayshid became the main transit point for refugees fleeing the conflict: thousands passed through but, at the time of writing, there remain several hundred Iraqis of Palestinian origin, who have been refused admission by both Israel and Jordan but are unable to return to Iraq, along with over a thousand Iranian Kurds stranded further east on the border, who refuse to return to either Iran or Iraq and have also been barred by Jordan. Both groups are in the care of the UN, pending some decision on their future.

From Ruwayshid, a dual-lane highway makes short work of the 79km to the border, which is better known by the name of the Iraqi border post **Turaybil** than by the Jordanian post of **Karama**. Baghdad is about 550km further east.

Burqu

The *qasr* at **Burqu** (pronounced with difficulty, along the lines of "beurkaa" rather than "berkoo") can be grouped – archeologically speaking – with the "Desert Castles" of Hallabat, Azraq and others, a small Roman fort occupied and expanded during the Islamic period. However, the ruins take a poor second place to Burqu's quite extraordinary natural environment, both on the off-road journey to reach the site and once you arrive: the *qasr* stands on the shores of **Ghadir Burqu**, a substantial lake some 2km long which is fabulous enough by itself, hidden in the depths of the desert, but which also serves as the lifeline and congregation point for an array of animals and local and migrating birds. Proposed to become a protected nature reserve under the aegis of the Royal Society for the Conservation of Nature (RSCN), Burqu is a wild and dramatic place, well worth the long and difficult journey. It lies at the focal point of desert tracks roughly 18km north of Muqat or 25km northwest of Ruwayshid, and is all-but-impossible to locate without the help of a guide with intimate local knowledge.

The **dam** 2km north of the *qasr* (which led to the lake's formation) and the jagged, broken-off tower which still rises above the ruined walls of the castle are thought both to have been constructed in the third century, possibly to guard the water source for caravans travelling between Syria and Arabia. Inhabited continuously during the Byzantine period – possibly as a monastery – Burqu was expanded and fortified by Emir Walid in the year 700 AD; an inscription dated 1409 might indicate occupation up to that date. The entrance into the *qasr* is on the north wall, which gives access to two **inscriptions** – one naming Walid – above the lintel of the room in the far left-hand corner of the rubble-strewn **courtyard**, next to a room with a pointed arch. In the opposite corner is a small, freestanding circular room with a cross carved into its lintel; next to it is the original **tower**, still standing to around 8m, with a tiny, easily defended door (now blocked) in one wall.

However, it's the enormous **lake** and its flora and fauna which most impress. The journey from Muqat to Burqu crosses a large, flat *qa*, from which subterranean water rises to form the lake, full almost year-round and bordered in spring by poppies, irises and other wildflowers. Gently lapping wavelets fringe the most incongruous beach you're ever likely to stroll on.

The projected nature reserve is to be centred on this mirage-like apparition, which stands between two very different habitats. To the east is a vast expanse of *hamad*, or stony desert pavement, covered with bushes and grasses in winter. To the west sweeps the black *Harrat ash-Sham*, a moonscape of basalt rocks ranging in size from a few centimetres to a metre or more across. The rocks make the *harra* impassable even for 4x4 jeeps: hunters cannot penetrate the area, turning it into a perfect wildlife refuge. **Gazelles** roam the *harra*, the last few herds surviving in Jordan, in addition to hyenas, wolves, red foxes, wildcats, caracals and hares, all of which were logged in an RSCN survey of Burqu. Birders, too, will be delighted: as well as regular sightings of sandpipers, larks, wheatears and finches, Burqu boasts herons, pelicans, storks and cranes, along with buzzards, owls, vultures and even the rare Verreaux's Eagle. Rumours, as yet unsubstantiated, persist among the locals of the presence of **cheetahs**.

Travel details

No timetables are in operation – most buses, and all minibuses and serveeces simply depart when they're full.

Buses, minibuses and serveeces

Azraq to: Zarqa (Old station; 1hr 20min).
Dayr al-Kahf to: Mafraq (Bedouin station; 1hr).
Hallabat to: Zarqa (Old station; 40min).
Khirbet as-Samra to: Zarqa (Old station; 30min).
Mafraq (Bedouin station) to: Amman (Abdali station; 1hr); Dayr al-Kahf (1hr); Ruwayshid (2hr 30min); Safawi (1hr 15min); Umm al-Jimal (30min); Zarqa (Old station; 30min).
Mafraq (Fellahin station) to: Irbid (New Amman station; 45min); Jerash (40min); Ramtha (30min).
Muwaggar to: Amman (Raghadan station; 30min).
Ruwayshid to: Mafraq (Bedouin station; 2hr 30min); Safawi (1hr 15min).

Safawi to: Mafraq (Bedouin station; 1hr 15min); Ruwayshid (1hr 15min).
Umm al-Jimal to: Mafraq (Bedouin station; 30min).
Zarqa (New station) to: Amman (Abdali station; 35min); Amman (Raghadan station; 25min); Karak (2hr 30min); Madaba (1hr); Salt (45min).
Zarqa (Old station) to: Ajloun (1hr 20min); Azraq (1hr 20min); Hallabat (40min); Irbid (New Amman station; 1hr); Jerash (45min); Khirbet as-Samra (30min); Mafraq (Bedouin station; 30min).

International buses

Mafraq (Fellahin station) to: Damascus (2hr 30min); Dera'a (1hr 20min).

Useful Arabic place names

Asaykhim	اصيخم	– Bedouin station	مجمع البدو
Azraq al-Janubi	الازرق الجنوبي	– Fellahin station	مجمع الفلاحين
Azraq ash-Shomali	الازرق الشمالي	Muwaggar	الموقّر
Azraq Wetlands Reserve	محمية الازرق المائية	Qasr Azraq	قصر الازرق
Baa'idj	الباعج	Qasr Hallabat	قصر الحلابات
Biqya'wiyya	البقيعاوية	Qasr Hraneh	قصر الحرانة
Burqu	برقع	Qasr Mushatta	قصر المشتّى
Dayr al-Kahf	دير الكهف	Qasr Tuba	قصر الطوبة
Dayr al-Qinn	دير القن	Qusayr Amra	قصير عمرة
Dulayl	الضليل	Ruwayshid	الرويشد
Hallabat al-Gharbi	الحلابات الغربي	Safawi	الصفاوي
Hallabat ash-Sharqi	الحلابات الشرقي	Shaumari Reserve	محمية الشومري
Hammam as-Srah	حمام السرح	Umm al-Jimal	ام الجمال
Jawa	جاوا	Zarqa	الزرقاء
Khirbet as-Samra	الخربة السمراء	– New station	مجمع الجديد
Mafraq	المفرق	– Old station	مجمع القديم

5

The King's Highway

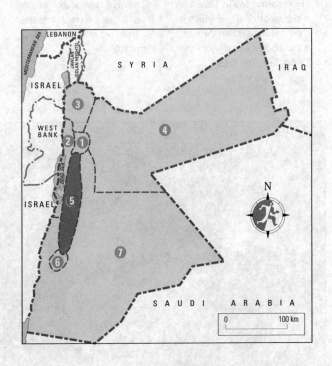

CHAPTER 5 # Highlights

✳ **Madaba** Amiable small town full of fine mosaics, among them a unique map of the Holy Land. See p.279

✳ **Mount Nebo** Awe-inspiring views from the mountain named in the Bible as the spot where Moses died. See p.289

✳ **Hammamat Ma'in** Take a dip beneath hot waterfalls as they cascade down through a barren desert valley to the Dead Sea. See p.293

✳ **Wadi Mujib** Jordan's Grand Canyon, a vast fold in the landscape now protected as a nature reserve. See p.298

✳ **Karak** Crusader stronghold, still within its original walls, perched on a crag above a busy market town. See p.304

✳ **Dana** Jordan's finest nature reserve, with walks, climbs and views to recharge the emptiest of batteries. See p.313

△ Shobak castle

The King's Highway

The **KING'S HIGHWAY** – the grandiose translation of an old Hebrew term which probably only meant "main road" – is a long, meandering squiggle of a road running through some of Jordan's loveliest countryside. It has been the route of north–south trade through Transjordan and the scene of battles since prehistoric times. **Moses** was refused permission to travel on the King's Highway by the king of Edom, and later, the **Nabateans**, from their power base in **Petra**, used the highway to trade luxury goods between Arabia and Syria (although located on the highway, Petra merits its own chapter, starting on p.323). When the Romans annexed the Nabatean kingdom, Emperor **Trajan** renovated the ancient road to facilitate travel and communications between his regional capital at Bosra, northeast of Mafraq, and Aqaba on the Red Sea coast. Early Christian pilgrims visited a number of sites on and off the road around **Madaba**, whose beautiful Byzantine mosaics still merit a pilgrimage today. The **Crusaders** used the highway as the linch-pin of their Kingdom of Oultrejourdain, fortifying positions along the road at **Karak** and **Shobak** – where extensive remains of castles survive – and also at Petra and Aqaba.

However, with the development by the **Ottomans** of the faster and more direct Darb al-Hajj (Pilgrimage Route), from Damascus to the Holy Places through the desert further east – and the subsequent construction of both the Hejaz Railway and the modern Desert Highway along the same route – the King's Highway faded in importance. Only tarmacked along its entire length in the 1950s and 1960s, today it is a simple road, often rutted and narrow, which meticulously follows the contours of the rolling hills above the Dead Sea rift. Linking a series of springs, and also following the line of maximum hilltop rainfall, the road runs through intensively cultivated farmland, and travelling on it today can both give you a glimpse of the reality of rural life for many Jordanians, and also open up possibilities for exploration of the entirely untouristed countryside. One particular draw is the spectacular **Dana Nature Reserve**, set in a deep and isolated valley, with good facilities for camping and hiking.

Transport practicalities

Whether you have a day or a week, the best way to travel on the King's Highway is by **rental car**, since, frustratingly enough, there is no public transport running the length of the road. All **buses** from Amman to towns along the highway start out on the faster, but thoroughly unpicturesque, Desert Highway and only cut west on feeder roads at the last moment. Thus, Karak-bound buses bypass Madaba, Tafileh buses bypass Karak, Shobak buses bypass Tafileh, and buses to Petra or Aqaba bypass them all.

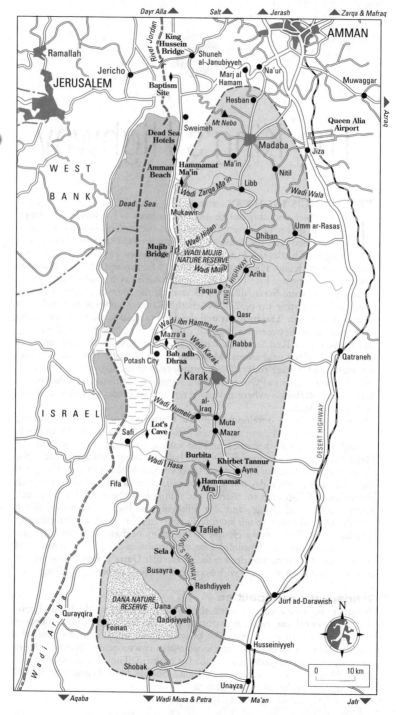

Public transport along the King's Highway is limited to a series of point-to-point local bus routes connecting towns and villages on the road. However, these local buses often don't run across governorate boundaries: no buses run directly between Madaba and Karak, or between Tafileh and Shobak, and to make these journeys you either have to switch buses several times in small villages or resort to **hitching**.

On the northern stretches of the highway, transport runs reasonably frequently and at manageable times of day: it's not too hard to hop a series of buses from Amman to Qadisiyyeh (via Madaba, Karak and Tafileh), although they stop on one rim of the Wadi Mujib canyon (halfway between Madaba and Karak) and start again on the other rim, so you have no choice but to hitch the bit in the middle. However, even if this journey were possible in one day – which is unlikely, since it involves at least six buses – you would have no time to stop to see anything on the way. **Overnighting** in Karak means you can at least enjoy the journey; additional nights in Madaba and Dana open up the possibility of making highly rewarding exploratory side-trips off the highway. South of Qadisiyyeh, public transport is almost nonexistent. From here to Wadi Musa/Petra, the only feasible option is to hitch, but there are enough pick-ups trundling from village to village that it's not difficult to get a ride.

Note the warning on p.158 concerning the various **scams** and cut-price deals operated by Amman hotels keen to service the market for King's Highway trips to Petra. The most reliable and best-value of these private bus services is operated by the *Mariam Hotel* in Madaba (see p.283).

Madaba to Wadi Mujib

Much as it did in antiquity, the initial portion of the King's Highway south of Amman runs past small farming villages interspersed among wide plains of wheat. The edge of the plateau overlooking the Dead Sea rift is never far from the road, and countless tracks lead off westwards into the hills teetering over the lowest point on earth. The largest town, and only worthwhile place to stay, is **Madaba**, capital of its own governorate. South of Madaba, the King's Highway meanders through several valleys draining rainwater off the hills; the most beautiful of these is **Wadi Wala**, the deepest and most dramatic, **Wadi Mujib**.

Madaba and around

The small, easy-going market town of **MADABA**, some 30km southwest of Amman, is best known for the dozens of fine Byzantine **mosaics** preserved in its churches and museums. An impressive sixth-century mosaic map of the Middle East takes top billing in package tours, but the town's narrow streets, dotted with fine old Ottoman stone houses and overlooked by the large Catholic Church of St John on the town's highest hill, lead to plenty of other, much more beautiful mosaics that are often ignored by visitors in a hurry to get to Karak. Excursions to the fabulous mosaics at **Mount Nebo** – from where

Moses looked over the Promised Land – and **Umm ar-Rasas**, as well as to the hot waterfalls of **Hammamat Ma'in** and King Herod's ruined mountain-top palace perched over the Dead Sea at **Mukawir**, make Madaba an ideal base for two or three days of exploration. Add to this easy access to the Dead Sea, the Baptism Site and Amman itself, and Madaba could easily work as a low-key alternative to basing yourself in the capital.

Some history

Madaba is first mentioned in the Old Testament as having been conquered – along with the rest of the land of **Moab** – by the Israelites, who then parcelled it out to the tribe of Reuben. The city was won back for Moab in the middle of the ninth century BC by King Mesha (as proclaimed in the famous Mesha Stele; see p.299), at which point the Israelite prophet **Isaiah** stepped in, prophesying doom: "Moab shall howl over Nebo and over Medeba: on all their heads shall be baldness and every beard cut off… everyone shall howl, weeping abundantly." After some further turmoil during the Hellenistic period, with the city passing from Greek hands to Jewish to Nabatean, the **Roman** Provincia Arabia brought order; by the third century AD, Madaba was minting its own coins.

Christianity spread rapidly and, by 451, Madaba had its own bishop. Mosaicists had been at work in and around the town since well before the 390s, but **mosaic art** really began to flourish in Madaba during the reign of the emperor Justinian (527–65). Towards the end of that century, Bishop Sergius oversaw a golden age of artistic accomplishment: surviving mosaics from the Cathedral (576), the Church of the Apostles (578), the Church of Bishop Sergius at Umm ar-Rasas (587), Madaba's Crypt of St Elianos and Church of the Virgin (both 595) and the Moses Memorial Church on Mount Nebo (597) – as well as, conceivably, the famed mosaic map of the Holy Land – all date from his period in office. When the **Persian** armies came through in 614, closely followed by the **Muslims**, Madaba surrendered without a fight and so retained its Christian identity and population; churches were still being built and mosaics laid for another hundred years or more. A mosaic discovered at Umm ar-Rasas mentions a bishop of Madaba as late as 785.

Madaba was abandoned during the **Mamluke** period and its ruins – by then strewn over a huge artificial mound, or *tell* – lay untouched for centuries. In 1879, conflict between Christian and Muslim tribes in Karak led to ninety Catholic and Orthodox families going into voluntary exile; they arrived at Madaba's uninhabited *tell* shortly after, laid claim to the surrounding land and began to farm. The **Ottoman** authorities in Damascus rubber-stamped the *fait accompli* but gave the settlers permission to build new churches only on the sites of previously existing ones. It was in 1884, during clearance work for a new church, that Madaba's fabulous **mosaic map of the Holy Land** was uncovered, closely followed by many more mosaics which lay in churches and houses all over the town. Scholars and archeologists arrived from all over the world to excavate in Madaba, and this continuous process still regularly uncovers mosaics and remnants of the past beneath the streets of the modern town centre.

These days the social and religious balance of the town is changing, in a slow urbanization process that has seen tens of thousands of **Muslim** families migrating from surrounding villages to occupy Madaba's suburbs and outskirts. Although **Christians** still comprise the overwhelming majority of inhabitants in the city centre (estimates put the proportion at over 95 percent), Madaba's total Christian population today is around 12,000 in a greater municipality that has ballooned to 100,000 or more.

Arrival, information and accommodation

Buses from Amman, Dhiban and elsewhere (there are no buses from Karak) arrive at the **bus station**, situated on the King's Highway about ten minutes' walk to the east of the town centre. The **tourist office** (Sat–Thurs 8am–5pm; ☎05/325 3563) is on Abu Bakr as-Saddeeq Street, alongside the Madaba Mosaic School, with free maps and helpful staff. The **tourist police** are generally always on duty outside *St George's Church*, and they also have an office about 100m north (☎05/324 1901). Madaba's main **post office** is in the centre of town (daily 7.30am–5pm, Fri until 1.30pm), on the same street as a handful of **banks**. A **taxi** across town should cost no more than 500 fils.

Accommodation

Heading Madaba's pack of decent, good-value mid-range **hotels** is the *Mariam*, the best two-star hotel in the country and – unusually – a place that is worth going out of your way for. It, and its competitors, all include fairly substantial breakfasts in their room rates; couple that with Madaba's proximity to Queen Alia International Airport (18km eastwards), and the town stands as an excellent alternative to basing yourself in Amman.

Black Iris North of town off Yarmouk Street ☎05/324 1959. Clean, spacious en-suite twins and doubles, quiet but less characterful than other places around town. ❸

Lulu's Pension A 10min walk north of the centre, opposite the large "JOLIFT" sign ☎05/324 3678, ☏324 7617. A cosy conversion of one floor of Lulu's own home, which offers comfortable rooms

---

Moving on from Madaba

From the **bus station** there are four bus-routes running to different points in **Amman**: more or less direct to Abdali, Raghadan and Wihdat stations, and a long way round to Muhajireen station, via Hesban and Na'ur. The last departs around 9pm. You can also bypass Amman: plenty of buses run to **Zarqa**, from where there are connections east to Azraq. In addition, buses run from Madaba over the crest of **Mount Nebo** and down to **Shuneh al-Janubiyyeh** in the Jordan Valley; to reach the **Dead Sea**, ask the driver if he'll go a bit further and drop you off at "Amman Beach", or just take a connecting bus to "Amman Beach" from Shuneh.

An alternative is to book a taxi at discount rates through the *Mariam Hotel* (see below) and share the cost between three or four passengers: the *Mariam* can do a return trip from Madaba to Mount Nebo, the Dead Sea and the **Baptism Site** at Bethany for JD20, including an hour at each site; from Madaba to the "Desert Castles" for JD35; from Madaba to the **airport** for JD7, day or night; and from Madaba direct to **Aqaba** via Wadi Araba, for JD50.

For full details of getting to Mount Nebo, Hesban, Hammamat Ma'in, Mukawir and Umm ar-Rasas, see the relevant accounts on the next few pages.

Along the King's Highway to Petra

For points south along the King's Highway, nearly all regular buses terminate in **Dhiban**, the last town before the dramatic gorge of Wadi Mujib. However, Charl al-Twal, the enterprising owner of the *Mariam Hotel* in Madaba, has started up his own **King's Highway bus service** between Madaba and Petra, departing from Madaba at 10am, stopping briefly at Wadi Mujib, then for an hour at Karak, arriving in Wadi Musa around 4pm. It runs each day that at least three people have **reserved in advance** for the journey (you don't have to be staying at the *Mariam*) – and only runs from north to south. His bargain fare is JD15 per person. To get to Petra more quickly, ask about the *Mariam's* service along the Desert Highway (JD13 per person).

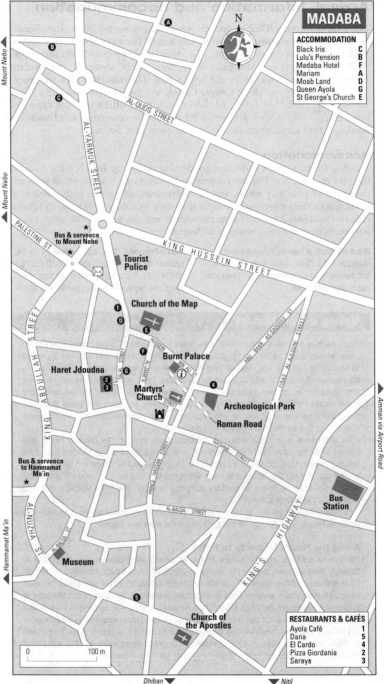

▲ Amman via Hesban

Mount Nebo ◀

Mount Nebo ◀

Hammamat Ma'in ◀

MADABA

N

ACCOMMODATION
Black Iris	C
Lulu's Pension	B
Madaba Hotel	F
Mariam	A
Moab Land	D
Queen Ayola	G
St George's Church	E

A
B
C

AL-QUDS STREET

AL-YARMUK STREET

PALESTINE ST.

Bus & serveece
to Mount Nebo

KING HUSSEIN STREET

Tourist
Police

Church of the Map

Burnt Palace

Haret Jdoudna

Martyrs'
Church

Archeological Park

Roman Road

ABU BAKR AS-SADDEEQ ST.

FIRAS AL-AJJOUNI STREET

Amman via Airport Road ▶

Bus & serveece
to Hammamat
Ma'in

PRINCE HASSAN STREET

HASHMI STREET

AL-BALQA STREET

KING'S HIGHWAY

Bus
Station

AL-NUZHA ST.

AL-BALQA ST.

Museum

Church of
the Apostles

0   100 m

▼ Dhiban   ▼ Nitil

RESTAURANTS & CAFÉS
Ayola Café	1
Dana	5
El Cardo	4
Pizza Giordania	2
Saraya	3

that are starting to look a little worn. Some are en suite, and there's a communal TV lounge and access to kitchen facilities. Go for the budget communal rooftop sleep-in during summer. ❸

Madaba Hotel Al-Jame'a Street ☎05/324 0643, ⓕ324 4367. Spartan place in the town centre, 100m south of the Church of the Map, with plain, basic rooms and shared bathrooms. Bed down on the shaded roof in summer to cut costs. ❷

Mariam Aisha Umm al-Mumeneen Street ☎05/325 1529, ⓕ325 1530, ⓔmh@go.com.jo, ⓦwww.mariamhotel.com. Best hotel in Madaba by a long way, family-run and located on a quiet street ten minutes' walk north of the centre. The rooms – spacious and bright, with en-suite bathrooms – are spotlessly clean, well kept and comfortable, with phones, fans and central heating. The lobby has a pleasant lounge area with TV, while breakfast (and other meals on request) are served in the restaurant or on the outside terrace: an open-air swimming pool with bar and restaurant was completed in 2005. The welcoming and knowledgeable owner, Charl al-Twal, is a mine of information on the history of Madaba (which features his own family prominently) and on travelling around Jordan. Ask about the bargain rates for local and long-distance taxis (including to and from the airport). Charl will knock 15 percent off all room rates if you show this Rough Guide when you check in, making it even better value for money. ❸

Moab Land Opposite *St George's Church* main gate ☎ & ⓕ05/325 1318. Another good choice, run by a friendly, helpful and accommodating Orthodox Christian family. Spotless, roomy en-suite twins and doubles have a nice attention to detail, some with balconies overlooking the street, and there's a great roof terrace for memorable breakfasts with a view out over the whole town. The only potential drawback is some road noise from the busy street in front. ❸

Queen Ayola Opposite the *Haret Jdoudna* restaurant and crafts complex ☎ & ⓕ05/324 4087, ⓦwww.geocities.com/queen_ayola_hotel_madaba. Small town-centre hotel with just eight decent en-suite doubles, some with balcony. ❸

St George's Church ☎05/324 4984, ⓕ324 1842. In an annexe beside the Greek Orthodox "Church of the Map" is accommodation intended for pilgrims, more specifically for those with a commitment to financially and spiritually benefiting the church and its affiliated school. The spick-and-span rooms – all of them en suite – are ranged around an upper-level gallery of a brilliant white internal courtyard more reminiscent of Tangier than Madaba. There is no charge, but you're expected to make a proportionate donation. Ask for Father Inikindios.

The Town

Although most visitors rush into Madaba to view the celebrated **mosaic map** and rush out again, the town is crammed with other mosaics, many of them more complete than the map and most more aesthetically pleasing. Within the central maze of streets is a large area of excavated mosaics dubbed the **Archeological Park**, while a small **museum** and the grand mosaic floor of the **Church of the Apostles** both lie a short stroll to the south.

As well as mosaics, Madaba is known for its **carpets**. If you're in the market for such items, you'll find that prices are more reasonable, and quality often better, than in Amman. Many places in the town still weave carpets on traditional upright handlooms, although these days all the actual weaving is done by Egyptian employees. Just beside the *Madaba Hotel*, a local old-timer oversees a continuously active loom, but your best bets are the shops on Hussein bin Ali Street. For other local crafts, **Haret Jdoudna**, a complex of small shops and restaurants set round an attractive, covered courtyard off Talal Street, merits a wander.

The Church of the Map

Madaba's prime attraction is a fabulous Byzantine **mosaic map** of the Holy Land, housed in the modern **St George's Church** (Mon–Thurs & Sat 8am–6pm, Fri 9am–6pm, Sun 10.30am–6pm; winter closes 5pm; JD1). Although hyped a little excessively – and thus suffering from over a thousand visitors a day in the high season – the map is well worth seeing, notwithstanding the cramped space inside the church itself and the echoing voices of all the tour guides.

Although there is no evidence of a date of composition, or the identity of the artist, the map was undoubtedly laid in the second half of the sixth century, in a Byzantine church that stood on the same site as the modern one but was possibly much larger; two of the original columns survive outside in the churchyard. The **map** is oriented to the east, its front edge being the Mediterranean coast, with north lying to the left. Its **size** and **style** both mark it out as special. What survives today are just fragments of the original, which comprised over two million stones, measured an enormous 15.6m long by 6m wide and depicted virtually the entire Levant, from Lebanon in the north to the Nile Delta in the south, and from the Mediterranean coast to the open desert. Other, simpler, mosaic renderings of cities and towns – and even mosaic maps – have been uncovered around the region, but the Madaba map is unique in depicting the larger towns and cities with an **oblique perspective**, as if from a vantage point high above to the west: what you see of Jerusalem, Karak, Gaza and Nablus is the outside of the western city wall and the inside of the eastern one, with buildings inside shown accurately in 3D-style, as if the mosaicist intended to produce a city plan.

Indeed, the whole, novel purpose of laying a map on the floor of the church may have been – in addition to glorifying God's works in the lands of the Bible – to better direct pilgrims to sites of biblical significance. Although there are some inaccuracies, the mapmaker has reproduced settlements and geographical features very precisely and, even by today's standards, the work is mostly cartographically correct. There are photos of the map and exhaustive historical glossaries at Ⓦ198.62.75.1/www1/ofm/mad.

Jerusalem

What you come to first, as you walk up the aisle of the church, is **Jerusalem**, the "centre of the world" and the map's largest city, oval-shaped and labelled in red Η ΑΓΙΑ ΠΟΛΙС ΙΕΡΟΥСΑ[ΛΗΜ] (The Holy City of Jerusalem). The six Byzantine gates of the city are shown in their exact locations and all survive to this day. At the northern edge of the city, marked by a tall column, is the **Damascus Gate** (in Arabic, *Bab al-Amud*, or Gate of the Column); the long, colonnaded *cardo maximus* runs from here due south to the **Zion Gate**. In order to show detail within the city as accurately as possible, the mosaicist opened up the street, turning the western colonnade upside down. A second, parallel street runs from Damascus Gate under an arch – still present today – to the **Dung Gate**, almost indiscernible in the jumble of detail at the southern end of the city. A short street branches off to **St Stephen's Gate** in the eastern wall, next to which lies the **Golden Gate**. In the western wall of the

---

The Miracle of the Blue Hand

St George's is the focus of Madaba's **Greek Orthodox** community, and services are held there every week, with carpets laid over the precious mosaic to protect it. One Sunday morning in 1976, during Mass, worshippers passed in front of one of the church's many icons as normal, looking at it and touching it. Later in the service, someone chanced to look at the icon again – a picture of the Virgin and Child, which had been in full public view for years – and noticed that it had suddenly "grown" a third, **blue hand**, unseen by the full congregation an hour or so before. No one had an explanation, and it was declared to be a miracle, the Virgin showing Madaba a helping hand. The celebrated icon, still with its blue hand, is now behind glass in the crypt; any one of the church guardians can take you down to see it and explain more of the story.

city, the only breach is for the **Jaffa Gate**, from which the *decumanus* (today's David Street) runs east to join the *cardo*, with a dogleg hooking south behind the Citadel. Of Jerusalem's many churches, the biggest is the Church of the Holy Sepulchre, a centrally located complex of buildings topped with a red roof and the Dome of the Resurrection. At the southern end of the *cardo* is the New Church of the Mother of God, with a double yellow doorway; this was consecrated on November 20, 542, which helps in dating the Madaba map. In the southwest corner of the city looms the huge basilica on Mount Zion, also with a double yellow doorway. Outside the walls to the southeast, a large patch of damage obscures everything up to the Dead Sea, but the four letters ΓΗΘC (GETHS) indicate the garden of **Gethsemane**.

The rest of Palestine

To the north of Jerusalem, the whole of the area outside the Damascus Gate is crammed with text identifying myriad biblical sites, including the portion of land allotted to the tribe of Benjamin following the Israelites' conquest of Canaan. A badly charred section conceals **Nablus**, identified as ΝΕΑΠΟΛΙC (Neapolis), seemingly as far north as the map shows; however, an isolated fragment between the pews against the left-hand wall of the church shows a patch of modern-day Lebanon, giving an idea of the full extent of the original map. To the east of Nablus, between the high ground and the sinuous curves of the River Jordan, lies **Jericho** (ΙΕΡΙΧω), shown face on, surrounded by palm trees. Nearby, exactly at the location of today's King Hussein Bridge, a small watchtower guards a ferry crossing, the boats hauled across the river by rope. A fish unknowingly swims downriver to a salty death in the Dead Sea, while another tries frantically to swim against the current. On the east bank, a gazelle is fleeing from a lion (obliterated in antiquity), showing the presence of considerably wilder wildlife in the Jordan Valley than survives today. Just below is an enclosed spring marked "Ainon, where now is Sapsafas" (ΑΙΝωΝ ΕΝΘΑ ΝΥΝ Ο CΑΠCΑΦΑC), the precise location of the rediscovered **Baptism Site** of Jesus.

West of Jerusalem are crowded more place names and biblical references, including, outside the southwestern corner of the city, the "field of blood" (ΑΚΕΛ ΔΑΜΑ), bought with Judas Iscariot's thirty pieces of silver (Matthew 27). The nearest major town is the unwalled Lod (ΛωΔ); just below, in large red letters, is marked the allocation of land to the tribe of Dan ([ΚΛΗ]ΡΟC ΔΑΝ). Below, and to the left of the patch of damage, is a tiny red-domed building, with the Mediterranean Sea beyond; this was one of the possible locations for **Jonah**'s being thrown up onto dry land out of the belly of the whale – ΤΟ ΤΥ ΑΓΙΥ ΙωΝΑ (The [sanctuary] of St Jonah). To the south, beyond the damaged area, lies **Ashdod** harbour, identified as ΑΖωΤΟC ΠΑΡΑΛΟ[C], with Ashdod town (ΑCΔω[Δ]) further inland.

To the south of Jerusalem, on the edge of the surviving mosaic, lies **Bethlehem** (ΒΗΘΛΕΕΜ), shown surprisingly small compared to less important towns; the mosaicist chose only to show the Church of the Nativity, isolated on a circular plain. Due south is the land of Judah (ΙΟΥΔΑ). Hard up against the pillar of the church is the sacred tree of Abraham (Genesis 18), identified as Η ΔΡΥC ΜΑΜ[ΒΡΗ] (the oak of Mambre); the small church just south of it lies over the Cave of the Makhpelah near **Hebron**. An isolated fragment of mosaic preserves part of the town of Ashkelon (ΑCΚΑΛω[Ν]) to the west.

The Dead Sea, Transjordan and the Nile

Central in the surviving fragments of the mosaic is the long, sausage-shaped **Dead Sea**, with shipping indicating trade links in antiquity. Of the two boats,

The mosaics of Jordan

Hundreds of floor-laid **mosaics** in stone have survived in Jordan, from a first-century BC example at Herod's palace at Mukawir (now on display in Madaba) through to pieces from the eighth century AD, when Christian mosaicists were still at work under the Muslim caliphate. Specific styles were used for places of worship and for civilian buildings, whether public baths, private mansions or the palaces and hunting lodges of the Umayyads. During the reign of the Byzantine emperor Justinian, for example, a retro taste for classical motifs was popular: many secular buildings were decorated with scenes taken from **Greek and Roman mythology**, with the Transjordanian mosaicists tending to work in small, demarcated panels rather than composing one tableau across an entire floor. Churches, of course, couldn't be decorated with the same pagan designs, but in addition to dedicatory inscriptions recording names of bishops and benefactors, and **Christian symbols** such as the lamb and the fish, **Classical-style personifications** of the sea, the earth and the seasons appeared on church floors throughout Jordan. These church mosaics served to dazzle and awe visitors to the house of God and, in an age of almost universal illiteracy, to teach the events of the Bible pictorially; the many representations of buildings and great cities may also have served as a rudimentary atlas.

Mosaic artists throughout the empire worked from **pattern-books** compiled in regional cultural centres, above all Constantinople. One result of this common artistic heritage is the predominance of **pastoral** scenes – which, in provincial backwaters such as Transjordan, also represented the reality of daily agricultural life for many people. The regularly recurring watery vignettes of ducks, boats and fish were rooted in a classical taste for representations of life on the **Nile**, and **hunting** scenes, often featuring lions, leopards and other extraordinary creatures, grew out of the Roman practice of capturing wild beasts for amphitheatre sports. In addition, Transjordanian mosaicists portrayed in detail a whole encyclopedia of **flora and fauna**, drawn from local experience, the tales of travellers (elephants, crocodiles and octopus), and the realms of imagination (sea monsters and phoenixes).

However, the controversy concerning the **depiction of people** which raged across Byzantium and Transjordan – then already in the control of the Muslim armies – in the eighth and ninth centuries led to many mosaics being disfigured. What was under attack, from **iconoclasts** both Byzantine and Umayyad, was, at heart, polytheism. For centuries, Christians in the East had been venerating religious images in paint, stone and mosaic in a way that more ascetic elements in the Byzantine hierarchy considered too close for comfort to antique paganism. In 726 Emperor **Leo III** banned the use of icons in worship throughout his empire. In Transjordan, though, with the Umayyads in control, what had as much practical impact was a parallel movement within Islam. The Prophet Muhammad is reported to have taught that God is the only creator; interpreting this to imply that human "creation" of images of living creatures was blasphemous, the Umayyad caliph **Yazid II** (719–24) issued a directive to destroy all depictions of people – and, by extension, animals – throughout the Muslim empire. With unequivocal orders from the highest religious and civil authorities, Transjordan's mosaicists had no choice but to set to work to obliterate with blank stones all images of people and animals in existing mosaics, sometimes with care, often in a panic: many of Jordan's mosaics today feature only surreal clouds of haze hanging over what were once portraits. Some mosaics survived unscathed by having been buried in earlier years; others, laid after the order was given, avoided the issue by remaining studiously abstract. After 120 years of bitter controversy, the Christian ban was rescinded, but the Muslim injunction remained and still applies today.

As a footnote to Jordan's mosaic heritage, thousands of glass mosaic tiles have been uncovered in churches everywhere from Jerash to Madaba, testifying to the former existence of large and lavish wall mosaics in **coloured glass**, the glory of which can only be imagined.

the left one is being rowed (its sail is furled) with a cargo of what seems to be salt. The right one has an open sail and a yellowish cargo, which might be wheat. The detail of both crews, though, has been obliterated by iconoclasts. On the northeastern shore of the sea are the hot springs of Callirhoë (ΘΕΡΜΑ ΚΑΛΛΙΡΟΗC) at the outflow of the Wadi Zarqa Ma'in, showing pools and flowing water. To the east, although the original map undoubtedly showed Philadelphia (Amman) and the mosaicist's hometown of Madaba, all that remains of Transjordan is a stretch of mountainous land reaching out as far as **Karak** ([ΧΑΡ]ΑΧΜΩΒ[Α] or Kharakh-Moba, the fortress of Moab), fortified and isolated on its hilltop. The deep east–west valley to the south of Karak, labelled as [Ζ]ΑΡΕΔ (Zared) is today called Wadi Hasa. On the southeastern tip of the sea, near Zoora (ΖΟΟΡΑ), is **Lot's Cave** (ΤΟ ΤΥ ΑΓΙΥ Λ[ωΤ]), a church commemorating the site where Lot was drunkenly seduced by his two daughters. The four letters **ΕΡΗΜ** are the beginning of the Greek word for "desert".

The final section of the map is the most difficult to relate to reality. Against the right-hand wall of the church curl the arms of the **Nile** delta; however, instead of flowing from south to north, the Nile is depicted as flowing from east to west. In order to squeeze the river onto his strictly rectangular map, and also so as to keep faith with the notion of all the Rivers of Paradise – the Nile being one of them – flowing from the east (Genesis 2), the mosaicist used artistic licence to twist things around. The major city of the region is **Gaza** ([Γ]ΑΖΑ), on the westernmost edge of the surviving map, intricately depicted with walls, towers, streets and buildings. To the south of Gaza is a two-line text in red describing "the border between Egypt and Palestine", a border which survives to this day. Over a dozen villages surround Gaza, which comprised the land allotted to Simeon (ΚΛΗΡΟC ΣΥΜΕ[ωΝ]). Of all the towns marked in the Nile Delta, only Pelusium (ΤΟ ΠΗΛΟΥCΙΝ), near modern-day Port Saïd, is of any size.

The Archeological Park

A short stroll round the back of St George's Church will bring you to Hussein bin Ali Street and the **Burnt Palace**. A sixth-century patrician mansion, the palace was destroyed by fire early in the seventh century; its large floor mosaics include an image of the Roman city-goddess Tyche and several hunting scenes. Also within this area is a swathe of second-century **Roman road** and, shielded behind a high wall pending negotiations between the Ministry of Tourism and the Greek Orthodox Church, the **Martyrs' Church**, which has fine floor mosaics (currently buried for protection from the elements).

Barely 100m southeast of the Burnt Palace is the very impressive **Archeological Park** (daily 8am–7pm; winter closes 5pm; JD3 ticket also covers entry to the Church of the Apostles and Madaba Museum). Comprising a linked complex of a large Byzantine mansion, a church and a small museum of mosaics, it houses some of the most striking mosaic images in the country and is well worth an hour or more. Left of the ticket office hangs a Hellenistic-period mosaic, the oldest discovered in Jordan, taken from Herod's palace at Mukawir. Walking right past more mosaics brings you to an open plaza; follow the catwalk over a stretch of diagonally paved Roman road (some 2m below the present road surface) to reach the well-worn mosaic floor of the ruined Church of the Prophet Elias, dated to 607/8, and, below it, the tiny Crypt of Elianos, from 595/6.

Cross over the Roman road again to the plaza and the marvellous **Hippolytus Hall** mosaic, housed beneath a well-designed protective hangar. Dating from the early sixth century, probably from the reign of Justinian, the mosaic lay on the floor of what must have been a breathtakingly lavish private house. Less than a century later, though, the house was demolished and the mosaics buried to make way for the construction of the adjacent Church of the Virgin. Closest to the doorway is a diamond grid showing birds and plants. Next to this, and damaged by the foundations of an ancient wall, is a panel depicting the myth of Phaedra and Hippolytus; an almond-eyed Phaedra, sick with love for her stepson Hippolytus, is supported by two handmaidens and awaits news of him with a falconer in attendance (the image of Hippolytus himself has been lost). Above is a riotous scene. To the right, a bare-breasted Aphrodite, sitting on a throne next to Adonis, is spanking a winged cupid with a sandal; all around, the Three Graces and a servant girl have their hands full dealing with several more mischievous cupids, one of which is upsetting a basket of petals. Outside the lavish acanthus-leaf border of the main mosaic – itself decorated with hunting scenes of leopards, lions and bears – are three women, personifications of (from the left) Rome, Gregoria and Madaba, seated next to a couple of hideous sea monsters.

The stepped catwalk leads you on to overlook the circular nave of the **Church of the Virgin**. Just discernible around the edge of the main mosaic are images of flowers dating from the construction of the church, some time at the end of the sixth century. Most of what is now visible, though, dates from an elaborate geometric reworking of the mosaic floor completed in 767, during the Muslim Abbasid period. Swirls, knots and endlessly twisting patterns encircle a central medallion, with an inscription urging the congregation to "purify mind, flesh and works" before looking on Mary. A second inscription says that the mosaic was laid "thanks to the zeal and ardour of the people who love Christ in this city of Madaba".

The catwalk delivers you to a small colonnaded courtyard next to the hangar, hung with more mosaics, some from nearby Ma'in. There are depictions of Hesban and Gadaron (Salt), but the most interesting piece is over in the far corner. A mosaic picture of an ox has been lovingly obliterated by a tree (all that remains are hooves and a tail); similar care was taken in disfiguring many of the mosaic images in and around Madaba, implying that a great deal of iconoclasm was effected by local artists working under orders, rather than by religious zealots charging through the town destroying whatever they saw.

The Church of the Apostles

At the corner of Nuzha Street and the King's Highway lies the **Church of the Apostles** (daily 8am–7pm; winter closes 5pm; JD3 joint ticket with the Archeological Park and Madaba Museum), housed beneath a large and graceful new arched building, another Ammar Khammash design.

The church itself was a huge 24m by 15m basilica with a couple of side-chapels, dating to 568, the high point of the Madaba school of mosaic art. The centrepiece of the mosaic is a personification of the sea, a spectacular portrait of a composed, regal woman emerging from the waves, surrounded by jumping fish, sharks, sea monsters and even an octopus. She holds a rudder up beside her face like a standard and is making a curious, undefinable hand gesture. The main body of the mosaic features pairs of long-tailed parrots; the acanthus-leaf border is filled with animals (a crouching cat, a wolf, a hen with her chicks) and boys at play. In the corners are distinctive, chubby human faces.

Madaba Museum

Just off Nuzha Street, to the southwest of the town centre, the small **Madaba Museum** (daily except Tues 9am–5pm, Fri 10am–4pm; JD3 joint ticket with the

Archeological Park and Church of the Apostles) is worth a quick look. Nestled in a residential courtyard, the museum buildings were formerly houses themselves and feature mosaics uncovered by the residents during modern renovation work. Next to the ticket office and down some steps is a partly damaged mosaic, featuring a naked satyr prancing in a Bacchic procession (although Bacchus himself is missing). Through an arch and to the right is the **al-Masri house**, with a mosaic showing a man's head and pairs of animals between fruit trees. Outside, steps lead down to the museum rooms, with pottery and coins discovered at local sites, but the most appealing exhibit is at the very back – the tiny chapel of the **Twal house**, laid with an exquisite mosaic floor featuring a lamb nibbling at a tree. Climb the steps back up to a quiet courtyard at the top, where there's a mosaic pavement from Hesban and peaceful open views across the roofs and fields.

Eating and drinking

The best **restaurant** in town – in fact, one of the best in the country – is the *Saraya*, in the **Haret Jdoudna** complex (daily 11am–3pm & 7pm–midnight; ☏05/324 8650, ⊛www.romero-jordan.com), about 100m south of the Church of the Map. The restaurant comprises two old houses beside each other, one with an elegant cross-vaulted interior dating from 1905, the other with its original colourful floor-tiles imported from Haifa in 1923; perhaps the most pleasant place to eat is in the quiet courtyard between the two. A mere JD8 or so will buy you a meal of superb Arabic food in a tasteful, atmospheric setting; cold *mezze* highlights are the *jibneh bil zaatar* (goat's cheese in thyme), the vegetarian *warag aynab* and excellent *muhammara* (JD1–2), while the hot *mezze* include stuffed mushrooms and *sambousek* (pastry filled with meat or cheese). There's a choice of chicken- or hummus-based *fatteh* (JD2.500), while kebabs cost around JD5. This is a popular out-of-town choice for gourmet Ammanis, and bookings are essential for Thursdays and Fridays. Downstairs, the more casual *Pizza Giordania* (daily noon–midnight) has great wood-fired pizzas for JD3. Both take credit cards.

For simpler fare, there are strings of cheap diners along Nuzha Street near the museum and Yarmouk Street towards *Lulu's*. The *Ayola* café, opposite the Church of the Map, has Bedouin-style decor and an English menu, but nonetheless draws locals for its good-quality snacks and drinks. Two large restaurants that are geared mainly towards tour groups are the *Dana*, just up from the Church of the Apostles (☏05/324 5749) – which does pretty good South Asian dishes, courtesy of the Indian chef – and *El Cardo*, opposite the Archeological Park (☏05/325 1006). Both do JD6 buffets of Arabic staples when there's a tour group in, and offer à la carte choices for around JD8 per head. An excellent small **bakery** can be found near the mosque on Prince Hassan Street and, Madaba being an important Christian town, you'll also see **liquor stores** everywhere (although barely any bars).

Mount Nebo

Northwest of Madaba, a series of peaks generally referred to collectively as **MOUNT NEBO** (in Arabic, Siyagha) comprise the single most important biblical site in Jordan, and one with a unique resonance for Jews, Christians and Muslims alike. Having led the Israelites for forty years through the wilderness, **Moses** finally saw, from this dizzy vantage point, the Promised Land that God had forbidden him to set foot in; after he died on the mountain, his successor Joshua went on to lead the Israelites into Canaan. In Christian and Jewish tradition, Moses was buried somewhere on or in Mount Nebo, but Muslims (who regard Moses as a prophet) hold that his body was carried across the river and placed in a tomb now lying off the modern Jericho–Jerusalem highway. The lack of earthly remains on Nebo, though, doesn't temper the drama accompanying a visit: the mountain, and the church on its summit, feel so remote – and the view is so awe-inspiring – that the holiness of the place is almost tangible. Besides, the marvellous **mosaics** on display in the church would be reason enough in themselves to visit.

The Moses Memorial Church

The focus of a visit is the **Moses Memorial Church** (daily: April–Oct 5am–7pm; Nov–March 7am–5pm; 500 fils). The first structure on this site may have dated from classical times, but by 394 AD it had been converted into a triapsidal church floored with mosaics. Major expansion work was undertaken during the sixth century, and over the subsequent centuries the building was added to until it became the focus for a large and flourishing monastic community; the monastery is known to have been still thriving in 1217, but by 1564 it had been abandoned. In 1933, the ruined site was purchased by Franciscans, who began excavating and restoring the church and the surrounding area. Today, Siyagha (originally Aramaic for "monastery") remains both a monastic refuge and the headquarters of the energetic Franciscan Archeological Institute (ⓦ198.62.75.1/www1/ofm/fai/FAImain.html).

The entrance is at the back of the church, but you should spend a little time absorbing the view first. From a cliff-edge platform beneath a huge, stylized cross in the form of a serpent – inspired by Jesus's words in John 3: "As Moses lifted up the serpent in the wilderness, so must the Son of Man be lifted up" – a panoramic view of the Land of Milk and Honey takes in the northern shore of the Dead Sea, the dark stripe of the River Jordan in its valley, Jericho on the opposite bank and, haze permitting, the towers on the Mount of Olives in Jerusalem amid the hills opposite.

As you enter the simple, stone-clad church, on your left, and a metre lower than the rest of the church, is the **Old Baptistry**, which boasts the most entertaining of all the mosaics in and around Madaba. Completed in August 531, it was rediscovered in 1976, when the mosaic which had been laid over it during expansion work in 597 (now hung on the wall) was removed for cleaning. The huge central panel features four beautiful and intricately designed tableaux. At the top, a tethered zebu is protected by a shepherd fighting off a huge lion, and a soldier lancing a lioness. Two mounted hunters with dogs are spearing a bear and a wild boar. Below, things are more peaceful, as a shepherd sits under a tree watching his goat and fat-tailed sheep nibble at the leaves. Closest to the catwalk, a dark-skinned Persian has an ostrich on a leash, while a boy next to him is looking after a zebra and an extraordinary creature that is either a spotted camel or a creatively imagined giraffe.

The main hall of the church is divided by columns into a nave and aisles, and mosaics are everywhere. In the aisles and between some of the columns survive fragments of the pieces laid in 597. To the right and left hang panels from the **Church of St George** at Mukhayyat (see below), showing peacocks, a lion and other animals. One, featuring doves and a deer around a date palm, dates from 536 and has, on one side, the name *Saola* in Greek and, on the other, either the same name in old Aramaic script, or – some historians claim – the word *bislameh* ("with peace") in Arabic; were the latter to be correct, this would be the earliest example of Arabic script found in Jordan, predating Islam by a full century. However, due to the similar formation of letters in the two languages, it's impossible to be certain.

In the far right-hand corner of the church, what was formerly a funerary chapel became the **New Baptistry** in 597. As you enter, a small mosaic panel to the right – originally laid on the threshold – wishes "Peace to All". Just next to the baptistry is a small modern **altar** with space for votive candles, decorated by a simple and strikingly beautiful mosaic cross, which hung in a room exactly in this location in the original fourth-century church.

As you leave, next to the door is a small display of books; to the left are notice-boards occupying part of the **Theotokos (Virgin Mary) Chapel**, which was added to the main building in the seventh century. Most of the floor is taken up with a mosaic carpet of plants and flowers, but the apse features a stylized representation of the Temple of Jerusalem and, to the left, a perfect and endear-ingly bright-eyed gazelle, complete with a little bell around its neck.

Around Mount Nebo

About 1km back along the road towards Madaba from Mount Nebo, a clutch of restaurants marks a left-hand turn leading steeply down the hillside to **Ayoun Musa**, the Springs of Moses, one of the reputed locations for Moses striking the rock and water gushing forth (the Ain Musa spring above Petra is another). The spring itself, marred by a modern pumping station, is overlooked by lush foliage and is set in beautiful countryside – the vineyards nearby produce some of Jordan's best wine – but aside from a couple of tiny ruined churches about ten minutes' walk beyond the spring, you'll find little of specific interest. All the mosaics discovered in the churches down here were long ago removed to Siyagha.

Back on the main road, about 1km further brings you to the village of Faysali-yyeh, and a right-hand turn to **Khirbet al-Mukhayyat**, site of the biblical town of Nebo and home to five ruined churches and yet another outstanding mosaic. At the first fork, the older road (left) will bring you, after about 2km, to a small car park at the foot of a small but steep hill; on the summit sits the **Church of SS Lot and Procopius**. A building was constructed in the 1930s to protect the large, almost perfectly preserved floor mosaic inside, featuring dozens of bunches of grapes, tableaux of vine-harvesting and musically accom-panied grape-treading, along with rabbit-chasing and lion-hunting. The most entertaining pieces are in between the column stumps: nearest the door are a fisherman and a man rowing a boat either side of a church, and two peculiar fish-tailed monsters, while opposite lie vignettes of geese and ducks in a pond full of fish and lily pads. In recent years, the roof has started to leak, and winter rains have damaged the mosaic; renovations are under way, meaning that you may have to admire the artwork from the doorway.

Visible on the hilltop beyond SS Lot and Procopius, the ruined sixth-century **Church of St George** occupies the highest peak on the mountain. Its mosaics now adorn the church at Siyagha, but the view from St George is breathtaking. There are three more churches dotted around the valley nearby (the guardian can tell you where), but none has mosaics *in situ*.

Practicalities

Buses and **serveeces** to Mount Nebo from outside the Bank of Jordan on Palestine Street in central Madaba normally only go as far as the village of **Faysaliyyeh**, 2km short of the Moses Memorial Church; there is no transport to either Ayoun Musa or Khirbet al-Mukhayyat. To get to Siyagha, you'll either have to walk 2km from Faysaliyyeh, hope the driver's willing to go the distance for 250 fils extra, or wait instead at Madaba bus station for one of the less frequent buses to Shuneh al-Janubiyyeh in the Jordan Valley, which run right past the gates to the Moses Memorial Church, opposite which is a **car park**. Getting a **taxi** to take you from Madaba to Siyagha, wait, and bring you back shouldn't cost more than JD4–5, a little more if you include other sites.

Siyagha isn't the end of the road, though you wouldn't want anyone but a close friend behind the wheel for the death-defying journey off the back of the mountain, plunging 1200m in a series of switchbacks down to a point on the Amman–Dead Sea road near the Dead Sea Junction. From Madaba, chartering a taxi for the return journey to the **Baptism Site** (see p.180), should you be willing to run the gauntlet of local driving methods on this road, will cost around JD20–25.

Hesban

Beside the modern village of **HESBAN**, 9km north of Madaba and about 22km southwest of Amman (signposted from Na'ur, off the Dead Sea highway), rises a huge *tell*, one of Jordan's most significant and atmospheric archeological sites but nonetheless rarely visited, despite interesting ruins and some good signage.

Remains uncovered on and within Tell Hesban testify to occupation from the **Paleolithic** Age onwards. In the thirteenth century BC, with the name **Heshbon**, it was "the city of Sihon, king of the Amorites" (Numbers 21). As the **Israelites** approached, they "sent messengers unto Sihon" seeking permission to pass through his territory "by the king's highway, until we be past thy borders". Sihon refused, and was defeated in battle by the Israelites, who then took up residence in Heshbon. After they moved on to Canaan, the city was fortified by the **Ammonites**, abandoned, and then re-fortified in the second-century BC **Hellenistic** period. The **Roman** historian Josephus named Hesbus, or Esbus, as one of the cities strengthened by Herod the Great; by the second century AD Esbus was flourishing, due mainly to its position at the junction of the Via Nova Traiana and a transverse Roman road connecting to Jericho and Jerusalem. From the fourth century onwards, the city was an important **Christian** ecclesiastical centre, and remained a bishopric until well after the **Umayyad** takeover. During the **Abbasid** period, after the eighth century, it became a pilgrims' rest-stop, and regained some significance as a regional capital under the **Mamlukes** in the fourteenth century. For half a millennium following, Hesban slumbered, only repopulated in the 1870s by the local **Ajarmeh** Bedouin; it remains a quiet agricultural village to this day.

Buses run to Hesban from Madaba and from Amman's Muhajireen station (via Na'ur); be sure to specify your destination, since most Madaba–Amman buses follow a different road. The *tell* is fenced, but the caretaker – a colourful character named Abu Noor – lives on site, and is happy to show visitors around. Teams from Andrews University in Michigan have been working here on and off since 1968 (seee ⓦ www.hesban.org), with their next season a six-week dig in June and July 2007. In the last few years, they have newly uncovered a network of Iron Age **caves** which riddle the *tell*, extending for 100m or more and penetrating on three levels deep beneath the surface, leading to all kinds of speculation concerning their possible connection to the residence at Heshbon of Moses and the Israelites; one particularly electrifying find was an unbroken pottery cup dating from 1200 BC – precisely the right period. The caretaker has the key for the cave network and some candles, and will help you explore beneath the surface. Just below ground level, excavations have exposed **walls** and a huge late Iron Age **cistern** capable of holding several million litres. On the summit are the remains and fallen columns of a clearly visible Byzantine

church dated to the early fourth century (its mosaic floor is now in the Madaba museum), as well as a Mamluke **mosque**, complete with south-facing *mihrab*, and **baths** with furnace and plunge pools. From here, panoramic views extend west to Jericho and Jerusalem, north into Gilead, east to the desert highlands, and south as far as Dhiban and even Karak, bringing home the strategic value of the site. **Caves** in the hillside across the valley, to the west of the *tell*, were used as a cemetery for a time, and during the last century as homes by the Ajarmeh Bedouin.

Hammamat Ma'in

Some 30km southwest of Madaba, at the end of one of the steepest, most tortuous roads in the country, the hot springs of **HAMMAMAT MA'IN** make for one of the best side-trips off the King's Highway. Continuously dousing the precipitous desert cliffs of the **Wadi Zarqa Ma'in** with steaming water – varying between a languorous 40°C and a scalding 60°C – the springs are very popular with weekend day-trippers. However, the site has been struggling for decades to make it as a viable holiday destination. In 1999 the French *Mercure* hotel group upgraded all facilities, but visitor numbers stayed low. The hotel was closed in 2005 for long-term renovation while politicians and business brains came up with a new plan.

Bureaucracy aside, the site's natural beauty is exceptional. The waters have been channelled to form two **hot waterfalls**, there are hot spa pools, natural and artificial saunas, full spa facilities at the hotel – but it's still not too hard to escape the melee and find a quiet, steamy niche in the rock all to yourself. If you're feeling energetic, **hiking** some or all of the way down the deep gorge to the Dead Sea is an exhilarating counterpoint to lying around in hot water all day. Bear in mind when planning a visit, though, that spring and autumn Fridays see the entire valley crammed with people, from gangs of rambunctious young lads splashing around to respectable family groups, with veiled women ducking fully clothed under the waterfalls.

The road through Ma'in

The road from Madaba passes first through fields and the small farming community of **MA'IN**; the village, perched on its *tell*, is mentioned in the Bible, and excavations in its Byzantine- and Umayyad-period churches revealed many mosaics, now on display in the Madaba Archeological Park. Beyond Ma'in, the terrain dries out, and the road begins to heave and twist around the contours of land above the Dead Sea. Thin tracks off to the left give innumerable options for picnic spots on slopes perched high above cultivated sections of the Wadi Zarqa Ma'in; to the right, the views over the desert hills down to the fairytale Dead Sea, luminous blue in a valley of brown, are incredible. The road keeps coiling and recoiling in steep switchbacks until it finally enters the barren, yawning gorge of the lower Wadi Zarqa Ma'in; it's only once you approach the resort on the valley floor that the humid lushness of this isolated spot becomes apparent.

Two small archeological sites can be visited near Ma'in village with your own transport. About 1km before Ma'in village, if you fork left at an avenue of trees, after about 5km you'll come to **Magheirat**. Lines of Neolithic standing stones crisscross the road here; up on the hilltop to the right is a largely unexcavated **stone circle** in a double ring, with some cultic purpose as yet undetermined. Back at Ma'in village, if you turn left and head south through orchards into open country – increasingly covered with white dust from a nearby quarry – you'll see, on the left in an unguarded field, a Neolithic **standing stone**

Hikes and gorge-walks from Hammamat Ma'in

With the reinvention of Hammamat Ma'in as an "Eco-Sports Park", partly under the aegis of the Royal Society for the Conservation of Nature (RSCN), it's now easy to indulge in a range of **hikes** and **adventure trips** in and around the Zarqa Ma'in valley. We've outlined some of the guided hikes below – for all of which you should book with the *Ma'in Spa* hotel well in advance – but it's just as easy to set off on your own for an exploration of the Upper Gorge, which extends for about 3km below the hotel; trails feature colour-coded markers. However, bear in mind that the terrain is difficult, and temperatures can soar in the sweltering, breezeless valley: **serious dehydration** can strike even the most experienced of walkers. You need to be fit, carry plenty of water and let the hotel staff know where you're going. Hiking in the rugged Lower Gorge, near the Dead Sea, which forms part of the RSCN Mujib reserve, is forbidden without a **guide**, both on safety and environmental grounds. In winter (Nov–March), the whole valley is prone to **flash-flooding**.

The star attraction is a **gorge-walk** from the *Ma'in Spa* hotel all the way down the Wadi Zarqa Ma'in to its outflow at ancient **Callirhoë** on the Dead Sea shore (see p.177), where King Herod soothed his many ills. This is an **extremely challenging** route, involving around six or seven hours of hiking and wading along the eight-kilometre canyon, sometimes using ropes to abseil down waterfalls. Most of the time you'll be walking in warm water, stepping on loose rocks in the river bed, but there are also deep pools and dense reeds. This is not a walk to undertake lightly! Reckon on an hour and a half to drive back to the hotel afterwards. The package, which includes a guide, water, lunch and return transport, is charged on a sliding scale: one person pays JD50, two people pay JD35 each, six people JD25 each, and so on. Adding on three hours' floating in the Dead Sea, courtesy of one of the big shoreside hotels, costs JD10 per person more. You may find that a couple of soldiers will come along too, for safety and security. It is unclear what impact the new **dam** at the western end of the gorge will have on water levels upstream or the viability of this walking route in future.

Alternatives include hiking a circuit through the Upper Gorge and back to the hotel via the hillside Bedouin Route. With a number of en-route variations, this can take anything from one to three hours; for the simplest package, two people pay JD15 each, six people JD11 each; for a more taxing route, two people pay JD25 each, six people JD19 each. It's also possible to trace an hour-long route on **donkeys** from the hotel up the cliffs above the waterfalls and round to the front gate; two people pay JD10 each, six people JD8 each.

The RSCN can take groups of four or more on a 4x4 trip from the hotel up a dirt track into the neighbouring **Wadi Mujib Nature Reserve** (see p.300) for a day of sightseeing – including Mukawir (see below) – plus hiking, swimming and bird- and wildlife-watching. A deal including return transport, an RSCN guide, water and packed lunch costs around JD40 per person for four people, JD35 each for six.

known as *Hajar al-Mansub*. From the road, it is just a monolith: if you view it from the other side, though, it was plainly carved in antiquity to be phallic. Theories abound as to its purpose and context: it's an incongruous sight.

Transport for Hammamat Ma'in

Virtually all local **buses** from Madaba, plus a few early-morning departures from Amman's Wihdat station, stop at Ma'in village, 8km from Madaba and some 21km short of Hammamat Ma'in itself; to go further, you'll have to cross the driver's palm with dinars. A **JETT bus** leaves Amman on Friday at 8.30am for the hot springs (JD5), departing for the return journey around 5pm; you can pick up this bus on its way through Madaba, but you need to book in advance.

The going rate for a **taxi** from Madaba to Hammamat Ma'in and back, with a reasonable wait included, is around JD15, or JD12 if you book through the *Mariam Hotel* (see p.283). You might also find one or two serveeces touting for business back to Madaba around 5pm on a Friday, but if you want to stay for sunset you should fix up a ride ahead of time.

The hot springs and spa complex

The whole valley has only one road in, across which has been positioned the **main gate** (daily 6am–4pm), where admission to non-hotel guests costs JD7 per person, covering entry to all attractions except those within the hotel itself. From the main gate, the road winds on for 1km down to the hulk of the four-star *Ma'in Spa Hotel* (☎05/324 5500, ⓕ324 5550; ❼-❾), closed for renovations at the time of writing, but formerly with fresh, pleasant, en-suite rooms, all with balcony, air con and only the sound of the waterfalls to disturb you. Just before you reach the hotel, facing it across the river is a more simple thirty-room family annexe dubbed *Beit Ma'in* (❹), with accommodation in singles, doubles and quads. **Camping** is prohibited.

The main gate officially forbids you to bring in your own **food and drink**, but this is loosely enforced and discreet picnicking is widespread. The only formal facilities for eating are at the hotel – a restaurant buffet (JD10 for lunch or dinner) or simpler fare at the eighth-floor café. The Drop & Shop supermarket, before the hotel, has nothing but cheeseballs, crackers and water.

The **hot waterfalls** tumble down off the cliffs to one side of the valley, steam rising from a series of pools below, where you can sit and enjoy a shoulder-pounding from the water. The waterfall nearest the hotel is public and open to all, while to the right of it is the fenced-off "family" waterfall, supposedly barred to single men and so a much better option for women, whether solo or accompanied – although you may find decently long shorts and a baggy T-shirt still attracting wolf whistles. Both these waterfalls are equally hot and equally explorable. Further down the valley, near the mosque behind the hotel, is the smaller, less crowded "Prince's waterfall", with open access. In the middle of the resort is an ordinary cold-water **swimming pool**, and up towards the main gate is the "**Roman bath**", with separate hot pools and steam rooms for men and women. The hotel pool is for hotel guests only.

Facilities within the hotel's international-standard **spa centre** (daily 8am–7.30pm) are extensive. The best options are their various day packages, all for about JD36, including combinations of mud facials, hydrojets, massages and dips in hot and cold pools. In the Beauty Salon, you can go for a body mud-wrap (JD16) or a mud facial (JD10), or plump for a half-hour regular massage (JD16) or shower massage followed by a scrub with Dead Sea salts (JD16). You'd do well to book in advance for these procedures, as well as for their multi-day treatment programmes (two days JD65, six days JD170).

The Dead Sea Panorama

Partway along the road from Madaba to Hammamat Ma'in, before you descend to enter the gorge of the Wadi Zarqa Ma'in, you'll spot a new road branching off across the hilltops to the **Dead Sea Panorama**. This complex, completed in 2005, houses a viewpoint terrace looking out over the Dead Sea and across to the hills of the West Bank, a small museum of local **fossils**, and an upscale **restaurant** and banqueting venue, all of it out in the wilds, miles from the nearest town. The road continues off the back of the mountain in a series of tight switchbacks down to join the Dead Sea highway near the luxury shoreside hotels.

At the time of writing, it was unclear at which times the restaurant would be open, or what else might go on up here. The best bet is that this will become a great place to stop on a tour of the attractions around Madaba: you could come up here after a dip in the hot springs at Hammamat Ma'in, or take a break here midway on a circular route between Madaba, the Dead Sea, Mount Nebo and the hot springs. A **taxi** from Madaba will likely cost around JD6, or double that if you ask him to wait for an hour and take you back.

Mukawir

The King's Highway heads south from Madaba through quiet, picturesque farmland for 13km to **Libb**, where a well-signed road branches right for a long, slow 20km across the windblown hilltops to the small village of **MUKAWIR** (pronounced "m-KAA-whirr"), views yawning away in all directions. The main reason for visiting is to make the short hike up to the isolated conical hill beyond the village, which is topped with the ruins of the **palace of Machaerus**, where Salome danced for King Herod, and where John the Baptist was beheaded.

During the first century BC, the hill was a stronghold of the Jewish Hasmonean revolt against the Seleucids, based in Syria, and was fortified to be a buffer against Nabatean power further south. In the last decades of the century, **Herod the Great**, king of Judea, constructed a walled citadel at Machaerus and developed road access to the site from the Dead Sea port at Callirhoë, 8km west, although trade on the King's Highway – just 22km east – remained under the control of the Nabateans. According to the Roman historian Josephus, it was at Machaerus that Salome danced for Herod Antipas, son of Herod the Great, and had the head of **John the Baptist** presented on a platter. Previously, Herod had married his brother's wife Herodias, in an act forbidden under Jewish law (Leviticus 18:16); when he was publicly accused of adultery by John, he'd had the troublemaker arrested and imprisoned at Machaerus. Some time later, at a birthday celebration in the palace at Machaerus, Herod had been so impressed by the dancing of Salome, Herodias' daughter, that he promised her anything she wanted. Salome, prompted by her mother, requested the head of the troublesome Baptist. Christian tradition holds that John was buried where he died, in a well-signposted **cave** near the hill, but Islam, according to which John (or **Yahya** in Arabic) is a prophet, keeps two shrines holy, one for his body (the same cave) and another in Damascus for his severed head, which was supposedly taken to that city and buried where the Great Mosque now stands.

A few decades after John's death, a Jewish revolt began against **Roman** rule. In 66 AD the rebels seized Machaerus from the Roman garrison, and held it for seven years, eventually surrendering when faced by Roman forces preparing to assault the fortress; in an almost identical situation at Masada, west of the Dead Sea, a Jewish resistance force committed mass suicide rather than submit. The Romans immediately moved into Machaerus, razed the buildings, massacred the local civilian population and departed, and the hill has remained quiet since.

Today, a visit to Machaerus is more likely to entice for the truly awe-inspiring views and the beautiful, rolling countryside, carpeted with wildflowers in spring, than for the archeology. Kestrels wheel against the Dead Sea haze above a handful of gleaming modern columns which sprout from the part-excavated rubble on the hilltop. Of the palace ruins, a few rooms are discernible, as are the remains of the Roman **assault ramp** on the far slopes of the hill and the line of an **aqueduct** across the saddle. A **mosaic** – the oldest discovered in Jordan – once lay in the baths complex, but has been removed to Madaba for display.

The Bani Hamida centre

The whole Mukawir area is the homeland of the **Bani Hamida** tribe, now well known in Jordan following the success of a highly publicized project to revive traditional weaving skills among the women of the tribe, simultaneously providing them and their families with an additional source of income and vocational training possibilities. On the outskirts of Mukawir village is the **Bani Hamida centre** (hours variable, but normally Sat–Wed 8am–3pm), sister outlet to the shop in Amman (see p.156), where you can buy beautiful rugs, wall-hangings and other knick-knacks. As you'd expect for high-quality handmade goods, nothing is cheap – decent-sized rugs start at JD150 – but you're free to watch the women weaving and there's absolutely no pressure to buy; however, if you fancy splashing out, you can be certain that what you're getting is the genuine article, and worth every penny.

Practicalities

Occasional **buses** run from Madaba to Mukawir, normally dropping off in the village. You may be able to persuade the driver to take you the extra 2km to the car park opposite the hill; if not, it's a pleasant walk. From the car park, a steep but easy fifteen-minute climb across the saddle and up some steps brings you to the hilltop ruins, known gloomily to the locals as Qal'at al-Meshneqeh, or the Citadel of the Gallows. A dirt track, passable by 4x4, connects Mukawir with Hammamat Ma'in (see p.293), and there's also a difficult **hiking trail** (see p.303) from Mukawir to Zara, but since both of these cross part of the Mujib Nature Reserve, you can only use them with accompanied by an RSCN guide.

Umm ar-Rasas

A tiny farming village on a back road midway between the King's Highway and the Desert Highway, **UMM AR-RASAS** is a minor gem, well worth a couple of hours' detour. The village is the site of the Roman garrison town of Kastron Mefaa, which developed during the Byzantine and Umayyad periods into a relatively important city, and large **mosaic** floors from two of its fifteen or so churches have been cleaned and protected for display. A short distance away is a striking Stylite **tower**. EU-funded excavation work is ongoing, and as a sign of its importance, Umm ar-Rasas was listed in 2004 as a UNESCO World Heritage Site.

If you join the local goats for a stumble through the ruins of the ancient city, only an arch or two poking through the acres of rubble give any indication of former urban splendour. The mosaics lie beneath a pale green shelter on the corner of the ruins furthest from the road. Entrance is to one side of the intricate mosaic floor of the **Church of St Stephen**, dated to 785, over 150 years after Muslim rule was established in Jordan. The apse has a dazzling kaleidoscopic diamond pattern swirling out from behind the altar, and the broad nave is framed by mosaic panels showing cities of the day: closest to the door is Jerusalem, with seven Palestinian cities below, including Nablus, Asqalan and, at the bottom, Gaza. On the far side are seven Transjordanian cities, headed by Kastron Mefaa itself, with Philadelphia (Amman), Madaba, Hesban, Ma'in, Rabba and Karak below. The central section is filled with scenes of fishermen, seashells, jellyfish and all kinds of intricate detail of animals, fruit and trees, although in antiquity iconoclasts blocked out virtually all representations of people. Against the far wall is an older mosaic belonging to the adjacent **Church of Bishop Sergius**, dated to 587. Its main feature is a rectangular panel in front of the altar featuring pomegranate trees and very wise-looking rams; on the other side of the catwalk, hard up against the exterior wall, a beautifully executed personification of one of the seasons survived the iconoclasts by having had a pulpit built over it at some point.

Attractive though they are, Umm ar-Rasas's mosaics are only half the story; if you've taken the time to visit, you shouldn't leave without standing awhile at the foot of the village's peculiar square **tower**, 1km away from the ruins and represented on the church floor by Kastron Mefaa's own mosaicists as an obviously important identifying feature of their city. Desolate, windblown and mysterious, the fifteen-metre tower (known in Arabic as *Burj Sam'an*) has defied explanation. It is solid, without internal stairs, yet at the top is a room with windows in four directions. Simple, almost rough crosses are carved on the three sides facing away from the city, but details of intricate and beautiful carving survive on the topmost corbels. Every indication would point to this being the Stylite tower of a Christian holy man; the fifth-century ascetic **Simon Stylites** spent 38 years atop a pillar near Aleppo, and a cult of pilgrimage grew up around him and later imitators who isolated themselves from worldly distractions in order to concentrate on their prayers. The foundations at the foot of the tower are of a roughly built church, and further away are cisterns and a three-storey building which may have been some kind of hostel for pilgrims come to pray in the presence of the Stylite. Today, almost wrenched apart by earthquakes, the sinister ruined tower is home only to pigeons and kestrels.

A footnote to the story of Kastron Mefaa concerns a prophecy heard there by the sixth-century Meccan holy man **Zeid bin Amr**, around the time of the birth of Muhammad. Islamic tradition relates that Zeid left Mecca to travel through Syria and Iraq on a quest to discover the roots of the religion of Abraham, questioning rabbis and monks in all major cities. On his arrival at "Mayfa'a, in the land of al-Balqa", a monk told him that a Prophet with the religion of Abraham would shortly come to prominence among his own people.

Practicalities

The only **buses** to Umm ar-Rasas run a few times daily from Madaba, on the back roads via **Nitil**. As they approach, they pass a small blue-domed mosque on the left. To visit the **tower**, ask to get off about 600m further, at the end of the row of buildings; from here, a road winds away to the left. The tumbled stones of the ancient city, as well as the shelter housing the **mosaics**, are clearly visible about a kilometre's easy walk away. If you're **driving**, turn off the road from Nitil at the post office 500m before the village's main T-junction (from where the Desert Highway is 14km east, Dhiban 16km west). From the post office, a track winds for 500m alongside the ruined city walls to the shelter.

Wadi Mujib and around

One of Jordan's most spectacular natural features lies midway between Madaba and Karak – the immense **Wadi Mujib**, dubbed, with a canny eye on the tourist dollar, "Jordan's Grand Canyon". The name, however, is well earned, as the King's Highway delivers you to stunning viewpoints on either rim over a vast gash in the barren landscape, cutting through 1200m of altitude from the desert plateau in the east down to the Dead Sea in the west. It is every bit as awe-inspiring as its Arizonan cousin and has the added selling-point of the memorable road journey winding down to the valley floor and up the other side. A large chunk of the surrounding territory now forms part of the RSCN-protected **Wadi Mujib Nature Reserve**, offering the chance for wilderness hiking and canyoning as good as any you'll find in the Middle East.

Dhiban and around

South of Madaba, the first of the series of large wadis slicing west–east across southern Jordan is the lush **Wadi Wala**, a little beyond **Libb**, pleasantly dotted with vineyards and shaded by groves of pine and eucalyptus. From the valley floor, you can drive west on a riverside road for some 15km into the quiet and beautiful **Wadi Hidan**. This road terminates in a dead end, but Hidan itself goes on to meet the Mujib river just before the Dead Sea; with a guide, it's just about possible to follow the deep river on foot for about 6km between basaltic cliffs up to the edge of an eighty-metre waterfall (which marks the start of an area off-limits to walkers), although you must then climb up the cliffside and make your way back to the road.

Back on the highway, when you reach the top of the southern slope of Wadi Wala, a stretch of the Roman Via Nova Traiana is visible on the valley floor behind. Some 10km further (33km south of Madaba), **DHIBAN** is the last town before the Mujib canyon. A signposted turn here heads east for 16km to Umm ar-Rasas (see p.297) and, after another 14km, the Desert Highway. Since there is no public transport through Wadi Mujib (although see p.158 and p.281 for details of private tours from Amman or Madaba), all **southbound buses terminate at Dhiban**. However, Dhibanis are well aware of foreigners' desire to travel through Mujib, and have a nice little earner going offering their pick-ups as taxis. Asking around at the handful of shops on

The Mesha stele

These days a largely unregarded village, in the past **Dhiban** was a large and important city, capital of Moab and mentioned many times in the Old Testament. In around 850 BC, a man named **Mesha**, described as a "shepherd king", liberated Moab from Israelite aggression, built a palace in Dhiban and set about refortifying the King's Highway against future attack.

Almost three thousand years later, in 1868, a German missionary travelling in the wild country between Salt and Karak was shown by Dhibani Bedouin a large basalt stone inscribed with strange characters. Unaware of its significance, he nonetheless circumspectly informed the German consul of his discovery, who then made quiet arrangements to obtain the stele on behalf of the Berlin Museum. However, a French diplomat in Jerusalem who heard of the discovery was less subtle; he travelled to Dhiban, took an imprint of the stele's text and there and then offered the locals a large sum of money. Suddenly finding themselves at the centre of an international furore over a seemingly very desirable lump of rock, the Bedouin refused his offer and sent him packing; they then did the obvious thing and devised a way to make more money. By heating the stone over a fire, then pouring cold water on it, they successfully managed to shatter it, and thus sell off each valuable fragment to the covetous foreigners one by one. Meanwhile, scholars in Europe were studying and translating the imprint of the text, which turned out to be Mesha's own record of his achievements, significant as the longest inscription in the Moabite language and one of the longest and most detailed original inscriptions from the biblical period yet discovered. The mostly reconstructed stele now sits in the Louvre in Paris; having become something of a symbol of national pride, copies of it are displayed in museums all over Jordan.

Dhiban's central roundabout for a ride through the canyon will quickly bear fruit; the going rate for a full car to **Ariha**, the first village on the southern rim, is around JD5, a little more if weather is bad. From Ariha, there are plenty of local buses south along the King's Highway to Karak.

Some 2km south of Dhiban, the vast canyon of the **Wadi Mujib** opens up spectacularly in front, over 500m deep and 4km broad at the top. Just over the lip of the gorge is a small rest stop and viewing platform, with tourist police on duty and a souvenir stall tucked surreptitiously out of sight. The dramatic canyon is an obvious natural focal point, and in biblical times, Arnon, as it was named, was the heartland of Moab, although with shifts in regional power it frequently marked a border between tribal jurisdictions; these days, it divides the governorates of Madaba and Karak. The sheer scale of the place is what takes your breath away, with vultures, eagles and kestrels wheeling silently on rising thermals all around and the valley floor to the right losing itself in the mistiness of the Dead Sea. The broad, flat plain of the wadi bed, now dammed, is noticeably hotter and creaks with frog calls.

Ariha, Qasr and Rabba

After snaking up Mujib's southern slope, the King's Highway emerges onto the flat Moabite plateau, fields of wheat stretching off in all directions. The first village on the southern rim, some 3km from the gorge, is **Ariha**, and from here the highway ploughs a straight furrow south through small farming communities to two towns nurturing minor remnants of a more glorious past. **Qasr**, 12km south of Ariha, boasts a Nabatean temple east of the town, while **Rabba**, 5km on, was a large and important Roman and Byzantine settlement – a fact celebrated by the authorities in the re-erection of ancient columns along the main street. The remains of a Roman temple sit gracefully to the west of the highway behind the modern bustle of the town. Midway between Qasr and Rabba, a side-turning gives access to hikes along the spectacular Wadi ibn Hammad (see p.309).

All the villages between Madaba and Rabba are too small to warrant even a falafel stand, let alone a restaurant: on a journey through, your only choices are to have a hearty breakfast in Madaba and hold out for lunch in Karak, or to bring along a **picnic**.

Wadi Mujib Nature Reserve

A sizeable proportion of the area between the King's Highway and the Dead Sea shore as far north as Hammamat Ma'in, and including the final 18km of the Mujib river, forms the protected **Wadi Mujib Nature Reserve**, created in 1987 under the control of the Royal Society for the Conservation of Nature (RSCN; Ⓦ www.rscn.org.jo). This swathe of diverse terrain extends from the hills alongside the King's Highway, at 900m above sea level, all the way down to the Dead Sea shore at 400m below sea level, and includes seven permanently flowing wadis within its 212 square kilometres. The biodiversity of this apparently barren area is startling: during ecological surveys of the reserve, four plant species never before recorded in Jordan were discovered, along with the rare Syrian wolf, Egyptian mongoose, Blanford's fox, caracal, striped hyena, two species of viper, the venomous desert cobra, and large numbers of raptors. In the mountains on Mujib's southern plateau, an enclosure established to breed the previously endangered **Nubian ibex** has resulted in a large number of animals, with some already released into the wild and others to follow.

However, problems persist, connected, as always, with the search for **fresh water**. In 1998, with little assessment either of environmental impact or of alternative water sources, the government approved plans to construct a dam of 20–30 million cubic metres' capacity across the Mujib, which would divert the river into a pipe system to supply agriculture and hotel construction on the Dead Sea shore further north. The dam has recently been completed; the resulting impact on the river's flow, oxygen levels, salinity and sediment, and damage to the ecosystems up- and downstream has yet to be assessed. Water levels in the Mujib River have been dropping consistently, from several metres deep in some places in the early 1990s to only knee-deep in the same places today; with the dam, it's possible that the whole of the Lower Mujib valley system may end up dry for most of the year, wiping out the majority of the flora and fauna.

For the moment, though, Wadi Mujib remains one of the most dramatic and unspoiled areas of natural beauty in Jordan, and is well worth the time and effort to experience.

Practicalities

The reserve is open all year round. The main **visitor centre** for the reserve is at the western end of the valley, down by the Mujib Bridge on the Dead Sea road (see also p.177): there is no walk-in information available at the King's Highway end of the valley, apart from a small RSCN office in **Faqua** village (☏03/231 3059), a little northwest of Qasr, but this is not geared up for general public enquiries. Contact the RSCN's Tourism Unit in Amman (see p.77) for all general bookings and information; for further advice or guidance try the mobile phone of the Mujib Tourism Manager (☏07/7742 2132).

The Mujib has several **hiking trails**, almost all of which must be booked in advance with the RSCN; admission to the reserve without permission is forbidden, both on grounds of safety and in order to safeguard the natural environment. Some of the trails are open in the summertime only (April–Oct); see below for details. Note that numbers allowed into the reserve are strictly controlled, and the guided hikes outlined below all require a minimum of five and maximum of 25 people to go ahead, within a limit of six trips in total per week. Guides are only available at certain times, so if you turn up on spec, you may find that you're not allowed into the reserve. In addition to hikes from **Hammamat Ma'in** (see p.294), turn to p.309 for details of treks nearby, including the route down the beautiful **Wadi ibn Hammad**.

The reserve's only **accommodation** is near the visitor centre, down on a quiet, north-facing beach on the Dead Sea, where the RSCN established in 2004 a small, ecologically sound experimental **campsite**, with showers, toilets and four-person tents designed to stay cool in the hot sun. Access, however, is difficult – it's set back from the road – and the tents proved to be unstable in strong winds. For now the campsite has closed, pending a redesign, but with advance notice, you may be able to wilderness camp in certain areas of the reserve. Check with the RSCN for full details.

Walks in the Wadi Mujib reserve

One of the Jordan's top adventure hikes is the trip along the **Mujib river**, most of which falls within the boundaries of the reserve; the full 36-kilometre trip from the King's Highway to the Dead Sea takes two days (April–Oct only), following the river with deviations at obstacles and passing through wild and varied scenery, but it's possible to avoid the initial stretches and make a day-trip instead, starting from the RSCN ranger post at **Faqua** village.

△ The Mujib gorge

As you descend below sea level on the trail from Faqua, the cliffs close in to the river's edge, and hot springs enter from each side. About 2km from the Dead Sea outflow, the extremely daunting canyon of **Wadi Hidan** enters from the right. It's in a protected area of the reserve; no visitors are allowed, but the Malagi Pools just upstream of the confluence are within the permitted area. Until 2001, when flash floods filled them with sand, these pools provided an exotic way to cool off, swimming in warm green water in a narrow, twisting, multicoloured canyon; it's fairly likely, though, that the next big flood will wash them clean again. The last 1500m of the journey passes through the stunning **Mujib Siq**, an ominous, narrow cleft through which the river runs over a twenty-metre **waterfall** and through pools to emerge at the Mujib Bridge: this is a unique canyoning adventure, involving swimming and abseiling with specialist equipment, but the alternative way out – hiking over the hills past the RSCN camp and the ibex breeding centre – is equally rewarding. With a guide, the trek from Faqua through the Mujib Gorge (and Siq, if that's your preference) and out to the Dead Sea road takes up to nine hours (JD40 per person, more with overnight camping). With notice, the RSCN can provide lifejackets.

The **Eagle's Nest/Malaqi Trail** (JD20 per person; April–Oct only) eliminates the long approach from Faqua. It begins from the Mujib Bridge, ascends past the ibex reserve, then descends to follow the river upstream to the Malaqi Pools and out again in around six hours. It's also possible to follow the **Mujib Siq Trail** (JD20 per person; April–Oct only) upstream from the Mujib Bridge to the base of the large waterfall, and back again in about three hours.

Another RSCN route is the guided three-hour **Ibex Trail** (JD8 per person; year-round), which begins a little south of the Mujib Bridge and heads up into the hills overlooking the gorge to Rayyashi, then on to the ibex enclosures to view the animals (by necessity from afar) and hear more about the breeding programme. There's also the tough 6km **Mukawir–Zara Trail** (JD20 per person; April–Oct only), descending 800m in altitude from Mukawir (see p.297), at 540m above sea level, down to Zara on the Dead Sea shore, at 261m below sea level. Reckon on at least four to five hours for the walk.

These and other walking routes in the area are described in more detail in Tony Howard's book *Jordan: Walks, Treks, Caves, Climbs, Canyons* (see p.496).

Karak to Shobak

The southern stretches of the King's Highway pass through an increasingly arid landscape dotted with lushly watered settlements. **Karak**, the most important town of southern Jordan, still lies largely within its Crusader-era walls and boasts one of the best-preserved castles in the Middle East. The deep canyon of **Wadi Hasa** to the south, overlooked by an extraordinary extinct volcano, runs a close second to Mujib for natural drama. From **Tafileh** a little beyond, the highway rises into the Shara mountains, well over 1500m above sea level (and considerably more above the deep Dead Sea rift to the west); up here are both the unspoiled **Dana Nature Reserve** and another Crusader castle at **Shobak**. A little way south, the dry, jagged mountains conceal ancient Petra (see p.325).

Karak

A small, busy town atop an isolated hill still encircled by Crusader walls, **KARAK** is the unofficial capital of southern Jordan. Roughly midway between Amman and Petra, it's also a natural place to break a journey along the King's Highway. The huge and well-preserved Crusader **castle** which occupies the southern tip of the hill is one of the finest in the Middle East, second only to Syria's Crac des Chevaliers for explorability.

As well as the King's Highway passing north–south at Karak, major roads lead east to the Desert Highway and west down to the Dead Sea road, where the ancient sites of **Bab adh-Dhraa** and, more appealingly, **Lot's Cave** (for both, see p.178) make a good day-trip. Both are fairly easily accessible by bus, but you should bear in mind that the climate down on the Dead Sea shore is much hotter and more humid than in the Karak hills. If you do make the trip from the cool heights of Karak, come equipped with food and water, and aim to avoid scrambling around in the killing noonday sun.

Some history

The hill on which Karak stands – with sheer cliffs on three sides and clear command over the Wadi Karak leading down to the Dead Sea – features both in the Old Testament and on Madaba's Byzantine mosaic map as a natural defensive stronghold. The **Crusaders** began building a fortress on a rocky spur atop the hill in 1142, boosting the natural advantages of the site by digging dry moats to the north and south and reinforcing the slopes with a paved glacis.

The castle's construction was initiated by the knights of the successful First Crusade, but its eventual downfall is inextricably linked with the personalities of those who came later, specifically **Reynald of Chatillon**. A ruthless warrior who arrived in the Holy Land in 1147 on the Second Crusade, Reynald was both vicious and unscrupulous, and it was specifically to avenge his treachery that the Muslim commander, **Salah ad-Din**, launched a campaign to expel the foreign invaders. In 1177, Reynald married Lady Stephanie, widow of the Lord of Oultrejourdain. Safely ensconced in Karak, he began a reign characterized by wanton cruelty: one of his more notorious pleasures involved encasing the heads of his prisoners in wooden boxes so that, when he flung them off the castle walls, he could be sure that they hadn't lost consciousness by the time they hit the rocks below. In 1180, he robbed a Mecca-bound caravan on the King's Highway in violation of a truce signed by King Baldwin and Salah ad-Din; Baldwin was unable to bring Reynald to heel, and Salah ad-Din was forced to swallow his anger until a suitable time for revenge could be found.

In November 1183, the wedding of Reynald's heir was celebrated within the walls of Karak castle at the very moment that Salah ad-Din and his army, having already invaded the town, were poised just beyond the north moat ready to attack. Lady Stephanie sent plates of food from the banquet to the Muslim army beyond the walls; in response, while his men were trying to bridge the moat and continuing to catapult rocks against the walls, Salah ad-Din enquired which tower the newly-weds were occupying. In an expression of his impeccable chivalry, he then ordered his army to direct their fire elsewhere.

Karak withstood that siege, but at the **Battle of Hattin** in 1187, the Crusaders, stymied by the strategic ineptitude of Reynald and others, suffered utter defeat. The victorious Salah ad-Din characteristically spared the king and the Crusader lords – all apart from Reynald, whom he personally decapitated. The besieged Crusader garrison at Karak held out for months; they sold their wives

The Crusaders in Transjordan

Following an appeal from the Byzantine emperor for foreign military assistance to defeat the Seljuk Turks, it took only a few years from the pope's first call to arms of 1095 for invading Christian European armies to seize **Jerusalem**. European-run statelets were set up in quick succession throughout the Levant – the Kingdom of Jerusalem, the Counties of Tripoli and Edessa, and the Principality of Antioch. One of the Christian lords, **Baldwin**, was crowned King of Jerusalem on Christmas Day 1100, and it was under his rule that the Crusaders began to realize the benefit of controlling the Transjordanian land route from Syria into Egypt and Arabia, in order to stand between the Muslim power bases in Damascus and Cairo and to be able to harass Muslims making the pilgrimage to the Arabian holy places. In 1107, simply the threat of attack by Baldwin's army persuaded a Seljuk force to flee their stronghold in **Petra**, and persistent harrying over a decade or more in the area around **Ajloun** successfully played havoc with established trade patterns in the region. In 1115, Baldwin crossed the Wadi Araba from Hebron with the intention of fully incorporating Transjordan into the Crusader realms, and began construction of a large castle at modern **Shobak**, which he named *Le Krak de Montreal* or the Fortress of the Royal Mountain. Establishment of a string of Crusader possessions soon followed, at Aila (Aqaba; including, possibly, a fortress on an island off Aqaba, which has not been conclusively dated), Wu'ayra and Habees at Petra, and Tafileh. However, the Lordship of Oultrejourdain, as it came to be known, was far from impregnable, and infiltration across the River Jordan by a Muslim raiding party in 1139 seems to have persuaded Paganus the Butler, by then the effective ruler, to move his power base northwards from Shobak. Construction of the massive fortress at **Karak** began in 1142, and twenty years later, with the addition of another citadel at Ahamant (possibly Amman), Crusader-controlled territory in Transjordan extended from the River Zarqa to the Red Sea, and from the Jordan Valley to the desert.

Such power was short-lived, however. Between 1169 and 1174, the Karak headquarters underwent four sieges, managing to survive partly because the opposing Muslim armies were divided. By 1174, though, Salah ad-Din had united the Muslim forces under his own banner, and began methodically to oust the Crusaders from Transjordan. Karak withstood two more sieges during 1183, but the tide was turning: the Latin armies were much depleted, and their young king, Baldwin IV, was dying of leprosy. In 1187, at **Hattin** near Tiberias, they were roundly defeated by Salah ad-Din, who executed the lord of Karak, Reynald, and soon after took Jerusalem. Wu'ayra and the great prize, Karak itself, capitulated in late 1188, and Shobak – the last Transjordanian possession – fell in the spring of 1189. The Europeans struggled on, but just a century later the entire Holy Land was once again under Arab rule.

and children in exchange for food, and resorted to eating horses and dogs, but surrender was inevitable. Karak capitulated in November 1188.

Over the centuries after the Crusaders departed, Ayyubid and **Mamluke** occupiers of the castle rebuilt and strengthened its defences. Remote Karak ranked last among the Syrian provinces of the Mamlukes, and the castle was used mainly as a dumping ground for disgraced sultans and officers.

Modern Karak

Under the **Ottomans**, anarchy was the rule rather than the exception in the lands around Karak. During widespread rebellion in 1879, Karaki Christians abandoned their town, moving north to settle among the ruins of ancient Madaba. In 1894, troops finally imposed order in Karak and, in an attempt to keep the town sweet, the Ottoman administration began to make monthly payments to the local sheikhs. However, official backhanders threatened the time-honoured status quo, and Karak's ruling families – among them, the Majali clan – began to foment rebellion against their overlords. In 1908 they rallied a local force and stormed Karak's government buildings, forcing the Ottoman garrison to seek refuge in the castle. After eight days, troops arrived from Damascus to put down the revolt: five rebel leaders were publicly executed in Karak, and the Majalis were declared outlaws. The Ottoman administration was swept away in the Arab Revolt of 1917–18, but Karak retained its reputation for political activism, and – a little ironically, considering the family history – the Majalis are today at the heart of the Jordanian establishment, boasting government officials and even a prime minister or two among their number.

Karak hit world headlines in 1996 when, under intense pressure from the IMF to reform economic policy, the government ended **subsidies** on grain. The result was an immediate doubling of bread prices. Discontent, especially strong in the poorer towns of the south, flared into open **rioting**. Government buildings in Karak were burned and looted, and tanks were deployed in an attempt to restore order. Curfews and broadcast appeals from King Hussein – to whom the rioters displayed unwavering loyalty throughout – eventually brought the situation under control, but the issues of economic liberalization and democratization were left largely unresolved. Karak remains both economically depressed and, with the continuing nationwide monopoly on power held by tribal notables, politically hamstrung.

Moving on from Karak

Buses and **minibuses** for **Amman**'s Wihdat station, Ma'an and Zarqa (all via the Desert Highway), **Tafileh** (via the King's Highway) and **Aqaba** (via the Dead Sea/Wadi Araba road) all operate out of the bus station, but only between 7am and about noon. You might be lucky and find a bus after that time, but don't rely on it. One bus may leave Karak around 3pm for **Wadi Musa/Petra**; it normally uses the Desert Highway (JD3), but on request the driver might agree to follow the King's Highway via Wadi Hasa, Tafileh and Shobak (JD5 or so). Buses north along the King's Highway, terminating in **Ariha** on the rim of Wadi Mujib, leave from a side-street in the middle of town; to get to Madaba from Ariha, you'll have to hitch through the canyon to Dhiban (see p.299), from where buses run on north.

Buses to **Mazra'a** and **Safi** on the Dead Sea shore leave from a different street corner in town and drive straight past Bab adh-Dhraa; those for Safi also go past the turn-off for Lot's Cave. It shouldn't be too hard to **hitch** a ride on these roads. Note that, whether by bus or in your own car, the road heading west from Karak for 26km down to the Dead Sea is one of Jordan's great **scenic drives**, especially in the afternoon, when low sunlight makes the walls of the steep Wadi Karak glow. There are still checkpoints down here, for which you'll need your passport.

With the dearth of public transport to **Petra** – most travellers' next major port of call – Karak's taxi-drivers are more than willing to help out. JD40 is the exorbitant going rate for a full car to Wadi Musa via the King's Highway, a two-and-a-half hour ride that admittedly would take considerably longer by other means. The local entrepreneur who owns the *Ram* hotel (among others) can help in fixing up a taxi ride, or you could just ask around at various taxi companies; those downtown are likely to be more amenable to bargaining than the sharper operators opposite the castle. The slow way of getting to Petra along the King's Highway involves a minibus to **Tafileh**, another to **Qadisiyyeh**, hitching to **Shobak** and a minibus or serveece into Wadi Musa. A faster but less picturesque route is with an early morning minibus to **Ma'an** along the Desert Highway and a minibus or serveece to Wadi Musa from there.

Arrival

The King's Highway makes a poorly signposted zigzag around Karak, and if you're **driving**, it's easy to get confused. At a T-junction 12km south of Rabba, just past the *Mujeb Hotel*, turning left will eventually deliver you after 34km to the Desert Highway at Qatraneh (see p.384), while turning right will lead you 4km through hilly suburbs to another T-junction at the foot of Karak castle. From here, the King's Highway heads left to Tafileh further south, while a right turn brings you spiralling up Karak's hill. The only road into the town centre is a poorly marked turning on the left just before an arch across this road at its highest point; heading straight on here leads down, eventually to the Dead Sea shore at Mazra'a.

Buses from Amman (via the Desert Highway), Ma'an, Tafileh, Aqaba and elsewhere arrive at the bus station, a dreary patch of open ground on a terrace below a residential neighbourhood. It's not easy to get to the castle from here, partly because there are no signs and partly because it involves climbing extremely steep slopes. With or without heavy bags, you might want to do your legs a favour and take a taxi.

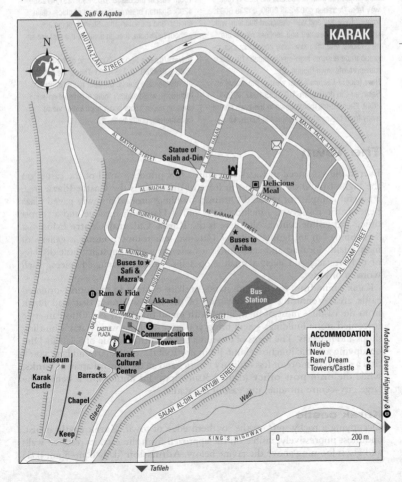

Accommodation

Karak stands in a prime position halfway between Amman and Petra, and has long been an overnight stop for travellers, yet even today the choice of **accommodation** is not exactly broad. Immediately after the peace treaty with Israel was signed, a handful of inexpensive hotels were flung up around the castle to meet the influx of visitors, and the small al-Shuhba supermarket even put up a sign in Hebrew welcoming Israeli tourists – something unheard of elsewhere in Jordan. However, the flood quickly slowed to a trickle and these days you could easily bargain a room for well below initial asking prices. One complicating factor, which rather undermines most bargaining ploys, is that the *Ram* and *Towers* hotels, as well as the al-Shuhba supermarket and the *Fida* and *Ram* restaurants, are all owned by the same man. The *Resthouse* – a long-standing tourist-class hotel in amongst the souvenir shops beside the castle – was closed at the time of writing, seemingly permanently.

Mujeb 4km east of Karak, at the junction of the King's Highway from Rabba and the Desert Highway from Qatraneh ☎03/238 6090, ☏238 6091. Impressively airy and well-designed building, with good facilities. Pleasant and spotless rooms are all en suite, and the reasonably consistent tourist-group trade ensures high-quality meals. No public transport into town though. ❹

New (aka *al-Kemmah*) Just west of the statue of Salah ad-Din downtown ☎03/235 1942, ☏235 3649. Ill-cared-for rooms down in the town centre away from the castle – cheapest in Karak. ❶

Ram/Dream Above the al-Shuhba supermarket, 100m east of the castle ☎03/235 1351, ☏235 4293. Spartan breeze-block kind of place, clean enough and unremarkable. Shared rooms are without bathroom, though some of the rest are en suite. ❷

Towers/Castle About 100m north of the castle ☎03/235 4289, ☏235 4293. This is the best of the inexpensive hotels. Cheaper rooms share a bathroom, while slightly more expensive en-suite ones on upper floors boast good valley views. Nonetheless, pretty basic. ❷

The Town

Everything you need in Karak is within a few minutes' stroll of the castle, on the highest point of town. Just in front of the castle is the **Castle Plaza** area, a tasteful complex of restored Ottoman buildings around a newly paved plaza beneath the castle walls, including the old al-Hammidi mosque and a tourist office and visitor centre. Also here is the **Karak Cultural Centre** (Mon–Sat 9am–5pm), an intriguing suite of Ottoman-era rooms housing a gallery of high-quality local art and crafts (most for sale), as well as, upstairs, little displays of old artefacts and even a small shop selling locally produced spices. Well worth a browse.

Karak's humdrum town centre stands in sharp contrast to the tourist-oriented castle area. Venturing down any one of the narrow streets that lead north from the castle – most of them lined with grand but grimy old Ottoman-style balconied stone buildings – will bring you nose-to-nose with Karak's bustling shops and markets. The focus of town is a big equestrian statue of Salah ad-Din, occupying a traffic junction about 400m north of the castle. Around here you'll find a clutch of more or less ordinary eateries and all the normal array of **banks**, while the main **post office** (daily 7.30am–5pm, Fri until 1pm) is behind the large city-centre mosque, just east of the statue.

Karak castle

Occupying a rocky spur on the southern edge of town, **Karak castle** is first, and most impressively, visible on the approach from the east, its restored walls and glacis looming above the ravine below. **Admission** (daily 8am–5pm; JD1)

5

Walks near Karak: Wadi ibn Hammad and Wadi Numeira

In addition to the magnificent hikes within the Wadi Mujib reserve (see p.301), there are two attractive **canyons** near Karak, outside the reserve, that are well worth exploring. You can easily arrange transport to their trailheads (unmarked) at Karak hotels or through the RSCN, and route-finding is not difficult – but you nonetheless need to treat this rugged landscape with respect, and should not undertake these trips without adequate experience and a knowledgeable guide. See p.76 for some names of specialist independent guides.

The full-day gorge-walk down the stunning **Wadi ibn Hammad**, 34km north of Karak, starts from a pool fed by a hot spring, accessed down a tortuous side-road midway between Qasr and Rabba. The canyon – briefly subterranean initially – extends for 12km down to the Dead Sea, 500m below, passing through beautiful mixed terrain, rich with palms, ferns and, in springtime, a breathtaking array of wild-flowers. The only obstacle is a five-metre waterfall, located about 2km east of the Dead Sea road; the path around it leads right, up the cliffs, before descending to follow the lower river bed out to the Dead Sea road, where you can pick up buses between Mazra'a and Karak.

Wadi Numeira, south of the village of al-Iraq, 34km south of Karak, is equally enjoyable. If you start from the end of the tarmac road in al-Iraq, it's a hike of 18km (8hr), but you can cover the first 5km of dirt track by 4x4, leaving 13km to do on foot (6hr). The route, which passes through the green canyon between barren mountains, climaxes in an impressive and extremely narrow 100-metre-high gorge, bringing you out onto the Dead Sea road midway between Mazra'a and Safi. Just before the finish, what was an easy two-metre step is now, thanks to 2001's flash floods, a three-metre vertical drop, for which a rope is advisable.

These walks, and many others in the area, are described in more detail in Tony Howard's book *Jordan: Walks, Treks, Caves, Climbs, Canyons* (see p.496).

is across a wooden footbridge spanning the moat from behind the Castle Plaza complex. The castle has seven separate levels, some buried deep inside the hill, and the best way to explore is to take a **torch** and simply let your inquisitiveness run free: it's quite possible to spend two or three atmospheric hours poking into dark rooms and gloomy vaulted passageways.

A good place to start is by heading up the slope once you enter, then doubling back on yourself into a long, vaulted passageway along the inside of the huge north wall built by the Crusaders. Down here, close to the original entrance of the castle in the northeastern corner, are a **barracks** and, on the right, the **kitchens**, complete with olive press and, further within, a huge oven. You emerge along the **east wall**, close to the ruined **chapel**. Over the battlements the restored glacis heralds a dizzy drop, and facing you is the partly complete Mamluke **keep**, the best-protected part of the castle. It's not difficult to climb to the highest point, from where there are scarily vertiginous views in all directions. In a sunken area between the chapel and the keep lie the remains of a Mamluke **palace**, while at the bottom of some steps just behind the chapel's apse is a beautifully carved stone panel. Of the two rooms opposite the panel, the one on the right features some reused Nabatean blocks set into the wall; next door, Reynald's extensive and suitably dank **dungeons** lead off into the hill. Back at the carved panel, a passageway to the left eventually brings you out, after passing another barracks, near the entrance. If you head down from here to the lower western side of the castle, you'll come across the **museum** (daily except Tues 8.30am–4.30pm), recently completely restored, and now offering fascinating background to the history of the castle and the local area. Equally interesting – if you can persuade the museum caretaker to unlock the door for you – is a restored Mamluke **gallery** nearby, running virtually the length of the west wall at the lowest level of the castle.

Eating and drinking

Karak being largely a Bedouin town, the choice of **eating** places is limited and pretty uninspiring (the locals tend to favour home-cooking), with a host of broadly similar traditional Arabic diners in the centre of town packed around 5 and 6pm for snacks and takeaways, and more or less empty by 8pm. Everywhere is open for breakfast, but generally closed by 9pm.

In plum position on the castle drag are the *Ram* and *Fida* restaurants, all very touristy, with identikit kebab and chicken dishes that can be easily bettered in more interesting places a little further into town. The Syrian run *Akkash / Al-Halabi* diner, just down from the *Fida*, is the height of friendliness and, although the simple fare is nothing to write home about, the cosy, cross-vaulted little den is an atmospheric place to sit and eat. Next to the equestrian statue of Salah ad-Din downtown, a Turkish restaurant and a *Mankal Chicken Tikka* dive are worth passing over for the much better *Delicious Meal* down the street, which does the best *shwarma* in town. At none of these places need you pay more than JD2–3 for a filling experience. The swankiest restaurant in town is within the Castle Plaza complex – a white-tablecloth place where meals are JD8 and upwards.

South to Shobak

The King's Highway floats along the wheat-sown plateau south of Karak for 10km before reaching **Muta**, best known today as the home of one of Jordan's leading universities, but also the scene, in 629 AD, of the first major battle between the Byzantine Empire and the nascent Muslim army on its first surge out of Arabia. On this occasion, the Muslims were routed, and its generals, including the Prophet Muhammad's adopted son Zaid bin Haritha and his deputy Jaafar bin Abi Talib, were killed. Some 3km south of Muta, in the town of **Mazar**, a large, royally funded mosque has been constructed over the shrines of Zaid and Jaafar; the small **Islamic museum** in the same building (daily except Tues 8am–2pm; free) is only of passing interest. According to legend, on his march north to Muta, Jaafar rested beneath the lone **pistachio tree** which survives today to the left of the highway some 5km south of Qadisiyyeh (see p.313); locals still bedeck the holy tree with pieces of cloth as expressions of their faith.

South of Mazar, the landscape becomes increasingly wild. The major natural feature here is the huge **Wadi Hasa**, replete with hot springs at Hammamat Afra and an ancient Nabatean temple atop Jebel Tannur. Further south, past the attractive regional capital of **Tafileh**, the hills rise further, to the RSCN nature reserve at **Dana** (see p.313), and on to **Shobak**, site of a ruined Crusader castle.

Khirbet Tannur

A little way out of Mazar, two roads, old and new, descend past the cultivated fields of Ayna village into the vast **Wadi Hasa**, a natural boundary which marked the transition from Moab into the land of Edom. Dominating the wadi is a huge and elementally scary **black mountain** – actually an extinct volcano

– which clashes so startlingly with the white limestone all around that it seems to be under a permanent, ominous cloud. The Nabateans clearly felt something similar, since they built, on the conical hill of Jebel Tannur directly opposite, a large temple complex, **Khirbet Tannur**, ruined today but still visitable.

As you rise out of the wadi bed, a broken concrete sign on the right side of the highway, 24km from Mazar, marks the track leading to Khirbet Tannur. This is passable for a little way by car, but eventually you'll have to get out and make the tough climb across a saddle and up the steep slope to the atmospheric ruins. The temple area dates from the second century AD, although some form of altar may have been constructed here up to two centuries earlier. Unfortunately, excavations in the 1930s carted off virtually everything of any interest, and all the carving and statuary that used to adorn the site now gathers dust in museums in Amman and Cincinnati. But, however hard it is to imagine the complete structures which once stood here, the windswept isolation of this rugged summit is able to resurrect the presence of the Nabatean gods more potently even than Petra's quietest cranny.

You arrive on the summit more or less where the Nabatean worshippers would have arrived: in front is a humped threshold, originally part of the entrance **gateway** to a paved courtyard. It's easy to make out the wall foundations of three **rooms** to the right, and although only random chunks of decorative carving survive, many of the courtyard's **flagstones** are still in place. Ahead is a raised platform on which stood the small **temple**, its entrance originally crowned with a large carved image of the goddess Atargatis bedecked with vines and fruit, now on display in the Amman museum. Within the holy of holies stood images both of Atargatis and the god Zeus-Hadad.

Hammamat Burbita and Hammamat Afra

Barely 2km from the Khirbet Tannur turning, the King's Highway is carried over Wadi Laban, a tributary of Wadi Hasa, on a small bridge; no buses follow the small turning off to the right side, but private transport can take you further along this narrow and winding side-road deep into the valley to reach a set of hot springs. Without your own transport, the only way to reach them is by taxi; the going rate from Tafileh is about JD12 round-trip. At the time of writing this side-road was closed, since facilities at both springs were under long-term renovation. It's worth asking around in Karak or Tafileh for the latest news before you head out here.

A turn-off after 7km leads down to peaceful **Hammamat Burbita**, in a broad and sunny part of the valley, with the river fringed by reed-beds and some cultivation. Unfortunately, the only access to the hot flowing water here is at one rather smelly pool under a tin roof above the reed-beds – until redevelopment, you're better off carrying on along the valley road.

Some 5km further, at the end of the road, is **Hammamat Afra**. The **hot pools** (four outdoor ones for men, one indoors for women) are set down in a gorge between high, narrow, rocky walls that cut out most of the direct sunshine, and are generally well maintained: this is a popular weekending spot for families from Tafileh and Karak, and if you arrive on a Friday you'll find the place quite crowded. The water is a striking rust-red colour from the high iron content, and genuinely hot: the last pool on the left – popularly known as the *megla*, or frying pan – is a broiling 52°C. The walls all along the narrow valley drip water, with mineral reds and mossy greens daubing the white limestone. Splashing barefoot up or down the warm river here is as much pleasure as flopping around in the pools with everybody else. There's a couple of small outlets selling snacks and cold drinks, but most people set up barbecues on the various terraces around the site.

Tafileh

South of Wadi Hasa, the King's Highway begins to climb into the Shara mountains, eventually reaching a small plateau where a road branches east (left) to the Desert Highway (if you're heading north along the King's Highway, the signposting at this junction is confusing and it's easy to lose the way). It was near here that, in January 1918, the only fully fledged battle of the Arab Revolt took place, Faysal and Lawrence's armies sweeping away an Ottoman force only to be halted in their tracks by heavy snow.

Some 25km south of the turn-off for Hammamat Afra, the picturesque town of **TAFILEH** comes into view, spread along gently curving terraces, with orchards of fruit and olives blanketing the hillside below. Although a governorate capital and a sizeable town, Tafileh has no specific attractions to make for (the signposted "castle" in the middle of town comprises a single, inaccessible tower, probably Mamluke), and you'll probably find yourself stopping only to switch buses. Along the main drag in the centre of town you'll find the **bus station**, from where you can depart, generally in the mornings only, to Amman and Ma'an (via the Desert Highway), Aqaba (via the Wadi Araba road) and Karak (via the King's Highway); buses to Qadisiyyeh depart from the main street 150m further on. If you're on a journey south, make sure to **set out early from Karak**, since arriving in Tafileh in the afternoon will leave you unable either to reach Petra or to get back to Amman by public bus before nightfall, and thus open to persuasion from the local taxi-drivers. Further along from the bus station, above a reeking chicken butcher, stands Tafileh's single **hotel**, the *Afra* (T03/234 1832; ●): bug-lovers will relish a night here. A handful of nameless diners serve basic Arabic **food**, the best of which is opposite the Qadisiyyeh bus stop; there are also large but rather uninspiring restaurants on the outskirts of town.

About 4km south of Tafileh is a turn-off westwards, signed for Aqaba and Fifa. This is the last surfaced road connecting the King's Highway and Wadi Araba until you reach Aqaba, and it offers some truly spectacular views out over Wadi Araba as it coils down to **Fifa** (see p.180), a little way south of the Dead Sea.

Sela

In the rugged hills south of Tafileh looms the remote mountain fastness of **SELA**, which offers a taxing but memorable hike up to a summit with magnificent views. The village of **Ain al-Baydha**, about 10km south of Tafileh, marks a turn-off heading steeply down the cliffside to the picturesque hamlet of **as-Sil**, with old stone cottages – not unlike Dana (see p.314) – clustering higgledy-piggledy on an outcrop. The giant sandstone mountain of Sela looms opposite the hamlet, on the other side of a deep ravine; as-Sil is just about accessible by ordinary car, but to go on you'll have to resort to 4x4 or your own leg-muscles. Although the route up to the top of the mountain isn't difficult, a **guide** is essential, since this is barren and inhospitable terrain. Your best bet is to start out early in the day, and ask around in Ain al-Baydha village: this will probably yield either advice or a guide. Alternatively you could consult the RSCN at Dana (see p.313) – staff here should be able to point you in the right direction.

A biblical account in II Kings narrates the story of the seventh-century BC King Amaziah of Judah, who attacked Edom, defeated a ten-thousand-strong army and seized "Selah", while II Chronicles says that, during the same campaign, Amaziah threw ten thousand captive Edomites off the "rock". Some archeologists have related present-day Sela with these events, citing the fact that the Hebrew word for "rock" is *sela*, but others have suggested that these events took place at the similarly remote, inaccessible mountain Umm al-Biyara at Petra, partly since the Greek word *petra* also means "rock". Neither case has been conclusively proved, and even the recent discovery of a worn **inscription** in Babylonian cuneiform, carved in a smoothed rectangle in the cliff-face on the side of the mountain of Sela (and just about visible to the naked eye from as-Sil), hasn't provided any further insight. The one-hour hike up to the summit from as-Sil heads down into the valley, then up via a Nabatean-style rock-cut stairway; once at the top, aside from exploring the various cisterns and chambers, you're rewarded with outstanding **views** over the rocky domes and towers of this folded landscape.

The hamlet and surrounding area were recently bought by the Ministry of Tourism, as part of their efforts to upgrade tourist facilities in the Tafileh area. It is proposed to turn the old cottages of as-Sil into a chalet-style hotel, with local people involved in projects such as producing traditional crafts and providing tourist services. With the failure of similar government wheezes at Umm Qais and Petra's Beit Zaman, and the proximity of the sustainable, sensitively developed nature reserve at Dana village (see below), it remains to be seen what form this project will take.

Dana Nature Reserve

Around 27km south of Tafileh and 22km north of Shobak, a steep road winds down off the King's Highway in Qadisiyyeh to the tiny village of Dana, at the eastern edge of Jordan's flagship **DANA NATURE RESERVE** (Ⓦwww .rscn.org.jo), which encompasses the breathtaking Wadi Dana and stretches as far as the Wadi Araba in the west. The village itself has been the scene of an extraordinary – and successful – social experiment conducted by the RSCN to rejuvenate a dying community by protecting the natural environment. Clinging to the edge of the cliff below the King's Highway, Dana is the starting-point for a series of walks and hikes through one of Jordan's few protected areas of natural beauty. Whether you put aside an hour or a week for the place, it's likely to charm you into staying longer than you intended.

The reserve's terrain drops from 1500m above sea level at Dana to below sea level west of Faynan, and its **geology** switches from limestone to sandstone to granite, ecosystems varying from lush, well-watered mountain slopes and open oak and juniper woodlands to scrubland and arid sandy desert. The list of **flora** and resident **fauna** is dizzying: a brief roundup includes various kinds of eagles, falcons, kestrels and vultures, cuckoos, owls, the Sinai rosefinch and Tristram's serin; wildcats, caracals, hyenas, jackals, badgers, foxes, wolves, hares, bats, hedgehogs, porcupine and ibex; snakes, chameleons and lizards galore; freshwater crabs; and, so far, three plants new to science out of more than seven hundred plant species recorded.

Practicalities

The only **bus to Dana** shuttles regularly to and from the village of **QADISI-YYEH** on the King's Highway above the village. Qadisiyyeh itself is connected by regular minibuses with Tafileh, but the section of the King's Highway to

The story of Dana

Dana is unique, not only in Jordan but in the whole Middle East – a positive, vision-ary programme combining scientific research, social reconstruction and **sustainable tourism**. For most of the twentieth century Dana was a simple farming community thriving on a temperate climate, three abundant springs and good grazing; indeed, some inhabitants had previously left Tafileh specifically for a better life in the village. But as Jordan developed new technologies and the general standard of living rose, a growing number of villagers felt isolated in their mountain hamlet of Ottoman stone cottages. Some moved out in the late 1960s to found a new village, **Qadisiyyeh**, on the main Tafileh–Shobak road, and the attractions of electricity and plumbing rapidly emptied primitive Dana. For many people, the construction of the huge Rashdiyyeh cement factory close by in the early 1980s was the last straw: with well-paid jobs for the taking, most locals saw the daily trek up from the village to the factory as point-less, and almost everyone moved to Qadisiyyeh.

Dana lay semi-abandoned for a decade or more, its handful of impoverished farm-ers forced to compete in the local markets with bigger farms using more advanced methods of production. This was what a group of twelve women from Amman discovered in the early 1990s as they travelled across the country to catalogue the remnants of traditional Jordanian culture. Realizing the deprivation faced by some of the poorest people in the country, these **"Friends of Dana"** embarked on a project to renovate and revitalize the fabric of the village under the auspices of the **Royal Society for the Conservation of Nature**. Electricity, telephones and a water supply were extended to the village and 65 cottages renovated. People started to drift back to Dana. The RSCN quickly realized the potential of the secluded Wadi Dana for scientific research; in a $3.3 million project funded partly by the World Bank and the UN, they turned the area into a protected **nature reserve**, built a small research station next to the village and, in 1994, launched a detailed ecological survey.

Continued grazing by thousands of domesticated goats, sheep and camels couldn't be reconciled with the need for environmental protection and so was banned; studies were undertaken into creating sustainable opportunities for villag-ers to gain a livelihood from the reserve. The ingenious solution came in redirecting the village's traditional crops to a new market. Dana's farmers produced their olives, figs, grapes, other fruits and nuts as before, but instead they sold everything to the RSCN, who employed the villagers to process these crops into novelty products such as organically produced jams and olive-oil soap for direct sale to relatively wealthy, environmentally aware consumers, both Jordanian and foreign. Medicinal herbs were introduced as a cash crop to aid the economic recovery, and the last Dana resident familiar with traditional pottery-making was encouraged to teach her craft to a younger generation. Dana soon hit the headlines, and in 1996 the RSCN launched **low-impact tourism** to the reserve, with the traditional-style *Guesthouse* going up next to the research buildings. Local villagers – some of whom were already employed as research scientists – now also work as managers and guides.

the south, between Qadisiyyeh and Shobak, has very little public transport. Hitching is one option, or bargaining hard for a **taxi** is another: a full taxi to Dana from Shobak or Tafileh shouldn't cost more than JD7, or JD12 from Wadi Musa. If you're **driving**, you might easily miss the turn-off for Dana village, which lies 3km south of the Rashdiyyeh cement factory: forget the big brown roadsigns signposting the reserve to the right (which indicate the turn-off confusingly far from the correct place) and look out instead for a small brown sign to Dana Village at the junction itself. Coming from the south, you need to drive all the way through Qadisiyyeh: the turn-off (left) is at the very top of the village hill.

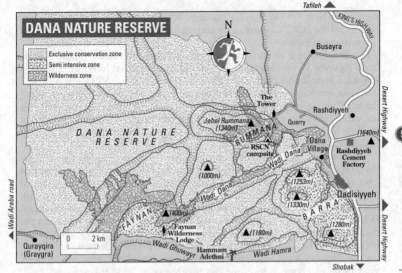

Map: DANA NATURE RESERVE

Legend:
- Exclusive conservation zone
- Semi intensive zone
- Wilderness zone

Tafileh
KING'S HIGHWAY
Busayra
Rashdiyyeh
Desert Highway
The Tower
Jebel Rummana (1340m)
RUMMANA
Quarry
(1640m)
DANA NATURE RESERVE
RSCN campsite
Wadi Dana
Dana Village
Rashdiyyeh Cement Factory
(1000m)
Qadisiyyeh
Wadi Dana
(1253m)
(1330m)
BARRA
FAYNAN
(400m)
Faynan Wilderness Lodge
(1180m)
(1280m)
Wadi Araba road
Qurayqira (Graygra)
0   2 km
Wadi Ghuwayr
Hammam Adethni
Wadi Hamra
Desert Highway
Shobak

On the way down to Dana, a **viewpoint** gives a tremendous panorama of Wadi Dana and the roofs of the old stone cottages of the village below. Further down, as you clatter down the steep cobbled street into the village, you come to a fork: a sign points left to the RSCN-run *Guesthouse*, and right to the *Dana Hotel* in the centre.

Entrance to the village and its immediate surroundings is free, but **admission to the reserve** (for hikes or in order to camp) costs JD5.

Private motor vehicles are banned within the reserve, which encompasses some 300 square kilometres of varied terrain. The large majority of it is an **Exclusive Conservation Zone**, where all access is forbidden. Limited areas around both campsites and along the valley floor comprise a **Wilderness Zone**, where access on foot is permitted along specified trails, sometimes only if you're accompanied by a guide. Two areas around Faynan and Barra are deemed **Semi-Intensive Use Zones**, where vehicle access is permitted on specified tracks (generally suitable only for 4x4), providing you've collected a permit in advance.

Accommodation and eating

Dana's **accommodation** – whether in a building or under canvas – isn't cheap but, considering what's been achieved in the village, the unparalleled atmosphere and the superb hiking on offer, is worth the extra and more. The lack of shops or diners means that, for **eating**, you must either take all meals at your hotel or campsite, or bring in supplies for picnics and self-catering; a mix of the two is in many ways the best solution. Women will experience no intrusive hassles at any of the hotels or campsites.

RSCN Dana Guesthouse

For its cosy atmosphere, simple comforts and an incredible silence, a night at the small RSCN-run **Guesthouse** (℡03/227 0497 or 0498, ℻227 0499, ✉dhana@rscn.org.jo; ❸–❹) is likely to be one of your most memorable in Jordan. Stay here a few days and let the atmosphere seep into your bones:

there's nowhere else like it in the country. Whatever you choose to spend here goes to aid the RSCN's work in protecting Jordan's natural environment – and is worth every penny.

The building and its furniture were designed by architect Ammar Khammash (ⓦ www.khammash.com) in a skilful and attractive blend of traditional Jordanian styles and a chic minimalism in stone and iron. All nine rooms, and the main terrace, overlook the full length of the still Wadi Dana: at night, lights twinkling on the Dead Sea and the call of nightjars echoing eerily up the valley make for an unforgettably serene experience. Queen Noor, wife of the late King Hussein, famously called the views "ten-star", and it's hard to argue with her.

The **rooms** – doubles, triples and one quad – are kept spotlessly clean by the cheerful and amenable staff, and most have a private balcony perched over the valley. You can pay less for a room with no balcony, or more to have the only room with an en-suite bathroom (all the rest share bathrooms), but should always **book weeks in advance**. Rates include a good breakfast. With notice, staff can lay on substantial lunches and dinners for JD6 extra per meal (or JD8 for a barbecue), and can provide hikers with a JD3 lunchbox of bread, meat, cheese, fruit, yoghurt and a drink. If you're arriving at Dana in the evening and want a meal laid on, you must either book it when you book your room or phone at least one day in advance to let staff know.

Alongside the *Guesthouse* is a **shop** (daily 9am–4pm) selling local products such as herbs, fruit and jewellery, as well as textiles, gifts and other handmade knick-knacks from RSCN projects around the country. Across the corridor from the shop is a **learning zone** – intended for kids – where interactive displays and pictures give a sense of Dana's natural context.

Other hotels in the village

With the popularity of the *Guesthouse*, some locals formed a **village co-operative** in the 1990s to filter business away from the RSCN. A leading light, Nabil Nwafleh, founded the simple *Dana Hotel* in one of the old cottages. Nwafleh then left the co-operative after his decision to create a second hotel sparked conflict. Now his ugly **Dana Tower Hotel** – built out of modern breezeblocks – juts crookedly above the otherwise entirely one-storey stone-built village, its windows pointing the wrong way for the valley views and its walls daubed with graffiti. Beds here are undoubtedly cheap (the showers and toilets aren't the cleanest), but the hotel is not connected with the RSCN or the village co-operative.

There is an honourable alternative to the *Guesthouse*. The **Dana Hotel** (ⓣ 03/227 0537, ⓔ sdqe@nets.com.jo; ❷), in the village centre on the left, is now back under the management of the co-operative, and has been sympathetically renovated with the help of the RSCN. It's an excellent, atmospheric little budget hotel, with simple rooms ranged around a quiet stone-flagged courtyard: two doubles, four quads and one six-bed dorm (all sharing toilets and showers) and two en-suite doubles. Staff are friendly, and happy to provide inexpensive meals and drinks.

RSCN Rummana campsite

The great Dana outdoors is best experienced by **camping**, but in order for the RSCN to control numbers within the reserve you're not allowed to pitch your own tent.

The RSCN's **Rummana campsite** (open March–Oct only) lies in the hills to the north of Wadi Dana. The walk to Rummana from Dana village is an easy couple of hours around the head of the valley. Coming **south** by car down the King's Highway, the Rummana turning is before Dana: turn right 22km south of Tafileh, just before the main road cuts through a small wood, at a blue sign for "Ain Lahda" and a small brown sign for the campsite. Coming **north** from Dana village, at the top of the access road turn left (up the hill) on the main Qadisiyyeh–Tafileh road, and follow this for about 5km and, just beyond where the road cuts straight through the middle of a small wood, turn left at a brown sign for the campsite. This brings you down below the level of the main road onto a wide, bumpy dirt road used by trucks; carry on, past a huge quarry on the left, and then down a signposted left turn. On this road, 800m beyond a lone roadside pistachio tree, three **wild cypresses** – marking the edge of Jordan's last wild cypress forest, now protected as part of the reserve – are visible silhouetted on a hillside over your right shoulder. A little further, at the entrance to the reserve, is the "**Tower**" – a small building with an office and a lookout terrace – where you must park.

A shuttle bus (actually a small truck) gingerly inches its way up and down the narrow, winding road between the Tower and the campsite, which is located in an idyllic spot at the foot of Jebel Rummana: this journey to and from the Tower (and, on request, back to the Dana *Guesthouse*) is free.

To stay at Rummana, you must **book in advance** through the Dana *Guesthouse*, letting them know when and how you intend to arrive, whether you want meals cooked, and so on. For single occupancy of a solid, roomy four-person tent, you **pay** JD18; for double occupancy, each person pays JD15; for triple JD14; for quad JD13. There are twenty tents. Prices include a mattress, blankets, a towel and access to a proper, clean toilet block with cold-water showers. Staff can prepare **meals**, but only for a minimum of six people; breakfast costs JD3, a hikers' lunchbox JD3, and full lunch or dinner JD6 (barbecue JD8). The Rummana campsite has excellent facilities, including a proper kitchen where you can cook your own meals with gas (access costs JD15, but there is no electricity).

RSCN Faynan Wilderness Lodge

Newly opened in 2005, the RSCN's **Wilderness Lodge** (book through Dana *Guesthouse*, see above; ❸–❹) stands at the lower, western end of the reserve at **Faynan** – designed, again by Ammar Khammash. This is desert terrain, hot, dry and dusty, and the solar-powered, environmentally friendly lodge is intended to be both a base for active exploration of the surrounding area and an isolated retreat for those seeking solitude. There is no access by paved road: the only way to get here is on foot from Dana (a five-hour walk) or with a 4x4 from the nearest villages to the west, **Qurayqira** (pronounced "graygra") or its neighbour **Rashaydeh**. From the turn-off on the Wadi Araba road about 135km north of Aqaba or 40km south of Fifa, a fairly decent road, passable by ordinary car, runs for 17km to Qurayqira and another 5km on to Rashaydeh, but there the road ends. From either village, you can ask around for a 4x4 ride on the 10km of desert track to the lodge itself.

There is electricity at the lodge (and even air-conditioning), but all the 26 rooms – designed in an attractive, spartan style and laid out on two levels around an internal courtyard – are lit only by candles set into mirrored niches. The walls are thick, and windows are either small or shielded from full sun, making the interior cool and pleasant in even the hottest weather. There's an attractive communal sitting and eating area, with a traditional oven for preparing meals, and the atmosphere of the place is bewitchingly calm, peaceful and contemplative.

As well as **walks** (see below), the RSCN is intending, in time, to open up eco-friendly **mountain-biking** and **off-road 4x4** driving routes in and around the Faynan area. In antiquity, Faynan was an extensive copper-smelting settlement; British-led archeological investigations to discover more about the site are ongoing. Today, too, Faynan is thriving: the local Azazmeh tribe of Bedouin are participants in a unique RSCN scheme to alter the rural economy to place greater emphasis on environmental protection. For years, their goats have been overgrazing reserve land and decimating the local flora, but rather than banning them – which would merely foment ill-will and shift the problem elsewhere – the RSCN is attempting instead to invest in them, fattening the goats in large pens outside reserve land and training local women to produce new craft items from **goat leather**; both projects mean that the goats sell for higher prices at market and that their owners can additionally raise the value of each animal by selling the hide for leather. Crafts made from Faynan goat leather are on sale in the Dana shop.

Walks in and around the Dana reserve

Once you arrive, it's worth stopping in at the RSCN-run **Guesthouse** – whether you're staying there or not – both for the views from their terrace and to get some firsthand **information** about the wildlife of the reserve from the experts. They have various leaflets detailing a number of walks and activities, and can provide a trained **nature guide** for any of the walks at a fixed rate: JD6 for 1–2hr, JD10 for 2–3hr, JD15 for 4–5hr, or JD30 for a full day, regardless of the size of the group. Many of the walks require you to take a guide, but there's a handful of routes on which you can strike out alone.

The handy spiral-bound full-colour "Wildlife of Dana" booklet, available at the Dana shop, names and details a range of resident mammals (with their footprints), birds and reptiles (note that most of the fauna in the reserve is nocturnal), as well as the more common species of tree, with photographs for identification.

Walks from Dana village

The most obvious walking route in the reserve is the magnificent **Wadi Dana Trail** (14km; 5–6hr) from the village along the downward-sloping floor of the wadi, an easy walk passing from the lush green gardens of Dana through increasingly wild and desolate terrain to Faynan. This can be done alone or with a guide. Another spectacular walk is the **Steppe Trail** (8km; 3hr; March–Oct only), a moderately difficult route that follows a contour around the head of the valley, passing first through the spring-fed terraced gardens of Dana and then beneath the massive escarpment to Rummana: this can be done in either direction, but only with a guide.

Another highly explorable area is a fifteen-minute drive south of the village (or a 2–3hr guided walk from Dana), where lush woodlands give way to networks of canyons and gorges cutting into the mountainous landscape. This is the starting-point for the superb circular "Mysterious Nabatean Tomb" route to **Shaq ar-Reesh**, a Nabatean mountain retreat that offers memorable views over Wadi Dana and the surrounding landscape. The walk, for which you must take a guide, is a fairly tough one, taking four hours for the round-trip; it begins easily enough in flower-filled meadows and quiet terraces, but involves a bit of scrambling and climbing through a narrow *siq*, cut by the Nabateans, to reach the spectacularly sited mountain-top, dotted with cisterns and water-channels. At the southern edge of the summit is a gully lined with trees and woody thorn bushes which conceal a Nabatean rock-cut tomb. Barra is also the start and finish for the guided circular **Water Drops Trail** (2km; 2hr 30min), heading out to the springs and ruins at Nawatef and back on a different route.

An alternative, difficult route down to Faynan is the beautiful but hard-going **Palm Trees Wadi Trail** (17km; 8hr) through the southern reaches of the reserve. This also starts from Barra, and passes between the red cliffs of Wadi Hamra before reaching the verdant oasis of Hammam Adethni and following flowing water all the way down to Faynan.

If you arrive in summer, you'd be unwise to turn down the chance for a guided **night walk** into the reserve, giving the chance to see the wadi come alive with wildlife. Dana village itself is also worth exploring, and the RSCN can easily set up a visit (the "**Traditional Tribal Arts Tour**") to meet with local farmers and visit the jewellery workshops, bakeries and fruit-drying centres.

Walks from Rummana campsite

Highly recommended from Rummana (open March–Oct) is the **Steppe Trail** (8km; 3hr) – see above – back to Dana, but a guide lives on-site at Rummana and can point you onto smaller and easier trails into the countryside around the campsite, including the easy **Campsite Trail**, a short two-hour self-guided circular walk exploring the natural surroundings. The moderate **Rummana Mountain Trail** (2.5km; 2hr) – either self-guided or accompanied – follows a trail through the juniper trees up to the summit of Jebel Rummana for the views down into Wadi Araba: it's also easy to spot raptors up here.

A short walk from the campsite is a **bird hide** overlooking a small pool – ideal for early morning observation of birds and ibex – or alternatively you can arrange for a guided **dawn walk** from the campsite to a nearby water source to watch the wildlife. Should you fancy stretching your legs instead of sitting on the shuttle bus, the walk back up to the Tower from the campsite takes about an hour.

Walks from Faynan lodge

Once you've arrived at the lodge on foot down the valley from Dana, your only realistic option is to stay here, unless you've arranged in advance a pick-up by 4x4 or are heading on with a guide on a longer walk. From the lodge, a guide can lead you on the two-hour **Faynan Copper Mine Tour**, a circular trail around the area's antiquities, including the Bronze and Iron Age copper mines, remains of Byzantine churches, a Roman tower and more. The return walk from Faynan to Dana along the wadi floor takes six hours or more, and is uphill all the way.

An alternative walk out of Faynan is to follow the Wadi Hamra route back up as far as the Adethni oasis, from where a difficult but spectacular trail branches off southwards to climb into the hills near **Shobak** castle (about 14km; 6hr).

But the most impressive long-distance trek is the route linking Dana village and Faynan with **Petra**, some 35–40km away. This taxing walk takes four days, with three nights spent camping in the wilds, and without a guide it's likely that you'd lose the way: there are no trail markers at all. The RSCN can organize this trip and provide a guide, but since the whole way bar the initial Dana–Faynan stretch is outside the reserve, you could just as easily arrange this in advance with an independent guide (see p.76 for some recommendations) or even on the spot by asking around in Rashaydeh or Qurayqira and negotiating a price. The walk takes you far from any beaten tracks, and you end up approaching Petra from Ammareen territory around "Little Petra" (Baydha):

this could be the finish line, or, if your guide is knowledgeable, you could continue on a little-used trail which circumnavigates the main entry routes into the ancient city and leads instead on a back route up to the Monastery for a visually momentous fifth-day conclusion to this epic walk.

Shobak castle

Perched dramatically like a ship on the crest of a hill, **Shobak castle** was the first to be built by the Crusaders in Transjordan (see p.305 for some Crusader history). In a more ruinous state than Karak castle, and much rebuilt by Mamlukes and Ottomans, it's nonetheless well worth an exploratory detour, and entrance is free.

As they are today, the **walls** and **towers** are Mamluke, and all the towers which stand have beautifully carved external calligraphic inscriptions dating from rebuilding work in the 1290s. As you enter, down and to the left is a small **chapel**, at the back of which are pools and channels of unknown usage. Below the chapel runs a long, dank and pitch-dark **secret passage**, which brings you out in the middle of the castle if you head right, and outside the walls if you head left. Back alongside the chapel is the original **gatehouse**, to the left side of which are two round wells which presage an even scarier secret passage – a dark and foul opening with, according to legend, 375 broken and slippery steps leading down into the heart of the hill. Even archeologists only got to number 150 or so before giving up, but legend has it that this was the castle's main water supply: somehow the Crusaders knew that by digging down so far they'd eventually hit water. A prudent "No Entry" sign now hangs over the staircase. The gatehouse gives onto a street, at the end of which is a building with three **arched entrances**, one topped by a calligraphic panel; up until the 1950s the castle was still inhabited, and this building was the old village school. If you head through to the back and turn right, a long vaulted corridor leads you out to the north side of the castle, and a maze of abandoned **Ottoman cottages**, beneath which is an exposed **Ayyubid palace** complex, with a large reception hall and baths. Further round towards the entrance stand the beautiful arches of a **church**, beneath which is a small room filled with catapult balls and chunks of carved masonry.

Practicalities

The castle lies 3km west of **SHOBAK** town, which is some 22km south of Qadisiyyeh. Minibuses and some serveeces run to Shobak direct from Amman's Wihdat station (mornings only) and from Wadi Musa (all day), but there is virtually no public transport from Qadisiyyeh. **No buses** run up to the castle, so without your own transport you'll need to persuade a taxi-driver to take you or face a stiff climb. A small **campsite** is signposted from the castle and the village: at around JD5 per person, it's not bad, but can get chilly.

Set in acres of lush orchards, Shobak is Jordan's leading producer of apples, but this quiet farming village has also been trying for years to reap some benefit from the tourists heading south to Petra. Aside from some excellent **diners** serving falafel on the main drag, its numerous **groceries** beat those in Wadi Musa on both price and quality: if you intend to picnic in Petra, you'd do well to stock up here in advance.

Travel details

No timetables are in operation: most buses, and all minibuses and serveeces, simply depart when they're full.

Buses, minibuses and serveeces

Ariha to: Karak (40min).
Dana to: Qadisiyyeh (10min).
Dhiban to: Madaba (40min).
Faysaliyyeh (Mount Nebo) to: Madaba (15min); Shuneh al-Janubiyyeh (45min).
Hammamat Ma'in to: Amman (JETT office; 1 on Fri; 1hr 45min).
Hesban to: Amman (Muhajireen station; 20min); Madaba (10min).
Karak to: Amman (Wihdat station; 2hr); Aqaba (3hr); Ariha (40min); Ma'an (2hr); Mazra'a (30min); Qasr (20min); Rabba (15min); Safi (40min); Tafileh (1hr); Zarqa (New station; 2hr 30min).
Madaba to: Amman (Abdali, Muhajireen, Raghadan or Wihdat stations; 30min); Dhiban (40min);

Faysaliyyeh (Mount Nebo; 15min); Hammamat Ma'in (50min); Hesban (10min); Ma'in village (15min); Mukawir (1hr); Shuneh al-Janubiyyeh (1hr); Umm ar-Rasas (50min); Zarqa (New station; 1hr).
Ma'in village to: Madaba (15min).
Mukawir to: Madaba (1hr).
Qadisiyyeh to: Dana (5min); Tafileh (40min).
Qasr to: Karak (20min).
Rabba to: Karak (15min).
Safi to: Aqaba (2hr); Karak (1hr).
Shobak to: Amman (Wihdat station; 2hr 45min); Ma'an (30min); Wadi Musa/Petra (30min).
Tafileh to: Amman (Wihdat station; 2hr 30min); Aqaba (2hr 30min); Karak (1hr); Ma'an (1hr); Qadisiyyeh (40min).
Umm ar-Rasas to: Madaba (50min).

Useful Arabic place names

Ain al-Baydha	العين البيضاء	Mount Nebo	جبل نبو
Ariha	اريحا	Mukawir	مكاور
Dana	ضانا	Muta	مؤتة
Dhiban	ذيبان	Nitil	نتل
Faqua	فقوع	Qadisiyyeh	القادسية
Faynan	فينان	Qasr	القصر
Faysaliyyeh	الفيصلية	Qurayqira	القريقرة
Hammamat Afra	حمامات عفرا	Rabba	الربة
Hammamat Ma'in	حمامات ماعين	Sela	السلع
Hesban	حسبان	Shobak	الشوبك
al-Iraq	العراق (جنب المؤتة)	Siyagha	صياغة
Karak	الكرك	Tafileh	الطفيلة
Khirbet al-Mukhayyat	الخربة المخيّط	Umm ar-Rasas	ام الرصاص
Khirbet Tannur	الخربة التنور	Wadi Hasa	وادي الحسا
Madaba	مأدبا	Wadi ibn Hammad	وادي ابن حمّاد
Ma'in	ماعين	Wadi Mujib	وادي الموجب
Mazar	المزار	Wadi Numeira	وادي النميرة

6

Petra

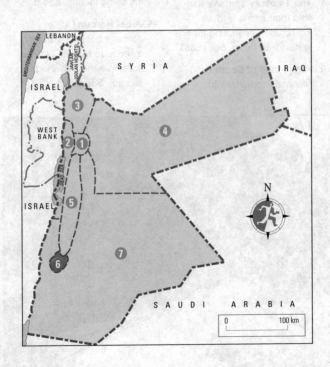

CHAPTER 6 # Highlights

* **Petra By Night** Magical late-night guided walks into Petra for traditional music and storytelling by candlelight. See p.346

* **The Siq** Dramatic entrance to the ancient city, through a high, narrow gorge. See p.350

* **The Treasury** Jordan's flagship monument, a towering facade dominating the entrance to Petra. See p.351

* **High Place of Sacrifice** Mountain-top altar with stunning views over Petra. See p.355

* **The East Cliff** A line of impressive royal tombs carved out of a cliff overlooking the city centre. See p.359

* **The Monastery** A long climb is rewarded with a close-up viewing of Petra's most imposing facade. See p.368

* **Jebel Haroun** One of Jordan's holiest sites, with a shrine to Moses' brother Aaron perched on a high summit. See p.371

△ The Treasury, Petra

Petra

Petra is incredible. Tucked away in a remote valley basin in the heart of southern Jordan's Shara mountains and shielded from the outside world behind an impenetrable barrier of rock, this fabled ancient city of ornate classical facades cannot fail to instil a sense of mystery and drama. Since a Western adventurer stumbled on the site in 1812, it has fired imaginations, its grandeur and dramatic setting pushing it – like the Pyramids or the Taj Mahal – into the realms of legend. Today, it's almost as if time has literally drawn a veil over the once-great city, which grew wealthy enough on the caravan trade to challenge the might of Rome: two millennia of wind and rain have blurred the sharp edges of the facades and rubbed away at the soft sandstone to expose vivid bands of colour beneath, putting the whole scene into soft focus.

Where Petra sits, in a valley basin between two lines of jagged peaks, there's only one route in and out, and that passes through the modern town of **Wadi Musa**, on the eastern side of the mountains. In the last few decades this town has grown to serve the lucrative tourist trade to Petra, and has all the hotels, restaurants and services you'd expect: there's nowhere to stay within the ancient city itself, and virtually nowhere to eat either. The single entrance gate into Petra is in Wadi Musa, but once you've crossed the barrier you're immediately thrown into the rocky landscape of the desert. There is no urban development of any kind within Petra, and the local culture is all rural. Spending a few days here is a constant to-and-fro – down-at-heel Wadi Musa providing all the necessities of life, and majestic Petra all the historical and natural drama.

Some history

In prehistory, the Petra region saw some of the first experiments in farming. The hunter-gatherers of the **Paleolithic Age** gave way, over nine thousand years ago, to settled communities living in walled farming villages such as at

---

Weather conditions

Petra is situated in the mountains, at around 1100m above sea level. In **spring** (March–May) and **autumn** (Sept–Oct) it is at least pleasantly warm, with highs around 25–30°C and virtually no chance of rain. In **summer** (late May–early Sept) it can be blisteringly hot during the day, perhaps above 40°C. However, with the altitude and the desert conditions, nights year-round are frequently chilly. In **winter** (Nov–Feb), Petra can be very cold, often not getting above 10–15°C during the day and dropping below freezing at night: rain is to be expected, and snow is not uncommon.

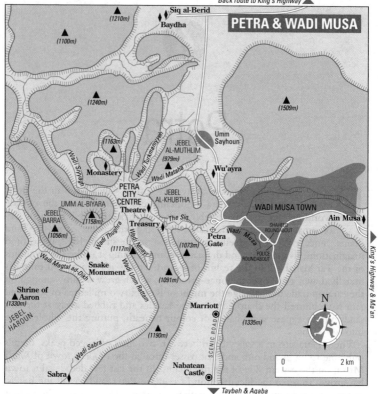

Baydha, just north of Petra. Nomadic tribes passed through the Petra basin in the millennia following, but the spur to its development came with attempts at contact between the two great ancient powers of **Mesopotamia** and **Egypt**. The desert plateaus of Mesopotamia, to the east of the King's Highway, were sealed off by high mountains from the routes both across the Naqab (Negev) to Gaza and across the Sinai to Egypt; somehow a caravan route across the barrier had to be found if contact was to be made. Petra, where abundant springs tumble down into the Wadi Araba through a natural fault in the mountains, was prime choice, marking the spot on the north–south King's Highway where an east–west passage could connect the two empires.

The first significant mention of Petra is in the Old Testament, as the **Israelites** approached **Edom** after their forty years in the desert. Local legend – running against the geographical evidence – maintains that it was in the hills just above Petra that God ordered Moses to produce water for the Israelites by speaking to a rock. Moses instead struck the rock, and the spring that gushed is today named **Ain Musa** (Spring of Moses), its outflow housed beneath a small domed building at the eastern entrance to the town of Wadi Musa. **King Reqem** of Edom (Reqem was the Semitic name for Petra, and he was probably just a local chieftain) refused permission to the Israelites to pass through his territory, but before they departed, Moses' brother Aaron (Haroun in Arabic) died, and was buried supposedly on top of **Jebel Haroun** overlooking

Protecting Petra

Petra's administrators have struggled to develop and also protect this unique site since the first Western tourists began to explore in the mid-nineteenth century. Even up to the 1970s, little or no overall planning control existed. UNESCO made the first move, adding Petra's eight hundred monuments to its list of **World Heritage Sites** in 1985; four years later a group of concerned local establishment figures set up the **Petra National Trust** (PNT; ⑩www.petranationaltrust.com), a not-for-profit NGO campaigning on issues of the environment, antiquities and the region's cultural heritage. Soon afterwards, Queen Noor brought local concern about the effects of unimpeded tourism growth and new building construction in Wadi Musa to international attention in a letter to UNESCO.

The debates that followed resulted in an alphabet soup of bodies being set up to oversee development. To start with, the **Petra Regional Planning Council** (PRPC) replaced the array of self-interested regional and national bodies that formerly held sway. The PRPC – comprising representatives from many government ministries as well as the PNT – began to implement coherent policies for development and infrastructure, and 1995 saw the launching of a joint UNESCO–PNT plan for the sustainable development of Petra (explained in detail on the PNT website). In 2001, reflecting the importance of Petra for the nation, and also the continued difficulty in reconciling the clashing interests of bureaucrats, environmentalists, business people and the local Bedouin, the government swept away the PRPC and created a new body under direct control of the Prime Ministry, the **Petra Regional Authority** (PRA; ⑩www.petra-pra.com.jo), funded from central government and from gate receipts. The PRA is also charged with addressing the most serious threat by far to Petra's integrity: **tourism**. Around 100,000 people visited Petra annually in the 1980s, rising by the year 2000 to half a million (with 83,000 in April alone). Some minor degradation of the site has already occurred, but restoration of the Siq and other areas is designed to halt any further damage before it occurs. A buffer zone of over 900 square kilometres of land, from Shobak to well south of Rajif, is formally protected, while a core 264 square kilometres is defined as the strictly regulated **Petra Archeological Park**. Drainage and sewage systems are now in place in Wadi Musa; new planning controls limit unsightly hotel construction; environmentally sound conservation of Petra's delicate masonry (and replacement of previous work done with unsuitable cement) is under way by a joint German-Jordanian team, who have invented a new porous, elastic mortar which can be injected into cracked stonework to reinforce it invisibly; and there's even reforestation of olive and pine trees, to halt desertification and beautify the site. Improved signage and trail development are on the cards in coming years, and eventually there will be controls to limit the currently unhindered freedom to roam all over the area.

And yet it's clear that further rationalization of control over Petra is still needed: currently jockeying for position are the **PRA** under the **Prime Minister**, the **Department of Antiquities** authorities who control the Petra Archeological Park, the **Ministry of Tourism**, the **Governor of Wadi Musa** representing the 30,000 local residents, and the various **NGOs**, headed by the Petra National Trust. The politicians are still mulling over how best to reconcile these frequently conflicting interests in the crucial years ahead.

Petra. A white shrine atop the mountain is still a site of pilgrimage for Jews, Christians and Muslims alike.

Just after 1000 BC, the Israelite **King David** moved to take control of Petra and the whole of Edom – by now rich on the proceeds of copper production as well as trade. His son **Solomon** consolidated the Israelite grip on trade and technology, and for fifty years diverted Petra's profits into his own coffers.

However, after his death, the Israelite kingdom collapsed and feuding erupted. Some Edomites withdrew to a settlement on top of the impregnable **Umm al-Biyara** mountain overlooking central Petra and to a village at **Tawilan** above Ain Musa. Fluctuations in regional power soon after led to Petra passing from Edomite hands to **Assyrian** to **Babylonian** to **Persian**: such instability left the way open for a new people to stamp their authority on the land and stake a claim to its future.

The Nabateans

The first mention of the **Nabateans** was in 647 BC, when they were listed as one of the enemies of Ashurbanipal, last king of Assyria; at that stage, they were still a tribe of Bedouin nomads inhabiting northern and northwestern Arabia. When the Babylonians depopulated much of Palestine during the sixth century BC, many Edomites came down from Petra to claim the empty land to the west. In turn, the Nabateans migrated out of the arid Arabian desert to the lusher and more temperate mountains of Edom, and, specifically, to the well-watered and easily defended prize of Petra. Whereas the Edomites had occupied the hills above Petra, the Nabateans quickly saw the potential for developing the central bowl of the valley floor. The migrants arrived slowly, though, and for several centuries it seems that most stuck to their Bedouin lifestyle, building little other than a temple and refuge atop **Umm al-Biyara**. However, displaying the adaptability that was to become their trademark, the Nabateans soon gave up the traditional occupation of raiding the plentiful caravans that passed to and fro in favour of charging the merchants for safe passage and a place to do business. It was probably around this time that the first organized, permanent trading emporium was established at Petra, and Edom became known as **Arabia Petrea**.

The Roman author Diodorus Siculus reports that the Greek **Seleucid** ruler of Syria, **Antigonus**, attacked Petra in 312 BC, both to limit Nabatean power and to undermine Ptolemaic authority. His troops sneaked in under cover of darkness, and found that all the Nabatean men were away. The Greeks slaughtered a few women and children and hurriedly made off with as much booty as they could carry – silver, myrrh and frankincense. However, someone managed to raise the alarm, since within an hour, the Nabateans were in pursuit. They rapidly caught up with the complacent army, massacred all but fifty, recovered the valuables and returned home. In true merchant style, though, the Nabateans instinctively recognized that war would do no good to their flourishing business, and so sent a mollifying letter of explanation to Antigonus. The general pretended to accept, but was secretly fuming; he let some time pass before sending another army against Petra. The small garrison they encountered, however, easily repelled the attackers. Comfortably ensconced in their unassailable headquarters, the Nabateans acted the wealthy tycoon: unruffled by the skirmish, they reached into their deep pockets to buy peace from the humiliated Greeks.

Over the following two centuries, the battling between Seleucid Syria and Ptolemaic Egypt for control of Alexander's empire enabled the Nabateans to fill the power vacuum in Transjordan and extend their kingdom far beyond Petra. By 80 BC they were in control of Damascus. Petra grew ever more wealthy on its profits from **trade**, standing at the pivots between Egypt, Arabia and Syria, and between East Asia and the Mediterranean. Traditional commodities such as **copper**, **iron** and Dead Sea **bitumen**, used for embalming in Egypt, were losing ground to **spices** from the southern Arabian coast – myrrh, balsam and frankincense, the last of which was central to religious ritual all over the

Hellenistic world. Pepper, ginger, sugar and cotton arrived from **India** for onward distribution. **Chinese** documents even talk of imports of silk, glass, gold, silver, henna and frankincense from a place known as Li-Kan, taken to be a corruption of "Reqem". Nabatean power seemed limitless, and even when **Pompey** sent troops against Petra in 62 BC, the Nabateans were able to buy peace from the Roman Empire for the price of three hundred talents of silver. Petran prosperity grew and grew.

Petra's golden age

The first centuries BC and AD saw Petra at its zenith, with a settled population of perhaps as many as 30,000. The Roman author **Strabo** describes it as a wealthy, cosmopolitan city, full of fine buildings and villas, gardens and watercourses, with Romans and other foreigners thronging the streets, and a democratic king. "The Nabateans," reported Strabo, "are so acquisitive that they give honours to those who increase their possessions, and publicly fine those who lose them." However, the writing was on the wall. The discovery of the monsoon winds had begun to cause a shift in trade patterns: overland routes from Arabia were being abandoned in favour of transport by **sea**. In addition, Rome was sponsoring the diversion of inland trade away from the upstart Petra, instead directing it into Egypt and via the Wadi Sirhan into Syria, presaging the rise of **Palmyra**. Pressure on Nabatea to come to heel was inexorable. The last Nabatean king, **Rabbel II**, tried moving his capital from Petra north to Bosra, but eventually had to strike a deal with Rome. On his death in 106 AD the entire Nabatean kingdom passed peacefully into Roman hands.

The Roman, Byzantine and Crusader eras

Under the **Romans**, Petra became a principal centre of the new Provincia Arabia, and seems to have undergone something of a cultural renaissance, with the theatre and Colonnaded Street both being renovated. The city was important enough to be visited by Emperor **Hadrian** in 130 AD, and possibly also by Emperor **Severus** in 199. However, the tide of history was turning, and by 300 Petra was in serious decline, with houses and temples falling derelict through lack of maintenance. Palmyra, an oasis entrepôt in the eastern Syrian desert, was on the ascendant, and sea trade into Egypt was well established; Petra was stuck between the two, and there was no reason to keep it alive. Roman patronage began to drift away from the city, and, sensing the party was over, entrepreneurs and merchants followed.

Petra's decline was drawn out. **Christianity** was adopted as the official religion of the empire in 324, but for many decades after that the proud Nabateans mingled elements of the new faith with remnants of their own pagan heritage. The massive earthquake of 363, according to the contemporary bishop of Jerusalem, levelled half of Petra, although the city limped on for another couple of centuries. In 447, the **Urn Tomb** was converted into a huge church, and both the lavishly decorated **Petra Church** and plainer **Ridge Church** were built within the following century or so. Nonetheless, by the time of the seventh-century Islamic invasion, Petra was more or less deserted, and the earthquake of 749 probably forced the final stragglers to depart the crumbling city.

On their push through Transjordan in the early twelfth century, the **Crusaders** built small forts within Petra at **Al-Habees** and **Wu'ayra**, though these were tiny outposts of their headquarters at nearby Shobak and were abandoned less than a century later. In 1276, the **Mamluke** sultan Baybars – on his way from Cairo to suppress a revolt in Karak – entered Petra from the southwest and proceeded through the deserted city "amidst most marvellous caves, the facades

Jean Louis Burckhardt was born in Lausanne, Switzerland, in 1784, son of a colonel in the French army, and became a strong-willed and energetic teenager. He travelled to London when he was 22 and shortly after came under the wing of the Association for Promoting the Discovery of the Interior Parts of Africa, which offered him the mission of discovering the source of the River Niger. Burckhardt accepted. Then, as now, Egypt was the gateway into Africa, and so he devised a plan to familiarize himself with Islam and Arab culture in preparation for the expedition. Journeys into the Middle East at this time were seen, with some justification, as extremely dangerous: the territory was virtually unknown and local people (few of whom had ever seen Europeans) were engaged in continuous tribal skirmishing and were highly suspicious of outsiders. While still in England, Burckhardt embarked on crash courses in Arabic, astronomy and medicine, and took to sleeping on the ground and eating nothing but vegetables to toughen himself up.

On arrival in Aleppo in 1810, locals immediately questioned him about his strange accent. Burckhardt told his cover story: that he was a Muslim trader from India and his mother tongue wasn't Arabic but Hindustani. Suspicion persisted, and he was pressed to say something in Hindustani, whereupon he let loose a volley of fluent Swiss-German – which seemed to satisfy the doubters. Burckhardt spent over two years in Aleppo, adopting local customs, taking the name **Sheikh Ibrahim ibn Abdallah**, perfecting his Arabic and becoming enough of an expert in Quranic law that disputes were often brought to him for resolution.

In 1812, Burckhardt set off for Cairo, recording everything that he saw and experienced in a **secret journal**: had he been found out, no doubt he would have been killed as a spy. Around Karak, he heard the locals talking of an amazing ancient city locked away in the heart of an impenetrable mountain. His curiosity was aroused, but there was no way he could openly declare an interest without bringing suspicion onto himself: a genuine devotee of Islam would know that such ruins were the work of infidels and of no concern. Burckhardt made up a story that he had vowed to sacrifice a goat at the shrine of the Prophet Aaron atop Jebel Haroun near the ruins: an unimpeachably honourable motive for pressing on.

As he and his guide approached Wadi Musa (then known by its old name of **Elji**), they were stopped by the Liyathneh tribe, camped near Ain Musa, who tried to persuade them to sacrifice their goat there and then, with the white shrine in plain view on the distant summit. But Sheikh Ibrahim insisted on going on, much to the irritation of his guide. They went down the steep hill, on into the Siq, and soon came up to the Treasury. Burckhardt, concealing both his excitement and his journal, somehow managed to make detailed notes and a sketch of the facade, and they continued throughout the city in this way, Burckhardt writing and sketching in secret, his guide becoming ever more suspicious. They reached the foot of Jebel Haroun as dusk was falling, and Burckhardt finally submitted to his guide's insistence that they make the sacrifice and turn back. He had seen enough.

After Petra, Burckhardt's adventures continued: he arrived in Cairo to prepare for his great African expedition, but quickly got tangled in bureaucracy. While cooling his heels, he travelled deep into Nubia, crossed the Red Sea to Jeddah (and was probably the first Christian ever to enter Mecca, where he made a profound impression on the religious judge of the city with his Quranic learning), and explored Sinai, but back in Egypt in 1817, he contracted dysentery and died in eleven days, with his journey to the Niger not even begun. All Burckhardt's journals were published after his death, *Travels in Nubia* and *Travels in Arabia* overshadowed by the news of his rediscovery of Petra, published in 1822 in **Travels in Syria and the Holy Land**. His **grave**, bearing his pseudonym Sheikh Ibrahim, is visitable in a Muslim cemetery in Cairo. Its existence shows that, far from being simply a game or ploy, Burckhardt's *alter ego* took on a genuine life of its own.

sculptured into the very rock face". He emerged from the Siq on June 6, 1276, and, as far as records show, was the last person, other than the local Bedouin, to see Petra for over five hundred years.

The modern era
On August 22, 1812, a Swiss scholar and explorer, Jean Louis **Burckhardt** (see box), entered the Siq in heavy Arab disguise in the company of a local guide. His short visit, and the notes and sketches he managed to make in secret, brought the fable of Petra to the attention of the world once again. In May 1818, two commanders of the British Royal Navy, Charles Irby and James Mangles, spent some days sightseeing in the ancient city, but it was the visits of **Léon de Laborde** in 1826 and the British artist **David Roberts** in 1839 that first brought plentiful images of Petra to the West. Laborde's engravings were often fanciful and cloyingly romanticized, but Roberts's drawings were relatively accurate. As well as helping to shape the legend of Petra in Western minds – **Burgon**'s oft-quoted line about the "rose-red city" (see the box on p.352) appeared within a few years – they also launched tourism to the place. The second half of the nineteenth century saw a steady trickle of earnest visitors, even though Petra was still a destination way off any beaten tracks, reached only with extreme hardship by horse or camel from Jerusalem. Serious archeological investigation began at the turn of the century, with specialists cataloguing all Petra's monuments in 1898 and producing the first accurate maps in 1925.

By this time, the Thomas Cook Travel Company had set up a camp in Petra for European tourists, offering the choice of tent or cave accommodation; until a regular bus service from Amman began in 1980, facilities around the site remained minimal. Wadi Musa town was a backwater, despite the designation of Petra as a national park. In the early 1980s, after protracted but fruitless negotiations, the government ordered the **Bdul** tribe (see p.358), who had been resident in Petra's caves for as long as anyone could remember, to move out to **Umm Sayhoun**, a purpose-built settlement of small breeze-block houses 4km from both Petra itself and the town of Wadi Musa. The prospect of electricity, running water, health care and better education for the kids proved irresistible, and, in dribs and drabs, the Bdul departed. Development of the site and archeological exploration then took off, and recent years have seen a host of new projects, ranging from ongoing digs at several sites to major engineering works to repave the Siq and beautify Wadi Musa town.

Wadi Musa

WADI MUSA is an anomaly, a dusty southern Jordanian town much like any other, given an unfamiliar twist with lots of signs in English, a huge number of hotels and a noticeable diminution in the usual hospitality towards foreigners. In sharp contrast to the rest of Jordan, where decency and respect are the unswerving norm, Wadi Musa shows an unusual tendency towards rip-offs, wheedling, and outright hassle, all too often overcharging and under-delivering. If you stay for a little while you may pick up on the town's rather sad air of powerlessness. This is epitomized by the local farmers and small-business-people who are well aware that their hands are tied (either by decision-makers who don't always put local interests first or by regional instability that can decimate the town's income for months on end), and exemplified by the jerry-built hotels serviced by bored, lonely guest workers from Egypt and northern Jordan, who see little of the whirlwinds of cash that blow into town with every tour bus.

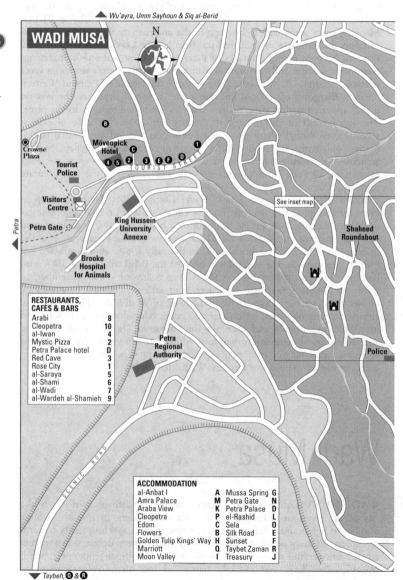

▲ Wu'ayra, Umm Sayhoun & Siq al-Berid

WADI MUSA

N

Crowne Plaza

Mövenpick Hotel

Tourist Police

Visitors' Centre

Petra Gate ⊕

Brooke Hospital for Animals

TOURIST STREET

King Hussein University Annexe

See inset map

Shaheed Roundabout

Petra Regional Authority

Police

Petra

RESTAURANTS, CAFÉS & BARS

Arabi	8
Cleopatra	10
al-Iwan	4
Mystic Pizza	2
Petra Palace hotel	D
Red Cave	3
Rose City	1
al-Saraya	5
al-Shami	6
al-Wadi	7
al-Wardeh al-Shamieh	9

SCENIC ROAD

ACCOMMODATION

al-Anbat I	A	Mussa Spring	G	
Amra Palace	M	Petra Gate	N	
Araba View	K	Petra Palace	D	
Cleopatra	P	el-Rashid	L	
Edom	C	Sela	O	
Flowers	B	Silk Road	E	
Golden Tulip Kings' Way	H	Sunset	F	
Marriott	Q	Taybet Zaman	R	
Moon Valley	I	Treasury	J	

▼ Taybeh, Q & R

Arrival

All roads into Wadi Musa meet just above **Ain Musa**, the spring in the hills to the east of Petra, marked by a small triple-domed building sheltering a rock – traditionally, the rock struck in anger by Moses – from beneath which the spring emerges. From here, the whole of Wadi Musa town is strung out for 4km along a main road which heads downhill all the way, eventually terminating at the ticket gate into Petra.

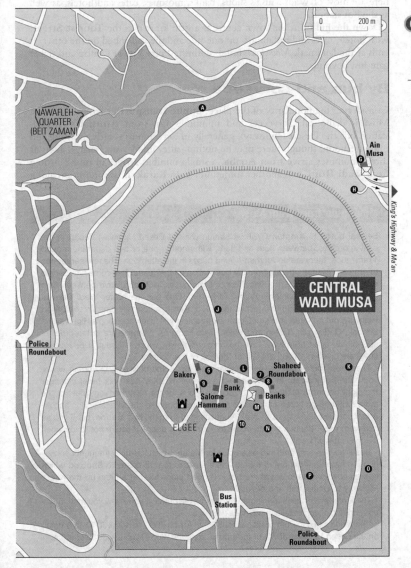

From Ain Musa the road heads down into Wadi Musa, with spectacular views out over the distant craggy mountains. Partway down is an intersection known as the **Police Roundabout** (Wadi Musa's police station is alongside it), from where a turn-off heads left through residential districts towards the neighbouring village of Taybeh and eventually out of town, passing big hotels such as the *Marriott* on the way.

The centre of Wadi Musa, just below the police intersection, is marked by the small **Shaheed Roundabout**, although there are no signs naming it (it's often dubbed the Central, or Midtown, Roundabout instead). Clustered near here are most of Wadi Musa's shops, banks, mosques, cafés and hotels, as well as the bus station.

Down the hill from the town centre is a strip known as the **Tourist Street**, with hotels, cafés and restaurants on one side and the valley bed on the other. It ends at the landmark *Mövenpick* hotel, with the Petra Visitor Centre and ticket gate just beyond.

By bus and serveece

Considering the popularity of the place, **public transport** provision for Wadi Musa is diabolical. Serveeces and minibuses run from **Amman**'s Wihdat station (via the Desert Highway), generally in two clumps – early morning and mid-afternoon, though there may be nothing after midday on Fridays. Two or three minibuses arrive from **Aqaba**, a single minibus arrives in mid-morning from **Wadi Rum**, and another sometimes from **Karak** in late afternoon along

---

Moving on from Wadi Musa

Several buses to **Amman**'s Wihdat station (via the Desert Highway) depart in the early mornings, between 6am and 8am, with another one or two departing around 11am–noon; there are no Amman-bound buses in the afternoon. The few **serveeces** to Amman (Wihdat) operate from the bus station on their usual first-come first-served basis, also in the early morning. Two or three buses to **Aqaba** leave between 6am and 8am, plus another one at around 3–4pm. One bus leaves for **Wadi Rum** at about 6am. Also around 6am, a bus leaves for **Karak**; it normally runs via the Desert Highway, but on request from at least six people it will follow the King's Highway via Shobak, Qadisiyyeh, Tafileh and Wadi Hasa. Fares for all these are in the order of JD3–3.500, apart from Karak via the King's Highway, which is about JD6. Journey times are given in "Travel details" at the end of this chapter.

These few routes are all very popular, and this is the only time in Jordan where you must **book seats in advance** for a normal minibus. Ask your hotel manager the night before to reserve you a place on a bus for the next morning: most of the more switched-on hotels can do this as a matter of course (the *Mussa Spring* and *al-Anbat* certainly know what's what). All buses start from the **bus station**, but if you've reserved a seat the bus should come to your hotel's door – if you're not ready when it arrives, it won't wait.

Buses leave hourly until mid-afternoon for **Ma'an**, which has fairly frequent connections to Amman, Aqaba and Karak. There are also regular buses to **Shobak**, which has no connections to anywhere but is a good place to start a hitch up the King's Highway to Qadisiyyeh and beyond.

There are fewer buses running on Fridays on all routes. If you know you must travel on a Friday, check details in advance with your hotel.

Chartering a **taxi** to Rum costs about JD25, to Aqaba JD30, to Karak JD40, to Amman on the Desert Highway JD50, or to Amman along the King's Highway JD80 or more.

with the private bus operated by the *Mariam Hotel* in **Madaba** (see p.281 for full details). More frequent minibuses arrive from **Ma'an** and **Shobak**, but these towns are hardly high on most visitors' agenda.

The **bus station** is in the centre of town, down the hill behind the main mosque about 300m south of the Shaheed Roundabout. Instead of being dropped here, you could ask the driver to let you out at the hotel of your choice along the way. In theory, the same thing happens in a **serveece**, but you're more likely to find that the driver "recommends" a particular hotel by taking you to the door. Feel free to accept or decline, but be aware that he does this to earn a commission from the hotel, who will correspondingly charge you a little more for your room. See p.158 for details of similar scams employed by some Wadi Musa serveece drivers.

By car

From Amman, the fastest route to Petra is 235km, safely driveable in around two and a half hours (without stops). Head south from 7th or 8th Circle on the **Desert Highway** past the airport: after 180km you'll come to the **Unayza** junction, which has a signposted turn-off to Petra. From here, a smooth, upgraded road takes you quickly and easily on to Wadi Musa through Shobak, partway along joining the King's Highway. Follow it straight all the way and it delivers you to Ain Musa. However, this is not the most scenic of approaches, and there is a much more beautiful **back road** which gives a better flavour of Petra's natural environment. About 16km south of Shobak town, you'll see a right turn signposted to Abdalih and the Ammareen campsite. This narrow, twisting road leads through the trees up to the crest of a ridge, where you suddenly get expansive views out over the valley floor and the jagged peaks beyond, including Jebel Haroun. Carry on down the other side (the straight line of a road visible on the valley floor points directly at a cleft in the mountains – this is "Little Petra"; see p.375). Take the signposted left turn just before you reach Little Petra (10km from the King's Highway), and you enter Wadi Musa the back way, passing through rolling desert terrain and the Bdul village at Umm Sayhoun before ending up, 8km on, at the *Mövenpick* hotel.

Coming **from Aqaba or Rum**, the left turn off the main highway, just as you crest the plateau at Ras an-Naqab, forms the southernmost stretch of the King's Highway and takes you across the rolling fields to the village of **Taybeh**; from here, the road, unofficially known as the **Scenic Road**, clings to the cliffside, passing several big hotels and some spectacular views over the Petra mountains until it arrives at the Police Roundabout in central Wadi Musa. Note that some **maps** mark a road into Wadi Musa from Gharandal, in Wadi Araba, via Dilagha: this is an unsurfaced road, and is only passable in a 4x4.

From Ma'an, the quickest route is the road through **Udhruh**, which meets the Shobak road just above Ain Musa: 33km in total.

Town transport

The only means of transport in town are **taxis**. The two main companies are al-Anbat (☏03/215 6777) and al-Hilali (☏03/215 6600); there are always plenty of taxis sharking around the streets. The standard flat rate for a ride anywhere in town – from the Petra ticket gate to Ain Musa or anywhere in between – is JD1 in theory, JD2 in practice; you'll have to bargain hard each time. The two-kilometre **walk** along the main road down from the town centre to the Petra gate is easy, but it's a rare individual who, after a day of walking in Petra, is prepared to walk back up the steep hill into town. Some hotels – in all price brackets – do **free transport** to and from the gate in the morning and the evening; it's worth checking in advance on timings and availability.

Accommodation

In keeping with Petra's status as Jordan's top attraction, Wadi Musa has **accommodation** to suit all budgets. There are around seventy hotels to choose from, many of them drab mid-range places flung up quickly without much attention paid to style or comfort: our recommendations pick out the best. Low-budget travellers are well catered for, with several recommendable places, and the few luxury hotels are acceptable, if rarely outstanding.

Wadi Musa's hotel prices are more open to **bargaining** than anywhere else in Jordan, especially in the low seasons (June–Aug and Nov–Feb). **En-suite bathrooms** are offered as standard in virtually all hotels, from budget upwards. Another feature of Wadi Musa is that all hotels have **rates** for room only, bed and breakfast, and half-board (breakfast and dinner), although meals in some of the smaller places can be skimpy: make sure you confirm what you want when you check in.

Campsite

The only **campsite** in the Petra area is the *Ammareen Camp* (☏07/9566 7771, ℻06/461 6787, ⊛www.bedouincamp.net), a Bedouin-style permanent encampment run by the Ammareen tribe, and located in a beautiful, quiet spot out near Siq al-Berid, or "Little Petra" (see p.375). It is well signposted from the King's Highway and in Wadi Musa: from the Little Petra access road, you turn off at the signpost and drive for 1km on a marked dust-track to reach the campsite, which is tucked away out of site behind a crag. A **taxi** here from Wadi Musa would cost about JD6.

The site has a series of long, low Bedouin goat-hair tents divided up into sections and given concrete floors: you sleep on reasonably comfortable beds with mattresses, and there is a block with proper, flushing toilets plus hot and cold running water. The big plus is that you are completely away from the hustle and bustle of Wadi Musa, nestling in amongst the mountains under a starry sky.

The basic rate for just sleeping here without meals puts it into the lower end of our ❷ bracket. With a day's advance notice the staff can lay on any meal you like: dinner and breakfast would add about JD15 to the basic rate. It's pricey, but the experience is wonderful – and being able to escape from Wadi Musa for a night or two is a great relief.

Budget hotels

The main thing to look out for in a **budget hotel** in Wadi Musa is **heating**: summer nights are cool enough, but all during winter and even as late as April, mornings and evenings can be very chilly. Most of these hotels have some double-bed rooms, but you won't find a soft mattress at any of them. **Location** is also an issue: the two best options (*Al-Anbat I* and *Mussa Spring*) are at the top of the valley, a long way from the cafés and shops in the town centre – you

Warning

Women travellers should be aware that some of the cheap hotels in the centre of Wadi Musa have had allegations of sexual harassment levelled at them, ranging from verbal coarseness to bedroom break-ins and, in one case, rape. All of the places we list are trustworthy and reliable; **if a hotel isn't reviewed here, it isn't worth your attention.** Male hotel staff have also been known to offer to show tourists some remote spot or great view, or invite guests to an evening meal at their special desert campsite. Women on their own in Wadi Musa should never accept such an offer.

may see this as a blessing, of course. They both offer free transport to and from the Petra ticket gate.

Incidentally, the large sign at Ain Musa pointing to the "Petra Youth Hostel" is misleading; the building, which in fact lies around 10km from the centre of town off the Scenic Road to Taybeh, is an institutional *Bayt ash-Shbab* (Youth Centre), and is not set up for tourists.

All these hotels are keyed on the **map** on p.332.

Al-Anbat I ☎03/215 6265, ℗215 6888, ℮info@alanbat.jo, ⓦwww.alanbat.jo. Great value, with friendly service, well-equipped rooms (in the main building and the four-floor rear extension) and a cosy atmosphere. Free transport to and from the gate, a place to pitch a tent and a good restaurant add to the appeal. There are more good rooms in the town centre at the *Al-Anbat II* annexe. ❶–❷

Araba View ☎ & ℗03/215 6107. Simple rooms, with Wadi Musa's best views from the rear balcony. Good value, but lack of heating lets it down. Go for the en-suite rooms on the upper floor. ❷

Cleopetra ☎ & ℗03/215 7090. One of the better cheapies, cleaner than most and reasonable value. Free transport to and from the gate. ❷

Moon Valley ☎03/215 6824, ℗215 7131, ℮moon-valley-hotel@yahoo.com. An excellent choice under fresh management, with a reputation to uphold, good facilities and information, and friendly staff. ❷

Mussa Spring ☎03/215 6310, ℗215 6910, ℮musaspring_hotel@yahoo.co.uk. Longstanding backpackers' favourite, situated right up beside Ain Musa, with friendly, efficient staff and a sociable atmosphere. Rooms are clean and comfortable, with phone and TV: singles, doubles

and dorms, both en suite and with shared bathrooms. "Student" rooms are the cheapest of the lot, and still better than at a lot of other Wadi Musa hotels. Rates include free transport to and from the gate, but breakfast is extra (JD1.500). With notice, staff can put together a reasonably substantial lunchbox for you (JD2), and the dinner buffet costs a bargain JD3.500. There's also a budget rooftop sleep-in in summer, laundry facilities and cut-price overnight camping trips to Wadi Rum. ❶–❷

Petra Gate ☎ & ℗03/215 6908. Funky and friendly backpackerish-style hangout, with a pool table and good dinners. ❶–❷

el-Rashid ☎03/215 6800, ℗215 6801, ℮rashid@joinnet.com.jo. Decent option overlooking the central roundabout, with very clean, cosy and quiet rooms. Excellent value. ❷–❸

Sunset ☎03/215 6579, ℗215 6950. The only remotely budget-like choice on the tourist strip close to the gate, but you pay for the location: rooms are all en suite but small and grimy, and dinner is JD5 extra. ❷

Treasury ☎ & ℗03/215 7274. Quiet place up dozens of stairs in a residential neighbourhood well off the main drag. Great views temper its characterlessness a little. ❷

Mid-range hotels

There's a huge number of **mid-range** hotels in Wadi Musa, almost all of them existing for tour-group business. Rates for individuals are frequently much higher but you can limit the damage by reserving well ahead; if you arrive without a reservation, it pays to shop around. Hotels close to the gate charge considerably more than those back in town.

All the places listed below accept major credit cards and are shown on the map on p.332.

Amra Palace ℡ 03/215 7070, ℻ 215 7071, ⓦ www.amrapalace.com. Decent, good-quality three-star hotel on a quiet backstreet in the town centre – big, too, with 72 rooms. It has air-conditioning, attractive pine decor and a lovely little palm-shaded garden, and there are plans to build a covered swimming pool. ❹

Edom ℡ 03/215 6995, ℻ 215 6994, ⓔ edom@go.com.jo. Three-star hotel that is the best value in this price range, with comfort, good service and some style. Prices can halve in the off season. ❺

Flowers ℡ 03/215 6771, ℻ 215 6770, ⓔ flowershotel@hotmail.com. Pleasant, comfort-able but cramped two-star rooms are slightly overpriced, but only because of the hotel's unbeat-able location, a short walk from the Petra gate. With on-the-ball management and a returning clientele of small-group hiking tour companies, it's popular and often full. ❹

Petra Palace ℡ 03/215 6723, ℻ 215 6724, ⓔ ppwnwm@go.com.jo. Rather pretentious pile on the main tourist strip down by the gate, lavish and sparkling on the outside, competent but humdrum within. All en suite, the rooms feature air con, mini-bars and the like, and there's a small swimming pool occupying an internal courtyard. Its location is the main attraction. ❺–❻

Sela ℡ 03/215 7170, ℻ 215 7173, ⓔ tariqsela -petra@yahoo.com, ⓦ www.sellahotel.com. Its 36 flamboyantly draped rooms are super-clean, cosy and reasonably priced. Very well kept, and open to bargaining ploys. A solid quality choice, also with a lift, but its location above the town centre does it down. ❹

Silk Road ℡ 03/215 7222, ℻ 215 7244, ⓔ petrasilkroad@hotmail.com. Characterful, pleasant hotel on the tourist strip down by the gate, frequently used by tour groups and excellent value for money. ❹

Luxury hotels

At the **luxury** end of the scale, two of Jordan's best hotels – the *Petra Mövenpick* and *Taybet Zaman* – compete with other big international chains such as Marriott, Crowne Plaza and Golden Tulip, some of them in the town centre, others out on the Scenic Road towards Taybeh.

All the places listed below accept major credit cards and are shown on the map on p.332.

Following the 1994 peace treaty with Israel, entrepreneurs quickly slapped a handful of luxury hotels onto the Scenic Road's hillside, with little regard for the environment, the views or basic engineering practice. Very soon it was realized that the road needed consolidation before it slipped into the valley: the works took three years to complete. Development was halted, but four blots on the landscape survived: the tacky *Grand View* (now suffering from subsidence and most of whose guest rooms face away from the view), the *Plaza* (taken over by Marriott), the undistinguished *Panorama*, and the *Nabatean Castle*, now under Mövenpick management.

Crowne Plaza ℡ 03/215 6266, ℻ 215 6977, ⓦ www.crowneplaza.com. A decent four-star hotel, located very close to the gate (a short stroll from the Visitor Centre), and a popular favourite with indi-viduals and upscale tour-groups alike. The design of the hotel is a bit old-fashioned (it was built in the 1980s), and rooms are comfortable but generic. It's worth visiting to hang out on their poolside, perched in front of the rocky ravines – especially at night when floodlights illuminate the mountains. Its *Guesthouse* annexe, sandwiched between the Visi-tor Centre and the gate, is less pricey, but is usually given over exclusively to tour groups. ❼–❾

Golden Tulip Kings' Way ℡ 03/215 6799, ℻ 215 6796, ⓦ www.goldentulip.com and ⓦ www.kingsway-petra.com. Classy four-star choice up at Ain Musa, with comfortable, spacious rooms and attentive service, although no free rides to the gate. An especially good choice in summer, when it can be noticeably cooler and more pleasant up here than down in town. ❻–❼

Marriott ℡ 03/215 6407, ℻ 215 7096, ⓦ www .marriott.com. An excellent five-star choice, located 4.5km from town high up on the Scenic Road, with spectacular views over the mountains. Public areas are comfortable but not excessively grand, and

About 11km south of Wadi Musa, the Scenic Road enters the quiet village of **Taybeh**, where, early in the 1990s, the company Jordan Tourism Investments was looking for some old buildings to renovate for hotel conversion. In consultation with the village council, the mayor of Taybeh offered his town – mostly modern buildings but with a crumbling Ottoman quarter on the hillside below – for the experiment on a profit-sharing basis. The residents of the old cottages were paid to depart, conversion began and **Taybet Zaman** was the incredible result, an environmentally sound, open-air luxury hotel, built to recreate the atmosphere of a nineteenth-century Jordanian village. Each old cottage is now a self-contained single or double "room", tastefully furnished and fitted out to international five-star standard; there are restaurants, bars, a pool, Turkish bath, shops and two heliports tucked away in different corners of the "village", which is separated off from the rest of workaday Taybeh by a high perimeter wall. The only thing lacking, of course, is any kind of original atmosphere, but certain things are impossible to recreate. Even if you don't stay, it's worth making it out here somehow, if only to savour a cold beer while marvelling at the audacity of it all. Local buses shuttle back and forth from Wadi Musa to Taybeh village for pennies; a taxi is around JD5.

Hoping to capitalize on such success, the same company took over the old Nawafleh quarter of Wadi Musa for conversion into **Beit Zaman**, a similar five-star hotel of refurbished stone cottages. Completed in 2000, its grand opening was scotched by the outbreak of the Palestinian *intifada* that autumn, and the virtually unused hotel remained closed in 2005 at the time of writing. It remains to be seen whether it will ever re-open.

---

there's a good swimming pool with a panoramic view across the valley. Rooms are good, with big windows, well-appointed bathrooms and large beds. Service is outstanding – perhaps the best in Wadi Musa. ⑦–⑨

Mövenpick ☎03/215 7111, ℱ215 7112, ⓦwww.movenpick-petra.com. One of the Middle East's finest hotels, superbly designed in traditional Damascene style right down to the last exquisite detail. The stunning four-storey courtyard atrium, with its mosaic-tiled fountain and palm trees, is perhaps the most striking public interior in the country, vying for gasps with the adjacent bar, its hand-painted walls inlaid with turquoise and gold leaf, and featuring hand-carved wooden screens and embroidered fabrics. The guest rooms are immaculate, service is calm, friendly and efficient, and the location – metres from the Petra gate – ideal. Don't miss the roof garden or the spectacular, and surprisingly affordable, buffet restaurant (see p.341). Its sister property, the similarly grand *Mövenpick Nabatean Castle*, located 6.5km out on the Scenic Road (and bookable through the main hotel), remained closed at the time of writing for long-term renovations. ⑦–⑨

Taybet Zaman ☎03/215 0111, ℱ215 0101. Award-winning luxury hotel built on the old Ottoman quarter of the village of Taybeh, 11km from Wadi Musa; see box for more information. All the spacious renovated cottages feature distinctive interior design and are equipped with every five-star facility; you couldn't want for anything more. ⑧–⑨

The Town

There's not a great deal to do in **Wadi Musa**. However, the local authorities have been trying to develop the place for years, and there is now, in the town centre, a little artisans' quarter of restored stone cottages – which had lain abandoned since 1950 – named **Elgee** (the original name for the Wadi Musa settlement). It can be pleasant to spend a bit of time wandering here, exploring the workshops and browsing amongst the moderately priced handicrafts and traditional jewellery.

Overlooking the Shaheed Roundabout is a small multi-level **shopping mall**, with a few clothes outlets and mobile-phone shops (and, on an upper level, the main **post office**). Down on the Tourist Street near the gate is a string of **souvenir shops**, selling postcards and trinkets as well as rugs and antiques; as you might expect, prices here are sky-high. One notable exception is the **Made In Jordan** gallery and gift shop, run by the Petra Moon tour company, which is located on the Tourist Street by the *Petra Palace* hotel; ask them for access. The crafts for sale here come from suppliers such as the Royal Society for the Conservation of Nature (RSCN), the Jordan River Foundation, the Noor al-Hussein Foundation and the Jordan Royal Ecological Diving Society (JREDS) – all of which employ chiefly rural women (in JREDS' case, the wives and daughters of Aqaba fishermen) to produce traditional crafts and handmade items of the highest quality. Also on show are pieces produced by individual artisans and artists from Wadi Musa and around Jordan.

The same building hosts the **Petra Kitchen**, an idea (also by Petra Moon) to give added perspective to a Petra visit. This is not a restaurant; rather, it is a way for a small number of visitors at a time to get hands-on experience of local culture by working with a team of Wadi Musa women to prepare ingredients, cook an evening meal and then eat together. For JD30 per

---

Petra tour companies and guides

Down on the "Tourist Street" near the Petra ticket gate are a trio of reliable, experienced and well-respected tour companies. **Petra Moon** (℡03/215 6665, ℻215 6666, ⓦ www.petramoon.com) and **La Beduina** (℡03/215 7099, ℻215 6931, ⓦ www .labeduinatours.com) both specialize in eco-tours and adventure tourism throughout southern Jordan, and, with notice, can arrange just about any event, anywhere, from mountain-biking to a silver-service banquet in the desert. Both concentrate on hiking-based expeditions, and can put together any number of routes around Petra, Dana and Rum, with guides and full trail support. A sample of other ideas includes a 2hr sunset horse-ride at Baydha, including a break for tea, for about JD25; a full day's horse-riding in the hills for two people, including a guide and lunch, for about JD230; or a five-night journey on horseback between Petra and Rum, complete with full support (meals, accommodation, guides, and so on), for JD800 or so. For about JD250, they'll organize a two-day camel trek for two people to Jebel Haroun and Sabra, including camels, food, camping gear and a guide. The third company in the trio is **Zaman Tours** (℡03/215 7723, ℻215 7722, ⓦ www.zamantours.com), offering similar experiences.

Three smaller operations, run by experienced individual guides in Wadi Musa and focused mainly on hiking and low-key wilderness exploration, are **Jordan Beauty Tours**, run by Sufian Amarat (mobile ℡07/9558 1644 or 7728 2730, ℻03/215 4999, ⓦ www.jordanbeauty.com), **Jordan Inspiration Tours**, run by Sami Hasanat (mobile ℡07/9555 4677, ℻03/215 7317, ⓦ www.jitours.com) and **Mahdi Hasanat** (℡03/215 7893, mobile ℡07/7742 7380, Ⓔ mhasanat18@hotmail.com, ⓦ mahtours.tripod .com). See details of some trips run by these guides at ⓦ www.jordanjubilee .com.

For an out-of-the-ordinary experience, contact the **Ammareen tribe** through their campsite at "Little Petra" (℡07/9566 7771, ⓦ www.bedouincamp.net; see also p.336): the website is very detailed, with material on Bedouin culture by anthropologist Rami Sajdi alongside details of a wide range of guided treks on foot and by camel through areas of Petra and southern Jordan little known to outsiders.

person, you get to see a demonstration of Arabic cooking, and then roll up your sleeves to start chopping, mixing and assembling a range of salads, soup, hot and cold *mezze* (starters), a main course such as *mansaf*, *maqlouba* or kebabs and Bedouin coffee and tea, the idea being that you learn new culinary techniques, handle unfamiliar products and break the social ice at the same time. The ingredients all come from Wadi Musa or the nearby Dana Nature Reserve; the tableware comes from the women's ceramics workshop at Iraq al-Amir near Amman; and the aprons, tablecloths and napkins were all hand-embroidered by women working with the Jordan River Foundation. To take part you must **book in advance** with the Petra Moon tour company (T03/215 6665, F215 6666, Wwww.petramoon.com) at least one or two days ahead. They can also extend the concept to run as a five-day **culinary course**, including exploratory buying trips around local markets and different menus each night.

Eating and drinking

For **eating in Wadi Musa**, most travellers stick with whatever's on offer in their hotel, although a handful of unabashedly overpriced town diners are worth checking out, and the *Mövenpick*'s buffet has to be seen to be believed. As usual, the only places for **drinking alcohol** are in the big hotels or a couple of specifically designated bars in town.

All places listed are shown on the map on p.332.

Arabi One of Wadi Musa's best local restaurants, located just up from the main roundabout. It's always busy, and does a wide range of Arabic dishes – all kinds of falafel, hummus, fuul, salads, kebabs and more, served with hot, fresh bread. The place is clean, staff are friendly, prices are low: a meal shouldn't cost you more than JD3. Daily 6am–11pm.

Cleopatra restaurant Not to be confused with the *Cleopatra* hotel, this is an OK diner, empty during the day but often crowded with *shwarma*-munching locals at night. Avoid the rather tasteless buffet meals, however. Daily 6am–11pm.

Mövenpick hotel T03/215 7111. The hotel boasts two different restaurants. The *al-Saraya* (daily 6.30–10.30pm) has a lavish buffet, from fresh vegetables wok-fried as you watch, through gourmet breads, superb kebabs, fresh fish and an array of salads to proper Black Forest gateau, everything top quality. It's not cheap (around JD16), but the quality and variety are excellent. For a cut-price deal of all-you-can-eat soup and salad ask the maitre-d as you walk in: when it's on, this can cost as little as JD6. When there is enough business – that is, when they have a tour group who aren't inside Petra – they also do a buffet lunch here (noon–3.30pm; around JD13). Alongside, but several notches up the scale, *al-Iwan* (daily 7–10.30pm) offers seriously sophisticated à la carte dining in a superbly designed space off the atrium for JD30 and up. In addition, the Mövenpick

bakery shop (daily 9am–7pm) boasts not only delicious fresh-baked wholegrain, nut and crusty white loaves, but also the best croissants this side of Beirut, a real espresso machine and Western-brand chocolate bars. If all this is beyond you, settle for Swiss ice cream or a milk-shake in the stunning atrium.

Mystic Pizza Amenable little place down near the gate, with pretty good pizza and pasta dishes for around JD4. Daily 10am–11pm.

Petra Palace hotel The town's liveliest bar (almost certainly because of its neon beer signs positioned prominently on the hotel strip by the gate), despite the fact that there are no beers on draught. Bottles of Amstel are around JD3.500, cans of Becks, Guinness or Kilkenny around JD5, or you could go for a bottle of a local brew, Petra – very strong at 8.0 percent, but only JD3 for a half-litre. Daily 2–11pm.

Red Cave T03/215 7799. A good choice, on the strip near the gate. The interior is large and cool, and the food is excellent, including – among many staple dishes – a Bedouin *gallaya* (rice with lamb or chicken in a spicy tomato/onion sauce). Reckon on a meal for around JD4. Daily 10am–11pm.

Rose City Restaurant Close to the gate, a basic, inexpensive diner with an all-day buffet and a handful of à la carte staples. Daily 6.30am–11pm.

al-Shami Excellent sweet and savoury pastries and *manaqeesh*, along with the usual staples, fairly priced. Daily 6am–11pm.

The only facilities for **eating** once you get **inside Petra** are expensive and/or of low quality. There are a handful of **tent cafés** along the path from the theatre to the Qasr al-Bint offering meagre buffets for JD6 or so, and inadequate JD4 "boxed lunches" (little more than bread, cheese and an orange) – poor sustenance for the amount of walking you're likely to be doing.

The only proper **restaurant** inside Petra is the canteen-style *Basin* (☎03/215 6266; daily 11.30am–3.30pm or so, depending on weather conditions), beneath shady tree cover opposite the Qasr al-Bint, owned by the *Crowne Plaza Hotel* and necessarily pricey considering they have to truck everything in. Buffet lunch costs almost JD9 (tax and service included), but, to be honest, the food isn't good enough to warrant the full shebang; lower your expectations and plump instead for salads and cold dishes only (JD6). It's not a bad idea to book in advance, since busy days can see tour-groups occupying every table. Their greatest service, frankly, is offering a cool, quiet corner where you can take the weight off your feet for the price of a coffee or a beer.

Your best option is to carry supplies with you for the day. Supermarkets and vegetable stalls in the centre of Wadi Musa can provide simple **picnic fare**, but nothing so energy-sustaining as nuts or dried fruit. The local bakers are up before dawn at the Sanabel Mechanical Bakeries just below the Shaheed Roundabout, doing the normal range of Arabic breads; for something different, try the Mövenpick's bakery shop, which does nutty wholegrain breads. Bear in mind that in the summer you'll need to be drinking four or five litres of **water** a day, possibly more; unless you can carry it all, you should budget on shelling out JD1 at the tent cafés for water or a soft drink to keep yourself hydrated along the way.

al-Wadi OK food, with good veggie choices, but more notable as the diviest bar in town, overlooking the central roundabout. Daily 6.30am–midnight.

al-Wardeh al-Shamieh A fine choice (also signed as *Shami Flower*), a friendly two-storey place in the town centre serving simple, good-quality Arabic food. Don't expect to pay the same price as the locals, however: an ordinary meal of hummus, chips and salad is likely to cost around JD3, twice that if you take a meaty main course. Daily 6.30am–11pm.

Listings

Banks You can change cash, traveller's cheques and get Visa advances at the Arab Bank (Sun–Thurs 8.30am–2.30pm, Fri 9–11am) in the Petra Visitors' Centre. Much the same services are offered at the Arab Bank, Housing Bank and Jordan Islamic Bank in the town centre (all Sun–Thurs 8.30am–1pm & 3.30–5pm), which all have ATMs.

Hammams Steam the day's dust out of your pores in a *hammam*, of which there are now a handful. In the town centre, the pleasant, salubrious but rather frenetic Salome (☎03/215 7342; daily 3–10pm; JD15) can do you the full sauna, massage, hot and cold shower treatment, as can the Petra Turkish Bath (☎03/215 7085; same hours; JD15). For an entirely different class of experience, check out the five-star *hammams* in the *Marriott* and at *Taybet Zaman*, both of them infinitely more regal and relaxed and not that much more expensive.

Hospital The large, well-equipped Queen Rania Hospital – with emergency facilities open 24hr – is located on the Scenic Road towards Taybeh, about 5km out of town.

Library With half a dozen books, the elegant, wood-panelled Burckhardt Library (daily 10am–10pm, roughly), on the mezzanine floor of the *Mövenpick*, barely counts as a place of study, but it's nonetheless a cool, peaceful spot for some quiet downtime and is just about the only place in Wadi Musa where nobody's trying to sell you something. One of the polished wood cabinets hides a free-to-use TV with satellite channels.

Pharmacy The Modern Petra Pharmacy (daily 8.30am–11pm), next to *al-Wardeh al-Shamieh* restaurant, has friendly, qualified English-speaking staff who give sensible advice.

Police In emergency, dial ☎191. Police are on 24hr, highly visible duty at Ain Musa and in most parts of the Petra ruins. Headquarters (☏03/215 6551) is off the Police Roundabout in Wadi Musa, where you can get your visa extended quickly and easily. There are also police offices next to the Petra ticket gate and at Al-Habees overlooking the Qasr al-Bint. English-speaking tourist police are available 24hr in their main office (☏03/215 6441) directly opposite the Visitors' Centre, and they're also on duty at the Visitors' Centre during opening hours.

Post offices There are three post offices in Wadi Musa, all open the same hours (daily 8am–5pm, Fri closes noon). Both the main town-centre office, just off the Shaheed Roundabout, and the branch office up at Ain Musa give small Wadi Musa postmarks, but the office 50m from the gate beside the police station is the only one with a Petra postmark.

Petra

After you've finished coping with the practicalities of bed and board in Wadi Musa, **PETRA** comes as an assault on the senses. As you leave the entrance gate behind, the sense of exposure to the elements is thrilling; the natural drama of the location, the sensuous colouring of the sandstone, the stillness, heat and clarity of light – along with a lingering, under-the-skin quality of supernatural power that seems to seep out of the rock – make it an unforgettable adventure.

Whether you're in a group or alone, you'd do well to branch off the main routes every now and again. These days, barring political upheavals elsewhere, Petra sees somewhere around half a million visitors annually – over two thousand daily, on average. The place is physically large enough to absorb that many people (although archeologists and environmentalists are both lobbying for controls on numbers), but the central path that runs past the major sights can get very busy between about 10am and 4pm. Taking a ten- or fifteen-minute detour to clamber around the rocks to either side of the path or explore interesting-looking side-valleys is a good idea, since not only does it instantly get you out of the crush, but it's also liable to yield previously unseen views and fascinating little carved niches or facades. All over Petra, the Nabateans carved for themselves paths and signposts, shrines and houses in what seem to us remote and desolate crags.

Practicalities

The **Petra Visitors' Centre** (daily 7am–10pm, with only security guards on duty after 5pm summer, 4pm winter; ☏03/215 6020), 50m from the gate, is the main office for help and information, with efficient, friendly staff and the tourist police on hand. Inside, there's also a **shop** for books, maps and souvenirs (same times). For advice on **eating and drinking** in Petra, see the box opposite.

One of the more unpleasant side-effects of the increasing popularity of Petra is the increasingly foul odour emanating from some of the ancient tombs. There are clean, well-maintained **public toilets** in the Visitors' Centre at the gate, in a converted cave more or less opposite the theatre, within the *Basin* restaurant and round the side of the Nazzal Camp building beside the Qasr al-Bint.

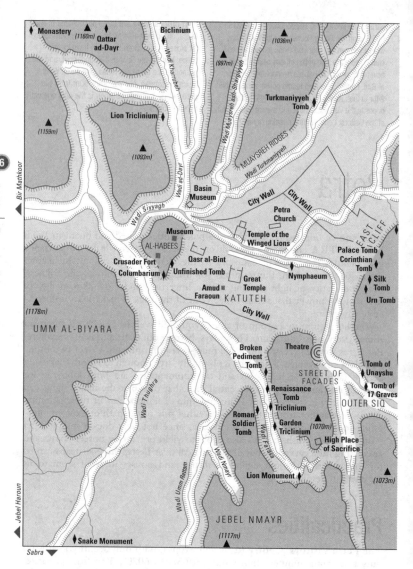

Tickets

All **tickets** are sold from a window beside the Visitors' Centre main door. Admission costs a mighty JD21 for one day, JD26 for two days, or JD31 for three or four days; this refers to blocks of consecutive days, with no chopping and changing allowed. Researchers and journalists pay full whack, students with valid ID and children under 12 pay half-price, Jordanians and foreign residents pay JD1, and only King Abdullah goes free. Tickets are dated, stamped and non-transferable (you have to sign multi-day passes and carry ID), and they're

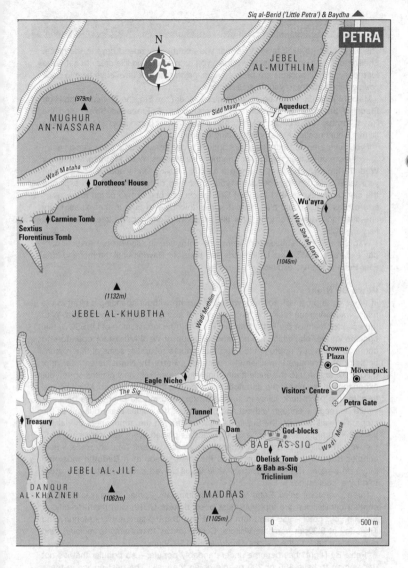

PETRA

JEBEL
AL-MUTHLIM

Sidd Maajn · Aqueduct

(979m)

MUGHUR
AN-NASSARA

Wadi Mataha

♦ Dorotheos' House

Wu'ayra

♦ Carmine Tomb

Sextius
Florentinus Tomb

(1046m)

(1132m)

JEBEL AL-KHUBTHA

Wadi Muthlim

Wadi Sha'ab Qays

Crowne
Plaza

Mövenpick

Eagle Niche

The Siq

Visitors' Centre

✚ Petra Gate

Tunnel

♦ Treasury

Dam · God-blocks

BAB AS-SIQ

Wadi Musa

Obelisk Tomb
& Bab as-Siq
Triclinium

JEBEL AL-JILF

DANQUR
AL-KHAZNEH

(1062m)

MADRAS

(1105m)

0 ——————— 500 m

checked at the gate, at the dam at the entrance to the Siq, and at varying points within Petra itself; even if you hike several kilometres out of the way to avoid the gate (some foolhardy folk endanger their lives doing just that), there's no guarantee a police officer won't pop up on some remote crag and ask to see your ticket. Even should you penetrate the mountain barrier, police stationed within Petra will certainly stop you when they see you walking in out of the desert. Note that Siq al-Berid ("Little Petra"), Baydha and, to all intents and purposes, Wu'ayra fall outside the (undefined) ticketed area, and so have free entry.

There's enough to explore in Petra that you could easily spend days in the place. Shelling out for a one-day ticket will have you running around like crazy to get value for money; if your pockets are deep enough, paying for four days buys time to pace yourself and explore to your heart's content.

Major **highlights**, which count as unmissable, are the **Siq**, the **Treasury**, the **High Place of Sacrifice**, the **Monastery**, a walk up the **Colonnaded Street**, and the **Royal Tombs**. With a break for lunch, and a little time for personal exploration, seeing all this would occupy a pretty exhausting ten-hour day.

If you have even one extra day, your options widen considerably. Choosing an entry or exit route other than the Siq for one trip – via **Madras**, **Wadi Muthlim/Mataha** or **Wadi Turkmaniyyeh** – can give you a feel for outlying landscapes. Depending on your taste for archeology or nature, you could then devote more time to exploring the city centre slopes and the East Cliff, or choose one or two of the many hikes and climbs. You should also budget some downtime to take in the extraordinary late-afternoon **views** from the Qasr al-Bint up the Colonnaded Street towards the fiery East Cliff.

With Siq al-Berid ("Little Petra") being free-entry, you should wait to take your half-day excursion to Wu'ayra, Little Petra and, possibly, Baydha until the morning after your Petra ticket has expired.

Petra By Night

In times gone by, a visit to Petra wasn't complete without spending a night in the ruins, wandering the rocky paths by moonlight and sleeping in a tomb cave. With the establishment of the Petra National Park and the intervention of UNESCO, this became impossible, which led an informal group of Wadi Musa tour operators to come up with a new approach to Petra that aims to recapture some of that romantic spirit of adventure – and largely succeeds. "**Petra By Night**" is an after-dark guided excursion into the ancient city that adds an entirely new dimension to your experience of the place; the **candlelit walk**, leaving the lights of Wadi Musa behind to enter the pitch-dark valley in silence (talking and mobile phones are banned), would be magical enough without adornment, but the guides really pull out all the stops. No walk through the Siq in daylight can match the atmosphere of walking through it at night, with only the light of candles placed every few metres to guide the way. The climax of the trip comes as you reach the still Treasury plaza, where candles throw flickering shadows onto the great facade as a **Bedouin musician** plays on a pipe. The magic lingers while tea is served and you listen to a **story** told by a local guide.

Three local companies, Petra Moon, La Beduina and Zaman Tours (see p.340 for contact details), run the trip; you must **book tickets** (JD12) with them directly, or through your hotel – you can't turn up and pay. The trip leaves every Monday and Thursday at **8.30pm** from the Visitors' Centre (arrive 15min early to register), and delivers you back to the Visitors' Centre around 10.30pm.

"Petra By Night" has become understandably popular – so popular that it's not uncommon to have 150 or 200 people doing the walk. The best advice in these circumstances is to stick right at the back of the crowd: if you ensure that you are the very last person in line, you'll avoid most of the chatter on the way down, and be walking through the Siq more or less alone in the moonlight. The Bedouin piper keeps playing until everyone has arrived at the Treasury, so you won't miss anything. Then there's nothing to stop you heading back early, before the crowd; this way, it's possible to find yourself the only person walking in the entire length of the Siq, alone, in silence, under the moon and the stars. It's a uniquely memorable experience.

For several years following the slump in tourism after 9/11, admission prices were halved to boost numbers. This policy was reversed in 2005, when it seemed clear that tourism was picking up. Should political instability in Jordan's neighbours cause another slump, it's possible that prices will be reduced again.

Round the corner from the Visitors' Centre is the **Petra gate**, the single public entrance into the site (open for admission daily 6am–5pm, winter closes 4pm; return permitted until dusk). Following increasing concern over the damage done by tourism, it is now forbidden for visitors to stay in Petra after sunset, and you'll be directed to start on the long walk out well in advance; it is, in any case, potentially dangerous to do some of the longer descents (such as from the Monastery or the High Place) in low light.

Guides

The Visitors' Centre is where you can hire a professional, accredited **guide**, at fixed prices (current rates are posted on the wall): a basic JD15 for a simple two-and-a-half-hour tour of the major sights, or JD35 for a genial, informative six-hour tour of the main central areas plus either the Monastery or the High Place of Sacrifice.

Although you can walk unguided to and from most of the main sights while staying this side of foolhardiness, there are still plenty of places in Petra where you definitely shouldn't venture without a guide. We've mentioned this in the accounts below where relevant. Aside from the dangers of twisted ankles (or worse) scrambling around rocky cliffs, once you leave the main routes it's easy to lose the path. A specialist guide for a day-trip to the summit of Jebel Haroun, or one of the other outlying attractions, will cost upwards of JD50.

Horses

The Visitors' Centre is also where you can book and pay for a **horse** to take you down to the Siq entrance, although at JD7 for a nine-hundred-metre walk, it's not much of a thrill. Bear in mind that, of this sum, JD5 goes to the owner of the horse (who is, almost without exception, not the person holding the reins) and JD2 goes to the Petra authorities. The only income gained by the handler is in tips.

It's forbidden to ride horses through the Siq, but a **horse and carriage** seating two can be taken all the way through the Siq to the Treasury for JD20 return – also bookable at the Visitors' Centre. These are officially reserved for the elderly and infirm, but in practice can be booked by anyone. The outbound leg is straightforward. For the return leg, there are always plenty of carriages waiting for business from tired sightseers as the afternoon draws on, but if you arrange with a particular carriage-driver to be at the Treasury at a set time for your return ride, he will turn up: his fee depends on it. Resist the temptation to copy the many weary visitors who just get into the first carriage they see; this a breach of honour, going back on the deal you made earlier in the day, and also leads to underhand competition between carriage-drivers to muscle in on each other's business. Ugly arguments over cash between two stalled carriages in the Siq are a feature of Petra afternoons. It is also possible to book at the Visitors' Centre for a carriage to take you all the way through Petra, past the Treasury and on down to the Basin Museum (JD40 return).

If you see a **horse** or **donkey** being mistreated, you can refer the matter to the Brooke Hospital for Animals (Sat–Thurs 8am–3pm; ☎03/215 6379, ⓦwww .thebrooke.org), an English-run charity located to the left of the gate.

The approach to the city

It's a walk of over 3km from the gate through to Petra's city centre, the gentle gradient of five percent concealing the fact that the drop in altitude (from 1027m to 861m) is equivalent to a 45-storey building – barely noticeable on the way down, but murder for tired thighs on the way back up. There are three main sections to the walk: the **Bab as-Siq** area, the **Siq** itself and the **Outer Siq**, which leads into the city centre past the Roman-style **theatre**.

If you have the option, you'd do well to start out as early as possible. The first tour groups set off by 8.30 or 9am, which brings them noisily through the echoing Siq to the Treasury as the sun strikes the facade (which you shouldn't miss). However, the experience of walking through the Siq in silence and alone is definitely worth at least one 6am start.

The Bab as-Siq

A modern gravel path – one side for horses, the other for pedestrians – leads from the gate down through a lunar landscape of extraordinary white rock domes and looming cliffs known as the **Bab as-Siq** (Gate of the Siq); the bed of the Wadi Musa, carrying water during the winter and early spring, curves alongside, with the offices of the Petra Regional Authority looking down from the clifftop high above. In all but the bleached-out midday hours, the light is soft enough to pick up earth tones of browns and beiges in the rock, but it's only with the last rays of the sunset that there's any hint of the pink that Petra is famous for.

Almost immediately, you can see evidence of Nabatean endeavour: three huge **god-blocks**, 6 to 8 metres high, loom next to the path just round the first corner, carved probably to serve as both representations of and repositories for the gods to stand sentinel over the city's vital water supply. Twenty-five such god-blocks exist in Petra, deemed by the locals to have been the work of *jinn*, or genies, and so also termed **jinn-blocks**; another name is **sahrij**, or water-tanks (ie tanks holding divine energy next to flowing water). The middle one has shaft graves cut into it, implying that it may also have served as some kind of funerary monument. Opposite the god-blocks are some caves, one of which has an obelisk carved in relief, representing the soul, or **nefesh**, of a dead person. Such carved shrines abound in every corner of Petra's mountains, and, for those with time to explore, the small side-valleys off this section of the Bab as-Siq are filled with tombs, water channels, niches and shrines: behind the blocks, the area of domes known as **Ramleh** is cut through by parallel wadis (one of which is Wadi Muthlim; see p.350), and is equally explorable.

The Obelisk Tomb and Bab as-Siq Triclinium

The first major Nabatean monuments are a few metres further on, and – being on an exposed corner – badly eroded. Although apparently the upper and lower halves of a single monument, the **Obelisk Tomb** and **Bab as-Siq Triclinium** may be separate entities, carved at different times. Above, four huge obelisks guard the entrance to a cave in the rock; such freestanding obelisks, as opposed to the *nefesh* in relief, are much like the god-blocks, both representing a god and storing divine energy in a material form. Between the four is an eroded figure in a niche, and the cave behind holds graves. The *triclinium*, or dining room, below is a single chamber with stone benches on three walls, for holding banquets in honour of the dead. On the opposite side of the path, 5m off the ground, is a bilingual **inscription** in Nabatean and Greek, recording that one

Nabatean religion

As much as they created a blend of Arab culture with Mediterranean, the Nabateans also blended inherited elements of the ancient **religions** of Egypt, Syria, Canaan, Assyria and Babylon with elements of the Greek and Roman pantheons, to create specifically Petran forms of worship.

Central to their religion was **rock**. Jehovah, the god of the Israelites, for example, was said to inhabit a blank rock called Bet-El, the House of God. This insistence on non-figurative representation was shared by many Levantine and Arabian peoples, and was passed on to the Nabateans (in stark contrast to the Egyptians' and Assyrians' lavish portrayals of gods and goddesses). Concepts such as "the Lord is my rock" also appear many times in the Old Testament, implying an extension of the "House of God" idea so that the rock actually represents the deity itself. Nabatean deities were thus often represented simply by squared-off rocks, termed "**god-blocks**". In addition, a later development gave the rock a third aspect: that of the altar, the contact point between the divine and the material.

At the head of the Nabatean pantheon was **Dushara**, "He of the Shara" (the mountains around Petra), later identified with the Greek god Zeus and the Syrian Hadad. The fact that his name is so closely tied to the locality indicates that he may originally have been an Edomite, rather than a Nabatean, god. To the Nabateans, Dushara was the sun, the primordial Light of the World, the Creator, and he was often represented by an obelisk – the visual materialization of a beam of light striking the earth. With the mingling of Semitic and Mediterranean ideas, Dushara also came to be associated with Dionysus, god of wine, and so began to assume human form, bedecked with vines and grapes (as at the Nabatean temple on Jebel Tannur).

At Dushara's side were **Atargatis**, the goddess of fertility, of grain, fruit and fish; **Allat** (which means simply "The Goddess"), who represented the moon; **Manat**, the goddess of luck and fate, suggested to have been the patron deity of Petra and possibly the goddess worshipped at the Treasury; and **al-Uzza** (The Mighty One), assimilated with the Egyptian goddess Isis and the Roman goddesses Diana, deity of water and fertility, and Venus, embodied by the evening star and representing spiritual and erotic love. Allat, al-Uzza and Manat are all mentioned by name in the Quran, implying that their cult was still active and popular in Mecca as late as the seventh century, the time of the Prophet Muhammad.

The Nabateans also had a plethora of smaller gods, including **al-Kutbay**, god of writing; **She'a-al-Qawm**, the patron deity of caravans; **Qos**, originally an Edomite god; and **Baal-Shamin**, a Phoenician god especially popular in northern Nabatea, who had a temple somewhere near the modern mosque in the centre of Wadi Musa town.

Abdmank chose this spot to build a tomb for himself and his children, although it's not certain that this refers to the monuments opposite.

Just past the Obelisk Tomb is a path leading to the hidden Petran suburb of **Madras**, tucked into the hills to the left (south), from where it's possible to cross the hilltops over the Jebel al-Jilf plateau, avoiding the Siq, to the top of the high, narrow Danqur al-Khazneh valley leading down to the Treasury; the views are stunning, and the sense of isolation is worth the scramble if you've already seen the Siq. However, the route is far from clear, relying on worn Nabatean rock-cut stairs, and you'll need a guide.

The dam and tunnel

Back on the path, the curving northern bank of the wadi is liberally pock-marked with caves and niches, round to the point where the path is taken over the wadi bed by a bridge and the Wadi Musa itself is blocked by a **dam**; this is almost exactly the same configuration as was built by the Nabateans in about 50 AD, and for the same reasons: to divert the floodwaters of the Wadi Musa away from the Siq so that the principal entry into the city could remain clear year round. It's here, at the mouth of the Siq, that all horse-riders must dismount and that entrance tickets will be checked. On the opposite bank of the wadi are four *nefesh* obelisks, one mentioning a man who lived in Reqem (Petra) but died in Jerash.

To the right, the Nabatean-carved, eight-metre-high **tunnel** – guarded by another, solitary god-block – enabled the floodwaters to feed into the **Wadi Muthlim** leading north around the gigantic Jebel al-Khubtha; today, this is an alternative way into Petra (see box).

The Siq

From the crowded, horse-smelly bridge, the path drops sharply down over the lip of the dam into Petra's most dramatic and awe-inspiring natural feature – the **Siq** gorge, principal entrance into the city, yet invisible until you're almost upon it. Overhead, the path was originally framed by an ornamental **arch**, which collapsed in 1896 although its abutments survive, decorated by the smoothed-out remnants of niches flanked by pilasters. All the way along the left-hand wall is a Nabatean rock-cut **water-channel**, and on the right-hand wall further along are the remains of terracotta pipes for water, both probably dating from the same time as the reorganization of the city water supply that prompted the

The Wadi Muthlim route

Although you should definitely follow the Siq into Petra at least once (and probably more than once, at different times of day), if you've allocated several days to a visit, the beautiful **Wadi Muthlim** is a wonderful alternative entry route through stunning scenery, peaceful and considerably easier than the twisting Madras path, but taking no less than two hours to deliver you to the Nymphaeum in the city centre. Due to the very real danger of flash floods, you shouldn't attempt it at all during the rainy season – roughly November to March – and even as late as May, there may be difficult-to-avoid standing pools of water harbouring water snakes: wading would be a big mistake.

Before beginning the walk, you can take a small detour from the dam to the **Eagle Niche**, set in the rocks 400m to the northwest. Cross the wadi over the roof of the tunnel and head left up the second side-valley; it's a short scramble over the smooth, hot rock up to a set of small niches carved in the right-hand wall, one of which features a strikingly carved eagle with wings outspread.

Back at the tunnel, Wadi Muthlim – full of oleanders, but with high walls cutting out all sound bar the occasional birdsong – is easily passable up to the remains of another Nabatean dam; beyond here, the path gets steadily narrower until you reach a point where a massive boulder all but blocks the way. It's possible to squeeze past, and the path continues to narrow until, with the wadi floor no wider than your foot, you reach a T-junction; arrows on the solid walls all around will point you left. This cross-wadi is the **Sidd Maajn**, equally narrow, but beautifully eroded by flowing water. As you proceed, seemingly moving through the heart of the mountain, you'll notice the Nabateans were here before you: there are dozens of carved niches, some featuring pediments, other curving horns. It's around here that the way might be blocked by rockpools. Eventually, you'll emerge into the open **Wadi Mataha** (see p.374), about 600m northeast of Dorotheos' House, and the best part of 2km northeast of the Nymphaeum.

building of the dam. At various points, you'll come across worn patches of the Roman/Nabatean road which originally paved the Siq along its entire length, in between stretches of newly consolidated pathway.

The Siq was formed when tectonic forces split the mountain in two. The waters of the Wadi Musa subsequently found their way into the fault, laying a bed of gravel and eroding the sharp corners into curves as smooth as eggshell, helped by the cool winds that blow in your face all the way down. The path along the wadi bed twists and turns between high, bizarrely eroded sandstone cliffs for 1200m, sometimes widening to form broad, sunlit open spaces in the echoing heart of the mountain, dotted with a tree or two and cut through by the cries of birds; in other places, the looming 150-metre-high walls close in to little more than a couple of metres apart, blocking out sound, warmth and even daylight. All the way down, high, narrow wadis feed in from either side, most of them blocked by modern dams (often set back to show the remains of the original Nabatean dams) to limit both flood danger and unauthorized exploration: once you're in the Siq, the only way is onward or backward. Dotted along the walls at many points are small **votive niches**, some Greek-style with pediments, others with mini god-blocks. After about 350m, a small **shrine** has been carved on the downhill side of a freestanding outcrop of rock, with two god-blocks, the larger of which is carved with eyes and a nose. A little further on, on the left-hand wall at a sharp right-hand bend, is a merchant in Egyptian-style dress leading two large **camels**; the water channel originally ran behind all five sets of legs, and it's just possible to trace the worn outline of the camels' humps in the rock wall.

When you think the gorge can't possibly go on any longer, there comes a dark, narrow defile, framing at its end a strip of extraordinary classical architecture. With your eye softened to the natural flows of eroded rock in the Siq, the clean lines of columns and pediments come as a revelation. As you step out into the daylight, there is no more dramatic or breathtaking vision in the whole of Jordan than the facade of the Treasury.

The Treasury

Perfectly positioned opposite the main route into Petra, the **Treasury** was designed to impress, and, two thousand years on, the effect is undiminished. What strikes you first is how well preserved it is; carved deep into the rockface and concealed in a high-walled ellipse of a valley (known as Wadi al-Jarra, "Urn Valley"), it has been protected from wind and rain from day one. The detailing of the capitals and pediments on the forty-by-thirty-metre facade is still crisp. The best times to view the Treasury are when the sun strikes it directly, between about 9am and 11am, and late in the afternoon, around 5 or 6pm, when the whole facade is suffused with a reflected reddish-pink glow from the walls all around.

The name "Treasury" is not Nabatean, and derives from the local name for such a seemingly inexplicable construction – **Khaznet al-Faraoun**, or Pharaoh's Treasury. Unaware of classical history, and unable to fathom why anyone should carve such a monument, the Bedouin of Wadi Musa tagged it as the work of the pharaoh, lord of black magic. In pursuit of the Israelites after the Exodus (the legend goes), the pharaoh was slowed down by having to carry all his treasure, so he created the Treasury at a stroke and deposited his riches in the urn at the very top of the facade, out of human reach. For centuries after Petra's abandonment, Bedouin marksmen tried to shatter the urn, and so release the treasure, but to no avail: their only success was in blasting chunks off the solid urn.

Petra colours

One of the most breathtaking aspects of Petra – for many people surpassing even the architecture – is its **colourful sandstone**, celebrated most famously in a particular tourist's memoirs almost 150 years ago. As the artist **Edward Lear** strolled up the Colonnaded Street on a visit in 1858, coolly noting "the tint of the stone... brilliant and gay beyond my anticipation", his manservant and cook, Giorgio Kokali, burst out in delight, "Oh master, we have come into a world of chocolate, ham, curry powder and salmon!" **Agatha Christie** preferred to see the rocks as "blood-red", and a character in her *Appointment with Death*, set in Petra, comes out with a line describing the place as "very much the colour of raw beef".

Unfortunately for posterity, however, the most famous lines on Petra's colours are rather less engaging. In 1845, **John William Burgon**, later to become Dean of Chichester, wrote in his poem *Petra*:

It seems no work of Man's creative hand,
By labour wrought as wavering fancy planned;
But from the rock as if by magic grown,
Eternal, silent, beautiful, alone!
Not virgin-white like that old Doric shrine,
Where erst Athena held her rites divine;
Not saintly-grey, like many a minister fane,
That crowns the hill and consecrates the plain;
But rose-red as if the blush of dawn
That first beheld them were not yet withdrawn;
The hues of youth upon a brow of woe,
Which Man deemed old two thousand years ago,

Match me such a marvel save in Eastern clime,
A rose-red city half as old as Time.

No advertising copywriter could have dreamt up a better final line, and Burgon's trite slogan has since hung over Petra like a bad smell: you'll be sick of reading the words **"rose-red city"** on every map, poster and booklet by the time you leave. Tellingly, Burgon had never been to Petra when he wrote it; he finally went sixteen years later, and at least then had the humility to write, if only in a letter to his sister, "there is nothing rosy about Petra, by any means".

Over the centuries, wind has rubbed away at the soft sandstone of Petra's cliffs to reveal an extraordinary array of colours streaking through the stone. The most colourful facades in Petra are the **Silk Tomb** and the **Carmine Tomb**, both on the East Cliff and bedecked in bands of rainbow colours, while the cafés on the path below are set in caves no less breathtaking. Elsewhere, the lower walls of the **Wadi Farasa** are streaked with colour, and the **Siq** cliffs are striped with everything from scarlet to yellow to purple to brown, to complement the green foliage on the trees, the pink of the oleander flowers, and the deep blue sky. The one place in Petra that's truly "rose-red" is the **Treasury**, lit in the afternoons by low reflected sunlight off the pinkish walls.

To the left of the facade, a set of stairs come down into the valley from the Danqur al-Khazneh area. Off to the right, a wall blocks the narrow north end of the Wadi al-Jarra; if you climb over the wall, then double back to scramble up the rocks, you'll reach a small, jutting plateau, with a perfect view from above of the Treasury and the whole bustling plaza in front of it.

The Treasury facade

The **carvings** on the Treasury facade, though much damaged by iconoclasts, are still discernible and show to what extent Nabatean culture was an amalgam of elements from the Hellenistic and Middle Eastern worlds.

The Treasury is normally dated to the first century BC, possibly to the reign of King Aretas III Philhellene ("the Greek-lover"), who brought architects to Petra from the centres of Hellenistic culture throughout the Mediterranean. Atop the broken pediments, framing the upper storey, are two large eagles, symbols of the Nabateans' chief male deity, Dushara (see box on p.349). In a central position on the rounded *tholos* below the urn is what's been identified as a representation of Isis, an Egyptian goddess who equated with the Nabatean goddess al-Uzza; in the recesses behind are two Winged Victories, although the remaining four figures, all of whom seem to be holding axes aloft, haven't been identified. Two lions, also symbolizing al-Uzza, adorn the entablature between the two storeys. At ground level, the mounted riders are Castor and Pollux, sons of Zeus. The parallel marks up the side of the facade, which occur in a couple of other places in Petra, may well have been footholds for the sculptors and masons.

One column is obviously new, a brick-and-plaster replacement for the original, which fell in antiquity. This neatly demonstrates one of the most extraordinary features of **Nabatean architecture**. A normal building that lost a main support like this would have come crashing down soon after; these Nabatean columns, though, support nothing. Like most of Petra's monuments, the entire Treasury "building" was sculpted *in situ*, gouged out of the unshaped rock in a kind of reverse architecture.

At the base of the facade, recent **excavations** into the four metres of gravel that overlie the original Nabatean surface revealed that the Treasury was carved above a line of older facades, also probably tombs, which are now viewable through a grille set into the ground.

Inside the Treasury doorway – unlike the scene in *Indiana Jones and the Last Crusade*, when Indy finds stone lions and Crusader seals set into the floor – there's only a blank **square chamber**, with smaller rooms opening off it, the entrance portico flanked by rooms featuring unusual round windows above their doors. Access to the interior has now been banned, but you can poke your nose in. The function of the Treasury is unknown, but a significant clue is the recessed **basin** on its threshold with a channel leading outside, clearly for libations or ritual washing. None of Petra's tomb-monuments has this feature, but the High Place of Sacrifice does, suggesting that the Treasury may have been a place of worship, possibly a tomb-temple.

The Outer Siq

From the Wadi al-Jarra, the path – known here as the **Outer Siq** – broadens and is lined with tombs in varying states of erosion. Steps lead up to a large cavern on the right, lined with benches inside and rather smelly. Opposite is a line of tombs at different heights, showing how the wadi floor rose during Nabatean occupation of Petra; most are badly eroded and give the peculiar impression that the classical facades are trying to push forward out of the soft rock but only half succeeding. One has the crow-step ornamental design that originated in Assyria and was adapted by the Nabateans to reappear in dozens of Petra's facades: a band of rising and falling zigzags running horizontally across the top of the facade. As the path broadens, in the corner of the right-hand cliff – pointed to by the terracotta pipe that has emerged from the Siq – the **Tomb of 17 Graves** is being restored behind scaffolding. If you look up and to the

△ Bust of Dushara

left of it, you'll spot one of the clearest examples of Nabatean facade-building; the **Tomb of Unayshu** (see p.359) presents a sharp profile of a clean classical facade facing left, carved from a rough outcrop of rock behind that looks barely capable of supporting it.

The path then opens out to the left to expose the **Street of Facades**, an agglomeration of dozens of facades carved side by side out of the rock on at least four different levels. Most are simple, cornice-free designs, probably some of the earliest carving in Petra. It's around here that you'll come across the first of Petra's many **cafés**, all of which offer water, shade and soft drinks.

The theatre

A few metres ahead sits Petra's massive **theatre**. Obviously classical in design and inspiration, it's nonetheless been dated to the first century AD, before the Romans annexed Nabatea but at a time when links between the two powers must have been strong. Though the Romans refurbished the building after they took over in 106, the basic design was still **Hellenistic**, with seats coming right down to the orchestra's floor level. As many as 8500 people could be accommodated, more even than in the vast theatre at Amman. Aside from the stage backdrop and the ends of the banks of seating, the entire edifice was carved out of the mountainside; one whole street of facades was wiped out to form the back wall of the auditorium, leaving some of their interiors behind as incongruous gaps. Much renovation work has been done here in recent years, in particular to build up the stage area, with its niches in front and elaborate *scaenae frons* behind (tumbled in the earthquake of 363), the high back wall of which would have sealed off the theatre from the street outside.

The path continues past **cafés** on both sides and even a set of clean **toilets** built into a beautifully colourful and tree-shaded cave, down to a point at which the Wadi Musa turns sharp left (west) into the **city centre** (see p.361). Way up to the right, a row of some of Petra's grandest monuments has been etched into the **East Cliff** (see p.359), while straight ahead the valley opens up towards Baydha, with the **Wadi Mataha** (see p.374) coming in from the northeast.

The High Place of Sacrifice route

A little before you reach the theatre, a set of steps leading south up a rocky slope to one side of a deep valley gives access to the **High Place of Sacrifice**, a diversion off the main path, but an unmissable part of a visit. Even if you have only one day in Petra, this is still worth the climb, about thirty or forty minutes with safe steps at all tricky points – there's no scrambling or mountaineering involved. You can return the same way, but steps also lead down off the back of the mountain into **Wadi Farasa**, forming a long but interesting loop that delivers you (after about two and a half hours) to the Qasr al-Bint. The breathtaking **views** and some of Petra's most extraordinary **rock-colouring** make the hike worthwhile, quite apart from the wealth of Nabatean architecture at every turn and the dramatic High Place itself. The path is well travelled, and you're unlikely to find yourself alone for more than a few minutes at a time.

The route up from the Outer Siq

The steps up are clearly marked, guarded by several god-blocks, and wind their way into the deep cleft of the lush and beautiful Wadi al-Mahfur; at several points, the Nabatean engineers took their chisels to what were otherwise impassable outcrops and sliced deep-cut corridors through the rock to house the stairs. The sign that you're reaching the top, apart from one or two impromptu cafés beneath bamboo shelters, is the appearance on your left of two very prominent **obelisks**, both over 6m high. As in the Bab as-Siq and elsewhere, these probably represent the chief male and female Nabatean deities, Dushara and al-Uzza, although far more extraordinary is to realize that they are solid: instead of being placed there, this entire side of the mountain-top was instead levelled to leave them sticking up. The ridge on which they stand is still marked on modern maps with the Bedouin name of Zibb Attuf, the Phallus of Mercy (often adapted to Amud Attuf, the Column of Mercy), implying that the notion of these obelisks representing beneficial fertility was somehow passed down unchanged from the Nabateans to the modern age. Opposite stand very ruined walls, the last remnants of what could have been a **Crusader fort** or a Nabatean structure. Broken steps lead beside it up to the summit.

The High Place of Sacrifice

As you emerge onto the hand-levelled platform atop the ridge, the sense of exposure after the climb is suddenly liberating. The **High Place of Sacrifice** (*al-Madhbah* in Arabic) is one of the highest easily accessible points in Petra, perched on cliffs that drop an almost sheer 170m to the Wadi Musa below. It's just one of dozens of High Places perched on ridges and mountain-tops around Petra, all of which are of similar design and function. A platform about 15m long and 6m wide served as the venue for the religious ceremonies, oriented towards an **altar**, set up on four steps, with a basin to one side and a socket into which may have slotted a stone representation of the god. Within the courtyard is a small dais, on which probably stood a table of (bloodless) offerings.

What exactly took place up here – probably in honour of Dushara – can only be guessed at, but there were almost certainly libations, smoking of frankincense and animal sacrifice. What is less sure is whether **human sacrifice** took place, although there is much evidence: boys and girls were known to have been sacrificed to al-Uzza elsewhere; the second-century philosopher Porphyrius reports that a boy's throat was cut annually at the Nabatean town of Dunat, just 300km from Petra; and at Hegra, a major Nabatean city in the Arabian interior, an inscription states explicitly: "Abd-Wadd, priest of Wadd, and his son Salim... have consecrated the young man Salim to be immolated to Dhu Gabat. Their double happiness!" If such sacrifices took place in Petra, the High Place would surely have seen at least some of them. It's also been suggested that Nabatean religion incorporated **ritual exposure of the dead**, as practised among the Zoroastrians of Persia; if so, the High Place would also have been an obvious choice as an exposure platform. You can survey the vastness of Petra's mountain terrain from here, and the tomb of Aaron atop **Jebel Haroun** is in clear sight in the distance.

The ridge extends a short distance north of the High Place, nosing out directly above the theatre, with the tombs of the Outer Siq minuscule below. From here, it's easy to see that the city of Petra lay in a broad valley, about a kilometre wide and hemmed in to east and west by mountain barriers; north the valley extends to Baydha, south to Sabra. It looks tempting to scramble down the front of the ridge, but there is no easily manageable path this way; it would be dangerous to try it.

The route down via Wadi Farasa

It's easy to go back the way you came, but the route down the western cliff of the Attuf ridge via **Wadi Farasa** (Butterfly Valley) is far preferable. The route leads directly straight ahead (south) as you scramble down from the High Place past the ruined Crusader walls, keeping the bamboo café on your right. After 50m you'll come to stairs winding downward to your right along the valley wall; the way is often narrow and steep but always clear. Note that it's also possible to descend via **Wadi Nmayr**, parallel to Wadi Farasa, but this is a very difficult, concealed path and should only be attempted with a knowledgeable guide.

The Lion Monument and Garden Triclinium

Part of the way down into the Wadi Farasa you'll come to the **Lion Monument** carved into a wall. This may have been a drinking fountain, since a pipe seems to have fed water to emerge from the lion's mouth. The creature itself, as on the Treasury facade, represented al-Uzza, and the monument was probably intended both to refresh devotees on their way up and prepare them for the ceremonies about to be held at the High Place. The precipitous stairs beyond, which give views of the monuments below, bring you down to the **Garden Triclinium**, a simple monument overlooked by a huge tree in a beautiful, hidden setting, which got its name from the carpet of green that sprouts in springtime in front of the portico. Two freestanding columns are framed by two engaged ones; within is a small square shrine. Stairs to the right of the facade lead to a huge cistern on the roof, serving the Roman Soldier Tomb below.

The Roman Soldier Tomb and around

A beautiful set of rock-cut stairs to the left of the Garden Triclinium brings you down to the complex of the **Roman Soldier Tomb**. Although not immediately apparent, the two facades facing each other across the wadi formed part of a unified area, with an elaborate colonnaded courtyard and garden between them, long vanished. The tomb itself is on your left, an orthodox classical facade with three framed niches holding figures probably representing those buried within; the interior chamber has a number of recesses for the dead. Opposite the tomb, with an eroded but undecorated facade, is a startlingly colourful **triclinium**, unique in Petra for having a carved interior. The walls have been decorated with fluted columns and bays, all worn to show streaks of mauves, blues, pinks, crimsons and silver. Why this *triclinium* was decorated so carefully, and who was buried in the tomb opposite, isn't known; even the name is only a supposition from the middle of the tomb's three figures, a headless man wearing a cuirass.

Stairs lead down over the lip of a retaining wall to the wadi floor, and it is around here that the colouring in the rock is at its most gorgeous. Plenty of tombs crowd the lower reaches of the wadi; one of the most interesting is the **Renaissance Tomb**, topped by an urn and with an unusual arch above its doorway also carrying three urns. Nearby is the **Broken Pediment Tomb**, above the level of the path, displaying an early forerunner of the kind of broken pediment found on Petra's grandest monuments, the Treasury and the Monastery.

Zantur, Katuteh and Amud Faraoun

As you emerge from the wadi into the open, you should bear in mind that you're still the best part of half an hour from reaching the main routes again. From here onwards, though, there's not a scrap of shade: you're exposed to the full force of the sun and are quite often walking in stifling breezeless dips

From time immemorial, the caves and dens of Petra have been occupied by one of Jordan's poorest and most downtrodden tribes, the **Bdul**. Surrounded by tribes living traditional tent-based lifestyles (the **Saidiyeen** to the south and west, the **Ammareen** to the north, and the **Liyathneh** to the east), the Bdul remain a community apart, looked down upon for their poverty, small numbers (only about three hundred families) and cave-centred lifestyle.

Most Bedouin tribes can trace their lineage back to a single founding father (whether real or fictitious), but mystery surrounds the origin of the Bdul. Some Bdul, naturally enough, claim descent from the Nabateans, but this may just be wishful thinking. Most claim that the name Bdul derives from the Arabic word *badal*, meaning to swap or change, and was given to the tribe after the handful of survivors of a massacre at the hands of Moses and the Israelites had agreed to convert to Judaism; at some point in the centuries following, the tribe converted again, this time to Islam. Much more plausible is the possibility that the Bdul earned their name from being a nomadic tribe that decided to settle in the ruins of Petra, changing their habits to suit a more stable existence.

The tribe comprises five branches. The **Judaylat** – meaning the stubborn or primitive – live around Jebel Haroun, many working as shepherds for the Saidiyeen. It was the Judaylat that Burckhardt came across when he passed through Petra; he wrote that their tents "were the smallest I had ever seen, about four feet high and ten in length. The inhabitants were very poor, and could not afford to give us coffee; our breakfast and dinner therefore consisted of dry barley cakes, which we dipped in melted goat's grease." The **Fuqara** – meaning the poor – are the source of the tribe's shamans, and are held to possess healing powers: they have the distinguished role of custodians of the shrine of Haroun. The other branches are less well demarcated. The **Mawasneh** and **Jamadat** are closely related to the Fuqara, and the **Samaheen** comprise a few families living in and around Mughur an-Nassara (see p.374).

The Bdul were slow to benefit from the growth in tourism in Petra, largely because of cut-throat competition with the more cosmopolitan and better-educated Liyathneh of Wadi Musa. When the *Resthouse* opened in the 1950s, Liyathneh were hired as construction workers, hotel staff, book- and postcard-sellers and even to provide horses for rides into Petra; their near-monopoly on tourist facilities in Wadi Musa has persisted to this day. Adding insult to injury, a USAID report dating from the establishment of Petra as a National Park in 1968 acknowledged that the Bdul held traditional rights over park lands, but nonetheless recommended that they be **resettled** elsewhere. This sparked a fifteen-year battle to oust the Bdul from Petra, which saw the tribe's traditional lifestyle of agriculture and goatherding decimated, income instead dribbling in from the refreshment cafés within Petra and the few individuals offering crafts and antiquities – real and fake – to tourists. In the mid-1980s, tempted by material comforts in the new, purpose-built village of Umm Sayhoun, many Bdul families finally left the caves of Petra for the breeze-block houses on the ridge. Some still herd a few goats, others cultivate small plots, but most Bdul are refocusing their energies on making an income providing services to tourists. You'll meet Bdul adults and kids in all corners of Petra, running the tent-cafés or offering tea and trinkets in the hills, and often happy to chat (in surprisingly fluent English). The "Bedouin named for changing", as archeologist Kenneth Russell dubbed them, are embracing change yet again.

For excellent background on the Bdul by anthropologist Rami Sajdi, go to ⊛www .acacialand.com – and also see Ruth Caswell's pages about the tribes of Wadi Musa, ⊛www.jordanjubilee.com/meetfolk.htm.

between hills. In addition, the path isn't immediately clear. You should bear a little right, initially keeping out of the wadi bed, and aim for the left flank of the smooth rounded hill dead ahead. This hill is **Zantur**, Petra's rubbish dump, and it crunches underfoot with fragments of pottery: as well as coarse, crudely decorated modern shards, there are countless chips of beautiful original Nabatean ware – very thin, smooth pottery that's been skilfully painted. As long as you don't start digging, you can take whatever you like.

Within metres are the remains of the house of a wealthy Nabatean merchant at **Katuteh**, suddenly abandoned for some reason (possibly, archeologists theorize, as a result of having the city's garbage dumped in the back garden). Swiss teams are currently excavating the villa.

The path eventually curls around to the western flank of the hill and **Amud Faraoun**, called Zibb Faraoun (Pharaoh's Phallus) by the Bedouin. This standing column, which must have formed part of the portico of a building – partvisible buried in the rubbly hill behind – now serves as a useful landmark and resting spot. Paths converge here from all sides; to the **southwest** is the main route into Wadi Thughra towards Umm al-Biyara, Jebel Haroun and Sabra; to the **west** is a path accessing a route up al-Habees; to the **northwest** are the Qasr al-Bint (see p.366) and the tent-cafés; and to the **northeast** a path runs behind the markets area of the city centre (see p.361), parallel to the Colonnaded Street.

The East Cliff

About 250m beyond the theatre, just before the Wadi Musa makes its sharp left turn, solid, modern steps lead to the **East Cliff**, looming up to the right above the whole of the city centre. This whole elbow of Jebel al-Khubtha is ranged with some of Petra's most impressive facades, collectively known as the **Royal Tombs**. If you have anything more than half a day in the city, you should fit them in; the climb is easy and the views are marvellous. From down below, in the direct, reddish light of late afternoon, the entire cliff seems to glow with an inner translucence, and is one of the sights of Petra. However, it's probably best to aim to be up here in the morning shadows, with the sun lighting up the valley and the mountains opposite.

From **right to left**, the first tomb on the cliff – separate from the big ones, and missable if you're short of time – is the **Tomb of Unayshu**, viewed in profile from the Outer Siq and easiest to get to by scrambling up the rocks opposite the High Place staircase. This is part of a complete Nabatean tomb complex, and features a once-porticoed courtyard in front, with a *triclinium* to one side. It is currently the focus of a project experimenting with different methods of stone preservation, and so may be obscured by scaffolding for some time.

The Urn Tomb
Heading north from Unayshu above the main path, past another well-preserved tomb facade, you join the modern steps leading from below up to the soaring facade of the **Urn Tomb**, with its very large colonnaded forecourt partially supported on several storeys of arched vaults. The Bdul know the tomb as al-Mahkamah, "**the Court**", dubbing the vaults as-Sijin, "**the Jail**". Whether it was later used in this way or not, the whole structure would seem originally to have been the tomb of somebody extremely important, quite probably one of the Nabatean kings – but who exactly isn't known. Set into the facade high

above the forecourt between the engaged columns are spaces for three bodies; this is a unique configuration in Petra, since such *loculi* are normally inside the monument, and they seem to have been placed here as an indication of the importance of their occupants. The central one – possibly that of the king himself – is still partially sealed by a stone which formerly depicted the bust of a man wearing a toga. The urn which gave the tomb its name is, as always, at the very top.

Due, no doubt, to its dominating position in the city's landscape, the tomb was later converted into a major church, possibly Petra's **cathedral**; the large interior room features, near the left-hand corner of the back wall, a Greek inscription in red paint recording the dedication of the church by Bishop Jason in 447 AD. Probably at the same time, two central recesses of the original four were combined to make a kind of apse, and myriad holes were drilled in the floor to support all the relevant ecclesiastical furniture: chancel screens, a pulpit, maybe a table, and so on. The **view** from the forecourt, which takes in the full sweep of the valley (and even the urn atop the Monastery), is one of Petra's best.

The Silk Tomb, Corinthian Tomb and Palace Tomb

Working your way around the cliff, you'll come to the **Silk Tomb**, unremarkable but for its brilliant colouring. The facade of the nearby **Corinthian Tomb** is something like a hybrid and ramshackle Treasury. It has the Treasury's style on the upper level – a *tholos* flanked by a broken pediment – but below, it's a mess, the symmetry thrown out by extra doors on the left. It has also suffered badly at the hands of the wind. However, such an exposed position on the corner of the cliff – directly in line with the Colonnaded Street – points to the fact that, like the Urn Tomb, this may well have been the tomb of another Nabatean king, visible from everywhere in the city.

Adjacent is an even more ramshackle jumble, the very broad **Palace Tomb**, boasting one of Petra's largest, and least comprehensible, facades. There are at least five different storeys, the top portions of which were built of masonry because the cliff turned out to be too low, and so subsequently collapsed. The unevenly spaced line of engaged columns on the second row clashes nastily with the orthodox lower level. Protected by the cliff, the extreme right-hand edge of the facade still has some sharply carved detail surviving.

The Sextius Florentinus Tomb, Carmine Tomb and the Khubtha High Places

From the Palace Tomb, tracks lead west towards the city centre, and northeast hugging the cliff round to the beautiful and peaceful **Sextius Florentinus Tomb**, positioned facing north where a finger of the cliff reaches the ground. Sextius Florentinus was a Roman governor of the Province of Arabia who died about 130 AD, and must have chosen to be buried in Petra rather than in the provincial capital of Bosra. The facade of his tomb, with a graceful semicircular pediment, is one of the most pleasing in the city. A few metres north, behind a tree, is the spectacular **Carmine Tomb**, girt with breathtaking bands of colour, but, by virtue of its position, hardly ever noticed. Wadi Zarnug al-Khubtha, which divides the two, holds a path which gives reasonably easy, if steep, access to little-visited High Places and a few scattered ruins perched atop the massive **Jebel al-Khubtha**, the main barrier standing between Petra and Wadi Musa town. The views from on top are tremendous – especially of the theatre – but you'd have to be keen (and sure-footed) to try it.

The path beyond Sextius Florentinus along the Wadi Mataha is described on p.374.

The city centre

As you round the corner of the path leading from the theatre, the **city centre** of Petra, focused along the Cardo Maximus, or **Colonnaded Street**, stretches out ahead, framed by the barrier range of mountains – and the flat-topped giant Umm al-Biyara – behind. Although there are excavations continuing on the flat, rounded hills to either side, the overall impression is of barrenness and rocky desolation; however, in Petra's prime, the landscape in all directions was covered with buildings – houses big and small, temples, marketplaces – all of them long

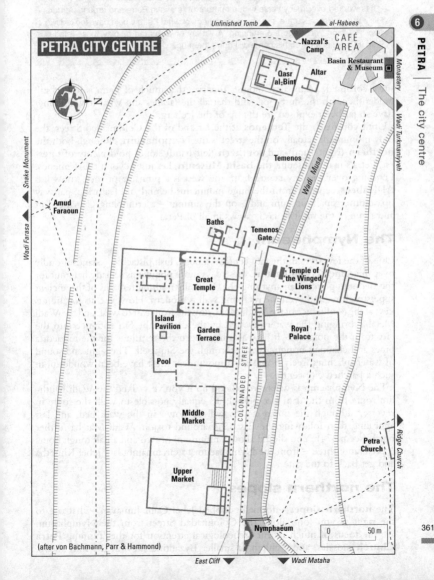

PETRA CITY CENTRE

Unfinished Tomb ▲   ▲ al-Habees

CAFÉ AREA

Nazzal's Camp

Basin Restaurant & Museum ▢

Qasr al-Bint   Altar

Monastery

Wadi Turkmaniyeh

Wadi Musa

Temenos

Snake Monument ▲

Amud Faraoun ▲

Wadi Farasa ▲

Baths   Temenos Gate

Great Temple

Temple of the Winged Lions

Island Pavilion

Garden Terrace

Royal Palace

Pool

COLONNADED STREET

Middle Market

Petra Church

Ridge Church ▲

Upper Market

Nymphaeum

0   50 m

(after von Bachmann, Parr & Hammond)

East Cliff ▼   ▼ Wadi Mataha

since collapsed. Many archeologists theorize that much of Petra is in fact still hidden beneath the dusty soil, and that all the facades and what few buildings have so far been exposed are the tip of the iceberg.

Until you reach the **Temenos** at the far end of the Colonnaded Street, the only monument actually on the street is the **Nymphaeum**, although both the **northern** (right-hand) and **southern** (left-hand) slopes hold plenty of interest. Petra's main museum, the **Basin Museum**, lies just beyond the Temenos. Looming over the city centre from the west is a pinnacle of rock known as **Al-Habees**, separate from the huge mountains behind and featuring, partway up, another small museum and – on the summit – a crumbling Crusader fort and some of the most fantastic views in all of Petra.

The Nymphaeum

One of the few trees in the city centre – a huge, lush pistachio – stands proudly over the ruined **Nymphaeum**, these days more popular as a shady hangout for the Bedouin police than anything else. Virtually nothing remains of the ancient superstructure, and even the retaining wall is modern. However, its location is key, at the confluence of the Wadi Musa, flowing from east to west, and the Wadi Mataha, bringing the water diverted by the dam at the Siq entrance into the city from the northeast. It may also have been the terminus for the terracotta pipes and channels bringing water through the Siq itself. The sight and sound of water splashing freely from such a monument must have been wonderful in such a parched city centre.

The Nymphaeum is where you'll end up if you've walked the Wadi Muthlim route from the dam (see p.350); it's equally possible to walk the route in reverse, although the initial stretch will be down in the wadi bed, and less appealing than following the East Cliff around to join Wadi Mataha further north (see p.374). You should allow a minimum of two and a half tough hours – preferably three – from the Nymphaeum to circumambulate Jebel Khubtha and get back to the gate.

The northern slopes

The **northern slopes** – formally dubbed Jebel Qabr Jumayan – that rise to the right as you look along the Colonnaded Street from the Nymphaeum are the focus of much recent archeological attention for the stunning **Petra Church** mosaics, and a clutch of smaller Byzantine sites on the hills above, as well as one of the city's longest-standing excavations, the **Temple of the Winged Lions**.

The Petra Church

Above and behind the Nymphaeum stands a modern shelter that was constructed in 1997 to protect one of Petra's most thrilling new finds, discovered only seven years before. The Byzantine **Petra Church**, as it's been unimaginatively dubbed, is a large tripartite basilica, roughly 26m by 15m, with three apses to the east and three entrances to the west, accessed from a stone-paved atrium. It was built in the late fifth century, and remodelled about fifty years later. Around 600 it was burned, and remained derelict until earthquakes shook it down shortly afterwards. Surviving in both aisles of the church, though, are superbly detailed **floor mosaics** depicting the bounty of creation, dated stylistically to the early sixth century. Much of the stone used to build the church was pilfered from the ruined Nabatean and Roman monuments all around, and now lies tumbled down the slopes in front.

The spectacular **south-aisle mosaics** are in three rows, the central line of personifications of the seasons flanked by rows of animals, birds and fish. From door to altar, the middle line features fishermen and hunters interspersed with Ocean (with one foot on a fish), a delightfully clear-faced Spring, and Summer with her breast bared and holding a fish. The **north-aisle mosaics** depict people and indigenous and exotic animals and birds, including a camel-like giraffe (much like a creature depicted on a mosaic floor in the Moses Memo-

The Petra scrolls

A hugely significant archeological find was made by accident in a storage room at the northeast corner of the Petra Church on December 4, 1993: archeologists stumbled on a cache of 152 **papyrus scrolls**, tumbled higgledy-piggledy from the shelves that presumably once carried them, which had lain buried beneath 4m of rubble. At the time of writing, analysis of the scrolls is still incomplete, but the preliminary results give tantalizing glimpses of life in Byzantine Petra, a period that is rarely accounted for.

The whole archive seems to have belonged to one Theodore, born in 514, who at the age of 24 married a young woman from a family already connected with his own by marriage in a previous generation. Theodore became archdeacon of the "Most Holy Church of NN in the metropolis" – presumably the Petra Church. Most of the documents date from a sixty-year period, roughly 528 to 588, and comprise property contracts, out-of-court settlements and tax receipts – not immediately gripping stuff, but providing a wealth of detail about everyday life. Transfers from one family to another of vineyards, arable land, orchards, living quarters and stables within a fifty-kilometre radius of Petra were all dutifully recorded. One man's will specifies that after his mother's death, all her assets were to be donated (presumably whether she liked it or not) to the "House of Aron", undoubtedly the Byzantine monastery newly identified atop Jebel Haroun. Farmers, tailors, doctors, slaves and soldiers are all mentioned by name, including one Abu Karib ibn Jabala, known to have been a military commander of the Arab tribes. However, Petra was decisively Christian at this time, and monks and priests feature prominently, not least a Bishop Theodore, who may have been the same Theodore who took part in a synod at Jerusalem in 536. Another reference is to a priest "of her, our All-Holy, Praised Lady, the Glorious God-Bearing and Eternally Virgin Mary", indicating that there may be a church to Mary yet to be uncovered in Petra. Only once the content of the scrolls has been fully published can investigation proceed any further, but this is just another sign that archeologists have only just begun to scratch Petra's surface.

rial Church on Mount Nebo; see p.289), a hyena, boar, bear and leopard. Archeologists also found thousands of gilded glass tesserae, indicating that lavish **wall mosaics** once adorned the church, and they managed to reconstruct – from more than a hundred pieces – a huge marble tub with panthers for handles (which now sits in the Basin Museum). At the rear (west) of the atrium is a superbly well-preserved fifth-century **Baptistry**, with a cruciform font surrounded by four limestone columns. The presence of such a large church so richly decorated – and the discovery of the Petra scrolls – merely highlights how little is known about Byzantine Petra, and how much awaits discovery.

From in front of the Petra Church, great **views** extend over the valley. To the left is the East Cliff; ahead is the Great Temple; and to the right you can clearly see the unusual Unfinished Tomb (see p.368), carved into the base of Al-Habees.

The Blue Church and Ridge Church

More recent finds shed a glimmer of light on the Byzantine period. On a ridge just above the Petra Church is the **Blue Church**, so named for its bluish granite columns. Not a great deal is known about this building, and work is ongoing. A short climb to the top of the hill that peaks behind the Petra Church will bring you to the austere **Ridge Church**, a much smaller building (some 18m by 13m) perched on a ridge at the northwestern edge of Byzantine-era Petra, overlooking the Wadi Turkmaniyyeh behind and the whole of the city centre in front. Dated to roughly the same time as the Petra Church, much of the church's interior paving survives, but there's no decoration. What's most interesting about the place is that archeologists found almost no remnants of the building's superstructure nearby, although they did find a hoard of water-washed stones in the church courtyard brought up from the wadi below. From this confusing evidence, they came up with an elaborate theory for the church's destruction. At a time of increasing political instability, they postulate, the Petrans deliberately dismantled the church – which lay hard up against the city wall – in order to use its stones as missiles against invaders approaching from below. When the church had been razed, they collected more stones from the wadi to hoard against future attacks, but these were forgotten as, possibly, the city was overrun from a different direction. Any truth in this tale has yet to be confirmed.

The Temple of the Winged Lions

Overlooking the Temenos Gate west of the Petra Church is the **Temple of the Winged Lions**, the principal building of the northern slope. It was named for unusual column capitals featuring winged lions (one of which is in the Basin Museum), but would – so the excavator suggests – have been more appropriately named the Temple of al-Uzza, for it seems to have been dedicated to her. Dated approximately to the early first century AD, the building – which must have been a major focus of the city's religious life – was approached via a bridge across the Wadi Musa, parts of which you can still see on the banks. The worshipper would have proceeded across ascending terraces, an open colonnaded courtyard and a portico into the temple itself, featuring close-packed columns and an altar platform. The floors were paved in contrasting black, brown and white marble, and the walls decorated with painted plaster; appropriately enough, archeologists uncovered both a painter's workshop – with paints and pigments still in their ceramic pots – and a marble-cutter's workshop adjoining the temple.

One of the most spectacular discoveries, also now on display in the Basin Museum, was a small rectangular stone **idol**, complete with a stylized face and a hole between the eyes (possibly for a set of horns, the symbol of the goddess Isis, to be inserted); the inscription along the base reads "Goddess of Hayyan son of Nybat". Adjacent to the temple to the east is a large unexcavated area of rubble deemed to have been a **royal palace**, also with a bridge over the wadi, but no work has as yet been done on it.

The southern slopes

From the Nymphaeum all the way along the paved Colonnaded Street westwards, columns on your left (south) stand in front of what have been dubbed Petra's **markets**, which remain in the preliminary stages of digging – all bar a site alongside the **Great Temple** further along, which has, in the last few years, been named as the **Garden Terrace**, once a fertile, leafy area flowing with water. Ranged along street level in front of the markets, to either side of the grand staircases, were small shops, which may have been refitted in the Byzantine period; some have been renovated, but work to excavate the market floors and outbuildings remains ongoing.

The Garden Terrace

Although there's not a great deal of above-ground evidence, the area alongside the Great Temple – formerly known as the Lower Market – has now been conclusively identified as an area of ornamental gardens, dubbed the **Garden Terrace**. It seems that this was laid out in Petra's "golden age" – the late first century BC – as a place of refuge in the city centre, tucked in amongst the grand temples and busy shops all around. In front, nearest the street, was a flat area that comprised the gardens themselves. Behind, occupying the whole southern area of the terrace, was a very large **pool**, 43m long by 23m wide (and about two and a half metres deep), surrounded by a colonnade. Occupying an **island** in the centre of the pool was a small, rectangular pavilion. The beauty of such a site can only be imagined.

The Great Temple

Alongside the Garden Terrace at the western end of the street, and accessed by a set of steps leading up from the street, is the late first-century BC **Great Temple**, or Southern Temple, an extremely grand affair, one of the largest complexes in the city at seven thousand square metres. Excavation work by teams from Brown University in the US only began in 1993, and is far from finished; you may be able to explore only part of the building.

Worshippers originally climbed a staircase from street level through a now tumbled monumental gateway onto the hexagonally paved **lower temenos**, featuring triple colonnades to east and west culminating in semicircular benched alcoves. The **temple** itself stands some 25m above street level, fronted by four enormous columns which were originally stuccoed in red and white. Within the *cella*, archeologists recently completed renovation of a small Nabatean theatre, or **theatron**, about 7m in diameter, which would have seated at least three hundred people, and might have been a council chamber. The whole building is extremely complex, set on different levels, with internal and external corridors flanking it on east and west. In addition, tumbled columns and chunks of architectural elements (many of them beautifully carved) all point to the fact that this was one of Petra's most important monuments. As yet, though, not even the deity who was worshipped here is known.

Scramble to the highest point of the walls for **views** west to the arches of the Crusader fort atop Al-Habees, north across the wadi to the Temple of the Winged Lions, behind which lie the valley tombs of Wadi Muaysreh ash-Shargiyyeh, and northeast to the Petra Church, with Umm Sayhoun behind it and Mughur an-Nassara to one side.

The Temenos

In most Roman cities, the main east–west and north–south streets ploughed straight furrows from city gate to city gate. However, as at Bosra, the heterodox Nabateans blocked off Petra's main street at one end and turned the area beyond – hard up against the mountain cliffs – into a **Temenos**, or sacred temple precinct. Framing the western end of the Colonnaded Street stand the partially reconstructed remains of the **Temenos Gate**, marking the end of the commercial sector of Petra and the entrance to the main area of worship. Sockets in the threshold indicate that great doors once closed off all three entrances of the gate; the floral frieze which survives on the easternmost facade of the gate was originally framed by freestanding columns which stood just in front and to either side.

As you pass through the gate, the impression remains of having left the city behind; the courtyard – occupied at the far end by, on one side, camels and, on the other, the bulk of a temple – is huge, paved and open, and at times of religious celebration would have been thronged with people. Low walls enclosed the Temenos on both sides, although the northern one has been eroded away by the waters of the Wadi Musa. Just inside the Temenos Gate to the south are three domed rooms tentatively identified as **baths**, only partially excavated. All along the south wall is a double row of stone benches, some 73m in length, leading almost up to the main feature of the Temenos, the Qasr al-Bint, the only freestanding monument as yet uncovered in the whole of Petra. Just visible from the Temenos, over the hill to the south, is the tip of the Amud Faraoun (see p.359).

The Qasr al-Bint

The **Qasr al-Bint al-Faraoun** – the "Palace of Pharaoh's Daughter" – is nothing of the sort. Its name derives from another far-fetched Bedouin tale of the pharaoh, who, it's said, after stashing his riches in the Treasury, and still desperate to let nothing slow him down in his pursuit of the Israelites, stashed his daughter away here for safekeeping. Interestingly enough though, an inscription naming Suudat, daughter of the Nabatean king Malchus II (40–70 AD), and probably from the base of a statue, was found on the steps; according to historian Iain Browning, this indicates that some link between the *qasr* and the daughter of a powerful man may not be so fanciful after all.

The building is a huge, square Nabatean temple, dating from the late first century BC, oriented to the north and facing a huge, freestanding altar, some 13m by 12m and at least 3m high. It is desperately in need of conservation, with deep cracks running crazily all across it, and its walls bowing alarmingly in places; UNESCO and a French team are currently engaged in conserving the building. The **altar**, clad in marble, showed a blank wall to the north, and was originally approached by steps from in front of the temple. From here looking back, the four gigantic columns of the temple portico, standing at the head of a broad staircase wider than the building and topped by an architrave and pediment, would have made a deeply impressive sight. The huge arch that survives today was probably only a relieving arch for a lower, horizontal lintel of the doorway into the *cella*, which spanned the width of the building and was lit by windows high up in each wall. Behind, the holy of holies was divided into three separate chambers, or *adyta*. The central one is slightly raised, and has engaged columns along the walls and another relieving arch overhead; this is where the god-block or cult statue would have stood. The temple's dedication is unknown, but Dushara is the most obvious candidate. Excavations in the altar courtyard in 1999 and 2000 went down to the level of the original paving, and uncovered an exedra, or recess, on the western side, which may have held a statue of the emperor. An impressive marble head found near the exedra is now housed in the Basin Museum.

Tent-cafés and **camel drivers** crowd the courtyard in front of the Qasr al-Bint, and this is the main rest area for gathering strength before you continue to explore or start the long walk back to the gate (which takes a full hour uphill by the most direct route through the Siq). In front of the *qasr*, a bridge crosses the Wadi Musa to the *Basin Restaurant* and museum; from the other bank, the **Wadi Turkmaniyyeh** dirt road (see p.374) wends its way out of the city to Umm Sayhoun.

The Basin Museum

Shaded by a prominent grove of trees opposite the Qasr al-Bint is the *Basin Restaurant* (see p.342) and adjacent **Basin Museum** (daily 8am–3.30pm; free), the latter definitely worth a quick look if only to give yourself a break from all the imposing architecture. It holds excellent informative noticeboards on Petra's history and geography (including a fascinating digression into the frankincense trade), as well as stacks of information about the Nabateans. Plenty of finds are on display from all periods of occupation at Petra, stretching right back to Neolithic times, among which Nabatean coins, pottery and some beautiful and delicate jewellery are by far the most engaging. Specific pieces that stand out are the small but extraordinarily powerful idol from the Temple of the Winged Lions, statues of Aphrodite and Dionysus, and the massive panther-handled marble tub from the Petra Church.

Al-Habees

The modern building next to the Qasr al-Bint – now used by the Department of Antiquities – is known as **Nazzal's Camp**, and was formerly Petra's sole hotel (of eleven rooms), built by the Nazzal family in 1943 on the site of Thomas Cook's old three-bed campsite established nine years before: early Cook's tourists were offered the option of sleeping instead in one of the caves cut into **Al-Habees** looming overhead. These caves are used now as storage areas and offices for the police, but one has been converted into a small **museum** (daily except Tues 8am–3.30pm, sometimes closed Fri; free), accessed up stairs in front of Nazzal's Camp and well worth a look. The chamber is crammed full of marvellous statuary, including busts of various Roman gods, an eagle with outspread wings perched on a thunderbolt (symbol of Zeus), and a headless statue of Hercules recovered from the theatre.

From the museum it's possible to follow the path around the mountain on the initial stretches of a processional way to the summit. A little way around is an open area overlooking the beautiful Wadi Siyyagh, with plenty of rock-cut caves – whether they're tombs or houses isn't certain – as well as a small **High Place**, in perfect isolation above a prominent crow-step facade and sunken courtyard in the so-called **Convent Group** of monuments. Beyond, though, the Nabatean stairway is worn and dangerous, and the best way up to the summit is now via a staircase on the southern flank of the mountain, for which you must return to Nazzal's Camp.

The Unfinished Tomb and Columbarium

Overlooking the rubbly hill directly behind Nazzal's Camp is one of Petra's most interesting monuments, the **Unfinished Tomb**. This is a part-complete facade, and shows how Nabatean craftsmen worked from the top down, scooping out the interior as they went. Beside it is the **Columbarium**, a strange monument covered inside and out with hundreds of tiny square niches that had an unknown function: the name literally means "dovecote", implying that each niche held a bird, but no dove could roost here and the niches seem too small to hold funerary urns, as has also been suggested.

The Al-Habees Crusader fort

To reach the **Crusader fort** on the top of Al-Habees, you should continue south up the rubbly hill from the Columbarium, and follow a sign pointing right, even though it appears to point at the blank rubbly cliffside. As you get nearer, you'll spot the modern, restored stairs which take you up to the summit; it's an easy fifteen-minute climb, although there is one wooden footbridge without railings on the way. A gate with a rock-cut bench marks the approach to the fort, after which you'll have to scramble over loose stones up to a gatehouse. From here, you must find your own way the last little bit to the top; steps rise at one point over the barrel vault of a small room. The layout of the ruined fort itself – only occupied for a few decades in the twelfth century – is jumbled and confusing, but the 360-degree views are quite stunning.

Wadi Siyyagh

Just to the north of Al-Habees, **Wadi Siyyagh** – which takes the waters of the Wadi Musa down to Wadi Araba – was formerly one of the most gorgeous and quiet short walks you could make in Petra. This was once an exclusive residential neighbourhood of the city, enclosed between high walls, and there are plenty of houses and tombs, a Nabatean quarry and a well to explore. However, the wadi is now a short cut for local people driving their pick-ups, and a cave near the eastern end is home to a **generator** that keeps the *Basin Restaurant* and the Department of Antiquities offices operational; the insane roar of the thing echoes for a good half-hour down the wadi, the first 150m of which are now also covered with litter.

Persevere with the walk, though, and after half an hour or so you'll reach the well-tended "Roman Gardens" (not Roman at all), now maintained by local people. Beyond, you'll find pools and waterfalls en route to Bir Mathkoor (see p.424) in the desert of Wadi Araba, 16km from Petra, but route-finding is not always obvious in this harsh terrain and some scrambling on steep cliffs is necessary; you should be fully confident in your skills, or hire a guide for the journey.

The Monastery

Petra's most awe-inspiring monument is also one of the most taxing to reach. The **Monastery** (*ad-Dayr* in Arabic) boasts a massive facade almost fifty metres square, carved from a chunk of mountain nearly an hour's climb northwest of the city centre, 220m above the elevation of the Qasr al-Bint. Daunting though this sounds, there are well-trodden steps the whole way, as well as plenty of places to rest; a tranquil holy spring two-thirds of the way up is almost worth the climb by itself. Even if you've had your fill of facades, the stupendous views from the mountain-top over the entire Petra basin and the Wadi Araba make the trip essential.

Whether you want to **ride a donkey** to the summit or not (prices are *very* negotiable), you'll most likely have to beat off the hordes of kids riding alongside offering them as "Air-condition taxi, mister?" Bear in mind that the archeological authorities would prefer that you walked: all those little hooves are seriously degrading the Nabatean-carved sandstone steps on the route up. Either way, by far the best time to attempt the climb is in the **afternoon**; not only is the way up mostly in shadow by then, but the sun has moved around enough to hit the facade on the summit full-on.

The route up to the Monastery

The route passes in front of the *Basin* restaurant and museum, and leads dead ahead into the soft sandy bed of the Wadi ad-Dayr. The steps begin after a short distance, and soon after there's a diversion pointed left to the **Lion Triclinium**, a small classical shrine in a peaceful bushy wadi, named for the very worn lions that flank its entrance. A small round window above the door and the doorway itself have been eroded together to form a strange keyhole shape. The frieze above has Medusas at either end; to the left of the facade is a small god-block set into a niche.

The processional way up to the Monastery is broken after another patch of steps by a sharp left turn where the Wadi Kharrubeh joins from in front; a little way along this wadi – off the main path – you'll find on the right-hand side a small **biclinium**, a ceremonial dining room with two stepped benches facing each other. Back on the path, after a step-free patch, the climb recommences. Some twenty or thirty minutes from the *Basin*, where the steps turn sharply left, you can branch right off the main path into a narrow wadi; double-back to the left, follow a track up and then right onto a broad, cool, protected ledge overlooking a deep ravine below. This is the **Qattar ad-Dayr**, an enchanted mossy grotto enclosed by high walls, completely silent but for the cries of wheeling birds and the continual dripping of water; it's a perfect spot for a picnic. Here, the one place in Petra where water flows year-round, the Nabateans built a *triclinium* and cisterns, and made dozens of carvings, including a spectacular two-armed cross.

As the steps drag on, the views begin to open up, and you get a sense of the vastness of the mountains and valleys all around. With tired legs, it's about another twenty minutes to a small sign pointing right to the **Hermitage**, a sheer-sided pinnacle of rock featuring a less-than-gripping set of caves carved with crosses. Another ten minutes, after a squeeze between two boulders and a short descent, and you emerge onto a wide, flat plateau, where you should turn right for the Monastery.

The Monastery

The **Monastery** facade is so big that it seems like an optical illusion – the doorway alone is taller than a house. A local entrepreneur has thoughtfully set up a café in a cave opposite: sink down at one of the shaded tables in front to take in the full vastness of the view. At first glance, the facade looks much like the Treasury's, but it's much less ornate; indeed, there's virtually no decoration at all. The name "Monastery" is again a misnomer, probably suggested by some crosses scratched inside; this was almost certainly a **temple**, possibly dedicated to the Nabatean king **Obodas I**, who reigned in the first century BC and was posthumously deified. Inside is a single chamber, with the same configuration of double staircases leading up to a cultic niche as in the Qasr al-Bint and the Temple of the Winged Lions. The flat plaza in front of the monument isn't natural: it was levelled deliberately, probably to contain the huge crowds that gathered here for religious ceremonies. You can pick out traces of a wall and colonnade in the ground to the south of the plaza, near where you entered. The opposite side (the left flank of the monument as you face it) has a scramble-path which can take you up to the **urn** on the top of the facade, which is no less than 10m high. Leaping around on the urn is a test of mettle for the local goat-footed kids, and some even shimmy to the very top; follow them with your life in your hands.

There are dozens more monuments and carvings to explore around the Monastery, not least of which is a cave and stone circle directly behind the refreshments cave. At any point, once you climb off ground level, the views are breathtaking. The cliff to the north (left) of the facade is punctuated for well over 100m with Nabatean caves, tombs and cisterns; some 200m or so north of the Monastery, you'll stumble onto a dramatically isolated **High Place**, with godlike **views** over the peaks down to the far-distant Wadi Araba, over 1000m below.

The only route back into Petra from the Monastery is the way you came up. Like all these descents, it's too rocky and isolated even to think about attempting it after sunset.

Further afield

There are plenty of sites of interest to explore beyond Petra's central valley. Although they're more difficult to reach, and generally have less striking architecture once you arrive, just the experience of hiking through Petra's incredible landscape is thrilling enough: all of these walks involve getting well off the popular tour-group tracks, and it's quite possible the only people you meet will be local families. Few visitors to Petra venture beyond the city centre sights, the High Place and the Monastery, but beyond them you'll be greeted by a panorama of barren peaks and wild canyons. All but experienced trekkers should take a guide to enter this wilderness.

Sites within striking distance are ranged along Petra's main valley to either side of the city, so we've divided the treks into two sections, namely **southwest** and **northeast** of Petra's city centre. **Siq al-Berid** (known as "**Little Petra**") and **Baydha**, some 9km north of Petra, are treated separately: they're accessible on long walks across country, but with the distance involved you're more likely to want to get to them on a half-day taxi excursion.

Southwest of Petra

Walking routes to the southwest of Petra begin from the Amud Faraoun; a path from there drops down to follow the main **Wadi Thughra** along the base of the cliffs, from which all the following sights can be reached. **Umm al-Biyara** is the flat-topped mountain overlooking the whole of Petra; a tough climb up steps delivers you to Nabatean ruins and the remains of a seventh-century BC Edomite settlement, and to vertiginous panoramas few people other than mountaineers ever get to experience. The **Snake Monument**, a single block carved as a huge snake, is over 2km southwest of Petra but on the flat. From there, a path branches out to the steps leading up the holy mountain **Jebel Haroun**, on the summit of which is the little white shrine visible from just about everywhere in Petra and Wadi Musa, the tomb of Moses' brother Aaron. Beyond the Snake Monument, **Sabra** is a southern suburb of Petra, mostly unexcavated and featuring a semi-ruined amphitheatre, a full day's hike on the flat through gorgeous open countryside.

Umm al-Biyara

Petra's hardest climb (other than off-route scrambling) is up **Umm al-Biyara**, likely to take a full hour from base to summit and requiring something of a head for heights: a couple of exposed scrambles might give you the flutters. You definitely need a guide, and should only make the climb in the afternoon when the east face of the mountain is in shadow.

As you head southwest from the Amud Faraoun, Wadi Umm Rattam comes in from the left after 350m; keep straight and, a little beyond, branch right (west) on a path directly towards a gully on the western edge of the massif, itself dotted all the way along with facades at different levels. The initial stages of the Nabatean **processional way** have collapsed, but a little to the south you'll find some modern steps, which lead you round to join the Nabatean path again higher up, part original, part restored. A little further is a sweeping hairpin ramp, deeply gouged out of the rockface to form a high corridor. Beyond here, the way is often eroded and, though there are some cairns to mark it, the drops are precipitous. You emerge at the south edge of the **summit plateau**, a scrubby slope that rises another 30m to the highest point on the northwest. The **Edomite settlement** is dead ahead, with many high dry-stone walls and corridors excavated; from the evidence of lamps, jars and looms, it seems that this community was a quiet, peaceful one, but it must have been important enough to receive a letter from Qaush-Gabr, king of Edom around 670 BC: his seal was discovered in the ruins. *Biyara* means "cisterns", and there are plenty up here, probably Nabatean. All along the eastern rim are ruins of Nabatean buildings commanding spectacular bird's-eye views over the Petra basin, 275 sheer metres below; the mountain vistas to the west, from the highest point of the plateau, are no less stunning. There are only two ways down: the fast way, and the way you came up.

The Snake Monument

The path to the Snake Monument is the same as for Umm al-Biyara in the initial stretches, except instead of branching off the Wadi Thughra you should keep going ahead through the undulating countryside. This was (and is) the main road into Petra from the south. After around thirty minutes or so you'll see a very prominent, top-heavy **god-block** atop an area of caves and tombs which has been dubbed the "Southern Graves"; these caves are still inhabited by Bdul families, so you shouldn't be exploring too inquisitively without being invited in. Poised above and to the left of the god-block, not immediately apparent, is the **Snake Monument**, a worn block carved with a large, coiled serpent overlooking the tombs and houses below. If you head another five minutes or so along the valley, you'll come to a flat area with trees that's been fenced around and cultivated; it's here that paths divide – south to Sabra, southeast towards the foot of Jebel Haroun.

Jebel Haroun

Jebel Haroun – Aaron's Mountain – is the holiest site in Petra and one of the holiest in Jordan, venerated by Muslims as the resting place of Prophet Haroun, as well as by Christians and Jews. There persists some local resistance to tourists casually climbing the mountain simply for the views, or to gawk (although this is much less of an issue than in former years): you should bear in mind that this is a place of pilgrimage. The trip there and back takes at least **six hours** from Petra city centre, involving a climb of almost 500m (a donkey can take you for all but the last twenty minutes), and you shouldn't attempt it without a guide, six to eight litres of water, some food, respectable clothing and a sense of humility. Don't bother if you're expecting an impressive shrine (it's small and unremarkable) or outstanding views (they're equally good from the Monastery and Umm al-Biyara). If you choose to visit, you should consider bringing a sum of money with you to leave as a donation.

Rosalyn Maqsood, in her excellent book on Petra (see p.496), explained the power of Jebel Haroun well:

Believers in the "numinous universe" accept that certain localities can be impregnated with the life-giving force of some saint or hero – transforming the sites into powerhouses of spiritual blessing. Traces of their essential virtue would cling to their mortal leavings even though their spirits had passed to another and better world. Holiness was seen as a kind of invisible substance, which clung to whatever it touched. So the virtues (the Latin word *virtu* means "power") of saints would remain and be continually renewed and built up by the constant stream of prayer and devotion emanating from the pilgrims who found their way there. These places are visited to gain healing, or fertility, or protection against dangers psychic and physical, or to gain whatever is the desire of the heart. Jebel Haroun is such a place... There is nothing there, really, and no one to watch you – so why should you remove your shoes, or leave an offering? Only you can answer this.

From the cultivated area near the Snake Monument, a path leads down into the Wadi Magtal ad-Dikh. A little beyond a cemetery on the right-hand side, and past a rock ledge called **Settuh Haroun** (Aaron's Terrace) at the foot of the mountain, where pilgrims unable to climb make an offering (Burckhardt slaughtered his goat here), there is a reasonably clear path up the mountain. Check in the tent at the bottom of the mountain whether the guardian will be around to open the shrine at the top; if not, you should collect the keys from him before heading up.

In 1997, archeologists revealed that a plateau just below the summit was the location of a **Byzantine monastery** dedicated to Aaron; excavations are ongoing under a Finnish team. The small domed **shrine of Haroun** on the peak was renovated by the Mamluke sultan Qalawun in 1459, replacing earlier buildings which had stood on the same site. Up until then, the caretakers had been Greek Christians, and it was in the late sixth century that the Prophet Muhammad, on a journey from Mecca to Damascus, passed through Petra and climbed Jebel Haroun with his uncle. The Christian guardian of the shrine, a monk named Bahira, prophesied that the boy – then aged 10 – would change the world. Today, pilgrims bedeck the shrine with rags, twined threads and shells, the Muslim equivalent of lighting a candle to the saint.

Sabra

At the zenith of its economic power, Petra must have been processing goods from dozens, possibly hundreds, of caravans, and it was obviously not desirable to have hordes of foreign merchants – not to mention camels, random travellers and all the hangers-on associated with the caravan trade – pouring into the city centre. The Nabateans therefore built for themselves "suburbs" on all the main routes into the city, where business could be done, camels fed and watered, and goods stored well away from the sensitive corridors of power. **Bir Mathkoor** (see p.424) in Wadi Araba was the western suburb dealing with trade to and

A two-day hike to Jebel Haroun and Sabra

A fascinating walking route from Petra involves a technically not too challenging twenty-kilometre, seven-hour trek over Jebel Haroun to the solitude of the Roman theatre in Wadi Sabra, beyond which is a palm-fringed spring, followed on the second day by a nine-kilometre direct route back to Petra.

Though the Sabra valley is obvious when looking south from the summit of Jebel Haroun (the route up the mountain is given on opposite), the best way into it is not. After you've returned down the zigzag path from the summit, note the small paths which lead southeast across the upper edge of the valley to a ridge on its far side. Follow this ridge down to reach **Wadi Sabra**, and continue down to find the **theatre** partially concealed by oleanders. The "**Waters of Sabra**" spring lies just beyond. There are rough spots for wilderness camping nearby. On the second day, the route back to Petra takes a direct line northeast up Wadi Sabra, following the main (right) fork of the watercourse where the valley splits. Finding your route only becomes tricky after emerging from the valley, 4km before Wadi Musa: your objective is clear but the way to it is not, and you're faced either with a scramble up the long hillside to the Scenic Road hotels, or devious route-finding along the lower slopes to arrive near the Petra gate. This is not a trek for the inexperienced, but anyone familiar with mountain terrain should be able to hike it with confidence.

from Gaza; **Siq al-Berid** (see p.376), the northern, for trade with Palestine and Syria; **al-Khan** (the area of the *Guesthouse* near the gate) may have been the eastern, receiving goods from the Arabian interior; and the southern suburb – with goods arriving from the Red Sea and Hejaz – was **Sabra**. Little has been excavated here, and the nine-kilometre walk from Petra could take two and a half hours or more, much more appealing as a day-long round-trip hike in open country than a ruin hunt.

There are two routes down to Sabra from Petra, both on the flat the whole way. The first, and more open, goes from the cultivated area near the Snake Monument, around the humped Ras Slayman hill and through the Ragbat al-Btahi pass between peaks before dropping to the sandy wadi floor; shortly after, **Wadi Sabra** joins from the left. As an alternative, you could head southwest from Amud Faraoun, then after 350m turn left (southeast) along Wadi Umm Rattam, which crosses to hug the eastern side of the valley below Jebel Nmayr; after a little less than an hour, aim right (southwest) to follow Wadi Sabra, which is eventually joined by the first path. A little ahead are the ruins of Sabra, set in beautifully green, rolling countryside well watered by a spring, **Ain Sabra**. On the left is a large rock-cut **theatre** with, above the auditorium, a large cistern that was used to provide a head of pressure for flooding the place so that the Nabateans could apparently indulge in mock sea battles. Ruinous evidence of the size of Nabatean Sabra is everywhere around – houses, monumental buildings, niches and several temples.

Continuing south from Sabra through the awesome **canyons** of lower Sabra and Tibn to the villages of Taybeh or Rajif is a more serious prospect and takes a further day or two. It's wild and magnificent country, only suitable for experienced trekkers or those with a knowledgeable guide. Routes are described in detail in Tony Howard's book on trekking in Jordan (see p.496).

Northeast of Petra

There are two main walking routes northeast from Petra, following the two wadis that join the Wadi Musa in the city centre. On the western side of the valley is the quiet **Wadi Turkmaniyyeh** – also often called **Wadi Abu Ullay-geh** – along the bank of which runs the only driveable track into and out of Petra (forbidden to the general public without written permission from the Wadi Musa tourist police, granted only *in extremis*). On the eastern side of the valley, the rocky **Wadi Mataha** hugs the east face of Jebel al-Khubtha, giving access to strenuous walking routes out to Wadi Musa town which avoid the Siq. Set in the heart of the lunar-looking domes behind the *Crowne Plaza Hotel* is the ruined Crusader fort of **Wu'ayra**.

The Wadi Turkmaniyyeh route

Joining the Wadi Musa between the Qasr al-Bint and the *Basin Restaurant*, **Wadi Turkmaniyyeh** is a very pleasant walking route to take out of Petra to the north, a small sandy valley with the hundred-metre-high jagged cliffs on your left contorted into weird shapes. There are two groups of tombs along the way: if you enter the **Wadi Muaysreh ash-Shargiyyeh**, which joins Wadi Turkmaniyyeh on the left barely five minutes from the restaurant, after about 350m you'll come to a dense gathering of facades; and five minutes further northeast along Wadi Turkmaniyyeh you'll see, ranged up on the **Muaysreh Ridges** to your left, plenty more, with niches, double-height courtyards and a tiny High Place dotted among them. Either of these areas would repay scrambled exploration, well away from the crowds; and both Wadi Muaysreh ash-Shargiyyeh and its neighbour Muaysreh al-Gharbiyyeh provide walks (7km; 2hr 30min) linking Petra with Baydha and Siq al-Berid, both of them emerging from Petra's valley onto a cultivated plateau 4km southwest of Siq al-Berid (which is concealed behind a small hill).

About 1km along Wadi Turkmaniyyeh from the *Basin* restaurant you'll see the facade of the **Turkmaniyyeh Tomb** on the left, with the entire bottom half broken away; at the time of writing, there was scaffolding in front for renovation work. Between the two pilasters is the longest inscription in Petra in Nabatean, a dialect of Aramaic, dedicating the tomb and the surrounding property to Dushara. All the gardens, cisterns and walls mentioned in the inscription must have been swept away by the floodwaters of the wadi, as, indeed, the facade almost has been.

From here, the road begins 1500m of tight switchbacks as it climbs the ridge to the police post on the outskirts of **Umm Sayhoun**, the breeze-block village constructed for the Bdul in the 1980s. Buses shuttle regularly from the village into Wadi Musa, about 4km away; they follow the road to the right, curling around the head of the valley and south past Wu'ayra to the *Mövenpick Hotel*.

The Wadi Mataha route

From the Sextius Florentinus Tomb (see p.360), a path hugs the Jebel al-Khubtha northeast along the broad **Wadi Mataha**. After 300m or so, you'll spot a complex of rock-cut dwellings known as **Dorotheos' House** set into the cliff on your right, so called because the name "Dorotheos" occurs twice in Greek inscriptions within a large, airy *triclinium* here. Opposite, on the western side of the wadi, are **Mughur an-Nassara** – the "Caves of the Christians" – a still-populated rocky crag dotted with dozens of tombs and rock-cut houses, many of which are carved with crosses (thus the name). The whole outcrop is worth exploring and commands an excellent view of Petra from the north. About 600m northeast from Dorotheos' House is the point at which the narrow **Sidd Maajn** joins the larger Wadi Mataha from the east.

There are two routes back to civilization from here, neither of them particularly easy, and both susceptible to flash-flooding in the winter and spring. First – and less complicated – is to follow the Wadi Muthlim route (see p.350) in reverse; this brings you to the dam at the mouth of the Siq. The other route is tricky and takes you into the heart of the mass of rocky domes west of Wu'ayra, where it's easy to get lost; from the Wadi Mataha, you should be certain you have at least two hours of good daylight left, or you may find dusk falling with you stranded in a hundred-metre-high blind gorge and nobody in earshot. From the Sidd Maajn junction, continue north only another 100m or so along Wadi Mataha, and scale the dark rusty rocks to your right. This ridge gives you a view down into the Sidd Maajn from above, and along the parallel wadis leading south away from you into the mountain. As you walk left (east), you'll spot – like an enchanted bridge – a Nabatean **aqueduct**, gracefully spanning a wadi below. You need to aim for the wadi which leads south-southeast into the domes from a point directly at the foot of the aqueduct; make a wrong move at this point, and you'll have trouble later on extricating yourself. This is **Wadi Sha'ab Qays** and, like all of the wadis hereabouts, is long, straight and perfectly still; tracks and fresh goat droppings are good signs that you're going roughly in the right direction. You'll have to scrape past woody oleanders rooted in the sandy bed, but the going is easy enough until you reach a gigantic boulder (featuring an endearing little niche) all but blocking the way. There's just enough room to squeeze through on the right. Much further along, you'll come across a Nabatean water channel, which you can follow all the way out of the domes and towards the *Crowne Plaza Hotel*.

Wu'ayra

On the edge of the domes, only about 200m east of Wadi Sha'ab Qays but utterly inaccessible from it, stands the Crusader fort of **Wu'ayra**. The ruins themselves are only of passing interest, but the location of the place is fairytale stuff, balanced on a razor-edge pinnacle of rock with sheer ravines on all sides and a single bridge giving access.

After King Baldwin led the Crusaders into Transjordan in 1115, founding their headquarters at Shobak, his forces rapidly set about consolidating their defences; Wu'ayra (called by them Li Vaux Moise, or "Moses' Valley") was one outpost constructed the following year, al-Habees another, with forts also going up at Aqaba and Tafileh. Wu'ayra was only briefly in Frankish hands, though: after some tussling over possession, Salah ad-Din seized control for good only seventy years later.

The fort is only accessible off the road towards Umm Sayhoun about 1km north of the *Mövenpick Hotel*, the spot handily marked out by a gaping rectangular tomb to the left of the road. Aim for a gap in the rocks about 10m left of the tomb, and you'll find the straightforward path down to where the **bridge** spans the chasm. The **gatehouse** on the other side, with benches and a graffitied niche, gives into the castle **interior**, rough, rocky and ruined.

Siq al-Berid ("Little Petra") and Baydha

Petra's northern suburb of **Siq al-Berid** is often touted to tourists as "**Little Petra**" – which, with its short, high gorge and familiar carved facades, isn't far wrong; however, although it's now consequently seeing its share of tour buses, the place retains an atmosphere and a stillness that have largely disappeared from the central areas of Petra. Adding in its location in gorgeous countryside and its proximity to **Baydha** (a rather less inspiring Neolithic village), it's well worth half a day of your time. Most travellers choose to visit by taxi, combining the two places with a quick peek at Wu'ayra (see above) on the way; the going rate for a full car from Wadi Musa there and back, with a wait included, is about JD10.

Siq al-Berid ("Little Petra")

The route follows the road north from the *Mövenpick Hotel*, past the Wu'ayra fort. Just beyond here, where the road curves left, you can park on the shoulder for one of Petra's best **views**, a breathtaking sweep over the central valley of the ancient city, with many of the monuments in view, dwarfed by the mountains.

Further on, past Umm Sayhoun, the road heads on across rolling, cultivated uplands that are breathtakingly beautiful after Petra's barren rockscapes. About 8km from the *Mövenpick*, a T-junction signs Shobak to the right (this is the back-route to the King's Highway; see p.335). The entrance to the **Siq al-Berid**, or "**Little Petra**", itself is about 800m to the left. You are now beyond Bdul territory in the lands of the Ammareen tribe; a signpost points off the Little Petra access road to the Ammareen campsite (see p.336). In front is a parking area, where kids hawk trinkets and guides offer their (unnecessary) services.

This whole area was a thriving community in Nabatean times, and there's evidence in almost every cranny of Nabatean occupation. Just before you reach the Siq entrance, there's a particularly striking **facade** on the right, with a strange, narrow passage for an interior.

As you enter, you'll realize why this was dubbed Siq al-Berid (the "Cold Siq"): almost no sun can reach inside to warm the place. It's only about 350m long, with alternating narrow and open sections, and differs from most areas of Petra firstly in the density of carved houses, temples and *triclinia* – there are very few blank areas – and secondly in the endearingly quaint **rock–cut stairs** which lead off on all sides, turning it into a multi-storey alleyway that must once have hummed with life. Feel free to explore on all sides; there are a few highlights, but every corner has something worth seeing. In the first open area is what was probably a **temple**, fronted by a portico, below which is a very explorable little rock-cut house. The second open area has four large **triclinia**, which could well have been used to wine and dine merchants and traders on their stopover in Petra. A little further on the left, stairs climb up to the **Painted House**, a *biclinium* featuring one of the very few Nabatean painted interiors to have survived the centuries, although much damaged. You might just be able to make out, on the ceiling at the back, a winged cupid with a bow and arrow; just above is a bird, to the left of which is a Pan figure playing a flute. The third open area culminates in rock–cut stairs which lead through a narrow gap out onto a wide flat ledge; the path drops down into the wadi (Petra is to the left), but you can scramble up to the right for some excellent views.

Baydha

If you emerge from the Siq al-Berid and head right on a track that hugs the cliff all the way round, after fifteen minutes or so you'll come to the Neolithic ruins of **Baydha**, which date from around nine thousand years ago, when the first experiments in settled agriculture were happening. There are two main levels of occupation: the first, from about 7000 BC, involved building a wall around what was formerly a temporary camping ground. The round stone houses inside were partly sunk into the ground and supported on a framework of vertical wooden posts (now rotted away). The occupants seemed to have farmed goats and possibly other animals, as well as cultivating a wide variety of cereals and nuts: querns, tools and stones for grinding and flints are dotted all over the site. After a fire sometime around 6650 BC, the village was rebuilt with "corridor houses", characterized by long, straight walls and large communal areas in addition to smaller rooms. Sometime around 6500 BC, and for a reason as yet unknown, Baydha was abandoned. Although the Nabateans later farmed the site, no one lived here permanently again.

Travel details

Minibuses and serveeces from Wadi Musa simply depart whenever they are full, with no fixed timetables.

Buses, minibuses and serveeces

Taybeh to: Wadi Musa (20min).

Umm Sayhoun to: Wadi Musa (15min).
Wadi Musa to: Amman (Wihdat station; 3hr); Aqaba (1hr 45min); Karak (via Desert Highway 2hr; via King's Highway 2hr 30min); Ma'an (40min); Shobak (30min); Taybeh (20min); Umm Sayhoun (15min); Wadi Rum (1hr 30min).

Useful Arabic place names

Ain Musa	عين موسى	Taybeh	الطيبة
Bir Mathkoor	بئر مذكور	Umm Sayhoun	ام صيحون
Petra	البتراء	Wadi Musa	وادي موسى

The southern desert and Aqaba

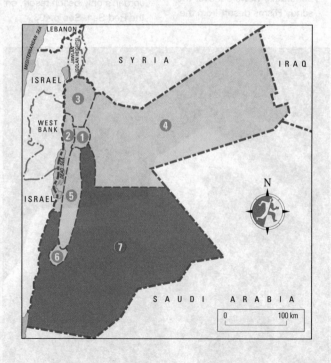

CHAPTER 7

Highlights

* **Desert driving** Three long desert drives capture the spirit and look of the Jordanian landscape: the Desert Highway from Amman, the Wadi Araba road, and, least travelled of all, the Ma'an–Azraq road through Jafr. See p.383

* **Ras an-Naqab** Legendary panoramic views out over the sandy Hisma desert from the edge of Jordan's highland plateau. See p.388

* **Wadi Rum** Rugged and majestic: simply one of the world's most alluring desert destinations. Towering cliffs, red dunes and sleeping under the stars. See p.388

* **Aqaba** Diving, snorkelling and year-round sunbathing at Jordan's only beach resort, on the Red Sea. See p.403

The southern desert and Aqaba

The huge eastern deserts of Jordan are mostly stony plains of limestone or basalt, but much of the **southern desert** to the south and southeast of Petra is sand, presaging the dunes and vast emptinesses of the Arabian interior. The principal town of the south, Ma'an, is eminently missable, but you shouldn't leave Jordan without having spent at least some time in the incredible desert moonscape of **Wadi Rum**, the haunt of Lawrence of Arabia and starting point for camel treks into the red sands. At the southern tip of the country, squeezed onto Jordan's only stretch of coastline, the peaceful town of **Aqaba** is a pleasant counterpoint to the breathtaking marine flora and fauna which thrive in the warm Red Sea waters just offshore.

Two of the three north–south highways connecting Amman with Aqaba are desert roads, and really only of interest as access routes to and from the south, so we've included them in this chapter. The easternmost of the three, the so-called **Desert Highway**, follows the line of the old Hejaz Railway and serves as a demarcation boundary between well-watered hills to the west and the open desert. The westernmost of the three is the fast **Wadi Araba road**, which hugs the Israeli border south of the Dead Sea. The middle route of the three and by far the most interesting – the King's Highway – is covered in detail in Chapter 5.

Transport is very straightforward. Plenty of buses run along the Desert Highway to Ma'an and Aqaba, and you can get connections from both of them to all other destinations in the region. Aqaba is also a major entry point into the country, with an international airport, a land crossing with Israel and a ferry port serving Egypt. The Wadi Araba road has only a handful of buses between Karak or Tafileh and Aqaba.

Destinations in the south are often less appealing than the journeys to get to them, and the freedom a **rental car** gives really comes into its own when you're travelling in the desert here. Being able to stop and walk even 100m away from the highway, to get a firsthand experience of the wide open vistas rather than having them just skim past a dirty window, is a fine way to get a taste of this incredible natural environment.

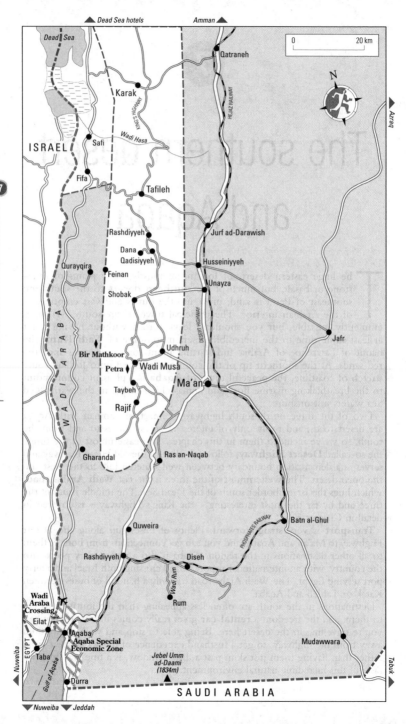

The Desert Highway

The fastest but least romantic of the three routes linking Amman and the south of Jordan, the **Desert Highway** can whisk you from the capital to Petra and beyond in a fraction of the time the same journey would take on the languorous King's Highway, but with a fraction of the interest. For the most part, the journey south is framed by bleached-out desert hills rolling off into the distance, the monotony broken only by feeder roads branching west at regular intervals to towns on the King's Highway – in north-to-south order, Dhiban, Karak, Tafileh, Dana and Shobak (all described in Chapter 5) and Wadi Musa/Petra (Chapter 6). The Desert Highway is the route followed by tankers and heavy lorries running between Aqaba's port, the industrial zones around Amman and Zarqa, and Baghdad; it may be a dual-lane highway but traffic can be relatively heavy. It is also the principal route connecting Saudi

The Hejaz railway

A plan for a **railway** to facilitate the Muslim pilgrimage was touted in the Ottoman capital, Istanbul, from the mid-nineteenth century onwards, and finally received approval from the sultan in the 1890s. At that time, a camel caravan covering the 1300km from **Damascus** to the holy cities of **Medina** and **Mecca**, in the Hejaz region of western Arabia, took the best part of two months, a difficult journey through harsh country that left the pilgrims vulnerable to exhaustion, disease and bandits. The train, it was proposed, would cut this to a mere three days. The route chosen for the rail line (and the adjacent **Desert Highway** that came later) followed almost exactly the pilgrimage route in use since the sixteenth century. By 1908, with good-will funds pouring in from all over the Islamic world, modern, comfortable carriages, a luxury Pullman car and even a rolling mosque complete with two-metre minaret were running three times a week along the full length of the line from Damascus to Medina, bringing new wealth and sophistication to villages such as Zarqa, Amman and Ma'an along the route.

During World War I, Faysal and Abdullah, the sons of Sherif Hussein of Mecca, and the British colonel T.E. Lawrence ("of Arabia"), organized the **Arab Revolt** in the Hejaz (see "Contexts", p.441, for more), and slowly moved north up the rail line, harassing the Turkish supply lines, blowing up trains and eventually taking Damascus. After the war and the collapse of the Ottoman Empire, the dream of pilgrimage by Pullman was as ruined as the track itself and, amid the political turmoil, money could be found to rebuild the line only as far as Ma'an. With its holy *raison d'être* negated, the railway lay semi-dormant for decades, and the only passenger services – between Damascus and Amman – came and went, subject to fluctuations in diplomatic relations. In 1982, a three-nation, three-year feasibility study on renovating the entire line came up with a projected cost of US$5 billion… and the plan was abandoned.

In 1992, a British advertising company hit on the idea of filming an ad for extra-strong mints on the old Hejaz steam locomotives, paying the railway handsomely for the privilege. More enquiries came in, and since then profits from passenger service have paled into insignificance beside the requests for **special charters** from diplomats and train buffs wanting nostalgic rides into the desert, and from film crews and tour operators capitalizing on the legend of Lawrence. Five-star package tours to Jordan now regularly include an afternoon of champagne and caviar on a steam-drawn Pullman, with the added "surprise" of a mid-desert Lawrence-style raid on the train by mounted Bedouin warriors. These days, the railway runs some seventy charters a year, which still generate much better profits than the diesel-drawn scheduled passenger services – but much less than the prosaic business of shifting freight for Jordan's heavy industries.

Arabia and the Gulf with the rest of the Middle East, and all summer long features a tide of big, well-suspensioned minivans packed with holidaying Saudi or Emirati families heading north to resorts in Syria or Lebanon. Most people prefer doing these huge cross-desert drives in the cool of the night, so you'll find services on the highway open until the small hours but often shut in the heat of the afternoon.

This route is older than it appears, as the road was built mostly along the line of the **Hejaz Railway** (see p.383), which itself shadowed earlier Ottoman **pilgrimage** routes through the desert from Damascus to Mecca. During the sixteenth century, the Ottoman authorities positioned tiny hajj forts roughly a day's journey (about 30km) apart all down the length of the route, to guard local water sources and to serve as accommodation for the pilgrims; some survive today, but almost all are ruined and/or inaccessible, the preserve of kestrels and archeologists.

Qatraneh

From Amman's 7th Circle, the Desert Highway (doubling up in its initial stretches as the Airport Road) heads more or less due south. After exits for the Dead Sea, then Madaba and then the airport itself, traffic swishes on south past the Mamluke fort at **Jiza** – now a Bedouin police station – and the infamous desert prison at **Suwaqa**. Just before Suwaqa, some 74km south of 7th Circle, is a small blue sign for Qasr Tuba pointing east into the desert; the dusty road looks enticing, and the ruins repay the effort needed to reach them (see p.255), but you need a 4x4 and a knowledgeable guide for the 54-kilometre desert journey.

Most buses take a break at **QATRANEH**, 90km south of Amman. This small, dusty town has made a living out of introducing roadside culture to Jordan, and a handful of generally decrepit and overpriced snack bars now line the highway, exploiting nod-and-wink understandings with bus operators to fleece hungry passengers. Rather than submit to the delights of stewed lamb or dry biscuits, you may prefer to tighten your belt. If you have your own transport, make instead for the excellent *Baalbaki Tourist Complex*, 9km north of Qatraneh (℡03/239 4156, ℻239 4090). Kept sparkling fresh and superbly equipped, it boasts the cleanest public toilets in the country (ask for the "Western toilets", which are usually kept locked), a basic canteen-style restaurant, a small supermarket, crafts from Bani Hamida, Beit al-Bawadi, the Noor al-Hussein Foundation and others (priced no higher than in Amman), a bookshop of sorts, a back garden shaded by olive trees, and nine comfortable, en-suite **motel rooms**, as well as three slightly more spacious **chalets** (all ❸).

Within the town, the small two-storey hajj **fort** (signed as Qatraneh Castle), built during the reign of the mid-sixteenth-century Ottoman sultan Suleiman the Magnificent, is situated by a wadi 300m west of the road and is in well-preserved condition. The guardian will probably be about to let you in (for a small sum), and a wander round the empty interior, restored in the 1980s by the Turkish government, makes for an atmospheric interlude.

The road to Karak branches west just beyond Qatraneh. Continuing south on the Desert Highway, the *Sultani Tourism Complex* (℡07/9556 1245), again complete with restaurant and souvenir shops, lies 23km south of Qatraneh, but there's little more to distract you from the journey south. Around Hasa, 27km further, are some phosphate mines; other major signposted turn-offs include those at **Jurf ad-Darawish** (69km south of Qatraneh) west to Tafileh; at **Husseiniyyeh** (83km) west to Dana and east to Jafr; and at **Unayza** (92km) west to Shobak and Petra.

Ma'an

MA'AN, 214km south of Amman, is the capital of the southern desert, a dyed-in-the-wool Bedouin town at the meeting-point of highways from Amman, Iraq, Aqaba and Saudi Arabia, as well as countless smaller roads and tracks from settlements dotted around the desert. A frontier staging-post from its earliest days, Ma'an only began to assert itself after the **Hejaz Railway** came through in 1904, transforming an isolated desert encampment into a thriving settlement. Even after the establishment of Transjordan, Ma'an lay in a grey area,

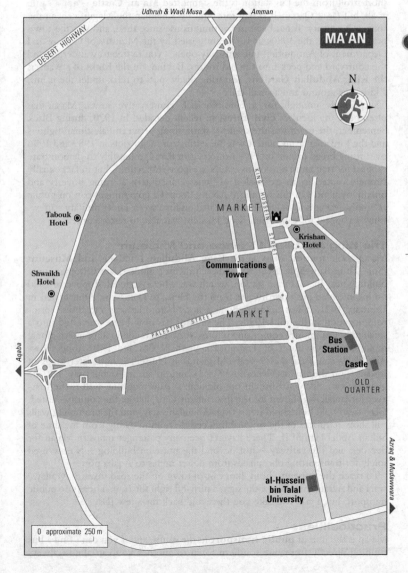

with closer links to the Hejaz region of northwestern Arabia than to Amman. These days farmers come in from all over the region to do business in the markets, and the al-Hussein bin Talal University brings a little student colour to the streets, but for the most part Ma'an is still a pretty lacklustre place. The Desert Highway bypasses the town, and there's little reason to visit other than to grab a bite or to change buses. The bus station lies on the edge of the **old quarter** of town, where Hejazi-style mud-brick houses cluster around palm-laden wadis, and shady gardens – sealed off from the outside world behind crumbling walls – make for a pleasantly cool retreat in such a hot, dry city. A short stroll from the bus station is the signposted **Ma'an Castle** – not a castle at all, but (as at Qatraneh) a hajj fort built by Suleiman the Magnificent in the sixteenth century. It has been in continuous use since then, and was the town prison as late as the 1980s. It is currently used by the Ministry of Culture and Department of Antiquities, but is usually open – you're free to wander around the courtyard and peek into the old rooms. Behind, on the banks of a wadi, is the **King Abdullah Gardens**, featuring shady spots to relax under the palms, a kids' playground and a small café.

Surprisingly enough for a blue-blooded, conservative town, Ma'an has often been the focus of **civil unrest** in recent decades. In 1970, during Black September, the town was the scene of skirmishing between Palestinian fighters and the Jordanian army, and it was the setting for major riots in 1989 and 1996 over rising bread prices. In 1998 rioting again flared, ostensibly to demonstrate support for Iraq amid tension over UN weapons inspections, but in fact equally strongly rooted in an expression of general discontent at rising poverty and unemployment. On this occasion, having flouted a government ban on public assembly, Ma'anis found their town sealed off for a week under military curfew. Only an appeal for calm from King Hussein was able to restore order.

The King Abdullah I Palace and Museum

Ma'an's sole touristic draw is the **King Abdullah I Palace and Museum** (Sun–Thurs 8am–5pm; free), a grandiose title for a modest, late-Ottoman stone building near the old train station, which was where Abdullah stopped in 1920 on his intended push northwards from the Hejaz to Damascus. After he left in February 1921, it was used briefly as a hotel before lapsing into disuse, prior to renovation in the mid-1990s. The interior has now been converted into a small museum, mostly comprising photos of Abdullah conducting international diplomacy as the Emir of Transjordan in the 1930s and 1940s (one shows Abdullah's son Talal and 9-year-old grandson Hussein – both later kings of Jordan – on the hajj at Mecca in 1944). Captions are in Arabic only, but the guardian can talk you through the highlights. Adorning one wall is the first-ever Jordanian flag, flown for the first time in 1918, before the country existed. Glass cases hold household items from Abdullah's stay, and the crumbling walls still show remnants of the original frescoed decoration dating from the time of Sultan Abdel Hamid II. There haven't been any passenger trains in Ma'an for decades, and the **railway** – just beyond the museum building – is now used solely for transporting phosphates from desert mines to Aqaba port.

To reach the museum, head 2km east of town on the road towards Mudawwara and Azraq, then follow the signed turn-off right for 1km. There's no public transport, but a taxi will take you there and back for a few JDs.

Practicalities

Ma'an is the hub of **public transport** in the south, and if you can't find a bus running directly from one southern town to another you can almost always find a connection from Ma'an instead. The **bus station** is 500m southeast of the town centre, and has reasonably regular services to and from Amman, Karak, Tafileh, Shobak, Wadi Musa and Aqaba, although things slow down noticeably after about 2pm. Less regular buses serve Diseh, near Rum, as well as the desert outposts of Mudawwara (on the Saudi border) and Jafr (on the Azraq road).

Of Ma'an's four spartan **hotels**, three pass muster. Best placed is the *Krishan* in the centre of town (T 03/213 2043; ●), basic but comfortable, with an atmospheric veranda but no fans. Out on the highway access road, the grimy *Tabouk* (T 03/213 2452; ●) and the much more welcoming *Shwaikh* (T 03/213 2428; ●) exist to serve Saudi families passing through, and both offer fairly decent rooms with or without bathrooms, all with the advantage of a fan.

The main produce **market** on Palestine Street is crammed to bursting with excellent-quality fruit and veg, and it's in the streets nearby (in the shadow of a huge communications tower) that life in Ma'an is at its most active, with a scattering of **shwarma** and **falafel** stands and pizza joints in between clothes shops and banks. A main reason for visiting Ma'an is to try and gain access to the dilapidated *Khoury Resthouse*, on the road which feeds into town from the north. This is the only **bar** in a very Muslim town, invariably with a couple of big old American cars out front, and makes for an entertaining diversion. Despite appearances, old Mr Khoury does a roaring trade selling excessively overpriced alcohol to overland travellers on their way through Jordan – JD5 for a small can of beer, JD10 for a big can, always with a mint or three to freshen the breath – but actively rejects any other custom by keeping the place locked and barking "Go away!" over the entryphone at visitors who rattle the door. If you make clear you're willing to shell out for a beer, he may let you into his Aladdin's cave of a bar, which is bedecked with fairy lights, dozens of ticking cuckoo clocks, fascinating junk of all kinds and patriotic photos of the Hashemite dynasty stretching back to the Arab Revolt. It feels like time has stood still in this odd place: the dust lies thick on the tables which, he claims very plausibly, haven't been sat at for years.

East from Ma'an

A junction 7km east of Ma'an town centre marks the start of two long, desolate roads through the desert. The main route is **southeast** to the Saudi border post of **Mudawwara**, and there are few reasons to venture onto this long, quiet road if you're not actually intending to cross the border – although if you have a 4x4, it's worth searching out a guide to help you navigate the three-hour, hard-to-follow route across the desert west from Mudawwara to Rum. Some 80km beyond Ma'an is a well-preserved station of the Hejaz Railway at **Batn al-Ghul**, while at Mudawwara itself, 113km southeast of Ma'an – also with a well-preserved station, now occupied by a friendly extended family – an old railway carriage blown up in 1917 by Lawrence and the Arab armies still rests near the disued tracks. Occasional buses run from Ma'an to Mudawwara. The Saudi border lies 15km beyond Mudawwara.

The other road from the junction 7km east of Ma'an leads **northeast** to **Azraq** (see p.256) and onwards towards Iraq, but the only buses along here terminate at **Jafr**, an amiable but rather dilapidated village 58km out of Ma'an. Although trucks to and from Iraq do pass this way, nobody else does, and getting stuck out here without a ride in the endless Plains of Flint under a scorching sun wouldn't be much fun. Jafr's only claim to fame is that it is set on the edge of a huge salt flat, smooth and hard as a tabletop, where in 1997 a British team clocked up an impressive 869kph in the world's fastest car, *ThrustSSC*, before going on to the Nevada desert to set a new world land speed record of 1228kph. A new road from Jafr heads past a large Jordanian airforce base west to Husseiniyyeh on the Desert Highway, but if you continue north without exiting at Jafr, the only thing breaking the long desert drive is a speed bump located outside a police post 71km north of the village. From then on, there's only the regular *tha-dum* of the concrete road under your wheels until you reach Azraq al-Janubi village, 209km north of Jafr. With a 4x4, you can follow the rough desert track 15km east of the police post to the remote settlement of **Bayir**, site of an ancient Nabatean fort and well – still used by the Bedouin today – and a more modern Arab Legion frontier post. The area is occasionally the focus of wilderness camping trips run by Jordanian adventure tourism operators.

South from Ma'an

The principal route from Ma'an to Petra (33km) runs from the centre of town across the Desert Highway and through **Udhruh**. Continuing south on the highway you'll pass another couple of exits marked for Petra (both of which meet the road from Udhruh just above Ain Musa), and then the *al-Anbat Tourist Complex*, another tour-bus rest stop. Just past here is the final turn-off for Petra, some 33km southwest of Ma'an; this is the start of the so-called "**Scenic Road**" which runs into Wadi Musa through Taybeh (see p.335).

A few hundred metres further, the Desert Highway reaches the edge of the highland plateau at **Ras an-Naqab**, from where the most stupendous panoramic views over the sandy desert suddenly open up in front of you. For many years, the stretch of road from here very nearly all the way to Aqaba was a narrow, potholed single-lane highway which used to see a horrendous number of crashes. It has now been upgraded, with two broad lanes heading down and three coming back up; however, the gradient is very steep – seven percent, or 1:14 – and you need to take care behind the wheel.

Once out of the hills, the highway scoots across the sandy floor of the desert, known in this region as the **Hisma**, with the sheer mountains of Rum clearly visible off to the left of the road for much of the way. Some 41km from Ras an-Naqab and a little beyond the village of **Quweira**, a clearly marked left turn at Rashdiyyeh points the way to Wadi Rum.

Wadi Rum

One of the most spectacular natural environments in the Middle East, the desert scenery of **WADI RUM** (pronounced to rhyme with "dumb", not "doom") is a major highlight of a visit to Jordan. The wadi itself is one of a sequence of parallel faults forming valleys in the sandy desert south of the Shara mountains. They are oriented almost perfectly north–south, shaped and characterized by giant granite, basalt and sandstone **mountains** rising up to 800m sheer from the desert floor. The rocky landscape has been weathered over the millennia into bulbous domes and weird ridges and textures that look like nothing so much as molten candle-wax, but it's the sheer bulk of these mountains that awes – some with vertical, smooth flanks, others scarred and distorted, seemingly dripping and melting under the burning sun. The intervening level corridors of soft red sand only add to the image of the

Lawrence of Arabia

Very few of the events concerning T.E. Lawrence and the Arab Revolt can be pinned down with any accuracy. The Arab protagonists left no record of their actions and motivations, and the single account of the Revolt is Lawrence's own, his famous **Seven Pillars of Wisdom**, written after the war, lost, rewritten from memory and published in 1926. By then, though, the image of Lawrence as a true British hero was firmly in place; he was almost universally seen as a soldier of integrity, a brilliant strategist, honest and courageous, who acted with genuine altruism in leading the Arabs to victory and was betrayed by his own officers. The image is a beguiling one, and stood the test of dozens of biographies. Even one of his closest friends describing him as "an infernal liar" didn't crack the facade.

But with the gradual declassifying of British war secrets – and dozens more biographies – elements of a different truth have slowly been taking hold. Lawrence was undoubtedly close to **British Intelligence**; indeed, even in his early 20s, Lawrence's work on an archeological dig in northern Syria may have been a front, enabling him to photograph engineering work on the nearby Berlin–Baghdad railway. His supposed altruism during the **Arab Revolt** seems to have been firmly rooted in a loyalty to his own country and a hatred of the French. During the Revolt, Lawrence was well aware of the Sykes–Picot Agreement that was to carve up the Levant, and seems to have wanted to establish Arab self-rule mostly to stop the French gaining any control. Although his own conscious betrayal of the Arabs racked him with guilt, he justified himself on the grounds that it was more important to defeat Germany and the Ottomans. Details have also emerged of Lawrence's dishonesty and self-glorification: biographers who have compared *Seven Pillars* to documentary evidence have regularly come up against inconsistencies and outright lies perpetrated by Lawrence, often for his own self-aggrandizement.

Lawrence is much less highly regarded in Jordan than in the West. He is today seen as an imperialist, who sought to play up his role in what was essentially an Arab military victory, achieved and led by Faysal. Although he pretended to have Arab interests at heart, in fact – as was shown by the events after the Revolt – his loyalty to British interests never wavered.

Nonetheless, as the years pass and the biographies pile up, the myth persists of Lawrence the square-jawed, blue-eyed buccaneering English Bedouin as portrayed by Peter O'Toole in David Lean's 1962 film epic *Lawrence of Arabia*. But in 1919, Lawrence's friend Colonel Richard Meinertzhagen recorded a conversation that they'd had about the text of *Seven Pillars*: "He confesses that he has overdone it, and is now terrified lest he is found out and deflated. He told me that ever since childhood he had wanted to be a hero. And now he is terrified at his brazen imagination. He hates himself and is having a great struggle with his conscience." This seems as appropriate an epitaph as any to a life still shrouded in mystery.

mountains as monumental islands in a dry sea. Split through by networks of **canyons** and ravines, spanned by naturally formed **rock bridges** and watered by hidden **springs**, the mountains offer opportunities galore for scrambling and rock-climbing, where you could walk for hours or days without seeing another soul.

However you choose to do it – and the best way is to book in advance for a one- or two-day tour with one of the specialist local guides listed on p.396 – you should clear at least one night in your schedule to **sleep in the desert** here. The sunsets are extraordinary; evening coolness after the heat of the day is blissful; the clarity of the desert air helps produce a starry sky of stunning beauty; and the tranquillity of the pitch-dark desert night is simply magical. It's an unforgettable experience.

Some background

Although an arid, open desert, the Rum area is far from depopulated. Wadi Rum and its surrounds have abundant fresh water, and, aside from the tents of semi-nomadic Bedouin scattered in the desert, there are a handful of modern villages in the area, including **Rum** itself in the heart of its eponymous wadi. There's also extensive evidence of past cultures, with plenty of **rock-carved drawings** and ancient **Thamudic inscriptions** still visible (the Thamud were a tribe, cousins of the Nabateans, who lived as nomads in the deserts of northern Arabia), as well as a single, semi-ruined **Nabatean temple**.

T.E. Lawrence waxed lyrical about the Rum area, describing it as "vast, echoing and godlike", and, appropriately enough, much of the epic *Lawrence of Arabia* was filmed here in the early 1960s, prompting tourists to visit in dribs and drabs during the years after.

However, until the late 1980s, Rum village was still comprised mostly of Bedouin tents at the end of a rough road, with a single radio-phone serving the lone Desert Patrol fort. In 1984, a British climbing team led by Tony Howard requested permission from the Ministry of Tourism to explore the possibilities for serious **mountaineering** in and around Wadi Rum. With approval and assistance from the Bedouin and the backing of the ministry, an excellent book on trekking and climbing resulted, which brought the area into the forefront of mainstream tourism for the first time.

Since then, the local Zalabieh and Zuwaydeh Bedouin – sub-clans of the great Howeitat tribe that is pre-eminent in the area – have established **co-operatives** to organize tourism. With the proceeds of their co-operative, the Zalabieh of Rum village built breeze-block houses and a school, and bought buses to link the village with Aqaba and Wadi Musa. The mid-1990s saw a tourist boom that has shown few signs of abating: during the peak months of March, April, September and October, the deserts around Rum can be thronged with visitors, a strange mix of budget backpackers, well-heeled groups bussed in on whirlwind tours, and serious professional climbers. Rum is now a **Protected Area** under the control of ASEZA, the municipal authority of Aqaba, and controls have been put in place to limit environmental degradation while allowing sustainable tourism to continue. Bureaucratic disputes aside, you'll quickly find that, however you manage it, escaping into the desert is infinitely more rewarding than staying for any length of time amid the tour-group hubbub.

Practicalities

There's only one **road** into Wadi Rum, signposted east off the Desert Highway at the village of Rashdiyyeh – 41km south of Ras an-Naqab and 42km north of Aqaba. This road, shadowed by a railway track, skirts the mountains and a couple of settlements for some 17km to a **checkpoint**; Diseh and a handful of other villages lie to the left, while the road ahead bends right into the long avenue of Wadi Rum itself. About 2km before the checkpoint, you'll see a sign pointing north off the road to the excellent camp and resthouse complex of *Bait Ali* (see p.398).

Transport

With most visitors booked on all-inclusive bus tours, there's very little **public transport** in or out of Wadi Rum; it's impossible to make a day-trip without your own transport, since few buses run after about noon. Bus service on Fridays is likely to be curtailed or non-existent.

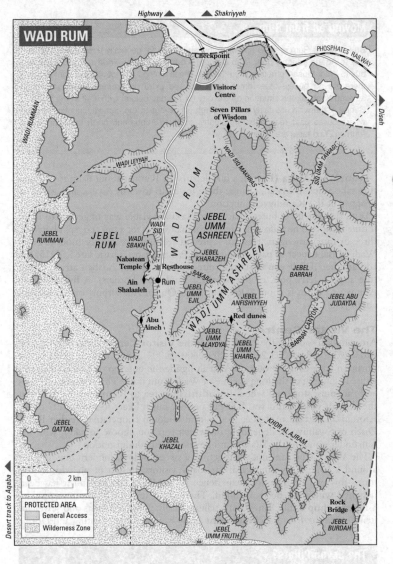

From Aqaba, there are minibuses to Rum at around 6.30am (although this is prone to cancellation), 11am, 1pm and 3pm. However, minibuses run more regularly from Aqaba to Rashdiyyeh and Quweira (both of them on the Desert Highway), and these can drop you at the highway junction at Rashdi-yyeh, from where hitching into Rum is easy: the standard price for a carload of people from the highway to Rum is about JD5. By the time you visit, you may find that the **railway line** – for years devoted only to phosphate trains shuttling between desert mines and Aqaba port – has been upgraded to take tourist passenger services, from Aqaba direct to Rum; at the time of writing, details remained sketchy.

Buses out of Rum are few and far between. There are generally three departures a day to Aqaba (roughly 5am, 7am & noon) – but only one on Fridays – and a single bus to Wadi Musa/Petra (roughly 8.30am). These timings are not reliable: sometimes there are no buses, other times there may be extra departures. You're strongly advised to check the situation on the day (or the day before) with staff at the Visitor Centre. Otherwise, it's fairly easy to hitch a ride out to the highway junction, from where buses pass reasonably frequently, south to Aqaba and north to Ma'an and Amman. **Taxi** fares are outlined below.

From Wadi Musa (Petra), a bus departs for Rum at about 6am; if you miss this, take a bus to Ma'an, change there for a bus towards Aqaba, and ask to be dropped at the Rashdiyyeh junction.

With the paucity of buses, chartering a **taxi** is a viable way of getting to Rum if time is short. The following are approximate fares for a full taxi: split between three or four passengers, this can represent reasonable value for money. From Wadi Musa, expect to pay around JD25. From Aqaba, a basic fare is JD15, but add another JD5 if you're starting directly from one of Aqaba's arrival points (the airport, ferry port, or the Israeli or Saudi land borders). A full taxi from Amman to Rum is about JD65, but from Queen Alia airport or Madaba it's about JD60.

The Visitor Centre

Around 4km south of the checkpoint is the **Visitor Centre** (daily 7am–10pm; ☏03/203 2918 or 203 2586 or 209 0600, ℉203 2586), built in 2004 at the northern edge of the Protected Area alongside the outcrop of Tell Hassan, just at the beginning of the long avenue of Wadi Rum itself. This is where all buses and cars must stop, and where the **admission fee** to Rum must be paid – at the time of writing this was JD2 per person, but is likely to rise to JD7 or so. Around 35 percent of it goes to the local Bedouin cooperatives (either Rum, Diseh or Swalhiyeen, depending on which trip you choose to take), with the remainder going to the Wadi Rum development administration.

The Visitor Centre is not unattractive, a sweep of low, modern buildings set around a large dusty courtyard; for many visitors, bussed in on whistle-stop tours, this will be their sole experience of the Rum deserts, and it has been designed with their needs in mind. There are a few small shops – including a **nature shop** (daily 8am–7pm), selling locally produced crafts and jewellery items – and the *Rum Gate* **restaurant** (daily 8am–4pm; see "Eating and Drink-

The Seven Pillars?

Although the free handout map, and almost all tourist literature, names the soaring pinnacles of rock directly opposite the Visitor Centre as the "**Seven Pillars of Wisdom**", this is a fabrication, made up in the last few years by some marketing executive to cash in on the legend of Lawrence. (Five of the pinnacles are in plain view; the other two are round the side.) Lawrence never mentioned this mountain, and took the title of his most famous work from the Book of Proverbs (9:1): "Wisdom has built a house; she has hewn out her seven pillars". The local Bedouin referred to this mountain as **Jebel al-Mazmar** long before outsiders had ever heard of Rum. It seems tragic that even they are now calling it the "Seven Pillars".

ing" below). Further round is an **Interpretation Hall**, for displays on Bedouin culture, local wildlife and protection of the desert environment, alongside a projection room showing a short **film** introducing Rum. You can also climb the two short towers across the courtyard, for eagle-eye **views** over the spectacular landscape.

Organizing excursions

Aside from **walking** solo, the only way to get out into the desert and see the sights is in a **4x4** driven by a local, or on a **camel**. If you've rented a 4x4 yourself, you really shouldn't head off into the sands hoping to navigate by **maps** alone – ours or anyone else's. To a foreign eye, these desert mountains, dunes and valleys soon all begin to look alike, and it's very easy to get confused and lost, to say nothing of becoming bogged down in soft sand.

The easy-to-overlook downside of 4x4 excursions, and, to a lesser extent, camel treks is that neither allows you to soak up the silence and isolation of the desert at your own walking pace. Hiring someone to drive your gear out to a camping spot in the desert while you take your time and walk, or arranging for a **one-way ride** by 4x4 or camel (either back to the Visitor Centre from an agreed landmark, or out to a particular spot from where you walk back), means you can both have your cake and eat it.

We've outlined a handful of the more popular and accessible sights around Rum, and also given a few pointers for **hikers** to get off the beaten track. However, our accounts are far from comprehensive; if you intend to stay in Rum for some time, or if you're at all serious about trekking (guided or independent) or climbing of any kind, you should seek out some of the excellent **books** by Tony Howard and Diana Taylor (see p.469): *Treks and Climbs in Wadi Rum Jordan* is a full-length paperback with detailed, technical route descriptions, while *Walks & Scrambles in Wadi Rum* is a slender booklet of short, easy-to-accomplish trips that is published in Jordan and widely available. Some of the routes from both are duplicated in their book *Jordan: Walks, Treks, Caves, Climbs, Canyons*.

Any of the routes in and around Rum can be easily strung together to form a two-, three- or four-day excursion, with intervening nights spent camping in the desert. There are also plenty of opportunities for journeys further afield, the most attractive of which is to **Aqaba**, the fifty- to seventy-kilometre desert track there covered in a day by 4x4, two or three by camel. Longer trips than this obviously have more appeal on camel-back, and it's possible to reach Mudawwara by camel in about four days, Petra or Ma'an in five or six.

Hiring drivers, camels and guides

With the exponential growth in visitors to Rum since the 1980s, the local Bedouin have almost completely given up keeping goats, and now make their living predominantly by providing **guide and driving services** to visitors. You should, however, be aware that strict rules surrounding guide services now apply – and the rules, as they stand, are not especially friendly to independent travellers.

If you turn up at the Visitor Centre **without a booking**, you have only one option. Large noticeboards by the ticket office describe a dozen routes in and around Rum by 4x4, and some others by camel, with prices for each. You simply choose which route you'd like to do, pay the fee, get your authorized ticket, and you're then assigned the next **driver** (or camel boy) in line. This can be a perfectly satisfactory way to explore the desert: the huge majority of the drivers, of whom there are dozens, are friendly, knowledgeable and

THE SOUTHERN DESERT AND AQABA | Wadi Rum

Excursions from the Rum Visitor Centre

Following is a list, correct at the time of writing, giving prices for the most popular **excursions** from the Rum Visitor Centre, bookable on a turn-up-and-go basis. All the longer journeys involve stops for intermediate sights such as the spring at Abu Aineh, small rock bridges, carvings or inscriptions, dunes and sunrise/sunset spots. Prices **by 4x4** are for a return journey in a full car, which can normally hold up to six passengers. Prices **by camel** are per person; for long journeys you should factor in food and drink for yourself and your guides, and also – if you're travelling one-way – the cost of getting the camels back to Rum from wherever you leave them. Chartering a camel to carry **luggage** only, so you can ride unencumbered on your own mount, commands the full per-person rate. If, however, you're walking or riding out to, say, a desert campsite, the rate for your gear to be driven out to you in a 4x4 is discounted (JD35 for the day, rather than JD50).

Excursions from the Visitor Centre are carved up into areas: "**Operator 1**" routes cover ground within the heartland of Wadi Rum; "**Operator 2**" routes are in more outlying (but not necessarily any less beautiful) areas to the north and east.

Route	Main destination	Distance/time	Cost
4x4 routes			
"Operator 1" routes by 4x4			
1	Lawrence's Spring	14km (1hr)	JD15
2	Khazali Canyon	30km (2hr)	JD20
3	Sunset sites (Rum)	35km (2.5hr)	JD25
4	Red dunes/Anfishiyyeh	40km (3.5hr)	JD30
5	Little Bridge	35km (3hr)	JD25
6	Lawrence's House	45km (3.5hr)	JD35
7	Umm Fruth bridge	50km (4hr)	JD40
8	Burdah rock bridge	60km (5hr)	JD45
–	Full day tour	65km (full day)	JD50
"Operator 2" routes by 4x4			
1	Alameleh inscriptions	15km (1hr)	JD15
2	Siq Umm Tawagi	18km (2hr)	JD20
3	Sunset sites (Diseh)	20km (2.5hr)	JD25
4	Burrah Canyon	40km (3hr)	JD30
5	Burdah rock bridge	50km (4hr)	JD40
–	Full day tour	60km (full day)	JD50
Camel routes			
"Operator 1" routes by camel			
–	Seven Pillars mountain	1hr	JD5
1	Nabatean temple (starting from Rum village)	30min	JD2
2	Lawrence's Spring	2hr	JD7
3	Khazali Canyon	4hr	JD16
4	Sunset sites	overnight	JD40
5	Red dunes	5hr	JD20
6	Burdah rock bridge	overnight	JD40
–	Full day tour	full day	JD20
"Operator 2" routes by camel			
1	Alameleh inscriptions	1hr	JD7
2	Sunset sites	1.5hr	JD10
3	Sunrise sites	1.5hr	JD10
4	Umm Salab	4hr	JD16
5	Burrah Canyon	8hr	JD20
6	Burdah rock bridge	overnight	JD40

professional. However, be aware that there is a difference between a driver – who may not speak English, whose car may not be the most comfortable, and who may not know many sites of interest – and a guide.

If you want the services of a particular **guide** (we've listed some recommended names below), then you must always **book in advance** by email or fax with that person at least **two days** ahead of your arrival, preferably longer – especially in the busy high seasons of April and October. Always state the name of your preferred guide clearly: email accounts and fax machines are often shared. If you do this, the guide is then entitled to meet you at the Visitor Centre (or elsewhere; some will meet you at the Rashdiyyeh junction on the highway on request), and escort you into the desert for your agreed programme. Otherwise, you may find that your preferred guide is unable to accommodate you, or that you have to pay for a driver to shuttle you from the Visitor Centre into Rum village in order to hook up with him. Guides are not permitted to come to the Visitor Centre to pick up tourists without a firm booking.

We've outlined the **cost** of the Visitor Centre's turn-up-and-go tours in the box. Programmes offered by private guides vary enormously, but a reasonable average for a basic overnight stay – a full day in a 4x4 visiting various desert sites and a night camping under the stars, with three meals and bedding facilities included – is around JD70–100, split between a full carload of passengers (up to four or even six people).

If you're intending to do serious, technical rock-climbing, then you should contact one of Rum's handful of UK-trained **mountain guides**, all of whom have full equipment and plenty of experience. A few other locals also guide rock climbs; like many Rum Bedouin they are naturally competent climbers, and have learnt rope techniques by climbing with experienced visitors. However, Jordan has no system of qualification for mountain guides: staff at the Visitor Centre can put you in touch with someone suitable, but you should establish his experience before agreeing terms. There is an informative leaflet on environmental and safety guidelines, *Climbing and Trekking in Wadi Rum Protected Area*, available free at the Visitor Centre.

Tribal territories

You should be aware that although the landscapes in and around Rum look similar, in fact there are three clearly defined tribal areas that intersect here. The officially protected zone of Wadi Rum itself, in and around Rum village, is the territory of the **Zalabia**. The area around Diseh village, east and northeast of Wadi Rum (including the easternmost part of the Protected Area) is **Zuwaydeh** land. North and west of Wadi Rum, around the village of Shakriyyeh, live the **Swalhiyeen** tribe.

As you approach the Visitor Centre, the jeeps parked outside the walls belong to the Zuwaydeh: they are permitted to follow routes only in the outlying "Operator 2" zone. Beyond the Visitor Centre, through the gateway, are cars belonging to the Zalabia; they stick to "Operator 1" routes in the central heartland of Wadi Rum. The Swalhiyeen get less of a look-in, but the excellent *Bait Ali* complex (see p.398), signposted north off the road a few kilometres before the Rum checkpoint, is in Swalhiyeen territory, and has guides for camel, horse and 4x4 trips in this less-explored area.

There's a great deal of jockeying for position among the tribes, with the Protected Area administrators bending over backwards to upset nobody (and thereby pleasing nobody either), but as an outsider you can, in effect, ignore all the demarcation lines. Although the legendary landscapes of Wadi Rum itself fall within Zalabia territory, there is nothing to stop you exploring further afield.

THE SOUTHERN DESERT AND AQABA | Wadi Rum

395

Recommended guides

Ali Hamad Zalabia ☏ & ⓕ 03/203 2574, mobile ☏ 07/9567 5327, ⓔ sun_rise_camp@yahoo .com. Jeep tours, hiking and some climbing and scrambling.

Atallah Sweilhin ☏ & ⓕ 03/203 3508, mobile ☏ 07/9580 2108, ⓔ rumhorses@yahoo.co.uk. Acknowledged specialist in horse-riding trips around the Rum area.

Attayak Ali and Attayak Aouda Mobile ☏ 07/9589 9723, ⓕ 03/203 2651, ⓔ bedouinroads@yahoo.com, ⓦ www.bedouin roads.com. Two friends who have set up together as "Wadi Rum Mountain Guides", offering a broad range of activities, including hiking, trekking, camel rides, jeep trips, scrambling and rock-climbing. Highly respected, extremely accomplished, and often booked solid.

Aodeh Abdullah Mobile ☏ 07/9561 7902, ⓔ aodeh25@yahoo.com, ⓦ www.aodeh.de. Good-value budget tours by jeep and camel, plus over-night desert camping.

Defallah Atieq ☏ 03/201 9135, ⓔ difallahz@yahoo.com. Experienced specialist in trekking and jeep trips, short and long.

Mattar Auda ☏ & ⓕ 03/201 9574, mobile ☏ 07/7747 2616. Trekking and hiking specialist.

Mohammed Sabah Al-Zalabeh ☏ & ⓕ 03/203 2961, mobile ☏ 07/7731 4688, ⓔ mohammed_rum@yahoo.com, ⓦ www.mohammedwadirum .8m.com. Specializing in cut-price jeep and camel trips and basic overnight desert camping.

Msallam Sabah Ateeg Mobile ☏ 07/9566 0362, ⓔ moslam_rum@yahoo.com. Jeep trips, hikes and camel-trekking, as well as specialist scrambling and rock-climbing.

Mzied Atieq Mobile ☏ 07/7730 4501, ⓕ 03/203 2819, ⓔ mziedco@yahoo.com. Mzied is a wonder-ful host, urbane, charming and exceptionally knowledgeable. He has many years of experience handling groups and individuals visiting Rum, and can offer a wide range of options for hiking, trek-king, camel treks and jeep trips, as well as over-night stays at his excellent permanent campsite in the deep desert, complete with running water and full facilities. Regularly fully booked.

Sabbah Eid ☏ & ⓕ 03/201 6238, mobile ☏ 07/7789 1243, ⓔ sabbah_azlapih@yahoo.com. Specialist in hiking, trekking and especially rock-climbing.

Saleem Ali al-Zalabia ☏ & ⓕ 03/203 2651, mobile ☏ 07/9529 8046, ⓔ saleemrum@yahoo.com.au. Jeep tours, camels and straightforward hiking.

Salem & Selim Lafi Mobile ☏ 07/9512 7148 or 9529 8046, ⓕ 03/203 2651, ⓔ rumtrekking@yahoo.com, ⓦ www.rumtrekking .com. Brothers working together on a range of jeep and hiking trips, including some climbing and scrambling.

Zedane al-Zalabieh ☏ & ⓕ 03/203 2607, mobile ☏ 07/9550 6417, ⓔ zedn_a@yahoo.com, ⓦ www .drschef.de/zedane. Budget-priced jeep trips and desert camping.

Accommodation and food

Facilities at Rum for **independent travellers** are not great: the whole system of tourism in the area is geared up either for large tour groups or for individu-als who have booked in advance for a tour with a specific guide; in the latter case, all your meals and accommodation will be part of the agreed programme and so taken care of by your guide. If you arrive on spec, you have two main options: the Rum Resthouse or Bait Ali – and it's not unknown for both to be fully booked. Bear in mind, too, the extremes of temperature: although it may be killingly hot during the day, nights even in summer can be chilly and, in winter, a dusting of frost isn't uncommon.

Once you've paid your admission fee at the Visitor Centre, you can cadge a lift on down the road, which continues south along the west side of Wadi Rum for another 7km into **Rum** village, with Jebel Rum rising to the right, Jebel Umm Ashreen to the left. The first building you come to, on the right-hand side, is the **Resthouse** (☏ 03/201 8867, ⓕ 201 4240; ❶), which formerly served the function of information centre, meeting-point, restaurant, café, campsite and social centre. These days, with most tourists remaining back at the Visi-tor Centre, it's quieter than it was, but it remains an atmospheric place for a meal – slightly overpriced, but excellent quality – or a quiet drink. Across the road from the Resthouse is a clutch of **local eateries**, the *Wadi Rum Bedouin Restaurant* among them, which provide inexpensive, basic Arabic food as well

Ruth Caswell, author of Ⓦwww.jordanjubilee.com, has been visiting and writing about Wadi Rum for the best part of twenty years. Here she sheds some light on the background of a generation of Bedouin who now make their living as tourist guides.

Two cousins I know, Muhammad and Mahmoud [names have been changed], who are guides at Rum, are both from the Zilabia tribe, a branch of the great Aneizat tribal confederation. Both of them were born in the mid-1970s, in the desert, in the family tent. When they were children they attended the army school in Wadi Rum, usually walking up to 10km in the mornings and then returning to the family camps in the afternoon (school finishes at about 2pm). Sometimes they rode a donkey, sharing it with their friends. After school and during school holidays they looked after their family's animals, often moving tens of kilometres across the desert in search of grazing. They learned to hunt for meat in the mountains, and to gather the medicinal herbs they found there. Both families had a number of goats, but they were (and still are) too valuable to be killed for meat except for special occasions.

The usual transport was by camel. Muhammad's father bought one of the first jeeps to be seen in Wadi Rum when Muhammad was 12 years old; they quickly realized that the jeep was more expensive to run than the camel was, so its use was strictly rationed. It certainly wasn't to be used for things like taking the children to school. Muhammad's family used to spend the winters sheltered in the Barra canyon; during the spring they made their way slowly across the desert, spending the high summers on a plateau across the border in Saudi Arabia. Then back again during the autumn. Mahmoud's father preferred to travel from east to west, from the Mudawwara mud flats to the Abu Aina spring in Wadi Rum.

It is not surprising that these men and their brothers and sisters know the desert and the mountains intimately, nor that they are good walkers.

Another trait that they nearly all share is complete independence whenever possible. Because they were not brought up to be able to call a doctor, a vet or a mechanic, they all know a fair bit about treating an injury or an illness, caring for a sick or injured animal or repairing a car. And so, even though young, they are confident in their own abilities in almost any situation. Most of the Bedouin guides in Wadi Rum have the same or similar backgrounds. The few exceptions are from the families that preferred to remain near to the fort in Wadi Rum that was built by the Desert Patrol and a sure source of water, rather than moving with the seasons. These people might know the deep desert less well than the others, but nonetheless all the Rum guides are still Bedouin to the core.

as a camaraderie with the locals that the Resthouse lacks. These are also good places to make contact with local guides for climbing or trekking excursions. The **Rum Gate restaurant** within the Visitor Centre is perfectly acceptable, with a few daily specials and all the basic dishes – again a bit overpriced, but with the benefit here of a terrace at the back for spectacular views out over the open desert.

Otherwise, the only viable option if you're determined to strike out alone is to bring in your own supplies for **picnicking**. There are a few small **shops** in Rum and Diseh villages selling bread, rice, pasta, canned food, dry biscuits, some basic veg, and so on, but as supplies and freshness can vary, it's advisable to calculate your food requirements prior to your trip and buy at least some essentials in Aqaba, Wadi Musa or Ma'an before you arrive. Your **water** needs while hiking and scrambling in this arid desert are of paramount importance (see p.46); if you carry nothing else, carry water.

The Resthouse also offers basic **accommodation**. The least expensive option is dossing down on a mattress on the roof (with blankets) for a few JDs. You can pitch your own tent on the sand behind the Resthouse, or use one of the tents already there, also for just a few JDs, with access to hot showers.

Permanent desert camps

A great alternative base to staying in or near Rum itself is the **Bait Ali Desert Camp** (☎ & ℉03/202 2626, mobile ☎07/9554 8133 or 7754 8133, ⓦwww .desertexplorer.net; ❷). It is signposted off the access road into Rum, 15km from the turn-off on the main highway and about 6km away from the Rum Visitor Centre on the north side of the protected area. The signpost leads you onto a desert track – passable with care in an ordinary car – round behind a rocky outcrop to the site itself. The public lounge areas, decorated in traditional style, are sheltered and cool but open to the elements, and include a circular dining and entertainment area, where lunches and barbecue dinners are served. There is also Rum's first **swimming pool** here, opened in 2005. For **accommodation**, there is a choice of sleeping under canvas in a well-equipped tent or a series of cosy, comfortable chalets. Toilets and showers are spotlessly clean.

Bait Ali is located within the territory of the Swalhiyeen tribe – who are quite separate from the Zalabia of Rum and the Zuwaydeh of Diseh, and so are able to offer unique trips by camel, horse or 4x4, at their own rates, into landscapes that most visitors don't get to experience.

There are several other **permanent camps**, most of them ranged around the base of Jebel Umm Bdoun near Diseh village. All are inaccessible by ordinary car: you'll have to arrange transport yourself. They all also generally restrict themselves to **group bookings only**, but you may be able to negotiate an overnight stay. A selection includes the *Jabal Rum Camp* (☎07/9557 3144, ℉06/439 7144), the *Captain's Camp* (☎03/201 6905 or 07/9551 0432, ℉03/201 6904) and *Hillawi's Camp* (☎ & ℉03/201 8867 or ☎07/9675 5600

Wadi Rum from above

Hot-air ballooning has now restarted at Rum after a gap of some years, and can offer one of the best ways of experiencing the grandeur of Wadi Rum's natural setting. You take off – generally at dawn, although there are some afternoon flights, depending on demand and weather conditions – from an area of smooth sand-flats near the *Bait Ali* camp, and float over the dunes and mountains for around an hour or hour and a half, with onboard refreshments. It is impossibly romantic – and comes with a concomitantly hefty price tag. The experience costs JD125 per person, with a minimum of five people needed for each flight.

Other aerial adventures include sightseeing in a **microlight** aircraft – a two-seater affair, where you sit behind the pilot for a thrilling low-altitude flight, often seeming to skim above the desert sands (up to 20min is JD25; up to 30min is JD40; up to 45min is JD75: up to 1hr is JD80). Alternatively, you can charter your own single-engined **Cessna** (with five passengers), or twin-engined **Islander** (with nine passengers), for a higher-altitude sightseeing jaunt over the desert, for as long or short as you like: the Cessna costs JD300/hr, the Islander JD500/hr.

All these are operated by the **Royal Aero Sports Club of Jordan** (RASCJ; ☎ & ℉03/203 3763, mobile ☎07/9574 1441, ℮rparaclb@go.com.jo, ⓦwww.fly.to/rpacj), which is based at Aqaba airport. Everything must be booked with them well in advance. They have also been known to run tandem **paragliding** above Wadi Rum.

or 9550 7315). All of these are huge places, catering for more than a hundred people each, sleeping in large tents on proper beds, with mattresses, starched white sheets and blankets. *Captain's* and *Hillawi's* in particular, when a big group is in, can feel almost like small towns in the desert, with electric lights strung across the mountainside above the camp, lights blazing in a series of long, low Bedouin-style tents, mountains of food cooking, music and dancing laid on as entertainment, and bathroom blocks complete with porcelain sit-down toilets in private cubicles, hot and cold running water, mirrors fixed to the walls… Jordan has worse hotels than these so-called camps! Rates for individuals are broadly similar – around JD25 per person for half board. A rather more low-key alternative is the quiet *Zawaideh Camp*, also near Diseh (℡03/203 4525 or 07/9584 0664), with basic facilities, a warmer, more personal welcome and rates roughly half those charged by their competitors.

Sights and walks close to Rum

Although the Visitor Centre is geared up to a set pattern of routes, you needn't feel restricted to just visiting named sites: if you have a couple of hours to spare, there's nothing to stop you striking out across the sands in whichever direction you fancy.

Crossing to the east side of Wadi Rum from the Visitor Centre immediately transfers you from tour-group frenzy into stillness and solitude; following the cliffs of the massif south for a few minutes will give you a more intimate flavour of the desert environment than a bouncing 4x4 ride ever could. In an ordinary rental car, as opposed to a 4x4, another way to lose the bustle is to drive out of Rum to the checkpoint, and then follow the Diseh road east, past the villages of Twayseh and Mensheer. The desert out here is just as explorable – and the views just as awesome – as in and around Wadi Rum itself, but remains virtually unmarked by foreign feet.

The outlines of routes given below assume a starting-point at the *Resthouse* in Rum village.

Jebel Rum

Walking alongside the telephone poles that lead away behind the *Resthouse*, within five minutes you'll come to a small **Nabatean temple** dating from the first or second centuries AD tucked up against the daunting cliffs of **Jebel Rum**, with Nabatean inscriptions on the walls and columns overlaid by later Thamudic graffiti. From here, a modern cylindrical water tank is in plain view a little way south; a safe and easy path leads from the tank up the hillside and around the cliffs above the mouth of a little valley, past springs lush with mint.

On the south side of the little valley, at the head of a Nabatean rock-cut aqueduct, is **Ain Shalaaleh**, a beautiful and utterly tranquil spot cool with water

---

Warning

It barely needs saying, but here goes: it would be **suicidally reckless** to tackle any of the mountain routes in and around Wadi Rum without a local guide. Walking on the desert floor is fine, but even then, if you choose to do a long-distance walk alone, you should register your intended route at the Visitor Centre and let staff know when you are planning to return. For multi-day walks, and all types of scrambling or climbing, it is essential to have a **knowledgeable local guide** with you, whether you're on your first or fiftieth visit: this is exceptionally harsh terrain and apparently safe rock can be treacherous.

△ The Desert Patrol

and shaded by ferns and trees, evocatively described by Lawrence in Chapter 63 of *Seven Pillars of Wisdom*. Nabatean (and modern) inscriptions are all around and there are stunning views out across Wadi Rum. Taking your time, you could devote a relaxing half-day to visiting these two places alone. Most camel- and car-drivers, though, can't be bothered with climbing the slope to reach the spring, and instead lead hopeful visitors – who may have negotiated for a trip specifically to see "**Lawrence's Spring**" – south along the valley floor to the rather mundane spring at **Abu Aineh**, which is marked by a tent pitched alongside an unromantic square concrete pumping block near a scree slope. Both are valid destinations, but the confusion has now become written into history, with the official map marking Abu Aineh as "Lawrence's Spring", rather than Ain Shalaaleh. It's as well to be aware of the confusion beforehand, and insist on Ain Shalaaleh, if that's where you want to go.

From Ain Shalaaleh, it's not hard to work your way east around an outcrop and south over a pass onto a path above the desert floor; about 500m further on, another pass to the right will deliver you to the Bedouin tent and spring at Abu Aineh – also easily reachable on a simple one-hour valley-floor walk 3km south from the *Resthouse*.

A much longer and more serious undertaking is to **circumnavigate Jebel Rum** – from the *Resthouse* to just beyond Abu Aineh, then north, passing to the east of Jebel Rumman and across a saddle into Wadi Leyyah – but this could take nine hours or more and is only for the fit. A much easier prospect is walking northwest from the *Resthouse* along the small, well-watered **Wadi Sbakh**, between the cliffs of Jebel Rum and the outcrop of **Jebel Mayeen**; you'll eventually have to make a short scramble over a saddle into the tiny, narrow **Wadi Sid**, often dotted with pools, from where a scramble leads down to the road a little north of Rum village, making a peaceful three-hour round-trip.

Jebel Umm Ashreen

The west face of **Jebel Umm Ashreen** – the "Mother of Twenty", named (depending on whom you talk to) for twenty Bedouin killed on the mountain, or twenty hikers swept away in a flash flood, or a crafty woman who killed nineteen suitors before marrying the twentieth – is pierced by a number of explorable ravines and canyons. Northeast of the *Resthouse*, between the highest peak of the Umm Ashreen massif and Jebel Kharazeh, is **Makhman Canyon**, explorable for about a kilometre along its length.

Directly east of the *Resthouse* is an enormous ravine splitting Jebel Kharazeh from Jebel Umm Ejil. Just beside it, a complex maze of canyons is negotiable all the way through the mountain. Once up and over a concealed gully alongside the ravine – the only way into the mountain – you emerge on a hidden plateau dotted with wind-eroded towers and framed by looming molten cliffs. Diagonally left is **Kharazeh Canyon**, and you can work your way along it for some distance before the cliffs close in. The main route follows the celebrated **Rakabat Canyon** southeast from the plateau, but path-finding is complex in this closed-in, rocky gorge, requiring plenty of scrambling up and down through interlinking ravines. You eventually emerge beneath the magnificent orange dunes of **Wadi Umm Ashreen**, from where you could walk south around the massif back to Rum village. To do the full ten-kilometre trip (which takes at least half a day), you need confidence on easy rock, a good head for heights and experience of route-finding; if in any doubt, take a local guide.

A different circumnavigation of Jebel Umm Ashreen – which avoids difficult scrambling but could involve as much as ten hours of hiking, some on soft sand – can be done by heading 8km north from Rum to **Wadi Siq Makhras**, which narrows as it cuts southeast through the massif, eventually delivering incredible views over the vast and silent Wadi Umm Ashreen. The twelve-kilometre walk from here south around the massif and back to the *Resthouse* can be shortened by navigating Rakabat Canyon from east to west. Other routes of 10–12km from the eastern opening of Wadi Siq Makhras involve heading northeast through Siq Umm Tawagi (see opposite) to get picked up in Diseh village, or southeast to camp overnight in Barrah Canyon. If you don't fancy such long hikes, you can arrange in advance to be picked up at any identifiable intermediate spot by camels or 4x4 for the return journey.

Longer trips from Rum

For those with more time to spend in the area, there are literally dozens of possible jaunts, whether you're into climbing and scrambling or would prefer to investigate inscriptions. The following gives an idea of what to expect from the more impressive sites, but again Tony Howard's *Walks & Scrambles* cannot be recommended highly enough for its clear and detailed route descriptions. These sights are far enough away from Rum that you'll almost certainly prefer to rent transport: by 4x4, a three- or four-hour excursion could whisk you round most of them and still leave time for the sunset; a stately tour by camel would take days.

South of Rum

About 8km south of Rum, on the desert track to Aqaba, rises **Jebel Qattar**, the "Mountain of Dripping", origin of several freshwater springs. A short walk up the hillside brings you to the largest spring, Ain Qattar, which was converted by the Nabateans into a well. Stone steps in an area of lush greenery descend into a hidden, underground pool of cold, sweet water, drinkable if a little mossy. South and west of Qattar, just off the Aqaba track in the beautiful hiking area around **al-Maghrar** are a handful of "sunset sites" (the places that give the best sunset views change according to the seasons), very popular spots for late-afternoon 4x4 excursions.

The titanic chunk of mountain opposite Qattar is **Jebel Khazali**, standing over the trails north through Wadi Rum and Wadi Umm Ashreen and south and east from the Arabian interior. It's supposedly named for a criminal, Khazal, who was pursued up to the summit and, with nowhere to run, leapt off, whereupon he miraculously floated to earth and landed unharmed. The mountain's north face is split by a mammoth canyon, entered by a ledge on the right, the inner walls of which are covered at different heights with stylized **Thamudic rock drawings** of people, horses and pairs of feet. It's possible to scramble your way up through the cool, narrowing ravine, dodging the pools of stagnant water, for about 200m until you meet unscaleable rock.

The area east and south of Khazali is full of small domes and outcrops, with a cat's cradle of wadis and hidden valleys running through and between the peaks. To the south, a small, easily climbed **rock bridge** rises from the desert floor at **Jebel Umm Fruth**, but for most trekkers the major highlight of the area – and, possibly, of the whole of Wadi Rum – is the large and impressive rock bridge perched way off the desert floor on the north ridge of **Jebel Burdah**. Best photographed from the east, the bridge is best scaled from the west; it's an easy but taxing and serious climb, especially if you're not that good with heights. Non-climbers should only attempt it in the company of a guide – preferably one who has a rope to protect the last few metres of climbing before the bridge, which is definitely dangerous and exposed. The sense of achievement at reaching the bridge, though, is marvellous, and the views are stupendous.

As an alternative to a guided ascent of Jebel Rum, which requires some climbing competence, a crowning glory of a visit would be the ascent of Jordan's highest mountain, **Jebel Umm ad-Daami** (1830m), some 40km south of Rum on the Saudi border – but, by all accounts, it's harder to find a driver who knows the way than it is to reach the summit. Once you've driven there, the scramble up the north ridge is straightforward, and the summit provides superb views over both countries. You can overnight in the desert, perhaps at a Bedouin camp among the beautiful **Domes of Abu Khsheibah**, midway back to Rum.

East and north of Rum

East of Wadi Umm Ashreen is an area of soft sand, with some scrambleable **red dunes** rising to 20m or more against the north face of Jebel Umm Alay-dya. Very close by, some of the best Thamudic carvings can be seen on **Jebel Anfishiyyeh**, including a herd of camels – some ridden by hunters, others suckling their calves – and some strange circle-and-line symbols. A little southeast, **Jebel Umm Kharg** has on its eastern side a small Nabatean structure, named – rightly or wrongly – Lawrence's House, which commands spectacular panoramic views out over the desert.

Further east lie Jebel Barrah and Jebel Abu Judayda, divided by the sandy, easily negotiable and deeply atmospheric **Barrah Canyon**, which winds between the cliffs for some 5km; this is an often-used overnight camping stop, the journey best done with camels. North of Barrah, between a group of three peaks, the hidden valley of **Siq Umm Tawagi** features plenty of Thamudic rock drawings, and is a good second-day route from Barrah to a pick-up point in Diseh village, about 15km north. From Barrah, it's also possible to round the Umm Ashreen massif and return to Rum.

For obvious reasons Rum has cornered the trade in desert adventuring in Jordan, but the wild landscape north of the nearby villages of Diseh and Shakri-yyeh is just as impressive and half as well known. Three easily accessible sites stand out to give a taste of the area. In the foothills just east of Diseh, at the base of **Jebel Amud** amidst dozens of Thamudic inscriptions, is a large slab of rock covered in lines and interconnected circles which, it has been theorized, is an ancient map – although what it refers to isn't known. About 6km north of Shakriyyeh are some amazing Thamudic drawings at **Abu al-Hawl**; the name means "father of terror" and suits well the extraordinary experience of coming across two-metre-high figures with stubby outstretched limbs carved into a remote desert cliff. About the same distance again north is a breathtaking rock arch at **Jebel Kharaz**. You could either take a half-day drive out to these two spots, or treat them as stop-offs on a long desert journey northwest to Petra or northeast to Ma'an.

Aqaba

At the southern tip of Jordan, glorying in the balmiest of climates and a beautiful setting on the shores of the Red Sea, **AQABA** is a perfect place to spend a few days underwater. Some of the best diving and snorkelling in the world is centred on the unspoiled **coral reefs** which hug the coast just south of the town. Whether you're an experienced pro or a novice paddler, getting into the clear blue water is a major priority: the sun-dappled vistas of coral and swarms of multicoloured fish cavorting inches below the surface are an engaging counterpoint to the nearby desert attractions of Petra and Wadi Rum.

In 2000, the **Aqaba Special Economic Zone** (ASEZ; Ⓦ www.aqabazone .com) was set up with tax breaks for business and all kinds of customs duties waived, in an attempt to encourage investment. It has been a wildly successful experiment, which has had a dramatic effect on what was, for years, a rather dowdy and uninspiring town. Nowadays business is booming, major construction

---

Developing Aqaba

With a fistful of tax breaks stimulating international investment into Aqaba, the range of ongoing projects in and around the city is dizzying. In recent years, the entire city centre has been rejuvenated, with new street furniture, public art and extensive re-planting of palm trees (after the palm groves that used to line Aqaba's shore had all been uprooted by previous, less visionary city authorities; see Ⓦ www.khammash. com/aqaba). New shopping malls, including the **Aqaba Gateway** (see p.412), the **City Centre Mall** (located a fair distance north of the centre) and the **Dream Mall**, have gone up, and the run-down Shallala slum district downtown – riddled with crime, drug addiction and prostitution – is to be razed, the population relocated, and a new **souk area** built in its place. The North Beach has got giant new **InterContinental** and **Kempinski** hotels, and the nearby site of the *Barracuda Beach* may not last, as the developers eye up such a prime beachfront location. Behind the Royal Palace complex is the site of the vast **Aqaba Lagoon**, a US$500m project to build a series of huge marinas inland from the beach, accessed by a channel which will also serve the projected Red Sea–Dead Sea canal (see p.173). Termed – perhaps inevitably – "an integrated multi-use leisure community", the lagoons will be surrounded by luxury residences and a string of four- and five-star hotels. Completion is scheduled for some time in 2012.

The South Beach, too, has its fair share of grand schemes, headed by the **Tala Bay Resort** (Ⓦ www.talabay.jo). Occupying the beachfront of Tala Bay, a sweeping curve of sand 15km south of Aqaba city centre, this is another millionaire's playground of luxury residences, a marina, golf course, aqua park and exclusive hotels, with the first phase of development already well on the way to completion. Other projects in the area include a **Dolphinarium**, partly to add a new angle to Aqaba beach tourism, and partly to act as a medical centre for children with special needs to swim with the dolphins; and the **American University at Aqaba**, a partner campus of the American University at Amman.

Future proposals include an ambitious scheme to move the entire **port** facilities several kilometres south, from their current position – stuck awkwardly between the town and the South Coast beaches – as far out of the way as possible, to the Saudi border area. This would free the current port location for further development, of course, but has major environmental consequences. Most of the coral reef beneath the port has been killed by marine activity over the years; moving it would firstly expose the dead area of reef – not especially attractive for beach tourism – and would also most likely kill off the section of reef wherever the port is rebuilt. Nothing has yet been decided – but with a future based on tourism, Aqaba's politicians are having to adjust their dreams to take into account environmental realities. In a move that is perhaps unique in the country, ASEZA's environmental commissioner has imposed a series of relatively stringent restrictions on developers, including a ban on construction within 100m of the high-tide mark and the requirement for a detailed Environmental Impact Assessment to be made for every proposed project. It seems as if Aqaba's development may be proceeding hand-in-hand with protection of its most valuable resource and asset: **coral**.

projects are under way, the city is looking good, its population is growing, and there's a fresh, new buzz in the air.

Sunseekers are now delivered direct to the beaches, thanks to a parallel growth in **charter flights** into Aqaba's international airport – chiefly Hungarians and Bulgarians up to now, with increasing numbers of Western Europeans. And yet, despite the recent appearance of package tourists flip-flopping through the town centre in shorts or bikinis, blithely ignorant of how many cultural taboos they are breaking, Aqaba's proximity to – and historical links with – Saudi Arabia make this actually one of the more socially **conservative** urban centres in Jordan. The contradictions between deep tradition, big business and mass tourism look set to give Aqaba a lively spin in the years ahead.

Another factor to reckon with is the extreme **heat and humidity**. During the four mild months around the New Year, a few days in Aqaba can pleasantly warm the chill of Amman from your bones (not for nothing does King Abdullah keep a winter residence here), but for the rest of the year, daytime temperatures damply soar. The four months of summer can be stifling, with July and August's fifty-degree days and thirty-degree nights too much to bear.

Some history

Aqaba has, for years, been utterly overshadowed by its huge Israeli neighbour Eilat, which was founded in 1949 on what used to be arid desert and is clearly visible sprawling around the opposite shore of the Gulf of Aqaba. However, Aqaba's location is much more naturally favoured than Eilat's: a series of freshwater springs barely a metre or two below the beaches has ensured almost continuous habitation of the shore at least since Nabatean times, although the town in or near Aqaba's position has confusingly changed names many times. In biblical times it was called Elot; through the Roman and Islamic periods this was adapted variously into Aela, Ailana or Aila. Aqaba means "alley", and is a shortening of the title "Aqabat Aila", which refers to the narrow Wadi Yitm pass that was the only route into the town through the mountains to the north.

One of the earliest references to the area comes in the Old Testament (I Kings). King Solomon built a large port at Ezion Geber "beside Elot on the shore of the Red Sea" both for trade and also to house his new navy. During the 1930s, excavations at **Tell al-Khaleifeh**, a little west of Aqaba, seemed to indicate occupation around the time of Solomon, but archeologists – hampered by construction of the modern Jordanian–Israeli border fence – later pinpointed occupation to have begun during the eighth century BC, much later than Solomon. Ongoing investigation is suspended while the *tell* lies in a militarily restricted zone, but nonetheless the real Ezion Geber must have been very close by.

The **Nabateans** controlled a series of ports from Aqaba all down the eastern Gulf coast. Aqaba's fresh water also ensured that the town became an important caravan stop for merchants arriving from Arabia, with routes leading north to Petra and Syria, northwest to the Mediterranean coast at Gaza and west across the Sinai desert into Egypt. A highway constructed by the Roman emperor **Trajan** in 111–14 AD led to Aqaba from his provincial capital at Bosra (Syria).

Recent excavations beneath the beach have revealed the world's **oldest purpose-built church**, dated to around 300 AD, putting meat on the bones of what little is known about Aqaba during the **Byzantine** period; the town was the seat of a bishopric and, on the basis of the ongoing digs, appears to have been of some importance. Aqaba was the first prize to fall to the **Muslims** on their military advance northwards in 630, and flourished throughout the early Islamic period, hosting an acclaimed theological seminary. By the tenth century, Aqaba was an important stop on the pilgrimage route to Mecca.

On their push into Transjordan after 1115, the **Crusaders** – led by Baldwin of Jerusalem – seized the town and built a castle, although no trace of it survives. In response, the Muslim resistance fortified a small offshore island, known to the Crusaders as the Île de Graye (today dubbed Pharaoh's Island), and within a century Salah ad-Din had retaken Aqaba on a campaign which eventually led to Jerusalem.

A small **Mamluke** fort on the shore was rebuilt in the early sixteenth century just before the **Ottoman** seizure of power, and its remains survive today. For three hundred years, Aqaba became again an important caravan stop, but the opening of the Suez Canal in 1869 dealt a death blow. For the first time, seaborne trade around the region, and between Europe and Asia, became an economically viable alternative to the camel caravans; equally, for Turkish and Syrian Muslims, making the pilgrimage to the Holy Places by sea through Suez was infinitely preferable to the arduous journey through the desert via Aqaba. The town's fortunes rapidly declined, and during the 1917 **Arab Revolt**, the forces of Faysal and Lawrence were able to surprise the small Ottoman garrison by approaching through the desert from the north: with all defensive artillery directed towards the sea, Aqaba fell with barely a skirmish. Ironically, when David Lean arrived in 1962 to stage the same incident for *Lawrence of Arabia*, he thought Aqaba looked wrong – and so departed to film the sequence in southern Spain instead.

Modern Aqaba

The sleepy fishing village was only dragged into modernity following a 1965 readjustment of the international border: Saudi Arabia got a patch of interior desert in exchange for Jordan's gaining an extra few kilometres of coastline and coral reef south of Aqaba. This made room for construction of full-size **port** facilities, and since then Aqaba has seen a resurgence in overland trade, although the camel caravans of antiquity have been replaced by a continuous stream of juggernauts: as well as being the sole outlet for Jordan's principal export, phosphates, Aqaba port has also become the transit point for goods trucked to and from Iraq. With the recent shift in priorities away from industry towards **beach tourism**, the dowdy, endearingly run-down Aqaba of old is being unceremoniously shouldered aside – and the longstanding **fishing** industry has been reduced to just a hundred individuals.

Arrival

The **highway** entering Aqaba from the north coils sinuously along the line of the Wadi Yitm, still today, as in antiquity, the only negotiable route through the craggy mountains that seal Aqaba off from the rest of the country. This road is often clogged with huge and slow-moving trucks, but two bypasses ensure that Aqaba town itself is free of them; the first leads behind the mountains direct to the Saudi border at Durra, and the second – just before entering the town itself – diverts truck traffic south to the port facilities. Between the two is a customs post marking the border of the Special Economic Zone; see p.42 for details of procedures on entering and leaving the zone. The highway heads on into the centre of town, connecting with the **Corniche**, or coast road; this hugs the shore right (west) to Aqaba's North Coast, lined with beach hotels; and left (east) to the longer South Coast, location of more hotels and beaches, plus the port and ferry terminal.

Minibuses from Amman, Wadi Musa/Petra, Tafileh, Ma'an, Quweira and Rum all arrive at the **bus station**, opposite the police station in the heart of town; those from Karak (via Safi) terminate 100m south of the bus station in a run-down residential neighbourhood, still within walking distance of the hotels. Of the express buses from Amman, **JETT** stop at their company's office on the Corniche north of the centre alongside the *Mövenpick*; **Trust** stop at their company's office in the centre opposite the *Aquamarina II City*; and **Afana** stop at the bus station.

Ferries and catamarans from Nuweiba in Egypt dock at the passenger terminal, 9km south of town. Arrival is straightforward, as is getting your visa. Taxis and serveeces gather outside the terminal gates to whisk passengers into town for around JD1 per person, or JD4 for the whole car. There are some bank counters in the terminal building, but you'd do better to change money in the town-centre banks or exchange bureaus.

The **Wadi Araba border** between Israel and Jordan (known in Israel as the Yitzhak Rabin or Arava crossing) is 5km north of Aqaba, off the Wadi Araba road. Border formalities are simple, and serveeces do the run into town for JD1–1.500 per person, or JD4–6 for the car. Alternatively, the **border tourist office** (Sat–Thurs 8am–2pm), as well as supplying maps and information, can order a taxi to whisk you directly to Petra (JD30) or Wadi Rum (JD20).

Aqaba's **King Hussein International Airport** is about 9km north of the city, also off the Wadi Araba road. To cope with the prevailing northerly winds blowing down the huge valley, all flights have to circle over the city in order to approach the runway from the south, in the process conveniently alerting Aqaba's taxi-drivers that business is to be done. Plenty gather to meet arriving planes, and the fare into the centre is about JD6.

City transport and information

City serveeces and minibuses generally serve only the residential suburbs, and by far the simplest way to **get around town** is on foot. Walking the length of the Corniche (from the *Radisson SAS* hotel to the fort) takes around half an hour. If it's too hot to walk, you need only lift a finger for a meterless **taxi** to screech to a stop for you; a ride within town shouldn't be more than 500 fils, but you might have to swallow your pride and shell out JD1. To reach the South Coast, **minibuses** depart regularly from the Corniche outside the fort all the way down the coast road to Durra on the Saudi border.

Aqaba's friendly **tourist office** (daily 7.30am–2.30pm & 4–6pm; ☏03/201 3731) is in the same building as the museum, about 750m southwest of the bus station, with free maps and plenty of good cheer.

Accommodation

Aqaba has seen a huge growth in **hotel** building in recent years. In 2004 the town had around 4400 beds; by 2007 that figure is projected to reach at least 11,500, with most of the expansion coming at the top end of the market.

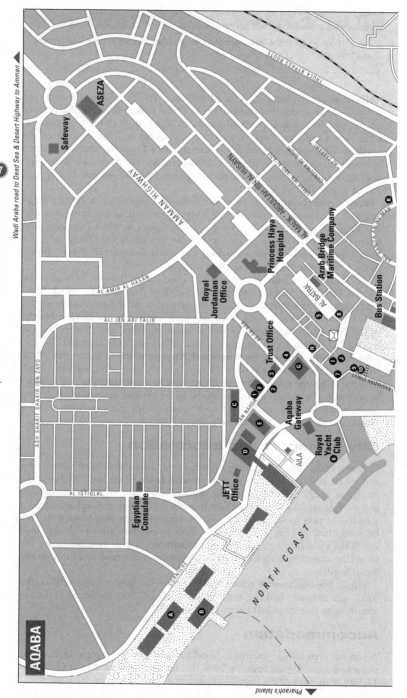

AQABA

Wadi Araba road to Dead Sea & Desert Highway to Amman ▲

Pharaoh's Island ▶

ASEZA

Safeway

AMMAN HIGHWAY

AL AMIR AL HASAN

ALI IBN ABI TALIB

ASH SHARIF SHAKIR IBN ZAYD

AL ISTIQLAL

Egyptian Consulate

CORNICHE

JETT Office

Royal Jordanian Office

Princess Haya Hospital

AL MALIK ABDULLAH IBN AL HUSAYN

JUKAZ IBN ABD AL AZIZ

TOWFUWFAH AL DHUMI

AZ ZABIKIWI

Arab Bridge Maritime Company

ABU HAYNA AL NISHAPURI

K

Bus Station

AL BATRA'

5

8

AS SADA

Trust Office

2 3

4

C

AN NAHDA

1 F

E

D

Aqaba Gateway

AILA

Royal Yacht Club

6

G

H

7

I J

9 10

BAGHDADAN STREET

NORTH COAST

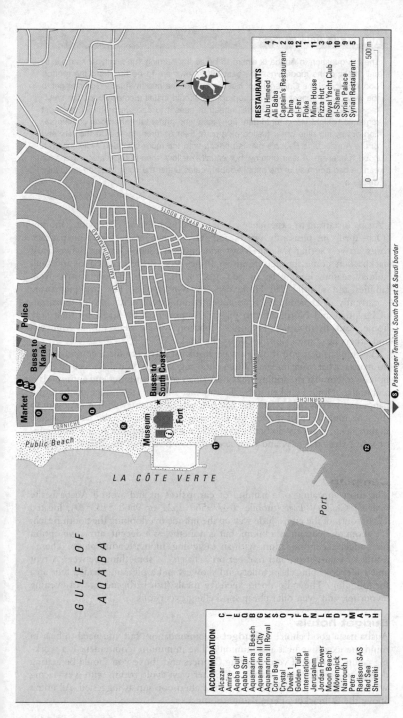

GULF OF
AQABA

LA CÔTE VERTE

Public Beach

Market

Police

Buses to Karak

Buses to South Coast

CORNICHE

Museum

Fort

Port

CORNICHE

AL AMIR MOHAMMAD

AL TA'AWUN

TRUCK BYPASS ROUTE

N

500 m
0

S *Passenger Terminal, South Coast & Saudi border*

ACCOMMODATION
Alcazar   C
Amira   I
Aqaba Gulf   E
Aqaba Star   Q
Aquamarina I Beach   B
Aquamarina II City   G
Aquamarina III Royal   K
Coral Bay   S
Crystal   O
Dweik 1   J
Golden Tulip   F
International   P
Jerusalem   N
Jordan Flower   L
Moon Beach   R
Mövenpick   D
Nairoukh 1   M
Petra   A
Radisson SAS   J
Red Sea   J
Shweiki   H

RESTAURANTS
Abu Hmeed   4
Ali Baba   7
Captain's Restaurant   2
China   8
al-Far   12
Floka   1
Mina House   11
Pizza Hut   3
Royal Yacht Club   6
al-Shami   10
Syrian Palace   9
Syrian Restaurant   5

Sunset in Aqaba

The big question in Aqaba is where to be as the burning sun finally sinks majestically behind the mountains. The best 360° views are to be had from the rooftop pool terrace of the *Golden Tulip*, but the bulk of the nearby *Aqaba Gulf* can get in the way of the sunset a bit. Photographers should install themselves on the west-facing roof of the *Petra* hotel well ahead of sunset to capture probably the most romantic twilight views in Jordan. For those who prefer late-afternoon contemplation of rippling blue water fuelled by a quiet beer or three, the bar at the very end of the *Aquamarina Beach*'s pier is perfect, with the more secluded *Mövenpick*'s a good runner-up. A less dreamy, but equally mellow, toes-in-the-water experience can be had courtesy of the hubbly-bubbly cafés under the palm trees on the public beaches.

Aqaba is starting to experience a year-round high season. The winter months (Oct–April) are pleasantly warm, and this is when many European package tours arrive. Spring (March–May) and autumn (Sept–Oct) are when most backpackers come through. Summer (June–Sept) is the main Saudi and Gulf holiday season, leading to an odd mix on the streets of conservative Arab families and scantily-clad Hungarian sun-worshippers. The hajj pilgrimage – currently in December – is an added complication, with tens of thousands of Egyptian and North African pilgrims stopping off in Aqaba on their way home. And the town can be booked solid on holiday weekends, as Ammanis and others head for a short break by the seaside.

The result is that you should always **book in advance** for accommodation, no matter what your budget. When choosing a room, you'd do well to factor in how to combat the stifling **heat** of Aqaba's spring, summer and autumn days and nights. Don't be taken in by the romance of a sea view, since the beautiful panorama **westwards** across the bay towards Eilat carries with it exposure to the scorching force of the sun for the entire afternoon. For the sake of a cool night's sleep, you may do better to choose a room facing east to the mountains or north over the city, and then keep the windows and the drapes closed all day.

Camping

The most appealing of a handful of **campsites** in and around Aqaba is the *Bedouin Garden Village* (mobile ☏07/9560 2521 or 9562 5133; ❷), located 12km south of the city, a little way up the hillside overlooking the South Beach. It's about as Bedouin as a bikini, but is nonetheless a decent, attractive option for budget accommodation, with an easygoing, hippyish atmosphere. There's a mix of two-person and five-person "chalets" – something between a tent and a teepee – plus clean toilets and showers and a pleasant, shaded tent area for lounging. They also do inexpensive meals (fish barbecues are an evening favourite), and even offer cheap snorkelling excursions.

Budget hotels

Aqaba has a good choice of **budget** accommodation, but you need to bear in mind the excessive heat and humidity. The minimum requirement is a working ceiling fan, but if you're paying ❷ prices and above you should be getting decent air-conditioning as standard. Either way, avoid rooms with west-facing windows, which get the full force of the afternoon sun as suggested. All hotels above the ❶ bracket offer en-suite rooms.

Amira Town centre ☎03/201 8840, ℗201 2559. Simple rooms are light, airy, no frills and sensibly priced. One of four hotels in this price range within 20m of each other on a backstreet near the post office (the others are the *Dweik 1*, *Nairoukh 1* and *Red Sea*). ❷

Aqaba Star Corniche, town centre ☎03/201 6480, ℗201 8147. Fairly good rooms with balconies overlooking the sea – but, unfortunately, the street as well. ❸

Dweik 1 Town centre ☎03/201 2984, ℗201 2985. Sizeable, comfortable rooms with TV are cleaner than the *Red Sea*'s next door, and considerably better value. ❷

International Town centre ☎ & ℗03/201 3445. Clean, well-furnished rooms on a backstreet behind the *Aqaba Star* that are comfortable, cosy and fairly good value. ❸

Jerusalem Town centre ☎03/201 4815. About as low as you'd want to go: basic, hot and grimy. Poor third-best to the *Petra* and *Jordan Flower* next door. ❶

Jordan Flower Town centre ☎ & ℗03/201 4378. Renovated, en-suite rooms aren't bad at all, and this is a good alternative to its popular next-door neighbours, with the option to pay a little extra for air-conditioning. ❶–❷

Nairoukh 1 Town centre ☎03/201 9284 ℗201 9285. A friendly choice, probably the best of the clutch of similar establishments alongside each other on this backstreet near the post office, with comfortable, clean rooms. ❷

Petra Town centre ☎03/201 3746. Longstanding backpackers' favourite, with friendly, understanding staff and a lift. Upper floors are reserved exclusively for foreigners. Rooms are clean, all have ceiling fans and many have balconies; in summer, avoid west-facing rooms. All rooms have optional air-con, which costs a few JDs extra. The shaded roof terrace has one of Aqaba's finest views, and opting to sleep on a mattress up here is a good choice for hot nights. ❶–❷

Red Sea Town centre ☎03/201 2156, ℗201 5789. OK place near the post office, with a range of different rooms (avoid the noisy ones at the back), well managed and popular with a backpacking clientele – but not such great value. ❷–❸

Mid-range hotels

Many **mid-range** hoteliers have gone to town on their lobby decor, but do less well when it comes to the rooms: in many of these places, a four-star reception desk preludes two-star facilities. Furthermore, sometimes as much as JD15 can separate rooms with a sea view from those facing the mountains. To add to the confusion, prices are subject to wild fluctuations depending on the season and current room occupancy.

Alcazar Town centre ☎03/201 4131, ℗201 4133, ⓦwww.alcazarhotel.com. A friendly, welcoming two-star hotel, well located in the centre, with individually decorated stone-floored rooms that are cool, airy and pleasant, set around a four-storey atrium open to the sky. Further attractions include the Seastar diving centre, one of the biggest pools in town and free transport and access to the Club Murjan beach complex on the South Coast. A characterful choice. ❸–❹

Coral Bay At the Royal Diving Club, 17km south of town ☎03/201 7035, ℗201 7097. Well-designed three-star hotel, with 69 rooms – most with a sea view – on a beautiful, quiet stretch of beach well away from the town bustle. Rooms are pleasant and have some character, and being within a few metres of the water's edge is a major plus. ❹–❺

Moon Beach Corniche ☎ & ℗03/201 3316. Rather incongruous block plonked down on the sands in front of the fort, decent enough, with generic midrange rooms and a substantial breakfast. ❸–❹

Shweiki Town centre ☎03/202 2657, ℗202 2659. Very large rooms are spotless and have good facilities. ❸–❹

Expensive hotels

Aqaba has seen a boom in both the number and quality of **luxury** four- and five-star hotels in the last few years – and the trend is set to continue. By the time you read this, there will be two new five-star beach resort hotels on the North Beach – an **InterContinental** and a **Kempinski**. Further west, the current *Barracuda Beach* area is due for conversion at some point into another large hotel, and the massive **Aqaba Lagoon** project, set back from the seafront behind the Royal Palace, will yield more hotel rooms. On the South Beach, there are plans for two new luxury hotels at the **Tala Bay** resort complex. See the on p.404 box for more on this.

Aqaba Gulf Corniche ℡ 03/201 6636, ℻ 201 8246. Landmark city-centre hotel which sees a lot of tour-group business – functional, generic and pleasant enough, but unremarkable. ⑥–⑦

Aquamarina I Beach Corniche, North Coast ℡ 03/201 6250, ℻ 203 2630, ⓦ www .aquamarina-group.com. Good-value beachfront hotel, with generally pleasant rooms of varying size, some with balconies over the sea. Also has its own patch of beach with bars galore, a diving centre and watersports facilities. Its popularity – both with tourist groups and with US Navy crews on shore leave – means that it's often full. ⑥

Aquamarina II City Town centre ℡ 03/201 5165, ℻ 203 2633, ⓦ www.aquamarina-group.com. Set back from the beach, with spacious, comfortable rooms that are better value than *Aquamarina 1*. Guests can use all facilities of the three *Aquamarina* hotels. ⑥

Aquamarina III Royal East of the centre ℡ 03/203 2634, ℻ 203 2639, ⓦ www .aquamarina-group.com. High above the town in a humdrum residential suburb, but offering stunning views from its airy, well-appointed rooms. All facilities at the other *Aquamarina* hotels are free, and shuttle buses link it to the town centre. ⑥

Crystal Corniche, town centre ℡ 03/202 2001, ℻ 202 2006. Classy choice in the heart of the town-centre action, very clean and stylish, with a range of large rooms and excellent facilities. ⑥

Golden Tulip Town centre ℡ 03/203 1910, ℻ 203 2845, ⓦ www.goldentulip.com. Occupying an odd building (begun as a shopping mall, then converted partway up into a hotel), this is a memorable, handsome hotel with a rooftop mini-pool that sizzles in summer, and a stunning five-storey atrium. All but ten of the 104 rooms have balconies, and those that don't are huge corner rooms. Also has several connected family suites. The detail and finishing can be a little lax, but prices are competitive enough to let you see past that. ⑤–⑥

Mövenpick Corniche, North Coast ℡ 03/203 4020, ℻ 203 4040, ⓦ www.movenpick-aqaba.com. Vast and lavish complex, variously dubbed by the locals "the fairy palace" for its twinkling lights and "the prison" for the curiously designed set of bars that slides across every window. Inside, it's airy, spacious and beautifully designed, with the pool placed up on a bridge over the road that connects the hotel proper (on the north side of the road) with the condominium section on the beach to the south. Rooms are very well appointed, with everything you'd expect, although some aren't as big as you might imagine. Four cafés, three restaurants and a pub fill out the facilities. ⑨

Radisson SAS Corniche, North Coast ℡ 03/201 2426, ℻ 201 3426, ⓦ www.radissonsas.com. Large hotel with its own pool and stretch of beach. Sea-view or land-view rooms are all luxurious to a fault, and service is swift and courteous. ⑨

The Town

Aqaba town centre is a dense network of streets and alleys clustered around the junction of the Corniche and the main highway from the north. Here you'll find the bulk of the town's smaller hotels, dozens of cafés and restaurants, the main produce market, access to the public beach and all of Aqaba's promenading, street-based nightlife. Aside from shopping, and checking out the multimedia extravaganza within the **Aqaba Gateway** mall, sights within the town are limited to a **Mamluke fort** and small **museum** to the south of the centre, and the open excavations of Islamic-period **Aila** to the north. All are worth checking out, although you'd do well to do any investigation early in the morning, before the sun has had a chance to turn up the heat. Aside from beach–bumming, Aqaba's only other land-based attraction is an **aquarium**, well south of the town in the Marine Science Station, housing examples of the local underwater fauna.

Aqaba Gateway: the "Jordan Experience"

Alongside the main traffic circle on the Corniche rises the **Aqaba Gateway** building, fronted most prominently with a *McDonalds*. This curious complex, located at the end of the highway from Amman as a point of welcome to the city, has a colourful history. It was conceived by Hollywood director Irvin "Shorty" Yeaworth (famous for 1958's *The Blob*) to be a mini-theme park, hosting costumed characters parading amidst a traditional-style souk of spices and jewellery. The complex was only part-completed when, in 2004, Yeaworth was killed in a traffic accident near Tafileh. Subsequently, the building works were rushed through and the retail units filled as quickly as possible – with the result that it has become just another mall, packed with fast-food outlets, albeit with a replica Arab dhow moored on a lagoon in the middle.

Nonetheless the complex is worth a visit, not least for Yeaworth's *pièce de résistance* (which survives him), the **Jordan Experience**, a multimedia extravaganza designed to showcase the country's attractions. From the ticket office waiting area, a guide leads you on a short tour through a darkened "siq", with spotlit displays and recorded voices telling stories of Jordan's past and present. Another door opens, and you are led through to what is – extraordinarily – **the world's largest motion-base cinema**, something akin to IMAX. The screen is big, with wraparound sound, while the movie itself (which lasts about twenty minutes) comprises footage of Jordan from the air, filmed from a microlight: as the camera angle shifts, so does the floor of the cinema, tilting on huge hydraulic supports from side to side, and forward and back, to match the pictures. It's most unusual; very kitsch, but hugely entertaining – and just as popular with visiting Ammanis as with European tour groups. At the time of writing, prices and English-language showtimes hadn't been fixed – the best advice is to go in person and ask for details.

Aqaba fort

Set in the midst of the palm-laden beach known as *La Côte Verte* (The Green Coast), Aqaba's Mamluke **fort** (daily 7.30am–sunset) is an atmospheric place for an hour's wander, cool, shady and cut off from the Corniche traffic behind thick walls.

The impressive entrance is flanked by semicircular **towers**, each bearing a calligraphic invocation to Allah; the arch that currently spans the gap between them is much narrower than the original, the line of which can still be traced. Overhead is a panel bearing the Hashemite coat of arms, installed following the ousting of the Ottomans in 1917. The fort was built in 1320; inside the gloomy cross-vaulted entranceway, a long **inscription** runs around the walls, celebrating renovations by the penultimate Mamluke sultan Qansawh al-Ghawni ("slayer of the unbelievers and the polytheists, reviver of justice in the universe") in either 1504–05 or 1514–15. A roundel commemorates further rebuilding work in 996 AH (1587 AD), by which time the Ottomans were in power.

Through a dark passageway (with mysterious, malodorous rooms off to either side) lies a domed area, beyond which opens the large, airy interior **courtyard**, dominated by a huge eucalyptus. This fort was the main focus of Aqaba's caravan trade for centuries, and rooms all around the walls – some of which have been restored – testify to its more hospitable function as caravanserai for much of its later life. The ruined section to the right as you enter the courtyard was destroyed mostly by shells fired from British gunboats during the Arab Revolt. Opposite the entrance is a concrete-and-plaster mosque; steps to the left of it can bring you up onto the highest point of the walls for a dreamy view through the palm trees and over the blue gulf waters.

Aqaba museum

Next to the fort is a small building housing both the tourist office and Aqaba's small but interesting **museum** (daily 7.30am–5pm; JD1). The collection demonstrates Aqaba's reliance on international trade over the centuries, with coins and pottery from Egypt (including a marvellous lustre-ware bowl from late tenth-century Fatimid Cairo captioned *Man with a Turban*), Iraq, Ethiopia and some exquisite tenth- and eleventh-century Chinese ceramics, a section of frescoes from Islamic-period Aila and a reconstruction of Aila's Egyptian Gate, Byzantine inscriptions galore, and the first milestone of the Roman emperor Trajan's Via Nova Traiana highway, discovered on the beach and inscribed "from the borders of Syria to the Red Sea". Excavations at Rum in 1998 uncovered three exquisite Nabatean figurines in bronze, also on display here.

The pleasantly shady building also served for a short time as the **House of Sheikh Hussein bin Ali**, Sharif of Mecca and the late King Hussein's great-grandfather. He spent six months here during 1924, in an attempt to dissuade his son, Emir Abdullah, from acceding to divisive British policy in the region; the 1923 Anglo-Jordanian Treaty had not only separated Transjordan from both Palestine and the Hashemite heartland of the Hejaz, but had also formally instituted Abdullah as emir over his father's claims. One room off the museum courtyard contains some remnants of Hussein's stay: huge *mensaf* platters, coffee grinders and pots, camel saddles and copperware.

Aila

Just north of the town centre, the open site of the Islamic-period town of **Aila** lies in an unromantic location, sandwiched between the Royal Yacht Club, the *Mövenpick* hotel, the Corniche road and the public beach. A wadi runs through the middle of the site, and the fenced-off grounds of the yacht club enclose most of the southeastern corner of the city, but the relatively small remaining area within the excavated city walls is well described on good information boards. Teams from Chicago still work here for a few weeks every summer.

A low reconstructed wall runs along the Corniche roughly in the position of the original: you enter the site through an open gateway which is also more or less where the original **Syrian Gate** would have met the road from the northeast. To the right, the foundations of towers projecting out of the city wall have been cleared; these can be followed down to the **Egyptian Gate**, the history of which reflects the history of the whole city. In the early Islamic, pre-Umayyad period, the gate was about 3m wide, flanked by the two semi-circular towers still apparent and featuring a round arch overhead. A stump in front is the remnant of a central column, built some time in the eighth century to narrow the arch. A century or two followed during which Aila was at its zenith; however, debris and rubbish from the burgeoning population dumped outside the walls caused the ground level to rise, the flanking towers were used as storerooms and shops further swamped the gate. Rebuilding work resulted in the current smaller, pointed arch over the gate, but Aila's days were numbered, and eventually the gate was sealed, serving only as a drain.

The street leading into the city from the Egyptian Gate has been cleared, and walking along it – well below current beach level – is a great way to get a feel for Aila, with simple shops and houses flanking the street (many bread ovens were discovered in the small residences here). Some 50m along the street, at the centre of the city, is the **Pavilion Building**, formerly a tetrapylon at the junction of four axial streets, later converted, during the ninth or tenth century, into a grand, two-storey residence (though the rooms seem tiny today). The minuscule square room in the nearest corner was a bath, and the interior of the building was a courtyard framed by rooms and open *iwans*.

A wadi cuts across the city just beyond the Pavilion Building, but the road from the Egyptian Gate would have continued straight across to the **Hejaz Gate**, now in the grounds of the yacht club opposite. Another road led from the Pavilion Building right to the **Sea Gate** and left to the Syrian Gate. Towards the Corniche, also on the banks of the wadi, lies a large building,

---

Aqaba's beaches

All the **beaches** in town, whether privately owned or public, are slim stretches of sand jammed with bodies from dawn to well after dusk; for peace and quiet, you'll have to head to the South Coast.

Aqaba's cleanest beaches, where foreign women will get no hassle whatsoever, are south of town at the **Royal Diving Club** (RDC; JD7, includes sunbed and towel) and **Club Murjan** (JD5); both of them also have a pool and changing areas. Both have a proper restaurant, and both operate private shuttle buses to and from the town centre (see "Dive centres", p.418). Until redevelopment beckons, the **Barracuda Beach** complex (☏03/201 9891) on the North Coast, beside the *Radisson SAS* hotel, is a good bet, a pleasant, well-designed place with beach bar, pool, sun loungers, beach volleyball and a small restaurant. The price of **hotel beaches** to non-guests is open to change, but you should expect to pay something between JD7 and JD15. Several of the big hotels do special deals on Fridays, covering access to the beach plus lunch and some **watersports** such as jet-skiing and windsurfing.

The **public beach** – comprising a long stretch from the Yacht Club all down the Côte Verte to beyond the fort – is quite a different affair. This is the best place to soak up a slice of local life: loosely partitioned cafés have been rigged up in the sand, with radios blaring, women sitting in the shallows fully clothed, hubbly-bubbly smoke wafting over everything, and square-eyed families glued to TVs balanced table-on-table within a metre of the lapping waves. Needless to say, this is not the place either for a relaxing spot of sun worship or for women to take a dip wearing anything less than an overcoat.

There are also dozens of **glass-bottomed boats** chugging around the public beaches sharking for customers, and they can be a mildly diverting way to check out the underwater scenery while still enjoying the wind in your hair. Plenty of people can fit on board, although it's worth having a look before you set off how sturdy the boat actually is when weighed down by ten or so bodies. A full complement of passengers should pay no more than JD10 per hour, although this may require some bargaining skills. Note that some disreputable boat captains have been known to dive down and snap off bits of coral to hand to their oohing-and-aahing clients. This is not only illegal but also kills a whole section of the reef. If it happens, you should refuse to pay for the trip and report them later to the police and tourist office.

anonymously termed on the noticeboards "The Large Enclosure" but now determined to be a **mosque**. Much rebuilding work makes it difficult to tell what's what, but a *mihrab* and a double row of columns along the south wall indicate a covered prayer hall, and the line of the external walls of the rectangular building can be traced. The huge size of this mosque relative to the area of the city shows the importance of Aila in its heyday, both in terms of its population and also as a centre of Islamic study.

Some 200m northwest of the site, in an open area behind the JETT bus station, excavations have uncovered the location of the earlier **Roman** and **Byzantine** settlement, including rooms, a stretch of city wall, cemeteries and – in a find which hit world headlines – remains of the oldest-known structure to have been designed and built as a **church**, dated to 290 or 300 AD (older buildings, in Syria and elsewhere, are known to have been converted into churches in the 260s). It was used for only a few decades before an earthquake in 363 caused it to be abandoned; sand quickly filled the interior, preserving the mud-brick walls up to a height of almost 5m.

The Marine Science Station aquarium

Some 10km south of the town, between the ferry terminal and the Royal Diving Club, is the **Marine Science Station** (run by Amman's Jordan University and Irbid's Yarmouk University; Ⓦwww.ju.edu.jo/mss), the only part of which open to the public is a small **aquarium** (daily 8am–5pm; JD2). Handy if you're unable to dive or snorkel, this gives the chance to check out firsthand the kind of fishy life that teems below the surface, although it is a little sad that these characters get to live out their days circling a tank while the vast clear gulf waters are merely a finstroke away. There's a short English-language video to watch, and the staff are happy to talk you through the varied collection of lionfish, parrotfish, moray eels and more, although the highlight (and a useful reference point if you intend to dive later on) is checking out a tank full of lethally poisonous stonefish – if you can tell them apart from the stones, that is.

Diving and snorkelling at Aqaba

Some of the best **diving and snorkelling** to be had in the world is packed along the slim 27km of coastline between Aqaba and the Saudi border, and the town has several professional dive centres providing technical assistance and a helping hand to pros and novices alike. If you've never been snorkelling before, Aqaba is an easier, and more instantly attractive, place to start than nearby Eilat (Israel) or Sharm el-Sheikh (Egypt), with the reef shelving gently directly from the beach, cutting out the need for boat entries. Diving beginners can go down accompanied by an instructor in complete safety, and for those with an internationally recognized diving qualification, there are some fourteen dive sites along the coast to choose from.

The major advantage of diving in Jordan rather than Egypt's Sinai coast or the handful of sites off Eilat is the almost untouched condition of the **coral**. Fish abound in greater densities elsewhere in the Red Sea (although you're still likely to come face-to-face with more marine life than you could shake a stick at) but Aqaba was a relatively slow and careful starter in specialized diving tourism, and so has managed to avoid severe deterioration of the reefs. Compared to the Sinai's two million annual dives, and Eilat's three-quarters of a million, Aqaba only sees about twenty thousand dives a year. Work by local environmental NGOs – principally the Jordan Royal Ecological Diving

Society, or JREDS (see p.77) – is raising awareness of conservation issues among local people.

The visionary **Red Sea Marine Peace Park** (Ⓦ www.marine-peacepark .org) was set up by Jordan in 1995, and soon joined by Israel, to protect the marine flora and fauna of the entire Gulf of Aqaba in an intended multinational co-operative effort. Coral conservation guidelines concerning correct diving procedures are already in place, and safe mooring buoys have been set up at all major dive sites to halt damage from boat anchors. International funding is forthcoming, and all that has to follow is Egyptian and Saudi implementation, but in the overheated political climate, the project has been renamed the **Aqaba Marine Park**, and cooperation with Israel has been suspended; the major issue of the moment is protecting Aqaba's fragile South Coast.

Wherever you choose to dive or snorkel off Aqaba, wide fields of near-perfect soft corals stretch off into the startlingly clear blue water, huge heads of stony corals growing literally as big as a house. Fish life is also thrillingly diverse, with endless species of small and large multicoloured swimmers goggling back at you from all sides. Butterflyfish, angelfish, parrotfish and groupers are all common, as are shoals of damselfish, jewelfish and even moray eels. Those who have had some previous experience of diving should not miss the chance to go down at **night**.

Dive sites

There are fourteen dive sites off Aqaba's South Coast, although, confusingly, different dive centres use different names for the same sites, and sometimes divide one site into two areas; we're adopting the names used by the Royal Diving Club (RDC; see p.419). If you intend diving or snorkelling, you should always consult with a dive centre in advance about the latest conditions; the account below – which covers the sites from north to south – is for general guidance only and not meant to be exhaustive.

Just south of the Marine Science Station's fenced-off area is the **King Abdullah Reef**, which extends for several hundred metres offshore and is good for snorkelling as well as diving; close by is the steeply sloping **Black Rock**, with a wide variety of massive hard corals and the added attraction of occasional turtle sightings. Some 4km north of the RDC and barely 50m from the shore lies the **wreck of the Cedar Pride**, a Lebanese cargo ship deliberately sunk here in 1986 as an artificial reef. Lying in 30m of water, it's now covered in soft corals. Very close by is the gently undulating **Japanese Gardens**, colourful and good for snorkellers.

A little further south, two of the most attractive sites in the whole Red Sea are the unmissable **Gorgonion I** and **II**, the reef gently inclining down to 30m or so with spectacular fish life and perfectly preserved coral growth of all kinds stretching off to all sides. A much-ignored site is the **Canyon**, with a shallow slope leading off for several hundred metres to a drop-off plunging over 45m,

Pharaoh's Island

About 17km southwest of Aqaba – and 250m off the Egyptian coast – lies a small rocky island known to Jordanians and Egyptians as **Pharaoh's Island** (Jezirat Faraoun), to Israelis as Coral Island, and to twelfth-century Crusaders as the Île de Graye. On their sweep south through Transjordan in 1115, King Baldwin's army built a castle at Aqaba, and, to counter the Frankish presence, Salah ad-Din's Muslim resistance fortified this barren islet at the head of the Gulf of Aqaba. Rising impressively from the craggy island, the **castle's** towers and passageways have been restored, but the main reason for coming is to **dive or snorkel** in the maze of reefs off the northeastern tip of the island. Currents are strong and the reefs labyrinthine, so it's best to explore only with the guide who accompanies the organized trip.

Pharaoh's Island lies in Egyptian waters and – since private sailing is forbidden in the gulf for security reasons – the only way to get there is with the day-trips run by a selection of Aqaba boat operators and dive centres. Whether you book with the *Aquamarina I Beach*, the RDC or the *Alcazar*, the price is the same. You need to reserve a place two days in advance to give time to organize a group visa. When enough people show interest (generally around half a dozen), a boat departs from the hotel at around 9.30am, arriving on the island at about 10.15am; you're back in Aqaba by 5.30pm. The JD28 price includes transport, visas, a full lunch, snorkelling equipment and a quick tour of the castle. It's not possible to leave from the island to the Egyptian mainland.

---

the whole slope split from the shallows outwards by a steep-sided ravine; its neighbour, the **New Canyon**, benefited from the sinking in 1999 of an old field tank, which created a barrier to encourage reef growth. **Blue Coral**, named for a bluish lacework coral found here, is a little south.

Just north of a fenced-off nature reserve, **Moon Valley** offers an undulating reef framed by sandy beds, and is also the entry point for the seven-hundred-metre **Long Swim**, taking divers or experienced snorkellers south beyond the reserve fence to the RDC's jetty, past patches of dense coral interspersed with sandy valleys. From the jetty itself, the **Aquarium** (to the north) and the **Garden** (to the south) are both superb for divers and novice snorkellers alike. Aqaba's southernmost dive site is appropriately known as the **Saudi Border**, only 300m north of the international frontier; once beyond the inshore shallows, you'll discover superbly preserved hard and soft corals, although the best of the reef is beyond snorkelling range.

Dive centres

Aqaba International Dive Centre Beside *Aqaba Gulf Hotel* ☏ & Ⓕ 03/203 1213, Ⓔdiveaqaba@yahoo.com. Daily 8am–9pm. A small centre, with a fairly standard range of options. Service is reasonable, and friendly.

Aquamarina Diving Club Corniche, North Coast ☏03/201 6250, Ⓕ203 2630, Ⓦwww.aquamarina-group.com. Daily 8am–6pm. Attached to the *Aquamarina I Beach* hotel on the sandy North Coast beach, but perhaps not as careful or forthcoming as the competition. Its location means that, even to do a spot of snorkelling, you have to be bussed or boated out to the coral reefs down the coast. Good enough for the basics – snorkelling and simple dives.

Dive Aqaba Opposite the *Golden Tulip Hotel* ☏ & Ⓕ03/203 4849, Ⓦwww.diveaqaba.com. Daily 8am–7pm. Rapidly earning a name for itself as one of the best dive centres in Jordan, run by a joint British–Jordanian team – friendly, knowledgeable, efficient and reliable. They run shore dives and boat dives, are closely involved with JREDS on environmental activities and the beach clean-up programme, and offer a range of PADI courses to suit all levels of ability. Highly recommended.

Coral conservation

Coral reefs are formed of millions of individual creatures called **polyps**, which come together to create a single, compound organism. The various species of polyp produce hard external skeletons, which remain intact after the polyp dies; sand and other detritus fill up holes and cracks, and the reef is built up little by little, with new corals growing on the surface of the stony mass. Some coral colonies are several centuries old. To avoid damaging the reefs:

• **never stand on the coral** – any kind of pressure can damage or kill the outermost polyps. If you opt for a boat dive, make certain that the captain ties up to one of the mooring buoys already in place all round Aqaba, and doesn't just drop anchor onto the reef. If he claims that his selected site has no buoy, then insist that you be taken instead to a site that does have one.

• **don't enter the sea from the beach** – the reef begins directly from the shallows. Instead, use jetties or boat entries.

• **never break the coral** – snapping off a particularly colourful bit of coral not only kills that section of the reef, it's also pointless: after a few days out of water, all coral turns grey.

• **avoid kicking up sand** – clouds of grit settling on the reef can smother the outer-most polyps.

• **don't litter, feed the fish** or **buy marine souvenirs**, such as corals, shells or starfish.

Royal Diving Club 17km south of Aqaba ⓣ03/201 7035 or 203 2709, ⓕ201 7097, ⓔinfo@rdc.jo, ⓦwww.rdc.jo. Daily 9am–8pm; Nov–Feb closes earlier. The only dive centre actually located on the reefs, expertly run, friendly and well equipped, whether you want to just hang out on their private beach, snorkel or dive. They have lockers, changing rooms, a pool, a restaurant and even the onsite three-star *Coral Bay* hotel (see p.411). You can rent a mask, fins and snorkel for the day very inexpensively, and this brings the bonus of access to their small jetty, which projects out over breathtaking coralscapes for the simplest of water entries. They have the full range of dive equipment for rent, and run a varied programme of day and night dives, as well as a fistful of PADI courses. Admission to the RDC beach (JD7)

includes a sunbed, towel, access to all facilities and also return transport from town: book your morning pick-up the day before with your hotel. The RDC minibus makes the return trip to town at lunchtime and again in the late afternoon. Alternatively, a taxi one way is around JD4.

Seastar At *Alcazar* hotel ⓣ03/201 4131, ⓕ201 4133, ⓦwww.seastar-watersports.com. Daily 9am–5pm. Friendly, professional and long-estab-lished dive centre in one of the town's best-known hotels, which uses the *Alcazar*'s private beach complex Club Murjan, down on the South Coast reefs. Snorkelling, diving and various courses are all on offer, and if you stay at the hotel, prices for diving and your room rate are both discounted. A shuttle bus runs between the hotel and Club Murjan several times a day.

Eating and drinking

Aqaba shakes a leg when the sun goes down, and many **restaurants and cafés** have tables either on balconies or out on the street for open-air evening consumption. If you're heading to Rum or Petra for a few days, you'd do well to stock up here on picnic supplies beforehand, since even basic food in both places is priced at a premium. Early in the morning, the fruit and veg **market** in the middle of Aqaba is a good place to pick up some bargains, but for range, quality, familiar brands and the odd discount deal you should copy the locals and head for the big Safeway **supermarket** (daily 7am–1am), north of the centre off the Amman highway.

Restaurants

The obvious thing to plump for when you're by the sea is **fish** – and there are plenty of places to oblige – but, although the creatures themselves are very fresh, so are the prices. A plate of good, but unspectacular fried fish (most often spiced red mullet served on rice as the dish *sayyadieh*) is rarely less than JD6 anywhere, and can be much more expensive.

At the bottom end of the market, the *Syrian Restaurant*, 200m east of the centre, is the best **Arabic diner** in town, although there are plenty of others clustered around nearby alleys. The best *shwarma*s and street cafés are opposite the *Aquamarina II City*, where you'll find the pleasant *Abu Hmeed* diner, a familiar *Pizza Hut* and two passable chicken tikka places. Raghadan Street in the middle of town is shoulder-to-shoulder Arabic restaurants serving simple kebab/chicken dishes (JD2–3 for a meal); the two best are the *Syrian Palace* and the *al-Shami* (aka *Upstairs*), but you'll pass half a dozen more as well.

Ali Baba Town centre. The most varied menu in Aqaba, with a full complement of OK *mezze* and Arabic main courses, as well as a good fish selection including a tasty fish curry. Simple fare can be had for simple prices, but larger dishes can push the bill up to JD8–10 per person. Serves beer. Daily 9am–11pm.

Captain's Restaurant Beside *Aquamarina II City* ☎03/201 6905. Large, bustling restaurant with a good reputation – and so often full. The fish is good, and you can also get dishes like pasta and all the normal Arabic staples at moderate prices. Daily 9am–11.30pm.

China 100m east of the centre. Climb to the top of the stairs for a surprisingly good Chinese, with a range of excellent soups and all the usual meat, chicken and veg dishes, plus sweet-and-sour fish. Good value at JD3–4. Daily 11.30am–3pm & 6.30–11pm.

al-Far South of the fishing harbour near the industrial port ☎03/201 3704. Classy, if rather bare, restaurant with a pleasant terrace well away from the central streets and so popular with holidaying Jordanian and other Arab families. The fish and *mezze* are good, if unadventurous. Moderately priced. Daily noon–midnight.

Floka Beside the *Golden Tulip* ☎03/203 0860. A rather good fish restaurant in the heart of the hotel district – don't be put off by the menu in Hungarian outside. Their *sayyadieh* is excellent, and a range of other, more familiar European dishes are well prepared and courteously served. A meal costs in the order of JD7. Daily 12.30–11.30pm.

Mina House A tiny boat moored beside the fishing harbour south of the museum ☎03/201 2699. Aqaba's only floating restaurant, in a perfect, peaceful location in shallow water and specializing in fish, squid and lobster. You pay extra for the location (upwards of JD9 per person) but the food is good; not the place for a cosy, private dinner, though. Daily noon–midnight.

Mövenpick hotel Corniche, North Beach ☎03/203 4020. Of the hotel's range of expensive restaurants, the stand-out choice is the *Red Sea Grill* (daily 7–11.30pm), a romantic, open-air spot overlooking the beach, serving up excellent fish and seafood. *Portofino* (daily 6.30–11pm) is another classy choice, within the main hotel building – an elegant setting for high-quality Italian cuisine, including wood-fired pizza. The *Palm Court and Terrace* (daily 6.30am–11.30pm) is the main hotel restaurant, serving good-value buffets at main mealtimes and à-la-carte fare in between.

Royal Yacht Club Off the main Corniche roundabout in the town centre ☎03/202 2404, ⊛www.romero-jordan.com. The best restaurant in Aqaba, calm, classy and air-conditioned, owned and run by *Romero* of Amman (a high recommendation) and with efficient, friendly service. Superb pasta and pizzas (JD3–4) are padded out with inexpensive *mezze*, but the highlight is the especially well-prepared fish (JD8). Also has a terrace overlooking the marina. Accepts credit cards. Daily 11.30am–3.30pm & 7.30–11.30pm; adjacent pool (JD5) and bar both daily 11am–midnight.

Juice bars and coffee houses

A little up from the *Crystal Hotel* are a handful of **juice bars**, complete with pavement tables, that can quench the most raging of thirsts with anything from plain orange juice to sensational mango–guava–strawberry–banana concoctions. Dozens of ordinary tea- and **coffee houses** all over town come into their own in the evening, when every empty car park and patch of waste ground is laid with chairs and a TV for locals to while away the twilight hours with coffee and a hubbly-bubbly or two. Cafés down on the public beaches give much the same service, with added palm trees and gulf views. After dark, half a dozen parlours on the honky-tonk strip in front of the *Petra Hotel* do a roaring trade in cups of super-sweet, strangely elastic Day-Glo **ice cream** that tastes a whole lot better than it sounds. For a real treat, drop into the *Mövenpick's* bakery shop (daily 8am–10pm), located on the hotel's main street frontage, for patisserie delicacies, genuine Swiss ice cream and proper espresso coffee.

Moving on from Aqaba

Suitably enough for a town at the end of the country, **transport** connections out of Aqaba are many and varied. As well as a good selection of buses around **the south**, there are fast bus connections and daily flights to **Amman**, ferry and catamaran services to nearby **Egypt** and an easily accessible overland crossing point into **Israel**. The bus services which formerly ran from Aqaba into Saudi Arabia are suspended.

Domestic destinations

There are plenty of fast air-con **buses** to Amman, from 7am until about 5pm; all cost around JD4 and take less than four hours. JETT (☏03/201 5222) has six or seven buses a day, departing from their office beside the *Mövenpick* hotel and dropping off at their building 1km uphill from Abdali in Amman. More modern, comfortable modern buses (all no smoking) are operated by Trust (☏03/203 2200) – also six a day – from their office opposite the *Aquamarina II City* hotel to their premises off Amman's 7th Circle. For either, it's advisable to book in person a day in advance, and check timings carefully. Both these companies follow the Wadi Araba/Dead Sea road northwards – good for the scenery, but they don't stop anywhere. Trust also runs three daily buses direct from Aqaba to **Irbid** (5hr 30min; JD6).

From the bus station in the middle of town, buses operated by Afana (☏03/201 6378) and ordinary minibuses (5hr; JD3) head to **Amman**'s Wihdat station via the Desert Highway, stopping off along the way when they're flagged down. Minibuses follow the same road to reach **Ma'an** and **Tafileh**. There are roughly three minibuses a day to **Wadi Musa/Petra** (8.30am, 10.30am & 12.30pm, although these timings depend on demand; JD3), interspersed with others which run via Rajif to **Taybeh** village, from where other buses run into Wadi Musa. There are also, in theory, four daily departures to **Wadi Rum** (6.30am, 11am, 1pm & 3pm; JD1.500), but if you miss these you could take one of the regular Ma'an or Quweira buses and hitch into Rum from the highway junction at Rashdiyyeh. Buses to Petra and Rum are less frequent on Fridays. Buses to **Karak** depart from a residential street 100m south of the bus station and head up the Wadi Araba road via Safi, past both Lot's Cave and Bab adh-Dhraa (see p.178).

A **taxi** from Aqaba to Wadi Rum costs about JD15, to Petra about JD30, to the Dead Sea or Amman upwards of JD70. At the time of writing, rumours were rife that the industrial phosphates **railway** that runs from Aqaba port into the desert via Wadi Rum would be converted to take tourist passenger trains; but details remained sketchy.

Royal Wings, with an office at the airport (☏03/201 4477), has two or three **flights** daily from Aqaba to Amman (JD35), either to Marka Airport or Queen Alia International Airport. You should check departure times in advance, either with Royal Wings or at the Royal Jordanian office (☏03/201 3781) on the

Amman highway beyond the Haya hospital; you can also buy tickets here, but it's normally no problem to turn up at the airport and buy as you board. Make sure to get a seat on the left-hand side of the plane for some spectacular Dead Sea views.

To Israel

The **Wadi Araba** border crossing into Israel (Sun–Thurs 6.30am–10pm, Fri & Sat 8am–8pm) – also known as the "Southern Crossing" – is down a side road off the Wadi Araba highway about 5km north of Aqaba. Serveeces (marked "Southern Pass Service") run from the bus station to the border for JD1 per person, or a taxi is about JD5–6. Procedures are simple and straightforward, and there's a JD5 **departure tax**. Free Israeli visas are issued on arrival. A taxi into Eilat is about NIS15 – or you can walk from the border about 500m to the Kibbutz Elot bus stop on the main road, from where you can flag down a bus for the last couple of kilometres into town. Note that during the Jewish *shabbat* – effectively from Friday 2pm until Saturday dusk – all Israeli public transport and many services shut down, and, in addition, the border may close altogether during Jewish and Islamic holidays.

Eilat is Israel's top holiday resort, characterized by ranks of luxury beachfront hotels, upfront hedonism and, at the lower end of the market, hustle. Sleeping on the beach is risky, but it's almost impossible to find a bed during the over-crowded peak times of Passover (around April) and other major Jewish holidays. Buses leave four or five times a day for Jerusalem or Tel Aviv (4–5hr).

To Egypt

The Arab Bridge Maritime Company (☎03/209 2000, ⓦwww.abmaritime .com.jo) operates the ferry and catamaran service to **Nuweiba**, 70km south-west of Aqaba on Egypt's Sinai coast. You can buy tickets for all services from the company's offices, either at the town-centre branch near the *China* restaurant (Sat–Thurs 8am–6pm), or up to an hour before departure at the passenger terminal itself, 9km south of town (daily 24hr; ☎03/201 3240 or 3891). Local buses from the Corniche outside Aqaba's fort to Durra on the Saudi border run past the passenger terminal for pennies; a taxi could whisk you there for JD4 or so. There are some ticket agents along the Corniche in town, but they offer no advantages over going straight to the horse's mouth. Alongside the terminal buildings is a duty-free shop (for departing passengers only) crammed with whisky, cigarettes and luxury goods.

The boats run to a notoriously unreliable timetable, and are often late. There's the choice of the slow **ferry** (daily 7pm; 3hr; US$22 in economy, US$30 in first-class) or the faster **catamaran** (daily 11am; takes 1hr; US$36/56). There may also be an additional ferry sailing at 1pm daily. Private vehicles are accepted on both the ferries and catamaran: the fare for an ordinary car is about US$110, or a 4x4 about US$150. You should add the port **departure tax** of JD5 onto all prices. Although it's possible to get an **Egyptian visa** on the boat, getting one ahead of time in Amman or Aqaba will save endless bureaucratic chaos.

At **Nuweiba port**, taxi-drivers do the eight-kilometre run into town for LE20 or whatever they can get, or alternatively you can hang around for the buses from the port straight to Cairo, which leave when they're full. There's plenty of accommodation in Nuweiba City and in Tarabeen, just to the north, or you can take a mid-afternoon bus to Dahab (LE10) or Cairo (LE60), among other places. There are also serveeces, for which you'll have to bargain hard.

When demand is high (during the summer, at the end of Ramadan for Eid al-Fitr, and around the hajj and Eid al-Adha), many more Aqaba–Nuweiba boats are laid on, both ferry and catamaran – and, in addition, catamaran service starts up between Aqaba and **Sharm el-Sheikh** (takes 3hr). This departs at noon, currently twice a week during these peak periods, for US$45 in economy or US$65 in first-class.

Crossing **overland** into Egypt via Eilat in Israel (see above) is much less time-consuming. From Eilat bus station, city bus #16 (NIS4) departs regularly to the Israel-Egypt border post of **Taba**, 6km south of Eilat. The border is open 24 hours a day, but a sizeable Israeli departure tax (NIS66 or US$16) plus an Egyptian entry tax (LE24) are disincentives to cross this way, as is the fact that you cannot get a full Egyptian visa on arrival at Taba, only a free Sinai-only visa, valid solely for the coast between Taba and Sharm el-Sheikh. If you want to travel on to **Cairo**, you must get an Egyptian visa in advance – easily done in Amman, Aqaba or Eilat. From Taba, 70km north of Nuweiba and dominated by a huge *Hilton* hotel and casino, buses and hard-sell serveeces run to all major Sinai destinations, as well as Suez and Cairo, in two clumps – at 10am and 2pm daily. To Dahab, for instance, the bus is around LE10, a seat in a serveece about LE50. Note that 4x4 vehicles are not permitted to enter Egypt either at Taba or at Rafah.

Listings

Airport Flight information on ☎03/201 4477.
Books and newspapers The Yamani and Redwan bookshops (both daily 8.30am–2pm & 5–9pm), within 10m of each other opposite the post office, have excellent ranges of English-language books and international newspapers – at a price. Redwan in particular stocks a broad variety of books on Jordan, the Arab World and Islam that can be hard to find even in Amman.

Car rental As well as international agencies, there's a handful of good local operators, but prices across the board are higher than in Amman. Most agencies offer 4x4s, but depending on size, age of the car and whether you want limited or unlimited kilometres, you could pay anything from JD35 to JD65 per day. Rum (☎ & ⓕ03/201 3581), opposite the post office, is the longest-established local outfit. Another good place to compare is Moon (☎03/202 2232, ⓕ201 9734), on the Corniche past the *Crystal* hotel. For one-way rentals to Amman or elsewhere, your best bet is Hertz, with an office opposite the *Aquamarina City* (☎03/201 6206, ⓕ201 6125, ⓔhertz@go.com.jo) and a desk within the *Mövenpick* (☎07/9565 9271): on rentals of three days and above, drop-off at any of their branches in Amman, Petra, the Dead Sea, or at Queen Alia Airport is free. Competition comes from Avis (☎ & ⓕ03/202 2883) by the *Crystal* hotel.

Consulate Egypt, Istiqlal St ☎03/201 6171, ⓕ201 5159, 15min walk north of JETT office. Visa applications Sun–Thurs 9am–3pm; collection is on-the-spot or after a short wait; one photo is needed (or they'll photocopy your passport photo instead).

Three-month tourist visas cost JD12 (single entry) or JD15 (multiple entry). "Sinai-only" visas, valid only for travel along the east Sinai coast as far as Sharm el-Sheikh (including St Catherine's), are issued free.

Hospital The Princess Haya hospital (☎03/201 4111), on the roundabout just north of the *Aquamarina City*, is one of the best in the country. As well as a 24hr emergency room, it's equipped with a modern six-person recompression chamber and has professionally trained staff to deal with diving accidents.

Mail The post office is bang in the middle of town (daily 7.30am–7pm, Fri closes 1pm). For sending valuables, you'd do better to trust international couriers such as Aramex (☎03/201 5352) or DHL (☎03/201 2039).

Police In emergency, dial ☎191. Headquarters of the tourist police are at the Wadi Araba border (☎03/201 9717). The main police directorate (☎03/201 2411) is on the highway north out of town, but a more convenient office for visa extensions is opposite the bus station.

Tour operators All over town you'll see outfits advertising trips to Wadi Rum; most of them, and the cheaper hotels, will show you photo albums of their adventures and glowing testimonials from happy customers. If all you want is to be driven to Rum, shuttled out to a campsite in the desert for tea and a meal, and then brought back in the morning – often, it seems, in the company of "guides" who speak little or no English – then these trips represent excellent value, costing as little as JD15 per person. For longer or more serious explorations, you'd do better going to one of the few professional tour operators. Quteish & Sons (☎ & Ⓕ 03/201 3882), advertised as "Wadi Rum Desert Services" and located on the stairs beside the al-Shami restaurant, is good, with extensive experience and impeccable standards. Hillawi Desert Services (☎ & Ⓕ 03/201 8082),

on the Corniche near the Aqaba Star hotel, is also excellent, and can arrange 4x4, camel, hiking and camping trips short and long. The Desert Guides, in the Alcazar Hotel (☎ 03/201 4131, Ⓕ 201 4133), has a range of excursions, as well as horse- and camel-back adventures all over southern Jordan.

The Wadi Araba road: Aqaba–Dead Sea

The road running due **north from Aqaba** along the floor of the vast **Wadi Araba** is much overlooked as a fast route back to the Dead Sea and Amman, but if you have your own transport it's much preferable to the tedious Desert Highway via Ma'an. However, you should bear in mind that, until you reach the Dead Sea hotels, there are only two turns off this road – after 179km to Tafileh and 224km to Karak. The only public transport that lets you hop on or off are minibuses between Aqaba and Tafileh or Karak.

There are few sights other than the scenery, which, at least in the southern parts, is marked by sandy desert. Local Bedouin tend to let their families of camels graze freely beside the road; the dunes and the camels, interspersed with acacia trees and framed by giant mountains on both sides, make a picturesque scene. At some points, the border fence with Israel is right next to the road, and traffic on the mirror-image Israeli highway on the other side is sometimes clearly visible, as are the fields of irrigated land cultivated by a string of desert kibbutzes.

At **Gharandal**, 70km north of Aqaba, the Chinese company who built this road left behind a pagoda as a memento; the incongruous object has since been turned into the weirdest police station you're likely to see. Some 40km further, there's the welcome sight of the Beir Mathkoor Café (☎ 03/206 3650), a **refreshment stop** and petrol station open all hours. Shortly after, a sign points off the road to **Bir Mathkoor**, which was the westernmost caravan suburb of Petra, tucked away in the mountains to the east of the road (you can spot the white shrine atop Jebel Haroun from here). The Nabatean ruins, however, are likely to inspire only the most enthusiastic of archeologists.

About 20km beyond Bir Mathkoor, the turn to Fidan and **Qurayqira** is passable in an ordinary car for 17km to Qurayqira village itself (pronounced "graygra") and for another 5km to Rashaydeh village – but there the road runs out. You'll need a 4x4 – or a lift from a local – for the extra 10km across the desert to reach the RSCN's Wilderness Lodge at the ancient copper-smelting site of **Faynan**, located at the western end of the **Dana Nature Reserve**. See p.313 for details of spending a night here, and the walking trails round and about.

Beyond the Qurayqira turning, another gently rising 35km of highway brings you to the edge of a scarp with the whole of the Dead Sea plain stretching in front. The small agricultural settlement of **Fifa** is at the bottom of the slope, with a signed turn-off climbing east into the mountains to Tafileh (see p.312).

The stretch from Fifa northwards is covered on p.180 as the **Dead Sea road**, which leads eventually to Amman.

Travel details

Since most buses and all minibuses and serveeces simply depart whenever they are full, regularity of service is indicated only when a fixed timetable is in operation.

Buses, minibuses and serveeces

Aqaba to: Amman (JETT office; 6 daily; 3hr 45min); Amman (Trust office; 6 daily; 3hr 45min); Amman (Wihdat station; 4hr); Durra (20min); Irbid (5hr 30min); Karak (3hr); Ma'an (1hr 30min); Quweira (45min); Safi (2hr); Tafileh (2hr 30min); Wadi Musa (1hr 45min); Wadi Rum (1hr).
Diseh to: Ma'an (1hr 20min).
Durra to: Aqaba (20min).
Jafr to: Ma'an (40min).
Ma'an to: Amman (Wihdat station; 2hr 30min); Aqaba (1hr 30min); Diseh (1hr 20min); Jafr (40min); Karak (2hr); Mudawwara (1hr); Shobak (30min); Tafileh (1hr); Wadi Musa (40min).
Mudawwara to: Ma'an (1hr).
Quweira to: Aqaba (45min).
Wadi Rum to: Aqaba (1hr); Wadi Musa (1hr 40min).

Domestic flights

Aqaba to: Amman (2–3 daily; 50min).

Ferries and catamarans

Aqaba to: Nuweiba, Egypt (2–3 daily; 1–3hr).

Useful Arabic place names

Aqaba	العقبة	Quweira	القويرة
Diseh	الديسة	Ras an-Naqab	راس النقب
Durra	الدرة	Rashdiyyeh	الراشدية
Jafr	الجفر	Rum	رم
Ma'an	معان	Wadi Araba	وادي عربة
Mudawwara	المدوّرة	Wadi Rum	وادي رم
Qatraneh	القطرانة		

Contexts

Contexts

The historical framework 429–458

Flora and fauna.. 459–465

Islam 466–470

Women in Jordan.. 471–473

Modern art 474–477

Writing from Jordan 478–491

Books... 492–503

The historical framework

The **history of Jordan** is a history of occupation. Never the seat of an empire, the country – known in the past as "Transjordan" (ie the land across the Jordan river) – has been stamped with the footprints of foreign armies and merchants since the pharaohs. Aside from brief flurries of political power in antiquity, the indigenous population, largely comprising Bedouin tribes, tended to live under the thumb of governors sent from Transjordan's larger and more powerful neighbours until independence in the mid-twentieth century.

Only relatively small parts of the country – the well-watered northern highlands and Jordan Valley – have ever been able to support large populations. Since prehistoric times, huge tracts of land to the south and east have received very little rainfall and have no rivers; only tiny populations of nomadic or semi-nomadic Bedouin have been able to live there. Thus the history of Jordan revolves largely around the history of the fertile north and west, the history of the desert surviving only in the culture and oral traditions of the Bedouin themselves.

The Stone Age: up to 3200 BC

During the **Paleolithic** period (c.500,000–17,000 BC), Jordan's climate was a good deal wetter than it is today, and what is now desert was then semi-fertile savannah. The local population of hunter-gatherer hominids, as well as foraging for wild plants, preyed upon the area's native big game, which included lions, elephants, bears and gazelle. Flint and stone handaxes from this time have been found all over the country, most significantly in enormous quantities at the **Azraq oasis** in the eastern desert.

Some time around 17,000 BC, at the beginning of the **Epipaleolithic** period, major changes took place in Transjordan. The previously nomadic hunter-gatherers began to make seasonal camps, broadened their diet to include small mammals and – most importantly – learnt how to domesticate goats and cultivate some wild grains, both of these advances providing a diet that was not only stable and assured but also nutritionally rich. These new proto-farmers, who used complex tools such as sickles and pestles and mortars, have left evidence of their building work all over Jordan: small, circular enclosures and huts solidly built with subterranean foundations.

From about 8500 BC onwards, during the **Neolithic** period, there were three profound shifts which fundamentally altered the pattern of life. First, responding to the introduction of new food sources from agriculture and animal husbandry, people began to opt for the certainties of community life, giving up their semi-nomadism and establishing permanent villages such as at **Baydha**, near Petra. The large Neolithic settlement at **Ain Ghazal**, northeast of Amman, was made up of many rectangular, multi-roomed houses, some with plastered floors. From the discovery here and across the region of skulls covered with plaster, their eye sockets stuffed with bitumen, it seems that one aspect of the new, comfortable Neolithic village life was veneration – or even worship – of the dead. The oldest statues in the world, dating from around 6000 BC, were uncovered at Ain Ghazal: one-metre-high androgynous figures with huge, painted eyes, now on display in Amman.

A second shift resulted from changing weather patterns: as temperatures rose, the eastern savannah dried out and became virtually uninhabitable. Desertification marked a clear distinction between Transjordan's arid east and fertile west, forcing most people to congregate in the western areas that, today, still hold the greater population.

But the most important innovation of Neolithic times was the discovery of how to make **pottery**. Around 5000 BC, potters arrived in Transjordan from the more advanced civilizations of Mesopotamia (the area between the rivers Tigris and Euphrates, in modern Iraq), and earlier Transjordanian efforts at making vessels from plaster were promptly abandoned as the new skill spread. By 4000 BC or so, during the **Chalcolithic** period, copper had been smelted for the first time for use in fashioning hooks, axes and arrowheads, and the new metal began to be used in conjunction with older technologies of pottery and flint-working to considerably improve the quality of life. People slowly began to turn their attention away from subsistence hunting and towards planned cultivation: olives, lentils, dates, barley and wheat were all common, as was sheep- and goat-breeding. The area's principal copper deposits were at **Faynan** in Wadi Araba, but the largest Chalcolithic village discovered in Jordan is at **Teleilat Ghassul** in the Jordan Valley, where mud-brick houses with roofs of wood, mud and reeds were constructed around large courtyards. Here, pots were decorated and of good quality, and woven baskets were sturdy. From the evidence of the village's huge and mysterious murals of masked figures, stars and geometric motifs, it seems that Ghassulian women decorated themselves with necklaces of shells and stones, and their men took some pride in their tattoos.

The Bronze Age: 3200–1200 BC

Capitalizing on the success and security of earlier villages, Transjordanian people developed more and more complex settlements in many areas of the country. Towns from the **Early Bronze Age** (c.3200–1950 BC), although still relying on copper ("Bronze Age" is a misnomer from the early days of archeology), often included the strongest defensive fortifications yet built, probably to keep the marauding nomadic tribes of the open countryside away. The tentative new technology of water management led to collection and some storage of supply against drier times. New customs of burial also developed, sometimes involving the digging of deep shaft tombs: at **Bab adh-Dhraa** on the Dead Sea, archeologists have uncovered over twenty thousand such shafts, perhaps containing up to a quarter of a million corpses in total. Other burial customs – possibly brought from Syria or Anatolia – involved the construction of dolmens (two or more huge stone slabs standing side by side and capped by another slab), which are now found dotted all over the hills and valleys of Jordan.

Elsewhere in the region at this time, the extraordinary innovation of **writing** was leading to the development of highly sophisticated civilizations. To the south, Egypt was unified into one kingdom, while to the north and east, Anatolia and Mesopotamia saw the rise of equally complex urbanized cultures. Occupying the area midway between the three, the simpler people of the Levant, who wouldn't start to use writing themselves for another millennium or so, fell into the role of merchant middlemen, and the first significant commerce began to flow between the great powers.

Around 2300 BC, many of the fortified towns in Transjordan were destroyed, although there is some controversy as to whether this was due to conquest by a new people, the Amorites, or simply an earthquake. A decrease in rainfall levels, though, coupled with a general rise in temperature, almost certainly played its part, and the fragile network of city-states across the region may simply have fallen victim to changes in climate and the regional power balance.

The years after 2000 BC – known as the **Middle Bronze Age** (c.1950–1550 BC) – saw trade between Egypt, Arabia and the great city-states of Syria and Palestine continuing to flow through Transjordan, generating wealth and facilitating the spread of ideas and culture. It was during this period that artisans mixed copper with tin for the first time; the resulting metal, **bronze**, made much harder and more durable tools and weapons than before. Transjordanian towns, such as Amman, Irbid and Pella (as well as Jericho, on the western bank of the river), built massive, banked earth ramparts, implying a need for security – as borne out by the eighteenth-century BC conquests of the Hyksos who overran much of the Levant. Probably nomadic herders from Central Asia, the Hyksos interrupted the steady indigenous cultural growth of Transjordan, replacing it with new, foreign elements. As well as importing a more graceful and technically accomplished style of pottery, they also introduced both horses and chariots to the Middle East.

Following the expulsion of the Hyksos around 1550 BC by the Egyptian Seventeenth Dynasty, Transjordan – and the rest of the Levant – saw an expansion of Egyptian influence during the **Late Bronze Age** (c.1550–1200 BC), especially under Pharaoh Tuthmosis III. Despite conflict further north, occupied Transjordan remained relatively peaceful and prosperous, and the presence of pottery from Mycenaean Greece and Cyprus indicates strong trade links across the Mediterranean and Aegean at this time.

By 1200 BC, however, the peace and prosperity of the entire eastern Mediterranean had been shattered, probably by the arrival of unknown invaders collectively termed "**Peoples of the Sea**", one group of whom, the Philistines, settled around Gaza, giving rise to the name Palestine. The principal cities of Greece and Cyprus fell to these foreigners, the Hittite Empire in Anatolia collapsed, wealthy city-states in Syria were razed, and the Egyptian occupiers of Transjordan retreated to face the onslaught at home. In addition, events surrounding a group of tribes known as the Israelites – about which ample, if contradictory, records survive – began to alter the power balance in Transjordan and Palestine.

Biblical accounts of the Bronze Age

At some undetermined time probably well before 2000 BC, Genesis records that **Abram**, a native of the city of Ur, in modern-day Iraq, travelled with his wife and extended family to Canaan (Palestine). After some years, the land – already home to existing tribes of Canaanites and others – was unable to support so many people, and bickering ensued between Abram's tribe and that of his nephew **Lot**. In an attempt to broker peace, Abram offered a separation: Lot would be given the choice of taking his tribe and flocks either east or west of the River Jordan, and whichever direction he chose, Abram and his tribe would go the other way. Lot chose to go east and pitched his tents at the southeastern corner of the Dead Sea. Abram went west and eventually settled near Hebron, meanwhile having a vision of God granting him in perpetuity the land that Lot had spurned.

After the adaptation of Abram's name to Abraham following another vision, Lot's home city of Sodom – and others nearby – were destroyed in a cataclysm visible from Hebron. The only survivors were Lot and his two daughters, who lived for a time in a cave in the desert. Fearful that their tribe would die out since no man had escaped with them other than their father, the elder of Lot's two daughters hatched a plan to get their father so drunk he wouldn't be able to tell who they were, whereupon they would seduce him and thus preserve the family. Everything worked to plan and both daughters gave birth to sons; the elder named her child **Moab**, and the younger **Ben-Ammi**, or "father of Ammon".

Meanwhile Abraham had had two sons, the first – **Ishmael** – by his Egyptian mistress Hagar, and the second – **Isaac** – by his wife Sarah. On Sarah's insistence, Hagar and Ishmael were banished to the desert, and the biblical record concentrates on Isaac's two sons, Esau and Jacob. (The Quran, though, concentrates on Ishmael, who had twelve children and died at the age of 137; Muslims and especially Arabs view him as their forebear and the hajj pilgrimage centres on commemoration of Hagar and Ishmael's banishment.) Jacob persuaded Esau to sell his inheritance for some bread and lentils and, by dint of trickery, also gained the blessing of his father to rule over his brother; the two then separated, Jacob fleeing to an uncle's house and after a series of visions changing his name to **Israel** (which means "he who wrestled with God"). Esau married into Ishmael's family and settled in the southern part of Transjordan, known as the land of **Edom**. Its southern neighbour **Midian** (modern Hejaz), and its northern neighbours **Moab** and **Ammon**, as well as Edom itself, were all established kingdoms by soon after 2000 BC.

The Bible makes no further mention of Transjordan until the **Exodus**, which occurred several centuries after Esau, although much controversy remains as to its exact date. The most accepted chronology places it during the reign of Pharaoh Merneptah (c.1236–1217 BC), but it may have been over two centuries earlier. The Book of Numbers records that, after expulsion from Egypt and several generations of wandering in the Sinai, the Israelites, an extended group of twelve related tribes descended from Abraham's grandson, Israel, arrived in the southern Palestinian desert near Aqaba, on a journey towards the lands west of the Jordan that had been granted by God to the tribal patriarch Abraham. The Israelite sheikh Moses and his brother Aaron had a vision from God instructing them to speak to a rock to produce water for their tribes; however, Moses instead struck the rock, and for this transgression both he and his brother were denied future entry to the Promised Land.

After Aaron's death on **Mount Hor** (possibly Jebel Haroun near Petra), the Israelites apparently followed the route of the present Desert Highway northwards. A little way north of modern Qatraneh, the Israelites defeated the **Amorites** in battle and destroyed their cities, including Hesban, Dhiban and Madaba. They proceeded north to Dera'a (just over the modern Syrian border), defeated King Og and returned to make camp in "the plain of Moab" opposite Jericho, probably near modern Shuneh al-Janubiyyeh. Much alarmed at the presence of such powerful newcomers on his borders, the king of Moab made a military pact with the kings of Midian, but after a seer prophesied only victory for the Israelites, the combined Moabite–Midianite forces lost heart, and were attacked and routed. Three Israelite tribes occupied Transjordan from Dhiban as far north as Gilead (the hills around modern Jerash) and the Golan north of Umm Qais. Moses then had several visions and, sometime probably around 1200 BC, at the age of 120, died on **Mount Nebo** near Madaba. Soon afterwards, his successor Joshua led the Israelite tribes across the Jordan into the Promised Land.

The Iron Age: 1200–332 BC

With the bulk of the Israelite forces safely on the other side of the Jordan, the years after 1200 BC saw a consolidation and development of the Transjordanian kingdoms of Ammon, Moab and Edom, all three of which lay on the lucrative Arabian–Syrian trade route for gold, spices and other precious goods. However, the times were anything but peaceful, and the three were constantly tussling among themselves and with the Israelites.

By about 1000 BC, though, the Israelites were strong enough to declare a united Kingdom of Israel; under **King David**, they expanded military control to encompass virtually the entire Levant and won several victories in Transjordan, not least against Ammon. Edom managed to regain some independence following David's death in 960 BC, but it wasn't until David's son **Solomon** died some thirty years later that the Israelite empire fell. The last vestiges of Israelite control in Transjordan were erased during the mid-ninth century BC, partly by the efforts of Mesha, apparently king of Moab, who recorded his victories on a basalt stone, the "**Mesha Stele**" (see p.299), set up in the Moabite capital, Dhiban. To the north, Ammon, centred on modern Amman, prospered, while to the south, Edom had developed great skill in mining and smelting copper and had major settlements near Busayrah, Petra and Aqaba, although much of the Edomite population may have been nomadic or semi-nomadic.

Just as Mesha was subduing the Israelites, in central Syria the **Assyrian** army's advance southwards had been halted – only temporarily though, since by the mid-eighth century BC Assyrian forces had captured both Damascus and portions of Israel. It was only by paying tribute that Ammon, Moab and Edom managed to retain their independence and continue to exploit the north–south flow of trade.

Barely a century later, in 612 BC, the Assyrians were themselves defeated by an alliance of Medes (from modern Iran) and **Babylonians** (from Iraq); the latter then took control in the Levant, considerably limiting the independence of the Transjordanian kingdoms and, in 587 BC, destroying Jerusalem and deporting thousands of Jews. Some fifty years later, chaotic Babylonian rule was overrun by the **Persian Empire**, the largest yet seen in the region. The Persians released the Jews from captivity in Babylon and permitted them to rebuild their temple at Jerusalem. The indignant Ammonites and Moabites took this to be a declaration of sovereignty and attacked, only to be repulsed by the direct intervention of the Persian leadership.

Two centuries of relatively stable Persian rule were brought to a swift end by the military adventures of the Greek general known as **Alexander the Great**. In 333 BC, at the age of 21, he defeated the Persian army in southeastern Turkey and proceeded to conquer the entire Levant and Egypt before heading east. At his death in Babylon in 323 BC, Alexander controlled an empire stretching from Greece to India.

The Greeks and the Nabateans: 332–64 BC

Alexander's conquest of the Persian capital Persepolis in 332 BC confirmed **Hellenistic** control over the formerly Persian lands of the Levant, and ushered in a period of dominance over Transjordan by Alexander's successors that lasted, with some turmoil, for three centuries. On Alexander's death, his generals **Seleucus** and **Ptolemy** divided the eastern part of his empire between them: Palestine, Transjordan and southern Syria went to Ptolemy, while Seleucus took northern Syria and Mesopotamia. Predictably, neither rested on his laurels, and bitter struggles for the upper hand ensued, with much of Transjordan caught in the crossfire. After more than a century of fighting, the Seleucids finally wrested Transjordan away from the Ptolemies in 198 BC.

Meanwhile, many new and rebuilt Transjordanian cities had been flourishing, including Philadelphia (Amman), Gerasa (Jerash), Pella and Gadara (Umm Qais). Unfortunately, later Roman, Byzantine and Islamic rebuilding at all these sites obliterated much of the Hellenistic work, and virtually the only Hellenistic monument to survive in the region is a lone palace in the countryside west of Amman, **Qasr al-Abd**.

Long before these events, and possibly as early as the sixth century BC, a nomadic tribe of Arabs had wandered out of the deserts to the south and taken up residence in and around Edom. Slowly these **Nabateans** had abandoned their nomadic ways and founded a number of settlements in southern Transjordan, northern Arabia and the Naqab (Negev) desert of modern Israel, probably using their position to plunder the caravans heading out of Arabia loaded with luxury goods. The Roman historian Diodorus Siculus, writing much later, describes "Arabs who are called Nabatei" occupying Petra around 312 BC (for more on Petra's history, see p.325). The Nabateans switched from plundering caravans to providing them with safe passage, and managed to remain largely independent throughout the Seleucid–Ptolemaic power battles raging all around.

With the Seleucid victory of 198 BC, trade again prospered in Transjordan and the Nabateans consequently began to expand their sphere of influence, absorbing as they went many Hellenistic influences which worked their way into the art and architecture both of Petra and of the outlying regions that fell under Nabatean influence. By 150 BC – and co-existing alongside Seleucid rule in western Transjordan – the independent **Kingdom of Nabatea** extended along a strip of eastern Transjordan as far north as the Hawran, and south into the Hejaz. The Nabateans were accumulating vast profits from trade across the Middle East in everything from Indian silks and spices to Dead Sea bitumen. The jewel in the Nabatean crown, though, and their greatest source of wealth, was a monopoly over trade in frankincense and myrrh. Both essences were central in religious ceremonies throughout the West and both were produced only in southern Arabia; transport overland from the Arabian coast terminated at the sole taxation and international distribution centre at Petra.

While the Nabateans were quietly amassing fabulous wealth, riots were breaking out in Judea to the west against Hellenistic rule. In three successive years – 167 to 165 BC – Jewish rebels defeated the Greek army four times. The Jewish leader **Judas Maccabeus** then invaded northern Transjordan. Although the Seleucids eventually won the area back, their empire was in terminal decline; less than a century later, Judas's successor was occupying the whole of Transjordan as far south as Wadi Hasa, with the Nabatean kingdom – by now distended to Damascus but still confined only to a slice of the country east of the King's Highway – remaining independent. With nothing appearing likely to put a stop to the growth of Nabatean wealth and influence, and faced by an increasingly unstable political situation, the generals of **Rome** decided that the time had come to impose some law and order in the east.

Rome and the Nabateans: 64 BC–324 AD

In 64 BC, the Roman general **Pompey** took Damascus and ordered Nabatean forces to pull back from the city. After proceeding to annex most of the region, Pompey showed his hand by sending a force to Petra specifically to subdue the Nabateans, but the Nabatean king was able easily to repulse the attack and dip into his treasury to pay the Romans off.

Pompey turned his attention elsewhere. The group of Hellenized northern Transjordanian cities that included Gerasa, Gadara, Philadelphia and Pella had been badly damaged under the Jewish occupation; Pompey restored their infrastructure and granted them some local autonomy. With shared cultural and economic ties, these cities – in a region of Transjordan known as the **Decapolis** ("Ten Cities"; see p.200) – agreed to pay taxes to the Romans and so retained complete independence.

In 44 BC, Julius Caesar was assassinated in Rome and the power of the Romans wavered. The **Parthians** – based in Mesopotamia and Persia – took the chance to attack, and the Nabateans sided with them; following Rome's reassertion of its power, the Nabatean king was forced to dip into his treasury again to placate the generals. The local Roman placeman, Herod the Great, twice attacked the Nabateans to ensure consistent payments, seizing control in 31 BC of a swathe of the Nabatean kingdom in Syria. By the time of Herod's death in 4 BC, Rome was in control of the region, with Transjordan divided into three spheres of influence: to the north, the Decapolis remained independent; Palestinian Jewish puppet-kings ruled central Transjordan (although Philadelphia remained part of the Decapolis); the south comprised the rump Kingdom of Nabatea, still nominally independent, though coming under increasing imperial pressure to submit to Rome.

Possibly as a tactical ploy, Herod the Great's successor, Herod Antipas, married a daughter of the Nabatean king Aretas IV, but soon afterwards divorced her, and married his brother's wife instead. Unable to ignore such an insult, Aretas sent an army against Herod and won, but showed magnanimity in withdrawing peacefully. A local holy man, John the Baptist, condemned Herod's incestuous marriage, was imprisoned at the royal palace at **Machaerus** and, at the behest of Herod's step-daughter Salome, beheaded.

Jewish uprisings in Palestine during the mid-first century AD gave a chance for the Nabateans to weigh in militarily and so restore amicable relations with Rome. The Nabatean king was personally present at the Roman capture of Jerusalem in 70 AD. Many Palestinian Jewish rebels sought refuge at Machaerus, but the Roman army razed the palace in 72 AD and slaughtered everyone inside.

It was clear to the Nabateans by this stage that their days of independence were numbered. A new trading centre far to the north, **Palmyra** – positioned on Roman-sponsored routes that were growing in popularity – was chipping away at Petra's business, and the Nabatean king Rabbel II, seeing Roman dominance all around, almost certainly made a deal permitting the Romans to annex the Nabatean lands peacefully. In 106, on Rabbel's death, the whole of Transjordan – with the exception of the Decapolis – was incorporated into the new Roman **Province of Arabia**, under the emperor **Trajan**, with a new capital at Bosra, in Syria.

From Trajan to Constantine: 106–324 AD

Almost immediately, Roman city planners, engineers and construction workers moved into Transjordan. Large forts were built near Karak, Petra and in the north to house the massed legions; Petra itself, along with Philadelphia, Gerasa, Gadara and other cities, was renovated and Romanized; and, by 114 AD, a massive new fortified road – the **Via Nova Traiana** – was in place, running from Bosra right the way through Transjordan to the Red Sea at Aila (Aqaba). Trajan's successor, Hadrian, paid the province a visit in 130, and, although he passed through Petra, his main port of call was **Gerasa**, by this time one of the most splendid of Rome's provincial cities. During the second and third centuries, Transjordan gained new social and cultural sophistication under the Romans, and prosperity rose to an unprecedented level. In 199, the emperor Septimius Severus toured the province with his Syrian wife; although many overland trade routes from Arabia had been diverted to Palmyra and seaborne trade along the Red Sea was flourishing, Petra was still important enough to merit a visit, and his family connection prompted Severus to devote extra energy to the upkeep of roads and infrastructure throughout the province. It was around this time that **Azraq**, at the head of a major route to and from the Arabian peninsula, was fortified for the first time.

Nonetheless, the desert fringes of the empire remained open to infiltration, and in 260, Persian **Sassanians** invaded from the north. Six years later, the Roman military commander of the region, based in Palmyra, was murdered, precipitating a rebellion throughout Syria led by Queen Zenobia. The strategic situation in the east was perilous enough to force the emperor **Diocletian** (284–305) to take drastic measures. Retaining overall command from his base in Turkey, Diocletian split the empire into eastern and western administrations under separate emperors, and then proceeded to strengthen the infrastructure of the eastern fringes, building forts and new roads, among them the **Strata Diocletiana** linking Azraq with Damascus. Meanwhile, with Palmyra's predominance annulled through its association with rebellion, trade through Transjordan once again began to flourish, and the Red Sea port of Aila took on a new importance.

On top of the military setbacks, a new force was beginning to make itself felt throughout the empire. The influence of **Christianity** went much deeper than the extent of its practice (by a mere fourteen percent or so of the empire's population) might show. The new religion – with its attractive doctrine of the equality of every individual soul – was uniquely popular, and the emperor **Constantine** had already converted by 324 when he made Christianity the official religion of the eastern empire. Six years later, he confirmed the eclipse of Rome by founding a new Christian imperial capital called Constantinople – today's Istanbul – in the east.

The Byzantine period: 324–636

The **Byzantine** period – so named because Constantinople had been built over the ancient Greek colony of Byzantium – drew together existing strands in the empire: long-lived Roman institutions coexisted with the new Christian faith, which flourished within a broadly Greek culture. In Transjordan, the period was characterized by a steady growth of population coupled with energetic construction projects and important artistic development.

Constantine's mother, Helena, started a trend of **pilgrimage** by journeying to Jerusalem in 326. It was around this time that the first church on Mount Nebo was built to commemorate Moses' death, and the area around Nebo and Madaba became the focus for pilgrimage in Transjordan. As Christianity became the mainstream religion of the country following the final divorce between Rome and Constantinople in 395, an enormous number of churches went up, often on the foundations of Roman temples and often decorated with ornate **mosaics**. Madaba, in particular, was a flourishing centre for mosaicists, especially during the reign of **Justinian** (527–65). Church building and mosaic art in Transjordan (see p.286) entered a golden age.

However, twin disasters were to bring both artistic development and, indirectly, the empire itself to an end. The first was **plague**, which struck Transjordan during Justinian's reign and wiped out much of the population. However, a far more sustained, if equally lethal, threat came from the dogged Persian **Sassanians**, who, in the sixth century, launched a series of raids against the Euphrates frontier, breaking through to sack Antioch (modern Antakya) in 540. There followed over eighty years of titanic, but inconclusive, struggle in Syria between Byzantium and Persia – Transjordan remaining quiet throughout – which was only ended by the emperor **Heraclius'** recapture of Syria in 628.

During the struggles (and unknown to either combatant), far to the south an Arab holy man named **Muhammad** had been gathering around himself a large band of followers following a series of divine visions. Initial sorties northwards had won over a few desert tribes on the southern frontiers of Transjordan but the **Muslims**, as they styled themselves, lost their first battle with Byzantium, near Karak in 629. Muhammad himself died in Mecca in 632, but his armies, led by Abu Bakr, the first caliph ("successor"), and fired by the zeal of a new religion, pushed northwards again, seizing Damascus from Heraclius in 635. On the banks of the River Yarmouk the following year, they defeated a Byzantine army exhausted from decades of war.

The early caliphs of Islam: 636–1250

After the Yarmouk victory, it took the Muslim armies barely ten years to entirely dismantle Byzantine control over the Levant, although the Byzantine Empire itself limped on for another eight hundred years. By 656, though, the whole of Persia and the Middle East was ruled from the Muslim capital at Medina. That year, the third caliph, Othman, was murdered; when his successor, Ali, dismissed many of Othman's appointees – including Muawiya, governor of Syria – civil war broke out among the Muslims, brought to an end only by negotiations held probably at Udhruh near Petra in 659. Ali was subsequently assassinated, and Muawiya, a member of the **Umayyad** clan, was acclaimed caliph in 661. This marked a schism in Islam, which persists today, between the **Sunnis** – the orthodox majority who accept the Umayyad succession – and the minority **Shi'ites**, who believe the succession should have passed instead to Ali, a relative of Muhammad's, and his descendants.

The Umayyads: 661–750

Muawiya's first, and most significant, decision was to relocate the Muslim capital away from the arid desert of Arabia to the vibrant metropolis of Damascus. At one stroke, Transjordan was transformed: not only was it on the direct pilgrimage route between the imperial capital and the holy sites in Mecca and Medina, but it also suddenly lay at the heart of a rapidly expanding empire, which, at its fullest extent, reached from India virtually to the Pyrenees. The Umayyad caliphs almost immediately began a vigorous campaign of extraordinarily accomplished monument building throughout the Levant, which included both the Dome of the Rock in Jerusalem and the Great Mosque of Damascus. At heart, however, they were desert people, and their most enduring legacy to Transjordan is a series of buildings in the eastern desert, now known as the "Desert Castles": some, such as **Qasr Hraneh**, served as focuses for negotiation with the Bedouin tribes of the area, while others – **Qusayr Amra**, **Qasr Mushatta** – were lavish country mansions or hunting lodges. Motivated less by adherence to Islamic orthodoxy than by older Arab notions of honour, loyalty and rule by negotiation, the Umayyads saw themselves as inheritors of the cosmopolitan Roman and Byzantine imperial legacy and had a lively aesthetic sense, valuing intellectual curiosity, poetry and wine in roughly equal quantities. Christianity was widely tolerated, and churches were still being built in Transjordan up to the middle of the eighth century.

Abbasids and Fatimids: 750–1097

However, followers of stricter interpretations of Islam eventually gained the upper hand, possibly aided by a devastating earthquake which struck the region in 749. A year later, Damascus fell to a new dynasty, the **Abbasids**, who immediately shifted the Muslim capital eastwards to Baghdad, a symbolic move embodying a fundamental rejection of the liberal Umayyad, Mediterranean, spirit in preference for straighter-laced Persian and Mesopotamian methods. Transjordan – instantly reduced to a provincial backwater – fell into obscurity.

During the ninth century, internal dissent whittled away at the power of the Abbasid caliphate, and by 969 a rival, Shi'ite-derived caliphate had been proclaimed in Cairo by the Tunisian **Fatimid** dynasty, who took control of Palestine, Transjordan and southern Syria soon after, destroying many churches and harassing Christian pilgrims. In 1037, Seljuk Turks took power in the Abbasid empire and within fifty years, ruling from Baghdad as sultans, had defeated both the Fatimids and the Byzantines to regain Transjordan for orthodox Islam.

These tides of Muslim conquest and reconquest sweeping the Holy Land, coupled with the anti-Christian feeling aroused by the Fatimids and, more particularly, a Byzantine request for military aid against the Seljuks, didn't go unnoticed in the West. In 1095 Pope Urban II, speaking in France, launched an appeal for a European force to intervene in the chaos in the Middle East, to restore Christian rule in Palestine and, above all, to liberate Jerusalem. This holy war was termed a **crusade**.

Crusaders and Ayyubids: 1097–1250

In 1097, an army of some 100,000 – comprising seasoned troops and peasant rabble alike – arrived at Constantinople; two years later, they seized Jerusalem, slaughtering every man, woman and child in the city. Within forty years, there was a strip of Crusader-held territory running from southern Turkey to Aqaba, part of it incorporating the Lordship of Oultrejourdain (Transjordan) with its two impressive castles at **Karak** and **Shobak** (for more on the Crusaders in Transjordan, see p.305). In 1144, local Muslim forces started to eat into Crusader realms in northern Syria, inspiring a wave of strong Muslim resistance to the invaders, led after 1176 by a Kurdish officer named **Salah ad-Din al-Ayyubi** – or, to European tongues, Saladin. Having already disposed of the Fatimids in Cairo (and by doing so uniting the Muslim world), Salah ad-Din turned his attention to the common enemy, routing the Crusaders on the battlefield in 1187 and rapidly retaking Jerusalem, coastal Palestine and Transjordan. After his death in 1193, his dynasty, the **Ayyubids**, ruled the Muslim forces from their power base in Cairo. Undaunted, waves of Crusaders continued to arrive from Europe over the next decades, and rule of Levantine coastal areas shifted to and fro.

Mamlukes and Ottomans: 1250–1915

The Ayyubids came increasingly to rely for their military strength upon a band of highly disciplined and trained slave-troops, known as "the owned ones". Most of these **Mamlukes** were Turks or Caucasians from southern Russia who had been bought at market; once trained, they were lavished with property, goods and women, their lack of local tribal allegiance guaranteeing loyalty to their master. In 1250, however, the worm turned: with the Ayyubid sultan on his deathbed, the Mamlukes seized power for themselves.

The Mamlukes faced their first challenge less than a decade after taking control. In 1258, a **Mongol** army under Genghis Khan's grandson Hulagu destroyed Baghdad and swept westward through Transjordan to Galilee, where they were halted by a Mamluke army. The victorious general, **Baybars**, claimed the title of sultan and proceeded methodically to eject the last remaining Crusaders from the Levant.

During the fourteenth century, the Mamluke unification of Syria and Egypt provided a period of relative peace for the embattled Transjordanian population, who resorted to their tried and trusted forms of facilitating north–south commerce and providing shelter to Muslim pilgrims. Another Mongol invasion in 1400 under Tamerlane overran much of Syria; Mamluke finances – which relied on the Red Sea shipping trade – were further undermined by the Portuguese discovery of a new sea route to India which circumnavigated Africa.

Meanwhile, in northwestern Turkey a new dynasty had been gathering power for more than a century, and, in 1453, these **Ottomans** seized Constantinople, erasing what was left of the Byzantine Empire. In a short campaign begun in 1516, the Ottoman leader **Selim the Grim** occupied Damascus, Transjordan and Jerusalem in quick succession, eventually suspending the last Mamluke sultan from the gallows in Cairo.

Ottoman expansion throughout the Mediterranean continued apace (halted only at the gates of Vienna in 1683) but although imperial architects lavished care and attention on Damascus and Jerusalem, Transjordan was seen as important only for being the area through which the road to Mecca passed; apart from small inns built along the pilgrimage route, the infrastructure of the country was allowed to fall into decline. Not so much governed as merely occupied, the people of Transjordan were largely left to themselves. Western European merchants, who had long been established within all the important trading towns and ports around the region, quietly but efficiently siphoned wealth away from the imperial coffers, and the empire slowly and majestically crumbled.

In 1798, **Napoleon Bonaparte** invaded Egypt, but lost power less than a decade later. In the 1830s, the new Egyptian ruler Ibrahim Pasha embarked on a military adventure through Transjordan and the Levant which looked poised to overthrow Ottoman rule altogether but for the intervention of the British, who preferred the presence of a feeble and ineffective sultan to that of an enthusiastic and powerful young general. Trade on the Red Sea was revivified by the opening of the Suez Canal in 1869, but the canal itself, which represented the fastest sea route from Europe to India, remained under sole control of the British, who were by now firmly installed in Egypt and nurturing imperialist designs on Palestine.

In the 1870s, Russian persecution of Muslims in the Caucasus region east of the Black Sea led to waves of refugees putting themselves at the mercy of the Ottoman authorities in Turkey, who dumped them more or less wholesale onto ships bound for Levantine ports. These **Circassian** and **Chechen** farmers settled throughout the region, working their way inland to godforsaken Transjordan and colonizing the long-abandoned ruins at Amman, Jerash and elsewhere, not without some initial conflict with local Bedouin. In a separate but contemporary development, Russian persecution of **Jews** in modern Poland and Lithuania led a few to seek refuge in the Levant, but this time exclusively in Palestine. Spurred on by the dynamism of these émigrés, Jewish thinkers and activists codified a philosophy of organized Jewish settlement of Palestine – **Zionism**.

The decline of the Ottoman Empire: 1900–15

By the turn of the twentieth century, there was a spate of railway building around the Levant. The French were establishing a network in Syria; the German Berlin–Baghdad railway had reached Aleppo; and in Palestine, the British had long been operating a line from Jaffa to Jerusalem. To counter this European influence, and in a dramatic bid to bolster his waning religious authority, the sultan announced the construction of an Ottoman-sponsored **Hejaz Railway** (see p.383), to run from Damascus south through Transjordan, terminating at the holy city of Mecca. Ostensibly, the railway was to serve as a means of transporting Muslim pilgrims, but the sultan also had an eye on facilitating the rapid mobilization of Ottoman troops should the Arab nationalism that was beginning to stir in the Hejaz come to a head. Transjordanian Circassian and Chechen labour was vital in the construction of the line – as were the thick forests around Ajloun and Shobak, felled indiscriminately for fuel. By 1908, the track had reached Medina, 400km short of Mecca, but a coup in Constantinople the following year led to seizure of Ottoman power by a group of secular Turkish nationalists, and the railway got no further.

On the outbreak of **World War I**, the puppet sultan sided with the Germans, bringing the Ottoman Empire into conflict with both Britain – eagerly eyeing the newly discovered oilfields in Iraq and Persia – and France. Turkification was proceeding apace, with a ban on the use of Arabic in schools and offices, arrests of Arab nationalist leaders in Damascus and Beirut, and, in 1915, the first of the twentieth century's genocides, when over a million Armenians were exterminated and thousands more dispersed throughout the Levant. Observing from Cairo, the British conspired on the best way to foment ill-will towards Turkish authority into full-scale rebellion. Negotiations with opposition leaders in Cairo and Damascus to involve Arab forces in a revolt against the Turks broke down, but contact with **Sharif Hussein**, the ruler of Mecca and self-styled "King of the Arabs", was more fruitful. Its consequences, and the events surrounding the end of World War I, have directly caused almost a century of war in the Middle East, and profound trauma, dislocation and conflict for the peoples of Transjordan and its neighbours.

British promises and the Arab Revolt: 1915–18

When the Ottoman Empire entered World War I, the sultan had declared a *jihad* (an Islamically sanctioned struggle) against the Western powers. Alarmed at the possible repercussions of this in Muslim areas under their control, the British were keen to enlist for their side the support of Sharif Hussein, an authoritative religious dignitary and direct descendant of the Prophet Muhammad. In 1915, ten letters, known as the **McMahon Correspondence**, passed between Sir Henry McMahon, British High Commissioner in Egypt, and Hussein, in which Britain pledged to support Arab claims for independence if Hussein sparked a revolt against Turkish authority. Hussein's initial claims were for an independent Arab state stretching from Aleppo to the Yemeni coast, but McMahon specifically countered this by stating that Arab claims were excluded from three areas: the districts of Basra and Baghdad in Iraq (which the British wanted for themselves), the Turkish Hatay region around modern Antakya, and – most significantly – "portions of Syria lying to the west of the districts of Damascus, Homs, Hama and Aleppo". Sharif Hussein took this clause to refer to Lebanon, and accepted the terms. Confident of British backing, he proclaimed Arab independence on June 16, 1916, and declared war on the Turks.

Meanwhile, the British had other ideas. Following negotiation with France and Russia, the secret **Sykes–Picot Agreement** of May 1916 carved up the Middle East into areas of permanent colonial dominance, riding roughshod over the promises made to Sharif Hussein about Arab independence. Under the agreement, France was handed power in southeastern Turkey, Lebanon, Syria and northern Iraq, Britain in a belt of land stretching from Haifa to Baghdad and the Gulf, with most of Palestine to be administered by an international body. The colonial powers told nobody of their plans (Sharif Hussein only learnt of them more than a year later). Also in 1917, in a letter addressed to a leader of Britain's Jewish community, which came to be known as the **Balfour Declaration**, the British Foreign Secretary Arthur Balfour wrote that "His Majesty's Government view with favour the establishment in Palestine of a national home for the Jewish people." Hussein had specifically agreed in the McMahon Correspondence to Arab claims being excluded from the "portion of Syria lying to the west of Damascus", and, in an attempt to cover their backs, British ministers later claimed that this clause referred not, as maps indicate, to Lebanon, but rather to Palestine. The Balfour Declaration thus completed an astonishing triangle of mutually incompatible promises and agreements made by the British government between 1915 and 1917.

The Arab Revolt: 1917–18

Meanwhile, still assuming wholehearted British support, Sharif Hussein – aided by two of his sons, **Abdullah** and **Faysal** – had launched the **Great Arab Revolt**. A ragtag army of some thirty thousand tribesmen quickly seized Mecca and Jeddah from Ottoman forces, and, in January 1917, local notables, as well as Britain, France and Italy, recognized Sharif Hussein as "King of the Hejaz", leader of the first independent Arab state. In its initial stages, the British lent their support to the Arab Revolt principally in the form of Second Lieutenant **T.E. Lawrence**, later mythologized as "Lawrence of Arabia" (see p.389). Charged with assessing the Arab leadership, Lawrence picked out Faysal as being the ablest of Sharif Hussein's sons. Leaving Abdullah to pin down a forlorn Turkish garrison in Medina, Faysal led an army northwards to the port of Aqaba, a strategic prize through which the Arabs would be able to receive weaponry and material support from the British Army in Egypt. Ottoman defences in the town, protected on two sides by arid mountains, focused all their attention on attack from the sea. Holed up to the south, Lawrence instead planned a looping overland route through the desert, and with a small force emerged from the mountains to launch a surprise attack on the town from the north. The plan worked, and Aqaba fell to Faysal on July 6, 1917.

Faysal's Arab forces then came under the command of the British general **Allenby**, who was leading several divisions from Egypt towards Jerusalem. The Arabs and the British worked their way northwards in concert, the Arabs using the old castle at Azraq as a base during the winter of 1917–18. After Jerusalem fell to the British, the Arab armies skirmished up the newly laid Hejaz Railway line, taking Ma'an, Shobak, Tafileh and Karak. Amman fell in the late summer of 1918, and the way was clear for the final assault on Damascus, launched that September from Azraq. On October 1, Faysal and Lawrence entered Damascus victorious, both of them instrumental in ending Ottoman rule in the Levant.

The establishment of the emirate: 1918–23

By now, the French (working to the Sykes–Picot Agreement) had designs on Syria and Lebanon, while both the British and Zionist Jewish immigrants (working to the Balfour Declaration) had designs on Palestine. When, in 1920, elected Arab delegates to the government in Damascus declared the Levant independent under King Faysal, and Iraq independent under the absent King Abdullah (who was at that time still in the Hejaz), both Britain and France came out in sharp denunciation. Within six weeks, administrative control – termed a "**mandate**" – over the Middle East was awarded by an international conference to the colonial powers, forming borders within the Levant for the first time and splitting Palestine and Iraq (awarded to Britain) away from Syria and Lebanon (handed to France). Faysal was forcibly ejected from Damascus by the French, and the British spent £40 million suppressing open rebellion in Iraq (more than four times the expenditure of the entire Arab Revolt). In Mecca, the stunned Sharif Hussein realized the extent of the betrayal. "I listened to the faithless Englishmen," he muttered to a group of confidants. "I let myself be tempted and won over by them."

Amid the tussling over Palestine and Syria, the position of Transjordan remained unclear for some time. Britain informed a meeting of sheikhs at Salt that it favoured self-government for Transjordan, but then did little to foster it. Further south, Arab discontent was growing at British and French duplicity, and, in late October, Abdullah left Mecca with an army of five hundred intending to liberate Damascus from the French. On November 21, 1920, he arrived in Ma'an to a rousing reception of Transjordanian sheikhs and Arab nationalists.

From Ma'an, Abdullah's path lay through British-held Transjordan, still neither part of the Palestine Mandate nor fully autonomous. To try and nip the rebellion in the bud, the British laid detailed plans for the **military occupation** of Transjordan, plans that were scotched only by a Finance Committee in London ruling on expenditure. With an army now grown to three thousand, Abdullah proceeded north without hindrance, arriving in the village of Amman on March 2, 1921, to cheering crowds of mounted tribesmen. Confronted by a *fait accompli*, but obligated to prevent attack on the French from British territory, the new British Colonial Secretary, Winston Churchill (accompanied by his special adviser T.E. Lawrence) proposed a separate British mandate to be established in Transjordan; in exchange for Abdullah's abdication of the throne of Iraq in favour of the exiled Faysal, Britain would offer Abdullah the temporary title of Emir (Prince) of Transjordan, until "some accommodation" could be made with the French in Damascus. With the knowledge that he was being brought to heel, Abdullah attempted at least to secure the unification of Palestine with Transjordan, but was told that Britain had other plans for Palestine which took account of Jewish national aspirations. Well aware that Transjordan was the best he and the Arabs were likely to get for the moment, Abdullah accepted.

The territory that Abdullah took control of in April 1921 was rugged, undeveloped and in a state of anarchy. The borders drawn by Churchill were more or less arbitrary, frequently cutting across tribal areas and grazing grounds in the far desert. The three existing Transjordanian governments – centred in Irbid, Salt and Karak – had virtually no authority and were overlaid by a patchwork of unstable local sheikhdoms jockeying for position with each other. The population numbered about 230,000, of which over 200,000 were Muslim Arabs, the remainder Christian Arabs and Muslim Circassians. Over half were **fellaheen**, or landowning tribal village-dwellers (there were only four towns holding more than ten thousand people); a quarter were semi-nomadic Bedouin concentrated in the north and west, and the rest were fully nomadic, relying on their livestock and on raiding the *fellaheen*, pilgrimage caravans and each other for survival. Amman was a town of some 2400 people. Political loyalties were rooted in tribalism, and although the population at large tended towards common aims – desire for an Arab ruler, hatred of the French for their destruction of the Kingdom of Syria, distrust of the British for their double-dealing – they lacked a collective voice. When Abdullah arrived, apart from a brief challenge from some petty potentates in Salt, he was accepted without question as a unifying leader.

For their part, the British wrote Transjordan out of the Palestine Mandate. On May 15, 1923, under an **Anglo-Jordanian Treaty**, the British formally recognized Abdullah as head of the new **Emirate of Transjordan**, describing it as a national state being prepared for full independence under the supervision of the British High Commissioner in Jerusalem.

Consolidation of the emirate: 1923–28

To the south, in Mecca, the fury of Abdullah's father Sharif Hussein at being supplanted was uncontrollable, and in January 1924, he left his power base in the Hejaz for Aqaba, where he ignored his son's, and British, authority and started to rule in his own right. It rapidly became apparent, though, that his dream of becoming sole king of the Arabs was as much in tatters as the Arab heartland itself. Syria was controlled by the French, who had carved Lebanon out of it; Iraq was ruled by one son, Faysal, Transjordan by another, Abdullah; Palestine was under the thumb of the British; and late in 1924 the Hejaz was invaded by forces of a fundamentalist central Arabian tribe led by **Abd al-Aziz al-Saud**, who shortly afterwards established the Kingdom of Saudi Arabia. As a crowning ignominy, the British insisted that Hussein be kept from interfering any longer, and the old man spent his last years in exile on Cyprus.

Meanwhile, Abdullah, free of his father's influence, set about consolidating power in his newly chosen capital of **Amman** (favoured over the fractious Salt). The 1920s and 1930s saw the forging of a cohesive political unity from among the disparate tribes, with one of Abdullah's earliest acts being the creation of an authoritative centralized security force; clinging to notions of pan-Arabism, he pointedly omitted any mention of its being Transjordanian, instead naming it the **Arab Legion**.

Throughout this period, a series of Anglo-Jordanian treaties guaranteed British funding for central government, with the payback of British advisers maintaining intimate contacts with Abdullah in the running of the country. A pragmatist, as visionary as he was realistic, Abdullah knew that the British still called the shots, and that without Britain – specifically, without military assistance and money – the emirate could never survive. By choosing his battles, and compromising where necessary, Abdullah was able to maintain progress towards his ultimate goal of independence, though his concessions to the British were profoundly to tarnish his reputation among Arab nationalists.

Some of the earliest challenges to his authority came from urbanized Syrians who had fled Damascus in 1920 to form **Hizb al-Istiqlal** (the Independence Party), intent on stoking in Transjordan a hotbed of nationalist activity against the French. Sophisticated and well-educated, they were scathing in portraying Abdullah as a British lackey, yet he actively sought to co-opt them into power, partly because at the time few Transjordanians had the calibre of education for governmental office, but partly because his pan-Arabist notions didn't allow him to reject any element of Arab opinion. During 1926 and 1927, Abdullah gave refuge to many Syrian Druzes fleeing insurrection against the French, yet received stinging criticism from nationalists for his lack of material support for the rebellion (despite the British grip on control of the Arab Legion). By militantly opposing compromise with the French ten years before, such hard-line nationalists had been the downfall of his brother Faysal in Damascus, and Abdullah was far too astute a diplomat to pay their carping much heed. Indeed British and popular Transjordanian hostility towards the "foreigners" installed in Amman led him to reshuffle Istiqlal party members out of power in favour of the newly formed, exclusively Transjordanian **Hizb al-Shaab** (the People's Party). To assuage growing popular discontent with the status quo, Abdullah rapidly promulgated the **first Transjordanian constitution** in 1928 and, a year later, representative elections to a legislative council placed Transjordanians in real power for the first time, quietening the mood in the country.

With his domestic affairs stable, Abdullah was able to turn his attention further afield – specifically to the increasingly fraught situation in Palestine.

Abdullah I and Palestine: 1920–39

Like most other Arab countries, Palestine had always had a small native Jewish community, resident for the most part in the towns, Arabic-speaking and culturally Palestinian. Since the 1880s, however, Jews from central and eastern Europe had been arriving in Palestine, many of them tough-minded nationalistic **Zionists**, for whom the area was not simply a holy land to be shared among religious communities but the rightful national homeland of the Jews of the world. As it became obvious that the Balfour Declaration was to become official mandate policy in Palestine, a **militant Arab reaction** to Zionism developed, denouncing both the mandate in general and Britain's perceived right in particular to hand the country over to the Jews. In Amman, Abdullah quickly grasped the political reality – principally that Britain was in a position to dictate its will and that at least some degree of Jewish immigration to Palestine was inevitable. He put forward the proposal that if the Jews were prepared to accept the extension of his own rule over Palestine, they would be left free to govern themselves with all civil rights guaranteed; this would not only secure the Jewish position in Palestine with minimum cost to the existing local population, but it would also enable Jews to settle in Transjordan, where they could contribute much-needed money and skills to the country's development.

However, amid the increasingly hot-headed politics of the time, such a vision was doomed to failure. The Jews wanted more in Palestine than mere political autonomy under a Muslim king, and rejected his proposals. Mainstream Arab opinion viewed Abdullah's plan as overly concessionary, and from this time on, doubts were laid in Palestinian minds as to Abdullah's rectitude and motives. Popular reservations were fuelled by the paramount leader of the Palestinians, **Hajj Amin al-Husseini**, Mufti of Jerusalem. A strict hardliner who refused to compromise an inch with the Jews, Hajj Amin led persistent calls for a complete ban on Jewish immigration and land purchase, ahead of a termination of British mandatory rule and declaration of Palestinian independence; he was aided by a silent alliance with the British, who had no desire to see Abdullah extending influence over a land he wasn't supposed to be ruling. Amman became the focus for the Palestinian opposition to Hajj Amin, which believed that the only way of saving Palestine for the Arabs was to cultivate British goodwill and offer limited concessions to the already entrenched Zionist settlers.

Throughout the 1920s and 1930s, anti-Zionist feeling among Palestinian Arabs exploded into violence, put down with increasing harshness by the British. Meanwhile, with the coming to power of the Nazis in Germany in

1933, Jewish immigration to Palestine increased dramatically, as did Arab attacks on both Jewish and British targets. From 1933 onwards, Abdullah began to appoint Palestinians to positions of power in Amman, but in such a charged political atmosphere, his pragmatism in backing both Arab dialogue with the Jews and Arab concessions to British dominance merely fanned Palestinian distrust of his motives. In 1937, a **Royal Commission** arrived from London to assess the political situation; the Palestinian leadership immediately boycotted the commission's proceedings, and under threat of arrest, Hajj Amin fled to Lebanon.

The build-up to World War II: 1937–39

War in Europe looked increasingly likely, and Britain now embarked on an attempt to secure its position in the Middle East, an area commanding vital land and water routes and, most important, harbouring oil. As an initial gambit, the Royal Commission report of 1937 recommended **partitioning** Palestine between Arabs and Jews, but this was rejected by the all-or-nothing Palestinian leadership. With war imminent, the British ruled out partition and instead, in May 1939, offered a sudden, dramatic turnaround in policy. On the table was **full independence** for Palestine after ten years, with severe limitations in the meantime on land transfers to Jews and with Jewish immigration permitted only subject to Arab approval. Victims of a mercenary U-turn, the Jews immediately rejected the proposal. In Amman, Abdullah hailed it as the best the Palestinian Arabs could ever hope to get, but his credibility in mainstream Palestinian opinion had been eroded too far. From exile, Hajj Amin denounced the deal as a British ploy, and his authority won the day.

Seeing reason dissipating before him, Abdullah wrote: "The pillars of Zionism in Palestine are three: the Balfour promise; the European nations that have decided to expel the Jews from their lands; and the extremists among the Arabs who do not accept any solution. So behold Palestine, breathing its last."

Independence and the loss of Palestine: 1939–52

World War II had little impact in Transjordan, other than to delay advances towards independence. However, Abdullah's Arab Legion served loyally and effectively alongside the British elsewhere in the Middle East, helping to retake Baghdad from the Axis powers in 1941 (which paved the way for the British victory at El-Alamein the following year), and helping to eject the

The Hashemites

The aristocratic Hashemite dynasty, headed by Jordan's King Abdullah II, traces its genealogy back at least to the Prophet Muhammad. An Arab chieftain **Quraysh**, claimed to be a descendant of Ishmael, and thus of Abraham himself, is said to have first arrived in Mecca in the second century AD. By 480, his family ruled the city. One of his descendants, **Hashem**, was the great-grandfather of the Prophet Muhammad, who was born into the tribe of Quraysh in Mecca in around 571. Muhammad's daughter had two sons, and the direct descendants of the elder son have been known as **"Sharifs"** (nobles) since that time. Different Sharifian families ruled the Hejaz from 967 onwards, with King Abdullah's own branch ruling Mecca itself from 1201 right through to 1925, when the Saudis seized control from Sharif Hussein.

King Abdullah is the 43rd-generation direct descendant of the Prophet Muhammad. You can find a full account of Hashemite history, including family trees going back 54 generations to Quraysh, at ⓦ **www.kingabdullah.jo**.

Vichy French from Syria and Lebanon. Abdullah deserved reward, and what he hoped for – as he had done for decades – was the throne of a new Greater Syria. However, neither the Syrians nor the Lebanese would accept anything other than independence now the French had been removed from power; and the king of Saudi Arabia, already faced by a strong Hashemite monarchy in Iraq, had no desire to see another on his northern borders (Britain and the United States were both aware by now of the vast oil reserves in Saudi Arabia, and were willing to bend over backwards to avoid upsetting King Saud). Syria and Lebanon were both granted independence, but Transjordan remained under British mandate until the 1946 **Treaty of London**, which granted the emirate independence, albeit with Britain maintaining a controlling presence. In May, the Transjordanian cabinet switched Abdullah's title from emir to king, and officially changed the name of the country to the **Hashemite Kingdom of Jordan**.

Meanwhile, the situation in Palestine had been getting worse and worse, with a flood of post-Holocaust Jewish immigration into the country and a simultaneous campaign of terror by underground Jewish groups aimed at the British. Early in 1947, Britain announced that it would unilaterally pull out of its Palestine mandate; in November, the UN approved a plan to partition Palestine into a Jewish and an Arab state, with Jerusalem administered internationally. The Jews were unhappy, having been denied Jerusalem, and mainstream Arab opinion was outraged at the whole idea of conceding any kind of Jewish state in Palestine. On May 15, 1948, the last British troops departed from Haifa. Highly efficient Jewish forces immediately declared an independent **State of Israel**, and woefully disorganized Arab armies, led by Jordan's Arab Legion, simultaneously entered the region intent on taking the land allotted to the Jews by the UN. By the time fighting ended in July, Jordan had occupied a swathe of the interior of Palestine, as well as the eastern districts – and Holy Places – of Jerusalem, although the entire Galilee region and the valuable fertile coastal strip, including the large towns of Haifa, Jaffa, Lydda and Ramle, had been lost to Israel. Hundreds of thousands of Palestinians fled, or were forcibly ejected, from towns and villages throughout the country, and most sought refuge in the Jordanian-held sector, known as the **West Bank**. Before the Israeli war, the kingdom's population had stood at around 435,000; four years later, it was 1.5 million, of whom two-thirds were Palestinian (including more than half a million refugees living in temporary camps).

Immediately following the hostilities, Abdullah came under severe criticism from around the Arab world, both for compromising with Israel on the West Bank armistice border and for his perceived desire to incorporate the Jordanian-occupied part of Palestine into his kingdom. A Government of All Palestine was set up in Egyptian-occupied Gaza to block Abdullah's claims, but, with the continued advance of Jewish forces, was forced to flee to Cairo and soon dissolved. In December 1948 Abdullah convened a meeting in Jericho of Palestinian notables to proclaim the absorption of the Jordanian-occupied West Bank into Jordan proper. In April 1950, Jordan formally annexed the West Bank under the guise of "**uniting the two banks**".

Following 1948, the newly formed **Arab League** had ruled that Arab countries should not grant citizenship to Palestinian refugees, lest the disowned and displaced should then lose their claim to their homeland. To this day, Palestinians who sought refuge in Lebanon, Syria and Egypt remain stateless and without rights. Jordan was the only Arab country to go against this policy; it formally resettled its Palestinian refugees, granting them (and, in fact, any Palestinian living anywhere in the world) full Jordanian citizenship and civil rights – as it still does to this day. Abdullah's policy enabled Palestinians in Jordan to pick up their lives again and start afresh, but it ran entirely against mainstream Arab thinking that refused to accept the fact of Israel's existence in Palestine. Citizenship notwithstanding, most Palestinians – in Jordan and elsewhere – felt betrayed by Abdullah's policies from as far back as the 1920s, and particularly by his perceived eagerness to absorb Arab Palestine under the Hashemite banner. On July 20, 1951, as Abdullah was about to enter the al-Aqsa mosque in Jerusalem for Friday prayers, a young Palestinian stepped up and shot him dead. A bullet intended for Abdullah's 15-year-old grandson, Hussein, ricocheted off a medal on the boy's chest.

On Abdullah's assassination, the throne passed automatically to the Crown Prince, Abdullah's 40-year-old son **Talal**, who at the time of his accession, was in Switzerland receiving medical treatment. Talal returned to Amman and took up his constitutional duties, but his increasingly erratic behaviour rapidly made it clear that he was unfit to rule. In 1952, under guidance from the Jordanian parliament, Talal abdicated the throne in favour of his eldest son, Hussein.

King Hussein's early years: 1952–67

Born in 1935, **King Hussein** was educated in Britain, at Harrow School and Sandhurst military academy. He succeeded to the throne before his seventeenth birthday, and was crowned king in May 1953. At this time, the Cold War was well established, and the new king found himself caught between a powerful Egyptian–Syrian–Saudi bloc on the one hand, closely allied with the Soviets, and on the other, the controlling British presence at the heart of his government pushing him towards the pro-Western Baghdad Pact (a British-designed defensive treaty against Soviet aggression, subscribed to by Iraq, Turkey, Iran and Pakistan). In addition, the events of 1948 had utterly changed the character of Jordan, and had thrown a cosmopolitan, well-educated and urbanized Palestinian population into the arms of an outnumbered Transjordanian population with an entirely different, rural and Bedouin-based culture. Most of the Palestinians yearned to return to their lost homeland, and were unwilling to follow the generally conciliatory and pro-Western Hashemite line; many favoured instead the **pan-Arabism** espoused by the charismatic Egyptian leader, **Nasser**.

Crisis loomed for Hussein in 1955 and 1956. In nine months, five prime ministers came and went; Jordan's initial declaration of Cold War neutrality wavered under British pressure to join the Baghdad Pact, but violent street protests in Amman in response prompted Hussein to peremptorily dismiss the English commander-in-chief of the Jordanian Armed Forces, **Glubb Pasha**, and replace him with a Jordanian. Nonetheless, anti-Western feeling continued to run high, especially after the British–French–Israeli invasion of Egypt during the **Suez Crisis** of 1956. A few months later, Jordan's pro-Soviet prime minister **Suleiman Nabulsi** terminated the 1948 Anglo-Jordanian treaty, and the British subsidy to Jordan was replaced instead by contributions from Saudi Arabia, Syria and Egypt (the last two soon defaulted). British troops left Jordan for good in July 1957. To make up the financial shortfall, Hussein requested aid from the US, which was granted; outraged, Nabulsi unsuccessfully attempted a coup. After accepting Nabulsi's resignation, Hussein took control of army appointments and ordered political parties and trade unions to be suppressed; all parliamentary elections – right through until 1989 – were conducted only under strict controls. The US weighed in with a declaration of its determination to preserve Jordan's independence, and when Syria overtly allied itself with the USSR in September 1957, US forces sent a large airlift of arms to Amman.

Throughout the 1950s Egypt and Syria, both then revolutionary republics, kept up a bombardment of anti-Hashemite propaganda, with Nasser's **Radio Cairo** particularly vocal in its championing of the cause of pan-Arabism to the denigration both of the Jordanian government and of King Hussein himself. On February 1, 1958, Egypt and Syria announced – to wild celebrations on the streets of Jordan as everywhere in the Arab world – their merger in a **United Arab Republic** (UAR); as a counter-move, two weeks later, the Hashemite monarchies of Jordan and Iraq announced their own merger in an **Arab Federation**. The latter body was to survive barely five months, however, the entire Iraqi royal family being slaughtered in a military coup in July. Tensions in Lebanon had meanwhile led to open Muslim insurrection in that country, supported by the new UAR, against the Christian-led and staunchly pro-American Lebanese government. Anti-Western feeling in the Middle East was at a peak, and the only obstacles most observers saw standing in the way of pan-Arab unity were the Lebanese Christians and Jordan's Hashemite monarchy. Few gave the latter much chance of survival.

The American response to the crisis was to bomb Lebanon and, in July, land Marines in the country. Meanwhile, the US administration had received a request for help from Jordan, which had run out of oil. However, with the revolutionary forces in Syria and Iraq sealing off their borders with Jordan, and the Saudi king in thrall to Nasser's popularity, the only remaining direction by which the US could deliver oil to Jordan was over **Israeli airspace**. Amazingly, Hussein applied to Israel for permission, which was granted, and the airlift commenced, to a barrage of scorn from all Arab sides. Soon after, to match the US landings in Lebanon, Britain flew troops into Amman to bolster the regime; they too arrived over Israel and the insults flew once again. Nonetheless, in Jordan, democracy had been sacrificed for stability, and Hussein's **security services** kept a tight lid on the simmering discontent. Palestinian-planted bombs exploded in Amman and, in 1960, the prime minister was assassinated, but a coup and repeated attempts on the king's life were foiled.

Opposition to Hussein slowly died down, not least because US financial aid – and substantial remittances from Jordanians working in the Gulf countries – were fostering tangible **economic development**: Jordan's key potash and phosphate industries were taking off, modern highways were being built for the first time, unemployment was down as construction teams greatly expanded East and West Bank cities, and tourism to Jordanian Jerusalem, Bethlehem, Hebron and the West Bank, as well as East Bank sites, was bringing in much-needed hard currency. Mutual ties with the Saudi Arabian monarchy were also strengthening in the face of strident Arab nationalism and communism elsewhere. Perhaps most important of all, Hussein came to the decision, albeit reluctantly, to approve the creation of a separate political entity to represent the Palestinians, the **Palestine Liberation Organization (PLO)**, founded in 1964. Its charter, in a specific rebuff to Jordanian claims on the West Bank, stated that it was to be the "only legitimate spokesman" for the Palestinian people. From the outset, however, King Hussein refused to permit the PLO to raise funds from Palestinians resident in Jordan, or the military units of the Palestine Liberation Army to train on Jordanian soil, indirectly pushing them towards pro-Soviet Syria.

The Six-Day War and Black September: 1967–74

During late 1966, relations with Syria deteriorated dramatically, and Jordan suspended support for the PLO, accusing its secretary of pro-communist activity. Syria and the PLO both made direct appeals to ordinary Jordanians to revolt against King Hussein. Clashes followed on the Jordanian–Syrian border, and PLO-laid bombs exploded in Amman. At the same time, skirmishes with Israeli troops and cross-border raids led Jordan to introduce conscription; the prospect of war with Israel seemed inevitable, but rather than isolate himself even more from his Arab neighbours, Hussein flew to Cairo in May 1967 to throw in his lot with Egypt and Syria.

On June 5, Israel launched a pre-emptive strike against its Arab neighbours. By the end of the **Six-Day War**, Jordanian losses were devastating: Israel was occupying East Jerusalem and the entire West Bank. From Syria it had seized the Jawlan (Golan Heights); from Egypt, the Gaza Strip and Sinai Peninsula as far west as Suez. In the eyes of the entire Arab world, this was an utter catastrophe: Egypt and Syria had lost relatively small areas of strategic importance, but Jordan had lost fully half its inhabited territory, a third of its population, its prime agricultural land and – most ignominious – control over the Muslim and Christian holy sites in Jerusalem. Up to a quarter of a million refugees crossed to the East Bank, putting the government, economy and social services under intolerable pressures.

The crushing defeat gave Palestinians in Jordan cause to believe that King Hussein and the other Arab leaders were unable or unwilling (or both) to liberate their homeland. King Hussein rapidly included equal representation from the East and West Banks in the National Assembly, but this was never going to satisfy Palestinian demands. The rift grew between the government and the Palestinian guerrilla organizations in Jordan, principally Fatah, led by **Yasser Arafat**, chairman of the umbrella PLO. After 1967, these groupings – funded by the oil-rich Gulf States and receiving arms and training from Syria – assumed effective control in Jordan's refugee camps, backed also by widespread grassroots support from Jordan's majority Palestinian population. A **fedayeen** ("martyrs") movement developed within the camps, which took on the appearance of a state-within-a-state, intent on liberating Palestine by their own independent efforts. The *fedayeen* took for granted their ability to overrule King Hussein in his own country, and launched military operations against Israel. The ensuing reprisals, however, caused extensive damage to the border areas – now Jordan's only remaining agricultural land – and seriously undermined any possibilities for a peace settlement with Israel, on which the country's long-term future depended.

Black September and its aftermath: 1970–74

Fedayeen opposition to the Hashemite regime, rooted in revolutionary social-ism, remained implacable. Confrontations flared in 1968, leading to serious street battles, and in June 1970, the Jordanian army mobilized on the streets of Amman to assert authority over the guerrilla movements. Arafat squeezed major concessions from King Hussein, who was forced to dismiss prime movers of the anti-*fedayeen* bloc from the army and cabinet; nonetheless, tension remained high, and there was at least one attempt on the king's life. In September, *fedayeen* **hijacked** three international aircraft to an airfield near Mafraq, ostensibly demanding the release of imprisoned comrades, but equally intent on embarrassing King Hussein in the eyes of the world and forcing the issue of the Palestinian revolution in Jordan. Once emptied of passengers and crew, all three aircraft were spectacularly blown up; the *fedayeen* then took over Irbid proclaiming a "people's government", and the country exploded into violence. By the end of "**Black September**", full civil war was raging, with thousands dead and injured, and the *fedayeen* claiming complete control of the north of Jordan. Documents released in 2001 reveal that King Hussein contacted London at the height of the crisis, requesting the British govern-ment to ask the Israeli government to bomb the pro-*fedayeen* Syrian army, which looked poised to cross the border and overrun Jordan. Such an unprec-edented request was kept top secret, and although the message was passed to the Israelis, no action was taken. Despite agreement between Hussein and Arafat to end the war in October, sporadic outbursts continued for months. Jordan's actions provoked bitter criticism from most Arab countries, but nonetheless, by April 1971, the Jordanian army had pushed the *fedayeen* out of Amman. Three months later, after a violent offensive on Palestinian posi-tions around Jerash and Ajloun, forces loyal to the king were back in control. The *fedayeen* fled to Lebanon to continue their fight (within four years, civil war had broken out in Lebanon as well). Palestinian commandos made three unsuccessful attempts to hijack Jordanian aircraft, and, in September 1971, members of the Black September faction of Fatah assassinated another Jorda-nian prime minister. Within Jordan, internal social divisions between Trans-jordanians and Palestinians were profound, and suspicion and resentment ran high on both sides.

King Hussein made an immediate attempt to regain Palestinian political cred-ibility by announcing in March 1972 his plans for a United Arab Kingdom, a **federation** of Jordan and Palestine, both regions to be near-autonomous but ruled by him from Amman. Criticism of the plan was almost universal, from Israel, from the exiled Palestinian organizations and from Egypt, which broke off diplomatic relations. A military coup in November was only just averted, and, in February 1973, leaders of Fatah were arrested on charges of infiltrating Jordan and sentenced to death (later commuted by the king to life imprison-ment). Jordan's isolation in the Arab world was almost complete. Nonetheless, Hussein attended a **reconciliation summit** soon afterwards with presidents Sadat of Egypt and Assad of Syria, which resulted in a general amnesty for all political prisoners in Jordan, including those Fatah activists sentenced months before. Jordanian security services and intelligence organizations were beefed up to deter dissident activity; political parties remained banned and the country had no elected parliament. Jordan stayed out of the 1973 Egyptian–Syrian **October War** (or Yom Kippur War) against Israel, but garnered little kudos for doing so.

The Rabat summit and Camp David: 1974–80

Throughout 1974, King Hussein attempted to preserve his claim over the West Bank, flying in the face of intense pressure from other Arab states and the increasing power and prestige of the PLO (in an unprecedented move, Yasser Arafat had that year been invited to address the UN General Assembly). In October 1974, at the **Arab Summit Conference** in Rabat, Morocco, twenty Arab heads of state passed a resolution recognizing the PLO as the "sole legitimate representative of the Palestinian people", and confirming its right to establish a national authority over any liberated Palestinian lands. King Hussein reluctantly agreed to this, thus effectively ceding Jordan's claims both to represent the Palestinians and to reincorporate the West Bank into the Hashemite realm. His authority, and what was left of his appeal, among West Bankers plummeted.

In 1974, both Egypt and Syria had signed disengagement agreements with Israel over the Sinai and the Jawlan respectively; in 1975 and 1976, King Hussein held secret talks with Israel over the West Bank, which later collapsed due to Israel's proposal to retain control over thirty percent of the territory. Post-Rabat, Jordan's relations with Syria were meanwhile improving, with trade and diplomatic links flourishing, but the new realities were thrown into turmoil by Egyptian President Sadat's peace initiative in visiting Jerusalem in 1977; Hussein tried to stand as an arbiter between Egypt and the rejectionist Arab states (led by Syria), while still demanding Israel's complete withdrawal from East Jerusalem, the West Bank and Gaza. Jordan joined the rest of the Arab world in scorning the US-sponsored Egypt–Israel **Camp David accords** of 1978, and, as a reward, was promised $1.25 billion annually by wealthy Iraq. Just prior to the formal signing of an Egypt–Israel peace treaty in 1979, King Hussein chose to demonstrate instead his commitment to the PLO by inviting Yasser Arafat on an official visit.

Throughout the 1970s, economic relations between Jordan and **Iraq** improved, with Iraq funding the expansion of Aqaba port and construction of major highways within Jordan. When Iraq invaded Iran in September 1980, launching the bloody **Iran–Iraq War**, Jordan benefited greatly from the passage of goods through Aqaba bound for Iraq, whose own port at Basra was rendered off-limits by hostilities.

The Palestinians and the first intifada: 1980–89

Since Black September, the PLO's bid for authority over Palestinians on the East Bank had – bizarrely – reinforced the stand of both Transjordanian and Israeli hardliners. The former had never viewed the Palestinians as true Jordanians anyway; the latter saw the Hashemite monarchy as the sole obstacle to annexation of the West Bank by Israel, and, under the slogan "**Jordan is Palestine**", pressed for a Palestinian revolution east of the Jordan, offering to help it along by expelling Palestinians en masse from the West Bank. Needless to say, this rapidly dampened Palestinian opposition to King Hussein in Jordan, and led to something of a *rapprochement*.

In 1982, the PLO was summarily ejected from its Beirut headquarters by the **Israeli invasion of Lebanon**, and sent into further exile in Tunis; humiliated, Arafat looked to King Hussein for some way to challenge Israeli hegemony. A series of talks between the two men took place during 1983; in the following year, Hussein reconvened the National Assembly, comprising representatives from both banks of the Jordan, for the first time since 1967, as a forum for discussion of moderate Palestinian opinion away from the extremist intransigence of the Syrian position. Israel even permitted West Bank deputies to travel to Amman. In March 1984, the first **elections** in Jordan for seventeen years (and the first in which women could vote) took place, although political parties were still banned and the eight seats up for grabs were East Bank only.

Less than a year later, in opposition to a widely denounced peace plan put forward by US President Reagan (who refused to talk to the PLO), Hussein and Arafat agreed to allow Jordan to start direct negotiations with Israel under UN auspices, on the basis of Hussein's formula of "**land for peace**" – that is, the return of lands occupied by Israel in 1967 in exchange for a comprehensive Arab-Israeli peace. Were this to have gone ahead, though, hardline Syria would have been completely marginalized in the region; Damascus therefore forced Hussein to drop the initiative, partly by a number of assassinations of Jordanian diplomats abroad, and partly by uniting the Abu Nidal Palestinian guerrilla organization with Arafat's main PLO rival, George Habash, to attack the accord. At the end of 1985, Hussein and Syria's President Assad issued a joint statement rejecting any direct peace negotiations with Israel; Hussein's motivation for this was also to put pressure on Arafat to accept **UN Resolution 242**, without which the PLO could gain no international credibility. "242" had been a thorn in the side of the Arabs since 1967, since it called ambiguously for Israel to withdraw from "occupied territories" (which could be taken to mean whatever anyone wanted) and referred to the Palestinians as "refugees", thus implying a denial of the existence of a Palestinian nation and the right of Palestinians to self-determination, and accepting the right of Israel to exist. Hamstrung by extremist attitudes embedded within the PLO, Arafat couldn't stop the PLO Executive Committee reiterating its opposition to 242 in December 1985. The following February, King Hussein severed political links with the PLO.

Although rumours of secret talks between Hussein and the Israeli Prime Minister Shimon Peres persisted through the mid-1980s, publicly Jordan continued to reject Israeli proposals for peace talks which excluded PLO participation. In November 1987, King Hussein managed to convene in Amman the first full meeting of the Arab League for eight years and, acting in the interests of Arab unity, was able to draw Egypt back into the fold after its expulsion for making peace with Israel. Following a two-year hiatus, cooperation between Jordan and the PLO recommenced.

The first intifada and Jordan's West Bank pull-out: 1987–89

In December 1987, an incident in the Gaza Strip sparked a widespread violent Palestinian uprising against Israeli occupation of the West Bank and Gaza, termed the **intifada**, or "shaking-off". Despite brutal security measures, Israel was unable to suppress the uprising, and, alarmed at the possibility of demonstrations turning violent, the Jordanian security services enforced their own clampdown on any shows of solidarity. The intensity of the revolt, as well as the Israeli response to it and the news that emerged of horrendous living conditions among Palestinians under Israeli occupation, alerted world opinion to the necessity of a comprehensive settlement in the Middle East. The US Secretary of State, George Shultz, shuttled around the region, but could only come up with a plan that not only refused participation by the PLO, but also neglected to address the Palestinian right to self-determination. This effectively guaranteed the plan's rejection by every Arab state.

In a momentous decision on July 31, 1988, with the *intifada* in full swing, Hussein announced the **severing** of all legal and administrative links between Jordan and the West Bank, stressing his adherence to the 1974 Rabat declaration. By doing so, he effectively ended Hashemite claims to Arab Palestine which had been playing beneath the surface of political machinations in the region since 1917. Hussein dissolved the half-Palestinian House of Representatives and dismantled Jordanian public services in the West Bank (Jordan had been paying teachers and civil servants there since 1967). The 850,000 Palestinians on the West Bank welcomed the clean break. However, with the departure of Jordanian staff, Israel immediately began restricting the activities of West Bank Palestinian institutions. Anti-Hashemite opinion cynically suggested that Hussein wanted to demonstrate the inability of the PLO to run public services and conduct international diplomacy without the backing of Jordan.

Shortly afterwards, on November 15, the PLO unilaterally proclaimed an independent **State of Palestine**, endorsing UN Resolution 242 and thus implicitly recognizing the right of Israel to exist (within its pre-1967 frontiers). Jordan and sixty other countries recognized the new state. The following month, Yasser Arafat renounced violence on behalf of the PLO in front of the UN General Assembly.

Democracy and the first Gulf War: 1989–91

In Jordan, the pull-out from the West Bank caused the value of the dinar to fall dramatically, and the austerity measures that followed resulted in **price rises** of up to fifty percent on basic goods and services. In April 1989, anti-government **riots** broke out in depressed southern towns such as Karak and Ma'an, particularly alarming because of these areas' traditional loyalty to the establishment. The prime minister and the entire cabinet resigned, and King Hussein announced that a full **general election** would be held for the first time since 1967.

The free election, held in November 1989, was contested mostly by independents, since the ban on political parties had not been lifted. Some 52 percent of the electorate voted – Jordanians of Palestinian origin were particularly under-represented – and 34 of the 80 seats went to Islamist candidates; a further 18 went to perceived "leftists". This strength of support for the opposition was surprising, not least because there had been some gerrymandering to ensure disproportionately large representation among traditionally loyal Bedouin rural areas.

Despite apparently improving political health, 1990 was a year of desperate crisis for Jordan. The dinar had lost two-thirds of its value in the two years since the pull-out from the West Bank, and unemployment was running at twenty percent. Fraud and embezzlement had been uncovered at the country's second largest bank, and the scandal had spread to the national airline and some 37 other companies. In addition, a huge influx of Jews into Israel from the former Soviet Union was resulting in ever more settlements going up on the West Bank and a consequent flood of Palestinians crossing the river into Jordan; with the West Bank Palestinians under almost continuous curfew, the *intifada* seemed to have fizzled out.

The first Gulf War: 1990–91

As the 1980–88 Iran–Iraq war juddered to a halt, it became clear that Iraq, which had received substantial loans from the Gulf States, was now in no position to repay them. President Saddam Hussein campaigned to have the loans cancelled, but **Kuwait** stood out by refusing to accede. This quarrel was complicated by a longstanding border dispute between the two countries – and by the fact that the disputed area was rich in oil. Penurious Iraq then also accused Kuwait and the UAE of producing oil above their quotas and of thus deliberately depressing global prices. Retaining his pan-Arab stance, King Hussein pressed for a resolution to the crisis by Arab mediation before an international crisis flared, but before steps could be taken, Iraq suddenly **invaded** Kuwait on August 2, 1990. An attempt to set up a pro-Iraqi regime failed, and Saddam Hussein quickly proclaimed the annexation of Kuwait to Iraq.

The UN Security Council imposed **economic sanctions** on Iraq four days later, precipitating a further crisis in Jordan. Thousands of Jordanian refugees returned destitute from Iraq and Kuwait, ending substantial foreign remittances to the kingdom and placing a huge burden on the country's social services; petroleum prices rose sharply, as Jordan's supply of free Iraqi oil (in return for loans during the Iran–Iraq war) dried up; fully a quarter of Jordan's export trade had been to Iraq, and this was terminated; and business at Aqaba port was cut overnight, as the road to Iraq was closed to trade.

It was clear that Saddam Hussein's actions flouted international law. King Hussein attempted to get the Arab League to mediate in the crisis, but he was countered by Saudi Arabia, Egypt and Syria leading calls for international action to proceed. In August, King Hussein started a round of peacemaking, intent on avoiding conflict in the Gulf. On September 23, he gave a televised address to the US Congress, urging withdrawal of the multinational force in Saudi Arabia. In November, he warned the World Climate Conference of the potentially disastrous environmental effects of war – borne out by Iraq's later ignition of Kuwaiti oil installations. The following month, he proposed a peace plan linking the Iraq–Kuwait dispute with the Arab–Israeli conflict, and advocating dialogue amongst Arab leaders.

His efforts proved fruitless: on January 16, 1991, **hostilities** began, sparking widespread anti-Western and anti-Israel demonstrations throughout Jordan. Saudi Arabia had halted oil supplies to Jordan in September 1990, and petrol rationing was introduced, which only bolstered pro-Iraqi sentiment. Arab popular opinion, outside the Arabian Peninsula, held that the US-led coalition was pursuing double standards, condemning Iraqi aggression against Kuwait, yet condoning Israeli aggression in the occupied territories; that the Gulf States were greedy, unwilling to share their new-found oil wealth with other Arabs; and that the West, by weighing in against Iraq, was supporting the oil-rich states against the poorer Arab states. In the region, King Hussein was highly regarded for being the only leader to articulate this opinion fully, although he was lambasted for it in the West. After hostilities ceased in March, the US Congress cancelled an aid programme in punishment for the king's stance. Kuwait regarded its sizeable Jordanian and Palestinian community as collaborators with the Iraqis, and expelled them all – about 300,000 people – to Jordan, a further burden on the country's social infrastructure.

Peace and crises: 1991–99

In 1991, the Royal Commission set up to regulate political life in Jordan drafted a new **National Charter**, endorsed by the king in June: as well as improving openness within government and easing bureaucracy, the charter lifted the ban on political parties, which had been in effect since 1963, in return for their pledge of allegiance to the crown. Martial law, which had been in force since 1967, was repealed. Jordan's first one-person one-vote, multi-party **elections** of November 1993 saw a 68 percent turnout, with by far the majority of candidates being independent centrists loyally backing the king, although the Islamic Action Front (the political arm of the Muslim Brother-hood) gained strong support.

New moves in the Middle East **peace process** were initiated by the US in Madrid in October 1991, and Jordan enthusiastically participated in a joint delegation with the Palestinians, thus relieving some of the US's lingering opprobrium towards the idea of Palestinian representation. Soon after inception, the peace talks hit deadlock, but, unknown even to King Hussein, Israel's new left-wing government and the PLO were engaged in secret talks in Oslo throughout the first half of 1993. That September, they emerged with a **Declaration of Principles** regarding Palestinian self-rule in the occupied territories. Soon after, King Hussein insisted that Jordan and the PLO sign agreements on economic and security co-operation, closely bonding the ongo-ing Israeli–Palestinian and Israeli–Jordanian peace talks together into a single framework.

On July 25, 1994, in Washington, King Hussein and Israeli Prime Minister Yitzhak Rabin formally ended the state of war that had existed between their two countries since 1948. A full **peace treaty** followed in October, opposed both by Syria and by Islamists within Jordan; President Clinton, however, immediately wrote off Jordan's outstanding debt to the US of $700 million. A clause in the treaty acknowledging King Hussein as the custodian of the Holy Places in Jerusalem initially brought complaints from the PLO that it under-mined Palestinian claims to the city, later mollified.

In August 1996, under intense pressure from the International Monetary Fund to institute austerity measures, the government ended **subsidies** on grain which were producing a ballooning economic deficit. The result was an immediate doubling of bread prices, and discontent, especially strong in the poorer towns of the south, flared into open **rioting**, which rapidly spread also to Amman. King Hussein suspended parliament and sent troops and tanks into Karak and elsewhere to suppress the disturbances, but the austerities remained. The election in 1996 of an extreme right-wing government in Israel, headed by **Binyamin Netanyahu**, brought the ongoing Middle East peace process to a grinding halt.

For many Jordanians, 1997 was a year of shattered confidence, as the country was exposed to a series of domestic and regional crises. Early in the year, a Jordanian soldier opened fire on Israeli schoolgirls visiting Baqoura in north-ern Jordan, killing seven. King Hussein attempted to mend ties with Israel by personally visiting the bereaved families, a gesture which inspired much admi-ration in Israel and much contempt in the Arab world (no bereaved Arab fami-lies have ever been consoled by an Israeli leader, the argument ran). Anti-Israel feeling surged in Jordan, and the soldier was spared the death penalty on the grounds of mental instability. In July, nine major political parties announced their intention to boycott the November parliamentary election, as a sign of their opposition to normalizing relations with Israel and as a stand against the election law, which, through gerrymandering, overrepresented the tribal and rural populations and underrepresented Jordanians of Palestinian origin. Diplomatic relations with Israel were almost terminated in September, after a botched assassination attempt in Amman by Mossad, the Israeli intelligence service, on an official at the Jordanian bureau of the Palestinian Islamist opposition group Hamas. Days before the Jordanian elections in November, Human Rights Watch issued a damning report on the state of human rights in Jordan. The elections themselves were held to be a whitewash, with extremely low voter turnout (just twenty percent in some Amman districts). Of the 80 seats, 62 were won by pro-government or independent centrist candidates; only 19 out of 524 candidates were women, none of whom was elected (the king later appointed three women to the Senate). A report from Jordan University showed unemployment in the country standing at a crippling 22–27 percent, double the official estimate.

Riots broke out again across the country in February 1998 after a rise in tension in Iraq over UN weapons inspections; a crowd of several thousand in Downtown Amman protested the US-led military build-up, and riot police were sent in to disperse them. Ma'an, a hotbed of dissent, was sealed off by tanks and placed under military curfew for several days.

The death of King Hussein

Throughout the 1990s, concern had been bubbling under Jordanian politics about the **health** of King Hussein. In August 1992, one of his kidneys was removed during an operation for cancer; spring 1996 saw an operation for an enlarged prostate, and during 1998 he underwent chemotherapy for lymph cancer. All these procedures were done in the US, his youngest brother, **Prince Hassan**, being sworn in as regent on each occasion. In October 1998, Hussein witnessed the **Wye River Accords**, guaranteeing Israeli withdrawal from more West Bank land in return for security safeguards from the Palestinians. (Two months later Israel suspended the agreement in the face of deepening domestic tension, and the Netanyahu government collapsed.) The king's appearance at Wye River, to free the negotiations from deadlock despite obvious physical frailty, inspired respect but also doubts about his ability to continue his public duties.

In January 1999, after six months of treatment in the US, Hussein flew back to Jordan and immediately took control of domestic affairs, although it was clear that his health was failing. In a controversially abrupt letter, published during this short stay, he removed Hassan from the **succession** after 34 years as Crown Prince, and placed in his stead his own eldest son, Abdullah. Within hours, Hussein had suffered a relapse and was rushed back to the US. Following an unsuccessful procedure, Hussein was flown back to Amman where he died three days later, on February 7, 1999, at the age of 63, having been in power for 46 years – one of the longest-serving executive heads of state in the world. His funeral drew worldwide media attention, with more than **fifty heads of state** in attendance. Even at a time of tragedy, such a turnout, demonstrating the international community's high regard for Jordan and its king, was a significant fillip to national confidence.

Jordan under Abdullah II

On the death of Hussein, a swearing-in ceremony confirmed the succession to **King Abdullah II**, who was crowned in July 1999. Abdullah was born in 1962 to Hussein's second wife, an Englishwoman, formerly Toni Gardiner, who took the name Princess Muna al-Hussein when she converted to Islam. He was educated at Oxford and Sandhurst; when he acceded, it was said at first that he spoke better English than Arabic. However, his prominent role in the Jordanian military ensured wholehearted support among East Bankers, while the fact that his wife, **Queen Rania**, is a scion of a notable Palestinian family from Tulkarm on the West Bank safeguarded his reputation among Jordanians of Palestinian origin.

In his first years in office, Abdullah has taken a relatively quiet role in regional and world affairs, preferring instead to consolidate his power at home and concentrate on domestic policy. Along with Mohammed VI of Morocco, who acceded to power in 1999 at the age of 38, and Bashar al-Assad, who took over the Syrian presidency in 2000 at 34, Abdullah has been hailed as representing a new, progressive generation of Arab leaders, committed to peace, economic liberalization and socially progressive politics. Unlike Mohammed and al-Assad, however, after a shaky start he has largely held true to these ideals.

Faced with continuing turmoil in Israel and Palestine, Abdullah has played only a minor role in suing for regional peace. With the election of the left-leaning **Ehud Barak** as Israeli prime minister in 1999, a new set of agreements were signed by the Palestinians and Israel, followed shortly after by the resumption of peace talks. Hopes were high for a comprehensive peace, but within months the Wye River Accords had collapsed following disagreement over the timetable for implementation, the Syrian presidency had changed hands and impetus was lost, and, in September 2000, the notorious right-wing Israeli general **Ariel Sharon** sparked outrage by touring Jerusalem's Haram ash-Sharif, the third-holiest site in Islam. Within weeks Sharon had won the Israeli elections, his bullish presence as prime minister effectively halting all progress in international peace negotiations and inducing Abdullah to postpone sending an ambassador to Tel Aviv. The **second intifada** which followed, incomparably bloodier than its forebear of the late 1980s, lasted for over four years, juddering to a halt in early 2005 following the **death of Yasser Arafat** in November 2004 and the election of **Mahmoud Abbas** as Palestinian president shortly after. Throughout, the uprising was supported almost universally by the Jordanian people and by such vocal bodies as Jordan's **Anti-Normalization Committee** (an informal grouping of activists which, among other agitation, published a blacklist exposing Jordanian politicians, writers and other public figures who have interacted with Israel). With a thawing of relations in 2005, Jordan finally sent an ambassador to Tel Aviv and, at the time of writing, its relations with all its neighbours, including Syria, Iraq and Saudi Arabia, are unusually warm.

Economic reform is where the new generation of Arab leaders have placed greatest emphasis, and where Abdullah has made most impact. Jordan has become the first country (other than Israel) to negotiate a **free trade agreement** with the US, approval for which was passed by the US Congress in 2001. Jordan now has several Qualifying Industrial Zones (QIZs), where goods are manufactured or processed jointly by Jordan and Israel for distribution to the US duty- and quota-free. Also in 2001, the low-tax Aqaba Special Economic Zone (ASEZ) was launched in an effort to attract investment to Jordan's Red Sea coast, with spectacular amounts of foreign investment flowing soon thereafter. **Privatization** of state concerns, such as Jordan Telecom and the airline Royal Jordanian, have proceeded apace; Jordan joined the World Trade Organization in 2000, and has hosted several full meetings of the World Economic Forum since; and in 2001, the national electricity grids of Jordan, Syria and Egypt were linked in an attempt to share the cost of electricity generation. A long-planned **dam** on the Yarmouk between Jordan and Syria was also due for inauguration late in 2005, after many stops and starts.

A sign of Abdullah's growing confidence in his own statesmanship came in 2004, when, for that year's Ramadan, he published the **Amman Message**, a communiqué drawn up with Muslim authorities to promote Islam as a religion of tolerance and moderation, specifically rejecting extremism as a deviation from Islamic belief. The accompanying press release talked of Abdullah's "determination to ward off Muslim image-tarnishing, marginalization and isolation and to assert what the world's 1.2 billion Muslims expect themselves to be: full partners in the development of human civilization, and in the progress of humanity in our age."

Prospects

For many people living in the Middle East, the "9/11" attacks on New York and Washington in September 2001 reinforced the urgency of establishing peace and prosperity in their region, and the general need for **dialogue** between the West and the Muslim world. In Jordan, as in virtually all Arab states, there is an increasing discrepancy between the motivations and preoccupations of government and those of the general population. The vast majority of Jordanians, with their deep and heartfelt tradition of hospitality, have no problem with their government's policy of maintaining warm relations with the West, as long as this is based on mutual respect and a fair crack at social and economic development. However, grand trade agreements notwithstanding, many people instead face unemployment and poverty, and feel that their beliefs and concerns are being slighted while injustice persists both at home and across the region. This alienates them not only from decision-makers in their own country but also from the source, as many see it, of their and their neighbours' cultural and political oppression – the West and, quite often, specifically the US. Radicalization often follows.

The principal challenge for King Abdullah, as for many Arab leaders, is to foster the rise of a practical, responsive **body politic** that is able, in Jordan's case, to incorporate strands of liberal democracy, homegrown tribalism and Islam, and give each an outlet for expression. Of equal importance is the development of a tolerant, participatory **civil society** to limit polarization and extremism. On both fronts, Jordan is generally held to be leaps and bounds ahead of most states in the region, but it is held back perhaps more than any other by the lack of progress on the key issue that casts a shadow over the whole region: a just and comprehensive resolution of the Israeli–Palestinian problem. Few prognoses in this regard are certain, apart from the increasingly obvious fact that while there is conflict – armed or otherwise – persisting in Israel and/or Palestine, there can only ever be limited and ultimately unsatisfying social, economic or political development in Jordan. It can fairly be said that both King Abdullah I and King Hussein recognized this fact and devoted their careers, and their lives, to addressing it. Hussein earned great respect abroad, and though he was often mistrusted by fellow Arabs, in Jordan he inspired love and loyalty in equal measure. A great deal of that goodwill has rubbed off on his son. Despite the fact that, having made a formal peace with Israel, Jordan must now take a secondary role in peace negotiations, it is clear that Abdullah has a substantial part to play, both in promoting regional stability and – under his universal feel-good slogan "**Jordan First**" – in creating a framework for sustainable economic and social development at home.

Flora and fauna

Jordan has a great variety of wildlife, not least because it lies at the cross-roads of the Mediterranean, Arabia and Africa. The deserts, which may initially look devoid of life, turn out to contain a rich flora and fauna especially adapted to the harsh environment, and there's even life in the Dead Sea – you just need a microscope to see the two species of bacteria which are known to occur.

Mosaics, rock art and frescoes paint a picture of Jordan's wildlife at a time when its significance was as a source of food and later sport. Ancient rock art in the eastern deserts depicts gazelles, ibex and ostriches, and stone corrals remain as evidence of systematic trapping by previous generations of Bedouin. Eighth-century frescoes at Qusayr Amra suggest that hunting game, such as the onager (a wild ass from Persia), was a great attraction for visitors from Damascus. These images also afford a glimpse of some larger animals which have subsequently become extinct due to excessive hunting and habitat destruction. It's hard to imagine today that leopards, Asiatic lions, cheetah, Syrian bears and crocodiles once roamed Jordan's deserts, forests and rivers. It's also hard to appreciate how quickly the thousands of gazelles present until the mid-1940s were reduced to near-extinction following the arrival of automatic weapons and motor vehicles; ostrich, Houbara bustard, oryx and onagers all went the same way.

For many years, Jordan's Royal Society for the Conservation of Nature (**RSCN**) has pursued a plan to **re-establish populations** of some of the country's extinct mammals back in the wild. Projects involving oryx, ostrich, Nubian ibex and fallow deer have reached the stage where healthy herds are awaiting release. However, most of the former ranges are at best occupied by goats and sheep, and at worst totally overgrazed, so finding suitable release sites, and policing them, may not be straightforward.

Major habitats

Jordan's varied topography, climate and geology interact to produce a patch-work of often tightly packed **habitats**: you can travel from pine forest to desert in an hour's drive. Broadly speaking, the country can be divided into four major regions: the rift valley, rift margins, highlands and interior deserts. Each of these contains a range of habitats which vary north to south, west to east and from low to high altitudes. In addition, there are habitats specific to the desert oases, rivers and coast.

From north to south, the **rift valley** comprises the Jordan Valley, the Dead Sea, Southern Ghor, Wadi Araba and the Gulf of Aqaba (before continuing on to the Red Sea and the East African Rift Valley). The whole valley is warm to hot, the only appreciable rain falling in the north, which is exposed to rainfall from Mediterranean weather systems and thus lushly vegetated.

The **highlands** constitute a spine of hills running north–south down the length of the country, dissected by major wadi systems flowing westwards. Terrain in the north, up to 1250m above sea level, comprises the country's richest agricultural land. Further south and east, a reduction in altitude and rainfall produces an undulating, steppe terrain (now mostly arable). The Shara mountains in the south, behind Petra, reach 1700m (considerably higher than any comparable hills to the west of the rift valley); their steppe habitat is unique in Jordan. Towards Aqaba, dissected granite mountains add further variation to this upland range.

Between the highlands and the rift valley, a deeply incised, west-facing escarpment contains some of the most dramatic of Jordan's scenery, including Petra and Dana. As you descend, habitats within this **rift margin** change with the drop in rainfall.

The interior **deserts**, covering eighty percent of Jordan's area, are typically rather flat, with geological variations controlling a complex pattern of fascinating habitats. Flint and limestone deserts predominate, with sand deserts decidedly rare. Of considerable interest is the basalt desert, a vast expanse of boulders harbouring a unique fauna adapted to live in this harsh, blackish habitat. The Rum desert is far from flat, with Jordan's highest mountain (1830m) among its towering peaks; the valleys in between these mountains contain the country's best sand dunes, largely stabilized with broom and other scrub. Much of the eastern desert's sporadic rainfall drains into mud flats or *qa*s which, for brief, irregular periods, support huge quantities of life, ranging from invertebrates to the birds that feed on them.

Water is a valuable resource in the region, and **rivers** are in short supply. Much of the flow of the Jordan River is now diverted to irrigate Israeli farms, and a mere trickle remains. Its tributaries are prime candidates for being dammed, and as a result, the future for riverine wildlife in Jordan looks uncertain. Azraq was a textbook **oasis** until water extraction put an end to the natural flow of its springs (see p.263). Other oases are small, such as those along the base of the rift margins and at Aqaba. The country's sewage treatment works effectively amount to man-made oases, and are surprisingly rich in wildlife. Jordan's few kilometres of arid, sparsely vegetated **coastline** are fringed by coral reef, before the seabed plunges to depths of over 500m.

Mammals

A little detective work is needed to spot Jordan's mammalian wildlife, as many of the larger animals survive only in the remotest corners and the smaller animals are typically nocturnal. Discarded quills offer the only clue that nocturnal **porcupines** have been through; the **Palestinian mole rat** gives itself away by leaving telltale molehills. The pine forests around Dibbeen are home to a small number of **Persian squirrels**, closely related to Europe's red squirrel, and even if you don't see one, you can look for the chewed pine cones they leave behind.

Excepting a chance sighting of **Nubian ibex** at Dana or a **Dorcas gazelle** in Wadi Araba, the largest mammal you are likely to see in Jordan is a **red fox**, not to be confused with the ubiquitous feral dogs; the few **wolves**, **jackals** and **striped hyenas** that remain keep well away from humans. Felines are represented by the wildcat and the **caracal**, both quite rare. Next largest is probably the **Cape hare**, which has evolved to become more rabbit-sized in the warm Arabian climate. But by far the most abundant are the varieties of **mice, gerbils, jerboas** and **jirds** – hamster-like rodents that make their home in desert burrows. A few **rock hyrax** – a burrowing rodent that's a close relative of the elephant, though just the size of a cat – remain in Dana and Rum. You may glimpse a **mongoose** scurrying along the bank of the River Zerqa.

The one-humped **dromedary**, the camel found in Arabia, has a history inextricably associated with that of the Bedouin, and it has been a beast of burden as well as a source of milk and meat for many thousands of years. All Jordan's camels are domesticated, any vestiges of wild stock having vanished long ago.

△ Caracals

Birds

Jordan has a lot to offer the birdwatcher: there are many resident bird species, some native to the Middle East, while others have European and even African affinities. Some species migrate vast distances to breed in Jordan, others winter here from points further north. Add to these the through-migration of literally millions of birds in spring and autumn – either dropping in for a rest or just flying over – and it is not difficult to imagine how 411 species have been identified in a relatively small country, with additional species being added each year.

Although some locals do **hunt** under licence from the RSCN, it is a relief that Jordanian culture differs from that of much of the Mediterranean, where birds are slaughtered in their millions using nets, bird-lime and the gun. Traditional Arab hunting with falcons (or even bringing falcons into the country) is also illegal, and it is regrettable that visiting hunters and falconers continue to have an impact by trapping migratory birds of prey in the eastern deserts.

Native bird species

Jordan has eight endemic Near East species – **sooty falcon**, **sand partridge**, **Tristram's grackle**, **Hume's tawny owl**, **Arabian babbler**, **hooded wheatear**, **Arabian warbler** and **Syrian serin**; their breeding ranges include Jordan's southern rift valley, rift margins and Rum desert. Of these, the starling-like grackle, with its orange wing flash and evocative whistling call, is the most likely to be seen.

Jordan's **deserts** are home to many characteristic birds. These include the many larks and wheatears, each of which is superbly adapted to its chosen habitat, such as **Temminck's horned lark** in the flat, eastern deserts, **hoopoe lark** in sandier areas and **white-crowned black wheatear** in the rockiest mountains. Although Jordan's national bird, the **Sinai rosefinch**, is only the size of a small sparrow, the male's vivid pink plumage evokes Jordan's rose-red city of Petra and the red cliffs and desert sands of Wadi Rum. Sunbirds are the Old World equivalent of the hummingbirds, and in Jordan the male **Palestine sunbirds** flash iridescent purple and blue as they hover, for example, by the borage flowers in the Dana campsite. The basalt desert is also home to a unique population of **mourning wheatears**, whose virtually all-black colouring better matches its surroundings.

Migrant and breeding bird species

Jordan's position at the crossroads between Europe, Asia and Africa results in a cosmopolitan bird community. Species such as **black-eared wheatear**, **woodchat shrike**, **hoopoe** and **black-headed bunting** have affinities with southeastern Europe. Jordan is on the southern extreme of several species' ranges, such as **blue** and **great tits**. The **Cyprus warbler** and **Cyprus wheatear** also have restricted breeding ranges, and occur in Jordan on migration. The African influence is less obvious, though many migrant species retreat to Africa in winter. Isolated pairs of the **Verreaux's eagle**, more at home feeding on hyraxes in east and southern Africa, are also found in Jordan.

The country also hosts several species that are globally or regionally threatened, including **griffon vulture** and **lesser kestrel** (which breed in Jordan) and **imperial eagle**, **Levant sparrowhawk** and **corncrake** (which are found in Jordan on migration or in winter).

Spring migration sees millions of birds returning from wintering in Africa to their breeding grounds in eastern Europe and western Russia, via the rift valley. Migrant **warblers**, **pipits** and **wagtails**, for instance, use every available scrap of cover in which to shelter and refuel, whether on a traffic island in Aqaba, a sewage works, a clump of bushes in the open desert or in the meagre shade underneath a parked car. From late February through to May, vast numbers of **raptors**, including eagles, buzzards, kites, hawks and falcons, use traditional routes over Jordan's rift margins, typically seeking out a remote hillside to roost overnight before continuing. The head of the Gulf of Aqaba is a migration bottleneck, and north from here they peel off to get to their specific destinations. In contrast, the migration front is much broader in autumn, when birds are not averse to stopping off to eat or drink.

In extremely wet winters, the inflow of the River Jordan into the Dead Sea gives rise to a layer of fresh water which persists for some time above the salt water before mixing; in these circumstances, it's possible to witness the rather incongruous sight of **ducks** swimming on the Dead Sea. **Herons** often gather at places like the Mujib delta to feed on the fish that die when they reach the saline water.

Insects

Insects abound in Jordan, and are particularly obvious in the hotter seasons. **Butterflies** are colourful and easy to spot, though, as with birds, where you are will dictate whether you see European or Arabian species. Representatives of the swallowtails, blues, coppers, whites, marbled whites, fritillaries, painted ladies and tortoiseshells all occur, some migrating in spectacular fashion in their hundreds of millions. One of the rarest and most beautiful of the migrant butterflies is the large orange, black and white **plain tiger**, which is commoner in some springtimes than others.

It is easy to see all shapes and sizes of beetles in Jordan – which is not surprising when you consider that around 1700 species have been identified in the country. The long-legged, black **pitted beetle** is one of the most obvious, as are **scarab beetles** and **dung beetles**. Large black **millipedes** are a feature of Jordan ruins, such as Jerash, and are disconcertingly crunchy if you accidentally tread on one.

Jordan has three species of **scorpion** (pale-yellow and black in colour), all of which can inflict sufficiently painful stings to warrant a visit to hospital. Unless you are particularly lucky (or unlucky), you're unlikely even to see one, unless you make a habit of turning over stones. Solifugids, or **camel spiders**, are formidable hunters, but are not venomous despite having a strong bite.

Grasshoppers, moths, dragonflies, solitary wasps, cicadas, locusts and praying and ground mantises are other obvious insects, with the list practically endless. Bluebottle-like flies are a pest especially in the hot Jordan Valley summer, and beware – they can bite. Mosquitoes tend to be more of an irritation than a pest or health hazard.

Reptiles, amphibians and freshwater fish

No desert would be complete without **lizards**. Around fifty species have been identified in Jordan, the largest of which is the **desert monitor**, reaching 130cm in length. There are nocturnal **geckos** with their stick-to-anything toe-pads, hammer-headed **agamas**, smooth-skinned **skinks** and long-tongued **chameleons**. In Wadi Araba, you may glimpse the 65-centimetre-long **spiny-tailed** (or **Dhab**) **lizard** – with its chunky, scaly tail – before it flees down its burrow. At Petra the dazzlingly turquoise male **Sinai agama** is one of the most eye-catching.

Snakes are a bit like the scorpions – much talked about and feared, but rarely seen. There are 24 species, including five that are venomous, particularly the **Palestine viper** and the **horned viper**.

Where there is water, **marsh frogs** occur in an extraordinary variety of colours and patterns, though it's easier to hear their rubber-glove croaking than it is to find them. There are a small number of freshwater **fish** in the River Jordan and its tributaries; however, the six species of fish which were introduced at Azraq have now perished with the decline in the oasis. On the mud flats, millions of dormant eggs hatch when the area floods, giving rise to vast populations of the small **killifish**, which provide a valuable food source to migrating birds.

Red Sea life

Rivalling even Sinai's famous Ras Mohammed reefs for variety and beauty of its marine life, the clear, warm waters of the **Gulf of Aqaba** host a fringing **coral reef**, among the most northerly in the world, which is particularly rich in coral and fish species. The shallow reef flat lies closest to the shore, but this soon gives way at the reef crest to the steeply shelving reef slope. Elsewhere, in sandy bays and at the head of the gulf, sea-grass beds host colonies of **garden-eels**. Looking themselves like blades of tall grass at first glance, these long sinuous creatures soon disappear into their burrows when approached.

Some one thousand species of fish occur off Aqaba, including the slimline **angel-** and **butterfly fishes**, coral-eating **parrot fishes**, predatory **groupers**, parasite-picking **cleaner wrasse**, shoals of red **jewelfish**, luminescent "**flashlight fish**", and the oddly shaped **box fishes**. Of the venomous fish, the **lionfish** is one of the most beautiful in the reef with its feather-like fins, whereas the **stonefish** is as ugly as they come, dull, bulky and covered in wart-like protrusions. Seeing a **turtle**, **shark** or **porpoise** off Aqaba requires a calm sea and a lot of luck; diving affords a better chance than watching from the shore or in a glass-bottomed boat.

Flora

For a country that is eighty percent semi-desert, Jordan's plant list is outstanding. Visit the higher ground in March or April, especially after a wet winter, and you will witness swathe after swathe of green, red and blue blanketing the hillsides.

On the downside, the desert landscape has changed dramatically following human introduction of sheep and goats, which has accelerated wind and rain erosion and desertification, putting tremendous pressure on the native wildlife. **Overgrazing** of the fragile semi-desert flora is ubiquitous, with the effects visible at Shaumari; compare the metre-high bushes inside the enclosures with the pitiful remnants outside. Many of Jordan's trees are grazed – the evergreen oaks, for example – and have responded by growing small, tough leaves at grazing height. Other trees are much hacked for firewood. Unusually heavy snow in the highlands can even snap mature trees under its weight.

Shrubs and herbaceous plants

Cyclamen are one of the earliest blooms, making their first appearance in late winter, followed by poppies, anemones and crocuses in March. Most of Jordan's 22 species of **orchid** flower in April in the highland forests in the northwest. April is also the optimum time to see the **black iris**, Jordan's national flower. One of at least four irises that are endemic to this region, it isn't actually jet-black, rather a very dark purple. The upland hillsides are often carpeted with low spiky bushes and aromatic herbs such as thyme and sagebrush (*Artemesia*). In summer, **thistles**, which grow in profusion and in great varieties, take on a new beauty as the six rainless months of fierce heat turn almost everything into a desiccated, buff-brown relic. However, some flowers do bloom at this time, for example the **sea-onion**, which carpets the flatter ground inside Petra and flowers in July; in autumn, **crocuses** add the only touch of colour when everything else is parched.

In early spring, if the ground warms up after winter rains, the **deserts** can become flushed with grasses and flowers, though this isn't on a dramatic scale and is often short-lived; if the sheep and goats don't eat the new arrivals, they soon succumb to the heat. White **broom** bushes line the wadis; a parasitic broomrape, the **cistanche**, is a spike of yellow in the semi-desert. **Desert melons**, found in the eastern desert, are poisonous and avoided by animals, and wild **capers** grow in the Jordan Valley.

Trees

Trees are largely restricted to the highlands, especially the Mediterranean regions of the northwest. Several species of evergreen and deciduous **oaks**, **Aleppo pines**, **carob** and **strawberry trees** can still be found in Jordan, along with fast-growing, introduced **eucalyptus**, **cypress** and **casuarinas**. **Almond** trees bloom early and **figs** grow wild near water sources in the hills. Ancient, gnarled **junipers** are characteristic of the Petra and Dana mountains. Natural **forest** remains only in parts of the northern highlands (mainly pines) and in the inaccessible mountain landscape around Dana and Petra (oak and juniper). Forests were undoubtedly more extensive in the past, and the operation of the Hejaz railway is often cited as a major destroyer of woodlands, which were cut down to fuel the trains; the Ottoman authorities even built a branch line to Shobak specifically to transport timber felled in that region.

On lower ground, **acacias** give Wadi Araba a distinctly African look, while palms are found by freshwater springs such as Aqaba and Azraq. Wadi Butm, at Qusayr Amra, gets its name from the Arabic word for the ancient **Atlantic pistachio** trees that line the wadi. Although not nut-producing, they provide vital shelter for much resident and migrant wildlife. Similarly rare is the **funeral cypress**, of which a small number of reportedly native trees remain near Dana.

By Ian J. Andrews

Islam

t's almost impossible to make any sense out of the Middle East – and especially out of Jordan – without knowing something of **Islam**. Well over
ninety percent of Jordan's population are Muslim, and the practice and
philosophy of Islam permeate most aspects of daily life. What follows is the
briefest of backgrounds; more detail can be found in the books cited on p.503,
and the websites on p.43.

Islam was the third of the great monotheistic religions to originate in the
Middle East, and places itself firmly in the tradition begun by Judaism and
Christianity: Abraham is seen as the first Muslim, and Islam itself is defined as a
reaffirmation, correction and consummation of the earlier faiths.

Islam was propagated in the seventh century AD by a merchant named
Muhammad from the city of Mecca, in the Hejaz region of what is now
Saudi Arabia. Muhammad is seen as the last of a series of prophets sent by God
to earth; among earlier prophets were Abraham, Noah, Moses, Solomon, Job,
John the Baptist and Jesus, whose messages, for whatever reason, had been lost
or corrupted over the centuries. Muhammad was sent to revive and refine the
words of past prophets.

The basic principles of Islam are that there is one God (in Arabic, Allah), and
he must be worshipped; and that Muhammad is his final prophet. The main
sources of the religion are the Quran (or Koran) – the revelation Muhammad
received during his lifetime – and Muhammad's own actions.

The Quran

Muslims regard the **Quran** (literally, "recitation") to be the word of God, as
revealed by the angel Jibril (Gabriel) to Muhammad from about 610 AD, when
Muhammad was about 40, until his death in 632. There is a noticeable difference in the style of the Quran between the early portions – which have the
ring of soothsaying about them, arising from Muhammad's early role as mystic
– and the later portions, which go into detail about the conduct of Muslim life,
as befits Muhammad's status as the leader of a large group of followers.

The principal emphasis of the Quran is on the **indivisibility of God**.
Human duty is to demonstrate gratitude to God by obedience and worship
– *islam* itself means "submission" – for he will judge the world on the Day of
Resurrection. Islamic concepts of heaven, as reward, and hell, as punishment,
are close to Christian ideas, although the way they are described in the Quran
is very physical, even earthy. God sent the prophets to humankind in order to
provide the guidance necessary to attain eternal reward.

The Quran is divided into 114 chapters, or **suras**. The first *sura* is a prayer
which Muslims recite frequently: "Praise be to God, Lord of the Worlds, the
Compassionate, the Merciful, King of the Day of Judgement. We worship you
and seek your aid. Guide us on the straight path, the path of those on whom
you have bestowed your Grace, not the path of those who incur your anger
nor of those who go astray." After this, the *suras* are in approximate order of
length, starting with the longest and ending with the shortest; many are patched
together from passages revealed to Muhammad at different periods of his life.

According to traditional Islamic belief, the Quran is the word of God which
has existed forever. It is unique, and is the miracle which Muhammad presented
to the world to prove his prophethood. However, not everything the Quran
reveals is comprehensible; the book itself declares that it contains "clear" verses

and "obscure" verses. On occasions, it appears to contradict itself. As a result, an elaborate literature of **interpretation** of the Quran developed, and early specialists put forward the idea that some revelations were made for a particular place or time and were cancelled out by later revelations.

The Hadith

The Quran provided a basic framework for the practices and beliefs necessary for Muslims, but it didn't go into much specific detail: of 6616 verses, only eighty concern issues of conduct. For precise guidance, Muslims also look to the example and habitual practice *sunna* of the Prophet Muhammad himself, as well as his words and actions. These were remembered by those who had known him, and transmitted in the form of reports, **hadith**, handed down within the Muslim community – *hadith* is generally translated into English as "**traditions**".

Although Muhammad himself didn't claim any infallibility outside revealing the Quran, Muslims around him seem to have collected these *hadith* from a very early time. Scholars soon began categorizing them by subject. It was obvious, though, that many of the reports of what the Prophet said or did weren't authentic; tales wove their way into his legend, and some of those who transmitted reports of his doings undoubtedly invented or exaggerated them. Scholars therefore developed a science of *hadith* criticism, requiring both specific content of what the Prophet is supposed to have said or done, and, more importantly, a traceable chain of transmission back to the Companion of the Prophet who had originally seen or heard it. Biographical dictionaries – to ascertain just how reliable a transmitter was – rapidly became a distinctive feature of Arabic literature. Two particularly refined collections of *hadith* from the late ninth century are generally held to have an authority second only to that of the Quran.

The pillars of Islam

Drawn both from the Quran and the *hadith*, there are five basic religious duties every Muslim must perform.

Statement of faith

Firstly, and most simply, is the **statement of faith** (*shahada*): "I testify that there is no god but God, and that Muhammad is the Messenger of God." If you say this with sincerity, you become a Muslim.

Prayer

A Muslim must perform formal **prayer** (*salat*) five times a day. Since the day begins at sunset, the five times are sunset (*maghrib*), evening (*isha*), dawn (*fajr*), midday (*duhr*) and afternoon (*asr*), the exact times set in advance by the religious authorities. Before performing the *salat*, a Muslim must be in a state of **ritual purity**, achieved by rinsing out the mouth, sniffing water into the nostrils, washing the face, head, ears, back of the neck, feet, and lastly the hands and forearms. All mosques, big or small, have ablutions fountains adjacent for worshippers to cleanse themselves.

The faithful are summoned to prayer by the **muezzin**; in previous centuries, he would climb the minaret of the mosque and call by shouting, but almost everywhere in Jordan this has now been overtaken either by a taped call to prayer or by amplification. Nonetheless, the sound has a captivating beauty all its own, especially down in the echoing valleys of Amman when dozens of mosques are calling simultaneously, repeating in long, melodious strings: "God is most great! (*Allahu akbar!*) I testify that there is no god but God. I testify that Muhammad is the Messenger of God. Come to prayer, come to salvation. God is most great!" The dawn call has another phrase added: "Prayer is better than sleep."

Once worshippers have assembled in the mosque, another call to prayer is given. Prayers are led by an **imam**, and are performed in a **ritualized cycle** facing towards Mecca without shoes on: standing with hands slightly raised, bowing, prostrating, sitting on one's haunches, and prostrating again. During the cycle, worshippers recite verses of the Quran, particularly the opening *sura*. Repetition of the cycles is completed by everyone turning and wishing peace on each other.

One way in which Islam differs crucially from Christianity and Judaism is that it has **no priests**. The *imam* who leads the prayers has no special qualification to do so, other than enough knowledge of the Quran to enable him to recite, or perhaps some standing in the local community. Anyone may lead prayers, and there is no claim to special religious knowledge or holiness marking out an *imam* from any other Muslim.

The midday prayer on Fridays is a special congregational prayer, and Muslims are expected to attend a large mosque of assembly, where a religious or political **sermon** is also given. The sermon must include a mention of the legitimate ruler – in fact, this is one of the traditional ways for a population to bestow legitimacy on a ruler. If the mosque is controlled by the government, the sermon is often used to endorse government policy; if it is independent, the Friday sermon can be used as a means to incite rebellion among the faithful. This is part of the reason why many political demonstrations in the Muslim world begin from the mosque after the midday prayer on a Friday.

Although it's preferable for men to pray together in the mosque, it's not obligatory, and you'll see many men throughout Jordan instead laying down a small **prayer mat** in their shops, or by the side of the road, to mark out a space for them to pray alone. Women almost always pray at home. Unlike in some Islamic countries, non-Muslims are permitted to enter mosques in Jordan, but only at the discretion of the officials of that particular mosque; however, you must always be dressed suitably modestly. If you're not praying, you don't have to go through any ritual ablutions.

A very common sight in Jordan is to see men holding strings of "worry beads", passing them rhythmically through their fingers in an almost unconscious action as they walk or sit quietly. The beads – *tasbih* or *subbah* – are **prayer beads**, and they always come in strings of 33 or 99, representing the 99 revealed names of God. As one passes through the fingers, the prayer is *subhanallah* ("Glory to God"); the next one is *al-hamdulillah* ("Thanks be to God"), the next *Allahu akbar* ("God is most great"), these three being repeated in a mantra until the cycle of 99 has been completed.

Alms

All Muslims who are able to do so should pay one-fortieth of their own wealth for purposes laid down in the Quran: for the poor, for those whose hearts need to be reconciled, for the freeing of slaves, those who are burdened with debts, for travellers, for the cause of God, and so on. This payment of **alms** is called *zakat*, literally "purification", and is primarily regarded as an act of worship: the recipients are less important than the giving, which is always done anonymously.

Fasting in the month of Ramadan

Ramadan is the ninth month of the Muslim year, and was the time at which Muhammad received his first revelation; it's a holy month, during which all Muslims must **fast** from dawn to sunset each day. All forms of consumption are forbidden during daylight hours, including eating, drinking and smoking, and any form of sexual contact. However, this is only the outward show of what is required; one *hadith* says: "There are many who fast all day and pray all night, but they gain nothing but hunger and sleeplessness." Ramadan is a time of spiritual cleansing.

As the Muslim calendar is lunar, Ramadan doesn't fall in a specific season each year: summer Ramadans in the Middle East, when the days are fourteen or fifteen hours long and the heat draining, can be particularly taxing, but Ramadan is an intense month at any time of year. Shops, offices and public services all operate limited hours. Families get up together before dawn for a quick breakfast (many people then go back to bed for another few hours' sleep). During the day, particularly late in the month, tempers can fray; there are even special judicial exemptions from certain criminal actions during Ramadan, which is seen as a time of particular stress. As sunset approaches, people hurry home to be with their families to break the fast, and after dark, a hectic round of socializing over large meals often brings distant relatives together for the only time in the year. Ramadan is much quieter in Jordan than, say, Egypt (where Ramadan nights involve huge, festive street parties), but nonetheless a special mood of excitement grips people all over the country. The month ends with a three-day festival, **Eid al-Fitr**, also a time for family get-togethers.

Pilgrimage

Mecca was a sacred place long before the time of Muhammad, its central feature the **Kaaba**, a fifteen-metre-high stone cube inset with a smaller, holy black stone. Islam incorporated both the Kaaba and a set of rituals involved with pagan worship at Mecca into its own set of rituals around the hajj, or **pilgrimage**, which takes place in the twelfth month, Dhul Hijja (a lesser pilgrimage, known as the *umrah*, can be undertaken at any time of year). Every Muslim who has the means must make the pilgrimage to Mecca at least once in his lifetime. These days, over two million descend each year on Mecca for the hajj from all over the world, and the Saudi Ministry of Pilgrimage has an organizational budget of some $300 million.

One of the buzzwords that has been latched onto by the Western media when reporting seemingly inexplicable acts of violence committed by Muslims is **jihad**. This is most often translated, with dramatic inaccuracy, as "holy war"; in fact, *jihad* simply means "striving". Early Islamic jurists divided the world into the domain of Islam (*dar al-Islam*) and the domain of war (*dar al-harb*) and posited that there could be truces between the two but never permanent peace. The Quran stipulates that it's the duty of every able-bodied Muslim to defend the *dar al-Islam* from attack, and *jihad* was thus applied in history to defensive struggle by Muslims against unbelievers; in World War I, for instance, the Ottoman caliph declared a *jihad* to defend the Islamic countries from the advancing British forces. These days, of course, all kinds of violent extremists fancy themselves to be acting in the name of God – and are able to parade learned clerics to endorse their bloodthirstiness – but true Islamic *jihad* is explicit in forbidding killing for the sake of religion. Wars of aggression, to force people to adopt Islam or over border disputes or nationalisms, explicitly do not come under the banner of Islamically sanctioned *jihad*.

In addition, military action is only the most extreme form of *jihad*, even if this is currently the most common way by which the word filters through to the West, in association with acts of violence committed by extremists claiming religious authority. Within the mainstream religion, *jihad* most often refers to a daily internal striving towards moral or spiritual goals, and is an entirely peaceful and reflective action. Sufis – mystical Islamic philosophers – even broke the idea down, placing emphasis on the "greater *jihad*", a struggle against one's base instincts, and downgrading the "lesser *jihad*", a struggle against unbelievers.

The Kaaba, now in the central precinct of the vast Grand Mosque at Mecca, is held to have been built by Abraham and his son Ishmael on the ruins of a shrine built by Adam, the first human. Male pilgrims wear only two lengths of plain, unsewn cotton cloth (symbolizing the equality of all before God); women veil their hair but must leave their faces uncovered, to express confidence and an atmosphere of purity. Everybody circumambulates the Kaaba seven times, emulating the angels who circle the throne of God, and kisses the black stone if they can. They go to the Well of Zamzam, discovered by Ishmael, and run between two small hills, commemorating the frantic running in search of water by Hagar – Abraham's concubine and Ishmael's mother – after Abraham had left them both in the desert. One day is spent on the arid Plain of Arafat, listening to sermons, praying and standing on the Mount of Mercy. All the pilgrims go to Mina, a suburb of Mecca, and hurl stones at three pillars, symbolically stoning the Devil. The hajj ends with the four-day festival of **Eid al-Adha**, celebrated throughout the Islamic world, when all who are able slaughter a sheep to commemorate Abraham's sacrifice – he was about to kill his son but God stopped him and provided a ram instead (Jews and Christians hold that the victim was to have been Isaac, but Muslims believe it was Ishmael).

There are often parties and celebrations to welcome home those who have returned from the hajj, and in Jordan you'll sometimes see murals painted by pilgrims on the outside walls of their houses, depicting the mosque at Mecca (with the Islamic symbol of the crescent often prominent), the Kaaba and other details of what they saw and experienced on their journey.

Women in Jordan

Jordan is considered one of the most progressive countries in the Middle East in terms of granting and ensuring **women** their rights. The constitution and other civil legislation permits women the right to receive an education, pursue work opportunities, travel freely, study abroad, own assets, choose their partner in marriage and inherit in accordance with the Shari'a (Islamic Law). However, there remains a substantial gap between legislation and its implementation; women's freedoms in general are confined to what is socially acceptable, rather than what is legally defined. Conservative traditions in both urban and rural areas deny women their legal rights, and Jordanian society continues to lack the maturity to accept women as equal to men.

As was the case not long ago in the West, many Jordanian women are raised from childhood with the belief that their lives ought to be dedicated to their husbands and children; indeed, it is not uncommon for a woman to have to choose her husband from a line-up of candidates handpicked by her family. Education and work are broadly considered male domains. Jordanian society's strict paternalism seeks, with good intentions, to protect women; however, it has caused their marginalization in society and severely limited their participation in decision-making outside the home. Just ten percent of the membership of political parties is women.

It is only very recently that Jordan has lifted **travel restrictions** on women. Previously a woman had to prove to the authorities that her father or male guardian had given consent for her journey abroad, and women still need their male guardian's or husband's consent to acquire a passport. Indeed, Jordanian society does not look kindly on women who travel alone outside the kingdom or who decide to leave their parents' home to live alone.

Nevertheless, things are changing: the 1990s in particular were a major turning-point in many areas, with women beginning to attain positions in more diverse fields of work and at higher levels. A UNIFEM report in 2002 found that ten percent of higher management positions in the public sector were held by women.

Education

Though the **literacy rate** among Jordanian women now stands at over ninety percent, some families prefer to marry off their daughters at a young age, thus forcing them to drop out of school; this happens either because family members fear their daughters might not marry later in life, or because these are large families economically burdened by the number of offspring. Many parents still prefer to invest whatever money they have in ensuring better education for their sons, enrolling them in private schools and then supporting their further education abroad. The establishment of the University of Jordan in the early 1960s, however, did bring more opportunities for women to pursue **higher education**; in 1965 Jordanian women constituted just nine percent of their graduating class, while today they more often than not enjoy slightly greater representation in higher education than men.

One of the biggest concerns for activists in Jordan is the portrayal of women in school **textbooks**, which remain male-oriented, generally depicting women as bystanders, housewives and as occupying traditional roles such as teachers and nurses. The government is becoming sensitive to this issue, and has promised a gradual modernization of the texts.

Marriage

Many families still raise their daughters from childhood to understand that their sole duty is to be virtuous and thereby secure a husband and a home; once **married**, the woman's task is seen as being loyal to, showing respect for and obeying her husband, while raising children properly. Many men are similarly brought up to expect obedient wives who will care for the home and children while they go out to work.

Women can legally tie the knot at the age of 15, men at 16. There is continuous social pressure for women to marry at an early age, in some cases to a man of her family's choosing (traditional families often aim to wed girls to their first cousins). If a woman reaches the age of 30 single, Jordanian society usually regards her as someone who will never marry or who no one will desire. Although the Shari'a stipulates that men are allowed to marry as many as four wives, this is uncommon in Jordan: only a handful of men take a second wife.

Virginity is regarded as the noblest virtue in a woman, and women are widely expected to be virgins on their wedding night. Men are not held to the same standards of propriety; on the contrary, they are expected to be experienced, and their masculinity is sometimes measured by the number of relationships they develop before marriage. If a woman is proven not to be a virgin when she marries, in many sectors of society she will most likely face a divorce; in extreme cases, she may be killed by her own family in what has become known as a "crime of honour", committed – often under a cloak of perceived religious sanction – to purge the family name and restore dignity.

Women face inequality in **divorce** procedures: while men can divorce their wives by sending them postal notification, or by repeating to them three times "*talaq*" (meaning "You are divorced"), it can take a woman a year or more to get a divorce in the Shari'a courts – if she can convince a judge that she has a case (often an extremely difficult task). Moreover, it's hard for divorced women to remarry, and generally socially unacceptable for them to live alone, so in most cases they are forced to return to their parents' home.

Employment

Though Jordan's constitution and labour laws have granted women equality in the workforce, women still face **discrimination** in recruitment and in wages. Employers refrain from hiring women to avoid legal obligations such as paid maternity leave, and it is widely known that many still fail to pay working women the legal minimum wage of JD85 a month. In 2004 an official report found that the average hourly rate of pay in the private sector was JD0.81 for men as against JD0.73 for women, and in the public sector JD1.26 as against JD1.10.

Jordanian women are most commonly **employed** in traditional "women's" occupations, such as nursing or education – jobs that are considered more socially acceptable and suitable for what is deemed to be a woman's nature. A handful of women have become pioneers in fields traditionally dominated by men: there is now a small group of women working in the public transport sector as drivers, and you might bump into female police officers directing Amman's traffic (a dozen comprised the first batch to graduate, in 2000). Nonetheless, the **participation rate** for women in the Jordanian workforce remains at just thirteen percent. In the **voluntary sector**, thousands of women have become members of the dozens of non-governmental women's organizations, in a bid to improve their lot and Jordanian society at large. These organizations are active in conducting all sorts of lectures, training, workshops and activities, aimed at informing women of their rights and lobbying the government; a few operate hotlines that offer legal advice and counselling to women.

Politics and the judiciary

Women gained the right to **vote** and to nominate themselves as candidates for the legislature through a Royal Decree issued in 1974; an amendment allowing women to nominate themselves for municipal councils followed eight years later. However, one intangible result of Jordan's patriarchal society is that generations of women have become dependent on their male guardians for the simplest matters: when it comes to the complexities of politics and voting, many women refer to their menfolk for guidance.

It was not until 1993 that the first female candidate, Toujan Faisal, was elected to the **Lower House** of parliament; a second became a member of the Lower House in 2001, though she was selected by the other members following the death of a sitting deputy. The forty members of the **Upper House**, or Senate, are appointed by the king, with the first woman deputy appointed in 1989. In 2003 the electoral law was changed to bring in a quota system for women, resulting in six women being elected to the Lower House and seven women being appointed to the Upper House. Denied men's business networking opportunities, female candidates face particular difficulties in supporting their campaigns financially in municipal contests.

The first time a woman was given a **ministerial portfolio** was in 1979, but it took almost twenty years before another woman gained such a position. Since 1990, six women have served as senior officials in various cabinets, including one who served as a deputy prime minister. In 2005, the Cabinet included four female ministers. In the **judiciary**, there are currently 26 women judges on the bench, among four hundred men.

By Rana Husseini

Modern art

Jordan has an active **contemporary art** scene, something of a surprise to many Western visitors. Darat al-Funun in Amman (see p.138) is one of the Arab world's leading centres for contemporary art and stands at the heart of efforts to nurture Jordanian artists in all fields.

Origins

The origins of modern art in Jordan – and, indeed, in all the Ottoman-ruled areas of the Levant – can be traced back to the **1798 invasion of Egypt** by the armies of Napoleon Bonaparte. For the first time since the Crusades, a European power invaded an Arab country not only militarily, but with a full complement of artists, writers and intellectuals in tow, introducing a completely new, European aesthetic to Cairo's – and the region's – urban intellectual elite, and, equally importantly, laying the foundations for a Western obsession with all things "oriental" that was to continue for the best part of two centuries. In 1867, **Sultan Abd al-Aziz** visited Europe, the first Ottoman sovereign to cross the boundaries of his empire for a purpose other than war. The firsthand knowledge he gained of European art, and the invitations to Istanbul he subsequently extended to a number of European artists, resulted in the opening, in 1883, of the Academy of Fine Arts in Istanbul, the first of its kind in the Islamic world.

However, little of the Istanbul enlightenment filtered down to Transjordan. At this time the area was still populated almost entirely by nomadic Bedouin, the regional capital Jerusalem was a town of a few thousand people, and Salt, the only settlement of any size east of the Jordan, was barely more than a village. The introduction during the 1880s by the **Ottoman army** of courses in drawing and topographical perspective for all officers as part of their training – although instrumental in introducing Western aesthetic styles to cadets from Iraq, Syria and Lebanon, who returned to sow the seeds of modern art movements in their home countries – had little impact in the impoverished agricultural and desert areas south of Damascus.

Art in the emirate: 1921–50

Jordan's modern art movement began with the nascent emirate in the 1920s, when a handful of artists came to live and work in Amman, their ideas and practice slowly attracting students.

The first figure to have a significant impact – and the first to live entirely as a professional artist – was a former officer in the Ottoman army, **Ziyaeddin Suleiman**, who moved to Amman in 1930 and spent the last fifteen years of his life in Transjordan. He had almost certainly taken art classes during his military training in Turkey – and possibly during a stay in Paris – and his unruffled, impressionistic style attracted much attention in the small world of Amman at that time. He mounted the city's first-ever solo exhibition, in 1938. Other individual artists such as **George Aleef** and **Ihsan Idilbi**, who drifted into the city at various times during the 1940s, gathered a small coterie of artists around them and ideas began to spread. The royal family were active patrons, acquiring many works by these early artists; art slowly found its way for the first time into the homes of Transjordan's noble families.

One result of the first **Arab–Israeli war** of 1948 was a blurring of the boundaries between specifically Jordanian and Palestinian art movements. Following the establishment of the State of Israel in Palestine in 1948, and the union two years later of the West Bank with the Emirate of Transjordan, many refugees from Palestine – artists among them – crossed into the territory of the newly expanded kingdom and either took Jordanian citizenship or began to consider themselves Jordanian. Artists resident on the West Bank often exhibited their work in Amman; those resident on the East Bank equally often in Jerusalem or Nablus. In addition, the Jordanian government employed a number of Palestinian artists to teach at schools, and some were given grants to study at art academies in Arab countries and the West.

Experimentation: 1952–67

In 1952, a group of artists – among them Ihsan Idilbi, Muhanna Durra, Rafiq Lahham and Valeria Sha'aban – founded the **Jordanian Art Club**, both to spread awareness of art among the general public and to encourage the growing number of amateur artists. In the same year, the Institute of Music and Painting was set up with similar aims. Although both institutions proved to be short-lived, their influence took hold, and foreign cultural centres in both Amman and Jerusalem began to exhibit works by local and foreign artists. A significant feature of the rapidly developing art scene at this time was the sizeable number of **women** involved, notably Afaf Arafat, Rebecca Bahu, Fatima Muhib and Wijdan Ali. Indeed, Arafat was the first Jordanian artist sent by the government to study abroad, at Bath in England.

During a stay in Damascus in 1955, Ihsan Idilbi had met and worked with the pioneer of Syrian **impressionism**, Michel Kirsheh, and on Idilbi's return to Amman, impressionism began to take hold as the dominant style. As the decade progressed, and more artists returned from academies in the West and, increasingly, from art schools in cosmopolitan Arab capitals such as Cairo, Baghdad and Damascus, **abstraction**, largely dependent on line and mass, began to take hold.

During the 1960s, the government began exhibiting the work of Jordanian artists abroad, most notably at the New York International Fair of 1965. However, the **Six-Day War** of 1967 fell like a hammer blow on Jordan and its maturing cultural scene. The West Bank was separated from the rest of the country; many Palestinian artists chose to emigrate and those who stayed became isolated. Amman and the whole of the East Bank area was flooded with semi-destitute refugees, and the bulk of governmental energy and funding was diverted to programmes of social welfare. Across the Arab World, subject matter in art shifted towards the expression of overtly nationalistic messages opposing the occupation, and with the intrusion of politics and military defeat into the everyday lives of the Jordanian population, art necessarily took a back seat.

Postwar development: 1967–89

It took fully five years for the Jordanian art scene to revive itself after the 1967 disaster. In 1972, the Department of Arts and Culture – headed by the long-established and influential artist **Muhanna Durra** – set up the first two-year foundation course in painting, sculpture and graphic art. Other well-established artists, including Durra and Rafiq Lahham, gave private instruction to students at their studios; in this undramatic way, Mahmoud Taha taught students how

A hit list of Jordanian artists

Nawal Abdallah (b.1951). Partly trained by Muhanna Durra, Abdallah is one of the leading lights of Jordan's contemporary art scene, her dynamic, abstract style based on the interplay of forms and dimensions.

Wijdan Ali (b.1939). A motivator of Jordanian art since the 1960s, Princess Wijdan was the recipient of London University's first-ever PhD in Islamic Art. Her best-known works, from the 1980s, are a series of shimmering desertscapes.

Omar Bsoul (b.1951). While still working as a barber in Irbid, Bsoul has carved a niche as one of the few naive painters in Jordan, producing strikingly patterned evocations of traditional life.

Muhanna Durra (b.1938). The pioneer of modern Jordanian art, responsible for introducing and developing cubist and abstract elements through his early works and studio classes. Although he is known for his character portraits, his later abstract work relies on shifting masses of colour.

Ali Jabri (b.1943). Mainly working in gouaches, watercolour, pencil and charcoal, Jabri has roamed the country to record mundane details of city and wilderness, in perfectionist and idiosyncratic style, on large diptychs and triptychs.

Ammar Khammash (b.1960). One of Jordan's leading architects and photographers, Khammash designed the *Resthouses* at Dana and Pella, and renovated Darat al-Funun, Madaba's Haret Jdoudna and the Umm Qais *Resthouse* (among other high-profile projects) using traditional methods and materials, often featuring his own wrought-iron, wood and stone furniture. He is also an accomplished watercolourist of city, village and rural landscapes.

Khalid Khreis (b.1956). A widely travelled painter, who has gathered research and experience from Cairo, Barcelona, New York and Mexico, Khreis's abstract and symbolic work is often lent a mystical quality by the use of calligraphy.

Rafiq Lahham (b.1932). A pioneer colleague of Durra, Lahham has experimented throughout his career with different styles and techniques, the most striking being a series of works on Jerusalem mixing arabesque figures with folk motifs and calligraphic script.

Larissa Najjar (b.1957). Born and educated in Moscow, Najjar works in sandstone, producing stylized and mellifluous sculpture portraits.

Ahmad Nawash (b.1934). A leading Jordanian painter of Palestinian origin, Nawash has a distinctive, almost infantile style, figures floating around the canvas in an often disturbingly sombre and despairing ambience.

Annie Sakkab (b.1969). A member of the new wave, painting monochromatic abstractions characterized by a sense of balance and design.

Mona Saudi (b.1945). The best known abroad of all Jordanian artists. Her speciality is abstract sculpture in stone, marked by smooth, intertwining figures often charged with emotion. A number of her works are displayed in public areas in Jordan, and one is on permanent display outside the Institut du Monde Arabe in Paris.

Suha Shoman (b.1944). From a family of artists, since the 1980s Shoman has concentrated on depicting Petra in an acclaimed series of expressively coloured abstract works.

Mahmoud Taha (b.1942). The leading Jordanian ceramicist; he also studied calligraphy in Baghdad and combines both skills in a blend of prehistoric, Islamic and contemporary design.

Fahrelnissa Zeid (1901–91). A cornerstone of Jordanian art, best known for her massive oil portraits and many large works in ink lovingly characterized by much intricate detail.

to use a kiln and single-handedly reintroduced **ceramic art** to Jordan after a gap of several centuries.

During the 1970s, art began to enter the mainstream of Jordanian society and to receive greater and greater recognition, aided by the decision of the renowned **Fahrelnissa Zeid** to move – at the age of 74 – from Paris to Amman. Zeid had studied and exhibited throughout Europe since the 1920s and was an artist of recognized talent; on her arrival in Jordan she became tutor to eight women, of whom four – Suha Shoman, Rula Shuqairy, Hind Nasser and Ufemia Rizk – went on to pursue art as a career. The **Royal Society of Fine Arts** was set up in 1979 as a private, non-profit organization to promote the visual arts in Jordan and the wider Islamic world: its principal achievement was the founding of the first art museum in the country, the **National Gallery of Fine Arts** (see p.139), which opened in 1980 and remains the premier establishment showcase for contemporary art in the country. The 1980s also saw art exhibitions travelling outside Amman for the first time, with shows in all corners of the country that allowed Bedouin and peasant farmers their first opportunities to view Western-style art. One of the breakthrough achievements of the Royal Society was a 1989 exhibition in London, which showed over two hundred works from the National Gallery of Fine Arts' collection.

Contemporary art

With greater and greater numbers of art students electing to work in Jordan, coupled with a meteoric rise in graphic and computer-aided design, Jordanian art expanded and diversified greatly during the 1990s, due also to the efforts of the charitable Shoman Foundation and, specifically, the painter **Suha Shoman**. After establishing a gallery and information centre in the late 1980s, the foundation inaugurated **Darat al-Funun** in 1992, comprising diverse exhibition halls, reference libraries and studios. In order to maintain a dialogue between Jordanian and foreign artists, each summer a different graphic artist takes up residence at the Darat, holding workshops and masterclasses. Pressure for exhibition space has also resulted in a boom in the number of **galleries** in and around Amman (see p.138), and Jordan's major banks and corporations have competed with each other to buy up works by local artists for exhibition in their headquarters and branch offices around the world.

Coming to maturity in an era where specific schools of style have been largely replaced worldwide by a spirit of individuality and personal experimentation, **contemporary Jordanian art** has few unifying stylistic features. The cosmopolitan nature of Jordanian society itself, coupled with the creative drive of a relatively small number of artists who feel themselves still to be pioneers, instead results in a wide spread of differing styles, with only occasional stylistic touches – such as the use of Nabatean motifs – identifying the work as Jordanian. The Islamic injunction against figurative art has shaped, but not cramped, Jordanian style, and you can find both abstract and representational contemporary art on show in Amman's galleries.

Writing from Jordan

Before the 1970s, very little **writing from Jordan** had been translated for publication in the West. Cairo and Beirut were the centres of literary debate in the Arab world and Amman was a backwater. However, with the surge of scholarly interest in the West in Arabic literature that began in the mid-1980s, far more writing from Jordan is now being translated into English, much of it under the aegis of PROTA (the Project for the Translation of Arabic), founded in 1980 by the Palestinian poet and critic Salma Khadra Jayyusi.

Native Jordanian literary traditions are oral for the most part, rooted in poems sung to a musical accompaniment and tales of tribal history; even today, research into this jealously guarded body of traditions – and attempts to catalogue and transcribe it – is in its infancy. By contrast, Jordanians of Palestinian origin draw on a rich written Palestinian literary culture stretching back to the beginning of the twentieth century.

Abd al-Rahman Munif

Abd al-Rahman Munif was born in Amman in 1933. After working for many years as an economist in the oil industry, he published his first novel in 1973. He is best known in English for his five-novel set *Cities of Salt* (1984–89), depicting the evolution of a desert kingdom resembling Saudi Arabia. In 1992, he was awarded the Sultan al-Uways Award, the Arabic equivalent of the Nobel Prize for Literature. He died in Damascus in 2004. The following is an extract from *Story of a City: A Childhood in Amman*, which was published in Arabic in 1994 and has since been translated into several major European languages.

Amman, the city and its people, was discovered by the child through the shock of death. … The monotonous sound of church bells in the morning created a sense of sadness and ending, affecting not only the dead person's family, or the religious community to which he belonged, but everyone, both Muslim and Christian. Muslim children had early memories of the questions they used to ask when they heard those bells: "Who is dead?", "Why did he die?", "Where do dead people go?"

When the ceremonies were over, the old, tired feet of the mourners would slowly trudge up the left side of al-Misdar hill [Jebel al-Ashrafiyyeh], accompanied by children, candles, the pale and weak ringing of the cemetery church bell and the priest, who shook with grief or out of habit. All this painted a heavy, cruel picture of death, affecting everyone in Amman, irrespective of religion.

The Muslim graves lay on the opposite side, across the road, visibly sloping to the west. They were more numerous and humbler than the Christian graves, with a few exceptions. Funeral processions used to arrive there more speedily, as though the pallbearers felt it necessary to carry out their duties as fast as possible, exactly as someone entrusted with a burdensome item would want to return it with the utmost haste. Despite the speed and simplicity of Muslim funerals, which expressed the inevitability and even the necessity of death, they struck fear into the hearts of children. Although that fear was concealed and the children pretended that they were unafraid, the terror did not disappear or wear off. Some would have nightmares and be jolted out of their sleep in panic. Others would hallucinate, screaming and crying.

Mothers and grandmothers were worried by such occurrences, dreading them. They would bring water to the children, saying prayers and reciting holy verses over their heads. They would insist that the child recite a *sura* from the Quran. If the child was too young to do this, he would be asked to repeat a few prayers, then say the name of God until he fell asleep.

The next day, the Cup of Terror had to be brought. A search for it would take place in neighbouring homes. It would usually be found in one of the Damascene homes. After being made to drink water from the cup three times, the terror of the previous night would disappear and things would return to how they had been before the nightmare.

Independence day was memorable in Amman. People went into the streets early. Those who found space on King Faisal Street near the spot where a platform had been erected at its intersection with Rida and Sa'adeh streets were lucky. When delegations from other areas and Arab countries arrived, the overcrowding, joy, goodwill and singing surged to unimaginable levels. ... People's faces and behaviour resembled those of children. They laughed and at times cried simultaneously. They were quietly dazed, then their shouting exploded for no clear reason. They were highly excited as memories, emotions and hopes which had formed in some mysterious way combined within their thoughts.

It was an exceptional day in the life of Amman. It was rarely repeated, and it said a great deal about people's dreams and ambitions, and also about their suffering.

The mounds of Jaffa oranges piled high in the vegetable market and other places during winter were a familiar sight in the 1940s. When the trucks arrived from Palestine and emptied their loads of oranges, a deliciously intoxicating smell permeated the souk, and everything was covered by the golden-yellow colour. Huge quantities arrived and anyone watching the sight of people buying and carrying vast numbers to their homes would imagine that they ate nothing but oranges. ...

When Grandmother saw oranges being brought home in large quantities, she looked at them happily. She would pick up an orange, rub it with a tender firmness and smell it as a mother does her newborn child. Before eating it, she would shake her head several times as she recollected, going on a journey in her mind, laughing as her face clouded over. Whenever she saw oranges she would ask herself aloud, "The scent of orange flowers gladdens the heart. If God does not prove me wrong, there is no better smell in the world. Why do the people of Amman not plant orange trees like the people of Baghdad?" ...

As for marjoram, thyme, olive oil soap, *k'naffy*, the sea, the Mountain of Fire in Nablus, they were all simply synonyms for the other side of the River Jordan. As soon as one of them was mentioned, it would evoke a series of endless associations. When the word "mujahideen" was spoken, an image leapt up of men with half-covered faces, living mostly in the countryside and in caves. Late at night, they moved from one place to another to fight the English and the Jews, who surrounded them completely. Those men were so strong, heroic and self-denying that every child hoped to be like them or to become one of them when he grew up.

The names of the cities across the River Jordan were many and ever-present, and they stirred the imagination. Sometimes, the names of cities in the other Arab countries were confused with one another or not easily remembered, but all the hands of all the students would shoot up when the teacher asked who could name five cities in Palestine. Voices competed, drowning each other out: Jerusalem, Jaffa, Haifa, Gaza, Lydda, Ramlah, Acre, Safad, Ramallah, Hebron ... Every student had more names!

Palestine was more than just a land and a people. In the mind of every Arab individual, it is a constellation of meanings, symbols and connotations which have accumulated and filtered down through several generations. In addition to its collective common significance, it also has a private significance to each person which may be mysterious and different but is very powerful. ...

Even before going to school, children were more familiar with the name "Palestine" than any other, as though they had imbibed it with their mother's milk. It had a special effect and evoked many shades of meaning. The first games improvised by the children were soldiers and robbers, and Arabs and Jews. The outcome of those games was always predetermined. The soldiers beat the robbers and the Arabs defeated the Jews. ... At school, during the earliest lessons and songs, patriotism in its highest form was embodied by the attitude to Palestine. Whatever differences people had, they did not disagree about the Palestinian cause.

[By June 1948, Amman] had already received thousands of refugees. It had not been nervous or frightened, but its anger had grown. It had waited for mid-May eagerly, the date on which the British forces would withdraw [from Palestine] and the Arab forces would go in. Amman licked its wounds, hid its pains and waited. The refugees themselves, despite their weariness and suffering, were full of confidence and optimism as they waited for that date. But after what happened, after the new losses and tragedies, after cities had fallen and large amounts of territory were occupied, great numbers of new refugees poured in and an atmosphere of misery, ill-will and suspicion prevailed. At the end of spring, Amman was full of wounds and bitterness. The horror and harshness of the shock left nothing untouched. No one could believe what had happened and life resembled a nightmare. Every individual was angry. ...

From that time onwards, the city became different. Its mood, the number of its inhabitants, its size and the depth of the anxiety and fear holding the city in its grip all changed. Events such as these cause people to grow old in a short, if not a record, time. Even the young boys, after these events, turned into men bowed down by worries and filled with questions. The adults, who had been contented and confident, suddenly became confused.

The tragedy left deep wounds. If some of them could be healed by time, the wounds of the spirit would never heal. They might disappear for some time, they might be forgotten, but they still exist, deep down. They continue to bleed, causing excruciating pain, tormenting body and soul. The torment cannot end unless the injustice is removed, the mistakes are rectified and relations are governed by justice, logic and the good of the generations to come.

Palestine is more than just a land and it is larger than one generation. It transcends armies fighting wars in which one army defeats another. Palestine does not concern only those who inhabit it, and is not an issue that can be determined by who defeats whom, or which side is more cunning than the other. Others from far away who are strong can intervene to change the course of things at one time or another. But those who are far away and are strong today cannot continue to be the deciding power, nor can they remain strong for ever. They cannot act for others, or substitute the movement of life, the strength of history and the power of geography. That is as impossible as trying to control the sun or the ebb and flow of the tide, or attempting to change the direction of the wind, the movement of the waves and the times of night and day.

Perhaps the Jews, using the Old Testament as their main argument, were able to "create" and impose a situation, benefiting from the advantages they had gained from the societies they came from, and from their relations with others. They capitalized on the weakness of the opposite side in the conflict. Although it remains weak and dazed, overwhelmed by backwardness and the harshness of the regimes that govern it, the other side will not remain weak for ever. It will not remain indefinitely servile, and its rulers will not be able to continue to impose whatever they want. The Arab side bases its claim on facts that are stronger than old papers and scrolls, and will not submit or surrender to the power that now prevails and the *de facto* situation that it is trying to impose.

The generation born into the eye of the storm may be carried by its winds towards this choice or that. The winds may blow it off course, especially since the older generation was not aware of what was being plotted and did not make ready. But the next generation, and the one after it, must take a look back, re-evaluate and learn from the mistakes of their predecessors, and from their anger as well, so that the balance can be changed and things can be corrected. Large-scale wars may be started, as they have been in many parts of the world during different eras, due to persistence of injustice and degradation. The coming generations will have to pay for the mistakes of those who preceded them, and blood will be the law that rules the region for a long time to come.

From *Story of a City: A Childhood in Amman* by Abd al-Rahman Munif, published by Quartet Books Limited, 1996. Translated from the Arabic by Samira Kawar. Reprinted with the permission of the publisher.

Janset Berkok Shami

Janset Berkok Shami was born in Istanbul and began to learn English when she was 12. She studied English literature at Ankara University and Queen Mary College in London, and has lived in Amman since 1951. More than twenty of her short stories have appeared in magazines in Britain and the United States, and her first novel, *Cages On Opposite Shores*, was published in 1995 by Interlink (New York). The following story, *Waiting*, first appeared in Mid-American Review, Vol XI No 2, 1991, and has since been translated into Arabic, Turkish and Swedish.

We are sitting in a coffee house one evening, every evening, in the dry, dusty well of central Amman surrounded by mountains and thinking. Thinking about the Israelis. What will they do next? Thinking about the Americans. Waiting for the calm face of their President to invade the television screen, waiting for his cautiously worded speeches. Waiting for help from our wealthier brethren, the other Arab nations.

Trying to figure out a way of putting two pennies over two pennies. Trying to discover a way of holding onto the two pennies, until we earn the next two pennies. The weight of four pennies in the pocket! Ya Allah!

I am a musician, so I need money to buy instruments. Without money, no instruments. Without instruments, no money. Similarities and contradictions interest me, because I am an Arab, a philosopher. I am an Arab because I am a philosopher. The daily parades of ruminating mouths on the television screen demonstrate that not all philosophers are Arabs. What is the world coming to?

The other night our group, "Pals from Palestine", had a piece of luck. A boy I knew from the Jebel Hussein refugee camp came up to our smoky table and said, "Look here, Yousef, I am going to get married tonight. How about some noise?"

He put it so aptly, that refugee boy who is all grown up now. What else do we do besides noise? Noise, noise, dusty noise all around!

What else can we do? See, I study accounting at a community college; I have no free time to practice during the day. Salah, the handsome keyboard man with the large head of curly hair, is a tile-fitter's helper. He mixes cement in the yards and carries it indoors. Each metal container he carried on his shoulder weighs ten kilos or more. Our drummer is an electrician. His big feet at the end of his skinny legs shuffle up and down his ladder all day long. He bores holes in walls and stretches wires through narrow tunnels inside them.

So, I tally and add other people's money on the strings of my guitar, at nights. Ali hits his sticks steadily on the same spots on his drums. The thin sticks are heavy hammers and the drumskins are newly painted walls behind the closing eyelids of his sleepy eyes. Salah's hands drop like blocks on the keyboard. The grey cement he carries stiffens his fingers and accumulates under his finger-nails.

We go and set up our equipment on the flat roof of the two-room house. The roof is a drop of water in a sea of refugee roofs. The refugee roofs of 1948 and the refugee roofs of 1967 extend to the edge of the hill rippling with their slightly alternating heights.

Our transistor size singer, Sameer, comes half an hour before the party starts, wearing his hundred percent polyester silk scarf. He lowers the stand of the microphone to his height and bends the goose neck down. He caps the microphone with an orange coloured sponge, a wind-screen, to tone down the hoarse sound which comes out of his throat when he sings. I line up my pedals side by side, starting from left to right: noise gate, screamer, distortion, phaser.

The Arab-disco music we play involves no risks. Our equipment protects us from listeners of yesterday and of today. The listeners fail to estimate our true musical competence. "How well he distorts the sound of his guitar," a young listener says about my playing. You see, my music is naturally distorted. But it is my prominently displayed distortion-effect pedal which makes the listener say that. My worn out guitar, covered by stickers of various music companies, is a Fender. A Fender by Fender, Made In Taiwan. It is a genuine imitation of the Fender of the USA.

The keyboard is a Hammond. An American instrument constructed in the up-to-date factories of the war-torn Korea of the past. Salah hands over most of what he earns from carrying buckets of cement as payments to the proprietor of the music store who sold him the keyboard. If he decides to get married within the coming three years, which he might as he already has a sexy girlfriend, the expenses of the wedding and setting up a house will stop the monthly payments. The proprietor of the music store will present the unpaid bills to the lawyer who takes care of such matters, and Salah will be taken to court. That will not change the situation much. If anything, it will help. He will pay nothing as the court sessions progress and the judge takes his time in reaching a decision. When it is over, he will be ordered to pay the total sum, but Allah Kerim! God is generous!

Ali's drum set was cheap. He bought it second hand, and paid in cash. Anyway Ali is an electrician. He makes more money than any of us.

We start our noise. First it whirls around, whirring like the new Jewish spy planes. That is the special trick of my guitar. Then the drum takes over, bringing heaven and earth over the heads of the unsuspecting listeners.

Suddenly, having spotted the approach of the bride on the arm of the groom, Sameer's booming voice joins in and the noise we produce becomes louder. The female relatives circle the couple. Inside the beaded décolleté dresses provided by the groom, their middle-aged breasts quiver visibly as they let out their customary ululations. Their ululations complement our music. Our music complements their ululations. We are one happy, unhappy, noisy family trying to forget tomorrow as we wait for miracles.

Then we start eating from the trays of *mansaf*. The groom, the boy of yesterday, tells us that he works at a foreign institute as a messenger. The building of this institute is next to another one. The objectives of both institutes seem almost identical to him. There is a narrow alleyway between them. Mahmoud carries important documents and reports from one building to the other. They pay him three hundred dollars a month for this service. He stresses the fact: they pay him in dollars. America is a great country, dollars never lose value! We, the musicians, including our singer, listen to him. We suppress the envy in our hearts as best we can. We congratulate him.

The colour of the lately grown-up, tall and handsome groom's suit is dove grey. Its material is a mixture of nylon and shiny polyester. His patent leather shoes with large plastic buckles remind me of those worn by pageboys in European television plays. His long black hair is parted in the middle. It is pasted to his head and cheeks with an oily pomade. His nose which appears from that flattened surface is sharp and shapely as the tip of an iceberg.

The dinner invigorates our music. Its pulsating rhythm lifts the young women out of their chairs, and brings them to the little circle of the dance arena. They tie colourful scarves around their hips and wiggle and shake everything moveable in their comely bodies. Their abandon to gaiety pushes from our minds the uncertainties of the future. Their sparkling eyes woo us from the alleyways of the past. Captured by the moment, imprisoned in the hollows of pairs and pairs of brown eyes, we breathe again. We rest in the present as long as the spirited dance keeps us whirling. Ali smiles with one gold tooth at the side of his mouth. Salah smiles with his even teeth and pink gums. I skip a note or two on my guitar while I desperately call self-control to my aid and hold my lips tightly clamped over a mouthful of stained teeth.

I miss the grand entry of the five policemen through the opening leading to the roof. But I witness the face-down fall of the tall policeman on the unevenly cemented floor. What tripped him were the water pipes which are laid out haphazardly on the roof. No harm comes to him. He stands up clutching the popped button of his tight uniform.

The other four policemen walk toward us with measured, dignified steps, and shout. First their leader shouts, then they shout in chorus. They take us by the arms and carry us off to some distance from our equipment.

People come up to the neighbouring roofs. "You were keeping us awake," murmur some voices apologetically. I try to figure out under which roof the guilty telephone hides. I try to imagine its colour. Red? Who put in the call? The father? What did he say to the policeman who answered the call?

The groom leaves his bride's side and comes to our rescue. He lunges at the tall policeman who still holds the button in his clasped hand. He sends him sprawling once again to the floor which loosens his grip on the button. This time it disappears. Does it go down the drain pipe? Perhaps! Who knows? Only Allah knows!

Two policemen grab the groom and push him towards us. His forcefully induced steps carry him right into the midst of our tightened front and his dove grey, nylon silk suit exposes our secondhand, *rababikia* clothes like a neon light.

The five of us, the musicians and the groom, and the five of them, the policemen of different sizes and the tall one with the missing button, march briskly to the police station. The five of us go further; we are taken on a journey to the crowded jail. They release us, the musicians, the next day, but they keep the groom. The groom who paid us for the noise we made, the groom who bought the dresses for the babyfaced bride's numerous sisters and aunts, remains in jail.

He sits in his small cell and thinks about the Israelis. What will they do next? He thinks about the Americans. What deflated words will come from the thin lips of their President? When he speaks, whenever he speaks, when he starts, "Peace in the Middle East is…", "is" is the only word he cares about. The word is a present tense form of "to be". Mahmoud was top of his class in English. He knows how to conjugate verbs.

I am a messenger.

You are a president.

Prophet Muhammad is the messenger of God.

We are the victims.

You are indifferent.

They are killing us. They are killing us with their rubber bullets. They are killing us with their tear gas. They are killing our youth. They are killing our dignity!

No help comes from conjugating the verb. No help comes from thinking about his babyfaced bride. So, he confines his thoughts to everyday concerns. He tries to figure out a way of putting two pennies over two other pennies. Who knows what the future will bring? He stops all kinds of thoughts and waits for his release. He waits.

His babyfaced bride serves coffee to her mother-in-law and listens to the old woman's nostalgia stream alongside her tears.

"Our tall wheat sways gently, in the past. Our heavy oranges pull the branches low, in the past. The harvest of our youngest olive tree fills knee-high jars, in the past. Our girls sing and dance, our young men curl their moustaches, in the past. Palestine glows, Palestinians thrive, in the past."

Sighs follow sighs, sighs follow sighs. A pair of dry hands draws circles and triangles in the air. Cones and pyramids in the air. The old woman waits for her son's return. She waits for a future which will twinkle like a million stars in Palestine's clear skies, in the past.

Fadia Faqir

Fadia Faqir was born in Amman in 1956. She gained her BA in English literature, MA in creative writing and doctorate in critical and creative writing at Jordan University, Lancaster University and the University of East Anglia respectively. Her first novel, *Nisanit*, dramatizing the Arab–Israeli conflict through the eyes of a Palestinian guerrilla, the woman in love with him and an Israeli interrogator, was published in 1987. This extract is taken from her second novel, *Pillars of Salt*. From 1994 to 2004 Fadia Faqir taught Arabic literature and Middle Eastern Women's Studies at Durham University in the UK. Her website is ⓦwww .fadiafaqir.com.

"Imam Rajab will ask you some questions. You answer yes," Daffash said as he twisted his moustache between thumb and forefinger.

I looked at the solemn faces of the men of the tribe.

Imam Rajab stood up with difficulty and said loudly, "Maha, daughter of Nimer, will you accept Sheikh Talib as a husband?"

My body grew lighter and lighter and began rising up, up towards the sky. I saw my mother's smiling face, my father's stick and Harb's arm. I would only place my head on Harb's strong arm. Daffash was rubbing his clenched fists. My voice was weak and thin when I said, "I want a sip of water."

Imam Rajab smiled, showing uneven brown teeth. Dark words could grind your teeth and tint them. "Daffash, she is shy. Let her have some water." I turned my back on them and went to the house, found a cup, marched out of the house, threw the cup on the soil, stuck the end of my robe in my trousers and ran, ran to the orchard.

Nasra was leaning on one of the orange trees talking to Murjan. She grabbed my hand and said in her shrill voice, "Quick, the mountains." The soles of my feet were blazing hot, Mubarak's crying filled the valley, the men would shoot me between the eyes if they caught me. Then, I could only hear the noise of my lungs rasping for air. Thorn shrubs, grass, dry soil and bugloss sped under my feet. Sweat trickled down my nose. We took one of the footpaths leading to the top of the mountain. Nasra was pulling me forwards. I felt very hot although the air was getting cooler. Murjan was right behind us. When we reached the top, I stopped and shouted to the wind, to the sick light of dusk. "No." I would not accept Sheikh Talib as a husband.

The jaws of Abu Auqab's cave were wide open. A lion ready to devour his prey. We entered the cave and threw ourselves on the rug-covered ground. My lungs felt as if they had been slashed by a dagger. Murjan and Jawaher had prepared the cave for us. A clay jar, a lamp, bread and some butter and dates. "Enough for a few days," Murjan said. "Close the entrance with the rock outside. I will keep an eye on the path leading to the cave. If you hear any noise, run south towards the Dead Sea. Do not stay here. If you hear voices, sneak quietly out of the cave."

"May Allah lengthen your life, my son," I gasped. Nasra brought a cup of water and told me to drink.

The foxes' barking and the howling of dogs besieged us in our cave. Nasra's face twitched under the dwindling light of the lamp. Sleep was far away from me. My heart quivered beneath my ribs. Mubarak. Would Tamam feed him, undress him, wipe his tears? I rocked and swayed my body to try to go to sleep. The rounded rock they pushed to lock the mouth of the cave seemed to crouch upon my chest. From now on, fear and exhaustion would be my sisters, my companions in the land of my tribe. No arrivals at all. The cave was dark, the rug I covered my body with was cold, my luck was scattered flour.

I was floating lightly between hazy clouds when Nasra shook my shoulder. "Wake up. Voices." We stood up and placed our ears on the ground. Faint sounds vibrated through soil and stone. "We must go." We pushed the rock slowly to one side and left the cave. A procession of torches climbed up the mountain like a glowing snake.

"Run."

Following the sounds of waves, we dashed to the south towards the hollow of the sea. Swishing waves crashed on the shore with all their might then retreated. My muscles ached, my eyes watered and the soles of my feet were bleeding. The running blood would leave a trace on the soil, would make it easy for the men of the tribe to find us. The salt covering the pebbles on the seashore rubbed into my cuts, inflaming them. Fire, fire, fire. The mother of Hulala was licking the soles of my bare feet. Nasra's back was stiff, my feet barely touched the ground, and the only sign of my being alive and running was the deep sound of drawn breath. The wings of darkness hid our figures, protected them, enveloped us like a kind mother.

The sky was a cloud of black smoke suspended over the open plain of the sea. Nasra guided me to a spring of fresh water flowing into the sea. "We will spend the night here." A warm breeze carrying the smell of carbon hit my damp face. Some faint lights were reflected in the water over on the other bank. Darkness and heat swathed the vast salt flats. I placed my head between my legs to let the blood stream down and push out the dizziness. When I closed my eyes I saw the smiling face of Harb, his warm hands pulling me closer and the water lapping my body gently. Had I – Maha the Indian fig, bitter like colocynth but patient – had I run away from my house? Was I really sitting on the salty stones, looking at the awesome hollow of the Dead Sea without the twin of my soul, without Harb, my beloved and the father of my son? Why did I leave my son with Tamam? Why did I...?

The darkness of the clouds descended and enveloped Nasra and me. The land-locked water held its breath and nothing moved on that vast coast except water from the mineral springs which gurgled out then glided down the cliffs to the black mirror. Mist lined the water, the rocks, the springs, making breathing impossible. The stink of acids and minerals rose up to the sky. I placed my head on a flat stone and tried to listen to the sound of fresh water streaming down to meet its death. A drop of fresh water in the vast salty sea. The sapless cloak of death shrouded the low land, the tops of mountains and even Jerusalem with its high minarets. I would try to go to sleep, I would try to shut my eyes like Nasra; I would try to forget about the pillars of salt under the water and the vipers lurking in the dark.

The sun rose, lighting up the white sky, scattering flickering beams on the surface of the calm water. The dawn transformed every grain of salt into a sparkling jewel, a precious stone. The sound of water swishing and hissing in the wind ebbed and swirled. Nasra was still asleep on top of the flat rock. In her black robe, she looked like a thin black lining of the rock. I filled my cupped hands with water and splashed my face. The bitter taste of minerals stuck to my tongue, to the rims of my eyes. A contraction in my chest told me that my son was crying. Whenever I thought about him, I felt it in my breasts. I stroked my nipples. He must be hungry. He must be crying. His tiny feet must be searching for a crack in the cliffs to fit into. Curse my heart which caught fire as easily as dry palm leaves.

Nasra woke up, stretched her hands and looked at the sky. Dangling her legs, she started blowing into her reed-pipe. She played sharp, bouncy tunes as a greeting to the morning.

"Nasra, sister, I want you to go to the village and bring me some news."

"Bring food?"

I looked at the dusty shrubs bravely sprouting on the banks of mineral springs. "Yes." Nasra leapt off the rock and washed her face. She stuck the end of her robe into her trousers and walked away. I watched her negotiate her way between the shrubs. When she had become just a crawling ant in the distance, I sighed and sat down. The heat started rising under the rude glare of the sun. My black robe absorbed the heat, stored the heat, baking my body inside. The swishing and hissing of the cool water filled my ears.

The translucent hands of the water waved to me, pulled me, held my wrists. The call of the sea was deep, husky, sad. My past. I untied my headband, flung the veil on a stone, then undid my plaits. I took off my tatty black robe, my trousers and my petticoat then stretched my naked body. My feet when plunged into the water welcomed the pleasant coolness. Whenever I dived in the Dead Sea my eyes hurt. The acids and minerals seemed to attack the tender tissues of my body. Must endure it till pleasure overtook the pain and I could see again. Fresh tears would wash out the salt. The lapping water, the wet hair and the bitter taste of minerals brought Harb back. First he kissed the right corner of my mouth, then the left corner, then the centre of my lips. I grabbed his shoulders and moved closer to him. When I enveloped him, curled around him with my being, he started crying like a baby. His expression was tender, was full of response. Receiving him was like coming home after a long sweaty day. My body tuned into a light pestle swiftly grinding coffee and cardamom in a mortar. Whispers and swishes. "Mistress of my soul, deer-eyes." I hugged myself tightly. Tears, emptiness and love. I dived to hold him, then floated. Murky green puddles followed by fresh air and dazzling light.

I thought I saw the crooked figure of Hakim. I wiped the water from my face. Yes, by the grey hair of my grandmother. He stopped, put his goat on the ground, then waved to me. His step when he continued walking was light as if he were only twenty years old. Holding his goat, he disappeared behind one of the high cliffs. I cried at the top of my voice, "Hakim." Nothing except the echo of my voice and the swishing of the waves. Maybe he could, with his rare herbs, cure my tired heart. "Hakim." Nothing except the echo of my voice breaking on top of the mountains.

The sun unchained its scalding flames and turned them loose in the plain of the Dead Sea. Sweat trickled down my face and my back. Two blurred crawling ants. Murjan and Nasra. Bearers of good news, I prayed.

"Peace be upon you," said Murjan.

"And upon you, my son," I said.

"Fine, Mubarak," said Nasra.

"Maha, my mother, your brother Daffash has taken possession of the orchard, the house and your son."

"Rooted out your vegetables, Daffash."

Grains of Dead Sea bitter salt lined my throat, stuck to my tongue, rimmed my eyes. "I am thirsty." Murjan handed me the waterskin. I gulped some water. Nasra offered me dates. I shook my head.

My orchard, the gem hanging on the valley's forehead. The golden dawn gently fingered the citrus trees and lifted them up, up to the sky and suspended them there. The icy water running in the old canal split the orchard in two and filtered into the soil, blunting the edges of the dry grains, making the whole area cool and damp. The scent of the blossoms carried me smoothly to another world. The cloud of perfume filled the valley. The clear water ran to the depth of my heart, wiped my tired soul clean and left me fragile, transparent.

Shielding my eyes, I looked at the sun. What was I, Maha, daughter of Maliha, daughter of Sabha doing there? How could I leave my son and house? I must fight Daffash. Slowly, slowly, I turned round and said in a determined voice, "I am going back to the village."

Nasra started slapping her cheeks and crying, "Crazy, Maha?"

Murjan gazed at the sea and said as if talking to the waves, "Do whatever you feel is right."

Straight backed, head held high, chin quivering, I marched across the vast plain. The few palm trees were like drops of fresh water in a salty sea. They could not change the plain to kind green. The forces of the pale desert triumphed over the bright green spots. A camel and a calf chewed and chewed the cud. Bringing the food back from the stomach and chewing it was useless for me. The banana plantation was the shortest cut to the village. A thorn pricked the sole of my foot. Nasra and Murjan tried to catch up with me.

Daffash, my brother, the son of my mother Maliha, my father Sheikh Nimer and the grandson of my grandmother Sabha swallowed the farm and the house.

I should have killed Daffash in the cave as he mounted Salih's wife. I should have pulled the trigger and shot him in the heart. I should have killed him before Nasra's tunes had lost their warmth. I should have shot Daffash before Nasra had lost her earring and the brilliance of her green eyes.

I pushed the headband up, wiped my sweat and continued marching towards the forgotten village which clung to the mountainside like a leech. Only two days and the village seemed older. Gloomy brown. Mud domes, mud walls, mud ears and eyes. I left the Dead Sea behind, roaring in its low land. The land belonged to me. Mubarak was my son, a piece of my heart. I planted the lemon and orange shoots, waited for three years, watered them until they threw their first crop. My fingernails were lined with soil, with dung and mud. I had dug, cleaned, uprooted. My brother's hands were clean, were never plunged into mud. The land was mine. It was better to be shot between the eyes than see the orchard withering away. I would prefer to lie in peace under the ground, entangled with the roots of my orange trees.

From *Pillars of Salt* by Fadia Faqir, published by Quartet Books Limited, 1996. Reprinted with the permission of the publisher.

Jordanian–Palestinian poetry

Of all Arab countries, Jordan has the closest links with Palestine and Palestinian culture, and many writers chose or were forced to take refuge in Jordan after the wars of 1948 and 1967. Following are four poems (all translated from the Arabic) by Palestinian writers with some close connection with Jordan – either as their birthplace, or as their present or former country of residence. All share common themes, evoked by Salma Khadra Jayyusi in her introduction to the *Anthology of Modern Palestinian Literature:*

"Modern Palestinian experience is harsh, unrelenting and all-penetrating; no Palestinian is free from its grip and no writer can evade it. It cannot be forgotten and its anguish cannot be transcended. Whether in Israel, or in the West Bank and the Gaza Strip, or in the diaspora, Palestinians are committed by their very identity to a life determined by events and circumstances arising out of their own rejection of captivity and national loss, as well as by other people's intentions, suspicions, fears and aggressions. There is no escape. For the writer to contemplate an orientation completely divorced from political life is to belie reality, to deny experience; for to engross oneself for too long in "normal" everyday experiences is to betray one's own life and one's own people. This means that Palestinian writers have little scope for indulging in escapism; they are compromised by the events of contemporary history even before they are born. The luxury of choosing one's past, of selecting memories, of re-arranging relations that transcend events and external circumstances, is not theirs; they have become permanent exiles, the prototype of the strangers of all times, struggling against obstacles of every kind and magnitude. But the greatest struggle and the greatest triumph of Palestinian writers lies in their refusal to become humanity's cringing victims during the second half of the twentieth century. While never ceasing to be aware of the particular predicament of their people, they exhibit a resilience that transcends tragedy and overcomes necessity. This has coloured contemporary Palestinian literature and directed its intention and tone."

Haydar Mahmoud

Haydar Mahmoud was born in Haifa in 1945 and has served as general director of culture and arts in Jordan and Jordan's ambassador to Tunisia. His collected poetry was published in 1990. This poem, *Two-in-One*, was translated by Salwa Jabsheh and John Heath-Stubbs.

One part of me is not
from the other part estranged,
although the whole wide world
against myself is ranged.

How can I cancel out
details of what I am
How can my pulse deny
pulse of its own bloodstream?

How can I myself
from my own self separate
when what within me is one
with that which is without?

One with myself, my eye
gazing sees only me
wherever I may go
it is myself I see.

Mureed Barghouthy

Mureed Barghouthy was born in 1944 and has spent all his life living outside Palestine. He left Egypt in 1979 after the signing of the peace treaty with Israel, and has since been living in Amman. This poem, *The Tribes*, was translated by Lena Jayyusi and W.S. Merwin.

Our tribes regain their charm:

Tents and more tents
tents of tranquil stone, their pegs are tile and marble
inscriptions on the ceiling, velvet paper covering the walls
the family portraits and "La Gioconda"
facing a tablet with inscriptions
to repel the evil eye
beside the diploma of a son
framed in gold, coated with dust.
Tents, and a glass window
it is the trap for young girls, who look out from it and tremble for fear
their young sister or brother might tell the grown-ups.
Vapour rises from the tea, whiskey and soda
and "I do not like wine" and "excuse me"
"did you manage with the fourth wife?"
Tents and more tents
the chandeliers illuminate opulent furnishings
flies of speech dance through them

in and out of brass gates draped with chains
Our tribes retain their charm
now that the tribes are out of date!

Abd al-Raheem Umar

Abd al-Raheem Umar was born near Tulkarm, Palestine, in 1929, and has spent much of his life in Amman, as a poet, playwright and political journalist. This is an extract from _The Siege_, which was translated by Sharif Elmusa and Naomi Shihab Nye.

The fathers would have built
a great wall between us and the road,
the waves of the vanquished sea
would have turned into stone,
had they known we'd become refugees.
Who could know our tents would be strewn
across the sands?

Long times passed, longer, long.
During nights of exile,
conquerors filed into our world.
Could our slender bodies ward them off?
Could we really have sung in such
interminable dark? We learned
the low hum of exile, nothing more.

Now Abel lies among ruins,
disintegrating, while a crow tells the tale
of a brother who killed his own.
Long times passed, longer, long
Conquerors filed past—
Kufr Qasim, Sabra, Shateela.★
And our own brothers, the ones
who speak our mother tongue,
had forsaken us.
Between the ocean and the gulf,
the gulf and the ocean,
between the weak and the strong,
the strong and the weak,
stretches the long arm of our siege.

★ In 1956, Israeli soldiers imposed a curfew on the village of Kufr Qasim, northeast
of Tel Aviv, while its inhabitants were out working in the fields; when the villagers
returned home unaware of events, the soldiers killed them for breaking the curfew.
Sabra and Shateela are the names of two slum areas in south Beirut, whose Palestinian inhabitants were massacred during Israel's 1982 invasion by Lebanese Christian
militias operating with the connivance of the occupying Israeli army.

Ibrahim Nasrallah

Ibrahim Nasrallah was born in the Wihdat refugee camp in South Amman in 1954, and still lives and works in Amman as a journalist and poet. His acclaimed novel *Prairies of Fever* (1985) has been translated into English. This poem, *The Hand*, was translated by Lena Jayyusi and Jeremy Reed.

It is the hand
day's beautiful branch
blossoming with fingers,
soft as the dove's cooing,
that neither catches the wind,
nor arrests the water.
But it takes in space
and embraces the earth
from the wild flower
to the palm tree.
It is the hand
comforts us when we are broken,
consoles us when we cry,
offers solace to our tiredness.
It is the hand
dream's miracle
legend of creation
columns of light
or a handful of embers
that quicken or subside.
It is the hand
a field, and a posy of children's songs,
and a planet.

The hand isn't a book, or lines.
Don't scrutinize the details
Don't read its silence
nor its contours
you will find nothing.
All the lines that have invaded it
all the bends
are our fault
from the first aberrations
to the advent of misery.
It is the hand
do not read it
read what it will write
read what it will do
and raise it
raise it
till it becomes a sky.

All poems, and the prose excerpt in the introduction, are from
Anthology of Modern Palestinian Literature, ed. Salma Khadra Jayyusi
© 1992 Columbia University Press.
Reprinted with the permission of the publisher.

Books

It can be difficult to find **books** focused on Jordan. Countless millions of words have been written about Palestine, Israel, Lebanon, Egypt and Syria, but Jordan is all too often relegated to patchy later chapters or a series of mentions in passing.

The selection of recommendations below is a personal one, and necessarily omits much. Lawrence's *The Seven Pillars of Wisdom* has appeal far beyond its worth, but if you want **fiction**, Fadia Faqir's *Pillars of Salt*, a brilliant tale of women resisting domination, or Mahmoud Darwish's *Memory for Forgetfulness*, a lyrical account of Beirut under Israeli siege, are both gripping. One of the best modern **histories** is Philip Robins' incisive *History of Jordan*, but – especially if you're travelling throughout the region – Albert Hourani's magisterial *History of the Arab Peoples* is unmissable. For history that reads like fiction, you should certainly make time for Amin Maalouf's marvellous *The Crusades through Arab Eyes*. The best one-stop take on why the region's **politics** is such a mess is Avi Shlaim's *War and Peace in the Middle East*. John L. Esposito's lively *Islam: The Straight Path* gives much readable insight into **Islam**.

In Britain, one excellent **bookseller** specializing in the Arab world is Al-Saqi (☏020/7221 9347, ⊛www.saqibooks.com). Saqi doubles as a **publisher** and has a diverse and fascinating catalogue; it also does worldwide mail order. In the US, Interlink Publishing (☏1-800/238-LINK, ⊛www.interlinkbooks.com) stands out for its broad range of translated Arabic fiction as well as books on Middle Eastern history, art and culture.

In most of the reviews following, **publishers** in the UK and US are listed; where they differ, they're given in the form "UK publisher/US publisher"; "o/p" signifies out-of-print. Titles marked ⊡ are particularly recommended. Books published in Amman are generally available only in Jordan.

Literature

With the paucity of **Jordanian literature** currently available in English, we've expanded horizons slightly in this section, not least because there's so much more available in English from **Palestinian writers**. As well as including some general anthologies of Arab writing, we've outlined works from three of the most important Palestinian authors, Ghassan Kanafani, Sahar Khalifeh and Mahmoud Darwish.

General

Inea Bushnaq (ed) *Arab Folktales* (Penguin/Pantheon). Delightful collection of translated tales, including a section of Bedouin stories entitled "Tales Told In Houses Made of Hair".

⊡ **Mahmoud Darwish** *Memory for Forgetfulness: August, Beirut, 1982* (University of California Press, US). Startling prose-poems, written as the Israeli army was laying siege to the city. Darwish is acknowledged as the greatest living Arab poet, and has published more than a dozen collections of poetry (his work appears in the two Columbia anthologies in this section); this, though, is perhaps the easiest way into his extraordinarily visceral and moving style.

Nur and Abdelwahab Elmessiri *A Land of Stone and Thyme* (Quartet). Digestible and well-chosen anthology of Palestinian short stories from the 1960s onwards, with all the big names present, including Liana Badr, Emile Habibi and Ghassan Kanafani.

Salma Khadra Jayyusi (ed) *An Anthology of Modern Palestinian Literature* (Columbia University Press, US). What it says, with poetry, fiction and personal narratives from Palestinians writing all over the world. Four poems by Jordanian-Palestinian writers from the anthology are reprinted on p.489.

★ **Ghassan Kanafani** *Men in the Sun* (Three Continents, US). Perhaps the best-known short story ever written in Arabic, about a journey across the desert from Amman to Kuwait, here translated along with six more. Kanafani was spokesman for the Popular Front for the Liberation of Palestine (and was assassinated at the age of 36), but his stories, far from being political diatribes, are tender, lyrical and superbly plotted.

Sahar Khalifeh *Wild Thorns* (Al Saqi Books/Interlink). Modern classic of Palestinian fiction, and a devastating view of life under Israeli occupation in the West Bank. A young Palestinian returns from abroad eager to take it all out on the occupiers, only to discover the reality of life among his compatriots is rather different from what he was expecting.

Modern Jordanian fiction

Diana Abu-Jaber *Arabian Jazz* (Harcourt Brace). Feisty, funny and touching first novel from Abu-Jaber, a Jordanian-American, about the life and daughters of a Jordanian widower transplanted to a poor white community in upstate New York.

Fadia Faqir *Nisanit* (Penguin). Powerful dramatization of the Arab–Israeli conflict through the voices of a guerrilla, his girlfriend and an interrogator, written in a raw, fractured style, describing violence, fanaticism and degradation through gritted teeth. Exhausting, and not easy to read.

★ **Fadia Faqir** *Pillars of Salt* (Quartet/Interlink). Exceptionally skilful and lyrical novel set in the cities and countryside of mandate-period Jordan, which manages simultaneously to champion both the rights of women and the traditional values of Bedouin culture. Two women, one from the city, the other from a Bedouin tribe, end up in Fuheis Mental Hospital after abuse at the hands of their male relatives; the fluid and compelling story traces the elements of their resistance to domination. See p.484 for an extract.

Abd al-Rahman Munif *Story of a City: A Childhood in Amman* (Quartet). Rambling tales of life in Amman in the 1940s, recalling the city passing from a period of bucolic innocence through World War II and the tragic loss of Palestine. Barely counting even as oral history, this is closer to fireside remembrances, padded out with digressions and family tales. See p.478 for an extract.

Abdelrahman Munif *Cities of Salt*; *The Trench*; *Variations on Night and Day* (all Vintage). Highly acclaimed trilogy of novels focusing on the corruption of traditional Arab values by Western influence, centred on the disruption caused in a fictional Gulf state by the discovery of oil. Munif's own close links with the oil industry, and his years working in the Gulf, give a uniquely insightful slant to his fictional indictment: all three novels were banned in Saudi Arabia and elsewhere.

Ibrahim Nasrallah *Prairies of Fever* (Interlink, US). Intense and bewildering postmodern novel by a leading Jordanian journalist. The protagonist, a young teacher hired to work in a remote part of the Arabian peninsula, is pronounced dead on page one; from then on, his struggle to keep a grip on his life shifts from past to future, from reality to hallucination, from human to animal.

Fuad al-Qoussouss *The Return from the North* (Ministry of Culture, Amman). Slow and careful evocation of the trials and tribulations of a rural Jordanian community in the 1930s, as it faces the rush to modernity of the newly founded emirate. Diverting and mildly entertaining, though the quality of the English translation is patchy.

Mu'nis Razzaz *Alive in the Dead Sea* (Ministry of Culture, Amman). Early novel from this doyen of Jordanian journalists, sarcastically criticizing the rise to power of the Baath Party in Iraq and Syria by charting the disillusionment of an intellectual departing his birthplace, Amman, for the city of his dreams, Beirut, only to

find his hopes shattered by the actions of those around him. If you can see through the lumpiness of the English translation, there's some beauty beneath, but the author's mingling of wakefulness, dreaming and hallucination doesn't aid the struggle.

Janset Berkok Shami *Cages on Opposite Shores* (Interlink, US). A longtime resident of Amman, Shami here concentrates on her native Istanbul during World War I. A modern Turkish woman, caged in an indeterminate present in a city symbolically divided between Europe and Asia, discovers diaries which reveal her grandmother's Armenian identity. In shimmeringly confident, poetic prose, the novel traces her exploration of her emotional and ethnic roots and her journey to the "opposite shore". See p.481 for one of Shami's short stories.

Travel

Early travellers

Gertrude Bell *The Desert and the Sown* (Virago/Beacon). Hard-to-read account of a 1905 journey from Jerusalem to Antioch, strewn with grating cultural assumptions about the people Bell meets. Although concentrating on the more populated and engaging lands in Syria, the book contains some interesting vignettes from Transjordan.

John Lewis Burckhardt *Travels in Syria and the Holy Land* (Darf, UK). Recent reprint of the original 1822 text, describing a massive jaunt around the Levant by a pioneer traveller and explorer (see p.330), who, partway through his journey, stumbled upon Petra. His style is surprisingly and refreshingly upbeat, bringing the wildness of Transjordan in this period very much to life.

Hon. Charles Irby and James Mangles *Travels in Egypt and Nubia, Syria and Asia Minor* (Darf, UK). Venerable tome from 1823, in which two British naval captains make their no-nonsense way through the Middle East, via Petra and Palmyra.

Selah Merrill *East of the Jordan* (Darf, UK). Reprint of one of the first truly comprehensive early modern surveys of the antiquities and peoples of Transjordan, conducted in 1875–77.

★ **Kathryn Tidrick** *Heart Beguiling Araby* (I.B. Tauris). Compelling and entertaining analysis of the enduring fascination of the English for Arabia over the centuries, focused on a detailed trawl through the life and works of Burton, Palgrave, Blunt and Doughty, plus sections on the early explorers and on Lawrence and twentieth-century Arabists.

Modern travellers

Michael Asher *The Last of the Bedu* (Penguin). Engrossing tales of epic desert travel, seeking to illuminate the myths surrounding Bedouin culture across the whole Middle East from Syria to Oman to Sudan. A rather treacly style and disappointingly skimpy look at the Bdul and Howeitat of Jordan don't detract from the author's uniquely insightful empathy with his subject.

Annie Caulfield *Kingdom of the Film-Stars* (Lonely Planet). Possibly the only travel book ever written solely about Jordan, and a light, chatty read. The author is whisked around the country to all the important places and some interesting family gatherings, against a background of her falling in love with a Jordanian man.

★ **Jonathan Raban** *Arabia* (Picador, UK). Engaging and deeply insightful tales of the Gulf States, Yemen, Egypt and Jordan in 1978 at the height of oil wealth, and before the Lebanese civil war and attempts at peace with Israel had had much impact on the Arab world. Much more than mere travelogue, the book is perceptive, fluently written and sympathetic, as relevant today as when it first appeared.

Bettina Selby *Like Water in a Dry Land* (HarperCollins). The famed solo traveller rides her bike quickly through Syria and Jordan in order to get to Israel. An occasionally acerbic manner doesn't detract too much from the freewheeling readability.

Specialist guides

Amman; *The Desert Castles*; *Jerash*; *Madaba & Mt Nebo*; *Pella*; *Petra*; *Umm el-Jimal*; *Umm Qais* (all al-Kutba, Amman). Series of pocket-sized booklets giving solid archeological and historical information for most major sites in the country. *Madaba*, *Umm el-Jimal* and *Umm Qais* are written by the archeologists who excavated the sites, and thus give particularly enthusiastic insight.

Ian J. Andrews *The Birds of the Hashemite Kingdom of Jordan*. The best ornithological field guide from a longtime leader of birdwatching tours to Jordan. Privately published in the UK by the author (ⓦwww.andrewsi.freeserve.co.uk) and also available in Jordan.

★ **Iain Browning** *Jerash and the Decapolis* and *Petra* (both Chatto & Windus, UK). Incomparably strong investigations into every aspect of the architecture, history and culture of Jordan's two premier ancient sites. In prose that's always very accurate but never turgid, Browning, an architectural historian, communicates a deep understanding and knowledge with zest, and the illustrations of what crumbling monuments might have looked like when new enhance site-wanderings enormously. *Jerash* hasn't been revised since 1982, less of a drawback than the fact that *Petra* is in a badly outdated 1989 edition.

Guy Buckles *The Dive Sites of the Red Sea* (New Holland, UK). Thoroughly comprehensive full-colour coverage of every site from Aqaba to Eritrea, packed with sensible advice, clear assessment of each location and some interesting background.

Herbert Donner *The Mosaic Map of Madaba* (Kok Pharos, Kampen, the Netherlands). Slim but intricately detailed analysis of the map, covering every inscription and place name and giving fascinating insight into context, history and sources. Available in Jordan.

Dawud M.H. al-Eisawi *Field Guide to the Wild Flowers of Jordan*. Exhaustive survey of the subject in English and Arabic by a professor of botany at Jordan University, complete with 488 colour photos. Privately published in Jordan by the author, and most easily available at the RSCN shops in Amman, Azraq and Dana.

Lankester G. Harding *The Antiquities of Jordan* (Jordan Distribution Agency, Amman). Written in 1959 by the then British director of the Department of Antiquities. The histories of the different sites are engagingly well written, and photographs often show that ancient sites have crumbled faster in the last few decades than in the previous few centuries.

★ **Itai Haviv** *Trekking and Canyoning in the Jordanian Dead Sea Rift* (Desert Breeze Press, Jerusalem). An excellent guide to a range of adventurous and often difficult routes in the mountains on the eastern shore of the Dead Sea. The maps and route descriptions are accurate and reliable, and the background information on culture and the environment is top-notch.

Tony Howard *Treks and Climbs in Wadi Rum, Jordan* (Cicerone, UK). Written by a professional climber with years of experience in Rum, and containing detailed rock-face plans and precise descriptions of equipment-assisted ascents, this is an invaluable full-length guide for dedicated pros. For most general wandering in and around Rum, the excellent booklet *Walks & Scrambles in Wadi Rum* (by Tony Howard and Diana Taylor; al-Kutba, Amman), available only in Jordan, is indispensable. See also Di Taylor and Tony Howard's book on walking in Jordan, listed below.

Rami G. Khouri *The Antiquities of the Jordan Rift Valley* (al-Kutba, Amman). Guide by one of Jordan's leading journalists and writers to every tell and wadi on the east bank from Shuneh ash-Shamaliyyeh to Aqaba, all with minute attention to detail. Authoritative, knowledgeable and specialized.

★ **Rosalyn Maqsood** *Petra: A Travellers' Guide* (Garnet, UK). Vivid and entertaining guide to Petra, featuring detailed walking tours and a comprehensive history, with much careful detail devoted to the religious and spiritual culture of the place.

Glenn Markoe & Glen W. Bowersock *Petra Rediscovered* (Thames & Hudson). Weighty, scholarly tome outlining recent discoveries from the various archeological digs at Petra, along with new research on the Nabateans and their capital.

Michele Piccirillo *Mount Nebo* (Custodia Terra Santa, Jerusalem). An excellent and well-illustrated guide to Siyagha, Mukhayyat and Ayoun Musa, with detailed and learned explication of the mosaics interspersed with biblical passages referring to Nebo, accounts of early pilgrims, maps, plans and photographs. Available in Jordan at the Moses Memorial Church itself.

Sue Rollin and Jane Streetly *Blue Guide Jordan* (Black/Norton). Exhaustive survey of Jordan's archeological sites.

★ **Di Taylor and Tony Howard** *Jordan: Walks, Treks, Caves, Climbs and Canyons* (Cicerone, UK). Published in the US as *Walking in Jordan* (Interlink). Outstanding selection of more than a hundred walking routes across the country. Taylor and Howard have been climbing and trekking in Jordan since 1984 (see above for their books about Wadi Rum), making this an invaluable companion if you're planning to head off the beaten track and explore independently.

Jane Taylor *Petra and the Lost Kingdom of the Nabataeans* (I.B. Tauris). An infectiously enthusiastic evocation of the history of Petra and wider Nabatean society, liberally scattered throughout with the author's beautiful photographs.

Don't be put off by its coffee-table format: this is a work as appealing intellectually as visually, penetrating the myths surrounding the Nabateans with clarity and providing unparalleled perspective for a visit to their capital.

Art, architecture, cuisine and local crafts

The Crafts of Jordan (al-Kutba, Amman). Introductory booklet guide, with good explanation of different techniques for everything from weaving and embroidery to sand bottling.

Madaba: Cultural Heritage (American Center of Oriental Research, Amman). Incredibly detailed account of a complete archeological and architectural survey of all buildings in Madaba, their history, past usage and present ownership. Accounts from early travellers to the town and information gleaned from old-timers build a complete picture of life in Madaba in the 1920s, 1930s and 1940s.

Wijdan Ali *Modern Art in Jordan* (Royal Society of Fine Arts, Amman). The first and only book on the subject, a learned, firsthand history lavishly illustrated with work from 72 Jordanian and Palestinian artists. The author, a member of the Jordanian royal household, is an artist in her own right and a world authority on classical and contemporary Islamic art.

Ammar Khammash *Notes on Village Architecture in Jordan* (Arabesque Int., Amman). The university thesis of this pioneering Jordanian architect (see p.476), but not half as intimidating as that sounds – this is actually light and interesting reading, exploring methods and styles of building and pottery design in small villages throughout the country.

Tess Mallos *The Complete Middle East Cookbook* (Parkway, UK).

Top-quality collection of recipes from Greece to Afghanistan that is perhaps the only book in the world to enthuse over Jordanian cuisine. All your favourite *mezze* are here, plus a recipe for *mensaf*; the photos are as mouth-watering as the text.

Michele Piccirillo *The Mosaics of Jordan* (American Center of Oriental Research, Amman). Eminently learned explication of every mosaic to have been uncovered in Jordan, with large, clear photographs of every one and massive historical detail. A huge and lavish volume, with a JD100 price tag to match.

Claudia Roden *A New Book of Middle Eastern Food* (Penguin). Food as cultural history; perhaps the most absorbing cookbook ever written and invaluable for getting a handle on the importance of food to Arab and Middle Eastern societies.

Peter Vine *Jewels of the Kingdom: The Heritage of Jordan* (Immel, UK). Superb survey of the country, well illustrated if a little dated by now. The history section is outstanding, and the section on Jordan's flora and fauna is the best introduction currently available; there are also very strong overviews both of cultural traditions and of more than twenty reproductions of Jordanian works of modern art. The best single bite at the whole country.

Sami Zubaida and Richard Tapper (eds) *A Taste of Thyme* (I.B. Tauris). Quirky, fascinating look at the centrality of food in Arab and

Islamic culture, delving into such topics as different methods of food preparation, the challenge repre- sented by Western fast food and the complements of colour and smell in the medieval Arab culinary tradition.

Coffee-table books

Cultural Treasures of Jordan (TURAB, Amman). Detailed and learned look at Jordanian crafts and traditional culture, from embroidery and styles of dress to music and coffee-making, illustrated throughout with colour photos.

The Holy Sites of Jordan (TURAB, Amman). Full details, lavishly presented, of all Jordan's holy sites, Muslim and Christian, ranging from sacred trees in the far desert to shabby city-centre shrines, and backed up by quotes and stories from the Quran and the Bible.

★ *Jordan: A Land for all Seasons* (Queen Alia Fund for Social Development, Amman). Stunningly beautiful panoramic images of Jordan's countryside taken by the royal photographer Zohrab Markarian, and embellished with quotes from world literature. Reverentially beautiful, but not at all easy to get hold of – try calling the Queen Alia Fund in Amman (☎06/582 5241).

Old Houses of Jordan (TURAB, Amman). Fascinating stories, and nice photographs, of the country's old emirate-period villas, concentrating on Amman, but with Salt and other places getting a look-in as well. Aside from the beauty of the architecture, and the gorgeous interiors, this also gives interesting background on the highest of Jordan's high society then and now.

Jane Taylor *Petra* (Aurum, UK). Slim, well-written work, with some engaging tales from the place and fine photos. Newly revised in a 2004 edition, available only in Jordan.

Jordan: history, politics and society

Raouf Sa'd Abujaber *Pioneers over Jordan: The Frontier of Settlement in Transjordan 1850–1914* (I.B. Tauris). Interesting but dry account of the first decades of settled life in Transjordan after centuries of nomadism, drawn from firsthand accounts of life on the Abujaber estate south of Amman (now the tourist village of Kan Zaman).

Uriel Dann *King Hussein and the Challenge of Arab Radicalism* (Oxford University Press, UK). Concise and pleasantly readable account of the turbulent years 1955–67, as Hussein scrabbled for a safe foothold in his own kingdom.

Graeme Donnan *The King's Highway* (al-Kutba, Amman). Slim and worthwhile general introduction to the history of Jordan from prehistory to the Arab Revolt, with well-sketched outlines of major events and some illustrations.

Beverley Milton-Edwards and Peter Hinchcliffe *Jordan: A Hashemite Legacy* (Routledge). Trenchant and readable overview of the recent history of the kingdom, including well-informed analysis of major events in King Hussein's reign and the prospects for the country under Abdullah II.

★ **Ghazi bin Muhammad** *The Tribes of Jordan* (TURAB, Amman). Slim but fascinating account of the nature of tribal society at the turn of the twenty-first century by a cousin of the king, former adviser for Tribal Affairs to

King Hussein, giving valuable insight into the Bedouin foundation of Jordanian society.

Queen Noor *Leap of Faith: Memoirs of an Unexpected Life* (Phoenix). A readable and inspiring account of Noor's extraordinary life, from her American origins as Lisa Halaby, to her long-lasting marriage to the late King Hussein.

Philip Robins *A History of Jordan* (Cambridge). An excellent recently published history, incisive and intelligent, which brings the story up to date with the first years of King Abdullah II's reign.

★ **Kamal Salibi** *The Modern History of Jordan* (I.B. Tauris). An outstanding and very readable account of the founding and development of the country from the Arab Revolt to the first Gulf War, by this leading Lebanese historian.

Avi Shlaim *The Politics of Partition: King Abdullah, the Zionists and Palestine 1921–51* (Oxford University Press, UK). Absorbing chronicle, in minute detail, of Abdullah's secret dealing with his neighbours to the west from the founding of the emirate to his assassination, that doesn't

shirk from pointing fingers. Rarefied, but of unique historical interest.

Andrew Shryock *Nationalism and the Genealogical Imagination: Oral History and Textual Authority in Tribal Jordan* (University of California Press, US). Surprisingly accessible anthropological tome examining the Bedouin's transition from oral traditions to written history, and the contradictions embodied in trying to pin tales down that have never needed pinning down before, while simultaneously not letting the mask of honour slip from the tribal visage.

Adaia and Abraham Shumsky *Bridge across the Jordan* (Arcade, US). Engaging tale based on personal memoirs of the friendship that developed between a Jewish master carpenter and Emir Abdullah, when the former was invited to Amman in 1937 to work at the Royal Palace.

Mary C. Wilson *King Abdullah, Britain and the Making of Jordan* (Cambridge University Press, UK). The standard work on Abdullah's role in the establishment of the emirate, a political biography showing the emir searching for a role beyond the confines of Transjordan.

The Middle East and the Arab World

General history

Warwick Ball *Rome in the East* (Routledge). Comprehensive and learned analysis of the social and cultural interaction between the Roman empire and the civilizations of the Near and Middle East, and how the latter had a much greater influence on the former than has generally been acknowledged.

A.A. Duri *The Historical Formation of the Arab Nation* (Croom Helm). Duri is a professor at Jordan University and expert on Islamic history; this is a suitably scholarly and

detailed work on Arab history since Muhammad.

★ **Albert Hourani** *A History of the Arab Peoples* (Faber/Warner). Essential reading – Hourani's wonderfully articulate and highly erudite prose draws threads through centuries of history, yet remains easily readable.

Terry Jones and Alan Ereira *Crusades* (Penguin/BBC Books, UK). If you don't know anything about the Crusades, this is the best place to start. Funny, sharp and only two hundred pages long, it covers everybody and everything, with at least one interesting nugget of digression on every page.

Elie Kedourie *England and the Middle East: The Destruction of the Ottoman Empire 1914–21* (Penguin). Authoritative and unsentimental assessment of British fingers in Middle Eastern pies.

T.E. Lawrence *The Seven Pillars of Wisdom* (Penguin). The old chestnut itself. Certainly not history, it is nonetheless the only firsthand account of the Arab Revolt, and is valuable for that. Otherwise, it's really rather dull, with Lawrence's pompous style showing its age badly, and his day-by-day recounting of battles, discussions, fights and intrigues wearing very thin very fast.

★ **Amin Maalouf** *The Crusades through Arab Eyes* (Al Saqi Books). Fascinating take on all the noble stories of valiant crusading normally touted in the West. Drawing on the extensive chronicles kept by Arab historians at the time, Maalouf paints a picture of a developed and civilized Arab society suddenly having to face the violent onslaught of a bunch of European barbarians fresh out of the Dark Ages. Superbly readable and endlessly intriguing.

F.E. Peters *The Hajj: The Muslim Pilgrimage to Mecca and the Holy Places* (Princeton University Press, US). Engaging look at the history of the hajj from the earliest written records through fascinating early photographs up to recent times.

Steven Runciman *A History of the Crusades* (Penguin). Standard three-volume work by the pre-eminent Western historian of the period, though probably a little stodgy to count as general background.

Contemporary politics and society

★ **Elizabeth Warnock Fernea and Robert A. Fernea** *The Arab World: Forty Years of Change* (Anchor). Intelligent and highly readable accounts of meetings with kings, sheikhs and ordinary people across the region over forty years of academic research – part travelogue, part social commentary, part oral history. The authors, both eminent anthropologists, give a marvellously human insight into daily life in the Arab world.

Thomas L. Friedman *From Beirut to Jerusalem* (Fontana). Thick memoir from the Pulitzer Prize-winning *New York Times* journalist, subtitled "One Man's Middle Eastern Odyssey". Friedman's description of his work first in Beirut (1979–84), then Jerusalem (1984–88), is human, funny, accessible but ultimately unsatisfying; his knowledge of political causes is profound, but he seems so much the estranged onlooker that little real insight filters through. Nonetheless, his evocation and analysis of the social diversity of Israel is startlingly good.

Fred Halliday *Islam and the Myth of Confrontation* (I.B. Tauris). Trenchant rejection of the prevailing notion among Western commentators that a "clash of civilizations" between Islam and the rest is nigh.

Jochen Hippler and Andrea Lueg (eds) *The Next Threat: Western Perceptions of Islam* (Pluto, UK). The blurb on the back says it all: "Enemy images tell more about those who produce them than about the real other." Fascinating insight into the consequences of Western governments' attitudes towards the Middle East, both for the perceived and, tellingly, the perceiver.

Fatima Mernissi *Islam and Democracy* (Addison-Wesley, US). One of the leading Arab feminists currently writing, and an outspoken voice in sociology and politics in the Arab world, Mernissi dissects why democracy hasn't taken root in the Middle East. Far from dry analysis, though, her writing – although translated – is engaging and empathetic. A compelling overview of the main issues.

★ **Margaret K. (Omar) Nydell** *Understanding Arabs: A Guide for Westerners* (Intercultural Press, US). Fascinating and extremely worthwhile cross-cultural handbook that gives a clear, objective presentation of Arab values, beliefs and perceptions in a number of different fields, contrasting them with those of Westerners and shedding rare light on the motivations and meanings that lie beneath the surface of Arab societies.

James Peters *The Arab World Handbook* (Stacey, UK). Well-informed digest of the principles of Arabic language, social etiquette and business methods for long-stay tourists, expats and business people.

Edward Said *Covering Islam* (Vintage). Shrewd investigation into how the Western media portray Islam, and where they got their ideas from about Islam being repressive and extreme.

★ **Edward Said** *Orientalism* (Penguin). Seminal study of Western attitudes towards the Arab and Islamic worlds that is both erudite and fluent. Said expertly picks apart preconception after preconception, taking Western ideas about the Arab East back to their foundations and exposing a tangle of shabby roots; not simple to read, but endlessly rewarding.

Avi Shlaim *War and Peace in the Middle East* (Penguin). Superb concise modern history of the region in 150 pages, concentrating on the period 1948–95. The perspective Shlaim brings to picking apart the clichés and rhetoric in order to get down to the plain sequence of events, and the plain motivations that led to them, is refreshing and illuminating.

Women's issues

Margot Badran and Miriam Cooke (eds) *Opening the Gates* (Virago, UK). Excellent one-stop anthology of Arab feminist writing over the last century.

Geraldine Brooks *Nine Parts of Desire: The Hidden World of Islamic Women* (Penguin). Hack dons a chador for a romp through the "closed" world of Middle Eastern women, on the way bumping into several notable figures, Queen Noor of Jordan among them. The interesting social criticism and details of a solo woman's journey, all catalogued with a journalistic eye, can't quite dispel the air of tabloidery.

★ **Elizabeth Fernea** *Middle Eastern Muslim Women Speak* (University of Texas Press, US).

Collection of biographical and autobiographical writings demonstrating a commitment to what the title says, and managing to come up with masterly social and cultural history. One of the stories is from a woman in a Bani Hassan Bedouin family settled in Amman.

★ **Judy Mabro** *Veiled Half-Truths: Western Travellers' Perceptions of Middle Eastern Women* (I.B. Tauris). Fascinating analysis of orientalist writings from the eighteenth and nineteenth centuries, examining the ways in which visiting Westerners portrayed Middle Eastern women – mostly in appallingly demeaning ways – and drawing lines towards more recent portrayals. Mabro's introduction to the subject is worth the cover price alone.

Fatima Mernissi *The Veil and the Male Elite* (Addison-Wesley, US). Convincing, lucid argument that the Quran and Muhammad himself stipulated direct, participatory equality between the sexes. Mernissi's *Beyond the Veil* (Al Saqi Books) – surveying Islamic attitudes towards female sexuality – is, if anything, even more compelling.

Palestinian politics and society

Laurie A. Brand *Palestinians in the Arab World* (Columbia University Press, US). Unique political history of the Palestinians in Jordan (and elsewhere in the diaspora) after 1948 as they built social and political institutions that later underpinned the drive towards statehood. Minutely detailed, and of highbrow appeal only, but no less interesting for it.

★ **Dick Doughty and Mohammed El Aydi** *Gaza: Legacy of Occupation* (Kumarian, US). Articulate and accessible account of three months spent living among Palestinian families in the Gaza Strip in 1993 by an American photojournalist; narrated with refreshing humanity and the clarity of a photographer's eye – invaluable for its insight into the nature of Palestinian society.

★ **Joe Sacco** *Palestine* (Fantagraphics). Extraordinary work from a pioneer of "graphic journalism", digging behind the media myths surrounding Palestinian society and culture to show the reality of life on the West Bank and in Gaza – but in "comic" picture-book form, drawn by hand with speech bubbles. Sounds trite, but is in fact wellinformed, accessible and startlingly effective. Two books (*A Nation Occupied* and *In the Gaza Strip*) have been reprinted in one volume with a new introduction by Edward Said.

Edward Said *The Politics of Dispossession* (Vintage). Just one of Said's many books on Palestine, all of them unrivalled in the quality of their research and lucidity of presentation. This one is more accessible than most, a collection of his political essays charting the Palestinians' struggle for self-determination from 1969 to 1994.

Graham Usher *Dispatches from Palestine* (Pluto). High-quality journalistic essays from a renowned commentator on Middle Eastern affairs, charting the rise and fall of the Oslo peace process.

Reference

Dilip Hiro *Dictionary of the Middle East* (Macmillan/St Martin's). Knowledgeable and generally impartial outlines of everything and everybody to do with the region, from "aal" to "Zoroastrianism".

Trevor Mostyn and Albert Hourani (eds) *The Cambridge Encyclopedia of the Middle East and North Africa* (Cambridge University Press). Weighty tome delving into every aspect of society, culture and politics in the region. Don't go looking for up-to-date material – the book was published in 1988 – but extensive sections on Islam and modern Islamic thinkers; Christians and Jews under Islam; Arabic, Persian, Turkish and Hebrew literature; Islamic art and architecture; and even Islamic garden design make for excellent library browsing.

Peter Sluglett and Marion Farouk-Sluglett (eds) *The Times Guide to the Middle East* (Times Books, UK). Admirably succinct and informed political surveys country by country, putting all recent events into a nutshell, but never neglecting context.

Islam

★ **Karen Armstrong** *The Battle for God* (HarperCollins/Ballantine). Sympathetic investigation of fundamentalism in Judaism, Christianity and Islam by this leading theologian, explaining crisply and authoritatively the roots, motivations and mindset of religious extremism. Her other works, all similarly brilliant, include *A History of God, A History of Jerusalem* and *Islam: A Short History*.

John L. Esposito *Islam: The Straight Path* (Oxford University Press). The best-written and most intelligent handbook to what Islam means, where it came from and where it seems to be going.

Majid Fakhry (trans.) *The Quran: A Modern English Version* (Garnet, UK). One of the most accessible of the many translations of the Quran. The ubiquitous Penguin version, translated by N.J. Dawood, is also good, but lacks some clarity.

Haifaa A. Jawad *The Rights of Women in Islam* (Macmillan/St Martin's). Slim but forceful debunking of supposed Islamic sanctioning of the repression of women. Close analysis of both the Quran and *sunna* shatters many myths.

Ruqaiyyah Maqsood *Teach Yourself Islam* (Hodder & Stoughton). The fundamentals of the religion presented in an admirably clear and accurate way, everything from pilgrimage and dietary laws to Green Islam and women's rights.

★ **Maxime Rodinson** *Muhammad* (Penguin). Fascinating and superbly researched secular account of the life and works of the Prophet, exploding many myths and giving Islam the kind of intelligible, human face it lacks in much Western writing. Recently removed from the curriculum of the American University in Cairo under direct pressure from the highest authorities of Sunni Islam, who tagged it blasphemous. Unmissable and unputdownable.

Faruq Sherif *A Guide to the Contents of the Quran* (Garnet, UK). Remarkably clear and sensible compendium of themes in the holy book, designed for novices to get a handle on what the Quran actually says.

Language

Language

Arabic 507

Useful words and phrases 508

A food and drink glossary 512

Glossary 515

Arabic

Many people in Jordan are fluent in English, and many more have at least some grasp of the basics. However, plain communication isn't necessarily the only consideration. Jordanian culture is deeply rooted in the verbal complexities of the **Arabic** language (see also p.88 on "Behaviour and attitudes"), and being able to exchange pleasantries in Arabic, or offer the appropriate response to a greeting, will endear you to people more than anything else. The most halting *"assalaamu alaykoom"* is likely to provoke beams of joy and cries of "You speak Arabic better than I do!"

Arabic is phenomenally hard for an English-speaker to learn. There are virtually no familiar points of contact between the two languages: the script is written in cursive from right to left; there's a host of often guttural sounds which don't appear in English and which take much vocal contortion to master; and the grammar, founded on utterly different principles from English, is proclaimed as one of the most pedantic in the world. It's said that, starting from scratch, Arabic can take seven times as long to master as French.

Briefly, the three forms of Arabic are:

• **Classical** – the language of the Quran, with many words and forms which are now obsolete.

• **Modern Standard** (*fuss-ha*) – the written language of books and newspapers, and the Arabic spoken in news broadcasts and on formal occasions. Identical throughout the Arab world and understandable from Morocco to Oman. Although most people can read *fuss-ha*, few ordinary people are completely fluent in it.

• **Colloquial** (*aamayya*) – umbrella term for the many dialects of spoken Arabic. In Jordan, as in all other Arabic-speaking countries, the colloquial language has no proper written form (although dialogue in plays and novels is sometimes transcribed from *aamayya*). Pronunciation varies not only from country to country but district to district, and people from Irbid may have difficulty understanding an Aqaba accent. Furthermore, the vocabulary and verb forms of Jordanian Arabic can be markedly different from the related Palestinian, Syrian and Iraqi dialects. Further afield, Algerian Arabic is about as incomprehensible to Jordanian-speakers as it is to English-speakers. If there is a lingua franca, it's Egyptian Arabic, radically different from other dialects but instantly understandable throughout the Arab world because of the prevalence of movies and TV soap operas emanating from Cairo.

There are no **phrasebooks** dedicated to Jordanian or Levantine Arabic, but as a handy second-best *The Rough Guide to Egyptian Arabic* covers essential expressions in Arabic script with phonetic equivalents, as well as dipping into grammar and providing a fuller vocabulary in dictionary format (English–Arabic and Arabic–English). Of **teach-yourself courses**, *Colloquial Arabic (Levantine)* by Leslie J. McLoughlin (Routledge; book and cassette) is almost the only one to concentrate specifically on the spoken dialect of Jordan. Well presented, manageable and very helpful, it needs two or three months of study end-to-end. *Nasr's Pocket English–Colloquial Arabic Dictionary* (Librarie du Liban, Beirut) is an indispensable little **dictionary** that gives everything only in phonetic transliteration from Levantine dialect. However, it's not at all easy to find, either in Jordan or internationally. The clearest introduction to writing and **reading Arabic script** is *The Arabic Alphabet* by Nicholas Awde and Putros Samano (Al Saqi Books/Lyle Stuart); with everything explained simply and carefully from first principles, this slim volume is invaluable for getting a handle on how the language works.

Pronunciation

Throughout this book, Arabic has been transliterated using a common-sense what-you-see-is-what-you-say system (see the introduction). However, Arabic vowel-sounds in particular often cannot be rendered accurately in English letters, and stress patterns are a minefield – both really need to be mimicked. Where two consonants fall together, pronounce them both: *hammam* means "bathroom", but *hamam* means "pigeon". The following are four of the most difficult common sounds:

kh represents the throaty rasp at the end of the Scottish "loch".

gh is the same sound as *kh*, but voiced: it sounds like the gargled French "r".

q represents a very guttural *k* sound made far back in the throat; in some Palestinian accents this becomes an unsounded glottal stop, while in Bedouin areas, many people change it into a straightforward hard *g* sound, converting "Aqaba" into "Agaba".

aa is especially tricky: constrict your throat muscles tightly like you're about to retch, open your mouth wide and make a strangulated "aaah" sound. Ridiculous as it feels, this is about as close as an English-speaker can get, and won't make Jordanians laugh. To keep things simple, the sound hasn't always been transliterated (it stands at the beginning of "Amman", for instance).

In this book, *ay* has been written where the Arabic rhymes roughly with "say", except where common usage dictates otherwise. Arabic *f* and *s* are always soft, and *r* is heavily trilled. Generally pronounce an *h* sound: *ahlan* (welcome) features a clear and definite exhalation of breath, as does *mneeh* (happy). The subtleties between the two different kinds of *s*, *t*, *d*, *h* and *th* are too rarefied to get into here. However, it's useful to know that the definite article *al* is elided into certain letters, known as "sun" letters: broadly *t*, *th*, *d*, *r*, *z*, *s*, *sh* and *n*. Thus *al-salaam* is spoken as *as-salaam*. All the rest are "moon" letters, and *al* remains unchanged in front of them.

Useful words and phrases

Where the form of a word or phrase differs depending on whether the speaker is male or female, we've shown this with (m) and (f): to say "I'm sorry", a man says "*mitaasef*", a woman "*mitaasfeh*". Where the form differs depending on who you're speaking to, we've shown the two separated by a slash, with the form for addressing a man first, thus: "*allah yaafeek/ yaafeeki* (to a woman)". Note also that all words and phrases ending *-ak* are for addressing a man; if you're addressing a woman, substitute *-ik*.

Greetings are often said in long strings, barely waiting for a response, while pumping your interlocutor's hand, and – if you're the same sex – looking him/her in the eyes. Old friends might also indulge in a complex ritual of double and triple kisses on both cheeks, but as a foreigner you won't be roped into this.

Greetings

assalaamu alaykoom	peace be upon you (all-purpose greeting in any situation, formal or informal)
sabahl-khayr	good morning (literally, "morning of abundance")
masa il-khayr	good afternoon/ evening
shoo akhbarak?	what's your news?
keefak?	how are you?
keef halak? (also keef il-hal?)	how's your status?
keef sahtak?	how's your health?
keef shughulak?	how's your work?
keef al-awlad?	how are the kids?
keef hal ahlak?	how's the family?
al-afyeh	wellbeing/good health
gawak	your strength (only in rural dialects)
shlawnak	what's your colour? (ie "how are you?"; only in rural dialects)
marhaba	hello (said by one already settled to someone arriving from outside)
ahlan	welcome (generally formal)
salaam	hi
tisbah (tisbahi to a woman) ala-khayr	good night
ma assalaameh	goodbye (literally, "go with peace")

Responses

wa alaykoom assalaam	and upon you be peace (the response to assalaamu alaykoom)
ahlan feek or beek (ahlan feeki or beeki to a woman)	it's you who are welcome (the response to ahlan)
marhabtayn or ahlayn	two hellos/welcomes [back to you]; responses to marhaba
al-hamdulillah	thank God (all-purpose response to any of the variations on "how are you?"; covers a range of moods from "everything's great!" to "can't complain" or even "not so good really")
hala	no translation; simply an acknowledgment of having been greeted
mneeh (m)/ mneeha (f) maleeh (m)/ maleeha (f)	I'm well I'm well; spoken mostly in rural dialects
(kulshee) kwayyis (m)/kwayyseh (f)	(everything's) good
(kulshee) tamam	(everything's) perfect
tayyib (m)/taybeh (f)	I'm doing fine
maashi il-hal	I'm OK
allah yaafeek /yaafeeki (to a woman)	May God give you health
sabahn-noor	morning of light (response to sabahl-khayr)
masa en-noor	afternoon/evening of light (response to masa il-khayr)
wa inta/inti (to a woman) min ahlo	the response to tisbah /tisbahi ala-khayr
allah ysalmak	God keep you safe (the response to ma assalaameh)

Basic terms

naam	yes
leh	no
maashi	OK
shukran	thank you
afwan	you're welcome
minfadlak	please
afwan; or lao samaht (samahti to a woman); both are used to attract someone's attention; *afwan* is also a casual apology (eg if you bump into someone)	excuse me
mitaasef (m) /mitaasfeh (f)	I'm sorry
insha'allah	hopefully, God willing
aysh ismak?	what's your name?
ismi…	my name is…
btihki ingleezee /faransi?	do you speak English/French?
ana biritanee/irlandee	I'm British/Irish
amerkanee	American
canadee	Canadian
ostraalee	Australian
noozeelandee	New Zealand
(if you're a woman, add -yyeh to the above)	
mabahki/mabafham arabee	I don't speak/ understand Arabic
ana bafham shwayyet arabee	I understand a little Arabic
ana mish fahem (m) /fahmeh (f)	I don't understand
shoo manato bil ingleezee?	what's the meaning of that in English?
mumkin, tooktoobliyaha lao samaht?	could you write it for me, please?
maalesh	never mind/forget it/it's OK/don't worry
mafee mushkelah	no problem
mittel ma biddak	as you like
ana khamseh wa- ashreen senneh	I'm 25 years old
ana (mish) mitjowez (m)/mitjowzeh (f)	I'm (not) married

rah nitjowez essenneh al-jay	we're getting married next year
mabrook!	congratulations!
allah ybarrak feek (feeki to a woman); the response to *mabrook*, but also used widely to acknowledge someone's kindness to you	God bless you
maandi awlad	I have no children
aandi walad/ waladayn /thalaath awlad	I have 1/2/3 children
yalla	let's go
ma dakhalak	it's none of your business
eem eedak	get your hands off me
utruknee le-halee	leave me alone
rooh	go away
mabaaraf	I don't know
mabagdar (aamalo)	I can't (do that)
shwayy-shwayy	slowly
bsooraa	quickly
hela	immediately
khalas	enough/finished /stop it
mish mumkin	it's impossible
ana taaban (m) /taabaneh (f)	I'm tired
ana mareed (m) /mareedeh (f)	I'm unwell
khuthni ala al-doktoor	get me to a doctor

Directions and travel

shmal/ymeen /dooghri	left/right/straight on
gareeb/baeed	near/far
hawn/hunak	here/there
wayn…	where is…
funduq Petra?	the Hotel Petra?
al-mujemma al-bussat?	the bus station?
al-mahattat al- sikkat al-hadeed?	the train station?
agrab mawqaf lal-servees?	the nearest serveece stop?

maktab al-bareed?	the post office?
makhfar al-shurtah?	the police station
al-bank?	the bank?
imta bitrik awwal /akher bus lal Amman?	when does the first /last bus leave for Amman?
hadal-bus birooh ala Jerash?	does this bus go to Jerash?

Banks, shops and hotels

masari	money or cash
maftooh/msekker	open/closed
imta rah yiftah?	when will it be open?
biddi asruf…	I want to change…
dollarat	dollars
masari ingleeziyyeh	British pounds
shikaat siyahiyyeh	traveller's cheques
kam dinaar rah aakhoud?	how many JDs will I get?
fee comishon?	is there a commission?
andak Jordan Times?	do you have the Jordan Times?
biddi…	I want…
ishi thaani	something else
ahsan min hada	better than this
arkhas/zay hada	cheaper/like this
kbir/zgheer	a big/small one
akbar/azghar	a bigger/smaller one
gadaysh hada?	how much is it?
mabiddi hada	I don't want this
ktir ghali	it's too expensive
andak ghurfeh fadiyyeh?	do you have a room free?
le-shakhs wahad	for one person
le-shakhsayn	for two people
le-thalaath ashkhas	for three people
bagdar ashouf al-ghurfeh?	can I see the room?
fee…	is there…
balconeh?	a balcony?
takht mizwej?	a double bed?
my sukhneh?	hot water?
hammam bil-ghurfeh?	an en-suite bathroom?
marwaha?	a fan?
hada mish nutheef, ferjeenee wahad thaani	it's not clean, show me another one

| fee hammam hawn? | is there a toilet here? |
| gadaysh al-layleh? | how much for one night? |

Numbers

Note that, unlike words, numbers are written from left to right.

sifr	٠	zero
wahad	١	one
ithnayn	٢	two
thalaatheh	٣	three
arbaa	٤	four
khamseh	٥	five
sitteh	٦	six
sabaa	٧	seven
thamanyeh	٨	eight
tisaa	٩	nine
ashra	١٠	ten
hidash	١١	eleven
ithnash	١٢	twelve
thalaatash	١٣	thirteen
arbatash	١٤	fourteen
khamstash	١٥	fifteen
sittash	١٦	sixteen
sabatash	١٧	seventeen
thamantash	١٨	eighteen
tisatash	١٩	nineteen
ashreen	٢٠	twenty
wahad wa-ashreen	٢١	twenty-one
thalatheen	٣٠	thirty
arbaeen	٤٠	forty
khamseen	٥٠	fifty
sitteen	٦٠	sixty
sabaeen	٧٠	seventy
thamaneen	٨٠	eighty
tisaeen	٩٠	ninety
miyyeh	١٠٠	a hundred
miyyeh wa-wahad	١٠١	a hundred and one
miyyeh wa-sitteh wa-ashreen	١٢٦	126
meetayn	٢٠٠	two hundred
thalaath miyyeh	٣٠٠	three hundred
elf	١٠٠٠	one thousand
elfayn	٢٠٠٠	two thousand
arbaat alaaf wa-khamesmiyyeh wa-arbaa wa-tisaeen	٤٥٩٤	4594

milyon	million
rube	one quarter
nuss	one half

Telling the time

gadaysh se'aa?	what time is it?
se'aa ashra	it's ten o'clock
ashra wa-khamseh	10.05
ashra wa-ashra	10.10
ashra wa-rube	10.15
ashra wa-toolt	10.20
ashra wa-nuss illa-khamseh	10.25
ashra wa-nuss	10.30
ashra wa-nuss wa-khamseh	10.35
hidash illa-toolt	10.40
hidash illa-rube	10.45
hidash illa-ashra	10.50
hidash illa-khamseh	10.55

Days and months

yom	day
layl	night
isbooa	week
shahr	month
senneh	year

imbaarih	yesterday
al-yom	today
bukra	tomorrow
essubbeh	this morning
baad edduhr	this afternoon
al-messa	this evening
al-layleh	tonight
bukra bil-layl	tomorrow night
essebt	Saturday
al-ahad	Sunday
al-ithnayn	Monday
al-thalaatha	Tuesday
al-arbaa	Wednesday
al-khamees	Thursday
al-juma	Friday
kanoon thaani	January
shbaat	February
athaar	March
nisaan	April
ayyar	May
huzayran	June
tamooz	July
aab	August
aylool	September
tishreen awwal	October
tishreen thaani	November
kanoon awwal	December

A food and drink glossary

Basic stomach-fillers

khubez	flat, round bread
falafel	spiced chickpea mixture, deep-fried; stuffed into *khubez* with salad to make a *sandweesh* (sandwich)
shwarma	shreds of lamb or chicken in *khubez*
fuul	spiced fava beans, mashed with lemon juice, olive oil and chopped chillis; side dishes include raw onion (*basal*), fresh mint and/or pickled vegetables
fuul masri	blander Egyptian-style *fuul*; without chilli but served with a dollop of *tahini* instead
hummus	dip of chickpeas mashed with *tahini*, lemon juice, garlic and olive oil
manaqeesh zaatar	small round of dough sprinkled with olive oil and *zaatar* (a mixture of dried

	thyme, marjoram, salt and sesame seeds), and baked until crispy
batatas	potatoes; by extension, French fries
tahini	sesame-seed paste
rooz	rice

Restaurant appetizers (*mezze*)

shorba(t addas)	(lentil) soup
s'laata	salad; chopped tomato and cucumber, invariably without lettuce
tabbouleh	parsley and tomato salad with cracked wheat
fattoush	Lebanese dish: salad with chopped parsley and squares of crispy fried bread
baba ghanouj	dip made from roasted mashed aubergine
moutabbel	*baba ghanouj* with added *tahini*
labneh	thick set yoghurt, similar to sour cream
shanklish	goat's cheese chopped with onion and tomato
warag aynab	stuffed vine leaves
kibbeh	ovals of spiced minced meat and cracked wheat
sujuk	fried spicy mini-sausages
mahshi	"stuffed"; by extension, a selection of stuffed vegetables such as peppers and aubergines
makdoos	pickled aubergine

The main course

mensaf	boiled lamb or mutton on rice with a tangy yoghurt-based sauce, pine nuts and spices
musakhan	chicken steamed with onions, sumac (a lemon-flavoured berry) and pine nuts, served on flat bread
magloobeh	literally "upside-down": Palestinian dish of chicken on steamed rice with strips of grilled vegetables
(nuss) farooj	(half-)chicken; usually spit-roasted
kebab	pieces of lamb or chicken chargrilled on a skewer with onions and tomatoes
kebab halaby	Syrian speciality: spiced minced meat char-grilled like a kebab
shish tawook	marinated chicken kebab
fatteh	spiced meat or chicken baked with rice, hummus, pine nuts, yoghurt or bread
mulukhayyeh	lamb or chicken stewed with a spinach-like vegetable
fasooliyeh	bean stew, often with chunks of meat or in a meat broth
mujeddrah	Palestinian dish of lentils, rice and onions
Daoud Pasha	meatballs stewed with onions and tomatoes
lahmeh	meat
djaj	chicken-meat
kharouf	mutton or lamb
khanzir	pork
kibdeh	liver
kelaawy	kidney
samak	fish
khoodar	vegetables
zayt	oil
meleh	salt
filfil	pepper

Arabic sweets (*halawiyyat*)

k'naffy	shredded-wheat squares filled with goat's cheese, smothered in hot honey syrup
baglawa	layered flaky pastry with nuts
gatayyif	pancakes filled with nuts and drenched in syrup
ftayer	triangles of flaky pastry with different fillings
hareeseh	syrupy almond and semolina cake
muhallabiyyeh	rose-scented almond cream pudding
Umm Ali	slice of corn cake soaked in milk, sugar, raisins, coconut and cinnamon, served hot
maamoul	rose-scented biscuits filled with dates or nuts
barazik	thin sesame biscuits
awameh	syrup-coated deep-fried balls of dough
asabya zaynab	syrupy figs
mushabbak	crunchy honey-coated pastries
karabeedj halaby	sugar-coated curlies
rooz b'laban	rice pudding with yoghurt
halwa	dense, flaky sweet made from sesame

Drinks (*mashroobat*) and fruits (*fawakeh*)

my	water
gahweh	coffee
shy	tea
naana/yansoon	mint/fennel (tea)
zaatar/helbeh	thyme/fenugreek (tea)
marrameeya	sage (tea)
babbohnidj	camomile (tea)
sahleb	thick, sweet, milky winter drink
haleeb	milk
tamarhindi	tamarind drink
kharroub	carob drink
soos	liquorice-root drink
luz	sweet almond-milk
aseer/koktayl	juice/juice cocktail
mooz	banana
boordan	orange
tfah	apple
njas	pear
grayfroot	grapefruit
jezer	carrot
manga	mango
jowaffah	guava
dourrag	peach
limoon	lemon (also drink)
aynab	grapes
karaz	cherries
rummaan	pomegranate
mishmish	apricot
teen	fig
battikh	watermelon
shimmam	melon
balah	crunchy unripe dates
tamar	soft ripe dates

Nuts, seeds and simple provisions

foustoug	peanuts
foustoug halaby	pistachios
boondoog	hazelnuts
luz	almonds
kashoo	cashews
bizr	dry-roasted seeds
zbeeb	raisins
bayd	eggs
zaytoon	olives
jibneh	cheese
laban	yoghurt
zabadi	high-fat yoghurt with cream
zibdeh	butter
asal	honey
marrabeh	jam

Glossary

The first list is a glossary of Arabic terms in common usage in Jordan. Common alternative spellings, as well as singulars and plurals, are given where appropriate in brackets. Afterwards is a list of English terms used in the guide to describe features of architecture.

Arabic terms

Abu Literally "Father of" used as a familiar term of respect in conjunction with the name of the man's eldest son, as in "Abu Muhammad".

Ain (*ayn, ein*) Spring.

Argileh (*arjileh, narjileh, nargileh*) Floor-standing water-pipe designed to let the smoke from the tobacco — which is kept smouldering by small coals — cool before being inhaled through a chamber of water. The sound of the smoke bubbling through the water gives the pipe its common name in Jordan of "hubbly-bubbly".

Bab Gate or door.

Badia Jordan's desert areas.

Bahr Sea.

Balad Nation or city.

Baladi Countryfied, rural.

Balqa (Balka, Balga) The fertile hill-country around Salt, west of Amman.

Bani (*beni*) Tribe.

Bayt (*beit, bait*; pl. *byoot*) House.

Bedouin (also *Bedu*) Generally refers to nomadic or semi-nomadic people who live in desert areas within a tribal social structure. Some Jordanian Bedouin tribes, however, have long been settled in towns and cities and, although taking pride in their Bedouin culture and ancestry, are indistinguishable in dress and lifestyle from urbanized Jordanians.

Bir (*beer*) Well.

Birkeh (*birka, birket*) Reservoir, pool, lake.

Burj Tower.

Daraj Flight of steps.

Darb Path or way — "Darb al-Hajj" is the ancient pilgrimage route from Damascus to Mecca, following the present Desert Highway.

Dayr (*deir*) Literally monastery or convent; by extension, a catch-all term for any ancient ruin of unknown usage.

Diwan Formal architectural space, not necessarily within a house, intended for tribal discussions.

Duwaar Circle (ie traffic intersection).

Fellaheen (*fellahin*; sing. *fellah*) Settled peasant farmers.

Ghor "Sunken land", ie the Jordan Valley.

Hajj (*haj, hadj*; f. *hajjeh*) The holy Muslim pilgrimage to Mecca and Medina; by extension, a title of respect, either for one who has literally made the pilgrimage, or — more commonly — simply for one who is of advancing years and thus deserving of honourable treatment.

Hamad Stony desert pavement.

Hammam (pl. *hammamat*) Turkish steam-bath; bathroom or toilet; or a natural hot spring.

Harra Rocky desert.

Hawran (Hauran) The basalt desert plains around Mafraq.

Imam Prayer leader of a mosque, cleric.

Iwan (*liwan*) Arched reception area at one end of a courtyard in traditional Arab architecture.

Jamia "Place of assembly", ie a large, congregational mosque.

Jawlan Arabic equivalent for the Hebrew Golan.

Jebel (*jabal*; pl. *jibal*) Hill or mountain.

Jellabiyyeh Ankle-length outer robe worn by men.

Jissr Bridge.

Keffiyeh (*quffiyeh, kafiya*, etc) Patterned headscarf worn by men.

Khirbet Ruin.

K'neeseh Church.

Manara Minaret, the tower attached to a mosque, from which the call to prayer sounds.

Masjid "Place of prostration", ie a small, everyday mosque.

Maydan (*midan*) Public square, or traffic intersection.

Mihrab Niche in the wall of a mosque indicating the direction of Mecca, and thus the direction of prayer.

Minbar Pulpit in a mosque, from which the Friday sermon is given.

Muezzin (*mueththin*) The one who gives the call to prayer.

Mujemma "Assembly point", used to describe an open-air bus or service station.

Nahr River.

Qa Topographical depression, pan.

Qal'a (*kalaa*) Fortress, citadel.

Qasr (*kasr*, pl. *qusoor*) Palace, mansion; by extension, castle, fortress or a catch-all term for any ancient ruin of unknown usage.

Qibla The direction in which Mecca lies, and therefore the direction in which Muslims pray.

Qubba Dome; by extension any domed building.

Quran (Koran) The holy book of Islam.

Qusayr (*kuseir*) Diminutive of *qasr*.

Ramadan Holy month in the Muslim calendar.

Riwaq Colonnade.

Sahra General term for desert; can also refer to sandy desert in particular.

Sharia Street or way.

Shari'a Set of laws based on Quranic precepts.

Shebab Literally "youth", but used most commonly where English uses "guys", as a casual term of greeting to peers.

Sheikh (*shaykh*) Tribal leader; consequently, mayor of a town or village.

Souk (*suq*, *souq*) Market or bazaar.

Tariq Way, path or road.

Tell (*tal*, *tall*) Hill; by extension, an artificial mound concealing ancient remains, resulting from the continuous collapse and rebuilding of settlements, one on top of another.

Umm (*um*, *oum*) "Mother of" — used as a term of respect in conjunction with the name of the woman's eldest son, as in "Umm Muhammad".

Wadi Valley or watercourse (also refers to dry or seasonal riverbeds).

Waha Oasis.

Architectural terms

Apse Semicircular recess behind the altar of a church.

Architrave Lintel resting on columns or piers, forming the lowest part of an entablature.

Atrium Open inner courtyard of a Roman villa; also the court in front of a Byzantine church.

Basilica Rectangular, apsed building; the earliest style of church.

Biclinium Room with two benches, often a banqueting hall.

Cardo Colonnaded main street of a Roman city; usually running north–south.

Cella Inner sanctum of a classical temple.

Corbel Projection from the face of a wall supporting a horizontal beam.

Corinthian Order of Classical architecture, identifiable by acanthus-leaf decoration on column capitals.

Cornice The upper part of an entablature; also a moulding running along the top of a wall.

Decumanus Main street of a Roman city; usually running east–west.

Engaged column Column attached to or partly set into a wall.

Entablature Element of Roman architecture positioned between the columns and the pediment; consists of architrave, frieze and cornice.

Frieze Part of an entablature between the architrave and cornice, often decorated with figures.

Glacis Slope below the walls of a castle, designed to be difficult to scale.

Hypocaust Roman heating system allowing hot air to circulate beneath a floor raised on small pillars.

Ionic Order of Classical architecture, identifiable by fluted columns with scrolled capitals.

Loculus Niche designed to hold a single body in a communal or family cave-tomb.

Machicolation A projecting parapet of a castle or fort often above a doorway with holes below through which to pour boiling oil, etc.

Narthex In a church, an area spanning the

width of the building at the end furthest from the altar.

Nave Central part of church, normally flanked by aisles.

Nymphaeum A Roman public fountain dedicated to water nymphs and decorated with statues.

Orchestra In a classical theatre, the semicircular area in front of the stage.

Pediment The shallow triangular gable over a door, window, etc.

Propylaeum Monumental entrance gateway to a temple precinct.

Scaenae frons The wall at the back of a stage in a classical theatre.

Squinch Small arch which spans the right angle formed by two walls, thus supporting a ceiling dome.

Temenos Sacred enclosure of a temple.

Tetrapylon Monumental four-sided structure supported on arches, usually at an important intersection of streets.

Tholos Round section of building surrounded by columns.

Triclinium Roman dining hall, most often with three benches.

Travel
store

Rough Guides travel...

UK & Ireland

Britain
Devon & Cornwall
Dublin DIRECTIONS
Edinburgh DIRECTIONS
England
Ireland
Lake District
London
London DIRECTIONS
London Mini Guide
Scotland
Scottish Highlands &
  Islands
Wales

Europe

Algarve DIRECTIONS
Amsterdam
Amsterdam
  DIRECTIONS
Andalucía
Athens DIRECTIONS
Austria
Baltic States
Barcelona
Barcelona DIRECTIONS
Belgium & Luxembourg
Berlin
Brittany & Normandy
Bruges DIRECTIONS
Brussels
Budapest
Bulgaria
Copenhagen
Corfu
Corsica
Costa Brava
  DIRECTIONS
Crete
Croatia
Cyprus
Czech & Slovak
  Republics
Dodecanese & East
  Aegean
Dordogne & The Lot
Europe
Florence & Siena
Florence DIRECTIONS
France

French Hotels & Restos
Germany
Greece
Greek Islands
Hungary
Ibiza & Formentera
  DIRECTIONS
Iceland
Ionian Islands
Italy
Italian Lakes
Languedoc &
  Roussillon
Lisbon
Lisbon DIRECTIONS
The Loire
Madeira DIRECTIONS
Madrid DIRECTIONS
Mallorca & Menorca
Mallorca DIRECTIONS
Malta & Gozo
  DIRECTIONS
Menorca
Moscow
Netherlands
Norway
Paris
Paris DIRECTIONS
Paris Mini Guide
Poland
Portugal
Prague
Prague DIRECTIONS
Provence & the Côte
  d'Azur
Pyrenees
Romania
Rome
Rome DIRECTIONS
Sardinia
Scandinavia
Sicily
Slovenia
Spain
St Petersburg
Sweden
Switzerland
Tenerife & La Gomera
  DIRECTIONS
Turkey
Tuscany & Umbria

Venice & The Veneto
Venice DIRECTIONS
Vienna

Asia

Bali & Lombok
Bangkok
Beijing
Cambodia
China
Goa
Hong Kong & Macau
India
Indonesia
Japan
Laos
Malaysia, Singapore &
  Brunei
Nepal
The Philippines
Singapore
South India
Southeast Asia
Sri Lanka
Taiwan
Thailand
Thailand's Beaches &
  Islands
Tokyo
Vietnam

Australasia

Australia
Melbourne
New Zealand
Sydney

North America

Alaska
Boston
California
Canada
Chicago
Florida
Grand Canyon
Hawaii
Honolulu
Las Vegas DIRECTIONS
Los Angeles
Maui DIRECTIONS

Miami & South Florida
Montréal
New England
New Orleans
  DIRECTIONS
New York City
New York City
  DIRECTIONS
New York City Mini
  Guide
Orlando & Walt Disney
  World DIRECTIONS
Pacific Northwest
Rocky Mountains
San Francisco
San Francisco
  DIRECTIONS
Seattle
Southwest USA
Toronto
USA
Vancouver
Washington DC
Washington DC
  DIRECTIONS
Yosemite

Caribbean
& Latin America

Antigua & Barbuda
  DIRECTIONS
Argentina
Bahamas
Barbados DIRECTIONS
Belize
Bolivia
Brazil
Cancùn & Cozumel
  DIRECTIONS
Caribbean
Central America
Chile
Costa Rica
Cuba
Dominican Republic
Dominican Republic
  DIRECTIONS
Ecuador
Guatemala
Jamaica

TRAVEL STORE

...music & reference

Mexico
Peru
St Lucia
South America
Trinidad & Tobago
Yúcatan

Africa & Middle East
Cape Town & the
    Garden Route
Egypt
The Gambia
Jordan
Kenya
Marrakesh
    DIRECTIONS
Morocco
South Africa, Lesotho
    & Swaziland
Syria
Tanzania
Tunisia
West Africa
Zanzibar

Travel Theme guides
First-Time Around the
    World
First-Time Asia
First-Time Europe
First-Time Latin
    America
Travel Online
Travel Health
Travel Survival
Walks in London & SE
    England
Women Travel

Maps
Algarve
Amsterdam
Andalucia & Costa
    del Sol
Argentina
Athens
Australia
Baja California
Barcelona
Berlin
Boston

Brittany
Brussels
California
Chicago
Corsica
Costa Rica & Panama
Crete
Croatia
Cuba
Cyprus
Czech Republic
Dominican Republic
Dubai & UAE
Dublin
Egypt
Florence & Siena
Florida
France
Frankfurt
Germany
Greece
Guatemala & Belize
Hong Kong
Iceland
Ireland
Kenya
Lisbon
London
Los Angeles
Madrid
Mallorca
Marrakesh
Mexico
Miami & Key West
Morocco
New England
New York City
New Zealand
Northern Spain
Paris
Peru
Portugal
Prague
Rome
San Francisco
Sicily
South Africa
South India
Sri Lanka
Tenerife
Thailand

Toronto
Trinidad & Tobago
Tuscany
Venice
Washington DC
Yucatán Peninsula

Dictionary Phrasebooks
Croatian
Czech
Dutch
Egyptian Arabic
European Languages
    (Czech, French,
    German, Greek,
    Italian, Portuguese,
    Spanish)
French
German
Greek
Hindi & Urdu
Hungarian
Indonesian
Italian
Japanese
Latin American
    Spanish
Mandarin Chinese
Mexican Spanish
Polish
Portuguese
Russian
Spanish
Swahili
Thai
Turkish
Vietnamese

Music Guides
The Beatles
Bob Dylan
Cult Pop
Classical Music
Elvis
Frank Sinatra
Heavy Metal
Hip-Hop
Jazz
Opera
Reggae

Rock
World Music (2 vols)

Reference Guides
Babies
Books for Teenagers
Children's Books, 0–5
Children's Books, 5–11
Comedy Movies
Conspiracy Theories
Cult Fiction
Cult Football
Cult Movies
Cult TV
The Da Vinci Code
Ethical Shopping
Gangster Movies
Horror Movies
iPods, iTunes & Music
    Online
The Internet
James Bond
Kids' Movies
Lord of the Rings
Macs & OS X
Muhammad Ali
Music Playlists
PCs and Windows
Poker
Pregnancy & Birth
Sci–Fi Movies
Shakespeare
Superheroes

Unexplained
    Phenomena
The Universe
Weather
Website Directory

Football
Arsenal 11s
Celtic 11s
Chelsea 11s
Liverpool 11s
Newcastle 11s
Rangers 11s
Tottenham 11s
Man United 11s

TRAVEL STORE

Rough Guides maps

Rough Guide Maps, printed on waterproof and rip-proof Yupo™ paper, offer an unbeatable combination of practicality, clarity of design and amazing value.

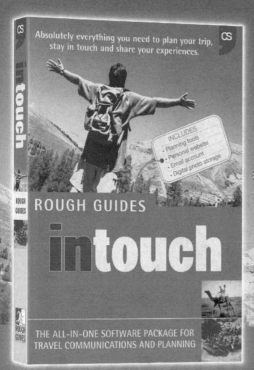

ROUGH GUIDES

not just travel

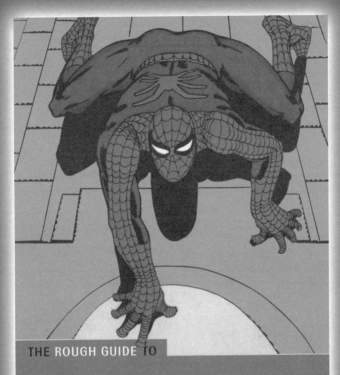

THE ROUGH GUIDE TO

Superheroes

THE COMICS ✱ THE COSTUMES ✱ THE CREATORS ✱ THE CATCHPHRASES

NOTES

NOTES

NOTES

NOTES

TRAVEL STORE

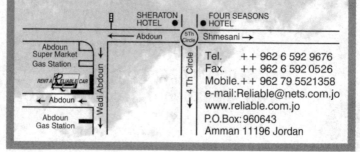

RSCN
Royal Society for the Conservation of Nature
www.rscn.org.jo

The RSCN is an independent voluntary organization devoted to the conservation of Jordan's natural resources. Under the patronage of Her Majesty Queen Noor, the RSCN was established in 1966 under His Majesty the late King Hussein. It is one of the few voluntary organizations in the Middle East with such a public service mandate.

Jordan's nature reserves
Jordan's nature reserves offer visitors a chance to experience the country's most beautiful landscapes, including stunning Dana and Mujib, Ajloun's oak woods, the desert grassland of Shaumari and Azraq's wetlands.

Beauty without crowds
In order to protect the environment within the nature reserves, the number of visitors allowed to enter each day is limited and cars must park outside.

Explore unspoiled landscapes
There are hiking trails for all abilities within the reserves – some are self-guided; others need an RSCN guide.

A sense of adventure
For small groups seeking a challenge, adventure treks can be arranged in the more remote corners of Jordan.

Support conservation
All the money visitors contribute through entrance fees, accommodation charges and buying crafts is used to further the work of the RSCN in protecting the wild places of Jordan.

Help local people
The RSCN has a policy to employ local people wherever possible and to create opportunities for them to earn a decent living income from the nature reserves.

RSCN, PO Box 1215, Amman 11941, Jordan
www.rscn.org.jo

RSCN tourism unit – tel: (+962 6) 461 6523 or 461 6483 or 463 3589, fax 463 3657, email: tourism@rscn.org.jo

Come and visit the RSCN's organic café in our Wild Jordan centre on Othman bin Affan Street, near 1st Circle on Jebel Amman.

AMMAN

JORDAN VALLEY
DEAD SEA RESORT & SPA
Marriott.

PETRA

TRAVEL STORE

small print and

Index

A Rough Guide to Rough Guides

In the summer of 1981, Mark Ellingham, a recent graduate from Bristol University, was travelling round Greece and couldn't find a guidebook that really met his needs. On the one hand there were the student guides, insistent on saving every last cent, and on the other the heavyweight cultural tomes whose authors seemed to have spent more time in a research library than lounging away the afternoon at a taverna or on the beach.

In a bid to avoid getting a job, Mark and a small group of writers set about creating their own guidebook. It was a guide to Greece that aimed to combine a journalistic approach to description with a thoroughly practical approach to travellers' needs – a guide that would incorporate culture, history, and contemporary insights with a critical edge, together with up-to-date, value-for-money listings. Back in London, Mark and the team finished their Rough Guide, as they called it, and talked Routledge into publishing the book.

That first *Rough Guide to Greece*, published in 1982, was a student scheme that became a publishing phenomenon. The immediate success of the book – with numerous reprints and a Thomas Cook Prize shortlisting – spawned a series that rapidly covered dozens of destinations. Rough Guides had a ready market among low-budget backpackers, but soon also acquired a much broader and older readership that relished Rough Guides' wit and inquisitiveness as much as their enthusiastic, critical approach. Everyone wants value for money, but not at any price.

Rough Guides soon began supplementing the "rougher" information about hostels and low-budget listings with the kind of detail on restaurants and quality hotels that independent-minded visitors on any budget might expect, whether on business in New York or trekking in Thailand.

These days the guides – distributed worldwide by the Penguin Group – offer recommendations from shoestring to luxury and cover more than 200 destinations around the globe, including almost every country in the Americas and Europe, more than half of Africa, and most of Asia and Australasia. Our ever-growing team of authors and photographers is spread all over the world, particularly in Europe, the USA and Australia.

In 1994, we published the *Rough Guide to World Music* and *Rough Guide to Classical Music*, and a year later the *Rough Guide to the Internet*. All three books have become benchmark titles in their fields – which encouraged us to expand into other areas of publishing, mainly around popular culture. Rough Guides now publish:

- Travel guides to more than 200 worldwide destinations
- Dictionary phrasebooks for 22 major languages
- History guides ranging from Ireland to Islam
- Maps printed on rip-proof and waterproof Polyart™ paper
- Music guides running the gamut from Opera to Elvis
- Restaurant guides to London, New York and San Francisco
- Reference books on topics as diverse as the Weather and Shakespeare
- Sports guides from Formula 1 to Man Utd
- Pop culture books from *Lord of the Rings* to Cult TV
- World Music CDs in association with World Music Network

Visit **www.roughguides.com** to see our latest publications.

Rough Guide credits

Text editor: Ella O'Donnell
Layout: Umesh Aggarwal
Cartography: Karobi Gogoi
Picture editor: Harriet Mills
Production: Katherine Owers
Proofreader: Karen Parker
Editorial: **London** Kate Berens, Claire
Saunders, Geoff Howard, Ruth Blackmore,
Polly Thomas, Richard Lim, Clifton Wilkinson,
Alison Murchie, Sally Schafer, Karoline
Densley, Andy Turner, Keith Drew, Edward
Aves, Nikki Birrell, Helen Marsden, Joe
Staines, Duncan Clark, Peter Buckley,
Matthew Milton; **New York** Andrew
Rosenberg, Richard Koss, Steven Horak,
AnneLise Sorensen, Amy Hegarty,
Hunter Slaton
Design & Pictures: **London** Simon Bracken,
Dan May, Diana Jarvis, Mark Thomas, Jj Luck,
Chloë Roberts; **Delhi** Madhulita Mohapatra,
Ajay Verma, Jessica Subramanian, Amit Verma,
Ankur Guha
Production: Julia Bovis, Sophie Hewat

Cartography: **London** Maxine Repath, Ed
Wright, Katie Lloyd-Jones; **Delhi** Manish
Chandra, Rajesh Chhibber, Jai Prakash
Mishra, Ashutosh Bharti, Rajesh Mishra,
Jasbir Sandhu, Animesh Pathak
Online: **New York** Jennifer Gold, Suzanne
Welles, Kristin Mingrone; **Delhi** Manik Chauhan,
Narender Kumar, Shekhar Jha, Rakesh Kumar,
Lalit Sharma, Chhandita Chakravarty
Marketing & Publicity: **London** Richard
Trillo, Niki Hanmer, David Wearn, Demelza
Dallow, Louise Maher; **New York** Geoff
Colquitt, Megan Kennedy, Katy Ball;
Delhi Reem Khokhar
Custom publishing and foreign rights:
Philippa Hopkins
Manager India: Punita Singh
Series editor: Mark Ellingham
Reference Director: Andrew Lockett
PA to Managing and Publishing Directors:
Megan McIntyre
Publishing Director: Martin Dunford
Managing Director: Kevin Fitzgerald

Publishing information

This third edition published January 2006 by
Rough Guides Ltd,
80 Strand, London WC2R 0RL
345 Hudson St, 4th Floor,
New York, NY 10014, USA
14 Local Shopping Centre, Panchsheel Park,
New Delhi 110017, India.
Distributed by the Penguin Group
Penguin Books Ltd,
80 Strand, London WC2R 0RL
Penguin Putnam, Inc.,
375 Hudson St, NY 10014, USA
Penguin Group (Australia)
250 Camberwell Road, Camberwell,
Victoria 3124, Australia
Penguin Books Canada Ltd,
10 Alcorn Avenue, Toronto, ON,
M4V 1E4 Canada
Penguin Group (New Zealand),
Cnr Rosedale and Airborne Roads,
Albany, Auckland, New Zealand

Typeset in Bembo and Helvetica to an original
design by Henry Iles.
Printed and bound in China
© Matthew Teller, 2006

552pp includes index
A catalogue record for this book is available from
the British Library.
ISBN 978-1-84353-458-7

The publishers and authors have done their best
to ensure the accuracy and currency of all the
information in **The Rough Guide to Jordan**,
however, they can accept no responsibility for
any loss, injury, or inconvenience sustained by
any traveller as a result of information or advice
contained in the guide.

5   7   9   8   6

Help us update

We've gone to a lot of effort to ensure that
the third edition of **The Rough Guide to
Jordan** is accurate and up to date. However,
things change – places get "discovered",
opening hours are notoriously fickle,
restaurants and rooms raise prices or lower
standards. If you feel we've got it wrong or
left something out, we'd like to know, and if
you can remember the address, the price, the
time, the phone number, so much the better.

We'll credit all contributions, and send a
copy of the next edition (or any other Rough

Guide if you prefer) for the best letters.
Everyone who writes to us and isn't already
a subscriber will receive a copy of our full-
colour thrice-yearly newsletter. Please mark
letters: "Rough Guide Jordan update" and
send to: Rough Guides, 80 Strand, London
WC2R 0RL, or Rough Guides, 4th Floor, 345
Hudson St, New York, NY 10014. Or send an
email to **mail@roughguides.com**.

Have your questions answered and tell
others about your trip at
www.roughguides.atinfopop.com.

Acknowledgments

The **author** would like to thank all those individuals throughout Jordan who were so willing to help, guide or offer support with such warmth and generosity. In particular: HE Mr Timoor Daghistani, Ambassador of the Hashemite Kingdom of Jordan in London; Mr Marwan Khoury, Ms Lana Hamarneh and colleagues, formerly of the Jordan Tourism Board, Amman; David Symes of JTB London; Mr Habeeb Habash and Mr Ghassan Nasser of ASEZA; Mr Ahmad Jabri and Mr Mahmoud Bdour of ASEZA's Wadi Rum team; Chris Johnson, Ghada al-Sous, Ahmad Zu'bi and colleagues at the RSCN; Ms Lama Nimr and colleagues at Marriott; Mr Mohammed Hallak and Ms Rohaifa Hallak of Reliable Rent-a-Car in Amman; Mr Najati al-Shakhshir of Hertz; Ms Shatha al-Qasem and Ms Jansate Ibrahim of Philadelphia Book Gallery, Amman, for all their hard work; Mr Mazen Kutob and Ms Lina Kutob of the University Bookshop, Amman, and family, for their generosity and kindness; Mr Charl al-Twal of the Mariam in Madaba; Kamel Jayusi, especially for unbending support most of the way down the Wadi Zarqa Ma'in; Khaled Odeh; Tony Durrant, Ros Hinchliffe and gang; Mr Mzied Atieg at Wadi Rum; Mr Tahseen and Ms Susan Shinaco of Bait Ali, Shakriyyeh; Mr William Sawalha and Ms Gill Balchin of the Alcazar Hotel, Aqaba; Kris Yeaworth at the Aqaba Gateway; Mr Samih Janakat and colleagues of the Royal Aero Sports Club, Aqaba; Mr Raed Abu Hayyaneh, Mr Abdelrazzaq Khwaldeh, Mr Ali and colleagues at the Dana Guesthouse; Mr Jihad Amarat of the Petra Visitor Centre; Mr Talal Falahat of the Petra Regional Authority; Mr Basel Ahmad for helping get me into the game; Mr Mehrdad Masoudi and colleague of Futbol Mundial; Mr Beder al-Adwan at the Baptism Site; Mr Ismael Helalat of La Beduina Tours, Wadi Musa; Ms Wendy Botham and Mr Eid Nawafleh of Petra Moon Tours, Wadi Musa; Mr Mu'anid al-Zuwaydeh and Mr Saleh al-Nu'imat at Rum; Mr Salem and Mr Hassan Redwan, Aqaba; Mr Stellan Lind, Mr Jeff Cullis and Mr Fawaz Zoubi of RACE, Jerash; Mr Salem Aoead and family at Mudawwara; and many more, too numerous to name.

At **Rough Guides**, grateful thanks are due to my hard-working, patient and skilful editor Ella O'Donnell.

Thanks are also due to Tony Howard and Di Taylor, Dr Fadia Faqir, Janset Berkok Shami, Rana Husseini, Ian Andrews, Jaap de Boer, Anna Hohler, Michelle Woodward and Karinne Keithley. I am fortunate to have had the friendship, guidance and insight of Jane Taylor through this and previous editions. Ruth Caswell's deep knowledge and infectious enthusiasm have been an inspiration. Thanks, too, to Jessica Jacobs, Madian al-Jazerah, Suhail AbualSameed, all at MEF, Samer and Amanda Kurdi and family, and Richard and Janet Adams and family. Above all, to Neville and Sheila Teller – and Han.

This edition is dedicated to Adam Katagiri, pilot.

Readers' letters and emails

Thanks to all those readers of the second edition who took the trouble to write in with their amendments, additions, new discoveries and accounts of their travels in Jordan. Apologies for any misspellings or omissions.

Thanks to: Florence Abubaker, Kahtan Alamery, Jane Craft, Emma Cramp, Jaap de Boer, Joanna Dench, Jonathan Fell, Bengt Furustam, John Gregory, Carrie Heffern, Sue & David Heyes, Hugh Hoffmann, Mark T. Jones, Jesse Kalisher & Helen Westwood, Suliman Khawaldeh, Jeff King, Petra Kopp, Michael Malenfant, Fiona Monteath, Douglas M. Nabhan, Alex Nikolic, Nabil Nwafleh, Geoff Payne, Helen Penaluna & Danny Davies, Marla Sanchez, Mark Steadman, John E. Terborgh, Paul Thompson, Christine Walton, Dophne Wong.

Photo credits

All photos © Rough Guides except the following:

Cover
Main front Dead Sea at sunset © Alamy
Small front top picture Mosaic from Apostles Church, Madaba © Alamy
Small front lower picture Red and yellow dates © Alamy
Back top picture Monastery, Petra © Alamy
Back lower picture Jerash city © Getty

Title page
Bedouin leaders at Dana Nature Reserve © Dave Saunders

Full page
View from jeep, Wadi Rum © Dave Saunders

Introduction
View of Wadi Rum © Bill Lyons
Carved heads © Jane Taylor
Aqaba at sunset © Michelle Woodward
Jerash Spring, St John the Baptist church ruins © Jane Taylor
Downtown Amman © Michelle Woodward
Jordan flag © Jordan Tourism Board
Blue Sinai lizard © Jane Taylor
Petra rock © Jane Taylor
Cracked earth © Bill Lyons
Black iris © Jane Taylor
Bedouin boy with camel, Wadi Rum © Dave Saunders
Baghdad Highway © Michelle Woodward
Nubian ibex on rocks © Jane Taylor
Drumming, Captain's Camp, Wadi Rum © Dave Saunders

Things not to miss
01 Wadi Mujib © H. Rogers/TRIP
02 Wadi Rum landscape © Lucy Davies
03 Baptism Site © Jane Taylor
04 Trekking © Jordan Tourism Board
05 Petra, Siq © Michelle Woodward
06 Petra, Treasury © Jane Taylor
07 Petra, Monastery © Michelle Woodward
08 Petra by night © Jordan Tourism Board
09 High Place of Sacrifice © Peter Wilson
10 Petra colours © Christopher Rennie/Robert Harding Picture Library
11 Madaba mosaic map © H. Rogers/TRIP

12 Qasr Hraneh © Michelle Woodward
13 Bedouin tent © Jad Younis
14 Red Sea diving © Jordan Tourism Board
15 Hammamat Ma'in © Christopher Rennie/Robert Harding Picture Library
16 Dead Sea © Jad Younis
17 Qusayr Amra © Jane Taylor
18 Bedouin camel race © Jane Taylor
19 Umayyad Palace, Amman © Allan Hartly/Travel Ink
20 Roman Theatre, Amman © Jon Spaull/Axiom
21 Dana Nature Reserve © Jane Taylor
22 King's Highway © Bill Lyons
23 Karak castle © Bill Lyons
24 Jordanian cuisine © Bill Lyons
25 Jerash © Michelle Woodward
26 Mount Nebo © Dave Saunders
27 Pella © Tony Howard
28 Burqu © Richard Adams
29 Umm Qais © Michelle Woodward
30 Jerash Festival © Bill Lyons
31 Qasr Azraq © Allan Hartly/Robert Harding Picture Library
32 Shaumari Wildlife Reserve © Michelle Woodward

Black and white photos
p.55 Downtown Amman © Tony Howard
p.102 King Abdullah Mosque, Amman © Dave Saunders
p.134 "Kaek" street vendor, Amman © Dave Saunders
p.170 Dead Sea © Jad Younis
p.188 Old house in backstreets of Salt © Michelle Woodward
p.196 Jerash, North Theatre © Dave Saunders
p.209 Oval Plaza, Jerash © Jordan Tourism Board
p.240 Serving coffee, Bedouin tent © Jad Younis
p.249 Umm al-Jimal camels © Jane Taylor
p.276 Shobak castle © Jane Taylor
p.302 Mujib canyon © Tony Durrant
p.324 Petra Treasury © Dave Saunders
p.354 Dushara bust © Jane Taylor
p.380 Local Bedouin leader, Dana Nature Reserve © Dave Saunders
p.400 Bedouin policeman © Jane Taylor
p.461 Caracals © Robert Harding Picture Library

SMALL PRINT

Index

Map entries are in colour

A

Abila.............................230
accommodation 60
adventure tours 75
aerial sports...................79
airport 112
Ajloun.........................214
Ajloun Woodland
    Reserve....................216
alcohol 68
Allenby Bridge, see King
    Hussein Bridge
American Express 52
AMMAN 101–67
    Amman.....................108
    Amman, Downtown 120
    Amman, Greater............108
    Abdali station 110
    Abdoun....................125
    Abu Alanda 143
    Abu Darwish mosque 142
    accommodation 119
    Ahl al-Kahf 143
    airline offices...................164
    airports.....................110, 112
    arrival 110
    art galleries 139
    banks 164
    bars..151
    bazaars 131
    books 156
    bus routes 116
    buses 119
    cafés 144
    car rental 111
    Cave of the Seven
        Sleepers....................143
    changing money 164
    cinema 153
    Circassians...................132
    Citadel........................133
    City Hall........................133
    coffee houses 144
    consulates......................164
    crafts 154
    cultural centres 164
    dance 152
    Dar al-Anda.....................139
    Darat al-Funun 138
    Downtown 128
    Duke's Diwan 131
    eating and drinking 143
    email................................165
    embassies 164
    fast food..........................150
    film 153
    galleries............................139

gold 155
hammam 140
Hejaz train station 114
history 104
hospitals..........................165
hotels 119
Husseini Mosque 130
information 115
Internet............................165
Jebel al-Ashrafiyyeh.........142
Jebel al-Lweibdeh............137
Jebel al-Lweibdeh............125
Jebel al-Qal'a 133
Jebel Amman 139
Jebel Amman 125
JETT office......................111
juice bars 144
Kan Zaman......................148
libraries............................165
Makan 139
malls.................................154
Marka airport 110
Martyrs' Memorial...........142
mosques 130, 142
museum, folklore 130
museum, national
    archeological 135
museum, popular
    traditions 130
music................................152
National Archeological
    Museum......................135
National Gallery of Fine
    Arts 139
nightlife............................151
Nymphaeum.....................131
Odeon 130
pharmacies 165
police 165
pubs 151
Queen Alia airport 112
Raghadan station............114
Rainbow Street 140
renting a car.....................111
restaurants....................145
Roman Theatre 129
Royal Automobile
    Museum......................142
serveeces 117
serveece routes 116
Shmeisani 127
shopping 153
Souk Sukkr 131
South Amman 142
stations 114
supermarkets 151
Sweifiyyeh church
    mosaic 141
taxis.................................118
Temple of Hercules 135

theatre..............................152
traffic 115
transport...........................115
travel agents 165
Trust office 114
Umayyad Palace..............136
visa extensions 165
visas 160
walking.............................118
West Amman....................137
Wihdat..............................143
Wihdat station.................111
Wild Jordan centre..........141
Amman Beach..............177
Anjara 218
AQABA........................403
Aqaba............................408
    accommodation 407
    Aila 414
    airport...........................407
    Aqaba Gateway 412
    Aqaba Lagoon 404
    arrival 406
    ASEZA..........................404
    beaches 415
    cafés 419
    car rental......................423
    city transport.................407
    consulate, Egyptian 423
    coral 416
    diving.............................416
    eating and drinking 419
    Eilat 422
    environment 404
    ferries 422
    fort.................................413
    history 405
    hospital 423
    hotels 407
    information 407
    Jordan Experience..........412
    mail................................423
    Marine Science Station
        aquarium.....................416
    market............................419
    museum 414
    Nuweiba 422
    Pharaoh's Island 418
    police 423
    post 423
    renting a car...................423
    restaurants....................419
    Sharm el-Sheikh 423
    snorkelling.......................416
    Tala Bay 404
    taxis...............................407
    transport..........................407
    visas 41
Arab Revolt..........389, 441
Arabic 92, 507

Arava crossing, see Wadi
   Araba crossing
archeology.........................92
architectural terms.......516
argileh.............................67
Ariha.............................300
Asaykhim.....................271
ASEZA...............41, 404
Ayoun Musa.................291
Azraq..........................256
Azraq............................259
Azraq Wetlands
   Reserve.....................262

B

Baa'idj..........................247
Bab adh-Dhraa..............178
Badia, Eastern..............266
Badia Research &
   Development
   Programme...........77, 267
ballooning.....................398
Bani Hamida tribe.........297
Baptism Site...............180
Baptism Site................181
Baqaa............................204
Baqoura........................230
bargaining......................82
Battle of Hattin.............304
Bayir.............................388
beaches, Dead Sea......175
beaches, Red Sea........415
Bethany, see Baptism
   Site
bicycles.........................60
Biqya'wiyya...................270
Bir Mathkoor.................424
birds.............................462
Black September..........449
books...........................492
BRDP...................77, 267
Burckhardt, J.L. 330
Burqu............................272
buses.............................54

C

Callirhoë.......................177
camels...........................75
camping..........................80
car rental.................57, 111
carpets..................82, 297
changing money.............51
chariot racing...............206

children.........................94
Church of the Map.......283
cigarettes.......................96
Circassians...................132
climate............................15
coffee.............................67
contraceptives................96
coral..............................416
costs...............................53
credit cards....................51
crime...............................81
Crusaders.....................305
currency..........................50
Customs..........................42
cycling............................60

D

**Dana Nature
   Reserve**....................313
Dana.............................315
Dayr al-Kahf.................269
Dayr Alla.......................191
Dayr al-Qinn.................269
Dead Sea...................171
Dead Sea......................172
Dead Sea Panorama....295
Decapolis.....................200
dehydration....................46
departure tax..................96
Desert Castles.............241
Desert Highway...........383
Dhiban..........................299
Dibbeen Forest
   Reserve.....................219
disabled travellers.........95
Diseh...........................390
diving............................416
doctors...........................49
dress codes....................84
driving............................56
drugs..............................81

E

Eastern Badia..............266
Eastern Jordan............242
eating..............................63
ecotourism......................75
Egypt, arrival from.........39
Egypt, travel to.....163, 422
el-Maghtas...................183
email...............................70
embassies in Amman....41,
   164

embassies, Jordanian....41
embroidery.....................82

F

Faqua...........................301
Faynan................317, 424
Faysaliyyeh..................291
Feinan, see Faynan
ferries....................38, 422
Fifa.......................180, 424
flag...................................9
flights
   from Australia...................34
   from Canada.....................32
   from Egypt........................40
   from Ireland......................28
   from Israel........................39
   from New Zealand............34
   from the UK.....................28
   from the US......................32
   within Jordan...................59
food................................63
Fuheis..........................189

G

Gadara, see Umm Qais
gay travellers.................88
Gerasa, see Jerash
gestures.........................89
Gharandal.....................424
Glubb Pasha.................447
gold..............................155
gorge-walking.......177, 294
greetings.......................509
guides......................80, 97

H

hajj...............................469
Halawa.........................216
Hallabat........................245
Hammam as-Srah........245
Hammamat Afra...........311
Hammamat Burbita......311
Hammamat Ma'in......293
harassment.....................85
Hashemites...................445
health.............................46
Hejaz railway................383
Hesban.........................292
hiking.............................77
Himmeh........................228

history of Jordan 429
hitch-hiking 56
homosexuality 88
hospitality 90
hospitals 49
hotels 60
hubbly-bubbly, see argileh

I

information 42
insurance 45
Internet 70
invitations 90
Iraq al-Amir 193
Irbid 220
Irbid 221
Islam 466
Islamic holidays 74
Island of Peace 230
Israel, arrival from 36
Israel, travel to 160, 222, 422
Israeli border stamps 37

J

Jafr 387
Jawa 269
Jebel Haroun 371
JERASH 198
    Jerash 202
    accommodation 204
    arrival 204
    Baths of Placcus 213
    Birketayn 213
    Cardo 208
    Cathedral 212
    chariot racing 206
    Church of SS Cosmas and
        Damian 213
    eating 205
    Fountain Court 212
    guides 204
    Hadrian's Arch 205
    Hippodrome 205
    history 199
    Jerash Festival 199
    macellum 208
    mosaics 213
    mosque 208
    museum 208
    North Gate 212
    North Theatre 211
    Nymphaeum 210
    Oval Plaza 207
    Propylaeum Church 210
    restaurants 205

    Sacred Way 210
    South Gate 206
    South Theatre 207
    Stepped Street 213
    Synagogue Church 213
    Temple of Artemis 210
    Temple of Zeus 207
    Visitors' Centre 204
    West Baths 211
Jerash Festival 199
Jerusalem, arrival from ... 36
Jerusalem, travel to 160
JETT buses 56
jewellery 83
jihad 470
Jiza 384
Jordan, central 278
Jordan Experience 412
Jordan River 185, 231
Jordan River crossing, see
    Sheikh Hussein Bridge
Jordan Tourism Board 42
Jordan Valley 191, 231
jordanjubilee.com 43

K

Kahf il-Messih 235
Kallirhoë, see Callirhoë
Karak 304
Karak 307
Karameh 191
Khirbet al-Mukhayyat ... 291
Khirbet as-Samra 244
Khirbet Tannur 310
King Abdullah II 456
King Hussein Bridge 36
King's Highway 277
King's Highway 278
Kraymeh 192

L

language 507
Lawrence, T.E. ("of Arabia")
    .... 256, 389
lesbian travellers 88
literature 478
Little Petra 375
Lot's Cave 178

M

Ma'an 385

Ma'an 385
Machaerus, see Mukawir
Madaba 279
Madaba 282
Mafraq 245
Magheirat 293
mail 69
Ma'in 293
maps 44
marathons 75
Mastercard 52
Mazar 310
Mazra'a 178
medical treatment 48
mensaf 65
Mesha stele 299
minibuses 54
modern art 474
money 50
Mosaic Map of the Holy
    Land 283
mosaics 286
Moses Memorial
    Church 290
Mount Nebo 289
Mshare'a 234
Mudawwara 387
Mujib 298
Mujib Bridge 177
Mukawir 296
Mukhaybeh 228
Muqat 272
Museum of Jordanian
    Heritage 220
Muslim holidays 74
Muta 310
Muwaggar 251

N

Nabateans 328
nargileh *see* argileh
nature reserves
    Ajloun Woodland 216
    Azraq Wetlands 262
    Burqu 272
    Dana 313
    Dibbeen Forest 219
    Mujib 300
    Shaumari 264
    Wadi Mujib 300
Nebo, Mount 289
newspapers 71
Northern Jordan 198
numbers 511

O

opening hours 73
organized tours 28

P

package tours 28
Pella 232
PETRA 325
  Petra 344
  Petra, city centre 361
  Petra area 326
  accommodation 336
  Ain Musa 333
  Amud Faraoun 359
  arrival 333
  Bab as-Siq 348
  Bab as-Siq Triclinium 348
  banks 342
  Basin museum 367
  Baydha 376
  Bdul tribe 358
  Blue Church 364
  Broken Pediment Tomb ... 357
  Carmine Tomb 360
  Colonnaded Street 361
  Columbarium 368
  Corinthian Tomb 360
  Crusaders 368, 375
  dam 350
  Dayr, see Monastery
  Deir, see Monastery
  Dorotheos' House 374
  Eagle Niche 350
  East Cliff 359
  eating 341
  Garden Terrace 365
  Garden Triclinium 357
  Great Temple 365
  guides 347
  Habees 367
  High Place of Sacrifice .. 355
  history 325
  Jebel Haroun 371
  Jebel al-Khubtha 360
  Katuteh 359
  Lion Monument 357
  Lion Triclinium 369
  Little Petra 375
  Madras 349
  medical facilities 342
  Monastery 368
  mosaics 363
  Mughur an-Nassara 374
  museums 367
  Nabatean religion 349
  Nymphaeum 361
  Obelisk Tomb 348
  Outer Siq 353
  Palace Tomb 360
  Petra By Night tour 346

  Petra Church 363
  police 342
  post 343
  Qasr al-Bint 366
  Qattar ad-Dayr 369
  Renaissance Tomb 357
  restaurants 341
  Ridge Church 364
  Roman Soldier Tomb 357
  Royal Tombs 359
  Sabra 372
  Sextius Florentinus
    Tomb 360
  Sidd Maajn 350, 374
  Silk Tomb 360
  Siq 350
  Siq al-Berid 375
  Snake Monument 371
  Street of Facades 355
  taxis 335
  Taybet Zaman 339
  Temenos 366
  Temple of the Winged
    Lions 364
  Theatre 355
  tickets 344
  Tomb of 17 Graves 355
  Tomb of Unayshu 359
  tour operators 340
  Treasury 351
  Turkmaniyyeh Tomb 374
  Umm al-Biyara 371
  Unfinished Tomb 368
  Urn Tomb 359
  Visitors' Centre 343
  Wadi Abu Ullaygeh, see Wadi
    Turkmaniyyeh
  Wadi Farasa 357
  Wadi Mataha 374
  Wadi Muaysreh ash-
    Shargiyyeh 374
  Wadi Musa 332
  Wadi Muthlim 350
  Wadi Sha'ab Qays 375
  Wadi Siyyagh 368
  Wadi Thughra 370
  Wadi Turkmaniyyeh 374
  Wu'ayra 375
  Zantur 359
  Petra By Night 346
Pharaoh's Island 418
phones 69
phrasebooks 507
poetry 488
police 81
post 69
press 71
public holidays 74

Q

Qadisiyyeh 313
Qal'at ar-Rabadh 214

Qasr 300
Qasr al-Abd 193
Qasr Azraq 261
Qasr Burqu 272
Qasr Hallabat 245
Qasr Hraneh 251
Qasr Kharana, see Qasr
  Hraneh
Qasr Mushatta 250
Qasr Tuba 255
Qatraneh 384
Queen Alia airport 112
Qurayqira 317, 424
Qusayr Amra 252
Qusayr Amra 254
Quweira 388
Qwaylbeh 230

R

Rabba 300
Rabin crossing, see Wadi
  Araba crossing
radio 72
Ramadan 64, 74, 469
Ramtha 222
Ras an-Naqab 388
Rashaydeh 317
Rashdiyyeh (Dana) 314
Rashdiyyeh (Rum) 388
Red Sea 403
religious holidays 74
renting a car 57, 111
renting a flat 122
restaurants 63
River Jordan 185, 231
road rules 56
Royal Aero Sports
  Club 79
Royal Family 445
Royal Society for the
  Conservation of
  Nature 77
RSCN 77
rugs 82, 297
Rum 388
Rum 391
Ruwayshid 272

S

Safawi 268
Safi 180
Salt 186
Salt 186

Sela..............................312
serveeces 56
service charges 53, 63
sexual harassment 85
Shaumari Wildlife
   Reserve......................264
Sheikh Hussein Bridge..38,
   236
Shobak........................320
shopping................82, 153
Shuneh al-Janubiyyeh... 191
Shuneh ash-Shamaliyyeh
  229
Siyagha, see Mount Nebo
snorkelling 416
Sodom and Gomorrah .179
Southern Jordan..........382
studying Arabic 92
Suf 204
sweets 66
Sweimeh.......................173
Syria, arrival from 36
Syria, travel to 162, 222

T

Tabqat Fahl...................234
Tafileh 312
taxes........................53, 63
taxis...............................59
Taybet Zaman...............339
tea..................................67
teaching English............92
telephones.....................69
Tell al-Khaleifeh 405
Tell as-Sa'idiyyeh..........192
Tell Dayr Alla................191
Tell Hesban..................292
Tell Mar Elias (Baptism Site)
  184
Tell Mar Elias (nr Ajloun)
  219
Thomas Cook................52
tipping 53, 63
tour operators
   in Australia 35
   in Canada.........................33
   in Jordan 76
   in New Zealand.................35
   in the UK 29
   in the US 33
tourist guides.................97
tourist information 42
trains.......................59, 383
travel insurance 45
trekking..........................77
Turaybil 272
TV 72

U

Udhruh...........................388
Umm al-Jimal 246
Umm al-Jimal 247
Umm ar-Rasas 297
Umm Qais 224
Umm Qais 227

V

vegetarians 65
Visa card.........................52
visa extensions.......40, 165
visas 40, 160

W

Wadi al-Yabis...............216
Wadi Araba...................424
Wadi Araba crossing 38
Wadi Butm....................253
Wadi Dana....................313
Wadi Hasa 310
Wadi Hidan...................299
Wadi ibn Hammad........309
Wadi Kharrar 180
Wadi Mujib 298
**Wadi Mujib Nature
   Reserve**....................300
Wadi Musa.................331
Wadi Musa....................332
Wadi Numeira...............309
Wadi Qwaylbeh 230
Wadi Rum 388
Wadi Rum 391
Wadi Seer.....................192
Wadi Shuayb 189
Wadi Sirhan..................256
Wadi Wala 299
Wadi Zarqa Ma'in 293
walking 77
   at Ajloun...........................217
   in Amman..........................118
   at Dana.............................318
   at Hammamat Ma'in 294
   near Karak.........................309
   near Petra 370
   at Wadi Mujib...................301
water issues 11
water-pipe, see argileh
weather...........................13
weaving 82
websites 43
West Bank, arrival from ..36

West Bank, travel to 160
wildlife 459
wiring money 52
women..........................471
women travellers 85
writing...........................478

Y

Yarmouk Gorge 229
Yarmouk University 220

Z

Zai National Park..........189
Zara 177
Zarqa 244
Zubia 216

Map symbols

Maps are listed in the full index using coloured text

Undisputed international border	Gardens
Other border	Campsite
Chapter division boundary	Internet access
Main road	Tourist office
Minor road	Gate
Tunnel/underpass	Bridge
Dirt road	Bus/serveece stop
Steps	Airport
Cliffs	Parking
Railway	Embassy
Path	Hospital
Wall	Post office
Ferry route	Mosque
Waterway and dam	Building
Mountain range	Church
Peak	Stadium
Swamp	Park
Oasis	Salt pan
Point of interest	Beach
Accommodation	Economic Zone
Restaurant/bar	